Empire of Magic

Empire of Magic

Medieval Romance
and the Politics of Cultural Fantasy

GERALDINE HENG

Columbia University Press • New York

COLUMBIA UNIVERSITY PRESS
PUBLISHERS SINCE 1893
NEW YORK   CHICHESTER, WEST SUSSEX

Library of Congress Cataloging-in-Publication Data
Heng, Geraldine.
Empire of magic : medieval romance and the politics of cultural fantasy / Geraldine Heng.
p.   cm.
Includes bibliographical references and index.
ISBN 978–0–231–12526–0 (cloth : alk. paper)—ISBN 978–0–231–12527–7 (paper : alk. paper)
1. Romances, English—History and criticism.   2. English literature—Middle English,
1100–1500—History and criticism.   3. Politics and literature—England—History—To 1500.
4. Literature and society—England—History—To 1500.   5. Civilization, Medieval, in
literature.   6. Imperialism in literature.   7. Crusades in literature.   8. Culture
in literature.   9. Magic in literature.   I. Title.

PR321 .H46 2003
820.9'001—dc21
2002034894

To Cecilia Heng, who made it possible;
Janadas Devan, who made it likely;
and
Shaan Heng-Devan, who made it worthwhile.

CONTENTS

❧

Acknowledgments

෬

This book, which began with two simple questions—why did the King Arthur legend survive (and not just survive, but *thrive*) for almost nine hundred years and what, exactly, is a romance, medieval or otherwise?—has been a while in the making, and the answers that have emerged (answers, also, to more difficult questions that inevitably came along) have surprised the author as much as anyone, at the many stages of making *Empire of Magic*. Throughout, key people enabled the project to begin, complexify, and come to fruition: my debt to them is what is recorded here. At every stage, also, generous interlocuters materialized to offer opportunities for public conversation and engagement, and to test arguments and ideas on a variety of audiences, in a variety of contexts: these good people and the venues they offered are individually acknowledged at the beginning of each chapter of this book, and I direct the reader to those pages as well.

Leah Marcus—who personifies, for me, intellectual magnanimity and integrity at its finest—believed in *Empire of Magic* from inception to end, was never skeptical of the project's increasingly larger and larger ambitions, and provided unfailing, essential support. Seth Lerer, Gene Vance, Tony Spearing, and Jane Chance were the generous medievalists who helped the project to begin, by helping me win crucial fellowship time at the Stanford Humanities Center in 1995–96, where the first chapter of *Empire of Magic* was written. David Wallace, Pete Wetherbee, John Ganim, Rick Emmerson, Carolyn Dinshaw, and Aranye Fradenburg were the medievalists who oversaw the project's conclusion, in 2001–2, with equally fine generosity. In between, Ellen Rooney and Elizabeth Weed offered a fellowship for the seminar on "Disciplinary Difference" at Brown University's Pembroke Center in 1997–98, where a community of scholars, theorists, and medievalists convened a fertile environment for the book's middle chapters. The last chapter was written when the inimitable Margo Hendricks convened the seminar on "Theorizing 'Race' in Pre- and Early Modern Contexts" at the University of California's Humanities Research Institute, in an environment that witnessed the pervasive influence of the incomparable David Theo Goldberg, and offered a residential fellowship in 2000. Various grant awards from the University of Texas at Austin's University Research Institute, Department of English, and the Harry Ransom Humanities Research Center from 1995 to 1999 furnished invaluable supplementary support.

Before *Empire of Magic* became an overriding obsession, my research at an earlier stage owed much to the ways I responded to the influence of Bob and Carol Kaske, Art Groos, David Wallace, Gene Vance, Jane Chance, and the intensely heady intellectual environment at Cornell University in the late 1980s. For many young women at Cornell's English department at the time, the example set by Dorothy Mermin, Laura Brown, Mary Jacobus, and Mary Ann Radzinowicz was formative in ways that would only be most importantly realized later in life. One legacy of a Cornell education—of a medieval and of a theoretical kind, intellectually and politically—has been the suggestion that in adventures of intellect and scholarship, as in communal life, the obvious, easier route is not always the one to take. From the directive to follow one's instinct and passion, even when what beckons looks strangely counterintuitive, I have learned much that has proven productive. In this, Bob Kaske's early insistence that everything one wrote should be held to exacting standards and "contribute to knowledge"—to use his expression—has been an important prompting.

At the University of Texas at Austin, my home institution, diverse colleagues very kindly read chapters, raised questions, and entered into friendly dialogue: among the most helpful have been Tom Cable, Jim Garrison, Denise Spellberg, Jim Wimsatt and Rebecca Beal, Betty Sue Flowers, Terry Kelley, Barbara Harlow, Evan Carton, Dolora Chapelle-Wojiehowski, Martha Newman, Alison Frazier, Lisa Moore, Ann Cvetkovich, Elizabeth Cullingford, Sue Heinzelman, Michael Adams, David Wevill, Michael White, Bill Kibler, Marjorie Woods, Jim Lee, Wayne Lesser, Al Martinich, and Tom Palaima. Both in terms of the book's ambitions, and the ways in which I imagine how medieval global realities and cultures can be taught and studied, I have also been sustained on campus by the steadfast wisdom of Jim Garrison, chair of the English department, and Tom Cable, senior colleague par excellence; by Rebecca Baltzer, Cyndy Talbot, Denise Spellberg, Janet Staiger, Shelley Fisher Fishkin, Gloria Lee, Roger Louis, Chuck Rossman, Linda Ferreira-Buckley, Rick Cherwitz, John Dollard, and Mia Carter; and by Richard Lariviere, visionary dean of Liberal Arts, and the peerless Terry Sullivan, former dean of the Graduate School and current vice-chancellor for Academic Affairs in the Texas system.

I am particularly grateful, also, to the superb team at Columbia University Press, who have gone the extra distance for this book. Ann Miller very deftly and ably acquired the manuscript in the course of chance meetings at conferences over two years, when I was undecided over the relative merits of individual presses, and shepherded the manuscript through the acquisitions process with remarkable efficiency. Her splendid successor, Wendy Lochner, has been everything that an author could wish, and more: her willingness to imagine possibilities and her resourceful effectiveness are an author's delight. The light, skilled touch of Rita Bernhard, copy editor extraordinaire, meant that *Empire of Magic* was not colonized by an empire of style—the nightmare of many who publish—and her friendship since has been a special gift. Anne McCoy's expertise and care in overseeing production bolstered confidence, and Linda Secondari's supervision of design went the extra mile in accommodating my preferences, for which I am grateful. I am also indebted to the readers of the manuscript who read four chapters in draft with scrupulous attention and generous decisiveness; and I was especially fortunate that the ideal graduate assistant, Peter Larkin, reappeared at the right moment to provide the meticulous, detailed attentiveness, at which Peter excels, to *Empire of Magic's* proofs and index.

Chapter 1 of this book was first published in *differences* 10:1 (1998): 98–174, and a draft of part of chapter 2 appeared in *The Postcolonial Middle Ages*, edited by Jeffrey Jerome Cohen (New York: St. Martin's Press, 2000). The friendly efficiency of librarians at the Perry-Castañeda and Harry Ransom libraries at the University of Texas, the Green Library at Stanford, the Rockefeller Library at Brown, and the Huntington and Newberry libraries has been a great help. In an earlier life in postcolonial Singapore—a place and time that have not ceased to shape my work, thinking, and commitments—Edwin Thumboo's interventions were crucial in securing vital, necessary protections and opportunities; I honor his generosity with gratitude. Koh Tai Ann, stalwart student of D. J. Enright, who helped me in my adolescent years to read William Empson's "Missing Dates," probably did not imagine that she would inaugurate, for that adolescent, all the later adventures in close critical reading; and Arthur

Lindley was my first Chaucer teacher. Of the many fine students I have been fortunate to teach, Suporn Arriwong and Erin McDonald are the two who have most enriched my life, always returning with their own gifts of instruction to surprise and delight.

My debts to the special friends who have continued to sustain a sense of home and community—far-flung though they are, across nation and world—are impossible to express with adequacy. My intellectual and personal life has been immeasurably enriched by the friendship of Sam Otter and Caverlee Cary, Bibijan Ibrahim and Harpal Singh, Dorothy and David Mermin, Leah and David Marcus, Philomena Essed and David Goldberg, Suvir Kaul and Ania Loomba, Marty Wechselblatt and Kathy Smits, Alison Case and James Pethica, Paul Sawyer and Wendy Jones, Chandra and Satya Mohanty, Walter Cohen, Sandra Siegel, Virginia Raymond and Tom Kolker, Amy Wong Mok and Al Mok, Dolora Wojiehowski and Eric Chapelle, Denise Spellberg, Gloria Lee, Lisa Moore and Madge Darlington, Chua Seok Hong, Woon-Ping Chin and Duncan Holaday, Minfong Ho and John Dennis, and their magnificent families. Before it had a name or shape, *Empire of Magic* glimmered in conversations in the homes of Sturges and Sara Cary, and Jeanne Otter, who did not live to see this project end, but who are remembered always for the living sense of home and community they embodied for those whose lives they so finely touched.

Finally, Cecilia Heng made it possible for me to work, when I was a handicapped person with a young infant, by giving unstintingly of herself for a long time. Janadas Devan's intellectual brilliance, conversation, good humor, and companionship are the bedrock context of every significant adventure of intellect in my adult life. George Heng and Geraldine Sng, C. V. Devan Nair, Dhanam Avadei, and Vijaya Devan, Mitra and Sabrina Devan, and their remarkable children, are important steadying and comforting presences. Last of all, and at the beginning of all things, Shaan Heng-Devan's irrepressible joyfulness, wise sense of mischief, and sheer logicality—and his impatience for Mom's book finally to be done, so that he might read it—are the sine qua non of my life and work.

Empire of Magic

In the Beginning Was Romance . . .

In Xanadu did Kubla Khan
A stately pleasure-dome decree:
Where Alph, the sacred river, ran
Through caverns measureless to man
Down to a sunless sea.

—"Kubla Khan," Samuel Taylor Coleridge

ROMANCE, OF COURSE, has no beginning, no identifiable moment or text in which it is possible to say, here is the location of the origin.

Before the Middle Ages, and the first usages of the Old French grapheme, "*romanz*," to signify an expanding category of fabulous narratives of a literary kind, something, we feel, existed that was already romance-like, that preceded the medieval concretions. Casting back in time, we speak of "Ancient" or "Greek" "romances, of the *Odyssey* (but not the *Iliad*) as a "romance," and of the "romances" of Alexander the Great that descend from the third century of the Common Era (or perhaps as early as the fourth century B.C.E.), as if we intuitively know what romances are, and are not. Yet there is a fringe of indecision: Are the fabulous Greek travel stories featuring the magical Wonders of the East, and especially India—the genre of the "Indika" of Ctesius and his literary descendants—romances?[1] Can *geography* and *place* be a subject of romance, along with human actors engaged in love, quest, and marvelous adventure?

Casting forward in time, past the Middle Ages and the revivals of medieval, and medieval-like, romances in the Renaissance, Enlightenment, Romantic, Victorian, and modern eras, can we say that certain kinds of narrative modes continue which we still think of as romance—specialized now into consumer categories like love stories, science fiction, westerns, fantasy, tales of travel, adventure, and exploration, new age fables—"magical narratives" (to use Fredric Jameson's naming) that make their way, in the new millenium, through a range of digital and electronic media, and a mutating spectrum of print cultures, where romances once traveled on handscripted vellum?

If romance did not begin in the Middle Ages, the genre is nonetheless so indelibly marked by the Middle Ages—when it was arguably the most prominent, sophisticated, and widely disseminated species of literary narrative—that romance seems virtually synonymous with medieval time itself, so that the entire Middle Ages, as John Ganim once put it, is characterized and depicted in later eras as if it were a romance.[2] One reason for that felt sense of intimacy between the genre and the period is possible to discover. If romance did not originate in the Middle Ages—if there never was an "origin" for romance—it had a powerful, distinct moment of *re-beginning* in early twelfth-century England: a conspicuous moment when a species of magical narrative coalesced in an extraordinary pattern, out of a field of forces in culture and history, to create an examplar for the romances that followed in the three hundred or more years to come, with an impact that ultimately traveled well beyond the Middle Ages itself.

I locate the point at which a narrative shaped itself into the pattern we now recognize as medieval romance in Geoffrey of Monmouth's audacious *History of the Kings of Britain* (*Historia Regum Britannie*), created around 1130–39: a moment that also witnesses the first appearance of King Arthur's legend in literary form in the West. Geoffrey's story is remarkable for many exemplary demonstrations: chief of which perhaps is how, in a resourcefully accommodating cultural medium, historical phenomena and fantasy may collide and vanish, each into the other, without explanation or apology, at the precise locations where both can be readily mined to best advantage—a prime characteristic of romance that persists henceforth. Geoffrey's exemplar materializes, I argue, as a form of cultural rescue in the aftermath of the First Crusade, a transnational militant pilgrimage during which Latin Christian crusaders did the unthinkable—committing acts of cannibalism on infidel Turkish cadavers in Syria, in 1098, with the attendant traumas of shock, pollution, and self-denaturing that accompany the violation of horrific taboos—and cultural fantasy was instantiated in order that the indiscussible, what is unthinkable and unsayable by other means, might surface into discussion.

Geoffrey's innovation shows how romance's preferred method is to arrange for an apparatus of the intimately familiar and pleasurable—figures of gender, sexuality, and varieties of adventure—to transact its negotiations with history, addressing what surfaces with difficulty, and exists under anxious pressure, through a loop of the familiar and the enjoyable: a lexicon that thereafter comprises romance's characteristic medium of discussion. Revealingly, Geoffrey's treatment of gender and sexuality also intimates that a homoerotic circuit, as much as the heterosexual dynamic organizing the surface narrative, animates and suffuses romance. Out of exigency, then, the *Historia* performs a dazzling cultural rescue by successively passing historical trauma through stages of memorial transfiguration, so that historical event finally issues, and is commemorated, as triumphant celebration in the form of a romance narrative in which the spoor of history and the track of fantasy creation become one, inextricably conjoined. The specific pattern instituted by the *Historia* suggests that one impulse driving romance is the discovery (and the making) of a safe harbor out of dangerous waters, in order that a *safe* language of cultural discussion accrues. The impetus of romance, the *Historia*'s illustration indicates, is toward *recovery*—not repression or denial—but surfacing and acknowledgment through stages of transmogrification, and the graduated mutating of exigency into opportunity.

The lexicon of romance having been secured by the *Historia*, and the operational modalities of cultural fantasy established, the topics of discussion treated by romance thereafter ramify. As contingencies arise, medieval romance resourcefully engages a variety of critical themes over the *longue durée* of medieval time. Among the genre's objects of attention are crises of collective and communal identity—the identity of the emerging medieval nation of England, or of pivotal racial groups, or even of Latin Christendom—as well as pressing economic, military, religious, and social conundrums of different kinds. The chapters in *Empire of Magic* are arranged to consider how types of romance respond to the demands of crisis, exigency, impasse and contradiction, and pressures of varying intensity, at significant junctures in medieval social and cultural history.

The story I tell of how romance re-forms itself, in its manifold apparitions through the long Middle Ages, suggests that one reason why romance flourishes but has been difficult to define with precision, or secure with demarcated borders, is that romance must be identified by the *structure of desire* which powers its narrative, and the transformational repetition of that structure through innumerable variations, rather than by any *intrinsic* subject matter, plot, style, or other content. In tracing continuities and breaks in the momentum of what impels romance through the Middle Ages, *Empire of Magic*'s procedure is not to declare and lay out its premises all at once at the beginning but to let the discontinuous story of medieval romances itself unfold through a range of genealogical moments that develop, and complicate, the delineation of romance desire.

Because *Empire of Magic* is not formally organized to elucidate or confirm taxonomies of romance content is not to say, of course, that romance in the Middle Ages *has* no repeating content at all. Much scholarship on medieval romance has been directed precisely at identifying the contents of romances, whether in the form of conventional subject matter (love, quests, giants, magic), or affective styles and trajectories (a dreamlike aura, or sense of "the marvelous," avoidance of final closure or heroic fatalism, fantastical landscapes or episodic progressions, or an economy of pleasurable delay and deferral of the end). Indeed, my selection of key romances as representatives of the principal constituencies of romance presupposes the necessity of intermittent, partial reiterations of romance content, with variation and change, over time, and thus also honors scholarly traditions of specification and classification that began with Jean Bodel's thirteenth-century taxonomies of romance *matière* in Europe.

In particular, after Geoffrey of Monmouth's critical instantiation of romance, *one* skein of magical narrative detaches itself, and, under the guiding genius of Chrétien de Troyes in the late twelfth century, dilates into an expansive constellation of romances that specialize in anatomizing and celebrating chivalry, a romance tradition that assumes enormous prominence in continental medieval European literature. So numerous and far-flung are the constituents of chivalric romance, it is easy to mistake the adventures of medieval knights and ladies as defining the entirety of medieval romance's interests, and postmedieval eras have sometimes synecdochically taken a sub-group of romances—chivalric romances—as the whole, vast, compendious universe of medieval romance itself. Despite the tantalizing fascinations of continental chivalric romances, however, I follow several species of medieval romance in this book.

If chapter 1, on Geoffrey's *Historia*, treats chronicle romances (romance in the mode of magisterial but fabulous history), chapter 2, on the boisterous romance of Richard Lionheart (*Richard Coer de Lyon* [*RCL*]), the immensely popular medieval cultural icon who was king of England, treats romances that existed in the Middle Ages as popular national fiction. Chapter 4 considers hagiographic and family romances in the form of the compellingly seductive Constance group of stories—romances that borrow from saints' legends, and may feature women and children, or families, rather than knights, at center stage—while chapter 5, on *Mandeville's Travels*, presents medieval travel narratives that are neither wholly fictitious, nor wholly factual, as a vital and important, if sometimes neglected, species of romance. Behind the subject matter occupying the foreground of romances like *Richard Coer de Lyon* and the Constance stories, moreover, lies other matter that these romances also engage: The emerging medieval nation of England is one critical focus; another is race and the emerging grammars of racial classification and hierarchy that appear in the process of nation formation. Chivalric romances, the best-known of romance types, are represented in chapter 3 by the scintillating Alliterative *Morte Arthure*, a fifteenth-century, late-medieval Arthurian story that measures the distance King Arthur and his knights have traveled since Geoffrey's Arthurian legend of almost three hundred years before, by showing how chivalric cultural fantasy responds to the encroaching end of medieval feudalism, and the inception of modernity, and modern times and people.

My fable of how romance effloresces at a particular historical instant, and remakes itself thereafter across a register of contexts—featuring women, children, nations, empires, war, races, classes, sexualities, modernity, travel, places, science, and geography, along with the conventional knights, ladies, love, and quests of chivalric tales—thus highlights a pattern of desire and an economy of pleasure that leave a characteristic footprint which can be glimpsed—briefly and discontinuously, appearing and disappearing in the wink of an eye—even when the grammars through which desire is expressed mutate and vary. Following the pathways of desire, in the countries of romance, my story also describes the pleasures afforded by romances of different kinds, in different temporal zones and formats, not as innocent, but as pleasures intimately folding into, and imbricated with, historical projects and agendas from which they are, at times, virtually inseparable.

Beginning with Geoffrey of Monmouth's literary experiment, *Empire of Magic* tells the story of how Arthurian romance, at the outset, collaborates with medieval Europe's earliest project of overseas empire, in the Levantine colonizations in Syria and Palestine that followed from the military-religious experiment known in the West as the First Crusade. I show how the installation of Arthurian romance furnishes the fledgling crusader colonies in the Levant with crucial cultural authority, even as the Levantine colonies furnish Arthurian romance with narrative *materia* in the form of ideas, plots, characters, constructs, affects, landscapes, and memory. I also suggest how Geoffrey's chronicle, *RCL*, the Alliterative *Morte*, and the Constance stories, when read together, can be seen to anchor the long and spectacular history of the crusades: from the first armed pilgrimage to the East in the eleventh century by the combined forces of Europe to the gradual supersession, in the late Middle Ages, of large-scale military incursions by cultural forms of empire.

Viewed through romance, we see empire installed in the eleventh and twelfth centuries as military and territorial domination through crusade. This devolves, in the thirteenth through fifteenth centuries, into empire-as-cultural-conquest—a domination expressed with particular vivacity through the missionary dream of conversion that is so seductively thematized in the Constance romances. Each representing a hinterland of other romances like and unlike itself, the *Historia*, *RCL*, the *Morte*, and the Constance stories ruminate over crusade history in ambitiously creative projects of rescue, critical commentary, nostalgia, and projective advocacy, and disclose how much European medieval romance, in its formative innovations and moments, owes to the history of the crusades in the Levant. The story of romance I tell is thus in part the story of medieval Europe's history of overseas empire-making, as seen through the diffractional medium of romance's involvement in projects of empire.

In offering *Mandeville's Travels* as the last segment of my book's meditation on romance, I suggest that at the end of the Middle Ages the momentum of empire-and-romance takes territorial form again. As new worlds enter the cultural imagination, technology and emergent mentalities enable travel to be configured as adventure, and the wonders of geography to be newly re-invested as magic—and travel romance moves to invite and urge territorial discovery, exploration, and settlement, thus presaging (and, as I show in chapter 5, impelling) the projects of power-knowledge-commerce-settlement that characterize the Renaissance to come.

Even as the genre conveys the changing impulses of empire, the romances considered by *Empire of Magic* also offer romance, simultaneously and in tandem, as a genre of *the nation*: a literary medium that solicits or invents the cultural means by which the medieval nation might be most productively conceptualized, and projected, for a diverse society of peoples otherwise ranged along numerous internal divides. The chapters on

Constance and *RCL*, particularly, show that impulses of nation and of empire are coextensive, mutually intelligible, and profitably cooperative, so that empire becomes an enabling condition of nation-making in the cultural imagination. The romances I consider, moreover, are specifically *English* romances, even when they have been written and disseminated in Latin and Old French, rather than Middle English dialects. The romances either first emerge in literary form in England (before their reproduction and dissemination throughout continental Europe, as with Geoffrey's *Historia*, written in Latin), or their instantiation of legendary motifs and plots amassed from elsewhere is uniquely concretized in England in a given form at a given moment, and specifically serves English sociocultural interests (as happens with Nicholas Trevet's *Cronicles*, written in Anglo-Norman French). Cumulatively, the Latin, French, and Middle English romances examined offer the resources of romance, in sum, as a genre of the English nation in the Middle Ages.

Hitherto, the *chronicle* has been assumed to be the principal medieval literary genre in which a country's identity is addressed or contemplated in narrative, just as the *epic* has been assumed to address the collective ethnic identity of tribes, the *chanson de geste* to address relations between monarch and retainers-in-chief, and romance to address the concerns preoccupying chivalric communities. My discussion of Geoffrey's *Historia*, *RCL*, and Chaucer's, Gower's, and Trevet's Constance stories shows how romance, by virtue of its popularity, special dispensations, and overarchingly wide address to a variety of domestic constituencies, uniquely subserves nationalist momentum, and nationalist requirements, in the projection of a national community and its future.

One formative moment in the emergence of the medieval English nation's identity, I argue, pivots on the manipulation of England's key internal racial-religious minority—its medieval Jewish community—an emergence assisted (as seen in the romances of *RCL* and the *King of Tars* treated in chapters 2 and 4) by romance's skillful elucidation of a discourse of racial difference and race-making. Allowing fantasies of race and nation to surface with remarkable freedom, and to flex themselves with astonishing ease and mobility, medieval romance becomes a medium that conduces with exceptional facility to the creation of races, and the production of a prioritizing discourse of essential differences among peoples, in the Middle Ages.

In this respect, though I have been discussing "history" and "culture" as if both were interdependent but distinct forces in a teleological dynamic, it is necessary to add that cultural performances of the kind enacted by and in medieval romance are, of course, also fully historical forces, in and of themselves. Romance projects of the kind I mention—projects of race-making and the culling of racial hierarchies, distinctions, and priorities; of imagining and projecting a national totality out of fragmentation and division; of resistance and opposition to the encroaching end of feudal time and feudal culture, and the incipience of modernity; and of exercising a will-to-power in geographically conceiving the world as the hinterland of Europe and the playground of the Christian faith—all show romance performing as historical actant. By intervening, persuading, influencing, judging, innovating, and deciding, romance has a hand in the shaping of the past and the making of the future.

Moreover, in the pre-electronic, pre-digital era of manuscript culture, something of the aggregated will and agency of whole communities of historical actors is realized and enacted in each romance that is selected to survive, by virtue of its popularity or felt importance, across the centuries, through manuscript copying, translation, redaction, preservation. Never the work of a sole authorial intelligence, even when an author's name, like Geoffrey of Monmouth's, can be attached, each romance treated in *Empire of Magic*—representing a concatenation of other romances that are somewhat like it, if never identically so—descends to us as the aggregated work of many minds, many hands, and many efforts over the centuries: as the material concretion of the collective will of cultural agents and forces acting over time to preserve, develop, and transmit a story felt to be important. Because it is the sedimented repository of what medieval culture has sought to retain across vast temporal divides, each romance that survives communicates the resultant aggregated will of a collective culture, and transmits the cumulative purposiveness of a diachronous endeavor in a way that is almost unimaginable to moderns habituated to the signed cultural works of mere single individuals.[3]

Finally, the allegory of medieval romance that I tell in this book also turns out, oddly but appropriately, to be the intermittent tale of *cannibalism* as a species of magical trope, and of Constantinople—fabled, eternal Byzantium—as a species of magical place. By a curious coincidence, cannibalism features as a principal or sub-theme in four of the major examples of romance I treat. Cannibalism is the anacrusis that breathes life into the annalistic and oral shards of a diffuse King Arthur legend that Geoffrey of Monmouth in twelfth-century England re-creates into a coherent fable, to bring romance newly to life again. In thirteenth- and fourteenth-century England, cannibalism supplies romance with a devastating means for a prime nationalistic joke, and a romance King Richard can organize a belligerent definition of English communal identity by presenting Englishmen as a unity of Christian military aggressors who gleefully gobble up the Islamic Levantine enemy as the main course at dinner—a colonial joke that also quirkily conjures, for me, the provocative instant at which an imperial England summons up, in literature, a colonial dish that will later be famously counterpointed, in English colonial societies farther East than Richard Lionheart's Levant, by another, favorite, colonial dish more decorously known as "curry."

In the early fifteenth century, cannibalism allows chivalric communities to address the unutterable through the body, acts, and power of a cannibal giant in the *Morte Arthure*, so that the obscene power of new capital, and a market economy's cash nexus, as well as a hugely profitable traffic in Christian slaves by Italian slavers—a heinous import/export commodity culture—can be anatomized, and shown to be complicit with the slow dissolution of masculine feudal identity under the new socioeconomic realities. And for late-medieval travel romance, cannibalism obligingly diffuses, National-Geographic–style, around the globe—courtesy of the field reports of "Sir John Mandeville," imaginary medieval anthropologist—to characterize foreign places and peoples in strategic exercises of cartographic ethnography. Romance itself, of course, is a species of pure cannibalism. At the end of the day, romance is, after all, the name of a desiring narrational modality that coalesces from the extant cultural matrix at hand, poaching and cannibalizing from a hybridity of all and any available resources, to transact a magical relationship with history, of which it is in fact a consuming part.

The genealogy of romance offered in *Empire of Magic* also finds that medieval romance, which has been held to be vague, dreamlike, and elusive in its depiction of place—evocations of locale in romance are said notoriously to suggest anywhere or every place—is no more evasive of geographical location than it is of history. The most vivid example of how the genre delivers a sense of place is shown in its distinctive relationship to a magical location that precedes, and haunts, medieval Europe, and Europe's capacity to envision aureal places, majestic grandeur, and a puissant past under threat: Constantinople. Across the centuries, romance summons up, again and again, Constantinople as a point of orientation. In the twelfth century, Byzantium is the glorious model for King Arthur's city, Caerleon, in Geoffrey of Monmouth's *Historia* (a seat later streamlined into the "Camelot" beloved of later ages). In the four-teenth century, the imperial lineage of Constantinople is where Nicolas Trevet plucks the names of his heroine, Constance, and her babe, Maurice, so that the mother may issue forth as an eponymous missionary heroine from the oldest of Christian empires—even when Trevet must pretend she is from Rome—and the son may seal his mother's success by consolidating the extension of Christian empire across ancient and modern time.

The fifteenth-century *Morte Arthure*, covertly replaying the infamy and glory of the Fourth Crusade's conquest of Constantinople—and Latin Europe's subsequent loss of the city back to the Greeks—also has Constantinople on its mind, as the fabled, fragile city comes under the shadow of an ascendant Ottoman Empire, in the aftermath of the failed 1396 Nicopolis crusade. "Mandeville," too, it seems, has an eye to Constantinople, even when seemingly most focused on the Holy Land and Jerusalem, and on the project of mapping a global imperium through an attentively roaming planetary survey. For collective identity, the *Travels* understands, is anchored *into* place by a sense *of* place, and Christian identity by a pivotal set of symbolic cities. Empires real and fictitious—the Great Khan's Cathay, or Prester John's India—can only be grasped through the old empire of Constantinople, queen of glittering cities and places in the country of romance. Though received tradition has it, then, that romance as fantasy evades place, as much as history, Constantinople, my story finds, is the locus that recurringly, resoundingly orients the narrational machine of dreaming geography.

POSTCRIPT: AFTERLIVES OF MEDIEVAL ROMANCE

Before the events of September 11, 2001, in an intellectual culture that now has the feel of a previous lifetime, it might have been productive to write an epilogue for *Empire of Magic* that speculatively ranged over some of the many, disseminating traces of medieval romance in postmedieval cultures: a discussion that might take in not only the self-conscious imitations and revivals of romance in the literary and cultural movements of postmedieval centuries—such as Spenser's *Faerie Queene*, the experiments of the Pre-Raphaelite Brotherhood, or Walter Scott's novels—but that would also consider how the unauthorized spirit and strategies of medieval romance might animate some of the populist subgenres of global mass culture today, genres that might be viewed as lively and vital, if prodigal, descendants of medieval romance, and whose transmissional channels in the twenty-first century are networks of electronic media and mass print distribution.

It is easiest to see, of course, how some of the purposes of medieval romance are revivified in literary romances that set out to imitate or recall the medieval: Romances like Tennyson's Arthurian *Idylls of the King*, for example, show how a medieval genre embedded within an older empire of culture can be reanimated to produce a flexible structure of ideological support and literary-theoretical justification to satisfy the needs of a new imperium—the British Empire of Victorian England—that would inherit the mantle of older civilizational culture through appropriable varieties of literature.[4] Beyond literary revivals and movements, however, also beckons a twilight landscape inhabited by cultural producers with no formal pretensions to literary culture, but who nonetheless hold the imaginative attention of immense—indeed, fully global—audiences distributed over unimaginable divides of class, race, nationality, and culture.

Jane Tompkins's study, *West of Everything*—on the favorite American genre of the "western"—evocatively suggests that filmic and paperback westerns alike, with their obsessive focus on death-encountering heroes, "big sky country," magnificent horses, wilderness, homosocial adventure, and musings on masculine identity and society, point to the resuscitation and adaptation of the genius of medieval romance for a rugged new American nation extending its borders and cities, meditating on its changing identity, naming its national values, and defining its native minorities. Janice Radway's *Reading the Romance* seems to pick up the psychological spoor of medieval romance when it discloses the desiring apparatus of modern mass-market "romance novels" aimed at pleasing a female audience who put their "romances" to a variety of significant uses (Chrétien de Troyes, we remember, designated Marie of Champagne as both audience and provocateuse for his creation of *Lancelot* in the late twelfth century, and the variety of satisfactions secured by medieval romance for its female audiences is still a lively theme in medievalist feminist scholarship today). Daniel Bernardi (*Star Trek and History*) and Micheal Pounds (*Race in Space*) are among those who study the cultural politics of race, gender, and empire in that most popular concatenation of late-twentieth-century travel romances, *Star Trek*, in its many incarnations on television and in film,

novels, and the scandalous unauthorized "story trees" created and compiled by *Trek* devotees, in the periodical format known as " 'zines" (or
"fanzines").[5] "Mandeville's" circumnavigable ocean, it would seem, with
its thousands of islands, all marvelous, finds its latter-day counterpart in a
navigable intergalactic continuum, with *its* wonders, cities, people, languages, technologies, and worlds; indeed, even the fortuitous erotic encounters between native women and the master-travelers who happen to
chance on them have resonant equivalents in this highly adaptive contemporary medium.[6] Arthurian romance seems also to have found science
fiction an appropriate channel for a kind of postmodern afterlife: Reviewing the comic book series issued as *Camelot 3000*, Charles Wood articulates
the freedoms and special dispensations available in this pop-cultural fantasy text in terms very like mine when I invoke the resources of medieval
romance.[7] It is possible to see how even the pleasure machine of cinema,
the most influential fantasy medium of narration today, is an apparatus
that inherits part of the legacy of romance.[8]

In the aftershock of September 11, 2001, however, it came slowly to
mind that the usefulness of understanding cultural fantasy's role in a *zeitgeist*—both the *zeitgeist* of the Middle Ages and today—exists with some
urgency also beyond the mediations of the culture industry and its politics of consolation and commercial dissemination. It has become clear, in
the year 2002 of the Common Era, that, contrary to prognostications, history has not, after all, come to an end; indeed, both history and the Middle Ages have returned, with a vengeance. Under the goad of a suddenly
renewed urgency to calibrate non-Western political and cultural mentalities that have never forgotten premodern history, Western intellectuals
who had believed that the political forces of empire-making and nation-
making only existed in the modern period now have less luxury to ignore
the medieval encounters of Christianity, Islam, and Judaism in the crucible of violent historical transformation. Not for nothing, then, are newly
hatched histories on Islam, the Crusades, and premodern "intercultural
relations" punctually appearing now at intervals.

Relegation of premodernity to a kind of cultural unconscious that
could be taken for granted has also meant other costs. For instance, the
panicked aftermath of September 11—when U.S. government agencies
floundered to grasp the group identity of the aggressor—revealed how in-
solvent our contemporary hypotheses of race had become, hypotheses that
had grown out of anatomizing and critiquing postmedieval racisms which
came to assume a position of primacy in entrenching concepts of race that

were no longer adequate to our twenty-first century conditions, and retarded the project of productive rethinking. Though we had dutifully echoed the axiom that race (like gender) was a construct, and not a system of somatic or biogenetic types, we had also tacitly continued to hold that racial categorizations always turned on the error of assuming the primacy of *biology* in the conferral of identity: If the definitional criteria used to identify members of a group were *cultural* criteria, then such acts of categorization, we thought, did not constitute racial acts, did not point to racial logic, nor produced races to order.[9]

While gesturing toward an acknowledgment that each deployment of racial categories was, in fact, a catachrestical instant—a moment productive of its own referent denoting what race might be within a particular context of use, and for a contingent purpose—we were simultaneously slow to admit the corollary implication that categories of race might then lack *any* specificity. We grasped that "race" was a portable, protean term, empty of stable referent, and without fixed dispositions in referencing, but a history of commitment to countering Enlightenment racisms posited on biology, anatomy, and color binarisms nonetheless raised biology to a position of central importance in deciding what constituted racisms and racial enactments: There evolved a concomitant reluctance to examine the ramifications of any recognition that the only referent of the term "race" was, in fact, its *function,* or *instrumentality* in a historical period.

That cognitive hesitancy, that lag, made it possible perhaps, among other reasons, to characterize certain historical periods—like the Middle Ages—as a kind of pre-political infancy, innocent of racial thinking or race-making (despite the otherwise retrograde character of feudal culture) because the master discourse ordering difference in the medieval period was, after all, *religion*: Religion was understood as properly belonging to the realm of culture, not biology, and culture did not produce authentic determinations of race nor racial formations. Whatever, then, medieval racisms-by-other-names might be called ("anti-Semitism"? "xenophobia"?), these names did not properly point to authentic, mature racial practices or race logic.

Since September 11, however, we have seen new definitions of race emerge pell-mell in practice—fantasy definitions flaunting a similarity to ideas on display in medieval romance—at airport security checkpoints, in the news media, and in public political discourse. Racial categories can now be, and have been, decided on the basis of religious identity (with "Muslims" at times defined as a race, even if, confusingly, African Americans—an older racial category—form the majority of U.S. Muslims). National/geopolitical origin can decide racial membership ("Middle Easterners" are sometimes grouped together as a race); and linguistic identifiers can also disclose one's race (Arabic-speakers might be assumed to be Arabs, though, confusingly, Christian Lebanese and Jews might also speak Arabic—cultural criteria, we note, sometimes clash in the new regimen of flexible definitions). Ever a moving target, "race" has emerged again—playing the role it had in the medieval literature I examine—as a thing that can be conferred on an individual by virtue of religious status, or membership in a community of culture, as much as by phenotype.[10]

In the palpable collapse between biological and cultural essentialisms as determinants of race, then—in the sudden demonstration that culture and biology might function very similarly in some circumstances, might be oddly interchangeable in how they are used, and might thus for all effective purposes be viewed as in-different—can be discerned also the return of the Middle Ages, and a medieval way of understanding human groups and of ordering and manipulating human differences in answer to exigent demands. To those who have held that races, racial practices, and race-making only began with the large-scale experiment of slavery in the fifteenth century and after, or with the advent of the modern state, or in the wake of scientific discourses on the body, the aftermath of September 11 returns the example of the Middle Ages. The making of races—the sudden entrance of specific groups of humans *into* race, through acts of identification and naming contingent on sociopolitical imperatives—returns this, our historical moment, to the medieval past, as it materializes the trace of the past in our present time.

Cultural fantasy does not evade but confronts history, as I show repeatedly through the chapters of my book. Fantasy engages with lived event, crisis and trauma, and conditions of exigency in ways that render intelligible to humans the incalculable and the incommensurate. In particular, as I argue in chapters 2 and 4, fantasy is unusually conducive to conceptualizations of race and race discourse: Race itself, after all, is a fantasy with fully material effects and consequences. Indeed, it is difficult to overestimate the material consequences of fantasy: Belief in the medieval fantasy of Prester John—I show in chapter 5—drove military field decisions that propelled the Fifth Crusade to abject failure in the thirteenth century; in the fifteenth century and after, the fantasy of John's existence beckoned to those who sought to open up new routes and territories, leading the way to settlement and colonization—new empires—in postmedieval eras. The fantasy of the medieval past itself, constructed and reinforced by postmedieval periods, delivers material effects: The fantasy of a pre-political, pre-racial, pre-nationalist, and pre-imperial time that is the Middle Ages—a zone of freedom evacuated of the dispositions bedeviling modernity and capital—has enabled the production of the very identities we know as modern, but at a distinct cost, and with material consequences for our understanding of race today.

Why, then, should medieval romance as cultural fantasy, and the cultural unconscious of modernity and postmodernity we call "the Middle Ages," matter? Or, to put it more tendentiously, why should a fictitious Muslim king whose skin color transmogrifies from black to white when he is Christianized, changing his racial markings and membership along with his religion, in a Middle English romance spuriously known as the *King of Tars*, matter, in the new dispensation of the twenty-first century, a time of cyberoptics, electronic warfare, and global flows of people, data, and capital? The answer lies in the spectacle of those who are busily defining race-and-religion once more for us—among a host of other definitions and calibrations—post–September 11, 2001.

In order for the present to pick its way, less than blindly, to the future—in order, perhaps, to have a future worth possessing—it is time, I think, to return to the past anew.

It has been suggested that romance is an evasion of history (and thus per-haps attractive to a people trying to evade the recent past). But I am more persuaded by arguments that find in it the head-on encounter with very real, pressing historical forces and the contradictions inherent in them as they came to be experienced by writers. Romance, an exploration of anxi-ety imported from the shadows of European culture, made possible the sometimes safe and other times risky embrace of quite specific, understand-ably human fears.

—Toni Morrison, *Playing in the Dark*

[Storytelling] is one of the most reassuring things. It seems its very basis is that it reassures you that there is a sense to things. . . . The story creates a form, and the form reassures [audiences] so that you can almost tell them any story. . . . there is something very powerful in stories, something that gives you security and a sense of identity and meaning.

—Wim Wenders, quoted by Tania Modleski,
differences, summer 1990

Historical trauma is transmitted complexly across generations.

—Peter Balakian, "A Memoir Across Generations:
Baby-Boom Suburbs, the Armenian Genocide,
and Scholarly Corruption in America"

CHAPTER I

⟦ꙮ⟧

Cannibalism, the First Crusade, and the Genesis of
Medieval Romance

ALMOST NINE HUNDRED years ago, between 1130 and 1139, the legend of
King Arthur erupted for the first time in full literary form in England,
elaborated out of hints and sketchy entries in written history and Celtic
legendary tradition by Geoffrey of Monmouth in an infamous, celebrated chronicle-history, the *Historia Regum Britannie*, or *History of the
Kings of Britain*.[1] Geoffrey's *Historia* was simultaneously celebrated and
infamous in part because its status as history was called into question,
then as now, by the pervasive aura that the *Historia* contrived of the fantastical, an aura more usually associated with the medieval literary genre
known as romance, than with historical writing.[2] Although the separation of genres distinguishing between the narration of history and the
narration of spectacular fiction was less secure in the twelfth century
than today (if such separation is secure today), conventions of historical
writing had nonetheless been sufficiently rehearsed by the twelfth century for historians among Geoffrey's near-contemporaries to respond

For their generous response to my argument in this chapter, I am particularly indebted to Leah
Marcus, Gene Vance, Sam Otter, Seth Lerer, Jane Chance, Barbara Harlow, Denise Spellberg,
Janadas Devan, Jim Garrison, Martha Newman, Elizabeth Weed, Ellen Rooney, Rick Russom,
Beth Bryan, Elizabeth Kirk, David Wallace, Sherron Knopp, Alison Case, Pete Wetherbee, Bio-
dun Jeyifo, Paul Sawyer, David Aers, and Susan Crane. Janadas Devan, in particular, saved the
argument from strategic error at a crucial early stage and was an essential presence through the
formative period of its conceptualization. Satya Mohanty and Pete Wetherbee rendered invaluable advice on the chapter's publication as an article. I am also grateful to audiences at Stanford,
Rice, Brown, and Cornell universities, and Williams College, for helpful responses to versions
of my argument. This chapter was written during an idyllic year at the Stanford Humanities
Center and first appeared in *differences* 10:1 (1998).

with "ambivalence," admiration, and outrage at the *Historia's* bold-faced inventions.[3]

It is because Geoffrey offers his narrative as a history—and invokes the authenticatory apparatus of historical narration, complete with the citation of earlier historical sources, provision of chronologies, onomastic and geographical descriptions, and a scrupulously causal and sequential recitation of Britain's past—that scholars today prefer to identify the emergence of medieval romance in general, and Arthurian romance in particular, with the more consistently fantastical creations of Chrétien de Troyes much later in the twelfth century (Chrétien's corpus was also written not in Latin but Old French or "Romanz," the language that subsequently came to lend its name to the genre). But scholars are generous in their agreement that romance *episodes* and *material* abound in the *Historia*, jostling ubiquitously against more palpably historical matter, and have been at odds to explain why romance in its earliest formations should thus mingle with history, beyond the simple consideration of adding to the historical text's appeal, even as it conspicuously undermines the historical text's claims to authenticity and authority.[4] Scholarly explanations have proliferated, most of which invoke Geoffrey's authorial ambitions, Norman patronage, and aims of ethnic and insular glorification.

To these critical accounts I would add another, of a differing but not inconsistent kind: an account that will address the articulation of fantasy and history in Geoffrey's text as varieties of cultural work negotiating—I will suggest—the shock of communal trauma in the period of European and Norman history preceding the *Historia's* appearance. Romance, I will argue, is the name of a developing narrational modality and apparatus in Geoffrey's text that coalesces from the cultural matrix at hand to effect specific forms of cultural rescue. The evolution of romance thereafter, through the Middle Ages and beyond, attests to the successful tenacity of the genre in harnessing the characteristic resources of a literary empire of fantasy, so that in the hands of able manipulators romance may offer a ready and—equally important—*safe* language of cultural discussion, and cultural transformation, in the service of crisis and urgent contingency. For the *Historia*, the special appeal and serviceability of romance-in-history is witnessed by the survival of an impressively large number of medieval manuscripts still extant today: 217 at latest count, in 1995, almost nine centuries after the *Historia's* popular and controversial inception.

THE VOCABULARY OF ROMANCE:
KING ARTHUR AND A TALE OF TWO GIANTS

Critics often agree that narrative interest in the *Historia* is organized to culminate in the appearance of King Arthur, whose life and achievements are typologically foreshadowed, biblical-fashion, by those of preceding British kings in the *Historia* and form the crowning fulfillment of earlier hints and guesses laid down as textual preparation for the Arthurian story that occupies one-fourth of the *Historia*'s narrative attention. Indeed, some have even detected a loss of textual interest after Arthur's exit from the narrative, after which, it is asserted, the *Historia* seems to wind fairly rapidly to a close. The performance of the Arthurian segment itself is marked by an extraordinary, fabricated tale of a double giant-killing enacted by King Arthur: a tale that eventually attracts the eye of every critic of the *Historia*, all of whom agree—even when they agree on nothing else—that the tale is an exemplary encapsulation of the quintessential features of romance. Perhaps the most memorable romance moment in the *Historia*'s Arthuriad, this drama of giant-killing would rapidly come to identify and inhabit the corpus of Arthurian romance after its creation, attracting attention and reworking, so that a version of it can still be found in Sir Thomas Malory's late-fifteenth-century prose romance at the close of the Middle Ages (*Works*, 1:54–56). The episode may be summarized as follows.

King Arthur, on his way to battle the forces of Rome, is temporarily diverted to Mont Saint-Michel to rescue Helena, an aristocratic maiden who is the daughter of Arthur's kinsman, Hoel of Brittany. The maiden has been borne away by a giant who has mysteriously emerged "ex partibus Hispaniarum"—generally translated as "from parts of Spain" ("from certain regions in Spain" [Thorpe, 237], "out of the parts of Spain" [Evans, 179], "from the shores of Spain" [Giles, 252]), despite the curious genitive plural of the place-name "Hispaniarum." The giant has already vanquished many would-be knightly rescuers by land and sea, casting down rocks on their ships like a very Polyphemus, and *eating* many captured knights while they were still half-alive (Wright, 1). Arthur defeats the monstrous cannibal in single combat, in a fight that is prefigured by an allegorical dream-vision. He arrives with only two companions at the giant's habitat on Mont Saint-Michel—too late to rescue Helena, who has mercifully died from terror as the giant was about to rape her—but successfully effects the rescue of Helena's aged nurse, a loyal crone who has been repeatedly raped by this barbarous savage ("inhumanus" [Wright,

1:118]). In addition to devouring humans, the giant is ostentatiously staged as a gory and hideous devourer of pigs.

After Arthur kills the giant with his sword Caliburn (the "Excalibur" beloved of Arthurian devotees) he has the giant decapitated, for exhibition of the monster's head to the king's army. In the aftermath Arthur reminisces: The monstrous strength of this giant of Mont Saint-Michel reminds Arthur of another giant Arthur had fought earlier in his career and also killed, "Rithonem gigantem in Arauio monte" (Wright, 1:119), which is usually translated as "the giant Ritho on Mount Aravius" (Thorpe, 240; see also Giles, 254)—a mountain that scholarship traditionally identifies as Mount Snowdon in Wales. Ritho had had a curious trophy, a cloak made from the beards of kings he had slain, and had demanded that Arthur skin off Arthur's own beard and send it to him. The giant had challenged the king to combat, on the terms that whoever proved the victor would have the beard of the vanquished and the cloak. Naturally, King Arthur had defeated Ritho and taken the giant's beard and trophy; till now, Arthur concludes, he had met no one more powerful. The king and his companions return to camp, the head of the giant of St. Michael's Mount is exhibited, and Arthur is praised as someone who has liberated the country from a great "maw"—that is, a bestial devourer (Wright, 1:119). Finally, a grieving Hoel has a church ("basilicam") built over Helena's grave, and to this day, we are told, the mountainous site has taken its name, "Helena's Tomb," from the maiden's tumulus (Wright, 1:119).

The source of this curious romance tale of two giants has sometimes been assumed to be Welsh or Breton folklore or local tradition (e.g., Tatlock, *Legendary History*, 203, 389), because of the Welsh (or Breton) elements that are an unquestionable part of the *Historia*'s fabric—a feature itself accounted for by the author's presumed ethnicity as a Welshman or Breton. It is on the basis of an assumed Welsh origin for the tale that "Mons Aravius," the home of the giant Ritho with the cloak of beards, has thus been cited in scholarly work—as recently as 1994 (Curley, 91)—as signaling Snowdon in Wales, although, interestingly, the episode of the two giants is in fact *missing* from the Welsh manuscript offered by Griscom and Jones as representing the Welsh and Irish manuscripts from which the *Historia* might supposedly have derived its materials (*Historia* [Griscom], 470–73).[5] Celtic provenance in this instance has been assumed, moreover, largely by default, in the apparent absence of other source evidence. That the *Historia* is the ground of a cunning hybridity of materials, all of which at different moments assume the character of a mask, has, however, been recognized. Where Geoffrey has openly declared a source as his authority, scholars have found none; where he has not acknowledged a debt, scholarship has discovered multiple instances of covert borrowing.[6] Critical analysis does well, therefore, to grant the *Historia*'s debt to diverse cultural materials: historical texts of the sixth to ninth centuries, such as Gildas's *De Excidio Britanniae* (On the ruin of Britain), Bede's *Historia Ecclesiastica Gentis Anglorum* (Ecclesiastical history of the English people), and the *Historia Brittonum* (History of the Britons), as well as a rich web of Welsh, Breton, biblical, and classical resources.

In that spirit of allowance, I want to suggest that folding into the vectors of the *Historia* meticulously mapped by scholarship is another, less commonly perceived layer of materials: a tissue of references deriving not from the distant past of Britain's history—the Celtic, Roman, and Saxon eras that furnish the surface limits of the *Historia*'s chronology—but from the events of the recent past of Geoffrey's time, from contemporary history. Though the *Historia* might deploy imaginative materials originally deriving from folklore, the Bible, or antiquity, its manipulation of its materials points well past their originary contexts, and toward the material reality of recent, disturbing historical events. That uncanny tale of the two giants issues less from the pressure of shadowy traditions than from an urgent residue of memory in active circulation in early-twelfth-century England and Europe, imported home from the shadows of the First Crusade. "Mons Aravius," I will argue, is merely a single node in an extraordinary mesh of coincidences in the *Historia* that can only be adequately read when we look in the direction of the Orient, and the territories and history of the First Crusade of European Christendom. In its skillful negotiation of history, memory, and cultural trauma, the story of two giants and mountains then becomes an allegorical performance of the very genesis of Arthurian and medieval romance out of the exigencies of historical occasion—a performance that signals how and why romance functions, and what romance is able to offer through the centuries that follow.

The story of King Arthur, I will show, begins in the East.

THE VOCABULARY OF HISTORY: THE FIRST CRUSADE AND THE NARRATION OF HORROR AND TRAUMA

In December 1098, seven months before the capture of Jerusalem by the militia of the First Crusade, Ma'arra an-Numan—a city in northern Syria—was sacked and its inhabitants put to the sword, one instance among many of the massacre of Muslims, Jews, and others enacted in the course of holy-war-cum-pilgrimage.[7] At Ma'arra, however, according to the three surviving eyewitness histories of the First Crusade written independently by Latin participants, the unthinkable happened: The crusaders roasted and ate the flesh of enemy corpses, an act of such unvitiated horror that all three chronicles are immediately driven to defend the cannibalism by invoking extreme famine as exigent explanation.[8]

Fulcher of Chartres's *Historia Hierosolymitana* (History of the expedition to Jerusalem) sounds a note of anguish in its description of the event:

> When the siege had lasted twenty days, our people suffered excessive hunger. I shudder to speak of it, because very many of our people, harrassed by the madness of excessive hunger, cut off pieces from the buttocks of the Saracens already dead there, which they cooked and chewed, and devoured with savage mouth, when insufficiently roasted at the fire. And thus the besiegers more than the besieged were tormented.[9]

The version in the *Gesta Francorum et Aliorum Hierosolimitanorum* (Deeds of the Franks and other pilgrims to Jerusalem), written by an anonymous crusader in the army of Bohemond, the controversial Norman leader of the Crusade, is more tersely brief and delivered without comment, though not without naturalizing explanation:

> While we were there, some of our men could not satisfy their needs, either because of the long stay or because they were so hungry, for there was no plunder to be had outside the walls. So they ripped up the bodies of the dead, because they used to find bezants hidden in their entrails, and others cut the dead flesh into slices and cooked it to eat.[10]

The narrative of the Provençal Raymond d'Aguiliers, the *Historia Francorum Qui Ceperunt Iherusalem* (History of the Franks who captured Jerusalem), details more explicitly the response of the crusaders and others who learned of the incident and reveals the consequences as the act reverberates in popular report, and the inhumanity of the Christians, attested by the marker of their anthropopagy, is confirmed through disseminating knowledge of their deed.

> Meanwhile, there was so great a famine in the army that the people ate most greedily the many already fetid bodies of the Saracens which they had cast into the swamps of the city two weeks and more ago. These

events frightened many people of our race, as well as strangers. On this account very many of us turned back. . . . But the Saracens and the Turks said on the contrary: "And who can resist this people who are so obstinate and inhuman, that for a year they could not be turned from the seige of Antioch by famine, or sword, or any other dangers, and who now feed on human flesh?" These and other most inhuman practices the pagans said exist among us. For God had given fear of us to all races, but we did not know it.[11]

Crusader cannibalism may also have erupted at Antioch, a few months before its advent at Ma'arra, but the documentary evidence here is of a less secure, more enigmatic kind, the principal evidence appearing in texts authored by cultural enemies of the Latins. Arabic chronicles by Ibn al-Qalanisi, Ibn Al-Athir, and Kemal al-Din, point to an outbreak of crusader cannibalism in Antioch after the capture and sack of the city in June 1098, following a debilitating siege of seven and a half months, when the occupation army found itself weakened by famine, demoralized by desertions and pestilence, and pincered between siege forces without—led by Karbuqa, atabeg of Mosul—and an undefeated Turkish garrison within that still held the citadel.[12] Another commentator hostile to the Latins memorializes the Antiochene cannibalism in suggestive if not entirely confirmatory terms. The Byzantine princess, Anna Comnena, writing a mid-twelfth-century biography of her father, Emperor Alexius I, features in her narrative a letter from Bohemond—a letter that has not survived, if it existed—in which Bohemond reports a devastating famine at Antioch, "a famine unsurpassed in living memory, so bad that most of us were even reduced to eating meats forbidden by the law" (Comnena, 358).[13]

The Latin participants themselves are reticent or equivocal on the subject of cannibalism at Antioch. A passage in the *Gesta* offering a long, poignant account of the horrors of the Antiochene famine ends on a cryptic note as the author rhetorically refuses or is unable to give a name to some crusader afflictions: "These and many anxieties and difficulties which I am unable to name [or mention, speak about: *nominare*] we suffered" (Hill, 62). Significantly, the *Gesta*'s admission of cannibalism at Ma'arra is also the most reticent among the Latin chronicles. One other eyewitness Latin source is important. A letter to Pope Paschal II, dated September 1099, from Laodicaea, and signed by three of the most prominent leaders of the crusading forces—Godfrey of Bouillon, Raymond de Saint-Gilles, and Daimbert, Archbishop of Pisa—confesses the famine at

Antioch was so extreme "that some might scarcely restrain themselves from eating human flesh" ("ut uix ab humanis dapibus se continerent aliqui" [Hagenmeyer, *Kreuzzugsbriefe*, 169]).

Curiously, in what seems here a report of self-vindication, an infinitesimal uncertainty creeps into the locution of these crusading leaders—an ambiguity pivoting on how the word "scarcely" (*uix*) performs. Suggesting (mostly) denial of wrongdoing, but also intimating the possibility of a tacit half-admission, "scarcely" here introduces a suspicion that hints at the authors' grammatical tact. Significantly, the letter confesses unambiguously to cannibalism at Ma'arra: "There was so great a famine in the army that the putrid bodies of the Saracens were now eaten up by the Christian people" ("Tanta fames in exercitu fuit, ut corpora Saracenorum iam fetentium a populo Christiano comesta sint" [Hagenmeyer, *Kreuzzugsbriefe*, 170]). That this necessary admission also troubled the Crusade leaders is detectable in a miniscule evasiveness here as well. The casual switching over to the passive voice at the point where the correspondents confess to the occurrence of cannibalism decides that those who cannibalize are displaced from their position as the grammatical subject of the main clause, while their victims—the rotting corpses of dead Saracens—occupy the foreground, presenting the imagination with an arresting spectacle that helps to retire the agency of the cannibalizing subject from the center of the addressee's attention.[14]

Ma'arra or Antioch: That a difference exists in the specified location of crusader cannibalism—the fact of cannibalism itself being the irreducible, repeating feature in the diverse documentary evidence of the period—is perhaps not so remarkable, given the vicissitudes of prolonged war, the many occasions of famine, vast cultural variation in narratorial methods, intelligibility, and purposes among the ethnic communities offering evidence, and the legendarily unscientific conditions of information retrieval in the Middle Ages. That being said, it is fair to add that scholars today might prefer to apportion more weight to the eyewitness Latin reports, since the enemy is likely to constitute an even less reliable witness of crusader atrocity than the crusaders themselves, whose reliability here at least extends to uncoerced if reluctant testimony of the guilt of their own community. The Latin narratives may also seem persuasive to some by virtue of their specular authority, as their cumulative and mutually corroborating testimony is evaluated. Finally, we might note that the ghastly, self-indicting nature of the offense possessed precisely the kind of memorable luridity that supported medieval habits of memory among the literate in the Latin communities.[15] Scholars agree, moreover, that the eyewitness Latin chronicles were written very soon after the First Crusade, when the memory of events would have been recent: Fulcher of Chartres is believed to have begun his between 1100 and 1102, a bare two to four years after Ma'arra (Munro, "A Crusader," 327; Runciman, 1:329; Peters, *First Crusade*, 23; Fink, 20); Raymond d'Aguiliers is thought to have completed his before 1105, and possibly as early as 1102 (Krey, *First Crusade*, 9; Raymond d'Aguiliers, *Historia*, 7); and a copy of the anonymous *Gesta* already appears at Jerusalem in 1101.[16] It is widely believed that the *Gesta* was begun at Antioch and perhaps completed as early as the end of 1099, after the battle of Ascalon—scarcely a year after Ma'arra (Hill, ix; Runciman, 1:328).

Whatever might seem authoritative or persuasive to a historian today, however, we can hardly deny that the material *facticity* of the cannibalism, in its minutiae of time and place, recedes from us, nine hundred years after the performance of the event. Furthermore, we have been taught to understand that an event is not itself necessarily or fully significative at the point of its occurrence: that events occur in historical time but are experienced as historical phenomena only by being placed in a signifying process determining their intelligibility. The phenomenality of crusader acts of cannibalism is thus realized at the precise moment of the passing of those acts into the discursive field of historical report, a practice that produces the meaning, and the existence, of those acts as historical occasions. Even as the facticity of the cannibalism is buried in, and dispersed across, the wavering details of time and place in late-eleventh-century Syria, therefore, the experienced reality of the cannibalism as a historical eruption is secured by the traumatic accounts of the eyewitness Latin documents that ostensibly function merely to report and witness. More than at any moment of their (f)actual occurrence, crusader acts of cannibalism were experienced as real after their inscription in the chief cultural documents of Crusade history and the crusader imaginary.

It is important to note, moreover, that the center of that experienced reality is the *trauma* which issues from anthropopagic atrocity: a trauma that slivers through the shock, torment, and anguish expressed by the narratives recording the drama of the unspeakable for peers and posterity. Though the taboo against cannibalism remains strongly in force in the twentieth-century West, it is virtually impossible for moderns to grasp the precise horror and dimensions of abhorrence, the trauma to the cultural imaginary of medieval Christendom caused by crusader cannibalism of the Muslim enemy. The crusaders were represented by their Pope as pilgrims enjoined to rescue from infidel pollution the sacred places of the Holy Land, not to visit the contagion of heathen pollution upon themselves. Death, including death by famine, was honorable, and repeatedly honored as martyrdom. Medieval Christians inhabited a world, moreover, in which eating was overlaid with sacramental, ritual, and symbolic significance, in which time itself was experienced as a pattern of fasts and feasts that shaped the liturgical year, with allowed and proscribed foods on particular days, occasions, and seasons: the regimen of a culture in which what one ate, how much or how little, and when, distinguished between sin and grace, orthodox and heretical practice, inclusion or exclusion in the fellowship of God and of Christian humanity. The apotheosis of that culture turned, of course, upon the symbolic eating of sacramental food, the body of the Eucharist—a sacred cannibalism, as the doctrine of real presence becomes consolidated in the eleventh and early twelfth centuries—the shared experience of which created and bound the identity of the individual Christian to a symbolic community that crossed divisions of country, region, ethnicity, family, tribe, caste, and race. Over and over, the crusaders describe themselves as a special transnational people defined by their religion and blazoned by the cross they bore: *gens Christiana,* a race/nation/community of Christian subjects constituting the privileged army of God (*exercitus Dei*).[17]

That eating God brought medieval Christians salvific reward was emphasized in doctrinal thinking from the mid-eleventh through the first quarter of the twelfth century, in the arguments of Lanfranc of Bec, Guitmund of Aversa, Alger of Liège, Rupert of Deutz, and others, doctrine shaped partly in response to the Berengarian controversy, but consolidating as a cornerstone of Eucharistic theology. Concomitantly, Eucharistic theology in the first decades of the twelfth century—as represented, for example, by Alger of Liège and Rupert of Deutz—stressed the *deification* secured by Eucharistic ingestion, an act that sealed the communicant's union with the Son and the Father. Twin convictions prevailed, then, in the late-eleventh and early-twelfth centuries, on what it meant to eat the flesh and blood of God: eating God would set one along the path of divinity, through union with godhead, as well as enact personal salvation.[18] In this context of what it meant to eat the living body of Christ, what might it mean to medieval Christians to eat the dead bodies of an infernal race—a race, moreover, whose practices and physical presence had been described, by Pope Urban II and the chroniclers, as polluting the holy places of Jerusalem? As a goad, the crusading address of Urban at the Council of Clermont in 1095, in the report of Robert the Monk, presents to the audience of clergy and laity the vision of an unbearable contamination: "Let the holy sepulchre of the Lord our Saviour, which is possessed by unclean nations, especially incite you, and the holy places which are now treated with ignominy and irreverently polluted with the filth of the unclean" (*RHC*, Occ., 3:728). In Baldric, Archbishop of Dol's account of Urban's homily, the medieval Pope describes Jerusalem as "reduced to the pollution of paganism and . . . withdrawn from the service of God" (*RHC*, Occ., 4:13). Fulcher of Chartres breaks into an ecstatic paean of rejoicing after the liberation of the Holy Sepulchre, and ends: "Cleansed from the contagion of the heathen . . . so long contaminated by their superstition, it was restored to its former rank" (Fulcher of Chartres, *Historia Hierosolymitana*, 305–6).[19]

Cannibalism per se was not, of course, unknown in medieval Europe. In the eleventh century, cannibalism attended famine in England in 1005 and 1069, France in 1031, and Europe in 1016 and 1022.[20] The eating of native European/Christian flesh was possibly less troubled by a problematics of bodily and spiritual pollution and injury to the imagined community of Christendom than the eating of foreign infidel flesh—at least, there is evidence to suggest that by the thirteenth century a regimen of excoriation and discipline might be imagined by a medieval pope and implemented for the infliction of this particular horror upon one's own kind.[21] But it has also been observed that the eschatological teleology of the Judaeo-Christian tradition functions to render cannibalism an especial abomination, committed on any race: "Ultimately the importance placed on the body led Jews and Christians to view human sacrifice and cannibalism with a fundamentally disproportionate horror" (Tannahill, 32); "Jews and Christians . . . are dedicated to the proposition that eating the dead is worse than murder" (34). Bynum points out that "cannibalism—the consumption in which survival of body is most deeply threatened . . . is the ultimate barbarism, the ultimate horror" for early Christians (*Resurrection*, 55): early Christian theorists decisively rejected any possibility that Christians might commit cannibalism.[22]

Even under the reified conditions of a uniquely sanctioned, doctrinally recommended Eucharistic cannibalism—the only circumstances in which human sacrifice and cannibalism are conceivable in Christianity, and conceivable *precisely* because of intensive mediation by a prolonged process of doctrinal reification strategically utilizing the attractions of paradox and contradiction—a residual unease might be sensed to persist: traceable, perhaps, in the periodic eruptions of theological dissent and heterodox repudiations that haunted Eucharistic discourse of the twelfth and thirteenth centuries.[23] The great texts of medieval literature, into which are encoded the responses of culture to a range of imagined conduct, confirm an overwhelming cultural revulsion to cannibalism. From the *Liber Monstrorum* and *Beowulf* in northwestern Europe of the eighth century to Dante's *Commedia* in the fourteenth-century Mediterranean, the flesh-eating cannibal is presented as a subhuman, grotesque demon: a misshapen Cyclops of hideous grisliness; nightmarish descendant of the line of Cain, like the bestial Grendel and his dam; or the monstrous, abhorrent devil himself, crushing sinners between his jaws and skinning them in the innermost circle of hell (*Inferno*, canto 34).[24]

Concomitantly, medieval texts of social history and popular tradition cannot conceive of the European Christian as a cannibal: Instead, they enact the supposition that the act of cannibalism decisively constructs a living creature as something other than Christian, European, or human. Charlemagne's twelfth capitulary, in mandating death for cannibalism, routinely equates the cannibal with the witch or sorcerer (Tannahill, 97); and Jews, in one late-twelfth-century incident at Bray, in France—an incident typical of the medieval blood-libel against the Jews—are accused of crucifying a boy to use his blood for their Passover bread (Tannahill, 95).[25] Even medieval Hebrew literature classes the cannibal with the magician (*mekhasef*) or witch (*mekhashefah*), who might be born with teeth and a tail (*Encyclopaedia Judaica*, 11:707–8). In fourteenth-century Scotland, wild men, savage tribes, or cave dwellers might be cannibals (Tannahill, 104); but the Hereford *mappamundi* of the late thirteenth century prefers to consign the race of anthropopagi safely to northeast Asia. Suggestively, Jon Block Friedman traces the hagiographic tradition of St. Christopher—whose legend had immense popular currency in Western Europe—back to a founding allegory in the Acts of Andrew and Bartholomew among the Parthians, in the Ethiopic *Contendings of the Apostles*, an allegory that features the repudiation of cannibalism at the point of entrance into the Christian community. A pagan cannibal called "Abominable" is converted to Christianity, ceases to be a cannibal, and is rewarded by the apostle Andrew with the new and blessed name of "Christianus" (Friedman, 70–75).[26]

Plainly, the record of the Middle Ages suggests that the charge of cannibalism is one of those instrumentally useful technologies of definition by which the malignant otherness of cultural enemies and outcasts can be established and periodically renewed. Witches, Jews, savages, Orientals, and pagans are conceivable as—indeed, must be—cannibals; but in the twelfth-century medieval imaginary, the Christian European subject cannot, and must not. Indeed, Latin, the language of Western European Christendom in the eleventh century, did not originally have a word for "cannibal" and needed to be furnished with one by the Greek: Literally a sin that could not be named, an obscenity that was nameless as well as unspeakable, cannibalism to the medieval Christian was that dehumanizing, monstrous condition which canceled out the coordinates of recognizably human identity, and reduced the sentient to the subhuman.

An atrocity that is conscionably unthinkable and that is not acknowledged by a language and cultural procedures for its discussion—only for its denial and evacuation from culture—soon ceases to be consciously thought and discussed. Accordingly, the eyewitness narratives record crusader cannibalism, then move on in silence, obligations to truth accomplished; the narratives greet only common-garden varieties of sin with discursive attention. Fulcher of Chartres inveighs against "avarice," "pride," "dissipation," "rapaciousness," and—Fulcher's bête noire—cowardice and desertion among the crusaders. Raymond d'Aguiliers thunders against "sloth and avarice," "despair," behavior that "displeased the Lord," "idleness and riches," "adultery," "sloth and fear," ignoring of God, "filthy deeds," and various unspecified sins. The *Gesta*—whose textual unconscious is the most perceptibly troubled by the cannibalism—weighs in against lust with Christian and pagan women. If the textual foreground of the chronicles is preoccupied with such commonly castigated sins as sexual misdemeanors, an oddly pervasive obsession with food nonetheless hovers in the recesses and interstices of the narratives: a fascinated obsession with the details, quantities, excess, or lack of food and drink, and a concomitant attachment to metaphors of ingestion, hunger, and devoration. The *Gesta*, whose description of the cannibalism at Ma'arra is the most compressed and taciturn of the three texts, never fails to observe punctually the presence or absence of food, or to mention famine, and, in one singularly vivid choice of figuration, describes the crusader forces as "thirsting and craving for the blood of Turks" (25).[27]

That the atrocity of cannibalism could not find adequate discursive voicing was consonant with the repeated and punctilious expression of concern with crusader sins. The crusade was "a religious expedition, undertaken for the sake of the souls of the participants as well as to free

Jerusalem" (Porges, 14); thus the participants' state of sinfulness or grace would consciously be scrutinized and periodically discussed. However, questions of morality were also necessarily subject to military imperatives of morale: "morale was vital," since its loss, in conditions of war, might mean "disaster, the destruction of the Christian army" (Porges, 9)—an army whose constantly thinning ranks, as Raymond's chronicle avers, had been further reduced by the popular report of crusader cannibalism.[28] A blockage to official discussion of the cannibalism in the three eyewitness chronicles also owes something to the fact that the patrons of the chroniclers were the great military leaders of the Crusade, with whom responsibility for the army of God ultimately rested. Fulcher of Chartres was chaplain to Baldwin of Boulogne, later count of Edessa, and subsequently the first crowned king of the Latin Kingdom of Jerusalem. The author of the *Gesta* was a subordinate, perhaps a vassal, of the Norman Bohemond, first prince of Antioch, who became legendarily famous throughout all Latin Christendom as a crusading hero, after his return to Europe and marriage to the daughter of the king of France. Raymond d'Aguiliers was chaplain to Raymond de Saint-Gilles, count of Toulouse, leader of the Provençals and close associate of the Papal Legate, Adhémar of Le Puys, and arguably the Pope's and the Byzantine Emperor's preferred delegate among the crusading barons. Indeed, since both Bohemond and Raymond de Saint-Gilles are consistently placed by a variety of reports at Ma'arra an-Numan, the integrity of the chroniclers is glimpsed in their very mention of crusader cannibalism at all.[29] Finally, even as the chronicles described the agents of Crusade history, to whom their authors were linked by bonds of dependency, vassalage, or patronage, they also explicitly functioned as the ideological instruments of their patrons and of ethnic partisanship. The chronicle of Raymond d'Aguiliers is unabashedly a narrative advertisement in the service of the Provençal cause, which it champions and promotes with unremitting energy; and the historian A. C. Krey ("Neglected Passage") argues that the *Gesta* expressly circulated in twelfth-century Europe as an ideological instrument in Bohemond's bid for self-legitimation and the legalization of his retention of the principality of Antioch.

One final aspect of the significance of crusader cannibalism deserves attention. In medieval culture, eating has *political* as well as religious valence, as amply demonstrated in the feasts hosted by the great lords of medieval history and literature, in which the display and conspicuous consumption of food function to mark the social status, economic position, and political or military power of he who provisions and he who eats. That eating is an exercise in power is visible even in sacramental communion—a cannibalism that guarantees the acquisition of divine power and status through union with godhead. The self-defilement and pollution enacted by crusader cannibalism of Muslim cadavers is, then, complexly overdetermined. While eating an infernal race might overwhelmingly invoke the horror of infernal contagion to medieval Christians accustomed to the sacred politics of eucharistic ingestion, the very act of eating your enemy is also a potent demonstration of political power. Indeed, the tremulous question posed by Raymond d'Aguiliers—a question, we note, he places in the mouths of the enemy—unites crusader cannibalism with triumphant military invasion: "And who can resist this people who are so obstinate and inhuman, that for a year they could not be turned from the siege of Antioch by famine, or sword, or any other dangers, and who now feed on human flesh?"

In the realm of the political, what after all is cannibalism but a hideously somatic literalization of the language of military conquest, which encompasses how successful conquerors swallow up and absorb unto themselves the land and possessions of the defeated? The eminently successful First Crusade installed the crusader states and fiefdoms of "Outremer" as colonies of Latin Europe overseas, in the territories of Syria, Lebanon, and Palestine taken from the Turks, Armenians, Jews, and Byzantines. The description of the crusader territories as the first colonies in the East created by medieval Europe's experiment with empire is not a taxonomic moment from recent history or political culture: no less than Guibert of Nogent, writing in the twelfth century, names the Latin Kingdom of Jerusalem a new colony ("novae coloniae") of holy Christendom (*RHC*, Occ., 4:245). Guibert's twelfth-century usage of the vocabulary of colonial conquest and settlement—vocabulary deriving, of course, from antique examples of empire—antedates, by more than half a millenium, Europe's "high-imperialist" use, in the eighteenth and nineteenth centuries, of the Roman Empire's example. As the historian Joshua Prawer notes, "The definition of the Crusades as a colonial movement . . . dates back several centuries to a time when this term had no pejorative connotation" (*Crusaders' Kingdom*, ix).[30] Divine sanction for the seizure and occupation of foreign lands issues from no less an authority than Pope Urban himself, in Robert the Monk's report of Urban's crusading address at Clermont:

> This land which you inhabit, shut in on all sides by the seas and surrounded by the mountain peaks, is too narrow for your large population; nor does it abound in wealth; and it furnishes scarcely food enough for

its cultivators. Hence it is that you murder one another, that you wage war, and that frequently you perish by mutual wounds. Let therefore hatred depart from among you, let your quarrels end, let wars cease, and let all dissensions and controversies slumber. Enter upon the road to the Holy Sepulchre; wrest that land from the wicked race, and subject it to yourselves (*RHC*, Occ., 3:728).

By the third book of his *Historia Hierosolymitana*, Fulcher is able to depict the Latin colonies in the Levant as blessed examples of successful colonial assimilation and governance, in an extraordinary narrative portrait that has no parallel before the recognized ages of modern European expansion:

> Consider, I pray, and reflect how in our time God has transformed the West into the East. For we who were Occidentals now have been made Orientals. He who was a Roman or a Frank is now a Galilaean, or an inhabitant of Palestine. One who was a citizen of Rheims or of Chartres now has been made a citizen of Tyre or of Antioch. We have already forgotten the places of our birth; already they have become unknown to many of us, or, at least, are unmentioned. Some already possess here homes and servants which they have received through inheritance. Some have taken wives not merely of their own people, but Syrians, or Armenians, or even Saracens who have received the grace of baptism. . . . One cultivates vines, another the fields. . . . Different languages, now made common, become known to both races, and faith unites those whose forefathers were strangers. . . . Those who were strangers are now natives; and he who was a sojourner now has become a resident. Our parents and relatives from day to day come to join us, abandoning, even though reluctantly, all that they possess. For those who were poor there, here God makes rich. Those who had few coins, here possess countless besants; and those who had not had a villa, here, by the gift of God, possess a city. Therefore, why should one who has found the East so favorable return to the West?. . . . You see, therefore, that this is a great miracle, and one which must greatly astonish the whole world. Who has ever heard anything like it? (Fulcher of Chartres, *Historia Hierosolymitana*, 748–49)[31]

Despite the "miracle" of successful overseas colonization accomplished by the First Crusade, however, the memory of Christian cannibals, officially lodged in the documents of the Crusade, seems to have remained; an anxious, undigested presence. Within a decade of Ma'arra, secondary historians in Europe, working at geographical and temporal removes from the events and personages of the Crusade, and thus free of the dependencies bedeviling the eyewitness historians, began to give the problem cultural attention. Of the secondary histories, possibly the most important and one of the earliest is Guibert of Nogent's *Gesta Dei per Francos* (1106? 1109?), whose advertised subject—the deeds of God through the medium of the Franks—hints at the palliative solution it would find. Guibert, who in his preface, and at the beginning of Books 4 and 5, discusses the problem of not being an eyewitness himself, equivocally and parenthetically admits the facticity of crusader cannibalism but makes the admission in such a way that the *rumor* of cannibalism is the impression that remains, and takes center stage—a rumor, moreover, that flatteringly expresses fear in the cultural enemy.[32] As Lewis Sumberg is prompted to remark, his mise-en-scène for the cannibalism intimates a smidgeon of anxiety: "The almost-frantic manner in which the Abbé of Nogent seeks to dispel this vicious *oui-dire*, would seem to suggest that it was generally believed by a large number of his contemporaries" (242).

More importantly, Guibert rehearses another solution to the problem, one that would ultimately find elaborate ramification in the crusade cycles of the *chansons de geste* or heroic epics of the late twelfth century and after.[33] The historian strategically introduces an internal difference into the army of God. Separating out a special category of the poor—called, he claims, "Tafurs" in a barbarian language or "Trudennes" by the Latins— Guibert presents this subaltern class of useful, ragged workers as that segment of the army which specifically commits the cannibalism at Ma'arra and anywhere else ("et sicubi alias"), a deed performed—he magnanimously adds—in secret and as rarely as possible (*RHC*, Occ., 4:242). To seal his association of cannibalism with these unfortunates, Guibert then offers an indelibly picturesque tableau in which "Tafurs" are shown to roast the body of a Turk in full, melodramatic view of the enemy. His conjuration of a shadow army within the main Christian army, set off from the larger body of crusaders by poverty and perhaps ethnicity, with blame assigned to that subaltern category of the poor thus produced, is perhaps a logical solution for a culture as stratified by caste as medieval culture.[34] The shadow army is even supplied with its own "king" of Norman origin, like Baldwin I of Jerusalem, but in inverted image—the "king" of the "Tafurs" is a rogue personage who has fallen in status, having become a foot soldier by virtue of having lost his horse ("ex equite tamen pedes factus"), and thus traveling in the opposite direction from Baldwin, who had risen to the kingdom from the County of Edessa by the accord and election of the council of Jerusalem, on his brother's death. The two parallel bodies of crusaders are contrastingly partnered, with Guibert volunteering that it is the "Tafurs," more than the great leaders of the crusading army, who are especially feared by the Turks (*RHC*, Occ., 4:242).

Despite Guibert's intellection, his crusading history visibly takes liberties with eyewitness evidence here, and at key junctures elsewhere. Guibert's baroque rendition of Urban's crusading address, for instance—an account deeply mired in its own elaborate understanding of Revelations' eschatological vision, splendid rhetoric, and highly involved logical and syntactical display—bears little surface resemblance to other extant accounts. His recapitulation of history, moreover, conspicuously tends to shift around responsibility among groups of historical actors. Where Fulcher's chronicle and the *Gesta* record, for example, that the crusaders cut open enemy bodies to search for bezants, Guibert has Muslims perform the inquisitional surgery instead on Christian victims.[35] Most tellingly, Guibert's singling out of a special subaltern category in conjunction with the cannibalism is not attested by either the eyewitness narratives or the crusading leaders' letter to Paschal, all of which assign blame, in no uncertain terms, to "*our* people," or "the *Christian* people" (my emphasis), a single body of crusaders sharing responsibility for atrocity as well as victory. This is not to suggest that, unlike Guibert, the eyewitness chronicles were blind to the poor in the Christian forces or to the heterogeneous composition of the crusading army. Fulcher discusses both the Latin crusaders and populations in Syria and Palestine by ethnicity and language, and Raymond d'Aguiliers gives the poor meticulous, frequent attention—without, however, any discovery of Tafurs or of a legend of cannibalism that is the specialized property of the Christian poor.

In the event, the materialization of scapegoats within the ranks of crusaders, though an intelligible innovation, seems not to amount to an adequate cultural strategy. Representing perhaps an intermediate stage of figural development between the eyewitness histories and the cultural negotiations to come, it is unsatisfactory to the extent that Guibert's intervention yet leaves the taint of a dehumanizing atrocity linked to recognizably Christian pilgrims on a spiritual mission of rescue: a reminder that even in the early twelfth century, the writing of history as a serious endeavor obligated to the attestation of veracity had conventions and circumscriptions that Guibert the historian was required ultimately to respect.[36] It remained for the unresolved matter of Christian cannibalism to be taken up again two decades later, by a historian-cum-romancer in Anglo-Norman England less bound by authorial decorum: Geoffrey of Monmouth.

History into Romance:
King Arthur Materializes at the
Vanishing Point of Historical Narration

Intensive historical writing follows "a crisis in national affairs" that alienates a people from its past, suggested R. W. Southern in his 1973 presidential address to the Royal Historical Society. Thus the Norman conquest of 1066, Southern reasons, was followed by a resurgence in historical narratives one generation later that worked to reinstall order and intelligibility by retelling the past. If invasion of the *domus* produces a disorder that requires one kind of cultural work, extraterritorial invasion—the invasion of foreign lands—requires another: especially when that foreign invasion also renders the invaders foreign to themselves, and denatured, by their own unrecognizable and self-transformative performance. It is possible to glimpse a fantasmatic hallucination of what the crusader-cannibals had become, one generation after their alienating offense, in Geoffrey of Monmouth's nexus of the Norman and European cultural imaginary: a distorted, miasmic giant in the Arthuriad of Geoffrey's *Historia*, a giant whose nightmarish cannibalism is the unmistakable mark of his disproportionate and inhuman monstrosity. In the hallucinatory figure of a giant in whom monstrosity and power—including the power to eat your enemy—are conjoined, atrocity and pollution can be seen to work their transformative power in dreadful tandem. The giant monster is shockingly and violently located where no monsters should be, suddenly materializing without explanation at a renowned pilgrim site in medieval Europe: Mont Saint-Michel, lodged in the pilgrim heart of Europe itself, a holy place whose very prominence retrieves the memory of another celebrated pilgrim territory where no monsters or monstrous acts should also have been. Named after Michael, the patron saint of warriors and a favorite of the Normans, Mont Saint-Michel in Normandy is magically a name that recalls war in tandem with pilgrimage, and serves as a fitting index to summon the memory of a crusading venture.[37]

It is commonplace, of course, to find cultural enemies depicted as giants—or cannibals—in the literatures of many nations and eras, especially in narratives of territorial invasion, conquest, and settlement.[38] It takes a crisis of subtle alienation, however, to produce *oneself* as a giant of monstrous proportions, requiring the intervention of a cultural savior plucked from the distant past (an older, intact representative of cultural identity) to rescue the contemporary past, and, with giant heroism defeating gigantic horror, restore proportionate dimensions, and thus secure the possession of a right-sized future. A crisis of subtle alienation requires, and discovers, a medium of subtle transformation: not the cultural mechanisms of history, with its known circumscriptions, but the powers of the magical genre of culture, known as romance.

The figural transformation effected in the Arthurian tale of St. Michael's Mount is aided by the fact that the crusaders were already giants of a physical and spiritual kind even before they were rendered disproportionate to themselves by their acts. Anna Comnena and Arab chroniclers exclaim over the—to them—impressive physical size of the Latins, Anna representing the Norman leader Bohemond as a veritable behemoth: "The sight of him inspired admiration, the mention of his name terror. . . . His stature was such that he towered almost a full cubit over the tallest men. . . . there was a hard, savage quality in his whole aspect, due, I suppose, to his great stature . . . even his laugh sounded like a threat to others" (Comnena, 422). According to the historian Orderic Vitalis, Bohemond was named by his father, Robert Guiscard, from the legend of a gigantic man called Bohemond ("fabula de Buamundo gigante" [Orderic, 6:71]), thought by Guiscard an apt name for "his own giant son" (Yewdale, 5). Anna reports with hostility that Bohemond's nephew, Tancred, also saw himself as "a mighty irresistible giant, with his feet firmly planted on earth" (Comnena, 440). The mammoth mission assigned to the crusaders by their Pope—a near-impossible undertaking against overwhelming odds—simultaneously conferred on this large body of Christians a certain moral and spiritual gigantism, a stature underscored by the crusading privileges, indulgence, and special protections bestowed by their Pope, and unavailable to lesser Christians.

If the cannibal of Mont Saint-Michel and King Arthur both constitute figurations of European culture imagined at its demonic and sublime extremes, a cleavage is also visible at the local level in the linguistic presentation of the monster's imagined origin. Geoffrey's giant has come to threaten Europe from out of "Hispania," curiously rendered in this episode of giant-killing as a genitive plural, "Hispaniarum"—a covert pointing, I suggest, to a double referent for the word, beyond the obvious referent of "Spain." Coincidentally, "Hispania" is also a geographical designation that routinely appears in the eyewitness chronicles of the First Crusade to signify the interior regions of Syria. Though sometimes given as "Spain" in translations, the crusading leaders' letter to Paschal announces, unmistakably, that the Christians "entered into the interior of Hispania" after the cannibalism at Ma'arra (Hagenmeyer, *Kreuzzugsbriefe*, 170) and before reaching Jerusalem; and Raymond d'Aguiliers' narrative plainly refers to the regions around Ma'arra and Antioch when it mentions Raymond of Toulouse's, and Bohemond's and Robert of Flanders's, foraging expeditions into "Hispania" for food (Raymond d'Aguiliers, *"Liber,"* 101; Peters, *First Crusade*, 153, 154; see also 159, passim). As Tatlock observes, the name "Hispania" is "often applied vaguely to Moslem regions in Asia Minor and eastward" ("Contemporaneous Matters," 219).[39]

Concealed in the genitive plural, then, lies a trace of the double origin of gigantic monstrosity. The cannibal comes from within Europe—ostensibly Spain—and also from the interior regions of Syria, from the territorial history of the First Crusade. Not only are the origins of the cannibal linked to Muslim-associated geography, but the giant is depicted in a grisly scene as devouring pigs: the most insultingly derogatory and offensive metaphor that Geoffrey's narrative can find with which to signify Muslims, since pork is a chief marker in Islam for unclean and forbidden meats, with explicit prohibitions in the sacred text of the Koran against its consumption (e.g., *Koran*, 2:3, 6:146, 16:115). To equate Muslims with pigs, moreover, reduces the detested cultural enemy to the level of the subhuman and bestial, and perhaps fugitively expresses, in a covert superscription, a wishful excision of atrocity.[40] For cannibalism is the single traumatic atrocity at which the crusade narratives evince real horror: Homicides and genocides are ideologically justifiable under the circumstances, and massacres of the enemy so bloody that the crusaders wade ankle-deep in gore—as had occurred at the conquest of Jerusalem—are merely described noncommittally, and even with approval, by the eyewitness chronicles.

But what of Arthur's memory of a *second* giant that he had earlier fought, Ritho "in Arauio monte"? Translations usually render the home of Ritho as "Mount Aravius"—signifying Snowdon in Wales, as we have said—since the two moments where the name of the mountain appears in the *Historia* (once in the accusative, "super montem Arauium" in the prophecies of Merlin, and once in the ablative, in the giant-killing), urge a second-declension noun of "Aravius" in the nominative. Observe, however, that if we were to treat "Aravius" not as a proper noun but as an adjective that declines identically to a noun—a grammatical alternative—

"mons Aravius" can plausibly be read as "the Arabian mountain," which would return the giant Ritho, like the giant of St. Michael's Mount, to an origin in the Orient.[41] This giant Ritho collected the beards of kings, which he wore as an insolent, emblematic trophy of his superordinate masculinity in overcoming monarchs, a superior species of men.[42] Commenting on the bizarre collection of kings' beards, Tatlock points to the perplexing fact that Normans of Geoffrey's period in fact rarely wore beards, as observed in the Bayeux tapestry and by William of Malmsbury (*Legendary History*, 349).

Indeed, beardless Latins (and especially the Norman Bohemond) were much remarked on in the Orient during the time of the First Crusade, since the beard functioned in the Levant then, as now, as an exhibitional symbol of masculinity—"the characteristic feature of a man, the glory of the face, the chief dignity of man," as the great Latin historian of Outremer, William of Tyre, intones (1:480).[43] Among hierarchical distinctions of dress and appearance introduced into the crusader colonies, Prawer ("Medieval Colonialism," 29–30) singles out the possession or absence of a beard as a powerful and highly visible separator demarcating native subjects (the ruled) from Latins (the rulers). In Europe, the beard also circulated as a symbol of racial-religious difference: Orderic Vitalis quotes Bishop Serlo of Séez in Normandy who, in preaching at Carentan in Easter, 1105, in the presence of Henry I, rudely likened bearded men to "goats" and "Saracens" (Orderic, 6:64, 66).[44]

Significantly, however, one renowned Norman king and crusader did wear a beard—which, according to a humorous anecdote, he was almost compelled to lose. William of Tyre reports that Baldwin, the first crowned monarch of the Latin kingdom of Jerusalem, successfully induced his father-in-law, the Armenian Gabriel, to part with thirty thousand gold bezants—coins, we note, that in the Orient were called "micheles" (see n. 37)—by claiming that he, Baldwin, had mortgaged his beard to his retainers as a pledge for the payment of their services: a beard which—now that he was in financially straightened circumstances—he was required to tender to his men, in fulfillment of his word. So horrified was the Armenian at the imagined injury to the symbolic manhood of his son-in-law, then Count of Edessa, that Gabriel parted with the micheles rather than allow the monster of economic duress to strip the emblem of masculinity off a redoubtable leader of men (William of Tyre, 1:478–81).[45] We might, then, read Arthur's anecdote of a second giant—a giant who only exists in the memory of a fictional king who, like the historical Baldwin, kept *his* beard and dignity—as furnishing a supporting layer of symbolic figuration. For not only does atrocity turn a man into a monster—and here, a personified monstrosity that collects the symbolic pelts of the defeated in the Orient as grisly trophies—but monstrosity redounds to destroy the visible honor, the manhood and dignity, also of Christian kings, iconic representatives of European culture at its apex. Arthur, who has aptly found these two giants the mightiest creatures he has ever fought, is summoned from an earlier cultural order to vindicate the humanity, masculinity, and cultural honor of Christian kings and knights, by his double defeat of symbolic beasts from the Arabian mountains.[46]

That Arthur is ostentatiously styled as a Norman king, presiding over a Norman court, is an old axiom of criticism on the *Historia*, antedating even the insight that Arthur's materialization as a cultural hero furnished the ruling elites of Anglo-Norman England with a cultural mythology rivaling in ideological magnitude the fabulous legacy of Charlemagne in France (Paton [Evans, xxi]; Gerould, 45; Southern ["Classical Tradition," 193–94]; Tatlock [*Legendary History*, 311]; see also Fleischman, 289). The various Anglo-Norman magnates to whom different manuscripts of the *Historia* are dedicated underscores, moreover, ambitions in cultivating not only individual patrons of proven munificence but more especially an attachment to the interests of a *ruling group* of Norman elites. Thus the conflicting dedications of the *Historia*'s manuscripts—variously to Robert, Earl of Gloucester, supporter of his half-sister, the empress Matilda, and her son, Henry of Anjou, for succession to the throne of Matilda's father, Henry I; to Robert and Waleran, Count of Meulan and sometime supporter of King Stephen, Matilda's cousin in the opposing camp of the royal succession struggle; and even, astonishingly, to both Stephen *and* Robert—are less perplexing when read as marks of the *Historia*'s shrewd evasion of political differences within the Anglo-Norman ruling caste and careful preferment of a cultural mythology that is serviceable to the group.[47]

The Anglo-Norman royal family and ruling caste were, of course, in the first rank of the military leaders of the Crusade, a movement dominated by the Normans of England, France, and Southern Italy. The eldest son of William the Conqueror—Robert Curthose, Duke of Normandy—was the highest-ranking Norman on crusade, and headed an Anglo-Norman contingent that included Stephen of Blois, husband to Robert's sister, Adela; Odo, Bishop of Bayeaux, the half-brother of the Conqueror; Robert's cousin, Robert Count of Flanders; Ralph de Gael, former Earl of Norfolk; Godehilde of Tosni, the first wife of Baldwin of

Boulogne; and other prominent members of the baronial families and landowners of Norman England (Tyerman, 15–16). More significantly, unlike Stephen of Blois, who infamously turned back at Antioch, Robert of Normandy and Robert of Flanders—often referred to collectively, in the *Gesta*, as "the counts"—returned from the Orient only after the successful close of the Crusade and were present at Ma'arra during the crusader cannibalism (Hill, 78; Ralph of Caen, *RHC*, Occ., 3:674; Albert of Aix, *RHC*, Occ., 4:448).

Intimate relations between the royal family of England and the politics and personages of the East continued after the Anglo-Normans returned. Robert of Normandy's sister, Adela, Countess of Blois, championed Bohemond's cause with her brother, Henry I of England, when the Prince of Antioch sought aid in Europe against the Emperor Alexius (Runciman, 2:48); and, according to Orderic Vitalis, she generously provisioned the marriage celebrations of Bohemond to the daughter of King Philip of France in 1106 (Orderic, 3:182). Her son, Stephen, King of England after Henry, married the niece of King Baldwin I of Jerusalem. In 1108 Robert of Normandy's son, William Cliton, a newly arrived crusader in the East, conducted a successful raid on "a wealthy Arab princess who was jouneying . . . from Arabia to Damascus" (Runciman, 2:97); William was briefly married in 1123 to Sibylla, daughter of Fulk of Anjou, the third King of Jerusalem. In 1118 Robert of Normandy's chaplain, Arnulf, crowned his career by becoming Patriarch of Jerusalem (David, 217) and, with Baldwin II, became instrumental in shaping political culture and policy in the Latin Kingdom (Runciman, 2:82–86). In 1119 the heir to the throne of England—William, the son of Henry I—was married to another daughter (Matilda) of Fulk of Anjou and Jerusalem. In 1128 Hugh of Payens, founder and Grand Master of Knights of the Order of the Temple in Jerusalem, visited England as Baldwin's representative on a recruitment and propaganda campaign (Tyerman, 23, Runciman, 2:179); and in that same year the empress Matilda of England married Geoffrey, the son of Fulk of Anjou and Jerusalem (Runciman, 2:178; Chibnall, 56–57), a crusading monarch who had given three of his children, at different times, to the royal family of England.

That a vigorous fascination with the Orient, and crusading lore, would persist and actively circulate in Anglo-Norman England in the opening decades of the twelfth century, with passage to and from the Holy Land, and close relations with the East—fueled moreover by "the widespread phenomenon of Crusade propaganda" which continually urged "European contributions of money and of men to support the newly-found Crusader states in the Levant" (Seidel, 383)—might reasonably be credited.[48] Copies of the *Gesta Francorum* were disseminated by Bohemond's supporters in 1105–6, to fan the legendary crusader's reputation and legitimate his claims to Antioch, according to the historian A. C. Krey ("Neglected Passage," 74–75). Fulcher's chronicle circulated in Europe, and was used as a source by Guibert de Nogent, Ekkehard of Aura, and Ralph of Caen, among others, for their own writing of Crusade histories. The *Gesta* found its way to England and was adjusted for Anglo-Norman reputations: Rosalind Hill notes that a revision of the *Gesta*, in a twelfth-century hand, promotes Robert of Normandy (Hill, xxxix), who is also promoted by an editor of the revision, whose work in three copies—all of English origin—survive alongside an abbreviated text of the *Gesta* in England that "shows its devotion to the Duke of Normandy still more" (xl).

The busy production, revision, and copying of numerous histories of the Crusade, in the first decades of the twelfth century—along with intercalations of Crusade material in biographies, national and regional histories, and texts of other kinds—suggest that the meaning and implications of the First Crusade had not yet settled, and were still being actively processed and pursued, when Geoffrey's *Historia* appeared. Inevitably, the First Crusade's image of military success—ameliorating the criticism that had attended the Crusade from its inception (Siberry, 190)—was soon tarnished and challenged by the tragic losses and humiliating defeats of the crusade of 1101 (Runciman, 2:18–31); after which, it might be assumed, the contest for the reputation of the Crusade might have taken on some urgency. It comes with little surprise, then, that in 1102–5, Raymond d'Aguiliers defensively declares that he is writing his chronicle to answer negative criticism of the First Crusade (Raymond d'Aguiliers, *"Liber,"* 35). It is in the context of such interventions that Geoffrey's *Historia*, dedicated to members of the Anglo-Norman royal family and their supporters, offers thus not only a national mythology of an imperial Arthur, but also the calculated romance of an Arthur who serviceably defeats monstrosities from a crusading history that is integrally intertwined with the Anglo-Norman past and present, the meaning of which continued to be revised, contested, and pursued.[49]

Why is Arthur, an obscure military hero briefly mentioned in the *Historia Brittonum*—the ninth-century chronicle that served as the "most important source" of Geoffrey's "elaborate construct" (Wright, "Bede," 31)—the chosen figure who is plucked from the distant past to serve the present? The *Historia Brittonum*, in reciting early insular history, mentions in passing a war leader ("dux bellorum") called Arthur who fought twelve battles against the Saxon heathen, with dramatic victories in the eighth and twelfth, and who carried the image of the Virgin Mary on his shoulders ("super humeros suos") in the eighth battle (J. Morris, 76).[50] This tantalizingly brief glimpse of an early Arthur is supplemented by an entry in the *Annales Cambriae*, or Welsh Annals, whose text appears with the *Historia Brittonum* in the crucial manuscript Harley 3859, an entry which enigmatically records that in the year 516 C.E., Arthur "carried the cross of our Lord Jesus Christ for three days and three nights on his shoulders and the Britons were the victors" at the battle of Badon ("Arthur portavit crucem Domini nostri Jhesu Christi tribus diebus et tribus noctibus in humeros suos et Brittones victores fuerunt" [J. Morris, 85]). A few more sketchy hints appear in this modestly rudimentary annalistic and chronicle vehicle: one section on the marvels of Britain mentions a dog, as well as a son, of Arthur ("qui erat canis Arthuri militis" and "filius Arthuri militis erat" [J. Morris, 83]), references in which Arthur pertinently features not as *dux*, now, but as *miles*—a lexical designation that, in the twelfth century of Geoffrey's era, though not in the ninth century of the *Historia Brittonum*'s, can suggest to an emergent stratum of military and cultural elites that Arthur might have been, like them, a knight.

The appeal of a cultural hero of shadowy origins, whose vestigial elaboration in the annalistic and chronicle record invites embellishment, need not be belabored, particularly if the cultural figure also circulated, as scholars believe, in stories of folkloric or popular tradition.[51] We see that the annalistic and chronicle Arthur, before his dramatic entrance into literary narrative in the medium of Geoffrey's *Historia*, already possesses irresistible, indeed indispensable, features: He is victorious against the enemies of Christianity and performs as a great warrior and military leader of men, like the barons of the First Crusade; he resembles a knight and might become, like Baldwin of Boulogne, a king; and, most indelibly of all, Arthur's identification as a Christian warrior takes dramatic, exhibitional form in the pious symbols he bears on his shoulders for inspiration or proclamation—his splendid display of what visibly resembles a crusader's cross.

That Arthur's campaigns in the *Historia* are invested with the aura of the First Crusade has been partly recognized. Tyerman, for instance, shrewdly notices that Archbishop Dubricius's speech to Arthur's militia, in the Saxon wars, presents Arthur's men as "marked with the sign of the

Christian faith (i.e., the cross)," and carries unmistakable echoes of Urban's crusading address, down to the offer of the Crusade indulgence and absolution (22). Tatlock notices the strange infusion of Muslim and Oriental kings, and their forces, into the ranks of the Roman army confronting Arthur, although "Geoffrey knew as well as we do that the Roman army in the sixth century was Christian," and concludes that Geoffrey "wished to secure for Arthur the nimbus of a crusader, which meant so much in the twelfth century" (*Legendary History*, 262).

But the depiction of Arthur in the *Historia* is not only as *dux bellorum*, a Christian leader of crusade-like forces against the Saxon and Saracen foe. Arthur is also newly deployed as a figure in *romance*, a strategy that shifts the commemoration of the Crusade, and the retrieval of crusading memory in the *Historia*, onto a different register. No explicit memorializing of the Crusade, or direct retrieval of history, occurs in the giant-killing episode: The defeat of the cannibal monster in the heart of Europe issues not from the wars of Christendom but from the urgent necessity of rescuing a single, helpless individual—an aristocratic maiden in peril.

A Definition of Romance: Gender, Magical Transformations, and a Language of Cultural Discussion

Medieval romance requires figures of gender for its narrational apparatus. Perhaps because gender, like romance, is a cultural invention that participates in both fantasy and reality, existing in oscillation between two modes, it lends—I will suggest—a ready and serviceable vocabulary to romance: a body of texts whose practices require an expressional medium that is able to perform the real as the fantastical, and the fantastical as the real, without the requisite necessity of explanation or apology. Following the *Historia*, in the full-length vernacular fictions of Chrétien de Troyes and others, it can readily be seen that gender acts as the special vocabulary of medieval romance, serving as the mediating and expressive terms that enable the articulation of urgent aristocratic concerns. In Chrétien's late-twelfth-century continental romances, and in chivalric romances of the thirteenth century, the romance system of gendered service—knights on quest, aiding maidens—makes available a fantasmatic consideration and resolution of critical feudal problems, and the vindication of the ideological apparatus and institutions of feudal knighthood.[52] Arthur's romance at Mont Saint-Michel in Geoffrey's early-twelfth-century *Historia* ushers in, then, willy-nilly, a prime instrument in the narrational machinery of medieval romance—the chivalric rescue of aristocratic maidens.

In this early, paradigmatic romance episode of giant-killing, the gender apparatus of medieval romance is already visible, and firmly in place: Helena, an aristocratic female victim, is the fetish and screen that occults an unbearable historical exigency even as she facilitates its articulation and surreptitious resolution through the giant-killing. As in later romances, the resolution enacted by the cultural hero is rendered as *incidental* to the objective at hand—the objective here being not defeating the memory of cannibalistic atrocity but saving a maiden—and thus a romance sleight-of-hand is accomplished while the readerly gaze is held by the female victim in the foreground. Indeed, we are generously given *two* female victims to consider, signifying the poles of youth and age, and thereby instantiating between them all womankind: a young maiden of aristocratic lineage, and therefore a valuable victim by virtue of class, youth, and sexuality; and her devoted old nurse, who is less valuable by virtue of age and presumptive social inferiority. In a romance performance of his own, Geoffrey chivalrously allows the aristocratic maiden to perish without sexual despoiling; the threatened body of the sexually endangered maiden evanesces before our eyes, as the narrative ruthlessly substitutes her old, socially inferior nurse as the scapegoat victim of repeated rape instead. Though the crone had earlier warned Bedivere, Arthur's companion, that the giant cannibal would destroy the flower of knightly youth—a warning whose meaning on the symbolic level, as much as the literal, is appropriately transparent—Helena's premature death shows how romance insists that it is *women*, after all, and not male elites, who truly figure the constituency at risk, and whose crises prompt and require splendid chivalric resolution by men.

Helena's youthful female body vanishes at her death, but her name is tropologically encrypted and resurrected later when her grieving father erects a memorial edifice over her tumulus. Indeed, Helena's bodily removal is necessary, in order that her *name* might be fetishistically enshrined—essentialized, purified, and emptied of any original reference—so as to serve as an ethereal cipher, or verbal relic, through which to index the newly transformed cultural memory that would henceforth issue as its appropriate referent. "Helena's Tomb," then, becomes the resounding cipher that invokes the place and moment in culture where a historical monstrosity triumphally metamorphoses into celebratory romance.[53] As a site of mourning without melancholia, Helena's Tomb marks the precise location in culture where historical trauma is successfully introjected and memorialized within the medieval cultural imaginary. Simultaneously the vanishing point of history and the instantiation of cultural fantasy, the moment is productive of, and defines, romance.

My description thus argues not that romance requires a forgetting, but that it circulates a remembering: that romance inaugurates not a hypothesis of burial and repression but of *transformation* through the strategic entrance and manipulation of difference. For the historical trauma here has not been buried so much as it has been metastasized and re-formed in order that it might be made harmless by being remembered *differently*, and famously, in the (lime)light of another place—the once and future European present—displacing the shadows of a lurking, Oriental past. St. Michael's Mount—now synonymous, we are told, with the name of Helena's Tomb—can be Mount Pilgrim writ large, a celebration of Christian and military space, offering a monument to memory that can be fearlessly exhibited to the public gaze. That this monumental transformation effected in culture requires as its foundational matter the dead body of a sacrificial child-maiden, the violation of an old woman, and the celebration of a monarchical conqueror merely testifies to the feudal politics of medieval courtly fantasy.

Thus analyzed, it can be seen that the Arthurian romance of the two giants in the *Historia* allegorizes, by virtue of its structure and operations, the narrational habits and modalities of romance as a genre. Deploying figures of gender as a means to discuss the virtually indiscussible, romance represents a medium that is neither wholly fantastical nor wholly historical, but in which history and fantasy collide, the one vanishing into the other, almost without trace, at the location where the advantage of both can most easily be mined. For romance does not repress or evade the historical—as has sometimes been claimed—but *surfaces* the historical, which it transforms and safely memorializes in an advantageous form, as fantasy. As surely as it is futile to repress the historical—for history itself has repeatedly shown that repression returns in ever more dangerous guises—it is equally futile and impossible to refute the fantastical (as the absurd twelfth-century spectacle of William of Newburgh sententiously attempting to rebut the *Historia*'s sensational fictions confirms). Negotiating thus history and fantasy to special advantage, the genre of romance offers the skillful manipulator an ideological medium of incomparable value.

Romance, of course, freely cannibalizes from extant cultural material—from bodies of older texts, floating metaphors and motifs, bits of tales,
legends, superstitions, mere hints and guesses—and organizes its hybrid
matter into a pattern and a structure that it instantiates at a particular historical moment. Romance thus is impure at its very emergence: an emergence "produced through a particular stage of forces" (Foucault, 148) and
designating "a place of confrontation but not . . . a closed field" (150), an
emergence that is not the *origin* of romance as such—the coming into
being of what has never existed—but a genesis, a re-patterning and re-
beginning that is constitutive of an exemplar. Just as we may only spo-
radically track, in disparate moments, the spoor of history in the operations of cultural fantasy, the rapid and massive ramification of romance
after the *Historia* also argues for the impossibility of tracing the chronology or unbroken evolution of medieval romance: Instead, what is available
to us is a rich genealogy, a ramifying web, through time, of exemplary romance moments and texts without an overarching trajectory toward teleological meaning and conclusion.[54]

The Empire of Magic:
Arthur's Empire, "Rome"/Byzantium, and
the Crusader Colonies of Outremer

From the very inception of the genre, Arthurian romance is imbricated in
the history of medieval European empire formation in the Levant: a colonial experiment for which the cultural rescue and popularity of Arthur's
deeds offer ideological support. Beyond the processing of a memory of
atrocity into monumental celebration, the story of Arthur's deeds in the
Historia furnishes as large a cultural aura and nimbus for crusading history as the aura of crusading history furnishes for Arthur's deeds in romance.
Arthur's aggressive empire formation—which has been read as culturally
justifying Norman territorial conquests of the eleventh century, including
the invasion of England—is also a literary homology for the experiment
in empire constituted by the crusader states of Outremer. Arthur's empire
is a virile and modern competitor to the exhausted empire of the Romans,
represented textually by the graybeard Roman emissaries to the youthful
Arthurian court.

The multiracial composition of the forces of "Rome" massed against
Arthur indicates, I suggest, that "Rome" in the *Historia*'s Arthuriad refers

as much to the Eastern Roman Empire that is the detested rival of the youthful crusader states in the Levant—twelfth-century Byzantium, or Constantinople—as to sixth-century Rome. The presence of Turcopoles, Cumans, Patzinaks, and other Oriental races in the polyglot Byzantine army was of traditional standing—but their presence in the Byzantine ranks mounted a cultural shock for the Latins of the First Crusade on their arrival in the East, for whom these races were the collective visage of the hated Oriental enemy. "Rome," significantly, was the name by which the Byzantine Empire—the historical descendent of the old Roman Empire—was known in the East, to Byzantines themselves, and to the native populations of the region. Anna Comnena routinely calls Constantinople "Rome" (e.g., 117), the Byzantine Empire "the Roman empire" (e.g., 119, 323), and her people "Romans" (e.g., 323, 338, 358). Arab chronicles call the Byzantines "the Rūmi" and the formerly Greek territory of Iconium or Anatolia in Asia Minor "the Sultanate of the Rūm." Even the Latin chronicles refer to Byzantium through a configuration of the Roman name, as "Romania."

Oriental kings and races are conspicuous in the "Roman" army of the Arthuriad: among them, Mustansar, king of the Africans ("rex Affricanorum" [Wright, 1:116]), Aliphatima, "rex Hispanie," the kings of Egypt, Babylon, Bithynia, Phrygia, Libya, and Syria, and the kings of the Parthians, the Medi, and the Iturei (Wright, 1:116, passim). Tatlock observes that these names, together with the kings of Greek lands mentioned, invoke not only the boundaries of the Roman Empire at its broadest but assemble a virtual cartography of the Orient, including the territories of the Byzantine Empire, in Geoffrey's day. Tatlock points out, moreover, that "Al-Mustansar" was the name of the eighth Shi'ite Fatimid Caliph of Egypt close to the time of the First Crusade (1036–94), while "Aliphatima" combines the names of the founders of Shi'ite Islam (the Islam of Egypt's breakaway Fatimid caliphate)—the prophet Mohammad's cousin, Ali, and Mohammad's daughter, Fatima, who married Ali ("Contemporaneous Matters," 207). Orderic Vitalis's own invocation of the very same names suggests that the combination of "Ali" and "Fatima" arrested the attention of more than one early-twelfth-century historian interested in Norman crusader history in the Orient (6:116).[55] Finally, Tatlock adds that "Leo," the name given to one of the two co-emperors of "Rome" in the Arthuriad, is coincidentally "that of the latest emperor at Constantinople (Leo I, 457–474) before the disappearance of the Western Empire (476)" ("Contemporaneous Matters," 215).

Tatlock takes the argument no further, but, in the narrative of Arthurian imperial conquest, "Rome," I suggest, functions much like the name "Hispania"—that is, as double-writing, a name twinning dual referents that command stereoptic, simultaneous attention. By Geoffrey's day, the Roman Empire in the East was viewed in the West with suspicion, contempt, and a hostility that amounted to loathing. Early in the twelfth century, Latin eyewitness chronicles and letters had held the Byzantines guilty of failing to fulfill the promises of assistance made by Alexius in the reconquest of Syria and Palestine, after the taking of Nicaea, a failure that seriously jeopardized the crusading mission at Antioch and elsewhere. As early as 1098, in fact, a letter to Urban II signed by the leaders of the Crusade, including Robert Curthose, casually damns the Byzantines as "heretics" (Hagenmeyer, *Kreuzzugsbriefe*, 164). Where a scant few years earlier Urban had emphasized at Clermont the commonality of Christians East and West, the crusaders' letter crudely points up the incommensurably schismatic and deviant character of Greek and Eastern Christians. The failed crusade of 1101, with disastrous massacres suffered by the Latins, was also blamed by its participants, predictably, on the Greeks. Finally, Bohemond's self-interested, wide-ranging campaign in Europe, to raise a "crusading" army against Alexius—a campaign that involved embassies to the Pope, the French king and nobles, and direct or mediated contact with Henry I of England—consolidated the negative image of the Eastern Romans in Western Europe (Yewdale, 106–9; Runciman, 2:48; Krey, "Neglected Passage," 69–70). The twelfth-century Norman historian Orderic Vitalis routinely disparages Alexius I, as does the otherwise magisterially judicious William of Malmsbury's *De Gestis Regum Anglorum*.

Geoffrey's *Historia* tellingly portrays Romans as cowardly, treacherous, disloyal, and militarily inferior and, even before the entrance of Arthur, had undercut its niggardly acknowledgement of even Julius Caesar's historical conquest of Britain with fantasy depictions of counter-conquests of Rome by Britons. Arthur's empire fulfills these earlier countervailing conquests, which it organizes into an intelligible pattern: the Arthurian empire, like the empire of the crusader states, is a newly arrived, virile alternative to the superannuated empire of the (Eastern) Romans, who are mockingly derided through metaphors of gender also used by the *Gesta Francorum*. In the *Gesta*, the Romans who are the rivals of the crusader colonies are mocked as an effeminate people ("effeminatis gentibus" [Hill, 67]); in the *Historia*, the Romans who are the rivals of the Arthurian empire are derided as the effeminate heirs ("muliebres"—womanish creatures [Wright, 1:128]) of a degenerate imperial legacy, who act womanishly, like women ("muliebriter" [Wright, 1:129]).

That romance supplies ideological support for empire formation is also suggested in the *Historia* at the level of narrative structure and plot. Arthur's empire is inaugurated soon after a romance interval of twelve years of peace, during which Arthur establishes an Arthurian culture of such supreme romance courtliness that its codes of dress and arms inspire international emulation and win a peerless reputation for Arthur's knights. Because of that peerless reputation, the romance logic of the *Historia* reasons, kings of kingdoms across the seas begin to fear Arthurian invasion, thus prompting Arthur to consider conquering all Europe ("totam Europam" [Wright, 1:107]). The campaign of imperial conquest immediately begins, and soon Arthur is the virtual master of Europe. Seamlessly, without hesitation, the courtly moment of Arthurian romance has opened into the military moment of Arthurian imperial invasion, the logic of the former driving the momentum of the latter, into which it vanishes without trace or apparent obstacle. At the inaugural moments of Arthurian romance, we thus find in operation violence of related kinds: the rape and sacrificial death of women; domination of racial and religious others; and aggressive empire formation. This critical nexus of violence lodged at the very genesis of medieval Arthurian romance—a contamination-at-origin—will be harnessed for strategic and political uses by both the producers and consumers of culture through the Middle Ages and beyond.

Arthur's now famous, ethically problematic birth in sin, treachery, and deception witnesses Arthurian romance's contamination-at-origin at the level of emblem. Romance themes, motifs, and structures in the *Historia*—which do not begin with Arthur but exist in minor key from almost the beginning of the *Historia*—are fulfilled, of course, with Arthur's entrance into the narrative.[56] But romance elements and moments in fact intensify earlier, with the entry of Merlin, the magus whose sensational prophecies signal a capture of the historical narrative by the magical aura of fantasy. The entrance of a magician and his magical words has the effect of suddenly transforming, magicalizing, the affect of the narrative: at once a vocabulary materializes that is full of lurid figures, fantastical allusions, and wild allegorical suggestiveness, giving free rein to a procession, in language, of dragons, giants, boars, snake-like women, lions, Arabs, Africans, and other such exotica, under the subtle rubric of prophecy.[57] In effect, Merlin's auguries cunningly devise an early form of the romance marvel, for their fantastical and exotic aura has performative value. Aurelius Ambrosius, pre-Arthurian King of the Britons, makes this plain when, desiring (to hear) marvels, he commands Merlin to speak of the future ("iussitque futura dicere cupiens miranda audire" [Wright, 1:90]), that is, to *perform* the marvelous by *speaking* of the marvelous.

In later literature, Arthur would make a similar equivalence between the marvel of listening to the performance of a story and the actual performance of a marvel itself, these becoming conventional and often interchangeable *topoi* in Arthurian romance. And Arthur himself would become a marvel. Merlin, a figure of the author in the Middle Ages (Bloch, *Etymologies*, 2) is more marvelously prophetic than either he or his author can possibly realize from the vantage point of 1130–39, when the magus optimistically proclaims, "[Arthur] will be celebrated in the mouth of peoples and his deeds will be food/nourishment to narrators of tales" ("In ore populorum celebrabitur et actus eius cibus erit narrantibus" [Wright, 1:74]).[58] In Arthurian literary history, the interventions of Merlin conjure so efficacious a magical aura that the magus is eventually imported into the constellation of Arthurian romance, with which he is not, in fact, initially associated.

Notwithstanding the durability of Arthur's legend, however, the formation of empire, whether in Arthurian romance or in the history of military Christendom, is an anxious experiment that is invariably subject to the reverse momentum of military reprisal. The fate of the militarily insecure fiefdoms of Outremer, geopolitically surrounded by the enemy and constantly vulnerable, was particularly dependent on the domination exercised by the ruling King of Jerusalem. In 1131 Baldwin II, last of the original barons of the First Crusade, and a military and political leader of shrewdly forceful character, died and was replaced by Fulk of Anjou, a king whose power and prestige were unhappily undermined by the reputed adultery of his wife with one of his younger nobles, with divisive consequences in the aftermath.[59] The *Historia*, composed sometime between 1130 and 1139, also records the departure of a crusader-like king, the fabled Arthur, after which, we discover, during the reign of the ineffectual Karetic (the historical Ceredig or Cerdic), an Islamic army of Africans is poised for invasion on the threshold of post-Arthurian Britain.

The *Historia*'s first mention of Muslims—Arabs and Africans—occurs in the prophecies of Merlin, where the presence of the exotic foe is insubstantial if startling, since they are merely figures that inhabit the histrionic register of mysterious, impressive-sounding prophecy. In the Arthuriad, however, Muslims amplify into kings of the Orient, leading armies against the Britons, and after Arthur's exit, and the mention of five kings in rapid succession, Muslims suddenly swarm and multiply, as an invading force of 160,000 Africans, led by an African king, materializes in Britain after conquering Ireland. The Muslims ravage fields, torch cities, destroy settlements, and submit people and priests to the sword or fire, in a hallucinatory reign of terror whose moments recall the Saxon or viking invasions, but whose explicit Islamicization here suggests nothing if not a counter-crusade (Wright, 1:133).

This reverse invasion, directed at the home country, the hearthlands of Britain itself, is developed from an episode in Gildas's *De Excidio Britanniae* (97–98), where, however, the invading force is, accurately, Saxon: The *Historia* rewrites history therefore, with deliberate calculation, by Islamicizing and Orientalizing the invaders, whom it projects, frighteningly, as a swarming vision of countless Africans led by a tyrant (Wright, 1:134). So horrific is the nightmarish counter-crusade of accelerating terror and chaos—even involving, as an authenticating gesture, the reverse-conversion of the nephew of the Frankish king away from Christianity—that the narrative breaks into a first-person voice whose histrionic tones recall not only Gildas but also Merlin's prophecies, bewailing the fate of Britons at the hands of the impious infidel (Wright, 1:133–34).[60] It would seem, after all, that Arthur's defeat of a monstrous cannibal settled only one half of a two-fold dilemma and that an intransigent horror of *pollution*—of an invasion of the communal body by foreign contaminants from without—still remained secreted within. We remember that the Christian cannibals had been tormented by their self-contaminating deed; and we see that the horizon of torment can be imagined as stretching beyond the boundary of the body envelope to envelop the borders of a living collectivity of bodies in Christendom.

The African invasion empties out the communal body, eviscerating Britain as the surviving remnants of the population disperse and flee, to find no safety elsewhere. Finally, the king of the Africans gives the portion of Britain called Loegria—England south of the Humber and east of the Severn—to the Saxons: Muslims, according to this romance, were responsible for the historical domination of England. Eventually Britain is peopled by mixed communities of Saxons and Britons, and the *Historia* attempts a final concretion of romance, designed to banish the phantom of pollution and restore the communal body to purity and health.

BRITAIN'S HISTORY AS FAMILY HISTORY; OR,
THE FAMILY ROMANCE OF BRIAN AND CADWALLO

The *Historia* offers "a romance" of two princes (Tatlock, *Legendary History*, 390), one Saxon, by the name of Edwin, and the other British, by the name of Cadwallo, both of whom are born of royal women at the same time, in the same household, and fostered together in intimacy through their infancy, childhood, and adolescence—a folkloric motif that drives narrative pretexts in romances and lays through the Middle Ages. In maturity, however, the two fosterlings become political enemies, as a result of intervention by Cadwallo's nephew, Brian, who pleads with the royal Cadwallo in an emotional scene not to grant Edwin the crown and legitimacy that the Saxon seeks, and thereby consolidate several generations of hated Saxon occupation of the island. In the struggle between Cadwallo and Edwin that ensues, the Saxon enlists the aid of a soothsayer-magus from "Hispania" ("auger ex Hispania" [Wright, 1:138], "magumque Edwini regis"[Wright, 1:140]) called Pellitus, an alter ego of Merlin, from either Muslim Spain or the East or both. Pellitus's powers are Merlin-like, in that he advises Edwin by forewarning him of approaching misfortune, but through distinctly Oriental skills and knowledges linked to astronomy/astrology and the flight of birds—mysteries that William of Malmsbury, in discussing Pope Sylvester II's travels for education in similar arcana, records as Saracen knowledges (Tatlock, *Legendary History*, 129 n. 65). After a defeat by Edwin as a result of magical foreknowledge, and a maritime catastrophe during which he loses his other ships, King Cadwallo of the Britons, Edwin's foster brother, is stranded on the isle of Guernsey with some companions, and falls ill from grief and anger, refusing all food. An extraordinary episode then follows.

Brian, who had been responsible for the falling-out of the royal fosterlings, is among Cadwallo's companions on the island. This nephew had first made his appearance in a bucolic idyll where Cadwallo had been lying in Brian's lap or bosom ("in gremio" [Wright, 1:137]): It was Brian's tears, trickling down upon the king's face and beard, and Brian's explanation for those tears—caused, he said, by grief at the Saxon occupation of their homeland, and Cadwallo's intention to honor the foreign barbarians by sharing kingship with Edwin—that had caused the rift between Cadwallo and his foster sibling (Wright, 1:137). Now, on the fourth day of his fast, Cadwallo is seized by the greatest yearning ("maxima cupiditas") for game ("ferinam carnaem"), summons Brian, and announces what he eagerly desires. Brian hunts for game throughout the island, but fails to find any, and is in the greatest torment at being unable to satisfy his lord's desire ("appetitum suum explere"), fearing that death would follow from Cadwallo's weakened condition. Then, in an inspired moment, Brian opens up his own thigh, slices away a piece of flesh from it, roasts the flesh on a spit, and takes it to the king, telling his uncle that the meat is venison ("et ad regem pro uenatione portauit"). Cadwallo eats, marveling that he had never discovered such sweetness in other flesh before. When he is sated, the king becomes more joyful and light-hearted, and after three days is wholly sound again (Wright, 1:138–39).

Almost unbelievably, we have here a *second* romance in the *Historia* in which cannibalism appears—but a cannibalism that appears in order to be inserted within a startlingly rescripted context. This time, a King of Britain is not produced to defeat the cannibal: He *is* the cannibal. Yet his cannibalism is not an atrocity, and does not turn the man into a monster of savage visage and proportions, because his cannibalism is inadvertent and involuntary, not of his will, and goes unrecognized by him. Instead— in a wonderful reversal of responsibility—the guilty culprit is *the victim*, and a victim, moreover, who is only guilty of loving concern for the cannibal, whom he instates as a cannibal by virtue of wishing upon him an offering of his own living flesh that heals. In this family drama of sacrificial food and love, offering and healing, the iconicity of the gift could not be more transparent: For in the family of Christendom, what other living, sacrificial offering of flesh and blood, lovingly made by a willing victim, and accepted by a weakened recipient, restores, saves, and heals? Revealingly, the economy of this eucharistic sacrifice that restores the body and spirit of the king, who is the human sign of the country itself, takes place entirely within the closed circuit of a family romance, involving neither outsider nor foreigner.

Strategically appearing toward the end of the *Historia*, the romance of Brian's eucharistic offering rescripts the historical paradigm of guilty Christians and foreign cadavers, dissipating the fantasy of fearful pollution by echoing the familiar, comforting affirmations of Christian ritual, as the romance remakes a traumatic atrocity safely and nobly back into sacred cannibalism.[61] At this vantage point two removes from the crusader cannibalism that occasioned the eruption of Arthurian romance, we see exemplarily how romance bypasses the paradigm of true and false to shift attention onto *representation as magical performance*: the subtly aggregational re-creation of a perilous thing in the direction and in contexts of ever-increasing safety. Evolving through modalities of mourning, transformation, exorcism, and celebration, the performative power of romance in the *Historia* becomes ineluctably irreducible, by this point, to its originary occasioning moment.

Brian's romance, then, closes the trajectory of Arthur's giant-killing and completes the literary evolution of a historical act originally performed on foreign and desanctified ground, by circling back home into the most familiar of sacerdotal rituals, performed on domestic terrain. Earlier, by alienating Cadwallo from Edwin, Brian had successfully expelled the foreigner who was intimately lodged within the bosom of the royal family and the bosom of Britain—an alien raised as twinned to the king, as a community of Saxon foreigners had been intergenerationally twinned with a community of Britons on native soil. Indeed, Brian's tribal and native patriotism has had the more personal effect of wresting the foster sibling Edwin from the affections of the king's very breast: For, in the course of reciting to Cadwallo the history of their *ethnos* as the country's history, while he was explaining the reason for his tears, Brian seems invisibly to replace Edwin as Cadwallo's chief companion. After the scene with the tears, the rupture between Cadwallo and Edwin is sudden, decisive, and final; and Brian assumes an increasingly larger and more active role in Cadwallo's and Britain's affairs. In a reversal of their original mutual affection, Edwin and Cadwallo then become linked by bonds of mutual hostility and enmity instead.

This peculiar triangulation of the affective flows interconnecting three men—Edwin, Cadwallo, and Brian—is highlighted by the oddity of the bucolic idyll in which the king had tenderly lain in the lap or breast of his nephew ("in gremio cuiusdam nepotis sui" [Wright, 1:137]). The features of the *tableau vivant* of king and nephew lying on a river bank might seem, at first glance, faintly familiar—though disturbed in present context by the scene's ambiguous affective status—since the tableau carries a faint trace of a trope of masculine relations in protofeudal culture, where a retainer's head might rest in the lap of his lord, a lord who is the symbol of hearth and home in the Anglo-Saxon military ethos. We find that comforting image, for instance, in the elegaic poem, "The Wanderer," where the speaker, shorn of a lord, wistfully retrieves a nostalgic memory of resting his head in the lap of his lord, who represents, in his culture, a loving and all-powerful paternal presence as much as a military leader. We might think to read Cadwallo's and Brian's idyll, then, as simply sketching a variant of old military relations, albeit mildly inexplicable in its reversal of positions between retainer and lord, a deviation from normalcy. There are, however, other correspondently odd moments in the *Historia*.

Framing the idyll, and the cannibalistic episode of the family romance, are two other telling descriptions of deviations from normalcy. Before Brian and Cadwallo appear, there is the mention of a sodomitical king, Malgo, who is described in glowing terms as handsomer than almost all the other leaders of Britain, powerful in arms, more generous than his predecessors, and driving away many oppressors—all the most prized qualities of a king—but who is then summarily dismissed by the narrative as hateful to God because of the pestilence of sodomy—despite, we note, his responsible provision of the kingdom with two male heirs, and an abbreviated empire that resembles a rudimentary version of Arthur's (Wright, 1:133). The depiction of Malgo strikingly reworks its sources, the *Historia Brittonum*, where "Mailcunus" is briefly mentioned but not characterized (J. Morris, 79), and Gildas's *De Excidio*, where "Maglocunus" is extensively vilified, not lingeringly admired, and where the vice of sodomy is more obliquely attached to him as one of many vices of a vilified king (102–5). In addition, after Brian's and Cadwallo's idyll, and the romance of the sacred cannibalism, there is a terse description, in a recitation of British history by Cadwallo to his foster father, the king of Brittany, of excessive sexuality indulged in by the Britons, of a kind unheard of among other peoples (Wright, 1:139).

The romance of sacred cannibalism is itself strange: It is staged as an impromptu drama that is triggered by the sudden, uncontrollable desire of a king, whose appetite must be satisfied if the king is to live. The mysterious and intense longing by which the king is suddenly seized, and Brian's fear that Cadwallo might die if his desire is not fulfilled, are symptoms that astonishingly echo those of the lover's malady, an affliction of heterosexual lovers last seen in the *Historia* afflicting Uther, whose desire for Igerne, described in terms that much resemble Cadwallo's yearning for another kind of flesh, results in time in Arthur's birth, and the birth of Arthurian romance. In this suggestive context, Brian's response—his offer of flesh from his own thigh—might be read, then, as encoding a homoerotic offer of some kind, an offer that cannot be rendered or accepted more explicitly in the circumstances of present narrative culture, as the narrative's dutiful condemnation of the otherwise much-admired sodomitical king, Malgo, shows.

As a euphemism for a sexual zone, the thigh has a long literary and mythological history, from the birth of the sexually ambiguous Dionysius to the sinful wound of the Fisher King in medieval Arthurian romance. Brian's offer of flesh from his thigh—an offer accepted and enjoyed, indeed, relished by the innocent Cadwallo—might suggest, then, that a covert sexual presentation, as well as a covert sacramental one, is being discreetly scripted into the scene, the one figuration dovetailing into the other. What else might be encoded here, in metaphors that seem simultaneously to wish to express and also conceal, can only be speculated on: For this symbolic exchange between men, it should be remembered, takes place within the ambit of royal family relations, and perhaps delicately, sympathetically, comments—in oblique, allegorical, and safe fashion—on the homoerotic culture that putatively inhabited the courts of William II, Robert Curthose, and select Anglo-Norman nobility of the late-eleventh and early-twelfth centuries.[62]

That a homoerotic exchange might be fugitively encoded into this romance would affect our understanding of the *Historia's* complex presentation of the operations of romance. The romance of Brian and Cadwallo, featuring good cannibalism, is, after all, propped upon the romance of Arthur's giant-killing, featuring bad cannibalism: The Arthurian romance, which itself offered a vocabulary for articulating the unutterable, has thus become the tacit lexicon through which the romance of Brian and Cadwallo might articulate—or at least suggestively sketch out the horizons of—its own unutterable concerns.[63] For in Brian's and Cadwallo's romance, desire can safely surface within an apparitional exchange between men to express or affirm a dynamic that might otherwise be impossible to legitimate in other contexts of dominant culture in the *Historia's* period.

In 1102, at the Council of London at Westminister, excommunication had been pronounced, by no less an authority than Anselm, on those who committed sodomy; by 1120 the Council of Nablus conjoined the forces of civil and religious authority in determining that death by burning was the appropriate legal penalty for those committing sodomy, inscripting into law for the first time in the medieval period the death penalty for that offense.[64]

The apparitional exchange here, occurring so early in the development of medieval romance, might suggest to us that the circuit of desire animating courtly romance—a circuit of desire that has always been assumed, in the literary history of romance, to be heterosexual—might be homoerotic, as well as homosocial in character, although expert at assuming heterosexual guise: or, at least, that multiply overlapping and overdetermined modalities of desire traverse medieval romance. Romance, of course, is a medium traversed by desire, which it thematizes, contemplates, and apotheosizes, even as it is powered by desire. Not least of these animating modalities, I am attempting to suggest, is the desire of culture to give voice to, and speak, its traumas in a safe medium.

But the story of Brian and Cadwallo is unfinished and does not end with the joyful and discreetly honorific exchange of flesh. While Cadwallo and Edwin are historical personages derived from a brief account in book 2, chapter 20, of Bede's *Historia Ecclesiastica Gentis Anglorum*—where, however, true to Bede's Northumbrian sympathies, Cadwallo is rendered as a barbarously and bestially savage rebel and usurper, and it is Edwin who is the lauded king—neither the salvific Brian nor the magician Pellitus is historical: Absent from the source text, they may be read as the *Historia*'s own deliberate invention. Indeed, "Brian" is a name that Geoffrey of Monmouth—whose principal dedicatee for the *Historia*, in an overwhelming majority of manuscripts, is Robert of Gloucester, Henry I's illegitimate son, who is one of two of the staunchest supporters of Henry's daughter, the empress Matilda—might well wish to commemorate in order to honor Brian Fitz Count, Matilda's other indispensable supporter who offered unwavering and staunchly loyal support (see, e.g., Potter, 90, 134; and William of Malmsbury, *Historia Novella*, 5, 35, 51). In the period of the *Historia*'s probable composition, "Brian" is not as common a name among the political figures of England as many others (e.g., the ubiquitous "Robert" or "William") and is therefore conspicuous; Brian Fitz Count, moreover, was a Breton who served the Norman royal family—an ancestry and a service not unlike Geoffrey's—and who had been raised in the court of the Norman king Henry I (Chibnall, 53), just as Cadwallo and Edwin had been raised in the court of the Breton king, Salomon (Wright, 1:136).[65]

Brian, the salvific agent who heals the king's body and eradicates the foreigner in the body politic, decisively exorcizes the last foreign contaminant in the collective body—Pellitus, the skulking magus from Muslim Spain or Syria, whose alien presence yet festers in the text, affecting the textual future, like Merlin or the shadow of the author, by magical foreknowledge of events that an augurer can avert or bring to pass.[66] Dressed as a humble pauper—recalling the Tafurs, perhaps?—Brian makes an iron rod ("baculum ferrum" [Wright, 1:140]) sharpened to a point and, with this pilgrim's staff ("burdonem"[Wright, 1:141]), stabs Pellitus with an upward thrust into the chest, as the magus walks among the poor, an assassination that the magician presumably was unable to foresee.[67] This vampire-like killing, involving an instrument faintly reminiscent of that famous, if controversial, Antiochene relic of the Crusade, the Holy Lance, is powerfully performed with the symbol of the pilgrim's staff that recalls and seals the best intentions of the First Crusade. The killing of this final specter of foreignness magically lays to rest, at last, all ghosts from the East. No more Arabs or Africans haunt the *Historia* thereafter, and national history is allowed to take its course without hallucinatory shadows from the Oriental past.

POSTSCRIPT: THE ONCE AND FUTURE TEXT, AND VARIATIONS ON A THEME OF CANNIBALISM

The *Historia*, which had begun with the journey of Brutus, the great-grandson of Aeneas and eponymous founder of Britain, from Troy, soon winds to a close with the death of Cadwallader, Cadwallo's son, after which the journey of the *Historia* itself famously begins—a journey through literary history, and cultural and national politics, that would take several centuries to complete. Kings of England would be drawn to the ideological usefulness of the Brut, as the genre of that vast, accumulating corpus of texts retelling the *Historia*'s invented insular narrative of Brutus, Arthur, and other kings would come to be called. An example of the Brut's ideological usefulness to English monarchy is Edward I's claim to England's sovereignty over Scotland, in a letter to Pope Boniface VIII in 1301, based on the "proof" of Albion's division among the fictive Brutus's three sons, a proof buttressed by the fictional Arthur's restoral of Albany or Scotland to Auguselus, who then putatively held the land from Arthur, as an underking (Keeler, 88, 130).

Literary scholarship has noted the ideological value of Arthur, who "gave the English a national hero, one of the Nine Worthies, and the type of the ideal Christian monarch" (Matheson, 265), and "Plantagenet, Lancastrian, and Tudor kings" were able to deploy Arthurian legend as "a convenient historical fiction to support the claim for a sovereign England," so that "several, including Edward I, Edward III, and Henry VII, clearly recognized and exploited its potential as political propaganda for their imperial ambitions" (Keiser, "Edward III," 37). Finally, as I argue in the next chapter, the foundational myth and regnal genealogy fashioned by the *Historia* devise an indispensable model, in culture, of an insular collectivity and political community that is specifically driven by continuity-through-disruption as its engine of historical development—thus producing the necessary conditions, and an indispensable matrix, for the future project of imagining England as a medieval nation.

The gigantic popularity of the *Historia*, whose narrative was sometimes retold in scarcely altered form, sometimes in expanded, abbreviated, revised, or vernacular formats, finally issued in a Middle English prose *Brut* that, in the fourteenth and fifteenth centuries, constituted "the most popular secular work of the Middle Ages in England, second in the number of surviving manuscripts only to the two versions of the Wycliffite translation of the Bible" (Matheson, 265). The proliferation of the *Historia*'s narrative has an apt, if ironical, consequence: "As new chronicles were written, they did not supersede the more popular of the older works, which continued to be copied and read. . . . By the end of the fifteenth century, it was forgotten that all such works had a single ultimate source in Geoffrey's *Historia*, and, as a result, the individual chronicles were seen as independent witnesses to the truth of Geoffrey's account" (Matheson, 263).

In the twelfth century, soon after the *Historia*'s creation, the "truth of Geoffrey's account" was translated, expanded, and selectively revised in 1155 by the Norman author Robert Wace, whose courtly *Roman de Brut* in the French vernacular, scholars agree, pushed the *Historia*'s materials further along the direction of romance, one track of which culminated, a decade and a half later, in the well-known Arthurian romances of Chrétien de Troyes.[68] Revealingly, Wace's usage of the *Historia*'s romances expresses the Norman's own tactful sense of the limits of reconfiguring historical subjects in romance form. Wace's patrons, like the *Historia*'s chief dedicatees, were Anglo-Norman royalty, but Wace, who—unlike Geoffrey—was himself Norman, and wrote in a vernacular familiar to Norman and Parisian courts alike, was more closely linked to the powerful than was Geoffrey by direct ties of patronage: We know that in 1160, after the completion of his *Brut*, Wace was commissioned by Henry II to write a history of the dukes of Normandy and, in 1169, was awarded a canonry at Bayeaux as a token of royal favor. Significantly, in his treatment of the romance of Arthur's giant-killing, Wace prefers to omit any mention of the fact that the giant of St. Michael's Mount is a cannibal: Between verse 11306 and verse 11307 of the *Roman de Brut*, where the description of the giant's cannibalism should be, is only pendant silence (Wace, 2:590). Even unconscious and involuntary cannibalism makes Wace uncomfortable; though not famed for its concision, his *Brut* elects not to have Cadwallo dwell on the sweetness of his nephew's flesh, nor does the text linger on the happy results of King Cadwallo's tabooed act (2:744).

If a cultural memory of cannibalism at which prominent Normans were present—or even the mere literary presentation of cannibalism—made the Norman Wace uneasy, the anonymous author of the First Variant Version of the *Historia*—whose text (largely an abbreviated recension of Geoffrey's) is witnessed by 8 of the 217 known surviving manuscripts and believed to be written almost immediately after the appearance of the vulgate *Historia*—is even more reluctant to repeat depictions of cannibalism than Wace.[69] The First Variant not only omits any mention of the giant's cannibalistic and Polyphemos-like qualities in the Arthurian adventure of St. Michael's Mount (Wright, 2:158), but excises even the episode of Cadwallo's inadvertent cannibalism (Wright, 2:181–82). So unaccommodating on taboo subjects is this anonymous reviser, that the First Variant even removes the suspiciously intimate details of the scene between Cadwallo and Brian on the bank of the river Douglas—the one in the other's lap/breast, the tears intimately touching the king's beard/face, and so on—and the acceptance of flesh from Brian's thigh: a decision, we might speculate, that might touch on the controversial nature of the twin subjects of cannibalistic atrocity and aristocratic homoeroticism in the culture of Geoffrey's era.

If the twelfth-century Norman Wace, and his courtly vehicle written with an eye to Norman royalty, are nervous at the mention of cannibalism (we are told that Wace presented a copy of the *Roman de Brut* to Queen Eleanor [La3amon, *Brut*, ll. 21–23]), La3amon's *Brut*—written in the thirteenth century or after, in the English language, rather than French, and clearly not intended as a courtly vehicle—does not share the cultural predicament of its parent source, the *Roman de Brut*. Finally, more than a century after Ma'arra, in a narrative intended for a class of folk who used the English tongue, rather than the French of courtly culture, and whose humble author was without known ties to powerful Norman patrons, the specter of cannibalism has no terrors for the writer—and La3amon's *Brut* has no difficulty restoring cannibalistic details to both the giant of St. Michael's Mount (*Brut*, l. 12816), and the fortunate Cadwallo (*Brut*, ll. 15248–76).

It remained, however, for an Arthurian text positioned toward the close of the Middle Ages to produce the most wittily sensational treatment of cannibalistic fetishism and giant consumption after Geoffrey's *Historia*. In the alliterative *Morte Arthure*, not only is the giant of St. Michael's

Mount a cannibalistic monster, but his cannibalism is gloriously lurid, detailed, and gory, surpassing even Guibert of Nogent's Tafurs. The *Morte* delights in its romance re-creation of crusading history: A Templar announces the giant's arrival to an Arthur dressed in a "jupon" from "Jerodyn" (Jordan); Arthur announces his quest as a pilgrimage, in a prolonged joke playing on pilgrimage and rescue; and, at last, the two giants—of St. Michael's Mount, and with the cloak of beards—are unmasked as a single monstrosity, whom Arthur defeats and handily emasculates, in revenge for eating Christians by the hundreds. In this magnificent text, written after the conquest of Constantinople ("Rome," in the *Morte*) by the Fourth Crusade, and the defeat of the massed European forces at Nicopolis, in the Ninth—and fantasmatically recounting, I argue in chapter 3, crusading history toward the close of the Middle Ages—we might say that Geoffrey's *Historia* finds its ultimate typological fulfillment.

But that argument, as the tellers of tales might have it, is another story.

It took considerable efforts of distortion to shape both the land and the people into a vision of a single community.

—Thorlac Turville-Petre,
England the Nation: Language, Literature,
and National Identity, 1290–1340

No other English King has shown so little interest in his realm or so little concern for its welfare as did Richard. . . . Nor, it is fair to add, has any other English King been so idolised by his people, both during his lifetime and afterwards.

—John T. Appleby, ed.,
The Chronicle of Richard of Devizes

Every student of the literature of the Middle Ages is aware that Richard I was a highly popular figure in medieval England, and that about the historical facts of his career there grew up with rapidity and luxuriance a considerable growth of romantic legend. As his fame challenged the pre-eminence of Arthur among British heroes, so his exploits, like Arthur's, multiplied and grew more marvellous in the imagination of the people.

—Roger Sherman Loomis,
"*Richard Coeur de Lion* and the
Pas Saladin in Medieval Art"

Chapter 2

༄

The Romance of England

Richard Coer de Lyon and the Politics of Race, Religion, Sexuality, and Nation

AT THE HEART of one version of the thirteenth/fourteenth/fifteenth cen-
tury romance, *Richard Coer de Lyon* (*RCL*)[1]—whose surviving Middle
English texts recount, in romance mode, the putative history of the Third
Crusade of Latin Christendom against the Islamic empire of Saladin in
the Levant—is a spectacular story of cannibalism performed by the king
of England, Richard I. During his siege of the Muslim-occupied city of
Acre, the story goes, Richard falls ill from the travails of his sea journey to
Syria, the unnatural cold and heat of the local climate, and the unsuitable
"mete and drynk" that his body endures on campaign (ll. 3043–48).
Richard's illness is historically documented; but what follows as cure in
RCL is purest romance. The anguished English crusaders and Christian
army pray for the king's deliverance, and then find an unorthodox solu-
tion that they claim is the work of Christ (l. 3066).

In his malady, Richard yearns for pork—animal flesh, I suggested in
chapter 1, that in medieval culture symbolically distinguishes Christians

Portions of this chapter were presented to audiences at the Pembroke Center, Brown University; the Center for Cultural Studies, University of California at Santa Cruz; a panel of the Middle English Division at the Modern Language Association's Annual Convention, in 1998; and
the residential seminar group, "Theorizing 'Race' in Pre- and Early Modern Contexts," at the
University of California's Humanities Research Institute in 2001. An early draft of the chapter
was published in Jeffrey Cohen's *The Postcolonial Middle Ages*. For their comments and help-
fulness with different parts of this chapter, I am deeply indebted to Penn Szittya, Michael Ragussis, Carla Freccero, Margaret Brose, Gail Hershatter, Chris Connery, Richard Emmerson,
Margo Hendricks, David Theo Goldberg, Karen Bassi, Sarah Morris, Ray Kea, Kristi Wilson,
Paget Henry, Lewis Gordon, and Philomena Essed. This chapter and the two following chapters were written in the course of a stimulating year at Brown University's Pembroke Center.

from Muslims, who are prohibited by religious orthodoxy from the consumption of swine's flesh. Since they are in Syria, Richard's men discover no pork anywhere to be had, but an "old kny3t" fashions an ingenious substitute: At the knight's detailed instructions and unbeknownst to Richard, the steward has a young, fat Saracen killed, opened up, and flayed; boiled with saffron and other spices, the freshly killed corpse is turned into a broth for the king's delectation.[2] The dish is offered as a tempting delicacy to lure back the king's appetite and for the food's specially curative, medicinal properties: Once supped, the king will sleep and sweat off his fever, and awaken restored, whole again (ll. 3077–3102). Not only does the planned cure perform with remarkable success but Richard devours his meal with greedy relish, eating faster than his carver is able to carve the human flesh for him (l. 3110), gnawing at the bones of his Saracen victim, and washing the whole down with plentiful drink (ll. 3111–12). Richard's folk are delighted at their kindly, healthful, and private joke at the king's expense— "His people turned themselves away and laugh" (l. 3114)—a collective prank that mightily restores the king's vitality, upon which Richard's people give thanks to "Jesus and Mary" for their help (ll. 3122–23). The point is clear: The king's cannibalism is authorized by God, no less. The healing cannibalism of the British king, Cadwallo, has now been spectacularly drafted into the legend of Richard Lionheart, celebrated king of England.

Shortly after boisterously returning to skirmish with the Saracens, Richard demands at supper "the head of that same swine of which I ate" ("þe hed off þat ylke swn / þat j off eet," ll. 3198–99), because, he says, he feels faint and fears the return of his malady. The cook at first resists but, threatened with the loss of his own head, returns on his knees with the black, grinning head of the dead (and eaten) Saracen, in a scene that triumphantly stages the horror of the head, its color difference, and its inhuman, devilish nature. Narrative attention zeroes in on the black face and black beard of the detached head, set off against white teeth that are bared by widely grinning lips (ll. 3211–13). Richard's response ("What devil is this?" l. 3214) is extravagant laughter. He had not known before, he exclaims, that Saracen flesh was this delicious: Now his army would never lack for food, since they were able, in any assault, to slay Saracens, and take their flesh to boil, roast, or bake, gnawing the flesh to the bones; never again would he and his men fear hunger, in their campaign of conquest in the Levant (ll. 3216–26).

What is extraordinary about this bizarre performance of cannibalism by a celebrated English king is less the cannibalism per se than the depiction of cannibalism *as a joke in a popular romance*—a joke that, like romance itself, has healing and aggressive properties; that is to say, a properly romance kind of joke, specially developed for its potentials in serving the cultural politics of romance. Pointedly, the joke here is attached to a historical English king to announce and embellish, not to condemn, his legend: Where Geoffrey's *Historia* in twelfth-century England had plucked two leaders from the shadows of the past—Arthur of Britain and Cadwallo—to banish the ghost of Christian cannibalism through the production of romance, *RCL* proudly celebrates a historical English king of recent vintage—one of the most admired of Christian warriors, crusaders, and medieval English monarchs—as a magnificent cannibal of a gloriously unapologetic, bellicose kind.[3] In the centuries between the occurrence of the historical cannibalism I describe in chapter 1—when the obscenity of Christians who eat human flesh is layered over by worse terrors of self-pollution and infernal contamination issuing from the cadavers they ingest—and the romance staging of a guilt-free, happy cannibalism performed with appetite by a Christian king of England in *RCL*, a discourse on cannibalism has plainly emerged in medieval culture.[4]

More importantly, *another* discourse has appeared, whose rhetorical force powerfully captures and organizes into orbit other discursivities in medieval culture: the discourse of medieval nationalism—a nationalist discourse different in organizational structure and governmentality from the post-Enlightenment nationalisms of mass movements and populist struggles but not different from later nationalist discourses in impulse or cultural imagination—and its working of England into a version of the medieval nation. Visible as early as Geoffrey's *Historia* are crucial moments in the foundational idea of medieval England as a nation-to-be. The *Historia* deftly offers an important precondition in imagining the possibility of national unity and continuity when it resolutely pronounces heterogeneity to be the stable, enduring condition of Britain's population: Ethnic communities of many kinds come from different parts of Europe to Britain's shores through repeated invasion or colonization; they settle, mingle, and are Christianized; and the disruptions in time feature, through the long view present in the *Historia*, as the very pattern of insular continuity itself, and thus the motor of historical development. The *Historia* demonstrates that, for *this* island community, invasion and conquest, and a hybrid, disparate population, do not feature as obstacles to the historical continuity and identity of the domus: *they are the specific pattern of continuity and identity for the domus itself.*[5]

The wildfire popularity of Geoffrey's Latin text in Anglo-Norman England leads us to an understanding of how profoundly useful, and ideologically valuable, such a view of continuity-through-disruption might be, to the descendants of the successful Norman invaders of Anglo-Saxon England, and the Norman ruling elites of Geoffrey's period and after. Medieval chroniclers of the twelfth century, as well as modern historians, demonstrate that Anglo-Norman elites already referred to themselves as "English" by the mid- to late-twelfth century, a century or so after the successful Norman conquest of 1066: references that suggest a view of themselves as essentially compatible and continuous with, the history of the land.[6] By giving Britain a regnal genealogy extending back to the glories of ancient Troy through Brutus, descendant of Aeneas—a genealogy anchored into place by key local monarchs such as King Arthur—Geoffrey's *Historia*, moreover, supplies a foundational mythology irresistible to insular monarchs and virtually ensures that the *Historia*, issuing the foundational myth of Britain, will furnish the conditional matrix for imagining England as well.

As a figure to express the overarching cohesion of the communal whole, the identity of a medieval geopolitical collectivity is crucially invoked by symbolic kingship—as the identity of the modern republican nation today might be invoked in flag or national anthem—and the coming to prominence of Richard Lionheart of England, in the footsteps of the legendary Arthur of Britain, is a logical moment in the creation of a medieval nation.[7] Chronicles amply document how Richard I of England is twinned with Arthur of Britain in the domestic imagination during Richard's lifetime and after: In his sojourn in Sicily, enroute to the Levant, Richard is even said to present Tancred of Sicily with Arthur's sword Excalibur, as a kingly gift—one purpose of the story being, no doubt, to announce Richard's possession of Arthur's fabulous legacy. For Arthur is to the foundational myth of Britain in the *Historia* as Richard is to the idea of England in *RCL*, a vernacular romance of the English nation fittingly organized around the icon of *its* king and *its* crusading enterprise, and one that repeatedly evokes Arthur as Richard's forebear in cultural mythology.[8]

As a popular Middle English romance materializing English nationalist feeling through the outline of crusade history, *RCL* is as culturally useful as Geoffrey's elite creation in Latin that materializes crusade history through a foundational romance of Britain—though useful, presumably, for an audience of a social class other than French- and Latin-using elites in the *domus*. Prominently, the consolidation of *RCL* as a literary text spans three centuries of collective authorship, as copyists, redactors, editors, and others cumulatively make its text: This most medieval of romances, whose creation richly exemplifies medieval textual culture and literary production at work, can be read only as a sedimented repository of cultural patterns, investments, and obsessions that were deemed important enough to be inscribed, and reinscribed, over a span of centuries—witnessed through the hands and intelligences that compiled its dual textual traditions—and not as the inspired autographic production of a single authorial genius, anonymous or attested by signature. Because the text of *RCL is* collectively produced, a reading of *RCL* is thus truly a reading of the sedimented locations of culture—of aggregated cultural markings felt by many to be necessary to lodge—over the long period that produced the distinctive spoor and text of this romance.[9]

That *RCL* was written *as* a romance—and not, say, an epic—also has significance for nationalist instrumentality. The characteristic freedom of romance to merge fantasy and reality without distinction or apology, and the ability of the medium to transform crisis into celebration and triumphalism, mean that romance has special serviceability for nationalist discourse.[10] In *RCL*, the skillful expansion of romance resources is witnessed when *humor*—exhibiting the joke as a centerpiece of attention, but also featuring puns, verbal boisterousness, lexical bellicosity, and exaggerated display—is explored, enlarging the narrative constituency of romance and the effectivity of the ideological medium. The selection of Richard I as the figure around which to exercise potentials inherent in the circuit of the joke is a particularly inspired decision. Not only is Richard an ideal historical king to figure the imagined community of England—among medieval kings, the aura of his personal magnetism, his massive stature as a crusading leader of Christendom, and his heroic reputation as a fearless military genius, can scarcely be matched—but Richard's love of, and supple facility with, jokes is also well attested by medieval chronicles, including Richard's historic use of the joke as a selective ploy in diplomatic negotiations with Saladin.[11]

Like the *Historia*'s creation of Arthurian romance to support the First Crusade and the empire of the crusader states of the Levant, *RCL*'s recreation of the Third Crusade functions to service rear-guard projects and fantasies of occupation-invasion. Fortuitously, the Third Crusade in many ways resembles the First—these two being also the only crusades to Levantine territory that can be deemed militarily and ideologically successful for Christendom—and irresistibly beckons to romance. However, unlike Geoffrey's *Historia*, which was completed while actual crusader colonies existed in the East, *RCL*'s fable of reoccupying the former sites of empire lost to Saladin's Islamic *reconquista* accumulates in the historical *absence* of any Levantine territory held by Christendom after the thirteenth century.[12] The romance of Richard thus demonstrates, in a different way from the romance of Arthur, the substitutive, performative character of the genre as an ideological instrument. *RCL* would also seem, by example, to urge a view of later romances as at once nostalgic and ominously projective: an interventionist moment in the long history of crusading ideology, *RCL* is an engaging specimen of that ideology by virtue of its boisterous romance humor, and thus perhaps rhetorically effective in an alternative way to earnest polemical tracts urging crusading.

Together the two romance texts of the *Historia* and *RCL* hold before our eyes a contention that, from the twelfth-century Latin foundation of Arthurian romance to the Middle English nationalistic romance of Richard/England in the next three centuries, the deep imbrication of romance with the project of empire stutteringly continues. Most importantly, by the time of *RCL* cannibalism has *explicitly* become the preferred trope, in romance, for figuring conquest and colonization: What was a mere hint in Raymond d'Aguilier's crusade history, and a problem for resolution in Geoffrey's romances in the *Historia*, has metamorphosed into a triumphant system of symbolism in the romance of England—where the most memorably indelible equation in literature between cannibalism, romance, and empire is spectacularly arranged.

THE THIRTEENTH CENTURY AND BEYOND: NATION AND ROMANCE IN THE EPISTEMIC CRUCIBLE

The thirteenth century—the period in which *RCL* was first begun, according to editorial traditions—is not only that century in which inscriptions of medieval nationalism begin to call attention to themselves in a pronounced fashion in the cultural documents of England. The thirteenth century, I suggest, is a remarkable period in medieval history that oversees a substantive epistemic transition and witnesses the emergence of a changing epistemic culture: a culture in which institutions of control are expanded, intensified, and refined through instruments of inquisition, regulation, and discipline that continue through the later centuries of the

Middle Ages. A symbolic moment of this transforming episteme is constituted by the Fourth Lateran Council under the presiding genius of Pope Innocent III in 1215, a council that generated *seventy* canons—more than double the number issued by any of the three previous Laterans of the preceding century, and more than triple those of Lateran I[13]—and representing a massive codification of rules on a vast array of subjects. There are canons setting out the doctrinal basis on which heresy would henceforth be prosecuted; canons mandating and schematizing the internal examination of the individual Christian subject through confession (after Lateran IV, it is routine to note, confessional manuals for clergy and penitents proliferate); canons governing marriage, excommunication, and the sacraments; canons instructing on the payment of tithes and taxes and the making of contracts; canons detailing the governance of clergy and clerical conduct, benefices, and parishes; even canons specifying conditions of appearance, dress, and distinguishing badges for racial and religious minorities living throughout Christendom (Schroeder, 560–84).

If Lateran IV furnished the ideological basis for disciplining the individual by searching out the secrets of conscience hidden within bodily interiors, the thirteenth century also infamously witnessed the rise and proliferation of another panopticonic institution aimed at viewing, examining, and controlling the insides of persons—the inquisition, whose methods of interrogation were designed to scrutinize the interior, even as its methods of evidence were designed to discipline the exterior by mapping the body's geography through exploration of the body's modalities of pain.[14] Close attention to the human microcosm was paired with concomitant attention to the macrocosm of Christendom-at-large. The early century saw an ominous expansion of the uses of the crusade— that military arm of Latin Christendom, comprising the combined might and armies of Europe—an institution originally designed by Pope Urban II a century before to pull together centrifugal forces in the *congregatio fidelium*. In the thirteenth century the crusade was for the first time turned against *internal* members of the *congregatio fidelium* itself: In 1204 the Fourth Crusade captured and eviscerated Constantinople, occupying Greek Christian territory for more than half a century afterward, and irreparably destroying thereafter the capacity of Eastern Christianity to continue in its centuries-long role as a bulwark against Islam in the Mediterranean; in 1208–29 the bloody, relentless persecution and massacre of Albigensians in southern France under the rubric of crusade was inaugurated. Just as the thirteenth century saw the Church's campaign against so-called schismatics and heretics crystalize in doctrinally and militarily innovative ways, it also witnessed efforts to contain and limit potential deviance by extending the supervisory umbra of the Church, as the rise of the mendicant orders in the first half of the century attests. The mendicants—a mobile, spiritual army of friars-at-large, undertaking the new, as well as older, religious duties—function, then, as a missionary presence of the Church in the field and an essential component of enforcement and ideological reproduction. Answering directly to the Pope, the orders supplied the ranks of papal inquisitors admirably: unlike older dispensations, their easy mobility in ferreting out heresy and heretics everywhere meant efficient deployment to new tasks. In philosophy and in cultural work, the impulse toward comprehensive containment, assimilation, and regulation finds the century engaged in producing *summae*—vast compendiums of knowledge aggregatively systematized; refining the procedures, dialectical methods, and evidential system of scholasticism; and amassing encyclopaedia-like literary compilations such as the interminable and definitive Old French Vulgate cycle of prose Arthurian and Grail-quest romances.

It is not a coincidence, then, that a century that saw interiors turned inside-out for inspection, and internal partitionings and divisions enacted in Christendom (a logical if ironic consequence of the Church's will-to-power and centralizing initiatives) should also witness a fractionalizing, partitioning drive at work in the European polity that powered nascent nationalisms.[15] The rise of medieval nationalism in the crucible of epistemic change is not—I will urge—merely conjunctural or accidental. In the thirteenth century, nationalist impulses in England had at hand examples, ideas, agents, and instrumentalities only vestigially (if at all) available earlier.

Among the instrumental regimes that developed in the episteme of the thirteenth century and after, I suggest, is *a racializing discourse* of biological and spiritual difference, posited on religion, color, and physiognomy, the intense and searching examination of which theorizes a taxonomy of essential differences among peoples, that sets the later Middle Ages apart from the earlier Middle Ages. I will argue that the emergence of a distinctly racial discourse, and racial thinking, in the thirteenth century—and continuing through the "long thirteenth century" of the Middle Ages before the onset of the Renaissance—specifically attests to the instrumentality of racial categories in the formation of a medieval nation. Before the grapheme "race" itself appeared in the English language, and even longer before the appearance of formal census inventories naming official categories of races, the hierarchical discourse of power that prioritizes among peoples on the basis of a taxonomy of essences—that is, what we would today understand racial discourse and racial thinking to position in culture—took root and was established in the long thirteenth century of the medieval period.

Medieval examples, I will show, instruct us that racial thinking, in premodern contexts, does not require races as such to exist a priori but will *produce* races at need, in answer to specific historical imperatives and occasions. One occasioning moment for the production of races, in the Middle Ages, occurs when the idea of the nation takes hold: when new subjects—national subjects—are projected and constituted by, for, and within a community, the intersection of "race" with "nation" becomes maximally visible. Without requiring to argue for the persistence of what Ann Stoler's Foucault calls a "transformational grammar" of race over the continuum of human history, it is possible to identify and locate the discontinuous traces and marks of racial thinking, and race-making, in premodern historical periods, by studying the *effects, uses,* and *targets* of discourses of power wielded by large communities possessing power. Contemporary critical race theory has shown that definitions of "race," in the event, ceaselessly shift, and alter, from the Renaissance through the twenty-first century: so that what constitutes "race" as a category has been contingently filled, at different historical moments, by naming women, slaves, people of different ethnicities, nationalities, and classes, religious communities, and groups of internal and external others as constituting foreign or problematic "races," in highly mutable classificatory systems. Indeed, what can be defined as a "race" is today still elusive and highly contested, as U.S. Population Census 2000's multiple and proliferating categories of racial self-identification (which subsume linguistic communities, and traditional ethnicities, under "races") has recently amply demonstrated.

In the medieval period, racial thinking, I will show, assumes the form of a parcel of tendencies within the impulse to differentiate that produces " races" at historical junctures when the national community-in-formation requires self-definition; and the effects, uses, and targets of racial thinking, and racial discourses of power, are visible in the treatment of specific groups of persons and bodies within the community. The medieval nationalism I discuss in this chapter does not, of course, issue in anything like a national republic nor a modern state, and not, I think—despite the con-

victions of a few highly respected medievalists—a "nation-state." Among
the distinguishing properties of the medieval nation is that it is always a
community of the realm, *communitas regni*. Leveling discourses cutting
across multiple divisions in medieval society, to imagine the nation as unified, cohesive, and stable, are nonetheless put in place under medieval nationalizing imperatives. An expressive vocabulary for imagining the nation
is established, and a linguistic medium—English—increasingly functions
as the equivalent of the nation's incipient modernity, especially from the
fourteenth century on. Through these and other processes, the figural status of monarchy, and the symbolizing potentials of the king, play a prominent role in imagining the nation (although, as chapter 4 will show, higher principles of civic and ethical justice, and civil consent, may contingently
take precedence over the usually useful symbolism of monarchy).

My discussion of *RCL* as an exemplar of nationalist romance in England from the thirteenth through fifteenth centuries thus has a number of
moments.

I begin from the critical commonplace that war, in medieval history
as in medieval romance, is a productive channel for nationalism and that
religious war—the crusade—is the productive channel for a nationalism
that, in the Middle Ages, is always and fundamentally traversed, determined, and articulated by religious investments: a specificity of medieval
nationalism. My discussion of a racializing discourse in England that answers to the interests of nation formation thus follows the example of
RCL by always reading racial difference—including depictions of skin
color and bodily markers, corporeal physiognomy—as intersecting with
religious difference: with Islam and Judaism, as racial thinking theorizes
an essential(ist) link that binds religion and physiognomy, in the identification of races. I indicate how the choice of Richard as an organizing
figure for the imagined community of the realm is not unproblematic,
given hints of sexual irregularity in Richard's history, and the medieval
epistemic tendency to conflate sodomy with heresy; I then show how a
romance written in English triumphantly harnesses English-language resources of humor for a brilliant and resoundingly nationalistic romance
solution. My selection of an English romance contends, thus, that the use
of English in medieval England is a bid for a linguistic modernity and a
linguistic nationalism that parallels and articulates the rise of the medieval nation. Finally, the choice of a *popular* romance as an exemplar—
RCL survives in seven manuscripts and two printed editions, and its narrative is traversed by utopian fictions of class unity and justice—intimates

the role of popular literary productions, and popular romances, in particular, in the discursive work of imagining the nation. For it is in popular, not courtly, romance that the impetus toward nation formation can be most readily read: chivalric productions being, above all, the ideological property of elites whose caste interests are typically overriding, and whose class culture touts chivalry as an international formation with loyalties that exceed the merely local or national. Though popular romances utilize conventions and topoi made conveniently familiar to all audiences by older modalities of romance, including courtly romance, the determinations of popular romance, I suggest, lie elsewhere, and allow the channeling of broader, deeper, and new—national—currents, forms of address, and experimentation.

Black Humor; or, The Color Politics of a Cannibalistic Joke: Nationalism, Colonization, Romance, and History

A joke that works begs to be told more than once, and the romance of Richard/England shows what can be gained when a successful joke is craftily repeated. With Richard's delighted discovery that Muslims can simultaneously be conquered and eaten in military assault (ll. 3220–25), the king's political strength, and his mastery and control of the Christian military forces, magically intensify: The crusading Orders, historically notorious for their belligerent independence and intransigent refusals of direction from all but their own leaders, become "*his* Templars . . . *his* Ospytalers" (ll. 3151–52; my emphasis), and the city of Acre instantly capitulates (ll. 3227–3340). With territorial digestion so felicitously accompanying alimentary digestion, a *second* episode of cannibalism naturally follows.

This second cannibalism, drawing out the implications of the first, is designed as a diplomatic exercise, carefully staged to bring home the full, intimidatory power of Christian military-gustatory aggression to Saladin's aged, aristocratic ambassadors. Richard invites Saladin's ambassadors to a state dinner and begins with an insult, placing the dignatories, not "on des" ("on the dais," l. 3451) or at the high table with the king and his chief nobles, as envoys from the great Saladin should be treated, but at "a sydetable" (l. 3446). For the meal's first course, Richard, who happens to have in captivity the sons of the kings of Niniveh, Persia, Samaria, Egypt, and Africa (ll. 3598–3603), has these scions beheaded, and their shaven and

plucked, cooked heads set before the Saracen diners who are their kinsmen. Each head arrives on a platter, piping hot, and is arranged so that
the face looks upward, with bared, grinning teeth like before, and bears
the name of the decapitated prince and his lineage labeled on its brow (ll.
3428–30)—every dish being set between two diners, in the grand style of
royal and ceremonial dinners in medieval literature and history. As the
horrified relatives weep over the beardless, hairless heads of their slain family members (l. 3466) and grow terrified for their lives, Richard's own dish
of Saracen's head, complete with label, is carved up for him by the royal
carver; and, before the horrified eyes of all, Richard the Lionheart devours
the flesh with "herte good" (l. 3481)—with a hearty, lion-sized appetite.[16]
Lest the meaning of this sublimely diabolical performance be lost on the
beholder, Richard commands the ambassadors to return to their master,
Saladin, with the message that Richard and his men plan to eat every living Saracen in Saladin's lands, and will not return again to England until
every Muslim inhabitant has been gobbled up (ll. 3555–62).[17]

This time around, the king of England emphasizes to the Muslim dignatories that his gustatory practices are not unique to himself but will be
the routine, identifying practice of a generalized commonality of peoples:
Englishmen. To an English Christian subject, Richard announces, there is
no flesh so nourishing as the flesh of a Saracen ("þer is no ﬄesch so no-
rysschaunt / Vnto an Ynglyssche Cristen-man . . . As þe ﬂesshe of a
Sarazyn," ll. 3548–52); in fact, what defines the Englishman—the national subject—is his delight in eating up the natives in his march of conquest
into foreign—international—territory. As Richard gleefully mimes that
foreign aggression through a cannibalistic joke, he perceptibly conjures up
a national collectivity of souls, materializes a unity of Christian Englishmen whose extraterritorial gustatory habits define their very identity.

The joke, meanwhile, taps conventions of humor that make the trans-
gression of taboos acceptable, narratable: Richard's barbarism in territorial and gustatory arenas can be overlooked, even admired, in the English
king's skillful manipulation of a joke's trajectory in overpowering limits of
permission, in the push for the punch line; so that the aggressive, nationalistic pleasure can be enjoyed with the full approval of conscience (it's
only a joke, after all). The meaning of Richard's grisly joke is not, of
course, lost on the graybeard ambassadors, whose powerlessness and fee-
bleness are silently echoed in the de-masculinized, plucked heads of their
murdered kinsmen.[18] In their subsequent report to Saladin—a report
that, in a double narration, performatively keeps the shocking scene be-

fore our eyes after the actual event has passed—the ambassadors speak directly to the territorial implications of a communalized English, Christian nationalism-cannibalism: Now that Richard has won Acre, they urge, he means to go forth to conquer lands east, west, south, and north—the entire Islamic world—and eat their children and themselves ("Now Richard has Acres wunne. / He has ment, ʒiff he may, go fforth / To wynne est, west, souþ, and norþ, / And eete oure chyldren and vs," ll. 3666–69). In devouring the heirs ("heyres") of Muslim kings and princes of the Orient (ll. 3658–61), English Christians will swallow up lineages and sweep away succession, consuming the future itself, in world domination.

A nationalistic joke, of course, is ideal for expressing international aggression, since aggression is precisely the point of its humor. A joke, as Freud once pointed out, cannily taps sources of aggressive pleasure when directed against others; a collective joke, moreover, bribes an audience "into taking sides . . . without any very close investigation" and works to draw "the laughers" over to one's side ("die Lacher auf seine Seite ziehen"), instantly uniting the collectivity of those who laugh, and share the joke (Freud, 8:103). Just as heads, in history and literature, are the trophies of military war in the Orient, jokes about cannibalizing the heads of the defeated are the linguistic trophies of an ideological war, as much a symbol of conquest in a military romance as a head itself. With humor, moreover, enemies—even the historically undefeatable Saladin, Salah ad-Din Yusof, Kurdish emperor par excellence, whose reputation for integrity, chivalric honor, dignity, and magnanimous invincibility, extended beyond the Levant into the heart of European culture and history itself—become magically vulnerable; history can be defeated with a joke.[19] And, thanks to the circuit of the joke in this romance, nationalist and colonial ambitions are exemplified as continuous—logically partnered with each other in the discourse of war and power. A joke is an entertaining and witty way of showing how "the 'national idea' flourished in the soil of foreign conquest" (Brennan, 59).[20]

As England's king, and the chief representative of the nation, Richard's mastery of ideological manipulation is glimpsed in how deftly he turns an initially affectionate joke against himself, in the first cannibalism, into a collective hostile joke against the enemy, in the second cannibalism—extrapolating, in the process, a community called "England," made up of "good," "English," "Christian men" who are defined by their appetite for Muslims. Before that moment where the collectivity of Englishmen is magically constituted in Richard's speech, however, first another defining instant has been necessary: a genetic moment when what is *not, and can never be,* English is conclusively identified. The basis of a communal English identity rests on that prior identification when Richard grasps for the first time that he has committed cannibalism: in the shock when the black face of the Saracen head, produced by the terrified cook, stares at him. Richard's gaze instantly takes in, and establishes beyond question, the simultaneous evidence of cannibalism and of racial-religious difference in what is undeniably a racial recognition: the instant in which the darkness of Saracen skin—a biological, genetic marker of racial difference—pulls into stark focus the Islamic otherness of the enemy, in opposition to English Christians. Next comes the Saracen's black beard, a sign of cultural difference—masculine physiognomy defined by religion and ethnicity—but a cultural alterity that signally acts to confirm the essential biological nature announced by the skin.[21] So important is this seemingly casual presentation that color is the first thing which we, and Richard, are forced to see, in acknowledging the victim: for the black face ("swarte vys" [l. 3211]), "blacke berd" and "whyte teeþ" (l. 3212), and widely grinning lips ("lyppys grennyd wyde" [l. 3213]) definitively establish the dead Saracen (and not the cannibalistic Christian king) as the "devil" ("deuyl" [l.3214]) that Richard immediately designates him.[22] Invisibly, via the visible intelligibility of color, a racial discourse has surfaced alongside the discourse of nationalism and colonization with which it is blended through humor—the racial humor of the collective national joke.

The cultural work performed by this black humor in the romance of England points back, it should be recalled, to a similar kind of work performed by one of the invasions depicted in Geoffrey's *Historia,* when the king of the Africans suddenly leads an invading force of 160,000 Africans into the hearthlands of Britain, issuing a campaign of terror that decimates the country and disperses the population. Unlike earlier and later waves of invaders/settlers, these Africans are *not* subsequently absorbed into the population of Britain—a population, I have said, whose changing composition and heterogeneity are vindicated as historically stable by eventual assimilation and Christianization, and thus constituting over time the engine of historical development in Britain's myth of foundation. We see, from the *Historia's* use of the Africans, that the offer of heterogeneity in the *Historia* is purchased at a price—at the cost of what is *not* assimilable: Muslim Africans. Thanks to the alterity of aliens who are truly unlike Europeans, other communal groups in Britain—Celts/Britons, Saxons, Picts/Scots, Irish, Bretons, and so on—seem less foreign, less different from one another, by the implied common denominator of color and Christianization. The horror of the Africans, who conduct counterconversion—having the nephew of the king of the Franks renounce Christianity—is the glue that holds together the ethnic multiplicity so necessary to the success of mythical foundation. But though the romance of Britain installs its foundational myth through Islamic Africans, it is only the much later romance of England that *explicitly* foregrounds what was merely embedded in the twelfth-century text: For *RCL* theatrically conjures with *blackness*, as well as with Islam, for *its* foundational fiction, performing a dramatic linkage of color, race, and religion—a construct of race-*as*-religion and religion-*as*-race—that typifies the racial discourse of later medieval epistemic culture.

To work its transformations, romance reprocesses history, making historical elements appear and disappear in romance narrative. The episode of the Africans, in Geoffrey's *Historia*, is transubstantiated from a source episode in Gildas's *De Excidio Britanniae* describing a *Saxon* invasion. In *RCL* historical moments gleam through the two cannibalisms: Richard was, in fact, recorded by chroniclers as recovering rather suddenly from his illness at Acre, after sweating off his malady (Richard of Devizes, 81); the English king did take enemy heads for trophies (*Itinerarium*, 251), and had the beards of antagonists who capitulated shaven off (*Itinerarium*, 201; Ambroise, l. 1948). The blackness of Saracen skin, as a visible marker of the devilishness and otherness of the enemy, is also historically remarked on (*Itinerarium*, 263; Ambroise places on record the loathly blackness of Saracens but omits devilishness [ll. 6215–18]); and dead Turks were desecrated by deliberately mingling and confusing them with swine's flesh/pigs' carcasses (*Itinerarium*, 412; Ambroise, ll. 11285–86). In *RCL* romance also repairs crusade history, offering the consolation of a literary narrative of success in the wake of desiccatory historical failure. In answer to the debacle of Hattin, where, in 1187, Saladin won a resounding victory over the combined Christian forces of the East, decimating the largest army ever assembled by the Latin colonies of the Levant, the romance plays up Richard's historically smaller victory at Arsuf (*RCL*, ll. 5151–52, 5169–70), a tactically dazzling but not decisive battle with few, if any, long-term consequences. To displace Saladin's historic recapture of Jerusalem—an inevitability that followed from Hattin—the romance offers up Richard's purely fictive conquest of "Babylon" (*RCL*, ll. 5824)—presumably, Cairo, symbolizing the Egyptian heart of Saladin's empire, and the territorial base from which Saladin's military and political campaigns originally began. Loss, failure, and absence in history thus engender success, victory, and presence in romance: a recipe for cultural fantasy's relationship to history that would endure till the late twentieth century's filmic re-presentations of the Vietnam War, "Rambo" diegeses, and beyond.

"There Be Jews Here"; or, How One Community Consumes Another in Nationalist Romance

But reading the sedimentations of history in *RCL*, we glean a suspicion of one more, important target of the cannibalistic joke lying hidden behind the target of the Saracen head—another racial-religious community of swarthy, bearded Levantines who are also imagined in medieval culture, particularly from the thirteenth century, as devilish, inimically hostile to Christians, and deserving of death, or a fate worse than death: the Jews.[23] If Richard's demand for a head on a platter seems uncannily to resemble typological revenge for the biblical decapitation of the forerunner and cousin of Christ, we recall that the killing of Jews was an integral part of crusade history, as well as the history of Richard's ascension to the throne of England. The so-called Popular Crusade of 1096, erupting after Pope Urban II's rousing exhortations at Clermont, showed how easily medieval modalities of thought made it possible to slide, ideologically, from one religious target to another—from the projected massacres of Muslims in the East, the enemy outside Western Europe, to immediate massacres of Jewish communities in the Rhineland, the enemy within Europe itself.[24] The very coronation of the famed English crusader-king in 1189 occasioned a slaughter of Jews at Westminster and London that spread months later to Lynn in Norfolk, Norwich, Stamford, and York—events celebrated by some twelfth-century chroniclers with as much relish as the slaughter of that other infidel enemy in Richard's campaigns (e.g., Richard of Devizes, 3–4; William of Newburgh, 1:294–99, 1:308–22; cf. Roger of Wendover, 1:166–67, 176–77).[25]

The political implications of the medieval capacity to think analogically are starkly visible in persecutory movements in which the targets of violence shift, spread, and stretch across a spectrum of nonidentical communities. Though David Nirenberg's fine study, *Communities of Violence*, argues for the local specificities of cause and effect in persecutory movements, its discussion of an example like the Shepherds' and Cowherds' crusades of 1320–21 ends up demonstrating how violence detours beyond its initial targets to absorb other targets and communities—finally subsuming Muslims, Jews, lepers, practitioners of sorcery—whose unlikeness and non-identity are bridged by habits of analogical thinking that catch at the underlying resemblance of these targets by virtue of the targets' alterity, their difference from cultural normativity: a thinking that enables targets to shift, substitute, and stand in for one another.[26] We should not be surprised, then, when we find Muslims acting strangely like Jews in *RCL*. The historical anti-Jewish libel of well poisoning, a libel that takes root in Chinon in 1320–21, and infamously recurs in Europe during the Black Death, is attributed here to Saladin, as if Jews and Muslims were identical:

> He leet taken alle þe cors,
> Boþe off dede men, and off hors,
> And caste into þe watyr off oure welle
> Vs to poysoun and to quelle;
> Dede he neuerre a wers dede
> To Crystene-men ffor no nede.
> For þorwȝ þat poysoun, and that brethe,
> Ffourty þousand toke her dethe. (ll. 2749–56)

> He ordered taken all the corpses,
> Both of dead men and of horses,
> And cast into the water of our well
> Us to poison and to kill;
> Did he never a worse deed
> To Christian men for any need.
> For through that poison, and that breath [of pestilence],
> Forty thousand took their death.

This depiction of Muslims as virtual Jews in the calumny of well poisoning is part of *RCL*'s narrative from at least the earliest surviving manuscript of the text, the fragment in the Auchinleck, dated circa 1330—about a generation after the expulsion of Jews from England in 1290, and the nearly simultaneous loss of the last crusader colony, Acre, to Muslims in 1291. Significantly, though awash with Saracens, *RCL* is ignorant about medieval Muslims and their religion: Islam is not a monotheism prohibiting deistic representation, but Saracen idols, gods, and temples abound; "heathen" and "pagan" are interchangeable synonyms; and the Islamic "gods"—Mahoun

(Mohammad), Termagant, Appolyn (Apollo), Jupiter—are conventions familiarized by the *chansons de geste*. Richard, a home-grown hero, resembles the Richard of medieval chronicles, but Saladin is a *chanson* villain who little recalls the noble emir of history. If this romance written in England is unfamiliar with the foreign enemies of Christendom it describes in Outremer—skirmishing with mere literary conventions in their depiction— what other enemies of Christendom might it be more familiar with, closer to home in England, who might come to mind in conceiving threats to *communitas Christiana* and English interests?

Despite the early Augustinian tradition of relative tolerance toward Jews in Christian communities, and protections occasionally extended by Pope, ecclesiastic, and Emperor, Christian polemicists from the twelfth century on increasingly accumulated arguments that positioned Jewish institutions, traditions, and practices as cornerstones on which the validation and consolidation of Christian doctrine and principles might be established. The rhetorical strategies of Odo of Cambrai, Guibert of Nogent, Rupert of Deutz, Petrus Alphonsi, Peter Abelard, and Peter the Venerable variously represented Jews as the antithesis of Christians, depicting Jewish rejection of the Incarnation as evidence of a literality—an incapacity for allegorical and figural thinking—that rendered the Jew subhuman, animal-like, through a lack in the faculty of reason (A. S. Abulafia, "Christian Imagery"). In the thirteenth century the ideological reduction of Jews to animality found hideous expression in the *Judensau*, the conflation of Jews with swine, tabooed animals in Judaism as much as Islam, in "portrayals of Jews sucking at the teats of a sow" (Cohen, *Friars*, 244; see also Fabre-Vassas, chap. 4). Also from the thirteenth century come confirmed blood libels against Jewish communities—the calumny that Jews murdered Christians, especially children, because Christian blood was consumed in Passover rituals—a thinly disguised accusation of vampiric cannibalism. A period of special epistemic virulence toward Jews, the thirteenth century issued the libel of Jewish Host-desecration— a libel which freshened the old tradition that Jews were the killers of Christ, by insinuating that Christ's deicide at Jewish hands was not only conscious but repeated postmortem through Jewish torture and destruction of the Eucharist.[27] A twelfth-century polemicist like Rupert of Deutz may have considered Jews, rather than Muslims, the antithesis of Christians, but the thirteenth century witnessed the consolidation of Jews as the standard by which contempt for enemies could be measured and fittingly expressed: Robert de Clari's chronicle on the Fourth Crusade's annexation of Constantinople reports that the Bishops of Soissons, Troyes, and Halberstadt, and the Abbot of Loos, vindicated Latin Christendom's attack on Greek Christendom as righteous by decisively dismissing the Byzantine victims as "worse than Jews" ("pieur que Juis" [72]).

In the new episteme, then, *RCL*'s two cannibalisms seem to serve up a special kind of punishment, and English Christendom's communal narration on what kind of justice Jews, as much as Saracens, deserve. For the killers of Christ who cannibalistically require Christian blood, what better desert could there be than the answer of Semitic heads on a platter, to be cannibalistically consumed in turn by Christian Englishmen? Moreover, the covert, second meaning of the cannibalistic scenes must be arrived at—can only be read—*allegorically*, since the decapitated heads in the foreground are ostensibly Saracen ones: Through allegory, then, a race believed incapable of grasping allegory—their defining difference from Christians, who are expert exegetical readers and manipulators of biblical allegory—may be fittingly humiliated. The polemical equation of Jews with carnality, animal senses, and the body, and the *Judensau*'s conflation of Jews with swine make Richard's desire for swine's flesh, and his eating of humans as if they were animals, grotesquely meaningful. Even the image of the grinning maws of Richard's victims has a counterpart in the *adversus Judaeos* tradition: Guibert de Nogent, for instance, counterposes a polemic around the "filthy gaping jaws" of the Jews, the "mouths which . . . mock the life-giving sacraments" (A. S. Abulafia, "Christian Imagery," 387)—mouths that are forever closed by their tortuous passage through Richard's purposeful joke.

That Jews, as much as Muslims, are the targets in *RCL*'s two scenes of cannibalism is aided by medieval Christendom's understanding that Jews collaborated with Muslims in Islamic invasions of Europe and Jerusalem. Oppressed Jews in Visigothic Spain were believed to have conspired with, invited, and assisted Arab and Berber invaders from the Mahgreb against the Visigothic Catholic monarch, Roderick, in the second decade of the eighth century (Watt and Cachia, 12, 14, 32; Cutler and Cutler, 93), a consequence of the fact that in Visigothic Spain after 589, Jews were persecuted, exiled, or forced to convert under Visigothic laws. Several thousand Jews were reputed to have fought alongside Abd-al Rahman and ten thousand Berbers, against Charles Martel, at Poitiers in 732. Closer to the crusades, "Adhemar of Chabannes (circa 1028) and the Cluniac Ralph Glaber (circa 1044), testify to the belief, widespread among the Christians of France, that the Jews were in league with the

Muslims and that the destruction of the Holy Sepulchre in 1009 by the
Fatimid Caliph of Egypt, al-Hakim, was a product of a joint Islamo/Ju-
daic conspiracy" (Cutler and Cutler, 87).[28] In Saladin's time, the closeness between Muslims and Jews was suggestively expressed when the
Kurdish ruler, on recapturing Jerusalem, brought in Jews to resettle the
holy city (Runciman, 2:467). The imagined co-identity of Christendom's enemies is symbolically expressed in Lateran IV's Canon 68,
which assigns a distinction in clothing to mark off Jews and Saracens
alike, collectively and together, from Christians, as if the two infidel nations were halves of a single body of aliens.[29]

If the medieval ideological mind is able to confuse Jews with Muslims,
RCL's obsessive description of the forcible mass conversions of Saracens
can be seen as more than just a simple fantasy. With seeming ahistorici-
ty, *RCL* offers conversion as a major objective of crusader colonization,
and virtually synonymous with territorial annexation itself: Mass conversion follows the conquest of Niniveh (ll. 5370ff.) and Babylon (ll. 5881ff.);
the crusaders demand conversion at Ebedy (ll. 4421–25); and, in a declaration of crusade policy, Richard orders Philip Augustus to put to the
sword everyone he finds in "Toun, cytee, and castel" who will not convert (ll. 3821–28), an imperative Richard repeats word for word to his own
army (ll. 3965–70). In *RCL*, territorial dominance is synonymous with
forcible conversion, and the alternative to conversion is death. History,
by contrast, shows Muslim conversion to Christianity in the Levant as in-
frequent, at best sporadic; enough of a novelty for it to be noticed, commented on, and recorded when it happened; and overwhelmingly dictated by the self-interest, ambitions, or faith of the individual. Though
occasionally urged by a voice or two in a religious tract, "Muslim conversion was not a mass phenomenon in the Crusading Kingdom" (Kedar,
82), and "religious conversion of the infidel was never proclaimed as an
aim" (Murray, 63). In fact, Levantine lore tellingly documents its opposite, the *prevention* of conversion: An infamous incident describes how
the Knights Templar undermine the prospect of mass conversion by the
Batinis (the Shi'ite Muslim group popularly known as the Assassins) to
ensure that the tax paid to the Order of the Temple by these Muslims inhabiting Templar-dominated territory would continue to furnish Templar revenues—an event that offers a revealing fiscal explanation for why
conversion should *not* take place in Christian-dominated Levantine territory. William of Tyre also records how, in 1154, when the fugitive son
of an Egyptian vizier fell into Templar hands, and expressed a desire to

convert, even learning Latin, the Templars preferred to hand the would-be apostate back to the Egyptians for sixty thousand pieces of gold instead. Most telling of all are the histories that document how Richard of England and Philip Augustus preferred to *end* Muslim conversions after their conquest of Acre, when the crusader kings discovered that the new Christians, on receiving freedom with Christianity, simply absconded for Saladin's camp.[30]

Medieval history shows that it is *Jews in Europe* who are forced to undergo conversion, or suffer death at the hands of Christians, more than Muslims in the Holy Land, and forcible conversion or death is a choice repeatedly offered to Jewries in medieval England, France, Spain, and Germany.[31] In playing thus with historical conditions that seem to vanish in medieval romance only to reappear, transformed, *RCL* hints at a curious parallel when it elects to articulate its theme of (Muslim) conversion with its theme of territorial dispossession and repossession in the Holy Land. For not only are Jews, the most prominent alien community in England, denied ownership of land in fee, while subject to forcible conversion or death in periodic eruptions, but an accident of economic history also made landless English Jews "the vehicle" and visible medium for the transfer of land ownership in England of the twelfth and thirteenth centuries (Pollins, 17)—and thus a figure of territorial dispossession and repossession in the home country of this romance.

Social historians have shown that Jewish moneylenders in England became associated with land, by serving as the means through which encumbered estates that passed as security through Jewish hands in financial transactions might be acquired by religious houses, secular groups, or great magnates with ambitions to extend their wealth or status through property holdings.[32] In the twelfth and thirteenth centuries, Cistercian and Augustinian houses (among them, Meaux Abbey, Malton Priory, Fountains Abbey, Waltham Abbey, Kirkstead, Biddlesden, Holy Trinity, Aldgate, and Healaugh Park), Premonstratensians, Gilbertines, Cluniacs, and Benedictines, acquired mortgaged properties through Jewish financiers (Richardson, 90–103), in a transactional system encompassing "so wide a geographical range and so many religious orders" (99) that it ultimately acted as a "solvent which broke down the apparent rigidity of the structure of feudal land tenure and facilitated the transfer of estates to a new capitalist class, the religious communities, or to new men who were making their fortune" (94).[33] By the reign of Henry III, cumulative land transfer through Jewish intermediaries had produced sufficient consequences in the loss of feudal dues and military service, and had so concentrated estates and military power in the hands of great landowners, as to subtract from the prerogatives of the Crown (Roth, *History*, 64). The Provisions of Jewry enacted by Henry III in 1269 specifically declared that "no debts whatsoever might be contracted in future with Jews on the security of lands held in fee" and "all obligations of the sort already registered were cancelled" (65); "the right to make loans on the security of real estate was from this period progressively restricted" (108).

The presence of a visible, economically active, yet unassimilated Jewish community in England living "cheek by jowl" with Christians (Stacey, 264)—a presence especially prominent in major cities like London and York, and in Eastern and Southeastern England—must have been a troubling focus in the social culture that conduced to the rise of the medieval English nation.[34] A persistent communal gaze and fixation is recorded in the ever-changing statutes, protections, and provisions imposed on English Jewry; the always-evolving basis of taxation and tallages applied to Jewish economic resources; and social eruptions of many kinds. Unlike national rivals across the sea or ethnic antagonists sharing a border with the English polity—the French, Irish, Welsh, Scots[35]—Jews constituted a resident alien community *within* England itself, as England was consolidating as a nation: an alien community whose existence and daily activities were intimately bound up with the economic and social life of the dominant community, but from which, nonetheless, they necessarily remained apart, by virtue of fundamental differences of race-religion.[36] That the religious, racial, and economic status of Jews were an obsessive target of attention for a medieval English society in transition, for English kings enlarging their fiscal and ideological resources, and prelates consolidating Christian doctrine, is attested by a series of evolving obsessions.

English economic dependence on Jewish mediation in financial transactions, and the crown's dependence on tallages levied on English Jewry (after Henry II dispensed with loans in favor of straightforward methods of fiscal extraction that required no repayments), meant that the association of Jews with profit and wealth drew as much inquisitive scrutiny as the threat of race-and-religion that Jews, as domestic aliens, were able to figure for the polity. Documents of debt to Jews and excitement over putative Jewish wealth featured as a prominent focus in anti-Jewish attacks, alongside religious conversion. Not surprisingly, in *RCL*, profit and conversion are linked themes. Richard warns Philip Augustus not to accept bribes of "gold, syluer" or any reward (l. 3824) proffered by desperate infidels: historically apt counsel to the king of France, since French Jewries largely escaped threats of conversion or death suffered by their coreligionists in the Rhineland in 1096 by buying off crusaders with large bribes. Though Richard insists that spiritual profit is the goal in this, the Third Crusade, Richard's own example shows how the fiscal resources of his victims at Babylon can profit Christians, so that "Erl, baroun, kny3t, and knaue, / Had as mekyl as þey wolde haue" ("Earl, baron, knight, and commoner / Had as much as they wanted" [ll. 5891–92])—a haunting reminder of how attacks against Jews in the wake of Richard's ascension festivities in England also profited the Christian benefactors of violence, especially would-be, self-described crusaders. Roger of Howden's chronicle tells of failed bribery, plunder, the killing of Jews, and the burning of records of debt to Jews, at York (3:33–34); Roger of Wendover recounts the slaying of Jews at Norwich, Stamford, and St. Edmunds by crusaders, and plunder and the burning of debt papers at York (1:176–77); William of Newburgh describes plunder at Lynn (1:308–10), plunder and killing at Stamford by crusaders for the expenses of Richard's Crusade (564–65), and even more massive plunder by crusaders for the same purpose at York, along with forcible and failed conversions and mass slaughter (566–71).

Just as Muslim infidels are plundered time and again by the English king and his cohorts in the crusading romance of England, Jewish infidels in England were plundered by English monarchs through tallages, time and again, when a crusade was declared in the twelfth and thirteenth centuries. Gervase of Canterbury reports a massive tallage on the Jews—sixty thousand marks—imposed by Henry II in 1186 to finance the Third Crusade (Roth, *History*, 17 n. 2; Richardson, 162; Tyerman, 79); a further ten thousand marks were demanded after the Saladin tithe was announced in 1188 (Richardson, 163), and two thousand more in 1190 (Tyerman, 79).[37] Jewish contribution in 1194 to the crusader Richard's ransom was at least three thousand marks (Richardson, 164). In 1237, "in the interval between two heavy tallages," the English Jewry was "commanded to make a gift of 3,000 marks to the Earl of Cornwall, the king's brother, for the purpose of his intended Crusade" (Roth, *History*, 44). After Henry III took the cross in 1250, a levy of ten thousand marks was ordered on the Jews in 1251 (Roth, *History*, 46); and the future Edward I's crusade in 1271 was largely financed by a tallage of five thousand or six thousand marks imposed on the English Jewry (Richardson, 214; Roth, *History*, 67):[38] "Between 1240 and 1255 Henry III collected more than £70,000 from the English Jews, at a time when the king's total annual cash revenues rarely exceeded £25,000" (Stacey, 270).

Other foreign themes in *RCL* are also acted out by domestic subjects in English history. At *RCL*'s romance banquet, Saracen guests are ostentatiously present, and princely Saracen victims are killed at Richard's command. Historically, Jews were ostentatiously required to be *absent* from Richard's coronation banquet, though they were soon also killed—it is thought—by the king's command (William of Newburgh, 1:294–95). Two of the Jews persecuted at the time of the banquet and shortly after—Benedict and Joceus of York—are likened by medieval chroniclers to princes who live in near-regal luxury, in homes likened to palaces (William of Newburgh, 1:312–13). Benedict of York was immortalized in chronicles as the Jew who was converted to Christianity during the attacks at Richard's coronation, and who subsequently reconverted to Judaism (Roger of Howden, 3:12–13; William of Newburgh, 1:295). Benedict's trajectory—from Judaism to Judaism, with a temporary detour through Christianity—queerly mimes the trajectory of the renegade at Orgulous, in *RCL*, who proceeds from Christianity to Christianity, with a temporary detour through Islam (ll. 4076ff., 4215–25). Even the labels on the Saracen heads at Richard's banquet, functioning as badges of identity for the Saracen victims, seem queerly to reproduce the Jewish "badges of shame," which also proclaimed identity and community filiation (and which, as specified by the Statute of Jewry of 1275 [Parkes, 395] were as large as labels: six inches long by three inches wide). Finally, if the romance Richard treats his Saracen victims as if they were not fully and autonomously human, and little more than chattel, we note that the historical Richard, as king of England, possessed English Jews by right, customarily, from the time of Edward the Confessor on, as legally the property or chattel of the Crown.[39]

The drama of conversion enacted by romance also speaks to an intimate fear generated by the presence of a domestic community of religious aliens in the English homeland, where intimacy meant that a certain blurring of religious identity was inevitable in the contact zone—a fluidity and exchange occurring when Christians and Jews met, overlapped, intermarried. Christian converts to Judaism in English society—no doubt as statistically negligible as Muslim converts to Christianity in the Holy Land—were a magnet for alarmist attention, especially when members of the religious community (always a benchmark and proving-ground for Christendom) chanced to be the new Jewish converts. In the twelfth century not only did the Christian wife of a prominent and wealthy Jewish financier, Jurnet of Norwich, convert to Judaism early in the reign of

Henry II (Roth, *History*, 10) but Giraldus Cambrensis describes in horrified detail the conversion to Judaism of two Cistercian monks (Jacobs,
283–85). In the thirteenth century a deacon who had converted to Judaism
and married a Jewess, after studying Hebrew, was tried in 1222 and executed by burning (Roth, *History*, 41); Robert of Reading, a Dominican
friar, was so "stimulated by his study of Hebrew literature" that he also
converted to Judaism, "assuming the name of Haggai and marrying a Jewish wife" (Roth, *History*, 83); and in 1274 "a number of prominent London Jews were accused of having abducted a woman convert and coerced
her to go overseas in order to revert to Judaism" (Roth, *History*, 83). Pope
Honorius's letter of 1286 to the archbishops of Canterbury and York gave
strong voice to papal alarm: "He pointed out the evil effects of free intercourse between Jews and Christians in England . . . the pernicious consequences of study of the Talmud . . . As though this were the most pressing business which confronted Christendom, he sternly called for
counter-measures, including sermons and spiritual penalties, to end this
improper state of affairs" (Roth, *History*, 77). *RCL*, patrolling its religious
borders with as fine a vigilance as its nationalist interests dictate, presents
religious conversion as occurring in only one direction: Muslims become
Christians, and even the renegade at Orgulous desires to reconvert to
Christianity, turning down territory and treasure in pursuing penitential
self-humiliations for his soul's salvation (ll. 4075ff., 4215–25). Any admission that Christians might voluntarily go over to an enemy religion must
occur offstage, earlier than the romance events depicted;[40] only conversions to Christianity are triumphantly shown in *RCL*, whose investment
in religion as a cornerstone of communal identity is never in doubt.

Because communal identity is not only defined against, but also always
in terms of, the other, and Judaism, in particular, continues as a remainder, a residue, in medieval Christian consciousness and culture—the sine
qua non on which the medieval Christian apparatus of belief is founded—
the insecurity of identity boundaries for medieval Christians in transition
is especially acute. Historically English Christians also depended, in entirely practical ways, on Jews for the support of their economic life, their
religious crusades, and a panoply of transactions in knowledge, culture,
and specialized services. In its manipulation of its internal minority group
of domestic aliens, therefore, the national community of the Christian
English produced, in the thirteenth century, a panopticon of laws, gazes,
and regulatory techniques that met at the locus of Jewish identity: lessons
in how to specify, and differentiate among, the races of local humanity.

Canons 67 through 70 of Lateran IV furnished an ideological guide of general principles for containment and control—specifying conditions under which Jews were required to tender tithes, refrain from public appearance on certain days of Holy Week, be prohibited public office, and exhibit differences of dress from Christians—but thirteenth-century England took the policing, marking, and scrutiny of Jewish activity and bodies to extraordinary lengths (Roth, *History*, 76). By 1218, a scant three years after Lateran IV, English Jews had to wear the infamous badge that publicly proclaimed them to be Jews, and therefore not a part of the rest of England's community. In 1222 the demand for public Jewish self-identification was repeated at the Council of Oxford, which specified the size of the badge for Jews of both sexes. In 1253 Henry III ordered the badge to be worn in a prominent position on the breast, and in 1275 Edward I's *Statutum de Judeismo* increased the badge's size, demanded that it be exhibited prominently over the heart, specified its color, and ordered all Jewish *children* above the age of seven to display the badge (Roth, *History*, 95–96).

If a whiff of communal hysteria seems to touch the obsession over the size, color, placement, prominence, and universality of the Jewish badge, we understand that the manipulation of domestic minorities is a formative moment in the self-construction of national majorities. Knowing who and what a racial-religious minority is, is an essential stage in knowing who and what a national majority is, and is not: the stable, legible categories of the one fiction enabling and stabilizing the categories of the other. Getting the lineaments of the two communities inhabiting the homeland fixed, visible, and clear is thus a project of some urgency, and in 1287, the Diocesan Synod of Exeter accordingly forbade Jews to employ Christian servants, hold public office, feast with Christians, attend Christians in the capacity of physicians, venture into churches, leave houses or even keep windows open at Eastertide, withhold tithes, or omit the wearing of the Jewish badge (Roth, *History*, 78): prohibitions, we note, that ruminated on and ramified the prescriptive strictures of Lateran IV.[41] Even as these prohibitions advertise the fears of religious authority, they also tellingly announce English Christian dependence on, and intimacy with, English Jews—a commingling in private and public life that disturbed the racial project of stable, known, and separate identities within England's borders.[42]

Beyond the policing of aliens *in domo*, a logical exercise in the regimens of border patrol is the attempted transformation of aliens into

Christians—confirming the centrality of the national community with recruits. *RCL*'s spectacles of conversion thus also eloquently speak to the
history of conversion enacted in the English homeland. While in twelfth-
century England inducements to convert to Christianity were usually sporadic—typically the spillovers of mob violence (laws ascribed to Edward
the Confessor technically placed Jews under Crown protection, as did the
laws of Henry I and charters granted by Henry II, Richard I, and
John)[43]—in the thirteenth century, under repeated papal and ecclesiastical attentions, the discourse of conversion systematized into formal institutions of recruitment that received the endorsement of English kings.[44]
Thirteenth-century England "was a world saturated with aggressive displays of Christian ritual," while "thirteenth-century [English] kings began
to confiscate Jewish synagogues and turn them into churches" (Stacey,
264, 265). In 1232, Henry III formally established a "Domus Conversorum" for Jewish converts to Christianity, and baptisms of converted Jews
were enacted before the king, "who took evident pleasure in naming the
new converts" (Stacey, 269).[45] Proselytization "was henceforth carried on
more and more systematically" (Roth, *History*, 43); correspondently a case
of conversion to Judaism in 1234 warranted trial before the king himself
(Roth, *History*, 53). In the 1240s and 1250s, Jewish converts to Christianity "may have numbered as many as 300 in a total Jewish population that
did not exceed 5,000 and that may have been as low as 3,000" (Stacey,
269). By 1280, Edward I required all Jews to attend conversionist sermons
preached at them during Lent to turn them from Judaism, "in accordance
with the Papal Bull *Vineam Sore* of the previous year" (Roth, *History*, 79;
see also Stacey, 267).

Edward's expulsion of the Jews from England in 1290 can thus be
viewed as a social and ideological, as well as economic, phenomenon. In
economic terms, the expulsion has been rightly read as the culminating
logic of a long process of systematic exactions that depleted the financial
resources of the Jews, rendering a Jewish presence no longer economically pertinent, but with profit accruing to the Crown from the expulsion. In
social terms, the eviction is legible as part of a processional logic of national consolidation that occurred in thirteenth-century England: a logic
that produces Jews as—despite all attempts at converting them—an ultimately unassimilable alien race, marked by their religion, history, practices, and intrinsic difference, and too intimately and dangerously interwoven into the daily life of the English communal body. The expulsion of
all persons of the Jewish race from England, then, renders Jews useful

through the very process of their excision from the corporate body, a corporate body whose identity could now emerge, whole. At least one scholar has shown how the removal of the Jews in England—an inconveniently present "Israel of the flesh"—facilitated the substitution of the *English themselves* as the new chosen community of God—an "Israel of the spirit"—as an emergent nationalist idea: a substitution that witnesses the cultural colonization of an old, familiar biblical topos for new, secular, and nationalist purposes, once Jews themselves, the old chosen people of God, were no longer present in the flesh to hinder imaginative reconfiguration in the nation's interest (Menache, "Expulsion," 360–63).[46] English Christians are the new chosen race of God, and Normans and Saxons are the appropriate races of England.[47]

After the expulsion of Jews from England in 1290, the *Domus Conversorum*, home for converts from Judaism, was converted into a residence for clerks of Chancery conducting government business in the last decade of the thirteenth century. The home of conversion then became, in the fourteenth century, "the recognized center for Chancery business, called the . . . Rolls House until the Public Record Office was built on the same site in 1845 and 1895" (Fisher, "Chancery," 874). With involuntary eloquence, the home where once-Jews were found became the official repository where the business of the new nation of England was recorded and kept, once Jews themselves were evicted from the national homeland. Emptied of Jews, the transitional meaning of the house of converts itself stabilized, like the races and identity of England.

If, in English history, the alien infidels at home live too close at hand, are too indigestible, and must be expelled, in English romance the alien infidels, safely at a distance across the sea, prove eminently digestible and become a welcome part of the English diet of jokes into which they are then incorporated. Historically the expulsion of Jews from England in 1290 is followed by the expulsion of Christians, in 1291, from the last crusader colony in the Levant, Acre—the place in *RCL* where Richard's first cannibalism occurs—twin absences that functioned to prompt, not deflect, literary improvisations in romance.[48] Romance, of course, is skilled at offering presence in the place of absence, a vocabulary for speaking difference differently, and for magical transformations: like the *Domus Conversorum*, romance is the perfect site for multiple conversions, in the making of a nation.

But if Jewish communities no longer existed in England after 1290, it turned out that the expulsion of Jews from England did not remove Jews from English culture or nationalist ideology at all: Communal fictions of Christian boy-martyrs supposedly killed by Jews for ritual, sacrificial, vampiric, or other purposes continued to be narrated—even, and especially, by Chaucer, late in the Middle Ages—thus keeping alive for the nation the instrumentality of Jewish difference and malignity "till . . . the Reformation" (Roth, *History*, 89).[49] Debts owed to Jews, and interest on those debts, remained on English minds, while individual Jews—or the apparitions of Jews—continued to be found in the homeland: in 1376 the Commons in Parliament complained that Lombard usurers "harboured Jews and Saracens in their midst" (Roth, *History*, 132–33; Richardson, 232), while the "*Domus Conversorum* founded by Henry III had never been quite empty. . . . Down to its decline at the beginning of the seventeenth century, there were always a few inmates to justify its existence" (Roth, *History*, 133–34). Apparitional and virtual Jews continued to be needed, after all; and, in the sporadic appearance and disappearance of Jews in fourteenth- and fifteenth-century medieval England, when a national English, Christian identity confidently makes its way in language and culture, medieval romance, and *RCL*, played its part.

A Tale about Tails; or, Speaking Otherwise of Richard: Puns, Sodomy, the Body, and Gender

Richard's definition of Englishmen as cannibals, in this romance, shows how an English community can be theorized, in the first instance, by exploiting the symbolizing potential of the monarch, who here demonstrably lends his cannibalism to a corporate definition of his people as Christian-English conquerors that uniquely devour territory and folk. Yet the selection of the charismatic crusader Richard to represent England in the romance of the nation, as Arthur had earlier represented Britain, is not without its problems. Medieval chronicles cautiously hint that the exemplary Richard I might have given himself over to unexemplary sodomitical acts and preferences. Roger of Howden, especially, documents a phase of excessive attachment between Richard and Philip Augustus of France in the summer of 1187, when both men ate from the same dish at the same table every day and shared the same bed every night, and the king of France loved Richard as his own soul (2:318)—actions repeated no doubt to send a political message to Henry II, Richard's royal sire (as John Gillingham astutely insists ["Legends," 62–63]), but nonetheless assuming the contours of a highly suggestive kind of affective intimacy.[50] Howden, who inveighs against the "filthiness" of Richard's life (3:74), also documents an incident in 1195 when a hermit turns up to chastise Richard vociferously, warn him to abstain from unlawful acts, and urge him to remember "the destruction of Sodom" and to fear the vengeance of God (3:288). The chronicler adds that the English king subsequently took back his wife and put away "illicit intercourse" (3:289). Though medieval chronicles are usually tactfully circumlocutory and oblique when attaching the taint of sodomy to historical monarchs and emperors, Richard's estrangement from his queen, Berengaria of Navarre, his banishment of women (along with Jews) from his coronation (Roger of Wendover, 2:i, 81; Roth, *History*, 19, citing Matthew Paris), and the near-absence of women on the Third Crusade (Tyerman, 61) are well documented.[51]

Equally well documented is the extent to which sodomy, "the sin against nature" (*peccatum contra naturam*), was abominated in medieval culture, first in theological and then in secular discourses and law (attentiveness that suggests, perhaps, the relative commonness of the sin as much as the panic it occasioned). That references to "Sodom" and "Gomorrah" are shorthand, in medieval culture, for same-sex copulation between men has been suggested in texts from as early as fifth-century Gaul (Jordan, 35) through Peter Damian's *Liber Gomorrhianus*, written in 1048–54 (and specifying in detail four kinds of sodomitical, same-sex copulatory acts among clerics), to the late fourteenth century and beyond.[52] The thirteenth-century law code drafted for Alfonso the Wise makes unusually plain the horizon of meaning for Howden's cryptic reference to the destruction of Sodom:

> "Sodomy" is the sin which men commit by having intercourse with each other, against nature and natural custom. . . . from this sin arise many evils in the land where it is perpetrated, and it sorely offends God and gives a bad name not only to those who indulge in it but also to the nation where it occurs. . . . Sodom and Gomorrah were two ancient cities . . . and so great was the wickedness of their inhabitants that because they engaged in that sin which is against nature, our Lord despised them to the point of destroying both cities with all their occupants. . . . From that city, Sodom, where God worked this miracle, the sin took its name and is called sodomy. (Boswell, 289)

Although Conciliar pronouncements on sodomy from the early twelfth century prescribed excommunication (Council of London, 1102) or death (Council of Nablus, 1120), it is from the thirteenth century on that sodomitical acts are prosecuted with virulence, with the first documented execution in Western Europe issuing from 1277 (Johanssen and Percy, 174). The dangerous association of sodomy with heresy later intensifies; indeed, the extirpation of the Order of the Temple initiated by Philip IV of France accused the Order's members of sodomy while expressively utilizing inquisitorial procedures, evidence, and methods developed for persecuting heresy.[53] Other cultural convictions prevailed to ensure that the stigma of same-sex activity would elicit revulsion: Scholars have noted the conviction in Europe that "same-sex love . . . was preached and practiced by Islam" (Jordan, 10) and that Muslims were particularly "given over to homosexual vices" (Johanssen and Percy, 172). The prophet Mohammad was depicted as a sodomite with both men and women (Daniel, *Islam and the West*, 142–43), while Alexius Comnenus was reputed to have written to Robert of Flanders on Muslim Turks sodomizing "men of every age and rank" (Boswell, 367–68). The Templars, a crusading Order founded to combat the armies of Islam, became vulnerable through even their agonistic association with Islam; in the early fourteenth century the agents of Philip the Fair accused the Templars of, among other heinous practices, the contamination of Oriental vice, sodomitical acts. In the thirteenth century, too, "heresy and sorcery began to be equated" (Bullogh, "Heresy," 196), bringing to crisis a nexus of inflammatory associations: sodomy-heresy-Islam-sorcery.

In negotiating the obstacles posed by Richard's life, the romance of England develops an arsenal of linguistic and rhetorical resources of extraordinary audacity, and like Geoffrey's *Historia*, *RCL* surfaces, transforms, and triumphantly celebrates, rather than denies. Boldly, with characteristic romance panache, *RCL* winks at the English king's sexual history: The larger-than-life romance Richard is superphallic, with gigantic weapons of war that improbably extend his body in hugely theatrical fashion. Richard has an exaggeratedly massive English axe, with an enormous head, forged in England, which lengthens in due course to become a poleaxe (ll. 6814ff.); his martial instruments include a stout lance with a stiff circumference of twenty-one inches for the tournament at Salisbury (286–88), a forty-foot long tree trunk (ll. 5559–60, 5689ff.) heftily overlaid with biblical overtones, and an all-piercing spearhead that is a divine gift for penetrating Saladin's armor (ll. 5573–75).[54] These superabundant projectiles that magnificently extend the reach of Richard's militant body as *vir* and *rex*, moreover, have as their intended objective a great many Saracen bodies—the preferred lodging place of the English king's fearsome, hyperpenetrating, and overphallicized weapons. Once we accede to the suspicion that an ingenious, and ingeniously fertile, variety of doublespeak inhabits *RCL*, this military arsenal, and a range of active verbs of penetration, describing Richard's vigorous motility (e.g., when the king typically "threst amonge the prese," l. 1934) instantly become palpable as a marvelously sexualized vocabulary of martial activity. Where Geoffrey of Monmouth magically negotiated a crisis with a fictive heterosexual adventure (the rescue of the sexually imperiled Helena on St. Michael's Mount), *RCL* offers the adventure of (hyper)sexualized language, and the glamor of the English tongue and its wit.

RCL's rhetorical strategy requires an admission that the community of Englishmen is vulnerable to sexual mockery because of the king, but the admission is a typically romance kind, and deftly routed, as usual, through a joke. Enemies are awarded boisterous varieties of double entendre, hooting rude metaphors at the English magically designed to strike Richard's men where it (so to speak) hurts them most:

> "Go hom, dogges, with your tayle!
> For all your boost and your orguyl
> Men shall threst in your cuyle." (ll. 1830–32)

> "Go home, dogs, with your tail!
> For all your boasting and your pride
> Men/We shall thrust in your fundament/your rear [end]."[55]

Among the sexual-martial-verbal assaults perpetrated in the narrative through dazzling shifts of gleeful humor and meaning, the use of the word "tail" features as a cunning tour de force (see, e.g., ll. 2124–25, 2158, 1960, 2006, 1878). Enemy references to "tailed" Englishmen in *RCL* allude to a legend of St. Augustine's mission in England (Broughton, 93–97): William of Malmsbury's *Gesta Pontificum*, in the twelfth century, recounts that God made unbelieving English folk who harassed Augustine to sprout tails, as a humiliating sign of divine rectitude—a story that must still be familiar to the audience of *RCL*, over the centuries, for the romance's spinning of the religious insult to work. Since only devils and beasts have tails, the incessant description, by their enemies, of Richard and all Englishmen as "taylardes" ("tailed ones") makes the English over into devilish unbelievers and bestial animals ("tayled dogges," l. 1878): truly an insult that cuts to the (tail)bone because it turns English crusaders into their avowed enemies—Muslims, Jews, heretics, sorcerers, and, thanks to the medieval analogical imagination, sodomites. Viewed "as allies of demons, devils, and witches" (Johanssen and Percy, 169), sodomites were, like Jews, "linked to bestial cruelty, to the loss of humanity" (Jordan, 17). Richard's reputed sodomitical taint, which spreads its shadow over Englishmen whose identity as a group is figured by their king, is thus partly if cunningly admitted when Richard comes to exemplify cruelty, inhumanity, and devilishness in *RCL*: The English king is called "a deuyll" by Saladin, after all, and Richard's relished cannibalism makes only too plain his demonic character and inhumanity .

But the tale of tails in *RCL* wags in different directions, and this romance written in English vauntingly exploits the resourcefulness of the language that will become the linguistic medium of modernity and nationalism in England: English. Mocked as "tayled dogges" by their enemies, Richard and the English dispose of each community of foes through a dizzying narrative display of puns that turns the tables on the enemy, and miraculously transforms a scandalous epithet into a badge of national unity and pride. Richard commands his men to hold up their manhood (literally, "holde vp your manshyppes," l. 1858) against the Greeks, whom the English then handily defeat; and a French "justyce" who derides Richard as a "taylarde" (l. 2006) justly turns tail and flees, with "Rycharde . . . soone at his tayle" (l. 2016)—a salty pun giving the Frenchman a turn at having a tail and putting Richard at his back, poised for an assault from the rear. In the melee, a knight arrives to give Richard good news about a strategic opening into which the English may easily enter without meeting resistance (ll. 1919–24), news described by this romance as "Tales in Englyssh" (l. 1916)—"Tales *on* Inglis," as the Auchinleck manuscript has it (my emphasis)—a slyly playful dig on multiple levels, including a covert boast that English tales, or romances, and not romances in French, will triumph in the (martial-sexual-literary) contest. We remember, moreover, that a "tail" is also a tallage, or a tax, and the English were, in fact, greatly entailed for the financing of Richard's crusade—through, among other means, the Saladin tithe (a tenth of revenues and movables [Douglas and Greenaway, 420])—as well as for Richard's subsequent ransom (one-fourth of the rents and chattel of laity and clergy [Clanchy, *England,* 138]), though most entailed of all in England, perhaps, were English Jews, another community of putatively demonic, bestial subhumans, who no doubt deserved their many entailments.

The play on "tails" thus cumulatively assembles a truly physical brand of humor, a rambunctious aggressivity in language that matches the bellicose physicality of the protagonist: a verbal equivalent to Richard's assaults and bodily banter. The dazzling puns, moreover, ensure that a physical body is always visible in the narrative's jokes and language, which are, in turn, sexualized by that constellation of references to the nether body and its functions. But if the puns make references to unnatural bodily acts briefly visible, they also alibi that visibility by locating it within a mechanism that simultaneously allows winking/pointing, and warding/holding off, defense: the punning joke. Humor in the joke allows an appropriate distance to be taken to the risky subject of unnatural acts, while puns arrange for a certain intermittency in grasping their subject—now you see it, now you don't—that does ideal service for romance. Sodomy, associated with crusades, Muslims, heretics, and also Richard, can be both admitted and hidden in the medium of the joke, which allows for the escape of a selective, disguised re-membering that speaks, but always and ever in safety.[56]

Johanssen and Percy remind us that sodomy had to be spoken of carefully in a culture where what they call "a sodomy delusion"—"a complex of paranoid beliefs invented and inculcated by the church"—persisted. The authors argue that the later medieval period saw "the formation of a linguistic code" of concealment, to avoid interception by "a hostile church and society" (171), with a concomitant "banishment of the subject from the realm of polite discourse":

Sodomy became invisible to the Christian mind, yet the object of a thousand fantasies. It was nowhere, yet everywhere threatened society with destruction. It was blotted out of the annals of the past, unrecorded in the present, forbidden to exist in the future. Yet . . . it existed silent and unseen, a phantom eluding the clutches of an intolerant world. This shift . . . to the frantic intolerance of homosexual expression has been a hallmark of Western civilization since the late thirteenth century. (175–76)

The "sodomy delusion" invokes the belief that sodomy "is so hateful to God as to provoke his retaliation in the form of catastrophes that can befall an entire community for the crime of a single individual in its midst" (172). The historical Richard's life, full of opacities and contradictions, also invites delusional musings: Why did God not reward such a heroic, legendary king with the culminating success of reconquering Jerusalem, after the sporadic military successes of the Third Crusade? Why was the returning crusader-king punished instead with the humiliation of prolonged captivity by fellow Christians, with the result that a terrible economic affliction—Richard's ransom—was subsequently visited upon his entire community, the kingdom of England?[57]

Sodomy, of course, "impairs and undermines the moral character of those who practice it" (Johanssen and Percy, 172), while "erotic disorder . . . is viewed as feminizing" (Jordan, 17). The masculinity of a king to whom the taint of sodomy has been attached might require insistent attestation, so that no trace of feminization might in any way contaminate his narrative character. Accordingly, we notice that in *RCL* all traces of the feminine are carefully evacuated from the life of this virile, militant English king. The romance Richard, unlike the historical Richard, does not have a dominant mother to whom he is inordinately attached and at whose court he is supervised to manhood as an Angevin-Poitevin princeling—the historical Eleanor of Aquitaine—but instead has for a mother a sweetly erotic if, alas, also demonic (because Oriental) Cassodorien of Antioch, whose disappearance through the roof of a cathedral one day at the elevation of the Host neatly removes her (and Richard's sister), romance-style, from the manly king's subsequent adult life (ll. 229–34).[58]

Margery, the German paramour whose brief appearance in the romance facilitates the exhibition of Richard's indomitability, fearlessness, and (hetero)sexual prowess and desirability while he is a captive—captivity, we note, is also a feminizing disorder—quickly disappears from the narrative the instant her usefulness is over (ll. 1237–42); and the romance Richard is not allowed the feminine presence of a wife. Even the jokes attached to Richard in the romance point to consciousness of gender trouble. A horse-trick conjured by the romance Saladin to humiliate the romance Richard refers to a most intimate kind of mother-son dependency, but a dependency ascribed to the English king's *horse*, a demonic animal, it seems, who is given to Richard by Saladin: Richard's stallion will betray its rider in battle, at the decisive moment, by going over to the enemy camp and kneeling down to suckle at its mother's breast when its mother calls. But the romance Richard, forewarned *chanson*-style by an angel, has his destrier's ears stopped up with wax so that the horse cannot hear or acknowledge the maternal animal, and so the tables are turned on Saladin, as the joke rebounds on its would-be perpetrator (ll. 5530ff.). This wonderfully expressive story of the mother-and-son horses seamlessly works a nugget of historical fact—a horse gift from the historical Saladin or his brother to the historical Richard—into a fabulous artifice that at once describes concern at the control that mothers have over the male military animal, and exemplifies the vanishing of history into romance within a single, memorably witty event. The story also faintly, usefully echoes Pope Honorius III's anxiety that Christian children should not have Jewish nurses, presumably because—as the horse-trick suggests—of the danger of a nurseling's intimate attachment, and thus allegiance, to nursing mother figures in the enemy's camp.[59]

In addition to the danger of feminization, the "moral character" of the sodomitic practitioner might be so reduced that one kind of sin against nature might lead to, become indistinguishable from, or be figured as another kind of unnatural sin: Like a sodomitical act, an act of cannibalism is also taboo, unspeakably transgressive, and an offense against nature. If eating, as Maggie Kilgour would have it, is uncannily like sex ("sexual intercourse . . . is often represented as a kind of eating. . . . Countless metaphors ally eating and intercourse" [7]), unnatural eating is uncannily like unnatural sex. Both forms of bodily disorder—disorders of appetite and of bodily desire—are marvelously expressed by the deliberate linguistic disordering and disarticulation performed by the rudely excessive joke. Jokes exist in *RCL*, of course, because humor is able to circumvent the "polite discourse" that prevents speaking of unspeakable subjects—cannibalism or sodomy, sexual or ethical taboos. Laws, regulations, and limits are bypassed at the triumph of the joke: a system of values is temporarily suspended; the ordinary is vanquished. Taking its lead from history, which also represents Richard as a superb manipulator of aggressive humor, this romance decides that a king whose appetites are extraordinary is aptly represented by his extraordinary talent for jokes and cannibalism. The unnatural constitutes Richard's larger-than-life personality and temperament, which only the linguistic loop of the joke adequately expresses and—as importantly—naturalizes for an English nation-in-process whose identity is necessarily a connective part and tissue of the identity of its foremost, legendary, cherished icon.

A Matter of England: Nation, Christendom, Language, "Class," and Other Romance Matters

Against contemporary theorization in the Western academy that locates the emergence of nations and nationalisms in modern, postmedieval periods of history—usually the eighteenth and nineteenth centuries—medievalists have struggled in recent years to outline specifically medieval forms of the nation, and of nationalist feeling and identification, even arguing for the rise of the nation-*state*, and statism, during the European Middle Ages itself.[60] Though the arguments are multifarious, occasionally contradictory, and undeniably *en procès*, a consensus has emerged that discourses of the nation in the medieval period, like nationalist discourses of the eighteenth and nineteenth centuries, hinge critically on Ben Anderson's famous formulation of the nation as an "imagined (political) community," while departing in local, period-specific details—political, economic, governmental—from nationalist formations in postmedieval centuries. Key to the notion of an imagined community, medievalist scholarship decides, is self-identification by a national grouping, especially in defining one's national community against large communities of others in oppositional confrontations over territory, political jurisdiction and dominion, and in warfare. Part of that self-identification involves a recognizably national form of address perceptible in the literary, historical, and cultural documents of a country in the various stages of medieval nationalist discourse. Equally distinctive is the production of a symbolic system that uniquely signals and presents a nation as occupying different cultural and symbolic space from others within transnational groupings such as Western Christendom. Finally, the role of language, geographical boundedness, and ideologies of solidarity that cut across competing, antagonistic interests among the social and economic groups in feudal society, are indispensable components of the nation-in-progress.

Medievalists have said that, from the thirteenth century on, discourses of the nation make themselves felt, and can be read without difficulty, in medieval England: It has even been suggested that "the establishment and exploration of a sense of national identity is a major preoccupation of English writers of the late thirteenth and early fourteenth centuries" (Turville-Petre, "*Havelok*," 121). Such discourses of the nation were aided by the boundedness of insular geography ("The sea defined the nation's territory" [Turville-Petre, *England*, 4]), despite (or because of) holdings in France by the English monarch and barony and England's annexations of territorially contiguous neighbors. Indeed, chronicle histories display a nascent sense of an "English" identity among Anglo-Normans from the end of the twelfth century—or even perhaps, as John Gillingham has argued, from as early as the mid-twelfth century ("Foundations," 54, passim). English military confrontations with the Welsh, Irish, Scots, and French in the twelfth and thirteenth centuries—when "English power . . . was institutionalised in Wales and Ireland" (Frame, 83)—deepened an emerging national community's projection of its difference from its contingent enemies. We are reminded that "the Magna Carta revolt, as it appears from an English perspective, was also a war of . . . the French, the Welsh, and the Scots against the English—and was so perceived at the time" (Gillingham, "Foundations," 63), while Henry III's struggles against Louis VIII of France "polarized the difference between English and French interests and encouraged a sense of apartness on both sides of the Channel" (Clanchy, *England*, 204). For Matthew Paris, the great nationalist historian, the struggles between England and France in the early thirteenth century assume the proportions of a contest between nations (Clanchy, *England*, 204; Turville-Petre, *England*, 3); it is Matthew Paris who, in the thirteenth century, renders England as a territorially distinct and bounded political and symbolic entity, in his detailed maps of England that produce the nation as a mappable collectivity with a known geography, occupying a distinctive, separate space of its own.[61] Despite the truism that " 'the nation . . . is an abstraction, an allegory, a myth that does not correspond to a reality that can be scientifically defined'" (Brennan, 49), the medieval cartographer's projection of a geopolitical category—territorial space coincident with the name of the nation, uniquely shaped and set off—is a powerfully performative moment, a moment that enacts and points to the performative character of nationalist discourse, and the power of such discourse to bring nations into being: "a dry, rancorous political fact" of national history is that " 'nationalism is not the awakening of nations to self-consciousness; [nationalism] *invents* nations where they do not exist'" (Brennan, 49). By the late thirteenth century the anonymous author of the *Cursor Mundi* easily names "ingland the nacione" and specifies the "Englis tong" as a unifying "speche" possessed by "englijs men in comune" (Barnie, 101).

In the fourteenth century Edward III's assertion of sovereignty over France, and his claim to the French throne over the Valois monarch's— the pretext that inaugurates the so-called Anglo-French war of a hundred years—merely brings to dramatic culmination, then, a long process of nationalist self-assertion at the expense of England's territorial enemies and neighbors. Thus the opening address of the chancellor to the parliament of 1376–77, in which that official rhetorically suggests that England, successor to the biblical Israel, was the chosen land and community of God (as witness England's victories in war), and Minot's prayer, "Now Ihesus saue all Ingland / And blis it with his haly hand," merely augment the sense that a culture had coalesced, by the later fourteenth century, that saw no difficulty in naming "England" as a distinctive national formation with a destiny in time and cultural history (Barnie, 103).[62] Fortuitously, for a popular English romance that would articulate its nationalism through the crusader rivalry of an English king, Richard I, and a French king, Philip II, the war in the later fourteenth century once more evocatively pitted an English Richard (Richard II) against a hated French Philip (Philip VI), in a richly symbolic coincidence. Richard II's father, Edward III, had even suggested to Philip VI another joint crusading enterprise of English and French armies against the Saracens.

A community that becomes a nation requires, as one of its necessary instrumentalities, a vocabulary of symbols that underpin the imagining of a national totality. Chief among *RCL*'s contributions to the vocabulary of national symbols is, of course, its spinning of a national insult into a shared communal joke with a touch of pride for Englishmen: We have seen how the folk epithet, *caudatus anglicus*, or "tailed English," is made over into a unifying resource to describe the English community's vaunt that they make their French counterparts turn tail in war (l. 2016), as well as give voice to the heavily entailed English community's plight in financing the Third Crusade and Richard's ransom. The bandying about of the epithet in different contexts thus produces a badge of identity that horizontally knits together the various English "taylardes," of high, low, and middling degrees, into community under a single, homogenized, and witty rubric. Just as you can tell an Englishman by his preferred diet of Saracen flesh, so can you tell him by his allegorical tail (tale) and mastery of English wit.

Other emblems include Richard's ax "that was wrought in England" (l. 6802) and the beehives Richard wields against the Saracens with jaunty impunity (ll. 2905ff.). The battle-ax—a terrifying weapon used only by the English king in *RCL*—was a favorite of Anglo-Saxon warriors: both housecarls, the elite professional guard of the thegn's *domus*, and the fyrd, or army of conscripts, are depicted in the Bayeux tapestry as wielding the battle-ax at Hastings; even the Anglo-Saxons of the Byzantine Emperor's Varangian guard legendarily wielded the weapon. The tapestry also depicts Duke William using the battle-ax, which Anglo-Normans continued to use after Hastings. Richard's ax thus economically unites two opposing military and political lineages, signaling their combination in the now-English king who deftly wields a cultural icon common to both (DeVries, 17–18). Richard's use of bees to attack Saracens has equally resonant cultural symbolism, since honey was to Western European domestic production what sugar was to the export culture of the Levant and Mediterranean. Egypt and Syria—Saladin's empire and the domicile of *RCL*'s Saracens—were great producers of sugar through the Middle Ages (even during the economic decline of the Levantine sugar industry in the fifteenth century) and supplied the demand of Western Europe for sugar long after the last crusader state had vanished (Phillips, "Sugar," 397; Abu-Lughod, 232; Ashtor, 15, 206–8, passim); by contrast, honey is Europe's export to Egypt and Syria (Ashtor, 17, 23, 146, 160, 161, passim).[63] The visibility of sugar as an export of the East guarantees that bees, honey, and hives would constitute an excellent symbolic marker for domestic culture in the West: when the king of England has hives hurled into Acre, then, and the bees stingingly harass the Saracens, a defiant statement of economic and ideological superiority is made of a distinctly vengeful kind—a thumbnail sketch of *translatio imperii*, the West's ascension to economic and cultural hegemony over the East, bitingly expressed. In case we miss the point, Christians themselves are later likened in *RCL* to swarming bees (ll. 5793–94). Richard's bees also, of course, aptly represent the English nation itself in miniature— bees being a traditional figure for the polity since the time of Bede—and the Middle English political poem, *Mum and the Sothsegger* makes plain that bees and the hive capture well the ideal polity in all its qualities of industry, skill, good governance, cooperative spirit, and harmonious loyalty under an ideal monarch who rules through reason, rightful judgment, and the united consent and contentment of the whole community (ll. 987–1043). In a single image, an ideological assertion of the nation's character and unity, and an indelibly memorable romance weapon, are simultaneously adduced. Richard's spectacular windmill that seems to grind men's bones instead of wheat or barley is an ideological boast, too, of a similar kind (ll. 2656–82). The first attested windmill in Europe is found in Yorkshire in 1185 (White, 87), and Ambroise's eyewitness account of Richard's crusade asserts that it was crusaders who constructed the first windmill ever known in Syria (ll. 3227–29). The English king's supernatural windmill, then, is a hyperbolic expression of English, and Western, technological superiority, rendered in the medium of a highly theatrical weapon of an unforgettable kind.

Although the form of the English nation, during the long period of *RCL*'s making, is that of the *communitas regni*, and England is an imagined political community of the realm, with the ruler at its apex—not a constitutionally driven modern nation-state, with state apparatuses—a specifically medieval form of nationalism nonetheless shows itself sensitive to the necessity of a broad impulse toward horizontal leveling in social relations, within the national community ideally conceived. In medieval and postmedieval nationalism alike, the drive toward horizontal linkages—a forging of solidarities with the vital "ability to rouse unlike peoples in dramatically unlike conditions in an impassioned chorus of voluntary cooperation and sacrifice" (Brennan, 45)—is essential to the would-be nation's internal cohesion. Revealingly, in the medium of popular romance, medieval nationalism is able to imagine a nascent impetus toward horizontal leveling under conditions of cooperative labor in the service of religious war. Clearly visible in *RCL*, a text that narrates nationalism in tandem with militant Christianity, is what might be called *a class dissimulation*: a projective discourse of baronial and monarchic subscription to equitable distributions of compensation for military labor. According to this popular romance, the English king and his knights are committed to the fair distribution of wealth among all Christian men, including commoners, boys, and servants.

Richard, as the king who figures the community, sets the example by sharing "gret tresour" (l. 5889) with all—"the high and the low" ("þe hyghe and þe lowe," l. 6527)—so that each had as much as he wished to have ("Had as mekyl as þey wolde haue," l. 5892), an example also scrupulously adhered to by Richard's lieutenants, Fouk Doyly at Ebedy (ll. 4605–8, 4676–77) and Sir Thomas of Multoun at Castle Orgulous (ll. 4287–94). It is commonality of membership in the Christian community, of course—and masculine military labor—that drives the utopian fiction that fair distribution is possible in feudal culture. Rewriting the history of the First Crusade, when the Christian poor died in droves during famine at the siege of Antioch, the rich of the Third Crusade in this romance charitably and equitably share their wealth during famine at the siege of Acre, so that the plight of both greater and lesser Christian folk ("þe more and þe lasse," l. 2873) is ameliorated. Significantly, as the crusaders are sharing in the spoils of their military labor, we notice that it is specifically only *English* Christians who are depicted as receiving their share of spoils—not French, Greek, or other Christians. In demonstrating how, under some conditions, membership in an overarching Christian community can subserve, rather than subtract from, nationalist impulses and discourses, *RCL* identifies the enabling possibilities of ideological manipulation in wielding religion as an expressly *national* resource.[64]

But the fair distribution of wealth set in motion by the English king also strongly suggests a *secular* fiction of utopian justice at work in this romance: a broadly national utopianism that exercises a broadly populist kind of justice. Richard's distribution of "great treasure" to all, both high and low, represents the medieval king as *directly* accountable to his populace—thus subverting the imported Norman-Angevin-Plantagenet feudal system in which the king had no direct political access to the population at large, but only an access governed by and mediated through innumerable layers of subinfeudation. By representing the medieval monarch as accountable directly to all his men, the class dissimulation in this popular romance slyly undercuts feudal modalities of hierarchy and the fossilized stratifications of power typical in feudalism—a dissimulation no doubt especially attractive in fourteenth- and fifteenth-century England, when social mobility is a channel of hope and opportunity for all but the *haute noblesse*. This populist representation is strategically aided by nostalgic echoes from an Anglo-Saxon past before the advent of Norman feudalism—a nostalgia located in Richard's English ax, for instance, a weapon that remembers Richard as a more Anglo-Saxon king than the Angevin-Poitevin princeling that the historical Richard in fact was, and in Richard's loud preference for Anglo-Saxon toasts ("Wesseyl," l. 6816). The suggestion of direct, popular justice also eerily recalls the popular communal justice directly available in the shire and hundred courts of preconquest Anglo-Saxon England, and that survived the fall, albeit altered, into the post-Norman era. If "justice" was the popular name for political power as it was exercised in the medieval period, as Perry Anderson has it, it is also the implied name of an operative modality in *RCL* that bears witness to a utopianized relationship between the English king and his national subjects: a justice that cuts across "the high and the low" and sets an example that is followed by the king's baronial commanders and knights, and thus a supremely useful fiction for the leveling discourse of the nation.

Of course, nationalist manipulations of this kind are marked by the very discourse of rampant militarism that they ride: In the same narrative breath that describes the sharing of wealth, we are told of the dispossession of the Islamic inhabitants of the Levant, as English crusaders are given Muslim property, lands, cities, and homes (ll. 4602–4, 4660–63, 4295–99), and the conquered territories of the East are repopulated by the English Christians of the West, who readily celebrate their triumphant share in colonization and empire formation. We are reminded, in *RCL*'s discourse of nationalism, that a nation secures its borders and identity in part by the aggressive outward extension and consolidation of borders; the romance example thus evocatively anticipates the postmedieval historical example of Victorian and modern imperial England.[65]

In the discourse of the nation, Middle English romances form a special category of cultural articulation, though an equally privileged literature is also, of course, that genre of English chronicle histories of England/Britain called the *Brut*, spawned from Geoffrey's Latin *Historia* and its French vernacular derivatives. Diane Speed and others insist that the medieval English romance constitutes a literature ideally consonant with and fully of "a type with the discourse of the nation" (146):

> It is immediately clear, merely from the overt subject matter, that a number of these romances belong in the discourse of the nation, that they have as a primary function a construction of England that articulates the partially conceptualized impulses observable in the new English-language writing of the preceding century. (145) [66]

Because the narrative address of large numbers of English romances seems to be either distinctively popular or national or both and to share a coherency of assumptions, conventions, and mutuality of reference, scholars have repeatedly argued that English romances, despite French counterparts or originals, effectively comprise a textual community of their own. The sine qua non of their textual communality is, of course, that the romances are written in *English*—not French or Latin, continental or international languages. The choice of English was a choice in favor of exclusivity, since English ensured that the romances addressed only an insular audience eschewing the outside, and all possibility of international reception: "The very act of writing in English," as Turville-Petre puts it, "is a statement about belonging" (*England*, 11),[67] about making a literature that will be accessible only to a national audience in England.

RCL, which begins by announcing its decision to narrate its tale in English because scarcely one among a hundred non-learned men can understand the tale in French (ll. 21–24), represents its choice of English as a populist move, a bid for the broadest possible address.[68] In its aggressive humor and puns, the romance brandishes its use of English in much the same way that the romance Richard brandishes his English battle-ax, windmill, and beehives. To insist on a world of difference between English and French in this romance, English is claimed as the language used by Richard's knights and Richard: When a knight brings good news about an unguarded gate that will give the siege army unresisted entry into

Messina, he emphatically brings the news to Richard as "Tales in Englyssh, stoute and bolde" (l. 1916). Good news comes in English—not
French—and no doubt this romance itself, dramatically also a tale in English, stout and bold, is part of the corpus of good news. Nationalist consciousness requires that the romance Richard *has* English, unlike the
French-speaking historical Richard, a king notorious for having spent a
mere six months in England in his decade-long reign, and his disloyal joke
that he would have sold off London itself had he been able to find a buyer.

The Plantagent king linked to the earliest public communication in
English is not Richard, but John's son, Henry III, whose confirmation of
the Provisions of Oxford in 1258 was issued in English in "the month of
October in the two-and-fortieth year of our reign" ("þe Monþe of Octo-
br' In þe Twoandfowertr3þe 3eare of vre crunínge" [Patent Roll, 43;
Henry III, m. 15., n. 40]; Ellis, 19). By proclaiming his confirmation not
only in French—the language of his baronial elites who had coerced
Henry into the Provisions—but also in English, the language of the other
social classes of his realm, Henry's act affords a glimpse of how English,
in the mid-thirteenth century, arcs across divisions of class and power, and
reaches into "every . . . shire over all the kingdom in England" ("æurihce
. . . shcíre ouer al þære kuneriche on Engleneloande" [Ellis, 23]). Post-
Henry, the romance Richard's association with English, not French, is
perhaps meant to recall Edward I, who, "facing the French attack in 1295,
accused the French of trying to exterminate the English language"
(Turville-Petre, *England*, 9)—a vilification that underscores the unifying
potentials of linguistic nationalism. The contention, in the parliaments of
1295, 1344, 1346, and 1376, that French victory in the Anglo-French wars
would "annihilate the English language" (Fisher, "Language Policy," 1169)
argues that English, by the fact that it was not the lingua franca of England's hostile continental competitor and enemy, came to be associated
with the nation itself.[69]

RCL's Richard at Jaffa even launches his attack against his foes with a
uniquely English joke, when he announces that he has come to drink to
his foes' health: "Wassail I shall drink to you!" ("Wesseyl j schal drynke
3ow too!"[l. 6816]). "Wesseyl," of course, descends from the Old English
"wes-hāl" (Middle English "wæs-hæil"), a greeting and toast unforgettably
depicted in Geoffrey's *Historia* as offered by Renwein, daughter of
Hengist (chief among the Saxon invaders of Britain), to the British king
Vortigern ("Lauerd king, Waesseil!" [Wright, 1:67]) to seduce Vortigern
and begin the settlement of Britain by Saxons. The romance Richard not

only knows his English history but represents himself, in a word, as aligned with English and England. Deliberately, in *RCL*, a linguistic and political history is retrieved that ignores the Norman conquest of 1066 and French rule.

In arcing back centuries to a language that is a memento of preconquest England, the romance breaks with the more recent, French-dominated past: a break that is necessary in articulating both national identification and a paradoxical modernity for English society. Nationalist momentum, it has been said, requires a strategic act of forgetting: "Forgetting . . . is a crucial factor in the creation of a nation" (Renan, 11), especially the willed forgetting of a minus-in-the-origin, the "deeds of violence which took place at the origin of all political formations" (Renan, 11). For the community of England to become English (again), one strategy in the *communitas regni* is to forget the king's continental descent through his parents Henry II and Eleanor of Aquitaine, his grandparents Geoffrey of Anjou and the Empress Matilda, and his great-grandfather Henry I's parent, William of Normandy, the invader of England, and to remember, instead, Richard's Anglo-Saxon heritage through his great-grandmother Matilda, Henry I's wife—a woman "descended from the stock of King Alfred" (Orderic Vitalis, 5:298–99) and "a kinswoman of King Edward [the Confessor]" (Anglo-saxon Chronicle, s.a., 1100), whose own mother, Margaret, had been the great-granddaughter of Edmund Ironside. A royal genealogy traced through the Saxon female line—while not unproblematic, like all gendered acts of remembering—bypasses the Norman invasion and represents the imagined political community as newly remade from the shards of an older past nostalgically retrievable in an array of linguistic and narrative artifacts, from weapons to lineages to toasts.[70]

In the fourteenth and fifteenth centuries, a bid for English is also a bid for a linguistic modernity from the languages available in England for use, including Latin and French. In that contest of languages, Latin—magisterial, scholarly, statutory, ecclesiastical—was irredeemably bound to ancient history, and church power, just as French—still preferred by the great nobles (as supposedly represented by their library collections [Shonk, 89; L. H. Loomis, "Auchinleck Manuscript," 155; Salter, 34–35]) and the language of law, government, and diplomacy—was bound to the history of an elite minority and insular colonization. Anglo-Norman, moreover, had increasingly assumed the status of a provincial dialect, a medium whose pastness was emphasized by the fact that the centers of French linguistic authority and vigor lay elsewhere, on the continent.[71] By

contrast, English, without the burden of association with French dominion, and derived from a pre-Norman era before the fall into French feudalism, could—in a period that was soon to exhaust feudalism—fortuitously be reinvested as the language most paradoxically allied to the
modern and the new: the language with the greatest potential for articulating new, broad-based currents of transformation channeling through
English society. Froissart's contention that "in about 1337 Edward III ordered the gentry and bourgeoisie of England to teach their children
French 'so that they would become better able and qualified for their
wars'" (Barnie, 98) expresses the common notion that it was English
which was the normative, everyday language of the commons: of bourgeoisie and gentry, social groups whose ambitions, capital accumulation,
and mobility were busily disrupting feudal certitudes and categories, and
powering the engine of England's economic modernity in the late Middle
Ages.[72] English was the language of an emerging new literature catering to
these urban interests and social classes—a linguistic community ably
tapped by Chaucer—and the tongue of a heterogeneous collectivity of
peoples that was assuming the proportions of a national formation. The
very diversity and proliferation of English dialects in the fourteenth and
fifteenth centuries, so memorably encapsulated in Chaucer's rueful fret-
ting over his text ("ther is so gret diversite / In Englissh and in writyng of
oure tonge" (*Troilus*, ll. 1793–94]), testifies to the health and sheer vitality of English, a language vigorously expanding its range and usages, and
active in its growth, resources, and dispersal. Significantly Caxton, England's first commercial print publisher (a man with a "sure sense of the
public's tastes, many parts of which he may well have solidified" [Rich-
mond, 7]) used the new, modern print technology for issuing books almost exclusively in English, himself translating work from Latin and
French into English for the purpose.

In 1362, as John Fisher points out, Parliament admitted for the first
time that it was addressed in English and passed a statute for court pro-
ceedings henceforth to be "conducted in English because the litigants
could not understand French" ("Chancery," 879); and "the parliaments
of 1363, 1364, and 1381 were opened in English" (880). Trevisa's "well-
known account of the revolution in the grammar schools" noted, in
1385, that "English was substituted for French as the language of instruction for Latin" (Barnie, 99). Fisher persuasively argues that Henry
V, early in the fifteenth century, saw that in English lay the linguistic future of the nation, and from 1417 till his death in 1422 used English "in

nearly all his correspondence with the government and the citizens of London and other English cities," setting an example followed by literary authors and "establishing English as the national language of England" ("Language Policy," 1171). Even earlier than this, at the end of the fourteenth century, Chaucer, in his "Treatise on the Astrolabe," was already referring to English as the king's language: "And preie God save the king, that is lord of this language" (ll. 56–57). In the contest of languages for priority in the fourteenth and fifteenth centuries, nationalistic literature in English played no small part, and linguistic modernity and linguistic nationalism coincide in the status of English as exercised in the discourse of the nation.[73]

RCL establishes English identity on the detritus of French identity: For, Saracens aside, the principal enemies of the English crusaders in this romance of England are plainly the French. Differentiated in every way from the English nation, the French in *RCL* are cowardly, greedy, sly, incompetent, covetous, and treacherous, and the English king finds that even his nephew, Henry of Champagne, a Frenchman—historically, Henry is de facto king of Jerusalem, by dint of marriage, though never crowned, and the son of Marie of Champagne, patroness of French romance—is no exception to the national character. The count of Champagne turns tail before Saladin's army, and Richard awards him a tongue-lashing that fastens on Henry's nationality as the focus of his cowardice (ll. 6705–10). The French monarch, Philip Augustus—Richard's negative foil—is condescendingly preached to and hectored by the English monarch like a subordinate, rather than co-equal leader of the crusading army. Predictably, the French king takes bribes from Muslims—who then turn around and despise his greed and cowardice in sparing their lives (ll. 4719–23, 4761–70)—while, by contrast, the English king converts or exterminates the enemy with gusto, brandishing his English ax and fighting on foot, like a true, stalwart Anglo-Saxon *drihten* (ll. 6150–51). Because of the obsessive narrative focus, even the English crusaders' skirmishes with the Greeks at Messina come to seem really battles with the French, who are mentioned more often than Greeks.[74] Nationalist romance is fortuitously supported by national history: not only does Philip VI, a fourteenth-century object of English hatred, bear an identical name to Philip Augustus, but in the thirteenth century Henry III's struggle against Louis VIII of France was represented by Pope Honorius III's legate, Guala, as also a de jure crusade. In 1217 the English forces "wore the white cross of crusaders . . . were absolved of all their sins before going into

battle, and recruits were described as converts"—an ideological triumph
for the English, since a crusade of English against French meant that the
French could be "considered infidels and . . . given no quarter" (Clanchy,
England, 203).

Among texts exercising the discourse of the nation, *RCL* ranks as one
of the most popular of English romances in terms of manuscript survival,
tying in a dead heat with *Bevis of Hampton* and the *Siege of Jerusalem.*[75]
After the advent of print technology, *RCL* continued to be chosen for
publication: Wynkyn de Worde, Caxton's commercially minded successor after 1491 at the Westminster Press, included *RCL* among his offerings
to customers in 1509 and 1528 (Brunner, 7); John Purfoot, a later publisher, secured a license for reissuing *RCL* in 1568–69, and manuscript copies
of *RCL* still circulated in the sixteenth century (a copy being owned by "a
certain James Haword" in 1562 [R. S. Crane, 7]). The popularity of *RCL*
may owe something to the romance's strategy of addressing the widest
possible audience among Anglophones, an address that "positions its audience as constituting a wide range of socio-economic levels" occupying
"something like the nation at large" (Speed, 152). *RCL* interpellates an especially broad range of social and economic constituents as an internal
narrative constituency, alongside the mandatory constituents of king,
courtiers, and knights: thus it is that servant boys ("knaue," l. 5891) receive
ample compensation for military labor alongside the barony and knights
("Erl, baroun, kny3t" [l. 5891]); and when the English king summons a
parliament, together with the barons, knights, and ecclesiastics who attend come also servants ("Seriauntes," l. 1267) and burgesses ("Burgeyses,"
l. 1266), whose attendance is specified and noted.[76] That both "the high
and the low" ("þe hyghe and þe lowe," l. 6527) feature in the romance partially explains how it is that the noble art of war, traditionally associated
only with the military estate of king, barony, and knights, can be described in *RCL* as a "mystere" (l. 3860)—a word whose denotational origins pointed to a craft or trade practiced by merchants/artisans/crafts-
folk/tradesmen, and the specialized organizations ("guilds") that
sponsored the membership of such folk to the freedom of cities like London, and city citizenship, with attendant rights and duties, as well as regulated training for apprentices, market monopolies, and financing for in-
dustries and community culture. Provocatively, the service obligations of
an older, traditional estate in feudalism are assimilated to the commerce-
craftsmanship of the emergent bourgeoisie powering the engine of civic
authority in major English cities like London. It would seem that *RCL*

found an audience across socioeconomic classes and constituents in Anglophone England during its long textual history: or at least that a linguistic co-optation of this kind, in which the noble art of war is rubricated as commercial craft—marking a class capture, in language, that is faithful to the new social realities—would afford pleasure to some of this popular romance's audience-communities.[77]

Scholarship believes, in the main, that medieval romances in English were read or listened to by a wide social spectrum ranging from lower nobility and gentry (a designation including knights, squires, *valetti*, yeomen, and free landowners in country and city alike) to mercers and burgesses (principally in cities); and the Auchinleck manuscript in which *RCL* appears may have constituted a single-volume library of texts for a wealthy owner or owners possessing something like mercantile status (Shonk, Pearsall, L. H. Loomis ["Auchinleck Manuscript"], Richmond, et al.). Thrupp estimates, from the evidence of male witnesses in a consistory court of Edward IV, that 50 percent of male Londoners of mercantile-craftsmen rank might be able to read English in the mid-fifteenth century (158); and among "the twenty odd books contained in sixteen bequests made between the years 1403 and 1483" in this class are included a Brut and two copies of a *Polychronicon*, testifying, perhaps, to a class interest in the history of the nation (Thrupp, 162–63). More than one scholar has argued that, in late medieval England, the cheap paper quartos of printed copies, "in which appeared such romances as . . . *Richard Coeur de Lion*, were undoubtedly meant . . . to circulate widely among a somewhat humbler public. Many of them were probably sold to country readers; peddled about by travelling booksellers, they were the true precursors of the chapbooks of the seventeenth century" (R. S. Crane, 9–10). The circumscriptions of documentary evidence mean that arguments on the audience and readership of Middle English romances remain necessarily circumstantial; nonetheless, *RCL*'s internal narrative evidence plainly suggests that the *fiction* of broad-based appeal is a useful construction.[78]

Furthermore, though I describe *RCL*'s utopian narrative premise of trans-class solidarity in war as an idealized dissimulation that subserves the overarching interests of a community in the grip of nationalization, late medieval English history in fact witnesses spontaneous occasions of contingent collaboration across social classes to meet military exigencies that threatened the formative nation. Thus in 1346, at the battle of Neville's Cross, "a hastily assembled body" of peasants, clerics, and knights fought side by side; and, in the south, merchants and churchmen spontaneously organized alongside knights "when the enemy suddenly appeared before Winchelsea, Rye, or Southampton" (Barnie, 106, 107). Indeed, concern "for England's security" would appear to have been an interest that traversed all social classes in the crucible of a nationalizing culture. A sense of national responsibility would appear to have fueled the sentiments of "Kentish peasants during the revolt of 1381" when, at "an assembly held at Dartford it was decided that 'no one who lived within twelve leagues of the sea should go with them, but should guard the coasts against enemies'" (Barnie, 108).

A context of spontaneous mobilizations organized around national rather than class interests imparts, then, some intelligibility to an extraordinary incident narrated in *RCL*. One of *RCL*'s innovations is a startling rescripting of a historical incident of enmity that erupts between Richard and Leopold of Austria. In chronicle accounts, Richard earns the detestation of Leopold by gratuitously casting down the duke's banners from the walls of Acre, where the banners of the triumphant crusading leaders are displayed after the city's capture (Richard of Devizes, 46–47). *RCL*, which has the confrontation occur at "Chaloyn" (l. 5951), does not have Richard gratuitously insult Leopold by an arrogant act but assigns *Leopold* responsibility for the hatred that, historically, brings about Richard's postcrusade capture in Europe by Leopold and prolonged incarceration. Unlike every single "king and emperor" present at "Chaloyn," who contributes to the collective labor of rebuilding the protective walls around the city by cooperatively and democratically hauling stones or mortar ("Euery kyng and emperere / Stones bare or mortere" [ll. 5969–70]), the Duke of Austria refuses to sully his hands with manual labor, haughtily declaring, "My father was not a mason or a carpenter, and even if your walls all utterly shake to pieces, I shall never help to make them" ("My fadyr nas mason ne carpentere; / And þou3 3oure walles al toschake, / I schal neuere helpe hem to make" [ll. 5978–80]). With purest fury, Richard then assaults the duke, hurling Leopold's banner in the river. The English king is fully justified, we are to understand, because of the duke's avowal of allegiance to his class, his boastful class insult, and his arrogant refusal to perform menial labor that he sees as beneath his class position. Remarkably, in order for Richard's indignation and retaliation to be received as just, the audience/readership for this romance must be willing to accept the fiction that manual labor is appropriate activity for dukes, kings, and emperors when an act of solidarity requires communal cooperation that cuts across all lines of social and economic division. In a culture where Froissart averred that one of Edward III's knights who was "a paragon of chivalric skill, valor, and beauty" would never be "accepted as a gentleman" because he had been the son of a mason (Thrupp, 309–10), and where "occupations were considered 'vile' if they involved manual labor or menial service" (306), the fiction of class solidarity through collective physical labor is a bold and daring fiction indeed.[79]

Indeed, bold and daring fictions, I have suggested, are the specialty of this romance, with its many experiments in service to the discourse of the nation. The nation itself—an experiment that has not yet seen its conclusion, despite twenty-first century transnationalism and the flows of global capital, cybernetic technology, and new populations of cosmopolites—is perhaps the boldest and most daring medieval fiction of all.[80] The production of "England" in English romances, literature, and culture, in the epistemic formation of the thirteenth century and after, is a catachresis so bold that it must infinitely, repeatedly, be defended, managed, argued, explored, and re-performed. That a celebrated English monarch and his crusade, cannibalism and conquest, war and jokes, Saracens, Jews, sodomy, and the English language and its fictions of class and identity should all be part of the arsenal of defense and argument, explanation and performance, merely suggests that romance is, in fact, a genre of the nation: a genre *about* the nation and for the nation's important fictions.

War (and other agonistic contests), not love, served to reveal the inner man, the stuff a free Greek male was made of.
—David Halperin, "Is There a History of Sexuality?"

The fact that the principal English strength lay in the massive use of the longbow, a weapon which was popular rather than aristocratic, led to the need to draw on the resources of every level of society, independent of juridical status, in order to recruit a sufficient number of highly qualified archers.
—Philippe Contamine, *War in the Middle Ages*

It is one of the unsolved problems of this puzzling work, that the criticism levelled against unjust wars does not diminish the poet's enthusiasm for the description of war.
—Karl Heinz Göller, "Reality versus Romance:
A Reassessment of the *Alliterative Morte Arthure*"

With the passage of time, cannibal stories . . . become intensely conventionalized, composed of a set of gestures that produce certain familiar . . . effects.
—Samuel Otter, *Melville's Anatomies*

CHAPTER 3

✑

Warring Against Modernity

Masculinity and Chivalry in Crisis; or, The Alliterative *Morte Arthure*'s
Romance Anatomy of the Crusades

IN MEDIEVAL ENGLAND, I have been suggesting, cannibalism and crusading warfare stalk the corridors of romance with a certain flourish. From
Geoffrey of Monmouth's *Historia Regum Britannie*, Wace's *Roman de
Brut*, and Laȝamon's *Brut* to *Richard Coer de Lyon*, and the Alliterative
Morte Arthure, cannibal plots, cannibal characters, cannibal jokes, and
cannibal obsessions dog the narratives, so that some romances seem willfully to outstrip their predecessors, doubling back on romance's field of vision with cunning, re-creative energy and ingenuity. We saw how, under
the exuberant attentions of nationalist cannibal enthusiasts, Geoffrey's
(bad) crusader-cannibal-giant from St. Michael's Mount and (good) king-
of-Britain-cannibal Cadwallo, are morphed in *RCL* into a single (good
and bad) behemoth of nationalist legendary history, the outsized canni-
bal-crusader-king-of-England Richard Lionheart.

As a latecomer to the scene of cannibalism, the Alliterative *Morte
Arthure* (henceforth *Morte*)—a romance arising in the last years of the
fourteenth century or the very first years of the fifteenth[1]—necessarily arrives in medieval England as retrospective theater, cannibal-wise, and
romance-wise, nearly three centuries after Geoffrey. This aesthetically superior elite romance—unlike Geoffrey's *Historia* and the popular *RCL*,

Audiences at the University of California at Santa Barbara in 2001, Vanderbilt University in
2000, and the thirty-second conference of the Center for Medieval and Renaissance Studies
(CEMERS), on the nine-hundredth anniversary of the fall of Jerusalem, at the State University
of New York at Binghampton in 1999, commented usefully on drafts of this chapter. Particularly helpful were the responses of Louise Fradenburg, Carol Pasternak, Leah Marcus, Jerome
Christensen, Regina Psaki, Barbara K. Altmann, Jim Garrison, and Dolora Chapelle Wojiehowski. Janadas Devan's critical attentiveness to the chapter was indispensable.

the complex, intelligent *Morte* exists only in a single manuscript—is by no means outclassed, however, in the genre of romance-and/as-cannibalism. For one, the *Morte* itself is a blatant and shameless cannibal. Its omniverous appetite for bodies of disparate matter—heraldry, law, diplomacy, government, cookery, nautical warfare, a spectrum of linguistic imports and innovations—has long served up a rich staple to fascinated scholars.[2] Beyond its penchant for promiscuous ingestion, the *Morte*'s avid assimilation of all the available attitudes toward war has also been appreciated: a smorgasbord of responses to warfare that ranges from sophisticated humor, tolerant irony, and mordant wit to savage critique, cynicism, and condemnation to glorious idealization, celebration, and advocacy of martial violence, even death, in the field of battle.[3] As anthropophagus and conundrum, the *Morte* has confounded scholars by its insatiable absorption of whole genres themselves, its greedy assumption of taxonomies, topoi, and stances from multiple literary genres into the ever-enlarging menu of chivalric romance.[4]

But what of the pièce de résistance, that episodic centerpiece of cannibalism made familiar by Arthurian romances with epistemological ambitions? Arriving late in the day, the *Morte*'s mise-en-scène at St. Michael's Mount produces cannibalism as a command performance, a performance commanded by received Arthurian literary tradition. Playing out a stagey theatricality, the *Morte*'s self-consciously sensational treatment is then, in part, a response to the potential awkwardness of fit between old and new, between inherited literary formulas and newly forming social conditions. Thus summoned, the *Morte*'s cannibalistic episode rises to the needs of its historical moment by a kind of cannibalistic camp whose deep seriousness requires that the force and ritual of its particular theater of the sensational be distributed differently from Geoffrey's and *RCL*'s.[5] At the end of the fourteenth century and beginning of the fifteenth, the needs of a chivalric institutional culture that occasion the fashioning of chivalric romance are shaped by the onset of what I will call "modernity"—a naming convenience to invoke, in shorthand, a panoply of effects, elaborated in the subsection "Warring Against Modernity," below, that exercise a large imagined impact on late medieval England.

While Geoffrey's cannibal plot, situated at an earlier juncture of the Middle Ages, begins the novelty of celebratory transmogrification for feudal elites, the *Morte*'s cannibal treatment, lodged at the later end of the Middle Ages, deferentially remembers the cultural work of elite predecessors. Indeed, the *Morte* demonstrates how well it understands the instrumentality of romance and cannibal stagings by performing a special repetition-with-difference, exercising its own cannibal moment to disclose the pressure nodes of chivalric vulnerability and crisis in its own historical instant. The *Morte*'s cannibal narrative is thus both encyclopedic in compass—a veritable *summa* of Arthurian giant/cannibal instantiations—and relentlessly probing in the diagnostic anatomization of constituent details: twin manifestations of late medieval epistemic forces operating in tandem, in the specificity of time and context. The cannibal grotesqueries are sublimely spun out at length, the romance seeming to evince a surgical fascination with its microscopic investigation of loathsome particulars. Sparing none, probing all, this late sequel is truly the apogee of Arthurian giant-killings and cannibal-pleasures. Together, the two cannibal episodes, Geoffrey's and the *Morte*'s, span crusading history and chivalric knighthood at the inception and eclipse of both these monumental traditions, in the interim of which, as *RCL*'s own cannibal plot intimates, whole medieval discourses, popular genres, and a medieval nation itself have arisen and ramified.

Introducing a Giant from Genoa: Conspicuous Consumption, and the Anatomy of Men and Monsters, in Late Medieval Cannibalism

By now, the narrative setting is duly familiar. King Arthur, on his way with knights and army to defy Rome's right to tribute and dominion over Britain and Britain's territories on the continent, crosses the channel and arrives at Barfleur, where continental allies mustered from fifteen realms await him. Here, Arthur is punctually summoned to a romance adventure with a cannibal giant who dwells on St. Michael's Mount, an occasion announcing the first martial action in the *Morte*. Yet at once a new character enters the cast: A Templar, no less, delivers the news of giant devastation (l. 841), and much of the news he delivers turns out to be, in fact, new news. For one, the threatening fiend is personified first as a *tyrant* ("teraunt," l. 842) even before it is registered as a giant. For another—and most surprisingly—the giant has come from Genoa, not "Hispania" (l. 843); later we will see that "Genoa" is the mysterious province from which, perplexingly, more giants issue to fight against Arthur's forces and alongside the enemies of Britain. The first mention of victimization by giant does not even feature Helena, niece of Duke Hoel, as the requisite romance maiden. Instead, we are told of an orgiastic genocide by eating: The Genoese giant has devoured more than five hundred people, and as many infants and freeborn children (l. 845) who are boys ("knaue childyre," l. 850).

This Genoese tyrant found his boy children in "the country of Constantine" (l. 848)—a pun that helps to materialize the Byzantine Empire, the country of Constantine the Great, whose territories are oriented by the eponymous capital seat, Constantinople—and has so decimated the country that he has left no family outside the "famous castles enclosed with walls" (l. 849). Lest we imagine that the name "Constantine" might only denote the Cotentin Peninsula in Normandy, the *Morte* incites a second orientation by pointing to the world-renowned fastnesses that identify Byzantium itself: the castle-complexes, with their massive walls, which had once supplied the impressive models that had prompted the post–First Crusade revolution in castle architecture in twelfth-century Western Europe.

Once the giant's provenance and his tramping grounds are established, the *Morte* can then go on to mention Helena and instantiate romance's time-honored maiden-as-victim pretext. Yet women have so little priority in the romance that this particular "Duchess of Brittany" (l. 852) is not even identified by personal name. Even her blood-kinship to Arthur evanesces, as inessential as her name, in the transition from *Historia* to *Morte*. Though sedimentations of crusader history are acknowledged in the totemic mention of Templar and Constantinople, we may be forgiven if we suspect that this romance's Genoese-style giant is no outdated, monstrosified crusader from the eleventh century. Instead, the *Morte* makes it plain that *Arthur* is the pivotal crusader in this text: Arthur, who obligingly conjures up an extended joke about his intention to "pass in pilgrimage secretly . . . to seek a saint . . . on St. Michael's Mount, where miracles are seen," (ll. 896–99) enjoys himself hugely when he represents his intended cannibal killing as a pilgrimage, and thus honors the ongoing metaphor of crusade-as-pilgrimage which had served Western Europe and Latin Christendom so well for centuries.[6]

Besides the metaphor-cluster of pilgrimage-saint-martyrdom (ll. 937, 939, 966, 969, 1066, 1163–65, 1168–68, 1221) that so delights Arthur, and later also Bedivere (ll. 1162–71), one other figural cluster is favored by the narrative to describe what this new cannibal operation signifies, a fiscal-juridical-diplomatic cluster that puns on the subject of treasure, law, and treaty (ll. 878–79, 991–92, 996). Underpinning it all is a strange circumstance that makes the double-talk possible in the first place: For besides being engorged with human victims, it seems, this giant is also engorged with gigantic wealth. The Templar declares that the Genoese tyrant possesses more florins than are found in France (l. 885); indeed, the giant has amassed far greater treasure by wrongful means ("vntrewely") than there was historically in Troy when Troy was captured (ll. 886–87). Money has been introduced into the scene of cannibalism: a modern development.

The giant, it turns out, is *an economic giant*: a fiscal monster who is vastly richer—and by extrapolation wields greater force—than the king of France. It is a Templar, significantly, who announces the economic monstrosity. As an Order, the Templars were themselves richer than any king of France, and intimately familiar with capital excess—master-bankers in Europe and the Mediterranean, it was the business of Templars to keep track of capital—here recorded as "florins" ("florenez" [l. 885]), one of the standard gold currencies in Latin Europe from the mid-thirteenth century on. The Templar also stresses that the tyrant's treasure is wrongfully acquired—constituting, thus, illegally derived wealth and positioning the giant as an outlaw, excluded from lawful society. Later we are told that exclusion is, in fact, preferred by the Genoese giant, for he is supremely confident and monstrously self-willed, asserting his identity with a vengeance, in a kind of giant self-fashioning. The giant can linger outside the bounds of law just as he likes, one of his victims declares, without the permission of any man, because he is the lord of his own domain (ll. 996–97). He is simultaneously an outlaw marginalized beyond the social polity—the giant's flesh is even anatomically described as recalling a "wolf's head" (l. 1064), "wolf's head" being a common metaphor for the medieval outlaw—and the independent lord of his own country, the center of power in his demesne, its "tyrant."

We see instantly that the *Morte*'s giant is different from his predecessors because he is at once a figure of economic monstrosity—of disproportionate wealth, wrongfully acquired—and a figure of superordinate independence: conditions that define him, in the feudal system, as a monster, as much as the unconscionable appetites for human flesh and taboo forms of sexual violence. Though he might superficially seem to resemble a feudal lord in his authority over his own territory, the giant in fact sets no store by feudal dispositions of land and estates ("For bothe landez and lythes full lyttill by he settes" [l. 994]), nor is he dependent on feudal rent as income ("Of rentez ne of rede golde rekkez he neuer" [l. 995]). Indeed, despite his ostensible residence at Mont St-Michel in northern France—a habitat and locale that is merely honorary—the giant

seems really to reside outside the traditional feudal hierarchy that characterizes Northwestern Europe's economic system. Enjoying freedom from
feudalism, the giant's exemption marks off yet another level of monstrosity in his identity.

Nonetheless, though he defies definition by the set terms of feudalism's
economic regime, the giant inescapably lodges in our mind as a medieval
imperialist, for he takes annual tribute from fifteen realms in the form of
their regnal kings' beards. Here we have again that infamous, bizarre cloak
of beards that was the giant Ritho's trophy in Geoffrey's *Historia*—a topos
now ineluctably interwoven into the tapestry of Arthurian romance and
too fascinatingly lurid, too rich in symbolic possibilities not to be rein-
voked. Accordingly, in the *Morte*'s transaction, this cloak-as-trophy becomes a highly and intricately specialized artifact. Not only does the garment have origins that advertise strata of crusading history (the cloak was
"spun in Spain . . . and afterward garnished in Greece" [ll. 999–1000), but
because the cloak is "bordered with the beards of noble kings" (l. 1002)
that can identify each tributary monarch through his hair color, the cloak
is now an anatomical map of all the territories under the giant's dominion
and sway: a highly colored-in map, in other words, of empire. So enamored is the *Morte* with this eloquent project of cartography-by-anatomy—
territorial space as body parts—that the *Morte*'s giant will take no other
coin than kings' beards for annual tribute at Easter eve (l. 1014). We are
told that the Genoese tyrant's vast economic accumulation and raw power
("he has more tresour to take when hym likes / Than euere aughte Arthure
or any of hys elders" ll. 1015–16]) effectively release him from the necessity to amass more fiscal capital, and confer on him a special privilege: the
freedom to manipulate symbolic capital instead.

We note, in this, that the *Morte* speaks its fascination with economic
accumulation, legality, power, and the might and movement of capital,
through a signifying vocabulary of gendered body parts—anatomical symbolization. The expressive framework which organizes that symbolic vocabulary into place is the riveting memory and history of the crusades.
Often, bodies that speak their meanings, and echoes from the crusading
past, coincide: that day itself, when Arthur arms for his giant killing, after
evensong, for example, his garments and armor simultaneously retrieve
geographical-historical coordinates from the crusades and produce an elite
masculine, military body whose ceremonial formality insists on its significance. Ostentatiously, Arthur's jeryn is from Acre (l. 903), and his jupon
from Jordan ("Jerodyn"),[7] while the scale-armor jesseraunt he wears serves

the double purpose of crusading nostalgia and emergent fashion: Scale armor is both a technological remnant, worn by Romans as the *lorica squamata* (DeVries, 56; Contamine, 178), by eighth-century Arabs and possibly Carolingians (DeVries, 60), in Spain between the tenth and twelfth centuries (Contamine, 187), and perhaps by Mongols (Contamine, 187), as well as newly fashionable again in fifteenth-century Europe.[8] Exquisitely ornamental as it is, Arthur's armor's concentration on upper-body details also materializes an impressively majestic masculine torso. An armored carapace of the well-shaped male military body at its most impressive, the armorial style also carries the history and future of other male military bodies of its kind. Arthur's armor, as it were, is corporate armor, a part incorporating the institution of the whole.

Once the king arrives at St. Michael's Mount, however, the story's attention swiftly shifts from the intact outer surface of the masculine body to a mutilated, split female bodily envelope and interior as the next spectacle. Though Arthur is accompanied to the adventure by the usual two companions, Kay and Bedivere, it is Arthur himself, in the *Morte*, and not Bedivere, who meets the crone who had been the dead maiden's foster mother and learns firsthand from her of the maiden's horrific bodily fate. For only in Geoffrey's *Historia* is the young female victim of romance at St. Michael's Mount spared the horror of monstrous rape and allowed to die inviolate; Wace and Laȝamon unsparingly enjoy the maiden's sexual despoiling before allowing her to perish from the violation. The *Morte*, in its turn, has the maiden brutally "slit . . . to the navel" ("slitt . . . to þe nauyll" [l. 979]) in the giant's sexual assault. With Arthur's male upper-body casing serving to frame the attention to bodies in this first, crucial adventure, the narrative counterpoint offers the first pathetically vulnerable body as female, gendered by its anatomical splitting. From the situated evidence of female vulnerability in the lower half of the human torso, we next move to the lofty subject of kings' beards and male vulnerability, as the old woman tells Arthur of the giant's hirsute garment. We grasp from her words that what menaces the best of fighting men is neither death nor sexual assault. True horror, for men, arises from the diminution of status-power, a frightening loss of control that renders them vulnerable to abject humiliation—a loss signaled in narrative as symbolic abdication of male bodily integrity.

That little allegory established, we are cunningly now sketched the location of menace. The first narrated scene of cannibalism proper is a microscopic description of the chopped-up bodies of seven boy children on which the giant has supped all season (l. 1025). Where eleventh-century eyewitness chroniclers had been transfixed by the spectacle of famished Christians desperately eating Muslim flesh half-raw at Ma'arra an-Numan, before the human meat was adequately roasted, the *Morte*'s cannibalism at St. Michael's Mount arrives not as primitive necessity but as a purposeful cultural ritual wrapped in all the trappings of civilization. For this cannibal is a veritable gourmand, who has his human victims delicately prepared in elaborate cuisinary arts for gourmet consumption: "chopped up in a serving-dish of chalk-white silver, with spiced vinegar sauce and the powder of precious spices" and honeyed spiced wines of Portuguese liqueurs (ll. 1026–28). This expensive, sensuous preparation of male children's flesh as fanciful cuisine assigns cannibalism to a specific cultural, discursive, and economic sign-system. Its conditions are no longer famine, urgent necessity, impoverishment, and wartime exigency, but a specialized aesthetic characterized by wealth, the rich resources of a consumer market, foreign imports that testify to networks of trade, and the pleasures and powers of artistic, *artful* preparation and consumption. It is the regime of culture, not the regime of instinct, that is emphasized here: the *Morte*'s obsession is with what culture and economic society, not nature, have accomplished in the late medieval period. The cuisinary morsel is exquisitely prepared, moreover, as a literary hors d'oeuvre, artfully designed to appeal to the mind, eye, and taste buds of consumers other than the giant—consumers, that is, of literature—and is saucy testimony to the favorite recipes of romance.

Three scenarios featuring body parts have now been exhibited to our eyes: Arthur's immaculate masculine upper body, swathed in protective shells of fabric and armor; the maiden's exposed, open, sexualized lower body; and seven defenseless boy children's once-bodies chopped up small—diced, cubed, spiced, peppered, and marinated to perfection.[9] The transposition—from male to female to children—has registered an alarming, progressive disintegration, a piecemeal, slowly intensifying dismantlement of the body. The stage has been carefully set for the giant's entrance—for the insertion, that is, of a body to end all bodies, the reconstitution and culmination of what we have thus far experienced.

When Arthur and we first catch sight of the giant, the creature is ostentatiously lounging around, casually lifting up a male human limb he is apparently about to devour. At once, the giant's own nether bodily regions attract our glance, as he warms ("bakes") his "back and his buttocks, and his broad loins" by the blazing fire (ll. 1045–48), apparently without breeches on ("breklesse hym semede" [l. 1048]), a wonderful vision of stereoptic obscenity that is simultaneously exhibited and withheld. For we do not know precisely what it is we see here, what is taking place before our eyes. We seem to have stumbled on a scene of cannibalism that is about to occur, and yet it seems a tease. Despite the stagey drawing out of the preparations for eating, and unlike chronicle accounts of crusader cannibalism and *RCL*'s unequivocal portrayals, no conclusive eating of humans has been glimpsed in *this* romance. Nor do we know, as he warms himself toastily by the fire, if the giant faces us, full frontally, or faces away from us, or even if he really is naked below the waist ("breklesse *hym semede*"; my emphasis). Indeed, beyond the narrative's communication of its fascination with the giant's nether quarters, we cannot tell what exactly the disclosure to our eyes entails.

But if obscene sex and obscene eating are evocatively conjoined here in what has been provokingly implied, we will soon learn that implied conjunctions, as well as provocative evocations, are this romance's *forte*. As an immediate spectacle, however, we are soon released into worse, as we are forced to see, this time with unpleasurable certainty, the lurid horror of livestock and men being skewered indifferently together on roasting spits (the Middle English "brochede" [ll. 1050, 1052], from the French, more feelingly delivers the spectacle than any modern English equivalent), and tubs "crammed full of chrismed children" (l. 1051), some of whom are also pinned together like fowl and roasted on spits turned by attendant ladies (ll. 1051–52). Whenever the narrative has troubled itself to insert gender into its story of St. Michael's Mount, we notice, the prospectively or retroactively cannibalized victims are invariably male: It is a "manns lymme" (l. 1046) that the giant raises by the haunch; it is boy children in the country of Constantine that the giant has stalked; it is seven boy children ("kanue childre" [l. 1025]) that he has fed on all season; and it is men ("beerynes" [l. 1050]) who are now turning on a spit strung along with cattle. Women are peripheral to the scene of eating or are consumed in a different way. Women function principally as sexual victims, servant-accomplices, or conscripts; or, like the crone who is the foster mother of the dead maiden, women merely witness, report, lament, and, on occasion, pray (ll. 1136–39), functions that are, in fact, remarkably like the functions women traditionally perform in medieval theaters of war.

At last, after the tense, cumulative piling on of the dehumanized, broken bodies of male adults and children massed as victims mingled with, and scarcely differentiated from, the carcasses of animals, we are finally awarded a description of the cannibal himself, as, of course, the manifest epitome of both man and animal conjoined. Climactically, the *Morte* assembles its giant as a menagerie of foul beasts pulled together within the approximate outline of a man, a lurid physical hybrid in whose anatomy man and animal uneasily shift and jostle together in in(de)finite combinations. Patiently the narrative inventories the giant's somatic features from head to foot, itemizing the many ghastly animals he resembles in teeth, ears, nose, gums, neck, chest, body skin, and mouth; his piglike greasiness and filth, body fat, matted hair, and broth-covered beard; the disgusting foam that spews from his maw over his face and forehead; his hairy shanks, limbs, shovel-footed feet, and so on (ll. 1075–1101).[10] The anatomization is patently concerned with telling the difference between a man and a monstrous assemblage of animal-like parts, through systematic notation of the body's composition. Whether it is possible, in this descriptive analysis, to locate the precise difference between man and beast in each part of the creature's body, the *Morte*'s practice here of lodging and reading significance in the corporeal body's constituents, through a procedure of anatomization, will henceforth become a habitual narrative practice of revelation in this romance.

The narrative scrutiny, within the giant's composite body, of creature parts that are not quite human, but seem, troublingly, to remember or partially recall the human, is paralleled by earlier narrative observation of what are unquestionably male human body parts that arrest instantaneous identification. We have seen that when the giant is first glimpsed, he is lifting up the thigh of a man's limb by the haunch (l. 1046), while men and livestock are stuck together on a spit alongside tubs "crammed with chrismed children" (l. 1051), in a scene not only of anxious excess (proliferating, anonymous, dehumanization) but also of subtle, pleasurable differentiation. Obscene and uncertain though we have said the spectacle has been, at first sight the giant has also appeared like a man, with "back," "buttocks," and "broad loins" that seem not unlike the lower human male torso he is apparently about to consume, and he is warming himself by a fire—a startlingly human and creaturely act, one that shapes itself in terms of familiar human gestures.

In some respects, moreover, the giant seems disturbingly *more* than a man, rather than less. When Arthur engages the giant in combat—which Arthur immediately does, after uttering suitable judgment and threat— the giant proves a formidable contestant, as durable as the best of Arthur's knights. Visibly an *übermensch* by virtue of size (he is five fathoms high, a

man to end all men) and possessing superior physical strength and endurance, the giant seems virtually indestructible, a superordinate battle
machine in the way that a knight should be but often is not, in history and
romance. When Arthur slashes into the giant's brain with his sword (l.
1113), the giant recovers and retaliates, so that the king then thrusts his
sword half a foot deep into the giant's haunch (ll. 1119–20), smites into his
opponent's entrails (l. 1122), and neatly slices off the giant's genitals, emas-
culating him (l. 1123). When the giant strikes back, Arthur slashes again
into his antagonist's body, eviscerating him in shanks or groin (l. 129) so
that the giant's "guts and gore gush out at once," spill onto the grass and
make the ground tacky and wet (l. 1130–31)—but still the giant lives on.
Opened up in innumerable parts, brain exposed, guts spilling out, genital-
less, the giant wrestles mightily with Arthur, the two opponents rolling fu-
riously on the ground, till the giant snaps three of Arthur's ribs (l. 1151).
During the struggle, the women on the crag tremulously intercede for
Arthur in prayer, and the king manages to bury his dagger ("anlace") up
to its hilt into the giant's body again and again (ll. 1148–49). This last
round of penetrations seems conclusive, but a shaky Arthur nonetheless
cautiously orders Bedivere to insert his sword into the giant's heart, as a
confirmatory gesture, and then to behead the giant and pike the head on
a stake—a final, indisputable, indispensable proof of conclusive organic
death. No other Arthur than the *Morte*'s has had to battle so hard, or so
long, to defeat his giant.

If we are uncomfortably pushed by the narrative portrayal of battle
into some confusion as to whether we are witnessing a duel to the death,
or a covert drama of sexual figures and sexualized actions passed off as
combat maneuvers, it is because the *Morte* is transfixed by the topography
of the giant's sex as an unequivocal location of his gender and resemblance
to the human. The text's voyeuristic absorption with the giant's genitals
stems from the narrative reasoning that the one part of the giant's anatomy that is palpably a man's—and not some appurtenance of amphibian,
fowl, fish, or mammal—has been ascertained in that most confirmatory of
manlike acts: the ritualistic commission of rape on a woman.[11] As a punitive sequel to the giant's illegal sexual violence, Arthur's exaction of judiciary violence is also accordingly sexualized. Though original to the *Morte*,
the shearing off of the giant's genitals, and closing in of the visual field on
the giant's haunch (l. 1119), groin or loins (l. 1129) in the zone of battle, is
by no means gratuitous. This sexualization of punishment has the immediate, telling effect also of sexualizing the combat with its many, adjacent

penetrations of the giant's body, and thus contingently eroticizes the terms, as well as the turns, of martial violence. Indeed, the shadowy mingling of sex, battle, and death in all the rounds of this combat has been as startling for its intermittent explicitness, as the conjoining of cannibalism and sex had been campily oblique in the giant's lounging scene. Obsessed with pinpointing genital masculinity as identity, the *Morte* has surfaced the relationship between martial and sexual affect. That adjacency of affect will play itself out again in other battlefields, with other fighting men, later in the romance.

The giant killing as martial combat is also exemplary in other ways. Subsequent events will show that any *one* of the dismemberments inflicted by Arthur on the giant will be enough to fell an ordinary knight. With the exception of the emasculation, the mutilations inflicted in the giant-killing in fact constitute prototype patterns in the *Morte* of opening up the male body in death on the battlefield. If most of the outside of the giant's body had seemed grotesquely inhuman and bestial, the opening up of his body—the spilling of the giant's insides—has shown that secreted within the hulking carapace of a visible menagerie of body parts are the soft, invisible insides of a man. In being opened up, turned inside out by Arthur's strokes, the giant has revealed that he is a man *within*, as he is a monster without. Worse yet, the giant's evisceration, dismemberment, and death suggest that it is *as a man*—not as a collective monster—that he is vulnerable. In one fell, memorable instance, the giant has shown that to be a man *is* to be vulnerable after all, to be soft inside an exterior shell, and to die.

That the *Morte* is vitally, urgently invested in probing the male body, inside and out, is palpable in the inquisitional investigation of bodies in this scene and later. Not only has a male monster's body been made to yield its secrets, in life and in death, but Bedivere's and Kay's systematic, almost surgical investigation of wounds on Arthur's body, after the giant-fight, attests to the continuation of narrative scrutiny, and the extension of that scrutiny to the body of a king—a royal knight, and attestably supreme species of fighting man. In a regimen that is beginning to feel faintly familiar, Kay and Bedivere probe the whole length of Arthur's body inside the casing of its armor, sensitively searching out the body's component parts. Arthur's haunch, shoulders, flanks, sides, skin, back, breast, "bright arms," loins, "bands of muscular tissue" (ll. 1156–59) are minutely examined; no inquisitor could be more thoroughly or painstakingly absorbed in comprehending the body's geographies of pain and wounding. In this post-battle absorption with Arthur's torso and members, none of the three men present seems to take further heed of the "chrismed children," the remains of the giant's anonymous human victims, or the plight of the nameless women survivors.

On St. Michael's Mount, all attention next turns to Arthur's rightful assumption of battle trophies—the giant's club and kirtle of kings' beards—as the victor briefly recites Arthurian literary history and crusader pasts by recalling an equally powerful giant from the mountains of "Araby"[12]—Geoffrey's "Mons Aravius" being plainly incommensurate, in this romance, with Mt. Snowdon in Wales. In a distinctly modern development that shows a fascinated interest in the fate of wealth, and the existence of a polity called "the commons," Arthur then gives instructions for the giant's treasure to be distributed to "the commons of the country" ("comouns of the contré" [l. 1215]) in such a way that no one will complain of his share ("none pleyn of thiere parte" [l. 1217]). By contrast to its express concern with distributing the giant's estate to its satisfaction, the narrative does not trouble itself to mention returning the survivors to their families or burial of the dead. For all its plaintive compassion for the giant's victims, then, this romance seems more eager to oversee the fate of his florins, through the route of monetary compensation and monarchic beneficence, than to oversee the fate of human remains or survivors.

That the *Morte* is preoccupied with men and knights—not dead duchesses—is reiterated by the utter lack of narrative interest in even the eponymous possibilities of the pilgrim site that had so engaged Geoffrey's fancies. Despite the fact that a church and monastery ("kyrke" [l. 1219]; "couent" [l. 1220]) are to be built there, the crag cannot be memorialized as "Helena's Tomb" because by no shred of narrative memory has the maiden's name been retained. Instead, the only line of figural continuity the *Morte* arranges is vested entirely between men. As Mary Hamel, the *Morte*'s latest editor, shrewdly notices, Arthur's assumption of the giant's cloak of beards effectively makes Arthur over into the giant's successor, in a chain of displacement and substitution that confirms Arthur as the latest personification of territorial dominance and tributary exaction.[13] Arthur's undisputed possession of masculinized symbolic capital—annual tribute from regnal kings, through the humiliating submission of a critical body part, their beards—conjoins supreme, superordinate, successful masculinity to conquest, empire, and domination. Apotropaically, to be a superior species of man in chivalric romance is to possess territory, wealth, and resources to distribute, and symbolic capital in the form of other men's bodies and their masculinity. In this late-medieval romance we are witnessing the emergent recognition, no less, that masculine power resides in the control of capital, in its symbolic as well as its fiscal forms. In the register of an elite feudal romance whose mission is the definition of masculinity and elite male identity, manliness—Arthur-style and giant-style—is defined as possessing tributary kings as one's virtual tenants-in-chief, in the perpetuation of militancy, occupation, and empire.

WARRING AGAINST MODERNITY: CHIVALRIC ROMANCE, SOCIOECONOMIC TRANSFORMATIONS, AND TECHNOLOGY

Chivalric romances are probably the best-known subset of medieval romances. Indeed, chivalric romances are often synecdochically mistaken for the full universe of medieval romance itself, thanks to the renown of Chrétien de Troyes, the voluminous prose of the Old French Arthurian vulgate cycle, the scintillating brilliance of *Sir Gawain and the Green Knight*, and the haunting nostalgia of narrative encyclopedists like Malory. Unlike other species of romances, moreover, medieval chivalric romance has the distinct advantage of close linkage to an identifiable social class. Its emergence in the third quarter of the twelfth century in association with the landless aristocratic "youths" tracked in France by Georges Duby has meant that chivalric romance can be readily read as a literature of self-fashioning and ideological mystification that has, from its earliest appearance, accommodated chivalric elites of varying seigneurial ranks in the Middle Ages. When late-medieval English society undergoes internal transformation of a kind that confounds seigneurial elites, then, two brilliant Middle English chivalric romances, *Sir Gawain and the Green Knight* (*SGGK*), and the Alliterative *Morte Arthure*, mount responses in defense of the elite culture and social class with which this subset of medieval romance has been associated for more than two centuries. Where *SGGK* transacts the changing meaning of elite masculine identity in England through a narrative apparatus featuring love, ladies, and leisure (see Heng, "A Woman Wants" and "Feminine Knots")—one of two time-honored trajectories in the country of chivalric romance—the *Morte* negotiates *its* preoccupations through that other chivalric route, the advocacy of martial action and male companionship. A text capable of critique as well as defense, the *Morte*'s brilliance, in part, lies in its extraordinary ability to lay bare the anatomy of defense, calling attention to its procedures of anatomization.

I discuss the *Morte* as a representative of chivalric romance, then, for several reasons.

The third section of this chapter ("A Virtual History of the Crusades") shows how a canny chivalric romance like the *Morte* can address the urgencies of a given historical present by meditative recourse to the long sweep of the past, and the full diachronic arc of historical and literary memory available in chivalry as an institution. Beyond its use of archival memory, the *Morte* also foregrounds certain key organizing structures and devices specific to the repertoire of romance, so that quintessential romance operations are accessibly close to its surface. The fourth section ("Priamus, Fortune's Wheel, and Genoese Giants") is thus able to suggest how romance descriptions of "chance" and contingency, and traditional figures like the goddess Fortune and her wheel, are articulated by the *Morte* with historical phenomena in ways that typically identify romance operations. The discussion, in this fourth section, of Genoese slavery and economic exploitation points to how critique is simultaneously asserted and disguised in romance, and how public secrets can be made visible, while being hidden, in romance narrative. Finally, the fifth section ("The Unmaking and Making of Men") indicates how chivalric romance understands individual, particular bodies to be related to social, corporate bodies, so that transitions and crises in the register of the social are played out and explored in the register of the corporeal. Ironically, the *Morte* has sometimes been thought by scholars to understand crisis only *too* well, for in dealing *with* crisis, the *Morte* has sometimes seemed to be a text *in* crisis, because it has seemed impervious to satisfactory scholarly taxonomization (Is it a romance? Fürstenspiegel? chronicle? tragedy?). But as a representative of its subset, the *Morte*'s limitations are as useful as its strengths. By considering the labor that the *Morte*, as chivalric romance, is *unable* to perform, the discursive work performed with ease by other kinds of romances is more readily grasped. I end this chapter, then, after a detailed consideration of what the *Morte* speaks with extraordinary eloquence, with what the *Morte* is unable to speak, in projective anticipation of a species of romances of a different order, which I consider in the next chapter.

In defending against the encroachments of economic modernity and its ramifications—the expansion of cash relations and intrusion of market forces, with concomitant diversifications in, and complexified relations between, the various strata of social organization—the *Morte* focuses on the social field that chivalric romance has known best, centrally featured, and faithfully served: knighthood. Though variously titled aristocrats appear in the text, the overarching descriptive category that has supreme and consistent priority in the *Morte* is "knight." The term "knight" is revealingly comprehensive and flexible in this romance, a title of honor that subsumes every rank from "kaiser," king, and great baronial magnates who are tenants-in-chief of the crown, to free gentles who may be lately dubbed in the field (such as Sir Cador's newly made knights in ll. 1738–42) or service officers who have performed largely administrative duties as knights (the "auditors" scorned by Sir Clegis in ll. 1672–73). The capacious elasticity of the definition acknowledges the variety within a late-medieval social stratum, and is insisted on precisely *because* knighthood as a category has opened up, ramified, and become labile, and thus socially problematic: a microcosm of the forces of complexification and change infecting late medieval English society.[14]

Forces of transition acting on knighthood and knights at the onset of late medieval modernity iconicize, then, for the *Morte*, the larger forces of transition sweeping through English society as a whole (for despite the Arthurian frame, it is contemporary "Ynglande," [l. 710] not antique "Britain," that is the focus).[15] Knighthood as such comes to represent the entire feudal structure under threat of erosion by modernity's wide-ranging impact. As feudal institutions, models, and systems come under pressure from within and without—operated on by economic, social, administrative, political, ecclesiastic, military, and technological transformations—the *Morte*'s defense of knighthood becomes a defense of feudalism itself, with its economic rewards for the traditionally privileged, its culture and hierarchies, its grand, mystified ideology. Feudalism is the territory that must be held in the war against modernity. And if the corporate body of society is the ultimate focus, the masculine body of individual knights is the intimate focus, the personal body marked by institution and gender being the lens through which the social and historical can be brought under examination. The knight's body is thus both the medium and the surface of scrutiny in narrative transactions—something to look at, and to look through, in an exchange that switches the attention back and forth, miming other kinds of exchange, circuits, and objects.

For chivalric romance, of course, to be truly a man *is* to be a knight. Other categories of feudal men and masculinity either fall outside the purview of the human—the *Morte*'s giant of St. Michael's Mount is poignantly damned as a "churl" ("carle" [ll. 1063, 1107, 1165]) or mere husbandman, smallholder-peasant, *rusticus*—or abut so negatively against the sublime normativity of knighthood that they are scarcely acknowledged, or are acknowledged only to be refused.[16] Where Geoffrey, Wace, and Laȝamon, for example, present twelve ambassadors from Rome, bearing the demands of the Roman Emperor to Arthur, the *Morte* presents one Roman senator accompanied by sixteen *knights* instead (l. 1491). Even Saracens and Romans alike—enemy hosts—are "cheualrye" (l. 1872). True to its time, and contemporary English stratifications, the *Morte* also carefully distinguishes between *kinds* and *degrees* of knights, singling out bannerets ("banerettez bolde" [l. 1424]) from bachelors ("bachellers noble" [l. 1424]), and knights who have recently been granted their arms (armigerous *parvenus*) from knights whose families have possessed their armorial bearings of old, for generations, through hereditary descent and noble lineage (ll. 1689–91, 1694–99).[17]

Such a fixation on distinctions in knighthood—and knighthood itself as a distinction—arrives at a historical moment when the utility and desirability of knighthood are undergoing challenge on multiple fronts. Historians have argued that perhaps as early as the thirteenth century, and more securely by the fourteenth, knighthood "was beginning to lose its significance as the common tie binding together higher and lower among the aristocracy . . . by a shared consciousness of noble descent and a common right to the hereditary insignia of nobility, armorial bearings" (Keen, *Chivalry*, 144). Whether the economic conditions for a true "crisis of the knightly class" were to be found in thirteenth-century England,[18] the monarchy's recorded practice of "distraint to knighthood"—the coercion of recalcitrants who were eligible, but declining, to become knights—supports the common view of historians that "the escalating cost of knightly equipment and of the ceremony of dubbing" (Given-Wilson, 18), and the "administrative burdens" of knighthood (Butt, 253), were "deterring a greater number of potential knights from assuming the honour" (Given-Wilson, 18).[19]

By the mid-fourteenth century, moreover, a "squirarchy" of esquires—a social category of men who were not knights but a chivalric diminutive who, though undubbed, often possessed holdings and economic assets approximately equal to those of knights—were not only members of chivalric Orders and participants at tournaments but were also newly armigerous, granted the right to possess and display coats of arms.[20] Revealingly, late-medieval English literature testifies to the competitive prominence and ubiquity of squires. In Chaucer's *Franklin's Tale*, for instance, not only does the squire Aurelius seem to possess substantial liquidity, parting with five hundred pounds in gold with ease (ll. 1571–73), but he also goes to some pains to show that a squire is equal to a knight in chivalric magnanimity, in manners as well as cash ("Thus kan a squier doon a gentil dede / As wel as kan a knyght" [ll. 1543–44]); Chaucer, of course, was himself an esquire but never a knight. In similar vein, we see the protagonist squire in *The Squire of Low Degree* spectacularly rising through the social hierarchy to become a king without ever having been dubbed, bypassing knighthood entirely, and seeming thus to render knighthood quaintly irrelevant.[21]

In the *Morte* an otherwise inexplicable, passionate outburst by Sir Clegis, a knight of Arthur's, who answers a challenge with an avowed declaration of the hallowed antiquity of Sir Clegis's family lineage in arms, thus seems specifically designed to address what might be called the challenge, from below, to hereditary status in arms. Sir Clegis—a name out of Arthurian literary history, perhaps, since it recalls Chrétien's "Cligès"—has himself twice issued Arthur's enemies a chivalric challenge (ll. 1651–52, 1681–82), when he is taunted by a Syrian king who replies with the requirement that Clegis's arms ("cote" and "creste" [l. 1690]) first be attested by lords, as hereditary arms ("armes of ancestrye" [l. 1691]) that are backed, in recorded documentation, with estates ("entyrde with londez" [l. 1691]). Since Clegis's chivalric invitation has been buoyantly expressed in tournament-like fashion (see Hamel, *Morte*, 307–8 nn. 1681–82, 1688–89), and since, by the late fourteenth century, armigerous squires are to be found at tournaments, the Syrian king's inquisitive insistence seems aimed at divining if Clegis is indeed an opponent of sufficiently high rank and thus worthwhile for a king to engage in combat. It is an inquiry that searches out and distinguishes knights of landed, ancient lineage—*maiores barones*, since "lordez" (l. 1690), i.e., nobles or peerage, must undertake the requisite attestation here—from mere wealthy squires.[22]

Clegis's own rude insult, first hurled at an enemy "earl" ("erle" [l. 1661]) a little before Clegis repeats his chivalric invitation, discloses yet another type of threat to chivalry, issuing from an additional quarter. Besides competitive pressure from a squirarchy, the prestige of traditional knighthood is also diluted when knightly ranks are replenished by knights who attest their class through the practice of arts of *peace* rather than of war, since knights in the late Middle Ages were often found busily distinguishing themselves in civil and administrative service: a suspicion Clegis surfaces when he insinuates that he can tell by his enemy's "carpynge" (l. 1672), that the enemy "erle" is really a mere "cowntere" (l. 1672) or auditor (l. 1673), someone who has served through competent desk labor, rather than heroic martial labor, attesting ancient descent (ll. 1672–73). Clegis's contempt for his opponent, an "earl," has a special biting edge, since "earl" is an old baronial designation, anteceding by far the new aristocratic titles of "duke" or "marquis" invented by monarchy only in the fourteenth century.[23] Clegis's ironical elaboration of his metaphor of accounting—Arthur, Clegis says, has already drawn up his business accounts ("araysede his accownte") and reviewed all his official records ("rollez") and will soon give a reckoning ("rekenyng") that his enemies will rue (ll. 1677–78)—adds to the felt presence, in the *Morte*, of a ubiquitous, necessary, and pervasive administrative culture underpinning all arrangements.

A vocabulary of administration—the accounting, recording, itemizing, and reviewing, of rolls, wills, lists, and diverse documents—and a lexicon of administrative officers and officialdom, of governmentality, suffuses the *Morte*. Not only is the work of parliament periodically invoked in this romance but Arthur, in appointing Mordred regent in Arthur's absence, uses the occasion to enumerate, in officialese, the various categories of chancellor, chamberlain, auditors, officers, juries, judges, and justices (ll. 660–62), for Mordred to supervise as chief executive officer ("sektour, cheffe of all oþer" [l. 665]) as he administers (l. 666) Arthur's possessions. If the requirements of late-medieval government are acknowledged in the *Morte* by the omnipresence of an administrative stratum, scripted into that acknowledgment is an intensifying recognition of a modern, immensely important avenue to advancement and power, outside the traditional avenue of martiality beloved by chivalry, in late medieval England. The giant of St. Michael's Mount, damned as a churl, is also twice dubbed a "maister-man" (ll. 990, 938) or leading official, his power acknowledged with a reference to administration.[24] Revealingly, when Mordred tries to decline Arthur's investiture of him as chief officer, the fosterling of Arthur's chamber (l. 690) pleads that administrative experience will not bring him the kind of honor bestowed by the theater of combat. "When others skilled in war are honored hereafter," Mordred pleads, "then I may in truth be valued but at little" (ll. 685–86). The *Morte*, we note, defends martial exploits as the true mark of worth and value for a man—the traditional route to power and honor—and downgrades, by comparison, excellence in administration or faithful government service as an inferior avenue of masculine advancement.

Sir Clegis's specification of ancient pedigree as a cornerstone of his knightliness—a defensive reflex to systemic accommodations in the composition of knighthood—is also fueled by other upstart ascensions: by the upward mobility, for instance, of wealthy merchants-turned-knights, "new men" of inferior social status but superior economic prowess, who jostle the ranks of knights of hereditary degree. One wealthy "merchant-knight" who attracted parliamentary attention for his massive loans to Edward III was the Hull wool trader Sir William de la Pole, who was made a knight banneret by Edward in 1355 and whose family subsequently survived in the male line for six generations. Sir William's son, Michael, not only served under Edward the Black Prince and John of Gaunt in the Anglo-French wars but became chancellor of England in 1383 and Earl of Suffolk in 1385, thus founding one of the great noble families of England, the earls and, later, dukes, of Suffolk, from origins in trade (Thrupp, 361; Given-Wilson, 49, 53; McFarlane, "Bastard Feudalism," 149).[25] The respect that accrues to economic power enables Christine de Pisan, a noted commentator on late chivalry, to remark that the great merchants of Venice and Genoa, who amassed enormous wealth, were dubbed, with good reason, "noble merchants" (154).

Sir Clegis's proud attestation of his insider status as a knight also provocatively calls to mind Froissart's description of Sir Robert Salle: "a paragon of chivalric skill, valor, and beauty" knighted by Edward III, who was nonetheless tempted by the rebels of 1381 to join them, because "being only the son of a mason, he [would] never be accepted as a gentleman" (Thrupp, 309–10). By contrast to Froissart's mason's son, when a little later in the *Morte* Sir Cador makes new knights on the battlefield (an old chivalric practice), the new knights just happen to be "heirs of Essex and all the East Marches" ("ayerez were of Esexe and all pase este marchez" [l. 740]). Thus the "newe men" (l. 1815) legitimized as knights in the *Morte* are, by a handy coincidence, really the old, familiar type of "new men." But even these newly made knights-who-are-landed-heirs do not measure up in battle with the enemy and have to be rescued by Sir Clegis, the knight of ancient pedigree: "If Sir Clegis had not come . . . Our new men had gone to naught" ("Ne hade sire Clegis comen . . . Oure newe men hade gone to noghte" [ll. 1828–29]).[26]

Historically, "new men" who are newly dubbed knights may resemble "John Philipot or Philpot, a prominent London grocer and alderman who was knighted in 1381," more than Sir Cador's landed heirs of chivalric romance. "Philipot was a man of some wealth, and in 1378 he equipped a fleet at his own expense and succeeded in capturing John Mercer, a Scottish pirate who had recently taken a toll on English shipping. This incident . . . made Philipot a national hero. . . . His popularity made him enemies among the nobility who were said to be jealous of the grocer's success in the pursuit of arms" (Barnie, 108). In history, if not in literature, it is the military *success*, not the military inadequacies of "new men," that gains them the attention of old knights. Indeed, the fact that in late medieval England "knighthood . . . was becoming increasingly a question of lineage" (Given-Wilson, 17) was "to some extent a defensive reaction to the dilution of the nobility's martial role in society. It was also a defence against the growing wealth of the merchant class" (Given-Wilson, 19). In the romance-belligerence of a Clegis protesting his lineage, and the exactitude of a Cador dubbing to knighthood the right kinds of new men, pulsate the uneasy currents of historical change. The *Morte*, we shall see later, will also address, creatively and at length, the diminution of knighthood's martial role.

Sir Clegis's insistence that ancient lineage is the essence of knighthood and chivalric conduct is discursively contested, moreover, by voices from other literary texts of the same proximate period as the *Morte*: The hag in Chaucer's *Wife of Bath's Tale*, for example, tendentiously reconstitutes knighthood as a more open category than Clegis's hereditary terms would allow. Reviving the antique Roman saying that true nobility consists not in blood but in virtue, the hag argues for a chivalry of *deeds*, not of inheritance, and maneuvers Christianity to support a position that would open up the ranks of chivalry to *anyone* who is virtuous, including an English grocer like Philipot or a mason's son like Robert Salle: "Chivalry/nobility is not only the renown of your ancestors," she tells the rogue knight-rapist she is educating, but "comes from God alone" ("gentillesse nys but renomee / Of thyne auncestres" [ll. 1159–92]; "gentillesse cometh fro God allone" [l. 1162]). Chaucer's hag's claim, which represents a legitimate category of opinion (see, e.g., *The Ayenbit of Inwyt*, ll. 87–88; and Christine de Pisan, 137–38), sketches a lively contest for social definition typical of the later Middle Ages, a period in which reduction in hereditary great nobility of the highest ranks was accompanied by expansion in the ranks of lower peerage and gentry, with concomitant stratifications and complexification of the expanding social classes.[27]

The evidence of cultural history, moreover, suggests that contests over social mobility, circulation, and definition in the period—a subject "distasteful to chivalric sensibilities" (Thrupp, 305) in part because it frequently pivoted on the fluidity and mobility of economic capital—often fought themselves out in the register of signs: for example, in heated disputes over coats-of-arms (such as the Scrope versus Grosvenor trial of 1386, to which

Sir Clegis's own attestation of ancient arms may allude [Keen, "Chaucer's Knight," 49–53; Hamel, *Morte*, 308 nn. 1694–97])[28] that required stringent adjudication and policing by professional heralds appointed to oversee and regulate the business of assignation, use, and genealogy in arms (Thrupp, 304–9). In the field of literature-as-cultural-insignia, the examples of late popular romances like *The Squire of Low Degree*, which ostentatiously features the upward mobility of a squire; of misfit knights like Sir Balin and Sir Dinadan in Malory's Arthuriad, who seem not to understand the chivalric performances required of them; or elaborately courtly romances like *Sir Gawain and the Green Knight* and the *Morte* itself—all demonstrate an avid interest in cultivating definitions of who, and what, a knight might be, or might become, in the late Middle Ages.

What a knight might be was complicated by yet another factor in late feudalism, namely, the expanded intrusion of cash relations—and, in particular, waged military labor at all levels—into the theater of war itself, an economic development rendered inevitable by the proliferation of war, and the repeated necessity of punctually recruiting both dependable armies of a certain size and the military commanders to lead them. Historically, the advent of "bastard feudalism" from at least the late thirteenth century, and perhaps earlier (economic historians have increasingly detected earlier evidence of encroachment), saw the gradual supersession of the old tenurial bond between lord and vassal, in which land held of a lord was repaid with obligatory military service—the traditional *servitium debitum* of feudalism—by waged contracts of retainer in military arrangements between master and man.[29] By the late fourteenth century through the fifteenth, a variety of such instruments of recruitment had emerged (letters patent, annuities, indentures of retainer for war, etc.), so that although the "great armies of the beginning of the Hundred Years War were . . . by their recruitment . . . very much a mixture" (Contamine, 155) in the first half of the fourteenth century, "the fourteenth century [also] saw prolonged periods of warfare, in which the fighting was done by contract armies within which there was an established system of . . . wage-rates" (Given-Wilson, 63). Froissart notes that, as early as the battle of Crécy in 1346, some who served "were obliged by homage to do so, others in order to earn their wages and money" (Contamine, 155), but "from the third quarter of the fourteenth century," during the Hundred Years War, "the core of the [English] army was formed by gathering retinues, of variable size, recruited according to the terms of contracts called indentures for war" (Contamine, 151).[30] "For [John of] Gaunt's expedition to France in

1373, there were gathered in this way . . . 28 leaders or captains of retinues: 13 Englishmen (three earls, seven bannerets, two knights and a clerk) and 15 foreigners. . . . These 28 retinues totalled 6,000 combatants" (Contamine, 151–52).[31]

If "indentures . . . were common to all great magnates in the fourteenth century" (Hicks, 78), efficient mobilization for war meant the necessary infiltration of money relations into all military ranks, a development whose economic logic can be detected as issuing from the market: "The general shift to pay is . . . better understood if it is placed in the wider context of the spread of wage labour" (Contamine, 164), a spread that signaled the beginnings of the transformation of feudalism into something else. The intrusion of market forces, moreover, intimates the ineluctable contamination of a once-pristine military romanticism eloquently enshrined in chivalric ideology. Where military elites might once have counted on fictions of exchange relations that enabled the positing of idealized, mystified notions of mutual obligation, protection, and dependence among social elites organized by subinfeudation into a hierarchy of land tenure and expropriations of peasant labor—a hierarchy in which military service functioned as an integral, organic, and ennobling component—the ugly specter of cash relations renders inevitable the corruption of fictions of piety, loyalty, regard, and ennobling service so essential to constructions of knighthood and knightliness.[32]

Historically, one manifestation of such corruption is the "degeneration of the notion of liege homage," an inevitable outcome of bastard feudalism, along with "the loss of that stability which the tenurial relation may be presumed to have maintained in earlier times" (McFarlane, "Bastard Feudalism," 31). Unlike traditional tenurial bonds, contracts of retainer may be "transient and fluctuating as retainers transferred from one connection to that of a competitor" (Hicks, 103), with "desertion or treachery" being acutely felt at times, especially under conditions of "competitive retaining" (103). Since indentures can be canceled "by mutual consent or one-sided action" (McFarlane, "Bastard Feudalism," 38), contracts of a contingent nature thus testify unblinkingly to a clear-eyed "calculation of mutual advantage" (39) that runs counter to time-honored chivalric sensibilities and pieties. When the "compiler of the *Brut* tells of one John Munsterworth who made a small fortune by defaulting on indentures negotiated with the king [i.e., Richard II]" (Barnie, 23), market-driven impulses can clearly be seen to take priority over traditional ties of loyalty, homage, duty, and service.

The *Morte* shows itself conscious of the instability and disruptive potential of competitive retaining, when it depicts Priamus's men, fighting under the banner of the Duke of Lorraine, defaulting on their contracts of retainer to Lorraine, once Priamus goes over to Arthur's forces, and justifying their action, in going over to the enemy, by announcing that Lorraine has not paid their fees for four winters (l. 2928) and their wages have been used up (l. 2930). Though the desertion of these de facto mercenaries ("sowdeours" [ll. 2925, 2938]), who suddenly "in default forsake their lord" (l. 2939), advantages Arthur's side in the immediate circumstances, their action registers an alarming fluidity and contingency of loyalties of which the *Morte* is acutely conscious, as demonstrated by the *Morte*'s careful narrative detailing of many, overdetermining justifications (the men are also following Priamus, their leader, who has switched sides for more chivalrous reasons, after being honorably defeated by Gawain). Not only are these treacherous retainers given several lines to utter, in justifying their betrayal, but their loud insistence that they might with "honor" ("wirchipe" [l. 2931]) go wherever they please—given exigent conditions of nonpayment for labor and the example of their leader, Priamus—suggests the kind of overprotestation that only underscores the threat they constitute to the stability of military allegiance, late medieval style. With a firm basis in cash relations, moreover, indentures, as can be seen from this example in chivalric romance, also dangerously blur the distinction between loyal retainers and mere hired mercenary troops.[33] Feudalism, in its military aspects, is shaken to the core by the adventitiousness of money.

Revealingly, the *Morte* finds it necessary to issue a late-medieval defense of liege homage, and a reminder of the traditional rewards of feudalism for male elites, when it has Sir Cador utter a quintessential summation of feudal ideology in its purest, unfettered form, a *grand récit* of feudalism, as it were, for chivalric combatants. Urging on his fellows, Cador (a figure from Geoffrey's *Historia* and thus recalling the earliest days of Arthurian romance) eloquently instructs his men to think on "the valiant prince who invests us ever / With lands and lordships . . . Who has dealt us dukedoms and dubbed us knights; / Given us treasures and gold and many guerdons, / Greyhounds and great horses, and all manner of festivities / Worthy of any man" (ll. 1726–31). Juxtaposing the older economic model against the advent of the newer, Cador's splendidly rousing advocacy of a purely feudal piety to be demonstrated by his men's military commitment to their lord is matched only by the equally splendid purity of the vision of feudalism he conjures for those men. On his part, Arthur affirms Cador's nostalgic vision of a pure feudalism by royally enacting economic feudalism in generous performances of his power as feudal monarch. On one notable occasion, Arthur spontaneously awards Toulouse, with all its taxes, appurtenances, taverns, dwellings, towers, et alia, to an unnamed knight, simply because the knight is the bearer of good news (ll. 1567–70), the very casualness of Arthur's generous gesture speaking volumes for the advantages of feudalism to elites. To a gathering of his own lords (l. 1594), Arthur reassuringly promises his deep life-long devotion ("I sall them luffe whylez I lyffe" [l. 1597]) and, of course, generous feudal estates ("landys full large" [l. 1598]), sealing, with a promise, the widening seam between feudal superstructure and base.

That it is feudalism, no less, which has to be defended from the encroachments of economic modernity and the market is unmistakable in Cador's speech and Arthur's enactments. Unlike the giant of St. Michael's Mount, whom Arthur supplants—a giant who scorns the feudal rents and estates that represent the whole edifice of economic feudalism (ll. 1994–95)—Arthur represents his own domination of conquered territories in the explicit terms of a feudal economy: as a repeating opportunity, under feudal economic conditions, for the extraction of rent, or seigneurial revenues, from successful conquest. The disputed tribute to imperial Rome, in the form of taxes putatively owed by Arthur, is also evocatively represented by the Roman senator, and Sir Clegis, in alternate turns, as "rents" that are either illegally withheld or rightfully claimed (ll. 103, 1680, 1667); Arthur's haughty reply to the Roman demand for tribute also reads the tribute as rent ("fermes" [l. 425]). When the subject of Roman ransoms is raised, the ransoms are, of course, to be paid from "renttez" (ll. 465, 1509, 1554); and even Mordred's later usurpation of the Arthurian desmesne is grasped by Arthur, and the messenger who brings the news of usurpation, as a theft of the "renttes" of the Round Table (ll. 3571, 3526), a theft that Arthur intends to punish swiftly so that he might return to receive the "rentis" of a newly reconquered Rome (l. 3587), the imagined enjoyment of which gives Arthur much prospective pleasure (l. 3215). If Arthur invariably describes subject territories in terms of the feudal revenues they will supply ("rente" [l. 2405]), Arthur's knights faithfully follow the king's example. Sir Cador, that redoubtable scion of chivalric feudalism, vows to repay the killing of his kinsman with "corne-bote" (l. 1786), that is, manorial rent paid out in the form of grain, a grim joke that allows Cador to pun on the name of his own feudal estate, Cornwall (Hamel, *Morte*, 310 nn. 1786, 1837). The ringing emphasis on feudal rents enjoyed by the militarily successful—renarrating, over and over, that model of successful exploitation enjoyed by landlords under economic feudalism—repeatedly recalls what is at stake, for chivalric combatants, in warding off incipient change.[34]

In field combat, feudalism's erosion was haunted by the strategic deployment and success of certain knightly elements in war who unquestionably fell outside the old tenurial bond: by, that is, the ineluctably useful presence of knight-mercenaries. Though mercenaries as individuals and groups were a feature of medieval armies from very early, the fourteenth century in particular witnessed the sensational rise to prominence of celebrated, infamous English mercenary knight-captains, who, during and/or after their participation in the Hundred Years War on the side of the English—a war that created the identities and careers of these often lowborn men-turned-knights—led renowned bands for hire called "free companies" seeking, and making, fortunes on the continent. The free-enterprise example of the most prominent of these mercenary knights and leaders—the likes of Sir John Hawkwood, Sir Robert Knollys, Sir Hugh Calveley—stood in direct contrast, by its clear-eyed pursuit of wealth and power through a kind of military rationality that has been read by historians as pragmatic, modern-style generalship, to the old-style chivalrous example of such splendidly romantic English hero-knights of the age as the Black Prince, Sir John Chandos, and Sir Walter Manny. The remarkable self-made success of knight-mercenaries (Sir Robert Knollys died in bed at his manor house at Sculthorpe, in Norfolk, around the age of ninety, after a profitable career; Sir John Hawkwood, the near-legendary leader of the White Company, and son of an Essex tanner and minor landowner, also retired comfortably and profitably in England, and even became the brother-in-law of Prince Lionel, younger son of Edward III, when both the mercenary and the royal prince married daughters of Bernabò Visconti, Duke of Milan) showed how knighthood might be disarticulated from one set of moorings and rearticulated within more modern configurations of economic opportunism (Contamine, 158–59). Mercenary armies, by virtue of their duration, also helped to point the way toward the more permanent standing forces of modern militarism, and away from the temporary armies of medieval feudalism, unmaking and remaking the institutions of military manhood in a future direction.

From the mid-fourteenth through the mid-fifteenth century, moreover, the composition of English expeditionary forces on the continent changed in yet another way. Contingents of archers came to prominence, eclipsing the use of infantry pikemen and spearmen in combat and, more pertinently, diminishing the absolute preeminence and domination of the battlefield by chivalry, as England learned increasingly to exploit the advantages of missile technology. The technological modernity represented by the rise to prominence of the longbow in late-medieval theaters of war has become a truism of military history, and it is now routinely grasped that "the longbow altered English warfare from the late thirteenth until the end of the fifteenth century" (DeVries, 37). Edward I took 10,000 archers with him in 1298 in his successful conquest of Scotland, and large contingents of effectively deployed archers were also represented in English victories by Edward III at Dupplin Moor in 1332 and Halidon Hill in 1333. As early as 1242 the Assize of Arms had already described archers as the second most important class of militia after knights (DeVries, 37), and Henry III's 1251 Assize of Arms also targets archery in a remarkable fashion (Oakeshott, 294–95).[35] In the early decades of the Hundred Years War, English longbowmen played a decisive role in the key English victories at Sluys, Crécy, and Poitiers, outperforming Genoese crossbowmen fighting for the French at Sluys and Crécy, and defeating waves of French knights sent by Jean, at Poitiers—in part by downing their horses, war animals integral to knightly identity and chivalric warfare. When the Black Prince invaded Castile in 1376, he brought 6,000 archers to Nájera, among which, according to enemy sources, "there were at least 3,000 each of whom was worth a Roland or an Oliver" (Barnie, 105). At the siege of Calais, Edward III had 20,076 archers (Bradbury, 95).

It thus comes with little surprise that by the fifteenth century, the English social classes who furnished the ranks of archers had begun to display a certain upstart competitiveness with knights, whom they imagined they resembled, in military importance: A group of English bowmen, shopkeepers of London Bridge organized by a grocer called William Steyde, jauntily styled themselves "Steyde's Knights," with Steyde's son even proudly bequeathing his "bowe called England" to a scrivener (Thrupp, 168). Recognition of the vital importance of missile technology, despite official adhesion to the glories of chivalric warfare and ideology—which dictated that honor accrue only from direct physical combat in which a knight's body was individually hazarded—was registered by no less a chivalric personage than the Black Prince himself, who ordered the forced labor of all fletchers in Cheshire in 1356 during a shortfall in his supply of arrows (DeVries, 39).[36] Froissart's claim that at the Anglo-French negotiations of 1393, the Duke of Gloucester boasted of his readiness to find

100,000 archers to follow the king of England testifies to a more than passing regard for the importance of English bowmen (Barnie, 127).

Despite the proven efficacy of the English longbow in fourteenth-century military engagements, however—and for all the resemblance that scholarship has sometimes detected between famous battles in the Hundred Years War and the *Morte's* supposedly faithful depictions of those skirmishes[37]—only one description of the terrifying efficacy of bowmen appears in the *Morte*: a romance in which it is knighthood, not emergent military technology, that determines the conditions of successful warfare. Like the portrayal of the fickleness of military retainers recruited under indentures, the chilling effectiveness of bowmen is shown, of course, to subserve Arthur's advantage. Because the bows are ranged on Arthur's side and against the enemy, the depiction of death-by-missiles can, in fact, be starkly unflinching: "With loosed arrows they shoot these men full vigorously, / Pierce with feathers through the fine mails— / Such shooting is evil that harms the flesh so, / That flew from afar into the flanks of steeds" (ll. 2097–2100).[38] Fine mail, we note, offers no protection from the deadly missiles, the horror of whose impersonal efficiency partly consists in their being able to be loosed from afar, reaching long-distance targets with no danger to the bowmen themselves and emphasizing the utter vulnerability of the horses on which knightly efficacy so depends. Evil, indeed, is such shooting. The arrows that strike, however, predictably strike only through enemy knights ("Duchemen" [l. 2101]) so that it is the enemy host who shrinks back from the onslaught, and scatters (ll. 2101–6); the isolated episode, moreover, is the sole narrative moment where knights are not the prime agents, but the fearful targets, of war. Only under exceptional, singular circumstances, and conditions specially advantageous to Arthur's side, can the technology, with its implications of class threat and difference, be safely considered. Staging thus a limited, carefully managed access to history, the description in this episode opens a window on the kinds of narrative witnessing available in romance.

Along with the enlarging role of English archers came experiments with another technology with scant respect for traditional categories of class privilege in warfare. Cannon and gunpowder were used by Edward III in his 1327 invasion of Scotland; and records exist of small cannon, together with gunpowder, in the Tower of London in 1338. "Not only did the English almost certainly set off powder and fire projectiles at the battle of Crécy (1346), but for the siege of Calais (1346–47) ten cannons, ribaudequins, lead-balls and gunpowder were despatched from London. A document dated 10 May 1346 speaks of 912 lbs of saltpetre and 886 lbs of sulphur [i.e., two of the requisite ingredients for gunpowder] bought from a London apothecary for the king's guns (ad opus ipsuis regis pro gunnis suis')" (Contamine, 140). At Crécy, guns may have been used on the battlefield deliberately "to cause panic" (DeVries, 145).[39] Whatever the circumstances, a table of weights of seventy-three cannons of various sizes, from 43–49 pounds to 665–737 pounds, manufactured for Richard II by William Woodward between 1382 and 1388, suggests a continuing English interest in developing this other form of missile technology (Contamine, 141). Significantly, a late-fourteenth-century medical encyclopedia by John of Mirfield contains, alongside information on the treatment of wounds, injuries, and diseases, a recipe for a "powder for that warlike or diabolic instrument that commonly is termed the gun" (Getz, 51. Hartley and Aldridge, 90). Though the use of cannon artillery in siege warfare would not be commonplace till the fifteenth century, the real century of gunpowder, "gunpowder weapons began to be delivered to castles and town walls by the middle of the fourteenth century" (DeVries, 264) as "the defence of castles was partially ensured by cannons . . . taking their place along with . . . other engines" (Contamine, 202); also "by the middle of the fourteenth century nearly every siege was accompanied by gunpowder artillery bombardment" (DeVries, 145), as "'an arms race' . . . affected every kingdom and principality . . . which would eventually lead to the so-called 'military revolution'" (DeVries, 145).

The advent of technological and economic modernity, however, colors in but a partial story of military crisis in the late fourteenth century. In the third quarter of that century, the French king Charles V, who succeeded the ineffectual Jean II, initiated new defensive strategies of "passive resistance" organized around stoic endurance of prolonged sieges, refusals of large-scale open field engagement with English armies, and dependence on naval strength in order to counter the pattern of dramatic English victories won through the *chevauchées* and pitched battles that had favored English forces and English technology in the opening decades of the Hundred Years War. The improved French strategies coincided with English problems: "After 1369 there is a distinct decline in the qualities of the armies, and especially of the commanders, which Edward III and later Richard II were able to put into the field," and "the great expense of the war in terms of payments for alliances, the maintenance of garrisons and the wages of troops placed an intolerable strain on [England's] resources at a time when national production and income were falling" (Barnie, 14).

If, in the late fourteenth century, the tide turned against the English in the Hundred Years War to the extent that—as has been claimed by historians—the "English military were no longer accounted the finest in Europe; in the 1370s and 80s . . . they were . . . heartily despised by their enemies" (Barnie, 27), the antiwar sentiments that swept through England as a result of these reversals often placed the blame at the door of *knighthood*: "Where, asks Bishop Brinton, is the might of England's chivalry, 'once powerful and beloved, now however feeble and disgraced'? The answer he finds typically in the decadence and injustice of the knightly estate" (28). While the French Charles V, "the humane hero of Christine de Pisan and Froissart and the 'greatest enemy of the king of England'" (28), is portrayed in Froissart's *Chroniques* as a kind of "precursor of the modern general" (30), the intransigence of English leaders—"Knolles (1370), Gaunt (1373), and Gloucester (1380)"—who would not, or could not, abandon the *chevauchées* and pitched battles, suggests an obtuse, outdated adherence to "a formula which had been so successful in the past" (29–30). The preference for aggressive devastation and large-scale offensive confrontations as field maneuvers was specific not to England or Englishmen as such, but to *class*. Indeed, the French king's successful "policy of passive resistance" had been strongly opposed by his own knights, "the conservative and impetuous chivalry of France who considered it 'a great disgrace' not to engage the enemy" directly and at full strength, in head-on field encounters en masse (29). On both sides, knights proved recalcitrant.

Finally, in the closing years of the fourteenth century, there unfolded a military drama of sensational import, which demonstrated, on an international scale, the consequences of European knighthood's adherence to old formulas. In 1396, during a period of truce in the Hundred Years War between England and France, the combined international forces of the last major European crusade set out, under papal injunctions, to defend the borders of Europe and to relieve Eastern Christianity and Constantinople from the invasion of Ottoman Turks under Bayezid I. The crusade was required by both the Roman and the Avignonese popes—the twin leaders of the divided papacy that loomed over Latin Christendom from 1378—and involved forces from France, England, Germany, Spain, Hungary, Wallachia, Transylvania, Bohemia, Poland, Italy, and elsewhere (Atiya, *Nicopolis*, 10, and *Later Middle Ages*, 440; Runciman, 3:455–61). At Nicopolis, the crusaders were utterly crushed in a resounding defeat that historians would later accept as rendering inevitable the fall of Constantinople to the Ottoman Empire in 1453. Prominent among the factors determining crusader failure were precisely the motivating values and field practices of that outmoded chivalric ideology responsible for military failures nearer home—an ideology that created fractious rivalry, disputes, and furious indiscipline among the knights of the van, each of whom was determined to outdo the others, as demanded by chivalric ideals of winning glory. Ideology also rendered inevitable the deployment of that superannuated formula of proud chivalric combat—massed heavy cavalry charges against the missile onslaught of Turkish foot archers and light cavalry— maneuvers in which the critical disadvantage of heavy armor in mounted and dismounted combat at the end of the fourteenth century was once again pathetically exposed.[40]

Though historians continue to argue over the details of European/Christian defeat at Nicopolis, a skein of agreement exists that the crusade was surrendered by the ideological folly and superannuated tactics and technologies of European knighthood: French knighthood, in the main—although an estimated one thousand English knights were also in the van, and some crusading leaders, like Enguerrand VII, Sire de Coucy, son-in-law of Edward III—typically had serial, mixed allegiances in the Anglo-French wars, as representatives of a class that traversed national loyalties.[41] Early in the Hundred Years War, English victory against French forces at Sluys (1340), Morlaix (1342), Crécy (1346), and Poitiers (1356) had, as we have seen, already suggested the lesson that medieval combat was in transition, caught in a modernizing phase in which the traditional military role of knights was progressively undergoing competition from, and gradual supersession by, alternative technologies and tactics represented in combat by men who were the social inferiors of knights. The debacle at Nicopolis, then, presented all Europe with a view of the drama of transition cast in the mode of crisis: what happens to knights and European armies led by knights when pragmatic transformations to modernity, in tactics, values, and leadership, are refused in the field. The subsequent enslavement of Christian survivors, the large ransoms of noble prisoners, the wanderings of survivors who trickled back home, and, finally, the horrifying ultimate defeat of that millenium-old bulwark of Christianity in the East, fabled Constantinople, only kept before the gaze of Christian Europe the fascination of the debacle as its aftermath continued to untwist and unwind, playing itself out.

The shock of Nicopolis loomed large for the implied future of traditional knighthood. To the specimens of elite masculinity for whom war furnished identity, knighthood was the very ground of masculine identity itself, and the theater of war and conquest, by association, was intimately continuous with the meaning of masculinity. In a revealing moment of pride in the *Morte*, King Arthur tells his knights, "You maintain *my manhood* on earth" ("My manhede ȝe mayntene in erthe" [l. 399; my emphasis]), because "you have, in knightly fashion, conquered all that now belongs to my crown" (l. 402). "Manhood"—successful military feudalism as individual and group identity—is precisely what is at stake in the struggle for territorial dominion between Arthur and the Roman Emperor Lucius. Arthur even explicitly tells Lucius's ambassadors that the Roman Emperor must meet Arthur in the field for the sake of Lucius's "manhood" ("manhede" [l. 434]), an assertion whose meaning none contests. Arthur's loss of his knights at the close of the romance, in the civil war with Mordred—the same knights who had "maintained" his "manhood by the might of their hands" and made him "manly on earth" (ll. 4278–79)—thus, to no surprise, un-mans the king and former conqueror, reducing Arthur to a "woeful widow who lacks her lord" ("wafull wedowe þat wanttes hir beryn"). With manhood gone, Arthur becomes a de facto woman who can only weep, curse, and wring her hands helplessly (ll. 4285–86), like the old crone-victim on St. Michael's Mount. The loss of knights in war—the loss of war itself—unmans a man who is a knight, fearfully turns him into a woman, a spectacle of abject reduction to meaninglessness. A crisis in knighthood, masculinity, and war is terrifying on all possible fronts.

A Virtual History of the Crusades: Knights, Just War, Masculine Identity, and Empire

And failures in masculinity, conquest, and knighthood are intimately connected to crusading history, which is the framing vehicle of the *Morte*. The late-medieval crusade, Maurice Keen has demonstrated, "was very much in men's minds in England, and was a live issue in political society, among the highest and most influential in the realm, in the late 1380s and 1390s" ("Chaucer's Knight," 57), and "crusading experience was spread through knightly society in widely different parts of the country" (53). Tracking several knightly families to crusades in Prussia, Tunis, Algeciras, Alexandria, Satalia, and Nicopolis, Keen places members of the royal circle itself at the crusading sites of Algeciras (Henry of Grosmont, first Duke of Lancaster and kinsman to Edward III, in 1343–44), Prussia (Henry Bolingbroke, John of Gaunt's son and future king of England, in 1390, 1392), and Nicopolis (John Beaufort, first Earl of Somerset, and Gaunt's son by Katherine Swynford, who also joined the Duke of Bourbon's crusade to Tunis in 1390 [56]). Keen makes plain that "crusading in this period" is less prompted by material profit—unlike "English knightly involvement in the Hundred Years war" (58)—than by *chivalric ideology.* English knights of the fourteenth century responded to the siren call of the crusade, risking "body and fortune" *because* the crusade "was still widely respected as the highest expression of chivalrous dedication" (60).

From its inception in 1096, the crusade had secured for knights the guarantee of an identity par excellence which sublimely married secular militarism to pious Christianity, affording knighthood both a manifest destiny and an ideologically impeccable alibi and spiritual genealogy for the vocation of violence. Pope Urban II's inspired theorization of a sanctified military invasion from slender theoretical conditions in Augustine's *City of God* (bk. 19, chap. 7), where the epistemological possibility of "just wars" is sketchily raised, presented the first military expedition to the East as a movement that would channel, and bring to ideal culmination, the martial energies of knights in Europe, whose professional identity and occupation were organized around an all-too-random, and all-too-masculine, destructive violence. According to the twelfth-century chronicle reports of Baldric of Dol, Fulcher of Chartres, and Robert the Monk, not only did Urban II preach the First Crusade in 1095 as an appropriate, indeed supreme cause for knighthood, but the pope insinuated, in his address at the Council of Clermont in 1095, that the knightly "pilgrims," as crusaders were called, should take, and hold, territory in the Levant:

> You, girt about with the badge of knighthood, are arrogant with great pride; you rage against your brothers and cut each other in pieces. This is not the (true) soldiery of Christ . . . The Holy Church has reserved a soldiery for herself to help her people, but you debase her wickedly to her hurt. . . . either lay down the girdle of such knighthood, or advance boldly, as knights of Christ. . . . restrain your murderous hands from the destruction of your brothers. . . . struggle for your Jerusalem, in Christian battle-line. . . . brandish your sword against Saracens. It is the only warfare that is righteous. . . . The possessions of the enemy, too, will be yours, since you will make spoil of their treasures.
>
> Baldric of Dol (Peters, *First Crusade*, 8–9)

Let those who until recently existed as plunderers, be soldiers of Christ
. . . let those who formerly contended against brothers and relations,
rightly fight barbarians.

> Fulcher of Chartres (Peters, *First Crusade*, 31)

This land which you inhabit . . . is too narrow for your large population;
nor does it abound in wealth. . . . Hence it is that you murder one another, that you wage war, and that frequently you perish by mutual
wounds. Let, therefore, hatred depart from among you, let your quarrels
end, let wars cease, and let all dissensions and controversies slumber.
Enter upon the road to the Holy Sepulchre; wrest that land from the
wicked race, and subject it to yourselves. That land . . . was given by
God into the possession of the children of Israel.

> Robert the Monk, *RHC,* Occ. 3:728 (Peters, *First Crusade*, 3)

Knights were the leading force in the crusades, which quickly spawned
three distinguished orders of knighthood which uniquely conjoined
chivalry and monasticism—the Templars, Hospitallers, and Teutonic
knights—orders that totemically exemplified in themselves the best intentions and potentials of knighthood fulfilled in a divine cause.[42]

The Templar in the *Morte* (l. 841), who comes to announce to Arthur
the misdeeds of that infamous Arthurian giant on St. Michael's Mount,
thus efficiently indexes crusading history in brief. The Templar's obser-
vant attention to the giant's illegal accumulation of gold coinage (ll.
885–87) even recalls the financial probity of the Templars and Hospitallers, international orders whose transactions in the movement of capital supported the trading institutions and economies of Europe, and European kings like Arthur, to no small degree. Arthur's joking
representation of himself as a pilgrim on a pilgrimage to a holy place accomplishes similar work. Generations of knightly crusaders in medieval
history, from the First Crusade on, embraced a view of themselves as pilgrims on a pilgrimage that would also require combat en route to the liberation of holy shrines. Even Guinevere's excessively emotional reaction to
Arthur's departure for war hauntingly echoes accounts, in crusade chronicles, of wives left behind—women who faint and fall to the floor, like
Guinevere (ll. 715–16), mourning the departing beloved "as if he were (already) dead," as Fulcher of Chartres has it (Peters, *First Crusade*, 37).

Appropriately, the *Morte*'s narrative begins with an extended prayer (ll.
1–11) and has knights repeatedly swear by "the holy Vernacle" (ll. 297, 309,

348, 386) to undertake war—St. Veronica's vernacle being a badge of pilgrimage that retrieves the memory of the *via dolorosa*—a ritual that recalls knightly vows sworn by another holy symbol from the *via dolorosa*, the cross, in undertaking war and pilgrimage.[43] The *Morte* is a romance in which the name of Christ and talk of war slide easily into one another in the same breath (e.g., ll. 257, 320–21, 397–98); where Templars (l. 841) or pilgrims (l. 3475) announce the most important news; and where a character who appears like a pilgrim on the outside turns out to be really a knight on the inside (l. 3511). The Janus figure of the pilgrim-knight in the *Morte* who announces that Arthur is conducting military expeditions *in the Orient* (l. 3502), when the narrative ostensibly depicts Arthur campaigning in Italy, shows us how, in the country of romance, the Orient can be anywhere, and everywhere—a virtual location for a virtual history of the crusades.

Most especially, the Orient is by the side of "Rome"—a name that in the *Morte* points both to Constantinople, or the Eastern Roman empire, and to papal Rome. Papal Rome is signaled in Arthur's projected overlordship of "Rome," a projection that constitutes a late-medieval English response to the papal schism of 1378—the fourteenth-century tragedy devised by contested Vatican politics of election and succession—so that the historical example of an Avignonese pope, from 1309 on, who favored French political interests, can be countered in romance by Arthurian English domination of the other prelate, the one in Rome, to deliver an imagined balance of international power. Historically, the metaphor of the crusade was pressed into service by the English to produce a more equitable equation between popes who favored opposite interests in the competitive wars of France and England: Henry Knighton's *Chronicon* (2:198–99) records the great excitement stirred up in England by the bishop of Norwich's, Henry Despenser's, "crusade" against the supporters of Clement VII, the "anti-pope" in Avignon, the large donations of money and treasure resulting from that excitement, and the crusade absolution and indulgences offered by the pontiff at Rome, Urban VI.[44] In the *Morte*, thanks to Arthur's dominion, England's forces have the Roman pontiff in their pocket.

In similar fashion, the Roman Emperor in the *Morte* commands the allegiance of numerous Muslim armies and sultans because, by the *Morte*'s era, history had witnessed the spectacular scandal of one later-medieval Roman Emperor's conduct and life. Frederick II, the Mozarabic Holy Roman Emperor who was literate in the Arabic language, versed in Arabic philosophy, poetry, and science, and had an Orientalized court in Sicily, was on friendly, even intimate, terms with prominent Muslim dignitaries, including the successor to Saladin's empire—al-Kamil, Saladin's nephew.[45] Frederick not only delayed, and attempted to discourage, the armies of the Fifth Crusade, but Arab chronicles depicted this Roman Emperor as warning the sultan, al-Kamil, of the advance and intentions of the crusaders, and frequently presented the emperor as a friend and ally of Muslims and Muslim interests in the Orient.[46] Accordingly, the Roman Emperor in the *Morte* has help from Alexandria, Damietta, "Babylon" (medieval Cairo), Egypt, Damascus, and Syria, the domains of Frederick's cultural compatriot, the Ayyubid sultan, al-Kamil. Frederick's son and grandson, in their turns as emperor, continued the Höhenstaufen example of cordial amity with Muslims. All three Holy Roman Emperors existed under papal excommunication for some part of their imperial reign: Not for nothing, thus, does Gawain in the *Morte* refer to the Roman Emperor as a "false heretic" ("fals heretyke" [l. 1307]) "who occupies in error the empire of Rome" (l. 1308), a reference that discloses the itinerary and operations of historical referentiality in medieval romance.

The *Morte*'s evocation of place-names ranging from "Prestor John's lands," Tartary, and Turkey to Rhodes and Cyprus, from Prussia and Lithuania to Greece and Macedonia, in fact, maps a virtual cartography, an atlas, of European crusading history (ll. 570–609). Damietta, Alexandria, "Babylon," the Nile, Africa, and Egypt were the destinations of the Fifth Crusade, and St. Louis's crusades (the Seventh and Eighth Crusades); "Prestor John" and the Tartars were names that featured prominently in the hopes, expectations, planning, and policies of the Fifth Crusade; while the corrosive ironies of the Sixth or Emperor's Crusade—an un-crusade in which Jerusalem was handed over as a diplomatic gift from al-Kamil to the emperor Frederick II, after an exchange of letters and embassies—are expressed in the "lordly letters" from the Roman Emperor to his Oriental allies in the *Morte* (l. 570).[47] The place-names "Prussia" and "Lettow" remind us that the *Morte* has not forgotten the crusades of pagan conversion conducted by the Teutonic knights on the northern European continent, crusades in which late-medieval English knights and barons, greater and lesser, participated, including the likes of Henry Bolingbroke, Robert Morley, Hugh Hastings, Lord Lovell, William le Scrope, Geoffrey le Scrope, Stephen le Scrope, Richard Waldegrave, William de Lucy, Richard de Beauchamp, Thomas de Beauchamp, Thomas Ufford, Humphrey de Bohun, John Montagu,

Thomas Holland, Hotspur, Thomas Percy, Thomas Erpingham, John Norbury, and John Waterton (Keen, "Chaucer's Knight," 51–56). "Rhodes" indexes the career and history of the Hospitallers, who head-quartered on the island and led repeated crusading skirmishes into the Levant after the territorial loss of all the crusader colonies. "Cyprus" was the seat of the Latin Kingdom of Jerusalem in exile, a territory that had been annexed for Latin Europe by Richard Lionheart during the Third Crusade, and considered by modern historians the single strategic gain of real value in Richard's crusade.[48] In addition, in the 1360s, "Cyprus" was a name that retrieved the crusade of Peter I, and the crusading history of the Lusignans, dynastic kings of Jerusalem-in-exile. The island played a strategic role, moreover, in negotiating the deliverance and ransom of European captives from the Turks after the debacle of the Nicopolis Crusade in 1396.[49]

Despite the *Morte's* promiscuous, free-ranging evocation of crusading history, however, and the poem's parade of Oriental exotica from "camels" and "cockadrisses" to place-names on the farthest reaches of the Western imagination, it is Constantinople—the "Rome" that Arthur conquers—and not Jerusalem, the Holy City lost to the infidels, that remains at the center of the narrative's secret consciousness, and situates the organizing axis of the narrative's world map. From the arrival of the "Roman senator" at Arthur's court, at the beginning of the *Morte*, through the adventure of Priamus and the dream of Fortune's wheel, up to the moment of the pilgrim-knight's appearance at "Rome," where Arthur has taken hostages and plans his coronation, key episodes in three-fourths of the romance are preoccupied with concerns affecting "Rome," as the Byzantine Empire called itself. Though more than a century and a half intervened between the Fourth Crusade's conquest of Constantinople in 1204 and the *Morte's* earliest possible beginnings, Latin Europe never forgot—nor was it allowed to forget—its extraordinary historical moment of glorious dominion coupled with unspeakable infamy in Constantinople: a moment that at once seemed to end, at last, the schism of Latin and Greek churches, doctrine, and Christendom, even as the Latin evisceration of Constantinople and its domains decisively ended the Byzantine Empire's centuries-long ability to stem the tide of Muslim conquest in the East, as the traditional bulwark at Christendom's frontier. Though the Byzantines wrested their empire back from the Latins (and the Latins' Venetian allies) in 1261, with the help of the Genoese (and "Genoese giants" always fight on behalf of "Rome," in the *Morte*), Constantinople never fully recovered from the Latin sack. The Byzantine capital was under siege by the Ottoman Emperor when the crusaders of 1396 arrived at Nicopolis; and, in the aftermath of Nicopolis, the Byzantine Emperor, Manuel II, was forced to swear allegiance to Bayezid. In 1399–1401 Manuel Paleologus "wandered from one court to another in Italy, France, and England" to plead for aid for Constantinople from the rulers of Europe (Atiya, *Later Middle Ages*, 15–16, 465), like a disinherited Priamus.[50]

At the end of the fourteenth century and the beginning of the fifteenth, a crisis in the meaning and future of knighthood coincided with the aftershock of Nicopolis—a crisis in contemporary crusading history—as well as that durable calamity in Latin Christendom which treated the faithful to the tired spectacle of two popes, concomitant divisions in loyalty, and prolonged directionlessness: a contemporary papal schism, from 1378, which no doubt helped to recall, to the historical mind, the earlier great schism in Christianity that had divided the Latin West from the Greek East in 1054. These parallels in fragmentation were possibly aided by the fugitive lure, repeated through the fourteenth century, of prospective reunion between Eastern and Western churches. From the Council of Lyons in 1274 till the loss of Constantinople to the Ottomans in 1453, one Byzantine Emperor after another—agonized by the empire's weaknesses and the predatory ambitions of both Latin Europe and the Muslim East—offered to submit the Greek church to the Latin, thus ending East-West division once and for all. The emperors Michael VIII, John Kantakuzenos, John VI, Manuel II, and John VIII all negotiated the submission of the Byzantine Empire's patriarchates and doctrine to the papacy, though equally frequent imperial changes of mind and policy resulted in more than one papal excommunication of Greek emperors, and the revival of papal preaching of a crusade against Byzantium, reissuing the specter of the Fourth Crusade (see Atiya, *Later Middle Ages*, chap. 11).

That one problematic might recall another in the late fourteenth century, with Constantinople occupying the attention of Latin Europe, and Nicopolis identifying the failures of chivalric warfare, is not difficult to imagine; linkages of this kind appeal and conduce to precisely the analogical and allegorical habits of mind that characterize medieval cultural thinking. Division and fragmentation in the spiritual and communal body of late-medieval Christendom, moreover, can be stirringly understood through the fantasmatic re-narration of a crusading war in which the very marks of division and fragmentation troubling both knighthood and Christianity, in the late Middle Ages, can be anatomically rendered on the bodies of knights. The visiting of concurrent, overlapping, and multilay-ered cultural crises on masculine anatomy—writing the troubles of the age on the organic male body—discloses a trafficking in reference that is char-acteristic of romance.

Ideologically, one of the justifications offered by the Fourth Crusade after the Latin conquest of Constantinople was the reunification of the Church, and the end of Greek deviation and heresy: another layer of sig-nificance embedded in the *Morte*'s declaration that the "Roman" (that is, Byzantine) Emperor is a "false heretic" ("fals heretyke" [l. 1307]) "who oc-cupies in error the empire of Rome" (l. 1308). Significantly, unlike the Arthur of Geoffrey of Monmouth's twelfth-century *Historia Regum Bri-tannie*—the *Morte*'s source for Arthur's invasion of "Rome"—the late-medieval Arthur of the *Morte*, when citing the three predecessors from whom he derives his authority to govern in Rome, does not list Belinus, Brennius, and Constantine the Great as his authorizing forebears. Instead, the *Morte*'s Arthur substitutes the emperor "*Baldwin*" (l. 277) for the em-peror Constantine, in that list of three. "Baldwin," we note, is the name of the conqueror of Constantinople in the Fourth Crusade: Baldwin of Flanders and Hainault, baronial leader and the first Latin emperor of Constantinople. In his list of Belinus, Brennius, and *Baldwin* as his impe-rial forebears, then, the *Morte*'s Arthur has found a romance way of say-ing that the historical precedent of the Fourth Crusade, which put a Latin emperor at Constantinople, is the authority that will legitimize Arthur's own reprise of that crusade.[51]

Arthur's crusade against the "Roman" Emperor Lucius, then, in-evitably carries with it the shadow of contradictions, and overtones of both celebration and repugnance. On the one hand, the "conquest of Constantinople . . . seemed to consummate and symbolize the triumphant vigour of Western feudalism," as Perry Anderson puts it (196)—one modality, and reassuring proof, of *translatio imperii*. The *Morte*, I have suggested, is avidly invested in vindicating and celebrating Western feu-dalism in its economic and military aspects. Nonetheless, despite Latin profit from Constantinople's treasures, the conquest of Constantinople was also ineluctably received as an example of a campaign that had gone awry, and evidence of martial energies that had been horribly detoured from their rightful objective—the recovery of the Holy Land from the in-fidel. The ruthless sack of Byzantium, whose civilized glories had been for many centuries a legend in the West (with Byzantium serving, I argued in chapter 1, as a model for the fictive splendors of Arthur's Caerleon or

Camelot), shocked and horrified many in Europe, furnishing the spectacle of a war machine that had run amok. The sober reaction of many contemporaries, including Pope Innocent III—who had urged and authorized that Crusade, and whose mixed reaction of shock, exasperation, and forced diplomatic tact is amply documented by papal letters—continued to wind its way through medieval criticism of crusading history, despite the call in 1281 by Pope Martin IV, after the Greeks had retaken their diminished empire, for a reenactment of the Fourth Crusade (Atiya, *Later Middle Ages*, 262). As a conqueror—and Arthur is called a "conqueror" many times over, in a compulsive refrain (e.g., in lines 26, 44, 132, 220, 232, 343, 680, 987, 1208, 1579, 1654, 2242, 2262, 2356, 2394, 2621, 2639, 3178, etc.)—Arthur is accordingly both admired and reviled, like the Latin conquerors of Byzantium. Arthur's uncontrollable destructiveness on campaign, after the defeat of the "Roman" Emperor—including gratuitous attacks on hospitals and churches—recalls the Crusade's swerving away from its legitimate objectives. Common to both the *Morte* and crusading history is thus a wanton, relentless destructiveness over "Roman" territory that raises the specter of war gone mad. The ambivalent double response of Latin Europe to conquest-turned-riot in the Orient makes possible, then, the "criticism levelled against unjust wars" that critics have discovered in the *Morte*, a criticism that nonetheless "does not diminish the poet's enthusiasm" for war and martial descriptions (Göller, "A Reassessment," 28), for, despite the excesses of its annexation, Constantinople or "Rome" was also a peerless prize to Latin Europe, and a triumphant reminder of the military hegemony of the West.

PRIAMUS, FORTUNE'S WHEEL, AND GENOESE GIANTS: AN ANATOMY OF ROMANCE ADVENTURE, NARRATIVE, AND FIGURATION

But the *Morte*'s imaginative mapping of Constantinople's meaning for the West does not pivot only on Latin Europe's historic claim, through conquest, over the Eastern Roman Empire. In the period contemporary with the creation of the *Morte*'s main text, the precariousness of Constantinople—an ancient, politically and militarily fragile empire existing in the shadow of an expanding, resurgent Turkish suzerainty under the Ottomans—was underscored by the debacle at Nicopolis, a precariousness that the latest crusade did nothing to dispel.[52] With a vanished Latin

Jerusalem still no nearer to territorial recovery, the Priamus episode in the *Morte*, in which Gawain meets and does combat with a wandering knight who is heir to the finest inheritance in the East but whose father must war constantly ("wyntters and ȝeres" [l.2599]), with sagacity ("weisely," l. 2599), as a "rebel" (l. 2598) to hold his lands ("his awen" [l. 2601]), suggests a sympathy to the threat of territorial disinheritance, and to the pathos of a proud prince from the noblest, oldest ancestry in the empires of Christian and classical history, who must wander in foreign ways and foreign wars.

Transported into a romance lexicon of adventure and chance encounter, Priamus, whose errancy might call to mind the Byzantine Emperor Manuel II's "mendicant pilgrimage" to the courts of "Italy, France, and England" in 1399–1401 to "rouse his fellow Christians to come to his aid and save . . . his Empire" (Atiya, *Later Middle Ages*, 16), is nonetheless still heir to Greek, Roman/Trojan, and biblical traditions alike (ll. 2602–5), as befits a prince of the Eastern Roman Empire.[53] Priamus's request for confession and final rites, after being mortally wounded by Gawain, "shows him to be a Christian," as Hamel observes, even if "his phrase 'thy Christ' hints at some kind of religious difference" (*Morte*, 340 nn. 2587–88). Priamus's religion, it has often been noted, seems strangely to echo, yet also to depart from, Gawain's Latin Christianity. Indeed, Priamus's allusion to the "Christ" of Gawain's church ("*thy* Cryste" [l. 2587]; my emphasis), and not the "Christ" of his own church, points to some of the oldest differences of belief in Roman and Eastern Christianity that centered on the figure of Christ: disagreement on the nature of Christ's godhead (issuing from the early fifth century), the use of leavened or unleavened bread in Eucharistic communion (prominent in eleventh-century disputes), and "the Latin doctrine of the 'Procession of the Holy Ghost'" from *both* the Father and the Son, as reiterated in "the insertion of . . . 'filioque' . . . into the Nicene Creed" (Atiya, *Later Middle Ages*, 267).

That Priamus is unequivocally a Christian, if not a Latin Christian, is seen when he swears by St. Peter (l. 2646) and invokes that saint's protection (l. 2724)—gestures that would be substantially meaningless for pagan, Muslim, or Jew. The question Gawain poses, in asking Priamus what doctrine or religious law Priamus believes in ("whate laye thow leues one" [l. 2593]), is therefore implicitly answered by the cumulative, if scattered, evidence of Priamus's replies. A conclusive answer is available, moreover, in the magic potion in Priamus's possession, a flask filled with the finest waters from the four rivers that flow out of the Earthly Paradise

("þe flour of the four well / þat flowes owte of Paradice" [ll. 2705–6]), a
paradise believed in the Middle Ages to be situated in the Orient, and the
ownership of which attests to Priamus's Christianity, even as it decisively
Christianizes the healing powers of the conventional magic potion of romance adventure.

Priamus's sudden entrance into the *Morte*, and the episode of his encounter with Gawain, has attracted critical attention not only because of its
odd intrusion into the body of the main narrative (an intrusion that in fact
merely continues the *Morte*'s exploration of the problem of Constantinople) but also because the episode features such quintessentially, even stereo-
typically, conventional romance *topoi*: for instance, the *locus amoenus* into
which Gawain rides, signaling Gawain's entrance into romance territory,
before being challenged by Priamus; the unknown challenger-knight who
turns out, after martial contest, to be a friend and ally; and even the magic
healing potion that is found as a narrative device as early as Chrétien de
Troyes's twelfth-century *Yvain*.[54] The *Morte*'s invocation of an Oriental
frame and provenance for these conventions, moreover, tellingly returns
romance to its earliest imaginative relations with the East.

In the present circumstances, the *Morte*'s reminder that a *locus amoenus*
is really a symbol of the terrestrial paradise is reinforced by the introduction of a vial of healing water from that terrestrial paradise itself—by the
provision of an ideal type that quietly interleaves the shadow of a Christian, and Oriental, provenance lurking behind all magic potions in romance. Furthermore, the coincidence here between a romance landscape
and a landscape in the Orient (the *locus amoenus* that convenes both romance geography and terrestrial paradise in the East) hints that other romance landscapes and settings might also owe the germ of their ideation-
ality to the Levantine East. Wastelands in romance seem curiously to echo
desert landscapes, for instance, while the unpredictability of a romance
vista—in which an enemy may lurk behind any rock or block any pass—
finds its topographical and geopolitical reality in the Levant of the crusader states, where crusading knights lived in absolute contingency, under un-
predictable conditions where they might suddenly face an enemy behind a
rock or at a pass. Even those delectably sexualized enclosed spaces narrated
with fine relish in European medieval romance—those isles and castles of
maidens, where nubile women exclusively and patiently await the knight-
adventurer's arrival and attentions—seem oddly reminiscent of the sexualized feminine enclosures of the Oriental harem (at least, as might be
glimpsed from the outside by male crusaders without privileges of access).

The absolute contingency represented by "the adventure" that may accost a knight, in an instant, in romance, is a condition not only historically found in twelfth-century medieval Europe in the errancy of knightly "youth" (*juvenes*) seeking opportunity, territory, heiresses, and advancement (Duby) but also—crucially—in the geopolitical environment of the Orient in which the crusader states maintained a precarious existence, an existence where randomness and contingency were the daily conditions of knightly life, along with sudden opportunities for seizing territory for occupation/possession, and the material sumptuousness and Oriental luxury, at many crusader courts, that constituted the rewards of successful adventuring.[55] Even the convention of the mysterious challenger-knight, who turns out to be an ally and prospective friend, has a counterpart in the labile military environment of the East, where the division between friend and foe was typically a shifting one, subject to the instability of temporary treaties and fluid alliances among warring sides, and someone who was nominally a foe or antagonist might turn out to be an ally and a friend in certain wars, under certain circumstances.[56] The exotic, the unknown, and the utterly familiar, are contradictions that meet not only in romance but also as indistinguishable conditions of crusading knighthood in the Levant for almost two centuries: Even the heiresses of romance have their counterpart in the heiresses of Jerusalem, Antioch, and the other crusader colonies, heiresses who simultaneously troubled and enabled dynastic succession in the Latin Kingdom.[57] Just as crusader-knights in the East saw their lives through the prism and conventions offered them by the chivalric romances of Europe, so, too, were the lexicon and narrative resources of chivalric romance likely enriched and shaped by the experience and legends of crusading knighthood in the East.

While the Priamus episode in the *Morte* frames a brief typology of the romance adventure, Arthur's dream of Fortune's wheel frames an allegory of how narrative functions in romance, and what narrative patterning accomplishes for romance ends. The two episodes are linked by the coincidence of strategic representatives among the Nine Worthies, in both Priamus's account of his lineage and Arthur's account of his dream: Alexander and Hector are named as two of the classical Worthies as well as Priamus's ancestors; Joshua and Judas Maccabeus, also Priamus's forefathers, feature as biblical Worthies; while Charlemagne, one of the Christian Worthies in Arthur's dream, is hinted at in Priamus's very name itself, "Priamon" being a knight who appears in the *Chanson de Roland* (l. 65). Though Arthur's dream cites Constantinople more obliquely than the

Priamus episode, the dream's referencing of the Fourth Crusade and its aftermath is no less inspired. Not only does the landscape in Arthur's dream
troll the Mediterranean for images—lions, vines, and grapes appear (ll.
234, 3242, 3243)—but, as Hamel points out, Fortune's offer of the orb of
rule to Arthur, an offer that presents the orb as an "apple" set with beautiful stones, enameled with azure, and with the earth painted on it ("a
pome pighte full of faire stonys, / Enamelde with azoure, the erth thereon
depayntide" [ll. 3354–55]), recites "'Mandeville's' description of the statue
of [the Emperor] Justinian in Constantinople: 'he was wont to holden a
round appell of gold in his hond. . . . This appull betokeneth the lordschipe þat he hadde ouer all the world þat is round'" (Hamel, *Morte*, 364
n. 3354). The glittering opulence of Fortune's visual appearance in the
dream, moreover, has the refractive feel of Byzantine art: Fortune is dazzling in silks of exotic, rare hues, and her breast gleams with brooches,
"bezants"—a Latin European reference to Byzantine gold coins—and
scintillating stones, so that she is literally limned in gold, glimmering in
variegated points of light and color (ll. 3255–57).

Though scholarship on this episode has centered on the fascination, in
medieval literature, with Fortune's wheel as a metaphor for change and
ephemerality, we note that Arthur's rise and fall on the turn of Fortune's
wheel in the *Morte* also specifically addresses his fate, in the crusading
frame of this romance, as the conqueror of the Eastern Roman Empire.
The moment of Arthur's triumph as Latin emperor of Constantinople,
holding the orb of dominion in his hand, like the Emperor Justinian's statue once had, is displaced in time by the moment of Arthur's fall from imperial rule, when he is crushed and broken under Fortune's wheel.[58] That
capsule figuration, I suggest, resonantly expresses both the sheer historical
chance—the triumphant good fortune—that wins the crown of Constantinople for the Latins, as well as renders intelligible the subsequent reversal
in Latin fortunes that returns Constantinople, fifty-seven years afterward,
back to the Byzantines—rendered, here, as the downturn of Fortune's
wheel. Fortune's wheel, palpably, is the *Morte*'s narrative device for organizing a description of historical processes that otherwise seem fearfully in-
coherent and uncontrollable: an organization that reassures by invoking
the simulation of control and coherency effected by literary narration itself.

The narratological work performed by Fortune's wheel, as a device of
meaning-making, is also available, of course, in the episodic structure of
chivalric romance itself: a structure that loosely strings together episodes
of often unrelated adventures to simulate, in narrative, the atomized ran-

domness of historical life, but whose mechanical action, as a narrational apparatus, also functions tacitly to impose the aura of a meaningful pattern on the very randomness it discovers and formalizes into narrative. Both kinds of narrational resource suggest that chance and contingency can be brought under a semblance of control, and acquire coherency, once randomness is processed as part of a narrative's design. Testifying to fundamental instincts within the drive to narrate, these romance mechanisms address the urgent desire and deep need to see structures intrinsically subtending the chaos of phenomenonality. Like the chivalric *aventure* that transforms fearful randomness into exciting opportunity for knightly ambitions and self-fashioning, "Fortune's wheel" names a device of meaning-making in romance that produces narrative sense out of radical contingency: and, in the frame of the *Morte*, issues the ultimate alibi for both the Latin/Arthurian conquest of the Eastern Roman Empire and the subsequent historical loss of the empire back to the Greeks. In its narrative performance, then, Arthur's dream of Fortune, in the *Morte*, functions less to predict, as dreams in Arthurian romance are supposed to do, than to *structure*: to offer a simulacrum of explanation that allegorizes the narrational modalities and purposive designs of romance.

The supervision of this narrational modality and the narrative ethics intrinsic to the motif of "Fortune's wheel" are, of course, aggressively gendered: Fortune, after all, is a woman and a goddess whose extensive personification in the *Morte* bears eloquent witness to the gender accusation residing at the heart of chivalric romance. Although the *Morte* understands it is social, economic, and technological change that threatens the structure of feudalism undergirding the institution of knighthood—an understanding acknowledged, as we have seen, in sporadic outbursts of class contempt by individual characters—the *Morte*'s ultimate subsumption of *all* change to the responsibility and charge of Fortune, depicted here as an all-powerful female figure who serially mimes the role of Everywoman, allegorically intimates that what undoes a knight and a man, in the final analysis, can be traced to his relations with, and dependence on, the significant women who structure his social, familial, and affective constellations. Fortune, as she is depicted in the *Morte*, ventriloquizes the performance of every woman of significance in a knight's life.

As Hamel observes with acuity, Fortune's mimicry of the solicitously intimate act of combing Arthur's locks for him, lovingly and attentively (ll. 351–52), casts her as Arthur's mother—a role also advanced in an earlier romance, the Old French *Morte Artu*, in which Arthur proclaims that

Fortune "'m'a esté mere jusque ici'" but subsequently behaves like "his stepmother" instead (Hamel, *Morte*, 364 nn. 3351–52). The goddess's offer of an apple to Arthur (l. 3354) and her urging the king to help himself to fruit from the apple orchard ("pomarie" [l. 3364]) that is a veritable paradise (l. 3365) also constructs Fortune as the immediate representative of that typological seductress, Eve: a disposition borne out when Fortune presents wine to Arthur, and requests a toast (ll. 3374–79), like the seductress Renwein before Vortigern, in Geoffrey's *Historia*—a text with which the goddess is familiar, as her words make plain.[59] Fortune is also a courtly mistress who offers Arthur "all likynge and luffe" (l. 3381) and the gift of a sword with shining hilts (l. 3358)—a precious weapon that, in romance at least, tends to issue from courtly mistresses and enchantresses alike, as Guinevere's gift of Arthur's sword, Caliburn, to Mordred reminds us in the *Morte*.[60] Finally, like Guinevere, the wife who inexplicably betrays Arthur after her extravagant display of tender emotion at Arthur's departure from court, Fortune also inexplicably discards Arthur, after her display of affectionate attention and regard—a betrayal made to seem all the more wanton, and sexual, like the wifely Guinevere's, by the graphic crushing of Arthur's haunches or hind quarters (l. 3389) and the breaking up of his lower bodily parts by Fortune's wheel.

Mother, Eve, seductress, courtly *amie*, wife: That the role of god, fate, or the author should be gendered in the text as female, and shown to exercise an absolute arbitrariness of power, confirms romance practices of alibiing masculine responsibility by recourse to a fantasy tradition that simultaneously blames women and registers an apprehensive suspicion of deep feminine power in intimate life. Romance's use of a lexicon and syntax of gender to transact its descriptions of social relations (and public performance) as *personal* relations, and private life, has been in service since romance's inauguration in Geoffrey's *Historia*, as we saw in chapter 1. In the *Morte*, we must understand, Arthur is forced to relinquish his imperial rule over the Eastern Roman Empire because *women*—Fortune, Guinevere—and the fosterling of Arthur's chamber, Mordred, betray him. In cultural fantasy, it seems, the political and public—everything important to male elites—*is* the personal.

Since political and public phenomena, in cultural fantasy, are focused through the lens of personal relations, the various crises afflicting knighthood, and the history of religious war in which knights feature so ideally, are then most movingly expressed in chivalric romance as crises of personal relations. Correspondingly, fragmentations in the social body and in social institutions are best articulated through individual bodies, and knighthood and crusading history are anatomized in the *Morte* by anatomizing the bodies of celebrated individual knights. When Gawain, a famed chivalric exemplar of the Latin West, wars with Priamus, putative heir of the imperial East, the bodies of both knights are mutually undone, opened up, and almost destroyed by the encounter of East and West in the field of battle. The micrological examination of their mutual fracture is as indelible as the macrological record of the Latin war against Constantinople; on knights' bodies, as in history, the harm accomplished is original, unique. Priamus's wound is so pronounced that "men might see his liver, with the light of the sun" (ll. 2560–61); Gawain loses so much blood through an open artery that "all his wits changed" (l. 2571) and no blood is left in his body (l. 2697). Only paradisial water from the East can heal the wounds of the warring encounter, an encounter that turns the East inside out, and vulnerable all the way through, while it supposedly drains away the lifeblood of the West and causes the mind to reel. When both knightly bodies are restored—by an act of personal plunder that is represented as a kind of semi-voluntary gift from the East—the movement of hegemony from East to West (*translatio imperii*) is expressed by Priamus's putatively voluntary self-conscription, along with his men, into the ranks of Arthur's host: a conscription, it seems, accomplished more by one knight's affection and respect for another (Priamus's for Gawain)—homosocialized personal relations—than by the West's macrocosmic victory in war over the East.

With bodies thus instrumentalized as the ground of public and political confrontation, it will come as no surprise that one set of vigorous antagonists to Latin Christendom and its knights—and especially to English crusaders—metastasize, in their romance figuration, into hyperbolic grotesques. "Genoese giants" proliferate in the *Morte*, beginning with the giant of St. Michael's Mount, and they are the special enemy of Arthur, the crusader-in-chief who not only handily emasculates the giant of St. Michael's Mount (thus asserting the normativity, and superiority, of English masculinity over monstrosities from Italian Genoa) but also decimates a group of sixty Genoese giants who align themselves on the side of "Rome" or the Eastern Roman Empire against Arthur's forces. But why should Genoese, as such, be figured as monstrous, when other enemies are not, and why should they be giants in this romance?

From the standpoint of Latin Europe, historians often agree, the role of the Italian republics—Venice, Genoa, and Pisa—in crusading history, and the history of the crusader colonies of Outremer, from the early thirteenth century on, appears an exemplification of infamy, betrayal, and utter Italian self-interest and economic realism on a mind-boggling scale: a role played out by the Italians to seemingly unimaginable extremes of cynicism in a cultural period when it is religious faith that furnished much of the volitional fervor, ideology, and energy of the crusading movement. Not only was the Fourth Crusade redirected to Constantinople by the Venetians—who were able to dictate the route and objectives of the crusaders because of massive crusader debt owed to Venice for the supply of ships, men, and provisions at exorbitant cost, under impracticable conditions of repayment—but the historical record argues that the detour of the Fourth Crusade was a deliberate Venetian policy stemming from the highly lucrative Venetian trade with Egypt, a trade that would have suffered disruption, to the mutual economic detriment of Venice and Egypt, from crusading warfare on the littoral and Mahgreb. Unsurprisingly, the chief beneficiaries of the historical outrage of the Fourth Crusade were Venice and Genoa. The Venetians were awarded three-eighths of Constantinople and the Empire by the new Latin conquerors, while the Genoese, rivals and competitors of Venice, established relations with the Greek empire in exile at Nicaea, an alliance that paid handsome dividends after the retaking of Constantinople by the Greeks in 1261, with the help of the Genoese.[61]

Genoese, then, in the Latin crusading imaginary, are ranged on the other side: allied with the Eastern Roman Empire and against the Latin Christendom represented in the *Morte* by Arthur and his forces. We have seen that for English crusaders the alliance of Genoa with "the other side" extended from at least as early as the Third Crusade, when the Genoese sided with Philip Augustus's candidate for the crown of Jerusalem over the English king's, Richard the Lionheart's candidate, Guy of Lusignan, who had the support of the Pisans. In subsequent crusades—such as Saint Louis's in the mid- and late-thirteenth century, and the 1390 crusade to Tunis undertaken by the Genoese to protect their trading rights—the Genoese were also allies of the French (Runciman, 3:260; Atiya, *Commerce*, 105; *Later Middle Ages*, 8). Not only do Genoese alliances with the French position the Genoese as ranged among the enemy, but in the fourteenth century Genoa also notoriously disappointed crusading hopes when it refused to help the 1365 crusade of Peter I of Cyprus and Jerusalem (Runciman, 3:443), leader of the house of Lusignan governing Latin Jerusalem in exile—a crusade in which the English themselves participated (Walsingham, 56).

Furthermore, from the second half of the thirteenth century, the Genoese, in particular—Christian merchants—supplied Egypt with European and other slaves for the Egyptian army. Ominously for crusading history, slaves imported for the Egyptian military came to form a core of career warriors singlemindedly trained from youth for the vocation of war, and some became the finest professional warriors in Egypt's standing forces. From the ranks of Egyptian military slaves, a line of Egyptian sultans themselves arose, creating an eponymously-named dynasty of slave-rulers—"Mamluks"—who replaced the Ayyubid sultans of Saladin's line by violent overthrow. Preceding thus the Janissories of the Ottomans by centuries, the Mamluks of Egypt were renowned for their ruthlessness, military invincibility (including excellent use of archery, the technological bane of knights, in the killing fields), their religiosity, and their mongrel ancestry: Baibars, the Mamluk sultan who defeated Saint Louis in two crusades, was said to have had blue eyes, the ostensible legacy of a European slave heritage.[62]

Despite papal bulls armed with the threat of excommunication prohibiting this monstrous, lucrative market in human merchandise that helped to man the ranks of the Muslim enemy with Christian slaves, among others, the Genoese dominated the slave trade to Egypt (Atiya, *Later Middle Ages,* 19, 482, passim; *Commerce,* 183–84; Phillips, *Slavery,* 104).[63] The Genoese not only exported slaves but also imported them into Europe: "Slaves were relatively inexpensive in the fourteenth and early fifteenth centuries, when the Genoese imported them in large numbers" (Huppert, 113).[64] In the horrid spectacle of the Genoese giant at St. Michael's Mount—a wealthy cannibal giant, trafficking in baptized human victims and illegally acquired gold—can be seen, then, the structures of romance figuration at work. Slavery, an outrage to civilization and banned by the church for its monstrous reduction of humans to commodities, finds suitably provocative expression in that other form of dehumanization: cannibalism. Significantly, part of the shock at St. Michael's Mount issues from the fact that the giant's victims are *Christians* and children,[65] especially boy children, from "the country of Constantine" (l. 848) where the giant's raiding has broken up families ("kynde" [l. 848]), in the searching out of valuable victims: A Greek slave, more valuable than an Albanian, Serb, or Slovene, was worth around ninety gold ducats to a Genoese slaver (Atiya, *Commerce,* 183). The distressing image of "chrismed children crammed into tubs" not only expresses human reduction to the anonymity of thinghood through the commodification enacted by slavery, but also articulates one form of consumption (the economic) in terms of another (the gustatory) and demonstrates, in action, romance's manipulation of proximate figural vocabularies.[66]

Impervious to law, the Genoese giant at St. Michael's Mount is an autonomous entity whose right to do as he pleases, unmolested, is conferred by the vast capital accumulation accruing from his wrongful transactions. In its anomalousness, the giant's independence hints at the autonomy of the Italian republics, whose quasi-capitalist economies and merchant-governments stood in startling contrast, in a still-medieval Europe, to economic feudalism and feudal hierarchies of rule: republics whose slightly monstrous models of entrepreneurial modernity, exercised by urban confederations, have already been read as monstrous throughout crusading history because of the economic self-interest jealously guarded by the Italians.[67] "Caffaro, the twelfth-century historian of Genoa" identifies an irony of Genoese history: the rise in tandem of "the first communal government" in Genoa and the simultaneous "departure of the Genoese fleet in support of the First Crusade" (Byrne, 139), a coincidence that connects the origin of Genoese crusading history overseas with the rise of the Genoese commune at home. The emergence and subsequent flourishing of Genoese trade in Syria, as a result of early crusading success and systematic, aggressive Genoese exploitation and defense of commercial privileges and rights granted thereafter, will guarantee the cannibal-giant of St. Michael's Mount his spiced luxuries in the culinary preparation of boys for dinner (ll. 1026–28).[68]

For the *Morte*, of course, "Genoese giants" is, in the final analysis, shorthand for *all* the Italian republics who grew wealthy by fattening on the fortunes and misfortunes of crusader-pilgrims whom they were believed to exploit: republics who were literally economic and trading giants in the Levantine Orient, Latin Europe, the Mediterranean, and the crusader colonies of Outremer. Significantly, the Italian republics were also active in the monstrously profitable trade in human, and Christian, commodities between East and West—slaves—a commercial trafficking particularly abhorrent, perhaps, to an English text accustomed to the absence of slavery in England for more than two centuries. Historians have repeatedly noted that all the Italian republics grew prosperous on their trade surpluses with the East, and sought every means to protect their *funduqs* in Alexandria, Cairo, and Islamic and Latin Syria from the disruptions to commerce caused by crusading warfare.[69] The "treaties" and "truce" that Arthur jestingly says, in full irony, he will seek with the Genoese giant of

St. Michael's Mount have fully historical counterparts in the trade treaties famously entered into by the crusaders of Outremer with the Italian economic giants, as well as by the Italians themselves with the Muslims of the East who were *their* trading partners, in relations of mutual aid and mutual economic interest that often functioned to the detriment of Outremer (Runciman, 3:361).

Perry Anderson observes that in 1293 alone "the maritime taxes of the single port of Genoa yielded 3 1/2 times the entire royal revenue of the French monarchy" (193). Communicated in the vocabulary of a romance knight—a Templar, say, who may be depended on to grasp fiscal matters with exactitude—we might see how it is possible that a thieving Genoese giant has amassed more florins than are available in all of France (Hamel, *Morte*, l. 885). Indeed, that there are florins in France at all owes something to the giant trade surpluses with the East enjoyed by the Italian republics, whose large role in making available gold coinage ("florins") in Europe is captured in the very existence of the giant's numismatic treasure. Although gold coins are minted in the crusader colonies of Jerusalem, Antioch, and Tripoli, from as early as the twelfth century, gold is not minted in post-Carolingian Europe (except in border-zone Sicily and Islamic Spain) until the mid-thirteenth century, with the appearance of the januarius in Genoa in 1251, and the florin in Florence in 1252 (P. Anderson, 193; Atiya, *Commerce*, 188–89; Bolton, 74–75). The "movement of gold from Moslem countries to the Christian . . . [and] further to the West" (Runciman, 3:363–64) becomes, then, one more indicator of the economic ascendancy of the West, *translatio imperii* in the channeling of precious metal to Europe, for coinage (P. Anderson, 193)—issuing, in late-fourteenth-century romance, as a Genoese monster's treasure horde that trumpets the existence, in Europe, of a gold standard that is at least partly financed by monstrous trafficking in human victims on the part of economic giants.[70]

Arthur's ironic jest about "treaties" with the Genoese giant of St. Michael's Mount also covertly refers, with grim humor, to other contracts, beyond trade, with Genoa and Venice—giant naval powers who had sea monopolies, along with Aragon, in the Mediterranean, and on whose ships the practicability of any later-medieval crusading venture depended—republics who struck tough, even apparently cruel bargains with crusaders, from the Fourth Crusade on, over ships and men.[71] The figuration of Italians as giants is likely colored also by the fiscal prominence of the Italian communities in late-medieval England, a prominence that some have argued signaled "the relative weakness of the local burgher class" in many towns, with the exception of London (P. Anderson, 195). Lombard bankers and mercantile financiers from a number of Italian cities, including Genoa, were highly visible in England, after historical events had done away with their chief competitors—Jews were expelled in 1290, and the Order of the Temple was extirpated after 1312—positioning the Italians as the most visible agents in financial transactions that were often understood (like trafficking in foreign exchange) to be usurious practices cleverly disguised to circumvent doctrinal prohibitions against usury.[72] Without their most visible, and highly resented erstwhile competitors in residence, Italian moneylenders and financiers nonetheless tellingly continued to be tarred with the earlier association, through their profession, with Jews. Almost a century after the Jewish expulsion from England, Lombard "usurers" continued to be linked with Jews in the English imagination, and in 1376 a complaint was voiced in Parliament that Jews were to be found harboring among the ranks of Lombards in England (Roth, *History*, 132–33; Richardson, 232). Not for nothing, then, is "Julian from Genoa," "a giant full huge" (l. 2889), vilified as an "errant Jew" (l. 2895) in the *Morte*, and overthrown on the field of battle by a "justice" called "Sir Gerard" (l. 2890). The destruction to which this particular Wandering Jew is sentenced is conveniently meted out by a knight representing justice, so that two communities conjoined in the person of a single giant—communities who had in common their substantial fiscal role in developing the medieval English economy—can be executed in one stroke by triumphant, judiciary knighthood.[73]

One Italian personage, in particular, might well be specially sedimented as a monster in the imaginary of the *Morte*: Gian Galeazzo Visconti, Duke of Milan, fleetingly appears in several places in this romance through variations of his title (Hamel, *Morte*, 267 nn. 324–332; L. D. Benson, 28), as the "Vicount of Rome" (ll. 325, 2050) or "Sire of Milan" (l. 3134), a consequence, as Hamel puts it, of "popular hostility" against the infamy of this notorious Italian lord.[74] Perfidiously, the Visconti had forewarned the Ottoman Bayezid of the Nicopolis Crusade, thus proving himself treacherous to Christians, some of whom became enslaved after the defeat at Nicopolis because of his perfidy (Atiya, *Later Middle Ages*, 9; Hamel, 267 nn. 324–32). The Visconti was also a notorious slave trader who had married a French princess, Isabel, daughter of Jean II. After Jean's capture by the English Black Prince early in the Hundred Years War, the French king's royal ransom was guaranteed by Gian Galeazzo's father—in a dowry of 600,000 gold florins promised to France for Jean's ransom in England—in exchange for Gian Galeazzo's marriage to the eleven-year-old royal child-princess of France. We cannot but notice that the Italian giant of St. Michael's Mount not only has more florins than are in all of France, but takes captive a French noblewoman of tender years who is the "flower of all France" (l. 860).[75] Significantly, in the *Morte*, the Italian giant's attitude to both France and Christendom is predatory: The Cotentin peninsula in Normandy and that other "country of Constantine" (848) are his hunting grounds for chrismed children whom the giant captures and treats like consumables, human livestock, or commodities waiting to be disposed of at leisure. Since the *Morte*'s geographical pun can signal both France and Constantinople, the "many Christians" in "Constantine's lands" (l. 1187) who are the giant's human prey also intercalates a reminder that Nicopolis—part of Constantinople's lands—became a supply ground for slavery, the other kind of consumption, in the aftermath of the failed crusade: a crusade whose failure was abetted by a notorious slaver's—the Visconti's—betrayal of the Christian forces to the Ottomans. Though Genoese giants are formidably ubiquitous enemies in the *Morte*, only one—the cannibal of St. Michael's Mount—is specially singled out for figuration as a monster whose treachery, vast wealth, power, loathsome lust, and gigantic appetite for acts of dehumanization— like the Visconti's—clearly fall outside moral, natural, and religious law ("owte of lawe" [l. 996]).[76]

The representation, in the *Morte*, of an economic giant as also a giant of the usual physical kind imparts a useful glimpse into the project of romance figuration. The representation turns a figure inside out: Secreted within an outsized brute is a giant economic monstrosity that is best investigated physically, it seems, rather than fiscally, although the one investigation cunningly leads to the other. We are pointed, thus, to a romance kind of irony suggesting that figures should be encouraged to dissolve, yield to self-disfiguration, even as we are duly encouraged, by their luridity, to scrutinize them. Where Gian Galeazzo is less obliquely hinted at in narrative, the hints are rather more deferential, offering references to the powerful Italian that are careful to qualify their implicit criticism, convey an aura of neutrality, or even to imply flattering respect (e.g., in l. 2050). Only the germ of a suspicion that an accusation might be lodged within the depiction of a giant whose acts mark him as monstrous, and thus unmitigatedly deserving of horror, releases other potentials. In order to read romance figuration in its multifold concretions, then, we must grant the ability of romance figures to dissolve into whatever is secreted within: the kernel of the historical that diffuses into the sensational, fantastical outer object we are proffered with casual nonchalance.[77]

The Unmaking and Making of Men: Defending Chivalry through the Body in the Late Middle Ages

But the monstrosified, hyperbolized body of the giant of St. Michael's Mount discloses yet another public secret of a medieval kind. The idea that the truth of a person may somehow be read on his body, or within his body, suggests a certain capacity, on the part of a narrative, to essentialize the body as the ground of reference and truth. In the *Morte*, where the knight's body is the microcosmic field in which a knight's institutional and ideological identity finds its expressive location, and where the public and historical sphere of knighthood may be read, the suggestion is readily embedded that a person *is* his body, and that the body is continuous with identity in some intrinsic, quintessential fashion.[78] The fourteenth century, after all, was a period in which attention to the body was highly specialized and marked in elaborate, newly modern ways. The visual emergence of the body, with the advent of tailoring and fitted clothes, and fashions toward tight hose, bright and variegated colors, sumptuous fabrics of different textures, pointed shoes, and so on, meant that the surface, shape, features, sensory zones, and contours of the body were noticed to an inordinate degree. The *Morte*'s close attention to the many details of armor—as, for instance, in Arthur's arming (ll. 901–13), and dissections of armor in battle (the eye slipping from detail to detail, e.g., in the unhinging of Gawain's shoulder-plate, back brace, elbow-cup, armplate, etc., in ll. 2565ff.)—scrutinizes the masculine body, since armor, even more than clothing, counterfeits the body and projects a surrogate body piece by piece. Simultaneously any consciousness of the body, in the late medieval period, when plague epidemics decimated perhaps a third of the population of Europe and distressing visions of corporeal infection, decay, and death were common, necessarily involved a consciousness of the body's vulnerability, its ease of disintegration, and its capacity for sudden disruption and death.

In the *Morte*, where sudden death comes through war, not disease, critics have observed that despite a certain critique of war scattered throughout the narrative—in the form of direct commentary on Arthur's wanton destructiveness during his imperial campaign or voiced in individual knights' complaints or neglected advice to Arthur—the romance nonetheless never tires of finding myriad ways to describe the dismantling of men's bodies in the battlefield and, indeed, seems to relish, even fetishize, its gift for vivid, highly memorable, even unique stylizations of death. In *chansons de geste*, the genre of narrative most commonly featuring descriptions of battlefield destruction, death comes in entirely conventional formulas—a knight typically dies vertically, through a downstroke that cleaves through his brain pan, torso, saddle, horse, and so forth, or horizontally, slashed sideways through the trunk of his body; even with variations on the theme, the parade of killing is fairly monotonous, and tiresomely predictable after the first few examples. The *Morte* does, of course, feature examples of crude, *chanson*-style vertical and horizontal slashing, but its specialty is to expose to the gaze the detailed interior and topography of the knight's body, part by part, and organ by organ.[79]

Disclosures are made of the spleen (ll. 2060–61), liver (ll. 2168, 2560–61), lungs (l. 2168), bowels/guts (ll. 1370–71, 2174–76, 2782), heart (ll. 1370–71, 2238, 2240, 2238, 2793), gullet/throat (ll. 1772, 3760), ribs (ll. 2060–61, 2271, 3843), belly/stomach (ll. 2075–77), skull (ll. 2228–29), nose (l. 2248), brain (ll. 2272, 2770, 3857), shoulders (ll. 2546, 4232), veins (l. 2571), neckbone (l. 2771), and flanks (l. 2781), to name but some of the body parts that attract attention. Equally extraordinary is the patient scrutiny of less commonly noticed features of the human torso, like the "slote" (ll. 2254, 2975)—the "slight depression or hollow running down the middle of the breast" (Hamel, *Morte*, 505, glossary) in the bony vertical divide of the sternum—and "feletez" (ll. 1158, 2174, 4237), "bands of muscular tissue, especially the loins" (444, glossary). As the body's topography, interior, and circumference are registered, the narrative seems to be accumulating a vocabulary to say, "this is what the body is made up of, inside and out, what it is, and how it comes apart: this is the physical sum and meaning of a man who is a knight."

The depiction of that body in its parts and sum, moreover, is not contextualized by a single kind of affect but arranges for a variety of responses, from humor or irony, to horror, to matter-of-factness, to pathos and poignancy. The delivery of that emotive range can be seen in a sublime set of lines that offers in narrative a kind of stuttering montage, a field version of the *danse macabre*: a tableau of "dying knights" who "lie wide open, thrown about on galloping horses," "wounds of goodly men, heaving sides," "faces hideously seen in tangled lakes," "all crushed, utterly trodden underfoot by caparisoned steeds," and "a thousand dead at once, for as far as a furlong" on "the fairest-appearing field of battle that has ever been pictured" (ll. 2146–52). In the depiction's staccato, pathos, horror, beauty, irony, and a kind of triumphant glory, even glee, are complexly conjoined from moment to moment.[80]

But even where the pathos of bodily vulnerability is the reigning affect, however, the descriptions of death on the battlefield are ultimately more reassuring than troubling to an elite social class whose entire profession has been organized for the practice of war. For in the narrative ideology of chivalric-heroic romance, the centrality of the knight's role on the battle-field is defined with utter clarity and affirmed at the moment when the knight's body is spectacularly and memorably undone in death. In ro-mance, death in battle performs and confirms the utter necessity, value, and existence of the knight as a history-making war machine; through death, the knight, as a history-making subject, is attested and vindicated. Horrible as the description of each individual dissection might be, the very variety of death that is pictured wards off the prospect of true vari-ety—the variety wrought by *change*, the momentum and inexorability of which are truly feared in this romance. By comparison, the arrival of death on the battlefield displays the continuing occupation of the knight in the central position in the theater of war, and ensures that knights are seen doing what they do best—dealing out and receiving death magnificently, chivalrously, heroically, and vindicating all the values of honor, valor, gen-erosity, glory, and piety enshrined in their ideological code. Multiplica-tion of an image, in this context, reassures by its very theatricality, repeti-tion, and variety.

Indeed, the dramatic theatricality and seemingly numberless ways in which knights are shown to die, delays a recognition that the battlefield deaths witnessed in the *Morte* are not, in fact, truly various. We scarcely see men being piked, for instance, or killed by arrows, in this romance de-picting war, although historians agree on the pivotal instrumentality of bowmen in all the major wars of the fourteenth century, including the Anglo-French Hundred Years War and the Nicopolis Crusade. We have instead, in the *Morte*, Arthur defiantly declaring before the walls of the city of Metz, where enemy crossbowmen are arrayed, that no "harlotte" (l. 2446) or lower-class scoundrel could possibly fell him with an arrow-shot—despite his deliberately making himself an inviting target, unarmed and dressed in bright clothing—since, as an anointed king and chiefest of knights, Arthur was, of course, invulnerable to the weapons of lower-class ruffians, an invulnerability that God himself would help to guarantee (l. 2446). Arthur's confident boast, uttered in response to one of his knights who aptly voices fear for the king's safety in the face of one of the most formidable of European weapons, directly contradicts well-known historical fact: Richard Lionheart, most brilliant of military leaders, and a redoubtable knight and king who was often associated with Arthur, was untimely felled by a crossbow shot at Châlus.[81] Though disdainfully dismissed by Arthur, however, knighthood's anxiety over bowmen discloses a momentary breach in the narrative, through which the efficacy of a technology that troubles knights can surface to be mentioned, but only in order to be dismissed. In the *Morte*, even the Saracen hosts—historically famed and feared as lightly armed, highly mobile horsed archers—fight exclusively like knights, and only with the weapons of knights, swords ("brandez" [l. 1861]) and lances ("castis in fewtire" [l. 1769]; "launce" [l. 1820]). Like European elites, the Muslims are also "cheualrye" (l. 1872); their foreignness does not admit military difference.

The *Morte*'s allegory of the body can now be summed up. First, in Arthur's arming, we see the identity of a knight literally organized around, upon, and through the male body, as the arming materializes a splendid bodily carapace, a simulacrum of a man who later materializes in the flesh, when Arthur's torso and members are systematically examined by Bedivere and Kay, after combat with the giant of St. Michael's Mount (a monster whose distended, grotesque bodily envelope defines *his* identity—specifying, through gross bodily hybridity and deformity, what is *not* a knight). Subsequently the elite body-machine, hazarded in combat, reissues knightly identity: Even when it is disassembled by knightly weapons, the anatomization of that noble subject of war, and of history, reinforces the identity, purpose, and centrality of the knight. Multiple images of mutilated and dead knights, then, only reconfirm the central importance of the knight in the theater of war, and are defended by the narrative's insistence that the warring contenders on every side, with few exceptions, are knights, and of superb prowess. That a knight is, in the last instance, not afraid of the body's destruction in war—the ultimate culmination and fulfillment of his identity—is aided by the crusading frame of this romance, with its references to the martyrdom that awaits the Christian knight who falls in the theater of war.

What, then, in chivalric-heroic romance, *are* knights afraid of, if not death in battle? Intriguingly, a shadow of a hint lurks in the humor of a joking dialogue that Gawain has with Priamus in the *Morte*, an exchange in which Gawain at first pretends not to be a knight but a mere servant of Arthur's chamber, a "knafe" tending to Arthur's wardrobe, and who was raised to the rank of "yeoman" at Christmas and given great gifts ("He made me 30mane at 30le and gafe me gret gyftes" [l. 2628]). When knights dissimulate their identity in the best tradition of romance encounters, the purpose of dissimulation is usually the gratifying self-aggrandizement that follows identity revelation—a *dénouement* often postponed by the narrative so that the surprise of revelation, and the admiring gaze upon the knight in his magnificent true identity, might be fully savored and enjoyed. The dynamic of Gawain's dissimulation here, however, takes a different route. Gawain does not pretend to be some unknown, or less distinguished, knight than himself—the convention established from Chrétien de Troyes's romances on—but introduces, instead, inferior social categories, "yeoman," and "knafe," and opposes these terms to "knight," thus drawing a clear distinction between social categories that are yoked by opposition.

Alarmingly, however, Priamus's immediate response suggests that he cannot tell, or cannot be sure, what, or which, Gawain in fact is—knight, yeoman, or servant—and thus hints at a possible slippage between the terms, and a miscarriage of the joke, for Priamus insists, "Tell the truth now, whether you are a knight or a knave" (l. 2637). Gawain's joke misfires if the distinctions between "knight," "yeoman," and "knave" in the late Middle Ages are not as secure or obvious as he supposes, and a clarification is actually needed to distinguish a representative of one social category from a representative of another. The joke is on *him*, not Priamus, if it is not blazingly obvious that he, Gawain, a magnificent exemplar of Arthurian knighthood, could not possibly be the "yeoman" or "knave" he sketches in jest.[82] The speed with which Gawain moves to rectify any intimacy or slippage between the categories registers a profound sense of narrative unease. In his very next words Gawain quickly reestablishes the grand coordinates of his famous knightly identity, immediately closing off speculation: "My name is Sir Gawain . . . Cousin to the Conqueror . . . Famous in his list, a knight of his chamber / And enrolled the most magnificent [noblest, wealthiest, etc.—"richeste" (l. 2641)] of all the Round Table. I am the douzepere and duke he dubbed with his hands" (ll. 2638–42). Plainly, that an English knight might be mistaken for an English yeoman, or worse, even for the briefest instant, is a troubling matter to knighthood in the late Middle Ages. It is change—social mobility and transformation, technological, economic, military change, agonizingly rep-

resented for Arthur by the turn of Fortune's wheel—and not spectacular
death on the battlefield, that an English knight in the late Middle Ages
fears and against which he must defend.

The End of the Line: A Family of Knights, Machinations of Desire, and the Ends of the Nation

In the *Morte*, the vision of a community of knights who live by, and loyally enact, Cador's idealized code of values finally crowds out the viability
of other groupings, relations, and affective ties. Family relationships of
every kind—except when they are entered as military relations in the theater of war—are shown to fail. Mordred, Arthur's fosterling and nephew,
betrays Arthur when Mordred is tested on the domestic front, a proving
ground the nephew had sought to evade, in pleading to be allowed to go
to war alongside Arthur. Dame Fortune's mothering—or stepmother-
ing—of Arthur proves fickle and treacherous, as does Guinevere's love for
her husband, a love that had been poignantly in evidence at her husband's
departure from home. Indeed, mother figures in the *Morte* are especially
powerless to protect: the crone who had been foster mother to the
Duchess of Brittany (l. 983) could not prevent her fosterling's rape and
death as the innocent victim of the giant of St. Michael's Mount; Guinevere, devoid of masculine protection after Mordred's death at Arthur's
hands, will presumably be as helpless to prevent the murder of her child
or children (ll. 3552, 3576, 3907) by Arthur's men, acting on Arthur's orders. Arthur's instructions to Constantine, the royal heir, to "go in a
manly fashion to Mordred's [and Guinevere's] children" and see that the
children are "covertly slain and [their bodies] slung into the water" (ll.
4320–21) typologically follow biblical and folkloric precedents of child-
and infant-killing, including failed infanticides associated with water and
secrecy. The irony of his instructions, furthermore—Constantine is told
to be "manly" in his performance of an act whose fundamental cowardice
is suggested by the necessity of concealment and dissimulation, an act
that will deny the child victims Christian burial—is underscored by
Arthur's own childlessness and failure at affective relations outside martial homosociality.[83]

The only family relations that are seen as deeply binding and true in
the *Morte*, then, are battlefield relations—the touching affection and loyalty between, say, fathers and sons who are comrades together or Arthur's

deep attachment to his nephew, Gawain, his greatest knight, an attachment mediated by Gawain's military value to Arthur. But even here feudal military allegiance takes precedence over, and indeed conditions, family allegiance, as Sir Idrus's loving and respectful monologue on his
father's wishes makes clear: The elder knight, Sir Ewain, orders his son,
Sir Idrus, to stand and fall loyally by their liegelord, Arthur, and no one
else (ll. 4142–54), in the field of battle, a command the son steadfastly and
movingly obeys, in a convenient overlap of filial and feudal obedience.
This depiction of family solidarity as military solidarity is only one mode
of the pervasive culture of military homosociality and affective homoeroticism in the *Morte*.

Tears shed by men, in this romance, are shed over other men; kisses
bestowed by men are bestowed on the bodies of their dead comrades.
Gawain weeps extravagantly over the death of an unnamed youth,
Arthur's squire (ll. 2962, 2965); Sir Cador kisses Sir Beril's corpse over and
over (l. 1779); even the villainous Mordred—whose subjectivity is portrayed with greater sympathy and sensitivity in this male-oriented romance than virtually anywhere else in Arthurian literature—weeps copi-
ously and compassionately for Gawain, though Mordred had himself dealt
Gawain's death blows (ll. 3886–91). Death in the field affirms, rather than
loosens, the affective ties of knighthood; the institution binds the living
and the dead tightly together by the recognition of mutual likeness and
identity, and a common understanding of why it is knights live and die.
In the common performance of masculinity in the field, homoerotic identifications available in group projects of war are allowed to surface: And
we see that in the sexual and affective economy of the *Morte*, the genital
masculinity represented by the giant of St. Michael's Mount is exchanged
for affective masculinity between men, circulated in performance as field
relations.

The most extravagant outpouring of passionate intensity is reserved for
Gawain, best of English Arthurian knights. Gawain's killer, Mordred, offers up an eloquent panegyric for Gawain's life, an exemplary chivalric
tribute that demonstrates how peerless knights should be eulogized, by
enemy and comrade (and enemy *as* comrade) alike. Arthur, in his turn,
faints and swoons in grief (l. 3969), passionately and repeatedly embraces
and kisses Gawain's corpse (ll. 3951–52, 3970), weeping all the while, till
his beard glistens with Gawain's blood (l. 3971). As if this visualization of
the blood bond between men (another kind of community of blood, a
military form of the *Blutsgemeinschaft*) insufficiently united the living with

the dead, Arthur reverently scoops up Gawain's blood with his hands (l. 3994), as he apotheosizes Gawain as a latter-day Christ who is possessed of sinless blood that should be enshrined in gold, like a relic from saint or deity (ll. 3991–92), and stores the blood in a helmet.[84] The lengthy eulogy for Gawain that precedes this reverent memorialization is uttered as a wailing, passionate, desperate keening by Arthur, a lamentation couched to fulfill the ultimate fantasy of every knight who desires his lord's acknowledgment of utter dependence on the corps of knighthood.

Through the figure of the dead Gawain, Arthur's testimony also assigns to knights all responsibility for the power and accomplishments of kings. Arthur attributes to Gawain all Arthur's success at arms, courage, honor, and martial "hardiness" (l. 3959) and all counsel, comfort, happiness, and hope of well-being. Indeed, Arthur wails, Gawain was worthy to be England's king, though Arthur bore the crown, and with his knight gone, the king's honor and war are effectively now ended (ll. 3957–64). The passionate testimony of the leader's reliance on his corps of knights is intensified manifold at the close of the civil war with Mordred, when a stupefied Arthur comes upon the bodies of each of his favorite knights in turn—"Ewayne," "Errake," "Cador," whom Arthur catches up in his arms, "Clegis," "Cleremonte," "Lothe," and "Lyonell," "Lawncelott and Lowell," "Marrake and Meneduke" (ll. 4262–67)—lays them down together, and gazes on their corpses like a man who no longer desires to live, and who has lost all joy (l. 4270). Staggering like a madman, his strength failing, Arthur looks up to the firmament, sways unsteadily on his feet, and falls in a swoon (ll. 4271–73). Returning to his senses, he utters a long eulogy to his dead men and concludes by taking his leave of all lordship, as all his joy ends (ll. 4288–90). Six centuries after the *Morte* was written, Klaus Theweleit's study of the diaries, journals, autobiographies, and letters of men in the *Freikorps*—private armies that roamed Germany in the aftermath of World War I, who became "the core of Hitler's SA and, in several cases . . . key functionaries in the Third Reich" (Ehrenreich, x)—suggests that Arthur's particular experience of intense emotive loss is not unique among field narrations, and is repeated in other, more modern contexts of report and representation. Theweleit notes the similar lamentation of "Freikorps-commander Mannsfeld"—"I simply can't live without my people . . . I can't live without my corps"—and concludes that the "end of the relationship to the troops is . . . [typically] depicted as the end of all relationships" (1:60). The reciprocal love between leader and men in the theater of war ("As the leader loves his men, so the . . . soldier loves his superior") "appears in one form or another" so that "in countless different forms, then, the activities of these men . . . are brought into association with the word 'love'" (Theweleit, 1:60).

Love, in the battlefield relations of the *Morte*, circulates within a world where real differences between men do not exist, where difference has, indeed, been held off: a world in which the activity of war brings intimacy and fusion to a corps of knights whose individual egos, boundaries, and identities are temporarily dissolved in the affective intensity of a glorious common purpose, a group communion of authorized violence. In the fantasy of war, love means the substitution of one man for another, in partnerships of mutual protection, sacrifice, and retribution exacted for one's fellows, and involving passions experienced *in extremis*. The generous surrendering of one's self, where necessary, for another who is like-self, and yet not, in the dance of chivalric identity relations, is part of the logic of love among men in the fantasy of war. Drawing close the circle of the military elect through the orchestrated furor of group violence, love, conducted under the banners of war, answers to the infinite desire for union, and an end to the ego's boundaries, with a specialized formulation. Unsurprisingly, the *Morte*'s accomplishment of war-as-fantasy conjures up a romance fusion that is not eroded, but rather climaxed, in death.

Arthur's extravagant outburst and eloquent tenderness toward the nephew who is eulogized as the king's best knight and warrior might be usefully contrasted, in its intensity, to the king's perfunctoriness with Guinevere, his wife, when she is deeply distressed at Arthur's departure from home. Though the queen is distraught—weeping and swooning, and kissing him—Arthur's efforts at comforting her merely take the form of perfunctorily telling her not to grieve ("Grefe þe noghte, Gaynour" [l. 705]) or grudge his departure, that her grieving wounds *him*, and that he cannot end her grief by changing his mind about departing for war (l. 705). The matter-of-fact response is quickly over, and Arthur turns directly to practical matters, the steward he has assigned for Guinevere and England (l. 709ff.). In stark contrast, Arthur cannot be drawn from his obsessive keening over Gawain; his heart almost bursts from grief (l. 3974), and when his knights chide him for excessive emotion, the king angrily responds that he will never cease until his brain or his heart utterly gives out (ll. 3981–82). Arthur's sanguinary memorialization of Gawain also reminds us that, unlike its source texts, the *Morte* chooses not to memorialize the maiden victim of St. Michael's Mount, and recalls how quickly, indeed, the Duchess of Brittany had been forgotten. Despite the chivalric requirement to honor and serve *women*—and Arthur's claim that he would rather have died than have let the Duchess of Brittany come to harm, had he known (l. 875)—we see that men's tears and emotions, in the *Morte*, are specially reserved for other men, and not for women.[85] Only women weep for other women in this romance (l. 951).

Indeed, the coincidence of martial and homosocial-homoerotic affects in the *Morte*, and the romance's relative lack of interest in heterosexual passion, recalls Freud's remark that "homosexual love is far more compatible with group ties" (or with "mass commitment," "group bonding," *Massenbindungen*) than heterosexual love (Freud, 18:141). In romance—a genre that, as discussed in chapter 1, concerns itself with the *safe* expression of risky passions—one party in the monogendered affective equation should be deceased before the intensest emotions of men for other men can be acted out, yet another way in which death can be useful to the institution of knighthood. Death allows the tenderness of men for one another to bloom, and come to fruition and intensest articulation. As the male beloved subject disappears into the arms of death, the loving subject who remains can speak and act his love: Arthur "sweetly kisses" (l. 3970) the dead Gawain lawfully, without self-explanation; the masculine speaker of love can even imagine himself in drag, as Arthur does, when he offers himself as a "woeful widow who is lacking her lord" (l. 4285), on the death of his men. The shadowy mingling of battle, death, and sexuality that had first congealed as a suspicion on St. Michael's Mount finds its proper culmination in the theater of war, in that intensely passionate tableau of the living and the dead locked in each other's arms.

If homoeroticism cannot be properly voiced or acted out till one of the masculine partners in knighthood is deceased, heterosexuality—nominally the theory of sexual relations that is featured in medieval romance—is featured in the *Morte* only to be defeated. When the topic of sexual intercourse between male and female is raised, the intercourse takes the form of unnatural, illegal, violent, or treacherous acts: brutal rape by a monster (the giant of St. Michael's Mount), potential rape by a military horde (the Arthurian army at Metz [ll. 3057–58]), or adultery, concupiscence, and sexual treachery (Mordred/Guinevere). Heterosexuality, it seems, either undoes a man (Mordred) or shapes a monster (the giant of St. Michael's Mount). For knights concerned with hewing to the chivalric code, *hetero*sexuality is tantamount to *hyper*sexuality: In the *Morte* it is war, and not heterosexual love, that truly *makes* a man. Or, put differently, it is love *of* war, and love *in* war, that is eroticized and made amatory. Knightly passion, between men, registers itself as an erotics *of* and *in* the killing fields of romance.

Finally, the elaborate anatomy of chivalry featured in the *Morte* has different dimensions, of which amatory homoeroticism is a part, not the whole. In the textual foreground, it is *social* identity, of course, that has priority over sexual identity. The urgency of the contest over social identity in late-medieval England, moreover, means that the *Morte* is alert on a variety of cultural fronts and sensitive to a range of cultural, social, and economic dispositions. The giant's cloak of beards, we have said, suggests that the *Morte's* economic unconscious is uncommonly attentive to the relationship between the power of fiscal accumulation and the power of symbolic capital. Since the giant monstrosity not only eats boys, rapes women, and vanquishes knights but also takes pains to acquire and cumulatively embellish a pivotal symbol of dominion over kings—the cloak of kings' beards—narrative recognition attests, at some level, the importance of controlling and manipulating symbolic capital. In the contest over social identity, we note, the *Morte's* own inventiveness, energy, and promiscuous eloquence are attractions that themselves feature as capital: the cultural capital mustered by chivalric romance on behalf of the social constituency it serves.

Nonetheless, at the end of the day, the code and community of knights sketched by the *Morte* ultimately disclose the limitations of a social constituency organized by class and vocational stratification alone—limitations that also determine the horizon of chivalric romances. The literature of a military caste with sectarian elite interests is finally unable to perform, symbolically or culturally, for anything larger than its bounded, stratified constituency and cannot express, say, the larger corporate life of medieval society as a whole. Chivalric romance, as Arthur's philosophers tell us, in the *Morte*, is to be "read by royal knights" (l. 3440); and, by narrative's end, the *Morte* has already taken its addressing of a subcommunity to its farthest potentials in the genre of elite romance. Unlike the popular romance of *Richard Coer de Lyon*, the *Morte* offers little sense of England as an overarching entity or nation; and though aspects of Arthur's wars might bear the occasional resemblance to the Hundred Years War between England and France, the *Morte* does not care to exploit differences between English and French to project an imagined collective unity binding together the English, as such: a greater priority, perhaps, for popular romance than elite romance. Indeed, "the intense caste solidarity" (Barnie,

82) of an aristocracy of knights historically tended to mitigate *against* the idea and formation of a national community: The "law of arms" and code of chivalry shared by English *and* French knights alike "transcended boundaries of [territorial] allegiance and nationality" (Barnie, 82–83).[86] If a larger collectivity that subsumes diverse interests, social classes, and groups is to be imagined—if the nation is to be figured—that figuration must emerge from elsewhere, and through other forms, than chivalric romances, with their well-defined system of priorities and defenses.

It is finally significant, then, in this context, that the *Morte* has no use for women or families in its narrative universe. The imagined community of Christendom, and of the nation, can be profoundly figured by women, children, and families, but it would take a different kind of romance, with a different purpose and affective constellation, to meet the particular challenge, and it is a challenge for another kind of story.

There is an "Oriental" tendency in all of us, which must be tamed if it can't be rooted out.

—Sheila Delany, "Geographies of Desire: Orientalism
in Chaucer's *Legend of Good Women*"

It is worth asking why the national novels of Latin America—the ones that governments institutionalized in the schools and that are by now indistinguishable from patriotic histories—are all love stories.

—Doris Sommer, *Foundational Fictions:
The National Romances of Latin America*

Family imagery, family models, in religious devotion and in daily experience: each echoed and reinforced the other. . . . Catherine [of Siena] would pretend her father was Christ, her mother our Blessed Lady, and her brethren the apostles. Catherine lived within two families.

—David Herlihy, *Medieval Households*

Custance is an apostle to the English and mother of a Christian emperor, as it were, in spite of herself.

—Winthrop Wetherbee, "Constance and
the World in Chaucer and Gower"

༄

CHAPTER 4

Beauty and the East, a Modern Love Story

Women, Children, and Imagined Communities
in *The Man of Law's Tale* and Its Others

IN THE "CONSTANCE GROUP" of medieval romances—a literary family in which Chaucer's *Man of Law's Tale* (henceforth *MLT*) is a senior member—a beautiful Christian princess from the East journeys far from her imperial family and homeland, in travels urgently begun and continued by desire: the amatory desire of men who want to marry and possess her; the hostile desire of royal queen mothers who want her away from their homeland; and, above all, the intense desire of fourteenth-century medieval culture and authors for her story. Wherever she goes—her narrative has two parts, two locales, in the East and in the West—the lovely innocent (whom I will call "Constance," though she also has other names) sets in motion a chain of events that culminates in the Christianization of a local populace and the disruption of local families, including the royal family that she re-creates as a new family system through Christianization. Women who do not intensely hate her, and wish her far from their countries, intensely desire her, and take her into the bosom of their home and family, into their very identity, even into their bed. In the first part of her

---

Audience response at the Thirty-Fourth International Congress of the Medieval Institute, in 1999, at a Comparative Literature medieval studies seminar at the University of Oregon, in 2001, and at Georgetown University, in 2002, where portions of this chapter were read, have contributed to the chapter's final shape. Pete Wetherbee's work on the Constance saga, in particular, urged the early asking of crucial questions whose ramifications are explored throughout the chapter. Gina Psaki, Ann Marie Rasmussen, Elizabeth McCartney, Louise Bishop, Warren Ginsberg, Lisa Wolverton, Penn Szittya, Michael Ragussis, Kelley Wickham-Crowley, and Joe Sitterson contributed helpful insights. This chapter, written during a fellowship year at Brown University's Pembroke Center, shows the influence of Ellen Rooney and Elizabeth Weed, and bears the imprint of ideas and formulations from Nancy Armstrong's *Desire and Domestic Fiction*.

story, the virtuous Christian princess (an aura of holiness, of divine protection and purpose, invests her sexual desirability) is childless; her marriage to a Muslim king—if indeed marriage occurs—remains circumstantial and likely unconsummated. (But in one revealing variant of the story,
we see what horror results when her marriage to a Saracen *is* consummat-
ed and a child is born from the union.) By contrast, the saintly princess's
marriage to a pagan king of Anglo-Saxon Northumberland, in the second
part of her story—her marriage, that is, to a representative ruler of England—creates a beautiful boy child from the union, a birth that consum-
mates the princess as a devout, Marian-style mother, and produces a new
royal family for Northumberland-as-England.

If the Constance romances seem faintly familiar as love stories—as
tales of masculine desire for beautiful, unknown women, *belles inconnues*,
who materialize to occasion adventures—the love and desire featured in
these stories are also estranged, denatured from their usual honorary status in chivalric romance, by the hagiographic nimbus surrounding the
Constance group. Midway through the tale of this traveling woman,
moreover, there is a palpable shift in the registers of desire driving the narrative, so that another form of desire suddenly coalesces around the
twinned figure of Constance and her babe, when they are victimized by
the machinations of unjust authority and set adrift together, away from
English shores, alone on the vast, vast sea: a poignant, floating tableau of
twinned human connection in its earliest, primary moment, around
which emotion strategically collects. The domestic, familial circuit of the
desire that condenses through this image of mother and child marks the
transfer of desire, then, to other cultural terrain, mid-story—to an affecting, sentimental scene of primitive community. For, in effect, the drifting
island of mother and infant who are mutually dependent and intercon-
nected sketches a human community in miniature, stripped to its essentials—a primary tribe of the most basic kind, in its first instance of creation—and narrates another story of love, and of community, in culture.

The woman from the East is sexualized insofar as she is repeatedly an
object of sexual desire, the desire of men for her; tellingly, desire *is* important to the narration of communities, families, and nations, however defined. More importantly, however—and, I will show, necessarily—Constance herself seems empty of erotic desire. Except for an erotics of
maternity, desire for her child, and Christian piety, Constance is an inviting cipher, a blank (Wetherbee, 69–74). The masculine desire that summons her and initiates her story is also shown, in present context, to initi-

ate violence—disruption—for families and communities, until heterosexual *eros* is suborned by other, larger, projects of desire. We see that because
Constance is desired by men she is twice set adrift at sea in a rudderless
boat, provisioned for years of drifting (in some versions), or without food
or water (in others); in its simplest sexual formula, masculine desire goes
awry and creates injustice. In the course of her second sea voyage, the saintly Constance is almost raped, a jarring recognition of the ultimate illegality and violence of a purely adventitious masculine desire. We are to understand that in hagiographic romance, the sexual formula and alchemy of
an erotic trajectory that has served medieval romance for centuries since the
genre's inception must give way to a different order of love.

Hagiographic romance has a use also for the intermittent glimpses of a
desire that tantalizingly circulates between and among women—the desire
of the Saxon woman Dame Hermengild *for* Constance, and *to be like*
Constance, and the intense negative affect aimed *at* Constance by the
Muslim and pagan royal mothers—which functions as a partial recognition of something provocative being located in narrative. The love story
into which the different forms of desire in the Constance romances fold is
not, however, simply a story of divine love, which would be the subject of
authentic hagiography depicting true martyrdom and sainthood, rather
than romance, a form that merely borrows from hagiographical resources
and affect. Divine love simply functions as an authorizing fiction, a protective cover, in hagiographic romance: the story that is told by the Constance romances merely applies the dominant authoritative discourse of its
time—religion—as its signature, its immanent sign.

Nonetheless, religion exercises the structures of power on which Constance's story is built. The power of religion to transform culture and civilizations—enacting the will of one society upon another—is presented in
the Constance romances under the sign of conversion. In hagiographic romance, religious conversion is a name for the will-to-power of a dominant
civilization and the inflicting of its practices, institutions, and cultures
upon a subordinate, recipient civilization, whose own native practices, institutions, and cultures are concomitantly weakened through the invasive
imposition. When Constance, a foreign beauty from an old empire, arrives on Muslim and pagan shores, bringing Christianity in her wake, and
reconfiguring, from within, the families of the nations who receive her,
she locates the entrance of a new instrument of empire particularly apposite for the late Middle Ages: a cultural hegemony that is the sign and type
of modern empire formations. Constance's story is the referent, then, for

a distinctly modern impulse of empire in the late-medieval period, and recognized in culture; the story identifies and seals the seam between old and new formations of empire, between territorial domination and hegemonic domination. Constance's nuptials with a symbolic local king pinpoints the moment of switching over—a moment that is contested by powerful local women who defend against the symbolic and material transmutation Constance enacts—and the nativity of Constance's babe makes visible, with sentimental effectivity, the efflorescence of a reconfigured—a new—local formation. Constance's romance, more than any other kind, simplifies the linkages between impulses of the nation and impulses of empire, and brings home, as it were—back to intimate locations of hearth and family—the dependence of one set of impulses on the other.

Like its heroine, Constance's story traveled far and wide in the Middle Ages, and was influential in literary culture, attracting the eye of major fourteenth-century authors in England and Europe. Significantly, England produced an important core group of Constance stories—an intertextual community put together by Chaucer's *Man of Law's Tale* in *The Canterbury Tales*, Gower's second exemplum in the *Confessio Amantis*, Nicholas Trevet's account in his Anglo-Norman *Cronicles* (the source for Chaucer and Gower), and the Middle English romances *Emaré*, and *The King of Tars*. Each story in that primary community of texts offers a full and substantial treatment of Constance and her babe; while in Italy, Boccaccio retained some of the story's lineaments for the *Decameron's* second tale of the fifth day, and *Florence de Rome* (or *Le Bone Florence of Rome*), attested in Old French, Middle English, and Spanish, emplots tantalizing features from the Constance story.[1]

The heroine's name itself is ironically inconstant: *Emaré*, often grouped with the popular, usually anonymous Middle English Breton lays, is a Constance romance, despite the titular character's name, "Emaré," and has been closely linked to Chaucer's *Man of Law's Tale*. The heroine of the Middle English *King of Tars* is, in fact, without a name, and the heroine is "Florence" in *Florence of Rome*; but both these romances offer versions of the Constance story, even if the unnamed heroine of *Tars* does not put out to sea and Florence of Rome does not bear a child till the very end.[2] Prominent in all the romances are collocations and adaptations of some of the following features: a woman who travels from one family, society, and country to another, often moving from East to West; a male infant born to that woman, an infant reputed to be (and in the version of *Tars* actually is) a monstrous creation; religious contests and alliances that are figured by women; desire, for which a price is paid; a narrative aura imported from hagiography and mingling *topoi* from saints' lives with conventions from secular fantasy; and imagined political, religious, and civil communities of various kinds, created by consent to ideals of social justice or by affective and ethical constellations.

What makes for the Constance narrative's widespread appeal in the European Middle Ages, especially in fourteenth-century England, so that the story entices the talents of authors—Chaucer, Gower—who would be read as negotiating the urgent social and historical forces of their time? Is the figure of a woman and the dyad of mother and child irresistibly malleable, and intrinsically inviting, for social, political, and religious discourses in late-medieval English and Christian society? For the genre of romance, whose innovations and expanding resources we have been tracking in the preceding chapters, what advantages are gained by featuring a *woman* at center stage, instead of the usual man or group of men—a woman, moreover, burdened with a child for part of her travels and her story?

The constituency of English romances that develops in the fourteenth century, featuring women, and sometimes, children—narratives we might call "family romances," to stretch and complicate a term—differs from the more conventional chivalric, monarchic, military, historical, or popular romances we have been considering, which feature men, in that the woman at the center never attempts anything like masculinized adventures of any kind: It is conventional feminine performance, not transgendered mimicry, that is desired of the heroine.[3] To examine the instrumentality and cultural politics peculiar to this species of "family" and hagiographic romance, I will consider that interlinked core of Constance romances in England—Trevet's, Gower's, Chaucer's, and *Emaré*—interleaving into the discussion Chaucer's *Clerk's Tale*, with its story of Griselda (another family and semi-hagiographic romance) and *The King of Tars*, to elicit the fullest achievements of the Constance group's effects for discourses of the nation, the imagined community of Christendom, and race and religion in the late Middle Ages.[4] Throughout, I stress the instrumentality of the discursive apparatus that is put together—the discourse assembled and the discourse enabled—by the Constance stories: a set of literary productions that forms a textual community of a certain kind in romance, a community that makes available special resources of particular efficacy for other communities—social, political, religious—in its historical period.

BEAUTY AND THE EAST: CRUSADES, RELIGIOUS CONVERSION,
AND THE EMPIRE OF CULTURE

Before there was Constance, another female figure in literature around
whom thoughts of conversion congealed was the beautiful enemy who was
a renegade to her people and her religion. Two hundred years before, or
earlier, the fantasy of the Muslim princess or queen who converts for the
love of a Christian knight, baron, or ruler, emerged with the First Crusade
and is closely linked with crusading heroes and crusade history: Orderic Vitalis's *Historia Ecclesiastica*, in the first third of the twelfth century, inserts
an entirely unhistorical episode into the life of Bohemond, the already
larger-than-life Norman crusader-baron and prince of Antioch, who, Orderic's fantasy claims, is released from captivity in Anatolia by the emir
Danishmend through the elaborate plots and agency of Danishmend's be-
sotted daughter, "Melaz" (5:359–79), a Saracen princess who is secretly a
Christian and a renegade (5:369) in love with Bohemond. The motif of the
"enamored Muslim princess," as the *topos* has been dubbed, occurs so regularly in *chansons de geste* and romance as to be utterly conventional (see,
e.g., de Weever); converted Saracen queens like Bramimonde in the *Chanson de Roland* and Orable in the *Prise d'Orange* of the Guillaume cycle of
chansons famously and early, but only typically, lead the cast.[5]

   In the early twelfth century, when the impulse of empire was satisfy-
ingly answered by military acquisition and political control of crusader
territories in the Levant, and economic exploitation of local resources—
raw power exercised in the first stages of colonization—mass religious
conversion was not writ large as part of the script or deeply embedded in
the agendas of cultural fantasy. Melaz, Fatima, Bramimonde, Orable,
Floripas, and their Saracen sisters tend to figure conversion as *individual*
occurrences, the behavior of memorable royal women who are valued as
much for their quirky spunkiness or their fantasized excess of libido, as for
their availability as cultural signs that witness, at the highest level, the superiority of the Christian religion. Significantly, the narratives within
which these quixotic Oriental women appear do not depict the nation of
Islam converting en masse because of the women's agency as figures of
conversion. To be sure, any conversion by a queen or princess to the religion of the conquerors attests a colonizing impetus at work in representation, but the historical epoch's principal preoccupations write that colonization as a private love story mostly involving the important, high-level
individuals who are the usual actors in elite cultural fantasy.[6]

When colonization is still available as successful territorial domination—when the West possesses a substantial physical presence in, and exercises a material impact on, the East—other modalities of colonization
are incipient, nascent, or potential, though they are never fully absent.[7]
Significantly, one modality of colonization that makes itself felt in culture
from the very beginning, as Jacqueline de Weever richly demonstrates, is
the whitening of the Muslim beauties, who are often explicitly depicted as
white- or light-skinned, like conventional European beauties, in a rhetorical system aimed at reducing the other to the same, the foreign to the familiar, by reproducing the other as really, flatteringly, oneself in other
guise, and hence a simple matter to assume to oneself, easy to assimilate
without exacting a cost, despite their names (e.g., "Melaz").

These important cultural predecessors are sisters to Constance, as it
were, in the skin. Under the skin, even if they turn out to be Constance's
fellow travelers in religion, they are Constance's opposite in nature. Utterly inconstant to their religious and political communities, and often slyly
treacherous to their families, these Saracen princesses tend to be written by
cultural fantasy as desiring, sexually aggressive agents, whose religious conversion is part of their bold enactment of their erotic attraction to particular Christian men. Part of the fantasy of empire, as colonial and conquest
literatures in later periods will amply teach us, is that the colonized, in the
form of their women, desire the colonizers: so that, as Benjamin Kedar
dryly puts it, "the sensuous Saracen maiden must have come to play a considerable role in the dream life of many a European knight" (84).

The literary example of these Muslim sisters to Constance, Oriental
women whose renegade status is registered in the very skin that betrays
them as betrayers, lodges useful instrumentalities in European culture. For
one, the women's enunciation of an erotic demand, and an erotics of conversion, insinuates the idea that desire, *eros*, mediates and articulates the
relationship between colonizers and colonized: that desire lubricates, and
is intrinsic to, the modalities of power that bind large communal groups
into mutual relationship, especially where the unequal possession of
power constitutes the organizing principle of relation. For another, the example of these libidinous Muslim women who convert "par amur"—out
of promptings of love and desire—declares the libidinal economy to be
both continuous with, and constitutive of, the political economy. And romance, as I urged in previous chapters, loves to depict the political *as* the
personal, and vice versa, a fondness to which even hagiographic forms of
romance are susceptible: With the sphere of private emotion and drives

overlapping the sphere of public institutions, including religion, the political and the libidinal are urged on us as inextricably and reversibly constitutive, as overlapping or contiguous categories.

Constance's story, maturing in Nicholas Trevet's *Cronicles* after 1334 in the form that influences Chaucer, Gower, and *Emaré*, manipulates these useful instrumentalities at a historical juncture that sees the necessary escalation of culture to a position of hegemonic supremacy. In the late Middle Ages, as historians have noted, theoretical and speculative literature on crusading—military and pilgrimage expeditions to the East—proliferated and flourished in Europe on an impressively grand scale, growing ever more complex in its recommendations, projections, and agendas, even as crusading—still an active ideal—was demonstrated, over and over again, with one expedition after another, to be inefficacious in permanently retrieving and retaining Jerusalem and the lost colonies of Outremer.[8] Philippe de Mézière's *Songe du Vieil Pèlerin* is only among the more renowned of polemical treatises that expansively contemplate and advocate crusading, treatises which in sum constituted a form of wistful dream-literature that made its way through European culture in the fourteenth century, after the loss of the last crusader colony, Acre, in 1291. Culture, as we have said, abhors a vacuum. Just as imaginary Jews multiply in literature, drama, and hagiography in England in the flagrant absence of an English Jewry after Edward I's expulsion of England's Jews in 1290, so also does Constance's story, in its mature form as a narrative of conversion and religious domination, seize hold of the imagination with vigor, once territorial domination had been evacuated. In the fourteenth century, when empire as territorial conquest and rule in the East is largely a memory and a dream—though still pusued with fervor, as all dreams and memories of power must be pursued—the impulse of empire shifts onto cultural terrain, which it seizes and holds as territory that is truly apposite to the new, modern era.

Conversion—*translatio*—in the Constance romances is a rich trope that exercises the full might, and powerfully nuanced authority, of religious discourse *as* cultural discourse: announcing, in effect, the arrival and existence of an empire of culture, and the workings of what we might today analogously think of as flows of "cultural imperialism," *translatio imperii*, in the register of romance. Constance effects group conversions of Saracens to Christianity, where her Muslim sisters-in-literary-history need not, because the history of military failure has shown that cultural capture is the game in town for the fourteenth century.[9]

There should be little doubt that what Constance accomplishes in her story is the enactment of a successful crusade, cultural-style, feminine-style. The hagiographic aura of the Constance romances, moreover, makes her feminized crusade over into a kind of sexual martyrdom for Constance, a martyrdom akin to the sufferings endured by heroines in hagiography who have no desire of their own but are sacrificed to the desire of others—men, kings, and, most of all, God—and thus borrows, for the Constance story, an added mantle of significance that appends Constance's sexual martyrdom to the martyrdom won by crusaders themselves, who are also, like Constance, travelers from their homelands suffering trauma, privation, and distress, in the service of God.

Trevet, Gower, and Chaucer all depict the Muslim Sultan's desire for Constance—the first royal male who longs for her is a Saracen—as documenting the triumph of Christian culture in performing not only the Sultan's conversion to Christianity but also the triumphant conversion of the natives to the Christian religion. Gower's narrator's Sultan arrives at the imperative of marriage-and-conversion on his own (ll. 620–29); Trevet's Sultan has to be helped to the recognition by negotiations at the state and papal levels (Bryan and Dempster, 166; Furnivall, 7), while the Man of Law's Sultan, badly afflicted by the lover's malady, explicitly understands that the marriage-cum-conversion he must undergo will be a form of capture: "I must be hers," he says ("I moot been hires" [*MLT*, l. 227]), "I may do nothing else." Though Constance is staged as a sexual, political, and religious martyr, a sacrificial lamb who pathetically goes to "the great Saracenland" ("la graunde sarazine" [Trevet: Bryan and Dempster, 165; Furnivall, 5]), "Barbarie" (Gower, l. 612), or "Syria" ("Surrye" [*MLT*, l. 134]) with reluctance, in tears, in utter wretchedness even, the narratives leave little doubt that a great religious and political victory has occurred with the sexual conquest of the Sultan by this maidenly innocent.

Bishops accompany Chaucer's "Custance" (*MLT*, l. 253) to the "Barbre nacioun" ("the Berber/barbarian/heathen nation" [*MLT*, l. 281]; Gower's and Trevet's Sultan gives hostages to the Christian Emperor, Constance's father (Gower, 632–33; Trevet: Bryan and Dempster 166; Furnivall, 7); and, most pointedly of all, in Trevet's *Cronicles*, Jerusalem is handed over by the Sultan to the Christians in exchange for the beautiful woman (Bryan and Dempster, 166–67; Furnivall, 7, 9). Trevet's account disentangles and surfaces most explicitly the crusading fantasy embedded in the Constance narratives, for after Constance leaves her family, people, and nation for the land of the Saracens, the Sultan relinquished the city of Jerusalem to the dominion of the Christians for them to inhabit, and granted liberty to the Christian bishops and to their clergy to preach, and to teach the peoples of his land the right faith, and to baptize, and to build churches, and to destroy the temples of Maumetry (Bryan and Dempster 166; Furnivall, 7, 9).[10]

We see that Constance's prospective union with the Sultan has achieved what a century and a half of crusades, after the loss of Jerusalem to Saladin, had conclusively failed to do: effect the successful transfer of the Holy City to Christendom, and purchase a workable peace that would guarantee "free passage to go freely and trade, and to visit the holy places of the Sepulcher, and Mount Calvary, and Bethlehem, and Nazareth, and the valley of Jehosephat, and all other holy places" (Trevet: Bryan and Dempster 166; Furnivall, 7).[11] Where large armies of men—kings, knights, barons, militant pilgrims of every class—have historically floundered, in waging war, a beautiful woman succeeds, wagering her sexuality, in cultural fantasy.

If the Constance romances make complacent the equation of war (a man's field of action) with sex (a woman's field of action), the conversion narrative in the Constance romances points with equal satisfaction to the transmogrification of large-scale, popular military enterprises into large-scale, popular *cultural* enterprises. The dream of re-creating a Latin empire in the East, given the *realpolitik* of the fourteenth century and after, translates, in the Constance romances, into a dream of religious conversion—European domination by cultural means. This importation of the impulses of empire into cultural production can be directly glimpsed in conversion narratives of the Constance variety after the westering of empire, or *translatio imperii*, had accomplished the economic ascendency of Europe. When the replication of colonial dominance in territorial and military terms falters, the preferred momentum of empire becomes cultural: ideological reproduction in the form of religious conversion.[12]

But why must the sexuality of Constance, the Christian princess who does not (herself) convert but who converts (others), be muted—unlike the sexuality of her Muslim counterparts—and a mere shadow or reflection of the desire of men (and women) who desire her? Leaving aside for the moment the medieval reverence for *ascesis* (an ideal inherited from the early church), and an antifeminist clerical and doctrinal tradition that discovered women as the site of too much sexuality conducing to sin (Jankyn, the clerkly husband of the Wife of Bath, typically names Delilah,

Deianira, Pasiphae, Clytemnestra, Livia, and Lucia, among others, as examples of excessive desire in women), we find that imaginative literature
occasionally—and chivalric romance frequently—enjoys suggesting that
good women might well be (to the delight of knights and others) desiring
agents. Hagiography, of course, follows the tradition of *ascesis* by vaunting
heroines evacuated of all longing except for the yearning after God. But
scholars have noted that Constance is not only stripped of carnal desire,
she is also granted an unusual degree of passivity, so that in some versions—Chaucer's is the prime example—the flatness of her characterization alienates our modern sensibility.

Trevet's and Gower's Constance is less passive by degrees than Chaucer's.
Trevet's Constance is a missionary, and thus highly educated, knowledgeable
in many languages (including, conveniently, Saxon English), and proselytizes
among merchant and noble alike (Bryan and Dempster, 165, 169; Furnivall,
5, 17). Palpably a female mendicant imagined by an English Dominican friar,
Trevet's Constance finds opportunities to work through the desire of others
for her, and she is capable of logical argument and of deploying a rhetoric of
emotions (and lies, where necessary); capable, also, of shoving a would-be
rapist overboard, into the sea.[13] Gower's Constance has at least a reassuringly humanized subjectivity as, in turns, a terrified victim, a tender mother, and
a wife, and displays some agency and forms of willed conduct. By contrast,
the Man of Law's Constance has been rightly read as an enigmatic cipher, a
self-masking blank for the fantasy of others, including her narrator (see, importantly, Wetherbee).[14]

Where the question of Constance's desire is concerned, a partial answer is to be found in the potentials of the Constance story for discourses
of empire and nation. A character in which desire is graphed not simply
as a gathering point, a mark for (the desire of) others, but is defined and
specified as intrinsic in the character (as with the Saracen princesses) en-
closes desire within a limit, a horizon that is determined by the desiring
agent's elaboration. To the extent that Constance is a blank, however, she
is, to my thinking, an invitation to write desire upon her, conducing to
the play of imagination. The very emptiness and availability of Constance
as a cipher attracts and invites response and a drama of speculation for audiences in and of the text; produces fantasy. While we are able to respond
with warmth to Gower's humanized Constance, and with admiration to
Trevet's erudite and plucky Constance, our responses are also framed by
the elucidations of these authors, by the lack of reticence that decides the
useful limits of fantasy.

Ironically, it is Chaucer's Constance ("Custance")—the blankest of blanks—who is the most effective writing surface for eliciting desire and fantasy, for reinscriptions of the character in different contexts. The desire to have her story, then—the desire that enables her story to be produced and manipulated—in part requires the eclipse of Constance's own desire. Characters, narrators, and authors desire Constance—act *on* her, desire *through* her, tug her story this way and that—in part because Constance's desire itself need not be negotiated, and operates as a soliciting blank. A Constance undistinguished by desire—and, I will show later, who signifies within a story-line that is also itself sparingly elaborated—is oddly useful to discourses of nation and empire. The less that is known about Constance, the more that can be gained with her story.[15]

But why does a *woman* occupy the center of fantasy in the Constance romances? For cultures in which masculinity is the dominant term in a normatively sexed drama of human identity, "woman"—allocated to the place of the other—functions as the locus of fantasy in the machinery of the psychic economy. Psychoanalytic theory teaches that the female is the means by which sexed and gendered identity—cultural identity—is organized, acquired, and maintained, however fictitiously or precariously, for the masculine subject. If masculine psychic identity, in its very construction and definition, is posited on, and derives from, manipulating "woman" in the drama of psychic fantasy, social life itself has traditionally shown that it, too, prefers to imagine its problems, and organize its imagination, through the signifying potentials of women, a habit of perception and manipulation that attests to an abiding conviction in many societies that women well serve to identify and locate the pressure points of collective culture. Women carry the burden of culture, then, on multiple levels. In literature, they constitute a figural presence through which the concerns, ideas, pressures, and values of a culture can be expressed, can signify. In history, women also implicitly or explicitly function as the touchstones and communicants of culture and cultural values: a fact registered in immigrant groups and settler colonies that begin to be seen as having a future and duration when women arrive to form families that entrench local existence, instantiating and consolidating community and continuity.

Medieval culture, then, merely replicates figural conventions when it deploys a gender system that sexes a land or city as a woman—Albin and Inge representing Albion and England (in the *Anonymous Short Metrical Chronicle*), for instance, or Emain Macha representing the eponymous site

in Ireland (Gantz, 129)—in narratives of settlement, origin, or rulership
where the rulers and settlers of territory are, of course, in the first instance
male.[16] If culture assigns genders to territory and rulership to describe the
libidinal cathexis between land and ruler, so also does culture assign gender values to geographical sites to describe the articulation of power binding disparate points on the map into intelligible relationship. Thus to the
West, the East, too, is a woman. Urban II, in Robert the Monk's report
of the pope's crusading address at the Council of Clermont in 1095, in recruiting knights and other militant pilgrims, is shown to display cunning
mastery of the motivational possibilities of feminine figuration, when the
pope blithely depicts Jerusalem and the Orient as a sensuous, inviting, and
fecund maiden in distress: a land "fruitful above others," a "paradise of delights," who "desires to be liberated," "asks succor," and "does not cease
to implore you to come to her aid" (Peters, *First Crusade*, 4).[17]

For those unmoved by the plight of nubile Oriental distress, Baldric of
Dol's account of the same historical occasion has Urban additionally pic-
turing the Eastern Church as a mother who needs rescue, a nursing mother, moreover, "who poured into your mouths the milk of divine wisdom"
and "from whom the joys of your whole salvation have come" (9). The
images that are set in play in these accounts of Urban's address milk the
erotic and affective attachments between the genders, between men and
women bound in heterosexual relations, in order to harness the power of
those libidinal attachments for political and military ends. Again, built
into the libidinal attachments organizing the genders is an unequal balance of power that allegorizes well the unequal geopolitical relationship
that is being sought in colonial movements.

That the East is a woman, therefore, owes little to Urban's unique genius. For a culture normatively organized as Occidental, the East orients
a fantasy function for the West that is proximately similar to the function
performed by "woman" in the sexed fabrication and maintenance of masculine identity. By virtue of its geographical distance and its mythological
proximity (in the European Middle Ages, after all, the terrestrial paradise
is found in the Orient), the East represents a space of special freedom and
fantasy within the Western imaginary: an exotic locale, safely elsewhere,
through which the European here-and-now may transact a variety of
imagined relations. Although cultural conventions that assign a sex to geography cannot, of course, be stable, in the cultural politics of romance,
geography and gender, sex and territorial space, neatly (if contingently)
coincide.

Constance, who is ostensibly Roman and Western European, comes with a halo of Eastern origins, as Trevet's *Cronicles* makes plain: Trevet's and Gower's Tiberius Constantius, "Roman emperor and father of the heroine, is a historical personage who reigned at Constantinople (not Rome), A.D. 578–82" (Schlauch, "Man of Law's Tale," 158), while "the name of Constance . . . suggests Constantia, daughter of Constantine (the Great)" (157), the imperial founder of Constantinople whose mother, Helena, is remembered in the name of Constance's cousin in Rome, a character called "Helen" in both Trevet's (Bryan and Dempster, 178; Furnivall, 43) and Gower's (l. 1200) stories.[18] The pretext that Constance is Roman and Italian, rather than Byzantine and Oriental, thus merely satisfies a cultural specification that this heroine of hagiographic romance should be an exemplar of Latin Christendom, for a fourteenth-century English audience, rather than a representative of deviant Greek Christianity with its schismatic heresies. In case the point is missed, *Florence of Rome*, an English romance of the fifteenth century, interleaves descriptions of its titular heroine's beauty with descriptions of the glorious beauty of Rome itself, a city the heroine is closely identified with; and both *Florence of Rome* and *Emaré* invoke the Latin Pontiff at regular intervals, to ensure we understand that it is Latin Christianity, and not the deviant Greek Church, which orients the religious culture and thus the normativity of their narratives.[19]

Nevertheless, *Emaré* very explicitly borrows the atmosphere of the Orient for *its* version of the Constance story, when the narrative repeatedly makes Emaré's cloak, sewn from a luxuriously exotic, embroidered, and bejeweled cloth from Babylon, into a synecdoche for Emaré herself, the luxuriantly beautiful and exotic wearer of the cloak. The interlocking of Western romance and Eastern locales surfaces in the very fabric of the cloth itself, which depicts famous Western and Eastern lovers from European romances visualized in the embroidery on the Oriental fabric's surface (*Emaré*, ll. 121–68). With the cloak wrapped around the heroine, desire for the woman, in the romance of *Emaré*, becomes indistinguishable from desire for the East, with its treasures and arts that are so intricately woven into the trophy of war that fits the heroine's body perfectly, a trophy that is an artifact of conquest and domination, and thus a symbol of Christian military might over the Orient. The King of Sicily ("Cesyle"), we are told, has wrested this artistic treasure from the Sultan of Babylon by "mastery" and "might" (ll. 172–74), and the king's son presents it as a tributary offering to the (Greek/Roman) Emperor, Emaré's father. This eminently legible garment—a priceless, peerless Oriental treasure created by a woman, an emir's ("amerayle") daughter—exhibits to all the men who rule kingdoms in the East and West the desirability of Oriental wealth and skill, and of the Orientalized female wearer who is indistinguishable from the exhibited treasure, as a prize.[20]

Nevertheless, the Eastern theme of Constance's origins (and Emaré's wardrobe) is cannily subdued and underplayed, receding into a background hum. When the story presents a Sultan as Constance's first ardent suitor, the heroine is instantly Europeanized instead by the presentation. That a Saracen should be depicted as uncontrollably desiring a Christian princess from "Rome," who is a virtual European, will strike no one as strange who is familiar with colonial and conquest literatures that depict native men as desiring the women of their colonizers: Racialized narrative encounters in which a fantasized inverse conquest, by the colonized, on libidinal terrain, gives symbolic utterance to the fears and desires of the colonizers themselves. The vaunted desirability of European colonial women (who are sometimes depicted as involuntarily attracting sexual violence by the colonized or, even worse, who are violated by their own sexual preference *for* the colonized) is moot testimony to the collective understanding that women are made to carry the responsibilities of culture on their bodies and in their sexuality. In the script of religion-as-colonization, Muslim and pagan men, of course, must desire Christian women; the medieval Constance narratives thus congenially depict a rich coincidence of *both* strains of desire, racial and religious, among the colonized, when they show the subjugation of Muslim royalty, abject with amorous longing for a Europeanized Constance, as a given.

But if the cultural invasion of Syria, Barbary, or Saracenland is accomplished through the figure of a woman—a reproducer of culture who carries the sign of reproduction in her very biology—the defense of Islamic territory and of the Muslim nation and religion is also mounted by a woman in the Constance narratives: the Sultan's nameless mother. As Constance is a woman who figures the powerful mobility of religious hegemony, the Sultaness (my naming follows the Man of Law's and Trevet's [*MLT*, l. 358; Bryan and Dempster, 167; Furnivall, 11]) is a woman who figures the power of a local culture to resist the foreign hegemonic invasion that Constance's arrival signals. This Saracen mother defends the nation of Islam's religious culture by sacrificing her own son and his retinue of converts to Christianity, even as Constance's father had sacrificed Constance to Christian ideological reproduction by sending his daughter forth as a missionary emissary.[21]

In the best biblical and chronicle traditions of massacres at feasts, the Sultaness has her son and his Muslim renegade cohorts slaughtered at a banquet she hosts, her actions earning her the swift, unmitigated censure of the narrators in the Constance story. Trevet, Chaucer's and Gower's source, foregrounds the unequivocally defensive nature of the Sultaness's act, mounted on behalf of her religion, "seeing that her religion/religious law was already on the point of being destroyed" ("veaunt que sa ley estoit ia en poynt destre destrute" [Bryan and Dempster, 167; Furnivall, 9]); but it is Chaucer's Man of Law who pays the Sultaness the compliment of condemning her as a "virago" even while he vilifies her as the "root of iniquity" and "a serpent under [the guise of] femininity" (*MLT*, ll. 359, 358, 360). Indeed, in usurping the functions of a man, acting mannishly and unnaturally for a woman and a mother, the Sultaness has also responsibly acted like the political and religious leader of the Islamic nation, by stepping into the role abdicated by her son, the colonized subject of his own irresponsible desire for a Christian woman.

Spared from the sword, Constance is set adrift on the sea by the Sultaness, and the woman from the East—the woman who *is* the East—washes up on English shores in Saxon Northumberland, where the first native she wins over to Christianity in pagan England is also—*voilà*—a woman, Hermengild, wife of the castellan who takes Constance into their household. In Trevet's *Cronicles*, Hermengild is so stricken with love for the foreign woman ("taunt fu de samour supprise" [Bryan and Dempster, 169; Furnivall, 15]) that she daily tells Constance there is nothing she would not do for the foreigner's sake, a declaration of love that Constance exploits by using the local woman's passion as a rhetorical wedge for evangelizing, and recruiting her to Constance's own religion. Constance's enunciation of her intention to recruit fixes the cultural capture of the native woman's identity with remarkable precision, as all difference of identity, and cultural distance between the two women, vanishes: "And since there is nothing that you will not do at my will," Constance tells Hermengild, "then you yourself will be such as I am" (Bryan and Dempster, 169; Furnivall, 15).

Hermengild's recruitment—accomplished explicitly, this time, by Christian overseas missionizing—is the critical gateway to a slew of further conversions: the religious recruitment of the castellan and his household, and, eventually, the recruitment of the king himself—a king who is the leader of his land—also through "great love (or passion)" ("grant amour" [Bryan and Dempster, 172; Furnivall, 25]) for the foreign woman.

Native culture in Saxon England has been rendered vulnerable to foreign cultural invasion, through a woman.

But if Constance is less covertly positioned now as a successful cultural contestant, seeking alliances and catechizing on behalf of her religion, it soon predictably develops, in this narrative diptych, that powerful resistance to the cultural conscriptions enacted by Constance is once again mounted by a symbolic woman: the formidable mother of the pagan king who weds Constance. Unlike the nameless Muslim mother who defends her nation and religion, the pagan English mother who defends both purity of royal lineage and religious fidelity in her homeland importantly has a name, Domild/Donegild (Trevet: Bryan and Dempster, 172; Furnivall, 27; *MLT*, l. 695).[22] Naturally, the unnatural Saxon mother-in-law is also vilified for her actions against Constance, who is, to her native eyes, a "foreign . . . creature" ("strange . . . creature" [*MLT*, l. 700]) of unknown lineage who is transforming the homeland's culture, household by household, and who has now borne a son, and thus planted the seed of cultural domination for future generations to come. Once again, Chaucer's Man of Law sees "mannysh" behavior in the mother's stratagems (*MLT*, l. 782)—usurpation of a king's function, from one point of view, or a ruler-like defence of the domicile and regnal *domus*, from another.[23]

With the Constance stories, late-medieval family/hagiographic romance has fascinatingly regraphed the historicity of Augustine's papally directed mission to England, to spread the Christian faith among the Anglo-Saxons, as a Roman/Greek princess's romance career of conversion, spontaneously accomplished through the private desire of others for her.[24] We also see in Constance's travel route, from the Mediterranean littoral to Western Europe, the plotted track of *translatio imperii*, and a fantasized retroactive projection, onto the Anglo-Saxon past, of an imperial genealogy and legacy for the kings of Northumberland. Geoffrey of Monmouth's twelfth-century fantasy of the imperial origins of Britain's monarchs has been matched, in the fourteenth century, by a late-medieval fantasy of imperial origins for Anglo-Saxon—that is, English—England. That the chief moments of cultural resistance, along Constance's itinerary, are also plotted through key (enemy) women speaks eloquently for the irresistibility of gender in romance figurations. Medieval romance, of course—as I argued in chapter 1—is a genre that finds in figures of gender strikingly conducive representational capital for its negotiations of the sociopolitical: negotiations that see, in women and their sexuality, the lineaments of a mobility that can be made to speak for a variety of issues and sociocultural contests.

Just as heiresses who represent territory are a plot staple of twelfth-century French romance—the period of the High Middle Ages, when crusades in the East and literature in the West dangled the lure of territory, represented by women, before the fascinated gaze of landless European chivalry—late-medieval English romances also feature women as representations that articulate contemporary obsessions over assets, cultural and financial capital, and socioeconomic advancement. We have seen that a Roman-Greek princess like Constance functions to figure the dissemination of religious hegemony and the economic ascendency of the West (the westering of empire) as conversion. We might also see, in such late popular romances as the *Squire of Low Degree,* that female characters—in the *Squire,* a princess of Hungary—can also serve to figure, and alibi, new capitalizations of wealth, and economic momentum and opportunity. In Hungary, it seems, it is a king's daughter's audacious desire that begins the economic adventurism of a modest representative of the middling gentry class (a "squire of low degree"), by starting him on the road to wealth and higher status with a capital supply of a thousand pounds, horse, armor, gold, and silver (ll. 252–54, 274, 574), and the proper instructions as to what goals he should achieve, and how. After appropriate narrative meanderings (during which *she*, not he, pays the price for the audacity to desire), the class representative's astoundingly passive adventure of upward social mobility is finally consolidated through marriage to her. Female erotic desire, having had suitable punishment dished out in the form of prolonged suffering by the heroine, is then fulfilled by securing male socioeconomic success with a lopsided marriage, in this romance's figural logic.

Even in chivalric re-creations like Malory's nostalgic compendium of late Arthurian romances, women locate and figure the pressure points of obsessions with wealth and power. The sheer ubiquity and omnipresence of quest maidens and enchantresses circulating in Malory's narrative—offering opportunity, accruing credit, and transacting a complex system of debt, repayment, and exchange in services—more than vestigially allegorizes the magical and otherwise invisible transactional power of *money*, and how money functions and flows in fifteenth-century English society. Through the agency of uncanny women who appear and disappear in narrative—bringing new power, presenting sudden opportunity, accomplishing a web of fluid, dynamic relations—the magic of money as an uncanny medium of circulation and exchange that produces tangible, material results can be intuitively rendered and grasped in the world of a chivalric narrative. Like the enigmatic magic of the Arthurian enchantresses, which also transacts tangible effects through intangible operations ungovernable by knights, cash and credit—under mercantilism, and in a universe of evolving financial instruments and relations—transact their effects in enigmatic exchanges that oft-times must seem sorcerously imponderable, arbitrary, and dangerously ungovernable by knights.[25]

Feminine figural performance in allegories of social and economic mobility in late-medieval romances trade, of course, on the traditionally anomalous and fluid position of women in the estates system of medieval feudalism—a system women were a part of and yet also undeniably apart from, in constituting a category of people who were both inside and outside the hierarchical orders structuring medieval society. With the unfixing of ranks and estates in late-medieval feudalism, and the advent of a proto-capitalism whose very conditions of existence were posited on, and reproduced, socioeconomic flux and mobility, the symbolizing usefulness of an identifiably female anomalousness and unfixability could, then, only intensify. In the labile, changing conditions of late-medieval feudalism, female figures suggesting volatility, by virtue of the traditional evasiveness of women's status—a slippery doubleness of social and economic positioning—must have seemed to answer well to expressional demands in the narration of a volatile process whose final shape and effects were yet unknown. The attraction of using female figures to give utterance to inchoate but coalescing ideas on the power of money, capital, circulation, and fluidity of status is easily intuited under the circumstances, and must have been considerable.[26]

Historically, at the same time, the prominence of female labor in certain English trades of the fourteenth century—such as the cloth industry—also raised the subject of feminized capital accumulation as a subset of the increased mobility, independence, and social circulation that followed from profitable labor, soliciting further the imagined association of women with wealth, and the power and portability convened by wealth. Literature throws up such memorable figures as the Wife of Bath, a former worker in cloth in whose person wealth, independence, and mobility expressly conjoin in volatile fashion. We note that *this* woman's economic mobility finds creative expression as an errant sexuality, freedom of movement, and penchant for pilgrimages—other mobilities—that happen to be financed by, and coincide with, her economic status. Indeed, the Wife of Bath's typicality, as an imaginary example of a successful female capitalist, might be feared as much as her supposed uniqueness in her time.

Significantly, guild-influenced or -controlled medieval drama found it
worthwhile and necessary to inveigh against women workers through an antifeminist rhetoric dressed up for the economically modern times: Noah's
wife, in the York and Wakefield cycles, for instance, is critiqued for refusing
to ascend the ark not only because she is a traditional figure of female dis-
obedience who is blindly bound to a rigidly pedestrian material realm but
specifically because—she says—she has "tools to truss," and is too dangerously and threateningly committed to her economic labor.[27] The productively profitable nature of feminine labor is registered by the fact that female
taxpayers of London in 1319 were largely "identified by name with a trade"
(Thrupp, 170), the "favorite trades" being "embroidery, the 'garnishing' of
cloth and wearing apparel with jewelry, and the manufacture of silk"
(170)—by coincidence or not, the very occupations at which Emaré, and the
emir's daughter who is Emaré's predecessor and alter-ego, excel, and for
which they are valued, in late-medieval English romance.[28]

The putative sexual mobility of women—dramatized so memorably in
the Wife of Bath's "wandrynge by the weye" (*Canterbury Tales, General
Prologue,* l. 467)—also plays into the equation when female figures are invested with allegorical significance in medieval romance. Medieval history,
literature, and canon law depict the sexual economy of women as trans-
gressively voracious in its processions of appetite, and its cunningly insistent passages—as, indeed, ungovernably mobile. Because of their imagined
sexual mobility (so conducive, in literature, to expressing mobility of other
kinds), medieval women were ritually forbidden to go on pilgrimages and
crusades, which, of course, did not prevent either an Eleanor of Acquitaine
or a Margery Kemp from following her desire—nor the ranks of nuns,
wives, laundresses, camp followers, aristocrats, and pious pilgrims whose
travels on crusade and pilgrimage are well documented.[29]

Revealingly, in contrast to history, the good Constance's travels in the
countries of hagiographic romance occur only in response to the desire of
others—desire for her, or that she leave their territory—and never issue at
her own initiative, pleasure, or the promptings of any perceptible sexuality on her part. Hagiography requires that feminine sexuality be stringent-
ly regulated, disciplined, and, preferably, effaced, and Chaucer's Man of
Law most congenially meets hagiographic obligations by leaching from
the heroine any taint or vestige of desire that might be even minisculely
suspected on Constance's part. In the marriage bed, the Man of Law's
Constance is the very picture of will-less and pleasureless conjugal resig-
nation, displaying an involuntariness that is almost tantamount to her sex-

ual victimization in a process that we would today call marital rape: "For thogh that wyves be ful hooly thynges, / They moste take in pacience at nyght / Swiche manere necessaries as been plesynges / To folk that han ywedded hem with rynges, / And leye a lite hir hoolynesse aside, / As for the tyme—it may no bet bitide" (*MLT*, ll. 709–14). This, then, is the price that is paid to have Constance be the ideal cipher, and for the story we have from the Man of Law, and Chaucer.

But one form of feminine sexuality is allowed Constance in all instances, which is required, in fact, by the story: a *reproductive* sexuality, the kind that transforms Constance from a solitary woman, who is the object of desire, into a tender, solicitous maternal subject. Significantly, the productive labor that hagiographic romance wants from a woman turns out to be *re*productive labor. While the economic labor of women may well be associated, in late-medieval Chaucerian England, with all the forms of mobility we have been considering, as we consider the utility and meaning of feminized figurations, the Constance romances show a canny understanding of just how much rhetorical force can be exercised by tapping into the deep cultural approval for traditional feminine roles, at *precisely* a time when traditional roles in social, economic, and occupational circumstances are rapidly undergoing change. Here, then, is revealed the power of a story that presents *a woman acting like a woman*, that invokes and exploits the "natural" role of a woman who behaves, not *contra Naturam*, like an ambitious economic agent or a virago, but like the Virgin Mary herself, whose own traditional delineation is affirmed by the elucidation of human surrogates who perform traditionally. In this story of love, it is Constance's reproductive sexuality that specifically induces the surfacing of another desire in narrative that must appear in the discourse of community: a desire depicted through the affecting, sentimental tableau of a mother and son upon the waters.

A FINE ROMANCE: WOMEN, CHILDREN, AND FAMILIES IN CHRISTENDOM AND ISLAM

Hagiography's gift to the genre of romance is a certain feminization and domestication of affect in narrative, and the center-stage role that can be played by a woman, and by domestic affection—sentimentality and melodrama, even—in plot. Women (and children) may feature, in this subspecies of romance, in a way that is not readily available in epic/heroic romances that depict war or in elite chivalric romances that depict the martial adventuring of individual (or a fellowship of) knights. In this, late-medieval hagiographic romance may well take its cue from a fourteenth-century historical phenomenon that David Herlihy, following André Vauchez, calls "the feminization of sainthood and sanctity" (*Households*, 129)—a statistical phenomenon in which the ratio of female to male saints increases exponentially from gender ratios of the same kind in earlier medieval periods (*Households*, 113)—a process that may have begun in the thirteenth century, but is certainly much in evidence in the fourteenth.

If sanctity and sainthood become associated with women in the late Middle Ages, and fuel the imagination of hagiographic romance, the metaphysic animating hagiography also allows for a certain expansion of the starring cast of romance characters to include women and children. For the model of relationship in a Christian metaphysic is the family: the Trinity as family, comprising Father, Son, and Holy Ghost, but also a trinity that, in the popular imagination, shades into the aureal image of the earthly Holy Family, another triad made up of the Christ child's human family members.[30] So persistently does a model of family underpin biblical narratives of all kinds that even the stern genealogies and tribes of the Judaeo-Christian Pentateuch are an agnatic history of the family as tribal community, a diachronic narrative of the family-tribe collected along the axis of patriarchal law and bloodlines.

Though Freud found his family romance in the stories of Oedipus and Moses, with their severe punishment of sons for sins against the father, the romance of the Holy Family plots a slightly modified trajectory of family associations. In this romance, an adult son voluntarily dies in cooperation with his divine father, a transcendent father absent from pedestrian daily life, while the human mother-son dyad, in scriptural and medieval cultural conventions, is little troubled by the prohibitive presence and censor of an earthly father. Despite the theoretical presence of Joseph, the foster father of Jesus in the Holy Family, it is the cult of the mother-son dyad, Mary and child Jesus, that was tenacious, widespread, and exercised a powerful hold on the imagination throughout the Middle Ages. Historians like Herlihy have found persuasive explanation for the totemic force of this enduring cultic phenomenon in the socioeconomic arrangements of the medieval family household, a household in which the (relatively young) mother was likely to be closer to her children than she was to her (relatively older) spouse, while the child was simultaneously likely to be closer to the maternal parent than to the father. Not until late in the Middle Ages, Herlihy suggests, did Joseph make much of an appearance in culture, and his cult, when it belatedly appeared, under prompting, might well have been the artificial manufacture of a few determined church ideologues: a reactive formation, perhaps, to counter the feminization of sainthood in late-medieval society (Herlihy, *Households*, 127–29).

By contrast to Joseph's delayed and assisted emergence, the organic popularity of the dyad of Virgin Mary and child Jesus attests the idea, in medieval Catholicism, that the primary family relationship is between mother and child.[31] As important as mariolatry—Marian devotion—was as a cultural phenomenon in the Middle Ages, Caroline Bynum and others have shown that motherhood was the overriding trope through which even celibate male officers of the church—bishop, abbot, monk, priest—recognized themselves and their pastoral mission (see Bynum, *Jesus as Mother*).[32] In the model of the Holy Family beloved to medievals, the third term, or paternal metaphor, that should enter to interrupt, and triangulate, the mother-child relationship constituted by the Virgin and Jesus is benignly filled instead by the role of the celestial Father-cum-impregnating-Holy Spirit, who exercises no domestic authority or prohibition in affective life: which is to say that in the romance of the Holy Family, a father is invisible, transcendent, and absent from the earthly realm of everyday emotions and everyday intimacy, absent from family life.

The Constance romances overwhelmingly bear out the primacy of the mother-child relationship as the fundamental and paramount family formation. Counterpointing Freudian scenarios of how sons must negotiate an entrance into identity through the violence of paternal prohibition against desire for the mother, the family unit of Constance and her son is not depicted as ever requiring paternal disruption or law for its teleological completion, nor does the infant abut against paternal will in his transition into his identity and cultural inheritance. Instead, adult males who try to occupy the position of an interrupting third term triangulating the dyad of mother and son are narratologically repulsed as outlaws—like the rogue knight and renegade who tries to rape Constance on her second sea voyage, when she is accompanied by Maurice, her child—or they are reprised as wholly temporary and contingent, like Aella, the Northumbrian king who is the biogenetic father of Maurice: a father absent for much of the story's time line and then quickly despatched through death, after the family's happy reunion, so that Constance may leave England and once more be with her son, as Maurice becomes the imperial heir in Rome, and subsequently emperor.

In medieval family/hagiographic romance, not only can you have your mother, and an empire, without punitive consequences—*without tragedy*—but your mother will be generously freed from her "thraldom" as a wife (*MLT*, l. 286) after her nine-month (Trevet: Bryan and Dempster 181; Furnivall, 51) or year-long (*MLT*, ll. 1143–44) conjugal reversion to your father, a gestation-length period beyond which the mother-son dyad may happily resume.[33] Not for nothing does the Roman senator say of Maurice, Constance's son, that the boy has a mother, but no father ("A mooder he hath, but fader hath he noon" [*MLT*, l. 1020]). Though the paternal post (in its harsh aspect of law-of-the-father) is left vacant for most of the story, however, the protective function and supplementary support rendered by paternity is thoughtfully allowed to be filled by more distant avuncular or grandfatherly figures—in the persons of the castellan/Constable who shelters Constance in England, and the Roman senator and his wife who house Constance and Maurice before their reunion with Aella and Constance's father, the emperor—and, ultimately, by Christ himself, as celestial father.[34]

The sine qua non in *this* family romance is, in fact, the imagined co-identity of mother and son, between whom little distance apparently exists. Maurice and Constance are so alike that they are virtual mirror images; and it is their deep likeness, their visual equivalence, that engineers the denouement of Maurice's recognition, first by Aella, then by Constance's father, who sees his long-lost daughter's face in his grandson's visage. "Now was this child as lyk unto Custance / As possible is a creature to be," the Man of Law tells us (*MLT*, ll. 1030–31); "he greatly resembled his mother" ("il durement resembla sa mere" [Bryan and Dempster, 179; Furnivall, 47]), relates Trevet's narrative, so that the boy's grandfather exclaims, "How marvellously this youth resembles my daughter Constance!" ("Com cel juuencel merueilousement resemble ma fille Constaunce!" [Bryan and Dempster, 180; Furnivall, 49]). Gower's narrator, Genius, perhaps best expresses the specular indivisibility of mother and son when he has Aella think to himself, on contemplating Maurice's face: "And in his face him thoghte als faste / He sih his oghne wif Constance; / For nature as in resemblance / Of face hem liketh so to clothe, / That thei were of a suite both" (ll. 1374–78).[35]

In suggesting that Maurice is Constance's flesh and spirit reembodied, rather than Aella's, the Constance romances, it seems, ignore received traditions in dominant culture that specify paternal parthenogenesis to reign supreme in matters of generation: the Aristotelian-influenced understanding that it is the man, and, even more importantly here, the king, and not his consort, who supplies the generative or active principle in conception, a biogenetic process in which a mother's contribution is usually traditionally minimized.[36] Instead, in the discourse resolutely established by the Constance group, the offspring of female reproductive sexuality is overwhelmingly the offspring of his *mother*. Biogenetically, in Maurice's self-identifying physical appearance; psychically and culturally, as the intimate nurturing and close instruction Maurice receives from Constance; in the father's disappearance from the son's life, and the representation of paternal return as a kind of hiatus in the mother-son relationship, after which that relationship easily resumes, romance trumps history and gives Maurice over to Constance, as her son, rather than his royal father's. Contrary to ruling biology, the Constance narratives resolutely elect to remain, and cavort, in the realms of the maternal imaginary.

The mention of Maurice's conception in the same narrative breath as the mention of Constance's wedding to Aella ("[he] wedded the maiden, who conceived from the King a male child" [Trevet: Bryan and Dempster, 172; Furnivall, 25]) also urges that motherhood, not wifehood, is the point of this marital union. The magic of sexual desire that produces marriage is magically transformed, in a quick turn of plot, into narrative desire for a family of mother and child. As if to confirm the urging, the king's mother's strategems soon isolate Constance and her infant from all human society, so that mother and child are all that remain to each other, as the two are cast adrift on a vessel that constitutes a time-honored allegorical convention for signifying trial, isolation, endurance, and divine agency and resolution in providential literature—a vessel on the waters.[37]

All narrative descriptions of mother and child at sea together are unanimously tender, even sentimental, in their treatment of the duo, happily locating parallels between this human pair and the divine family of Madonna and child Jesus—an allegorical similitude the *Man of Law's Tale* particularly exploits, in having Constance implore the Virgin for aid in terms that make parallels of shared plight and suffering impossible to evade (*MLT*, ll. 841–54). Constance is also shown, like the Virgin Mary in the sublime yet creaturely tradition of the medieval *Virgo lactans*, rising to the medieval maternal ideal of nursing her own infant, even in the exigent circumstances of their exposure at sea (Gower, ll. 1978–79; *Emaré*, ll. 657, 661–63).[38] Her tender ministrations to her infant, described with small differences from text to text, specify the human bonds of care and affection that bind the two together, and create human community.

At this quintessential moment of paired survival, when the simple society of Constance and Maurice together suggests both the Holy Family,
and a human family stripped to its basic, essential conditions, an allegorical structure may be sensed at work in the mutual interdependence of
mother and child, each of whom is intimately tied to the other, whom
s/he needs for sustenance and existence. Gower's Constance, careless of
her own life, sees her survival as imperative to ensure the survival of her
son (ll. 1071–79), while Emaré, who is afraid of the sea, finds in her nursing of her child the strength and distraction that help her to survive (ll.
655–57, 661–69). The *Cronicles*'s Maurice, at two years of age, helps his
mother's survival by serving as a pretext for her lies, when the would-be
rapist boards their vessel, enabling the vital delay and distraction that allows Constance to push the man overboard (Bryan and Dempster,
175–76; Furnivall, 35, 37). We are offered, in the interdependence of the
family constituted here by mother and son, a picture of the first, vital
community into which the human subject enters: the most basic and fundamental communal unit that ensures survival, relation, and meaning for
the human individual.

We also see in no uncertain terms that Constance, in moving from
one civilization to another, is consistently depicted as moving from one
family to another: from her own, imperial Byzantine family to the family of the Islamic Sultan and his mother and court; and thence to the
pagan English household of the castellan/Constable and Hermengild, in
Northumberland, and the royal family of Aella and Domild/Donegild;
thereafter Constance and Maurice, themselves now a family unit, travel
to the family of the noble "Roman" senator and his wife who are Constance's kinfolk, until Constance is able to reconstitute her family circle
of Constance-Maurice-Aella (the royal family of Christian Northumberland), and Constance-Maurice-Tiberius Constantius (the imperial family of "Roman" Christendom).

By a curious turn of cultural logic, then, the nations and religious
civilizations that Constance encounters in her travels are constellated in
these romances as *families*. Contests between religious laws and communities are also constellated as contests between, and within, families:
as inter- or intrafamilial struggles. Constance's family—Christendom—
sends her forth to win over the Islamic nation, which is represented as a
family deeply divided by Constance's entrance. Constance's arrival in
Syria/Barbary/Saracenland undoes from within the Muslim royal fami-

ly of Sultan and his mother, and an intrafamilial struggle ensues, which the Sultaness temporarily wins. In defending the *ummah* of Islam against the Christian intruder into the *domus* and domicile, the Sultaness must destroy her own integral family unit—an ominous portent of the future destruction of her kingdom-cum-religious community that will be visited by Constance's avenging family-cum-Christendom.[39] Later, in pagan England, Donegild defends *her* religious community and household from the Christian intruder also by dividing up a family, the family formed by Constance-Maurice-Aella, and thus denying her son, Aella, his son, Maurice.[40]

Why families? Christian tradition and allegory, of course, privilege the family as a narrative model; the family *in* Christ is a logical and mystical extension of the family *of* Christ, a logic and mystery intensified by persecutions visited on early Christians, the closeness of whose bonds in suffering constructed the family of Christendom in affective, as well as spiritual and organizational, terms. Accordingly, the Constance stories make it plain that Christendom *is* a family in medieval English romance.[41] Trevet's *Cronicles*, after depicting God's intervention to defend Constance in a moment of trial, has Him announce (in Latin, *ex caelo*) that Constance is "filiam matris ecclesie," "the daughter of mother church" (Bryan and Dempster, 172; Furnivall, 25). Picking up his cue, the Man of Law has the Virgin Mary protectively oversee and shape the ecclesiastical daughter's destiny, to save Constance from the would-be rapist and bring her safely home again, and "out of woe" (*MLT*, ll. 920ff., 950–52, 977–78), back to Christendom and the bosom of the family that originally sent her forth. But if the church is the institutional mother and the Virgin Mary the divine mother, Constance is the human mother whose affectionate, protective relationship with her child allows the imagined community of Christendom to come to fruition in the most immediately accessible, and poignantly intimate terms, as a family.[42]

Once configured, this model of the family as the first human community becomes immensely portable and resonant in the lexicon of romance-as-community-narrative. For if the family can figure the imagined community of Christendom, it can also serve to position and facilitate the narration of other imagined communities as well: and the usefulness of a constituency of family-cum-hagiographic romances in late medieval England becomes clear when we consider the instrumentality of their service to discourses of the medieval nation.

The Family of the Nation: Imagining the Medieval
Community through Maternal and Family Relations

Historically, the moments at which the feminine and the maternal are most prominently vocalized in culture often arrive as moments in which the conditions of nationalism, or early nation formation, are being researched or assiduously advanced in social collectivities. I have argued elsewhere that a nationalist imaginary at key junctures requires figures of maternity and family to instantiate concretions of feeling and thought whose momentum cannot be easily harnessed by other means. Thus it is that postmedieval, modern nations-in-making conjure with the idea of a "mother country" or "motherland" (for a people to defend or separate from), an originary "mother culture" (to establish descent, return, or the necessity of breakaway revitalization/modernization), or a "mother tongue" (a unity of speakers to vocalize collective identity). The vocabulary of gender may also instantiate family figures of related kinds: "founding fathers," "sons of the soil/land/nation," "brothers-in-struggle" (a variant of the more military "brothers-in-arms"), "the brotherhood of man," "sacrificial sons," "women and children," and so forth.

Nations are, of course, abstract entities that are notoriously difficult, if not impossible, to imagine *ex nihilo*, without exemplars; and the emotions and ideas that must collect, in order that the imagined community might be generated, require for their organization models of interrelationship and meaning of widespread familiarity and immediacy. A family, by the very nature of its existence as the first society into which the human subject enters, serviceably provides a ready-made cluster of associations, memories, roles, and affects that can be usefully channeled by social discourses on behalf of larger formations. Symbolic identities, positions, and roles from family life mediate, then, the emergence of a consciousness that can be mustered for national impulses; often the symbols appear at a formative stage, and are periodically resorted to thereafter when the nation's collective identity needs to be recalled, freshened, or redirected.[43]

The nexus of family figures thus produced form a matrix, in culture, that proto-nationalist discourse, or the imagined community of the nation, may tap for its expressional vocabulary both at a nascent stage and thereafter—a flexible cultural trove that performs alongside the more obvious forms of collective mobilization and transformation. Even today, centuries after the creation of the United States, arguments over the American nation—its meaning, future directions, its very identity—invariably take the form of an urgent contest over the symbolic terrain of "family values," while prominent families, like the Kennedys, seem to the nation to identify its best aspirations and ambitions, its utopian self, in some resonant, if also quasi-subliminal fashion: the romance of the Kennedy family, and their Arthurian "Camelot," seeming to guarantee, for example, that the U.S. national narrative is cast as romance, and not tragedy.[44]

Coincidentally, the medieval church, which also taps the symbolizing potential of family roles, relationships, and identities in efforts to unify the far-flung, diverse Christian community and to express pastoral care and feeling, has been seen by historians like Bartlett as also tapping into the resources available to nationalist culture, impulses, and discourse before, during, and after the rise of nations in Europe. The medieval Church functions, as it were, like a nation; or, to put it another way, Church and nation are much alike in fostering particular cultures of ideology and motivation. In the Constance romances, we have seen how Christendom, Islam, and the pagan community of English Northumberland are characterized as at once religions, lands, communities, and families, with no distance apparently existing to distinguish the separation of categories whose usefulness for cultural fantasy lies in their flexible similitude.

Constance's reproductive sexuality and maternity devise a special kind of productive hypothesis, then, for a nationalist imaginary, a hypothesis with two stages. The first stage begins when a foreign princess, representing an ancient empire, marries a local king of England, and symbolically creates a royal-imperial tie, through love and conjugal union, which links the local domicile to the ancient civilization of "Rome"/Greece. With the conversion of the king as a condition of marriage, Constance's arrival on English soil thus issues, in effect, a narrative of re-origin for the local community: a community that now gains new life and identity by its entrance into Christianity, marked by the new religious culture that has overtaken its king and key households in the land. The moment of modernization established by transforming pagans into Christians is consolidated and given a future with the birth of a boy-child who links two dynastic houses, royal and imperial, in the West and in the East, creating a new blood pedigree that will furnish an impeccable future genealogy for the re-imagined local community.

In the way it unobtrusively performs a myth of re-foundation—of a new, alternative starting-point—for what will eventually be the Christian England that will emerge in Trevet's, Chaucer's, and Gower's time, Constance's story functions like the Christian counterpart, for fourteenth-century

England, of Geoffrey of Monmouth's classical foundational myth of Britain from Troy, in twelfth-century Anglo-Norman England: one explanation for the popularity of the later, as well as the earlier, story. In its first stage, then, the productive hypothesis engineered by the Constance story in the fourteenth century argues for the importance of imagining a new beginning for the English community's past, and, simultaneously, also argues for the importance of establishing that newly re-modernized community as nonetheless also existing in integral continuity and unbroken progression with ancient, time-honored civilization, a civilization with the halo of empire.[45]

A Roman/Greek princess who Christianizes, marries, and becomes the mother of a child, Constance ideally embodies past, present, and future, all rolled into one beautiful emblematic bundle through the twists and turns of desire. Because the re-foundation of a community is always a catachrestical moment—a moment of bringing into being what had not existed before, with all the anxieties that attend (self) invention—the communal rebirth can be staged with resonant reassurance by figuring it through the traditional symbolism of reproductive maternity, the maternity of an iconic woman. Also because it is a catachrestical, and therefore an anxious, moment, the new beginning—a break that marks an entrance into modern time—has to be paradoxically presented as really continuous with older time, with the authentically ancient past, in a fictive time line that presents the modern as essentially continuous, and in conformity, with premodernity.[46] For a nationalist imaginary, the most useful narratives are those that tell of the break which establishes the newly modern community, and yet manage to claim and retain for the new community the magisterial authority of the past, in a willed double gesture of recitation.[47]

We see, through the Constance romances, that desire and fantasy are deeply implicated in imagining communal formations. In these romances, one form of desire seems to induce another, so that desire mutates and proliferates productively. Domesticated through marriage, sexual desire becomes harvested in the Constance story as an erotics of maternal desire which itself comes to teleological focus in a desiring family narrative; slippage in the chain of desire arranges, finally, for the interwoven, multiple strands of desire animating the plot to be placed at the service of a communal narrative. In the order of the imagination, moreover, the rhetoric of love for a homeland that is larger than tribe, region, or city requires a degree of fond fantasy—a way of imagining associative relationship and close bonds among people with little in common—which can be evoked through *eros*, and the idea of home and family, since lovers and family members are, after all, traditional signifiers of belonging (and of longing).[48]

For those not repulsed by Freudian logic, "das Heim," the home, also leads back to the mother's body and to her reproductive sexuality, to the womb that is the first home of all, and the anchor of every impulse of belonging. An imagined sense of connectedness, of associative relationship, rooted in land and figured in family, therefore inevitably takes the form of a story of love. Desire—erotic, familial—functions, then, as "shorthand for human association" (D. Sommer, 32); and desire, it has been argued, is "the underlying principle of all social formations" (32). The Constance romances enable us to see that many kinds of desire feed into the national story: the private desire of a king; the solicitude of the loving mother; the intense compassion that the local populace show Constance and her babe when this family of two is unjustly persecuted; even, in the first originary instance, the passion of one woman for another woman, when the native Hermengild is won over by the foreign Constance.[49]

The second stage in the Constance story's productive hypothesis is reached when the various forms of personal and private love are taken up and translated into an intense and shared public passion that erupts when the plight of Constance and her child is disclosed to the public. Trevet's *Cronicles* shows us that a surge of popular feeling forcefully arises and gathers momentum, once the maltreatment of Constance and Maurice, engineered by Domild but blamed on Aella, becomes known, a feeling that spontaneously organizes a mass critique of the king by all peoples in the land, "rich and poor, old and young" living in urban centers, even as it coalesces around the figure of mother and infant:

> And so much grief and crying and weeping was in city and town, by rich and poor, old and young, when they heard the sorrowful news, that no heart can comprehend it; for all the people lamented her. . . . everyone cursed King Aella.

> (E taunt de dolour e crie e plour fu en cite e ville, de riches e pouerez, veuz e joeuenes, quant oyrent de la dolorouse nouele, qe nul qoer ne le puet comprendre; qar toute gentz la weymenteient. . . . al rei Alle touz mauudisoient. [Bryan and Dempster, 175; Furnivall, 33])

The very mariners who tow Constance's and Maurice's ship out to sea are grief-stricken, feelingly commend Constance to God, and anxiously pray that she may return again to the land with joy ("qe vnquore peust ele a joie a la terre retourner" [Bryan and Dempster, 175; Furnivall, 33]), a comment on the king's injustice. As collective emotion masses around Constance and her babe, the universality of feeling against the hapless king is so overwhelming that the narrative tells us Aella and his army are forced to travel by night because of the hostility of the united populace, a populace whose strength of response on behalf of mother and child subjects the king to gross humiliation and public abuse:

> And as the King went his way through cities and towns, by day, in England, men and women came against him, children and old folk, and reviled him with crying and reproaches, throwing on him and his men mud and ordure and great stones, and women and naked children showed him their *derrière*, in scorn.

> (Et com ly rois erra soun chemyn par cites e viles, de iour, en Engletere, luy vindrent encountrauns hommes e femmes, enfauntz e veilars, e le reuilerent de crie e ledengge, gettauntz sur lui et les seuns tay e ordure e grosses peres, e femmes e enfauntz deuestuz par despyt luy moustrerent lour derere. . . . [Bryan and Dempster, 176; Furnivall, 37])

In this astonishing portrait of group unity, where women and children insult their king with the eloquent mockery of their rear ends, we are shown romance operating in cultural narration's most active mode: as a participant in cultural history, a history that the interventions of romance help to shape. For the supremely important, overriding suggestion here— what I have been calling the productive hypothesis that romance makes available—is that *immense group power resides in consent, as opposed to coercion.* Coercion, a ruler's prerogative, is what has created here the pathetic spectacle of a victimized woman and infant whose victimization the community of the ruled vehemently opposes, and to which it spontaneously and overwhelmingly reacts. By contrast to the power of coercion vested in the traditional institutions of a kingdom, the wave of opposition that washes over the startled king discloses the power of public consent to a view that is freely assumed and arises organically from the community, without force. Notably, if "politics is a process of discussion that demands dialectic, public criticism of public proposals . . . a way of ruling divided societies without undue violence" (Hannaford, 10, quoting Bernard Crick), then progress is made toward accomplishing a national politics in a community that is as divided as late-medieval England, when the drama of public criticism is rendered in so visible and unexceptionable a form—as it is here—through a collective critical response deemed impeccably just.

We have seen that in a popular romance conventionally featuring a male hero at center stage, like the Middle English *Richard Coer de Lyon*, the idea that disparate classes, ages, and orders of people can unify if there is an overriding cause had required rousing elements of crusading warfare, foreign soil, overseas military invasion, and a foreign enemy (the Duke of Austria) to accomplish. In pointed contrast to *RCL*'s military forms of class dissimulation, the Constance group brings the important fiction of collective unity—the projective idea, critical to proto-nationalist discourse, that universal interests exist that can cut across stratifications of caste/class in feudal society—closer to hearth and home, back to domestic soil. The Constance story suggests that unity may be an organic community response to the victimization of two innocents symbolizing domesticity and family, a woman and infant who figure continuity with ancient civilization as well as a new beginning in the land.

That "the land" which the Constance narrative has in mind is really the proto-nation of *England*, and not merely sixth-century Saxon Northumberland, is seen in the slippage that occurs when the *Cronicles* tells us Aella travels through *England* and is reviled throughout the domain.[50] Our story's insistence that a universal response can be culled from diverse communities and sectors of the public—men and women, children and old folk, rich and poor, in city and town—issues a cultural signal, detectable also in other non-elite Middle English romances at this time, that cues us to the project of representing an emerging polity, and political relationships, among diverse strata of society not linked by blood or obvious common interests.

The fiction of associative unity is most explicit in Trevet's narrative, but the Constance family of texts in general share the strategy. Though the *Canterbury Tales* commonly depict heterogeneity in popular opinion, for instance ("diverse folk diversely they said" is a common note in the *CT*), the *Man of Law's Tale* shows "yonge and olde" alike weeping, "whan that the kyng this cursed lettre sente" (*MLT*, ll. 819–20), so that even the constable, who is the king's agent and surrogate, supplicates God in consternation, asking how He can allow "wikked folk" to "regne in prosperitee?" (*MLT*, l. 816). In *Emaré*, too, neither old nor young can stop weeping (ll. 610–11); there is "sorow and mych woe" when the heroine and her child board the ship, and people weep and wring their hands (ll. 637–39). As the ship departs, men collapse and faint on the sand, weep bitterly again, and condemn Emaré's treatment, saying, "Accused be evil deeds" (ll. 645–48), a dangerously treasonous-sounding judgment, given the popular conviction that the evil deed at hand issues from the king.[51]

In *RCL*, the figure chosen to represent the imagined community of diverse classes of Englishmen is the obvious and traditional one: a crusader-king at the apex of English society. The *Cronicles*, however, shows what can be gained when tradition is displaced by hagiographic romance's preference for a woman and infant at center stage: a special brand of horizontal leveling arranged through a critique of kings imagined as tyrannous. In the spectacle of a monarch who is abjectly humiliated, brought low, by his people for acts of social injustice so that he is forced to travel covertly by night, under cover of darkness, like an outlaw or a common thief, to conceal himself from the censure of a united populace, the right of a people to accuse a king over an issue of social justice becomes the ideational cement of mass unity denominating the common interest of all groups. Part of the foundational myth supplied by the arrival of Constance and Maurice for a proto-nation-in-making is precisely this important universalizing fiction of an emergent discourse: the hypothesis that a community of people can unify for an innate principle of social justice that not even a king may gainsay—a communal act conveniently vindicated, in narrative, by Constance's hagiographic and imperial status. In medieval discourses of the nation, universalizing fictions only assume ever greater authority when they are backed by Christianity and a dream of continuity with empire.

For the nationalist imaginary, the insight that power resides in *consent,* not in coercion, is a triumphant and powerful, indeed a key, moment. Representing an insight into the kind of bonds that must unite the would-be nation, this particular enabling fiction displaces power away from kings and onto the collective will of the community. In addition, collective will is here usefully essentialized—romanticized by romance—as organic to the people, and not imposed from above nor canvassed. In the scenario given to us by the Constance group, behind the story of an imagined community lies the story of a collective power that organically manifests itself and strategically—unthreateningly—appears to have no ostensible force at all, because the power in this story only seems forceful to those who consent to it. Issuing by itself, uncoerced, the power of the community that is enacted in the harassment of a king enforces none who do not consent; and the immense force that a collective feeling, universally felt, possesses, the power it is able to muster, thus appears not under any recognizable aspect of force at all.[52]

Avant la nation, it seems, national subjects are imagined to emerge, who are linked by key recognitions of what constitutes justice and common interest, in a context suffused with intimations of how a relationship to power might be reimagined. The fecund soil that delivers the emergence of national subjects is, naturally, the will of the people expressing itself in response to an affective symbol of human community under duress. We see how a fantasy such as this tacitly institutes and advances, while it purports merely to represent, important ideas and formulas in cultural thinking, laying the groundwork for the kind of imaginative understanding that conducts the emergence of nations. What I have been calling "thinking" need not, of course, surface to consciousness, as such, for group or individual in the late-medieval English community. Indeed, of tendencies in the cultural imaginary, scholars remark that "no one . . . need be conscious of these forces in order to be caught up in them, in fact it helps to be *not* conscious of them" (MacCannell and MacCannell, 218).

Here again is explanation for why desire should not be located in Constance, as much as it should be spied in characters who are *not* Constance—who are outside her and constitute her audience—for passion settled on these others, and read there, offers medieval readers valuable sites of identification: an identification that productively helps to engineer consent (and a consensus) among the audience *of* the texts, by manipulating the audience *in* the texts. From the cipher that is Constance (a zero to be filled in) and the parsimony of her story, multiple invitations radiate and beckon. For the purposes of a nationalist imaginary, a sketchy character and story line exercise special stimulus, solicit cultural participation, to fill in the blanks. Indeed, in this respect, a fully developed story and complex characters shut out, rather than invite in; the popularity of the Constance saga, and the number of writers' talents it attracts (each with his or her own audiences), suggests the importance of not overelaborating any narrative that would be useful to the nation.

WHY GRISELDA IS PATIENT; OR, RE-IMAGINING THE MEDIEVAL COMMUNITY THROUGH FIGURES OF CLASS

The story that the imperial princess, Constance, and her native-born babe make available to nationalist impulses satisfies one urgent requirement in myths of re-foundation, but at the expense of another requirement. The role of an imperial princess from ancient civilizations reassuringly offers a fiction of continuity in the moment of offering, too, the fiction of a new beginning. But the figure of a high-born princess can ultimately do little to suggest how the traditional divides of medieval society might be crossed—a future that must be imaginable if a nation is to be accomplished—beyond the exquisite moment of collective response galvanized spontaneously on her behalf. Another key family romance, then—also featuring a woman and her offspring—must step in where the Constance story does not go: Griselda's story, in the *Clerk's Tale* of the *Canterbury Tales*, also offers the lesson of "an allegorical relationship between personal and political narratives" (D. Sommer, 41), and re-imagines the medieval community anew, but *specifically in the social-economic categories impossible to depict* under the enabling conditions of the Constance saga.

Like the narrative of Constance, Griselda's is also a domestic story of a persecuted innocent, a story with equally wide currency in the fourteenth century, and rewritten many times.[53] The English account of this particular family romance, the Chaucerian Clerk's, is as important, in different and related ways, as the romance of Constance. Here, too, the idea of a re-beginning for an imagined community appears—though following the story's Italian literary sources, the community is ostensibly that of Saluzzo, in northern Italy, instead of medieval England—and a population unites with a single voice, on significant occasions. Here, as well, a political fable is couched as a domestic fable; and a woman and her reproductive sexuality again stage the public conundrum and drama of community.

The re-origin imagined by Griselda's story is a radical one: the idea that a village woman representing the lowest socioeconomic rank can ascend to rulership through male desire for her and, in the process, produce a future in which heirs of mixed-class ancestry—socioeconomic mongrels—can rule without objection or censure. Though the Clerk does not say whether Griselda is of free or unfree status, the repeated attention to her abject poverty and the radical humbleness of her station and bloodlines (Griselda's father is the poorest man in a humble village of poor folk) makes the marriage of the Marquis, Walter, with the villager, Griselda, a fantasy which insists that centuries-old class hierarchies can be ignored, and set aside, if conditions of virtue, justice, and worthiness warrant change, thus awarding this tale a visibly allegorical status in late-feudal society.

To authorize the union of classes across a socioeconomic chasm, and render union imaginable, religion and individual moral worth—of the kind advocated by the hag in the *Wife of Bath's Tale*—are specifically invoked for the woman representing subalternity. Griselda is outlined, like Constance, as virtuous (and virtuously beautiful) beyond the ordinary and, like Constance, also in such terms as to make her resemblance to the Virgin Mary impossible to miss.[54] Religion, again, helps to make a new kind of society imaginable, a society in which a class hybrid like Griselda's and Walter's son can ascend to rulership, in his time (*Clerk's Tale*, ll. 1135–36), and be praised as morally superior to his father, the traditional aristocrat, in the treatment of *his* spouse (*Clerk's Tale*, l. 1138), while the boy's equally hybrid sister is able to marry one of the worthiest lords of all Italy (*Clerk's Tale*, ll. 1131–32). And, once again, a narrative of community depicts desire as mediating the relations of power between groups of unequal status, this time articulating the dramatically unequal relationship between class communities in medieval society.

If we look at the structure of the Griselda story, which imagines a society in which the poorest and humblest villager succeeds in spreading her biogenetic stock among the rulers of Italy, we understand why it is that Griselda must be made to suffer so in her marriage to an aristocratic husband who torments her with unspeakable "tests" of her patience, constancy, and obedience: For the structure commands a narrative price that is paid for with Griselda's suffering. The spectacle of innocent and steadfast wifely pathos, then, distracts attention away from Griselda's ascent, and the ascent of her children, up the feudal hierarchy, while pity for the staunch heroine attenuates the threat of her low-born family's admission to power and authority. Finally, as our gaze is held by the sensational spectacle that concentrates intense affectivity in the foreground, the admission of Griselda's children to rulership unobtrusively arrives as a fait accompli.

Once we look past the melodrama of masculine sadism and feminine endurance—Walter deprives Griselda of the childhood of her children and has her believe that they have been put to death at his command; repudiates her as a wife in favor of a projected marriage with their own daughter; and obscenely makes Griselda prepare the household, chambers, and "beds" (*Clerk's Tale*, ll. 960, 975) for her putative replacement's arrival—we are able to discern, in the overarching organization of the narrative, that the terms of the feudal contract between ruler and ruled have been radically rewritten with the introduction of Griselda. Here, then, is another cipherlike saintly woman desired by a male ruler, a woman who is again empty of all desire of her own but for a maternal love she involuntarily betrays, as it were, against her will, and that derives from her successful reproductive sexuality.

At his end of the new feudal contract, Walter's depiction argues for the inadequacy of traditional rulers, who are critiqued through Walter's behavior. Praised only conventionally and perfunctorily, this dynastic-aristocrat-as-ruler is never complimented without simultaneously being criticized. When he first appears, he is so absorbed in hunting and hawking—the usual aristocratic pastimes—that he lets his responsibilities slide, for "on present pleasure was all his thought" (*Clerk's Tale*, l. 80). Walter has to be politely urged by his people to marry in order to assure continuity of government through an heir. His decision to marry a low-born woman, in response to that popular urging, seems, then, a halfway-spiteful reaction to being reminded of his duties—duties that Walter is apparently willing to fulfill but apparently not in the way his people expect.

Deliberately, the marriage is cast, from its very beginning, in terms of a contract in which the husband has the absolute authority of a feudal overlord who is not checked by parliamentary, juridical, or indeed any law external to his will. Griselda, his humble subject, is installed as a feudal subaltern bound to servile obedience by the contractual terms of the union to which she technically, if fearfully, consents.[55] The conditions of Griselda's subjection in marriage echo and exemplify Constance's insight that "women are born to thralldom . . . And to be under man's governance" (*MLT*, ll. 286–87): an insight that argues for the uncanny resemblance between an enserfed underclass in feudal society and the position of the woman within the bonds of marriage. The analogy here between marital and feudal "thraldom" is deliberately exaggerated for the purposes of cultural fantasy, so that Griselda swears absolute obedience and asks nothing in return, not even sustenance, in the unequal "alliance": the oddly political description Walter applies to his impending marriage. Here, once again, a libidinal economy is depicted as coterminous with a political economy, and the two systems are symbolically partnered as mutually constitutive, mutually expressive, analogues that find appropriate articulation in domestic space: in the public-private arrangement known as marriage.[56]

What does a narrative accomplish when it depicts feudal relations and the feudal economy through a symbolic marriage? Griselda, the low-born subject Walter chooses, is soon praised, after her marriage, in terms that give us to understand that it is *she*, and not the natural aristocrat, Walter, who is the ideal governor of the people. This woman of "low degree" (*Clerk's Tale*, l. 425) knows how to promote the common good, we are told ("The commune profit koude she redresse" [l. 431]), wisely ensure peace when there is "discord" or "rancor" "in al that land," and unite people and

bring them to agreement with wise words and judgments of "greet equi-
tee" or fairness, so that men think she is sent from heaven to save people
and right every wrong:

> Nat oonly this Grisildis thurgh hir wit
> Koude al the feet of wyfly hoomlinesse,
> But eek, whan that the cas required it,
> The commune profit koude she redresse.
> Ther nas discord, rancour, ne hevynesse
> In al that land that she ne koude apese,
> And wisely brynge hem alle in reste and ese.
>
> Though that hire housbonde absent were anon,
> If gentil men or othere of hir contree
> Were wrothe, she wolde bryngen hem aton;
> So wise and rype wordes hadde she,
> And juggementz of so greet equitee,
> That she from hevene sent was, as men wende,
> Peple to save and every wrong t'amende.
>
> (428–41)
>
> Not only this Griselda through her wisdom
> Knew all the accomplishments of housewifely duties,
> But also, when that the occasion required it,
> The common good was she able to redress.
> There was not discord, rancor, (n)or heaviness
> In all that land, that she knew not to appease,
> And wisely bring them all to rest and ease.
>
> Though that her husband were absent at once,
> If gentle men or others of her country
> Were wroth, she would bring them to unity;
> So wise and ripe words had she,
> And judgments of such great equity,
> That she was sent from heaven, as men thought,
> People to save and every wrong to amende.

Even as Griselda is described as a tireless advocate of the common weal,
a force for peace and concord, and the embodied guarantor of public wisdom and justice, we are not allowed to forget that she is equally gifted at

fulfilling domestic duties of home and hearth, and all wifely responsibilities ("al the feet of wyfly hoomlinesse"): The good wife vanishes into the
good administrator of the public realm, without difference, and the two
roles are shown here as compatible, natural, and coterminous. Low-born
Griselda, depicted in the extraordinary role of public administrator and advocate ("when the circumstances required it" and when "her husband was
absent") is praised far more warmly in the story than is Walter, depicted in
his public role. It seems that the lowliest subject may know better than the
ruler, and perform more admirably, and morally, when the opportunity for
such performance arises in the public sphere.[57]

The political allegory set in place by Griselda's example is aided, I have
said, by narrative invocation of Griselda's likeness to the Virgin Mary—a
sanctified and traditional figure of intercessory agency—though Griselda's
actions push, in their consequences, far beyond mere traditional wifely intercession with her husband on the people's behalf.[58] Indeed, Griselda acts
in place of Walter, not through him, but like a surrogate or regent; and it
is very noticeably only *her* public activity that is singled out for extravagant praise. When Walter is not lauded in turn (except for his "prudence"
in marrying such a remarkable woman), the fantasy of class equivalence—
or, rather, the fantasy of underclass superiority—in matters of competen-
cy is unavoidable. Indeed, the representative of the underclass in this
feudal-marital arrangement is glorified at the expense of the traditional dynastic ruler, who appears the less worthy by contrast.

Moreover, like Constance, Griselda occasions a unity of response
among the community at large, for people unanimously love and value
her: "to every creature she has grown so dear" ("to every wight she woxen
is so deere" [*Clerk's Tale*, l. 400]); "if one spoke well [of her], another said
the same" (l. 417); "each loved her who looked on her face" (l. 413); and a
diversity of people, "men and women" alike as well as "young and old,"
are drawn to her from beyond even Saluzzo, as her reputation spreads (ll.
418–20).[59] The unanimous popular opinion on Griselda's behalf positions
her, in the political allegory of this romance, along similar coordinates as
Constance (the lowly Griselda even seems to the populace to have been
"nourished in an emperor's hall" [l. 399] like the imperial Constance).
The web of textual relations between the two sets of family romances can
also be glimpsed when Emaré, in the Constance group, makes Griselda-
like claims to putatively low birth, in dissimulating her own imperial identity ("he weddede so porely / on me a sympull lady" [*Emaré*, ll. 631–32]).
And like Griselda, Florence of Rome, another saintly Constance model,

also shows *her* spouse how to behave correctly, as a ruler should (*Florence*, ll. 2134–36).

The modernized community that begins in the radical break from the past instituted by the symbolic union of the ruler with a woman of "low degree" (*Clerk's Tale*, l. 425), in the Griselda story, also enshrines continuity, alongside modernization, by not breaking with the feudal model of governance in its fundamental structure. Though Griselda's stock comes to rule Saluzzo and marry into the highest dynastic houses of Italy, the community that is imagined as flexibly allowing for extreme social mobility is still a community of the realm—or, rather, in this instance, still a marquisate—and not a republic; the polity remains, that is, a recognizably medieval (and not a modern) imagined political community, by necessary design.

The Clerk's Griselda story, moreover, shows a discretionary tact—or a loss of nerve—when it depicts the populace as also capable of being deceived and swayed by Walter in his machinations against Griselda. The people initially champion her vociferously, as one of their own, when Walter first begins his series of sadistic torments (ll. 722–31), condemning the ruler's arbitrary tyrannies out of hand (ll. 722–31); eventually, however, they are tricked, along with Griselda, into believing Walter's lies (ll. 750–51); and, finally, they are made to approve Walter's repudiation of Griselda in favor of a new wife (ll. 750–51, 985–94), a development that allows the Clerk to editorialize, in the style of Shakespearean drama, on the fickleness of the commons (ll. 995–1001).[60] This necessary moment—a moment of appeasement and a sop to those who may object to any depiction of a sainted populace united behind their own—in turn gives way to Griselda's movingly reproachful advice to Walter not to treat his next wife in the same fashion, when Griselda accurately calls the marquis' so-called "testing" of her virtue and worthiness by its proper name, and judges both his conduct and the man by characterizing his victimization of her as "tormentynge" (l. 1038).

Since she is the iconic representative of the feudal underclass, Griselda's "tormentynge" by her ruler-husband is consistently played out in class categories. As preface to each of his abominable cruelties, Walter explains, in exquisitely brutal, excruciatingly clear detail to Griselda, that he acts against her only and directly because of her class status. When Walter takes Griselda's infant daughter away from her—a deed that follows promptly on the heels of narrative acclaim of Griselda as a faultless administrator of the public good (and concomitant narrative silence on Walter's qualities as a ruler)—his act is contextualized by him as a class disparagement and appeasement. Walter says that his nobles contest the ruler's union with a woman of "poor estate full low" (l. 473), so that the projective infanticide of Griselda's firstborn is represented as a palliative to elites who have the ruler's ear, an act of solidarity with his own class, in its contempt for hers. After Griselda's son is born and weaned from the breast at two years, Walter enlarges the fictive class objection to encompass the will of putatively all the populace—he refers to them twice as "my peple" (ll. 625, 634), never thinking to share or expand the first-person genitive, in rulership—for the low-born blood that flows through the infant must be destroyed, it seems, lest it contaminate the dynasty of rulers (ll. 631–33).

Bereft of her children, who embody in their double inheritance the utopian future of a community stratified for centuries by socioeconomic caste-class, Griselda is all that remains of the utopian promise of this class-blended family, when Walter announces his repudiation of her, again specifying, as his moral and legal authority, the unbridgeable class chasm between them. In a shameless narrative twist that inverts their class statuses, Walter represents himself to Griselda as being unfree to choose his own wife, because "great lordship" puts him in "great servitude in sondry ways" (ll. 797–98)—"I may not do as every plowman may," he says, a little belatedly, "My people constrain me to take / Another wife" (ll. 799–800). With over-the-top irony, the marquis brutally dares to suggest that the plowman represents the class of people in feudal society who are truly free, while the ruling seigneury live in pitiable bondage and constraint. Walter's words trace yet another level of irony in expressing the political unconscious of the period, moreover, for the marquis' selection of a plowman to figure the class that he asserts is truly free, while remaining unfree, is particularly apposite in the post-1381 political community of Chaucerian England, after plowmen had been valorized over gentles in the political and economic struggle of the Peasants' Rebellion.[61]

Throughout, the narrative shows Griselda fulfilling her part of the feudal-marital contract in spirit and letter, and in the full public eye, even as Walter is seen to lie, cheat, twist, deceive, and thrash about willy-nilly, mongering for a pretext for his class abominations. When, with further ironic cruelty, Walter tells Griselda to take back with her the "dower" that she had brought to him in marriage—and the narrative has already shown us that Griselda had come with empty hands, since Walter had had her exchange the rags on her back for fine clothing of his provision at the door of her hut—Griselda reminds him (thrice) with full dignity that she had brought her "maydenhede" with her (ll. 837, 866, 883). Those of high degree in feudal society, it seems, have possessions—wealth, *culture*—whereas those of low degree have *nature* and biology; but a woman who symbolically represents the lowborn can point to the stray gift of female anatomy that signifies so much and so little at the same time, her virgin's hymen that belongs to *both* nature *and* culture (as Griselda's carefully chosen words, and Marian iconography, indicate so well).[62]

Because the iconographic status of their marriage requires that the making and breaking of contracts between Walter and Griselda be publicly attested, at her departure the woman of low degree publicly undresses to her "smock"—payment that Walter agrees to tender in exchange for her hymen, "faith," and nakedness (l. 866)—"before the folk," who then follow her, weeping, to her father's house, a public mourning for a failed social experiment (ll. 890–91, 894–97).[63] When Walter later requests Griselda's temporary return to his house, to supervise and direct arrangements for the bridal festivities with which he plans to receive her replacement, he drives home to her again his commitment to traditional class divisions and stratifications, and the primacy of the feudal status quo, when he specifies that Griselda see to it that everyone is to take his place at the dinner table, in seating arrangements and service, according to his proper "estate" (ll. 957–59), according, that is, to exact and proper hierarchies of class.

Clearly, Griselda's story—a crossover class fantasy exploring the cultural conditions under which a different kind of overarching community can be envisaged and authorized—exercises many cautions, along with the narrative opportunities it dares to seize. The absolute freedom of Walter's authority as ruler is carefully exaggerated, for instance, as is the ruler's penchant for self-willed, arbitrary, and extreme conduct, since exaggeration allows bad behavior by rulers to be the more easily criticized, even by agents in Walter's pay, like the ill-famed "sergeant" (ll. 519, 524) who begs Griselda's forgiveness for bereaving her of her infant at the "pleasure" and orders of lords (ll. 526–31).

We note that the narrative takes the long view in presenting change: Though all occurs at Walter's will and dictates in the short term, once Griselda, the subaltern, has paid the price of her "tormentynge," her unorthodox social ascent is vindicated beyond question, and the narrative indicates that the next generation is fully secure, and can reap the benefits of Griselda's labor. No one questions the right of Griselda's son to succeed Walter as marquis; no further mention is made of any shameful or lowborn heritage, bloodlines, descent, or innate unworthiness to rule. Indeed,

Walter's bad behavior has so eclipsed all else in the diegesis that the only memory which is retained of the family past is the memory of Walter's tormenting of Griselda; admirably, the son did not put *his* wife to great trial, we are told. In identical fashion, the socioeconomic relocation of Griselda's daughter is also fully secure and beyond question: The daughter, like the son, has been gently raised, and no one seems remotely interested to assert the primacy of nature over nurture.

The Clerk's tale of Griselda would have lost much of its potential as a story in which individual desire subserves communal allegory had its focus remained exclusively with the feudalized marriage of Walter and Griselda. But the story also takes pains to establish Griselda *as a mother*—tapping the cultural authority of Marian iconography, in this—even as it exploits the pathos of a family divided by a father's ruthless will. The extent to which the story implicitly condemns Walter is suggested to the degree that his wife explicitly recalls the Virgin, in her loving maternity: as Griselda bids a pathos-filled farewell to her first babe, she invokes Christ, whom she sees in her infant, when she says to the child, "this night shall you die for my sake" (l. 560).[64] In recalling the sacrifice represented by the Christ child in Christianity, Griselda's loving surrender of her child is also an exemplar for a spirit of sacrifice essential to, and that must be embraced by, an imagined community of the nation: "a spirit of sacrifice that would be unimaginable from the kind of cost-benefit calculations that self-conscious ideologies assume" (D. Sommer, 37) but that must be willingly borne by all, whenever necessary, for the greater good of an overarching community. Unlike the "competitive comparison between nationalism and religion" (40) in postmedieval culture, medieval culture in the form of Griselda's story registers only the overlap of religious and nationalist modes of feeling in modeling family affections and maternal behavior.

Griselda's attachment to her children, and to her maternity, despite Walter's theft of her children's childhood from her, is carefully emphasized. Each time the sergeant comes for her infants, Griselda pitifully begs him to try to ensure the babies' burial, so that their bodies might not be desecrated by predatory beasts or birds (ll. 569–72, 680–83), choosing her words carefully in order that she remain faithful to her contracted agreement with Walter. The feudal underclass, we are given to understand, is represented admirably by this woman who still exercises her intelligence and remembers her fealty to her troth under great distress, and in extreme conditions. Even when Griselda no longer has any children at home, her maternity lingers like a scent about her. When Walter submits his wife to

public exhibition in her smock, "with head and foot all bare" (l. 895)—a
mode of sexual humiliation, pandering as it does to the voyeuristic pruri-
ance enabled by her public undressing—Griselda's emphasis on the
"maidenhead" she has gifted to Walter in marriage, and the impossibility
of its return, brings into proper focus her status as the mother of their children and emphasizes the *reproductive* aspects of feminine sexuality. Finally, even Griselda's request for clothing to cover her nakedness is couched
to remind Walter of her maternity, for she asks for clothing to cover her
"womb" (l. 887). When Griselda's children are returned to her, all grown,
she faints, embraces, kisses, weeps "ful lyk a mooder" (l. 1084), calling to
them, bathing their faces and hair with her tears, and holding on to her
children so tightly that even when she faints it is scarcely possible to ex-
tricate her children from her embrace (ll. 1102–3).[65]

Encoded into both the stories of Griselda and Constance, then, is the
quintessential, often underemphasized role of *emotion*—passion and intensity—in narratives of community, including the spontaneous materialization of group emotion gathering to a point of consensus. Though the
status of emotion in nationalist and community discourses is seldom fully
disclosed or acknowledged, the play of affect in assisting the success of
such discourses should not be underestimated. A politics of emotion undergirds the nationalist imaginary itself, and strategic collocations of emotion, strategically deployed, usually punctuate the momentum of *all* successful nationalist and community discourses. Pervaded by sentiment and
pathos, milking conventions of *eros*, sublimity, and melodrama we see that
Griselda's and Constance's communal-national narratives also find their
precise emotional center, their exactly useful iteration, at the nexus of
family identity.

Not by chance, then, do Constance's and Griselda's narratives point inexorably to the same space in collective and personal consciousness where
intimate associations are forged: to that mental territory where the mystifi-
cations and misrecognitions occur that make identifications with others
possible, so that people are knit into bonds of intimacy, relation, and
union. For not only do individuals fall in love, touch the mystical, worship
God, and become utterly devoted to their children, in that discontinuous
continuum known as the imaginary, but nations and communities that require for their collective existence the same experiences of intense identification, relationship, and union also play out their necessary mystications in
the same imaginative location. The useful forces of mystification and identification that drive passionate love affairs and family relationships also

drive the passionate conception of utopian projects like the imagining of an integral community—the love affair, or the family, of a collectivity knit together by a linked species of longing and drive toward belonging.[66]

With Constance and Griselda, the story of passionately, sentimentally imagining community is, then, almost complete but for an epilogue that treats a strategic kind of emotional omission.

A Race of One's Own: Family Figures in Discourses of Color, Difference, and Community

If a narrative of community like Griselda's story negotiates class division and hostility through an allegory of marriage and generation, the pivotal status of women and children in representing an imagined medieval community healed of the annihilating effects of differences assumes a special significance when we consider not only Griselda's and Constance's *success* in constituting symbolic families for "Saluzzo" and "Northumberland" but also Constance's *failure* to constitute a family of any kind in Syria, Barbary, or "Saracenland." Indeed, though scholars sometimes assume that Constance first marries the Sultan of the generic Islamic nation and later marries King Aella of pagan Northumberland, the sequence of events in Trevet's and Gower's accounts of the Constance story makes plain that, despite Muslim conversion to Christianity and the religious conquest signaled by Constance's arrival on Islamic shores, Constance's marriage to the Sultan never, in fact, happens.

In the *Cronicles*, the Sultan's mother asks for and receives from her son the honor of hosting "the first feast *before* the nuptials" ("la prime feste auant les esposailes" [Bryan and Dempster, 167; Furnivall, 9; my emphasis); and, since the Sultaness then has nearly everyone but Constance massacred at this early banquet, we may safely assume that no nuptials actually take place.[67] In similar fashion, the Sultan's mother in Gower's *Confessio Amantis* also asks for the "ferste feste" at Constance's "welcominge" (ll. 670–71); we may assume that no marriage occurs either in Genius's narration. Though Chaucer's *Man of Law's Tale* obscures the chronology of events—we are told only that "the tyme cam" for the feast (*MLT*, l. 414)—there is no mention whatsoever of nuptials in Syria, in clear contrast to the unequivocal occurrence of marriage between King Aella and Constance in England: "And after this Jhesus, of his mercy, / Made Alla wedden ful solempnely / This hooly mayden" (*MLT*, ll. 690–92).

Needless to say, Constance also has no children with the Sultan. Despite the heroine's conversion of Muslims to Christianity, the Constance romances show no interest whatsoever in imagining a re-beginning for the Islamic nation and its people as a newly (re)formed Christian community, suggesting the unimaginability—the unspeakability—of the project. If anything, we see in these romances the *impossibility* of re-beginning in the Orient: Genocide follows massacre, so that we are left to wonder (those of us who are so inclined) if anyone remains alive in Syria at narrative's end. First, the Sultaness eradicates all trace of Christianity and Christians in the land with her bloody massacre of Christians and Muslim converts to Christianity, including her own son and his council/court/retinue. Subsequently, Constance's father, the "Roman" Emperor, completes the ethnic and religious cleansing by having the Sultaness and the local populace of Muslims eliminated (in Trevet's narrative, more than eleven thousand Muslims are slaughtered; in Gower's, no one of "all that alliance, / By whom the treason was encompassed" (ll. 1184–86) is spared the sword; while in the *Man of Law's Tale*, the Christians "burn, slay and bring [the Syrians] to evil fortune / Full many a day" (*MLT*, ll. 964–65).

The abrupt truncation of the story in Syria, and the elimination of much of or all the local populace, brings into stark relief the paired difference between the story in Syria and the story in England/Northumberland in the Constance narratives. The twinned structure of episodes in the two locales is impossible to miss; each episode has a scheming mother-in-law, a king who desires to marry Constance, and the faithful theme of conversion, in a specially plotted bipartite doubling. One nation in the diptych is embraced, Christianized, and given a symbolic royal family; the other nation is held off, refused, and its populace is apparently decimated. Why the difference? Why does the Constance story not allow Constance and the Sultan to marry and to produce a child who symbolizes their union? In the contest of religions, what is there to choose from between paganism and Islam? And why is Northumberland privileged over Syria?

A hint of an answer appears when we interleave into our reading the final member in the core group of Constance romances, the Middle English *King of Tars* (*KT*), a romance that also issues from the fourteenth century and features conversion to Christianity through the agent of a Christian princess.[68] In this romance, the nameless princess (her father is the titular "King of Tars") does, in fact, marry the Sultan of Damascus—and, indeed, marries only the sultan; there is no secondary episode in England—and the marriage does, in fact, produce a child. Where, however, in the other members of the Constance group, the Christian union of Constance and Aella in England produces Maurice, a beautiful child who resembles his beautiful mother ("a beautiful child and large, well begotten, well born"; "beautiful and graceful" [Trevet: Bryan and Dempster, 172, 176; Furnivall, 27, 37]; "In all the world . . . / There was never a woman who brought forth / A fairer child" [Gower, ll. 1245–47]; "that fair child" [*MLT*, l. 1018]; "A fair child born and a handsome"; "noble was that child" [*Emaré*, ll. 503, 507]), the marriage of the princess of Tars to the Muslim Sultan of Damascus hideously brings forth a shapeless lump of flesh: insensate, inanimate, and with neither "blood" nor "bone" nor "limbs" (*KT*, ll. 579–82), a true monstrosity.

In the other narratives of the core Constance group, of course, the Saxon King Aella's supposition that a monstrous creature has been birthed from his nuptial union with the foreign princess, Constance, rests on a lie—an epistolary fabrication fashioned by his demonic queen mother, whose artful epistolary monstrosity discloses her to be the true monster in the family. By contrast, the hideous lump of bodily matter that does result from the nuptial union of the Christian princess of Tars with the Muslim Sultan of Damascus is no libelous fable concocted by a devilish mother-in-law but a monster of the flesh, in the flesh: the physical embodiment of an obscene marriage in which the Christian princess has done the unthinkable, either because she pretends, outwardly, to convert to Islam, the infernal religion of her husband, the Sultan (*KT*, ll. 604–5), or because she joins with a Muslim without first converting him to her religion, or both. The inescapable, explicit lesson in this representational script of hideous birth is that religion, which we had assumed to belong purely to the realm of culture, can shape and instruct *biology*: a startling logic suggesting that secreted within the theory of religious difference in this tale is also a theory of biological essences seemingly indivisible from religion.

Despite the ostensible undecidability at issue here—is it the Muslim man's (de)generative seed that fashions the monster which is birthed? Or is it the horrifying spectacle of a Christian princess's avowed conversion to Islam (however feigned) that has issued *par consequence* a fleshly horror? Is it the intimate metaphysical mingling of the warring essences of Islam and Christianity in the conjugal bed that so misshapes the essence of the infant flesh thus produced? Or should we understand that the princess's act of conversion has deeper and more tenacious consequences than she comprehends, when she later denies its validity?—religion seems, in all instances, to answer as the operative category of difference that is fore-grounded. The suggested plot in which religion features as the main actor and agent then appears, in outline, to be straightforward: For when the senseless lump is baptized by a priest and given the name "John" (on the feast day of the Baptist), it instantly transforms into a little infant, "with life and limb and face" as well as "skin and flesh," an infant who is now conventionally the fairest child ever born (*KT*, ll. 775–76, 778, 781). Christianity, it seems, possesses a spiritual essence with the power to reshape biological fleshly matter and, we must assume, also to confer a divine soul in the process of making a human being.

We might be led to believe, then, that Islam itself, or the hybridity of Islam-plus-Christianity, or perhaps the princess's terrifying public act of betraying the Christian faith, procures a monstrous lump of flesh, whereas Christianity in the pure elicits a beautiful little child. Religion seems the sole determinative ground of contestation, issuing each twist of plot in the struggle for dominion and hegemony between forces: For, in this romance, it is the Christian princess, and not the infatuated sultan, who first begins as the cultural conscript, a sexual victim given over by her disempowered father to the Muslim conqueror whose puissance extends to his demonstrable ability to force *her* conversion to *his* religion (a conversion actualized in gesture and ceremony, if apparently not in the innermost sanctum of the victim's consciousness) before the tables are turned by the lesson of progeny.

The assertion in literature that physical matter can be interfered with and ontologically rewritten—changed in essence and composition—by religious conversion is a peculiarly medieval one. The *King of Tars* shows medieval romance to shape a theory that an essence resides within Christianity that has the power to trump ordinary human biology, a hypothesis aided here by textual exploitation and adaptation of hagiographic themes. (In authentic hagiography, of course, if not in hagiographic romance, a Christian princess would choose martyrdom and death over any false public conversion.) That is, in the medieval theory evinced by this romance, religion and physiognomy exist in a volatile relationship in which religion is the dominant term, the term that possesses the authority to define and produce a master taxonomy of physiological differences.[69] In the *King of Tars*'s representation of this odd medieval hypothesis of the essentialist power of Christianity to bestow bodily configurations, religion has moved from the realm of culture per se to inhabit a twilight, interzonal space in which culture *and* biology overlap: Christianity, in this context—when

functioning as a master discourse in the making of essential differences—
operates as a discourse of *both* culture *and* biology.

Powerful and provocative as the statement of religious essentialisms is,
it also has a useful, complicating secondary moment. Following the mirac-
ulous transformation of the lump of flesh into a child, at baptism, the Sultan in his turn converts to Christianity, and his physical form, too, is
changed, but with a pivotal difference. The Sultan's original skin color,
which is "blac" (*KT*, l. 799) and "foule" (*KT*, l. 393), "blac & loþely" (*KT*,
l. 928), becomes "Al white" and clear without any taint (*KT*, ll. 929–30).[70]
To overdetermine the point, the romance insists: *"chaunged was his hewe"*
(*KT*, l. 945; my emphasis). Thereafter, the newly whitened Sultan, at the
behest of his Christian wife—a princess whose own whiteness of skin has
been trumpeted early, and repeatedly, in this romance—conducts crusading warfare against all Saracens who will not convert to Christianity. In his
crusade, Muslims "all and some," "old and young" are "hounds" or dogs
(*KT*, ll. 169, 743, 1097, 1176, 1181), their conventional opprobrious sobriquet in *chansons de geste*. The blackness of Saracen skin is specifically remarked—pointed to—and blackness is not a personal, individual characteristic but a collective biological attribute, the racial feature that
demarcates and identifies a people: "Thirty thousand there were taken / Of
Saracens both blackish-blue and black" ("blo & blac" [*KT*, ll. 1225–26]).

The romance's most haunting evocation of Saracens as black and inhuman is evoked even earlier, in a dream that the princess has had, a hallucinatory nightmare in which a hundred black hounds (*KT*, ll. 423–24)
and three devils with swords (*KT*, ll. 431–34) materialize before her threateningly, while one black hound, in particular, presses on her a violence
that is a thinly disguised euphemism for sexual force, a rapelike assault
that is patently also mustered as religious coercion (*KT*, ll. 425–29, 442);
for even when war is available, romance speaks its obsessions, after all, in
sexualized vocabulary and in sexual terms. After her traumatization, the
black hound, following her, speaks to her in man's form, dressed "in white
clothes" like a knight (*KT*, ll. 448–51), addressing her as "my sweet creature" and telling her not to be afraid of Tervagant or Mahoun, for Christ
would help her at need (*KT*, ll. 452–56). When the princess awakens from
the dream, "al naked" in bed (*KT*, l. 460) and prays, the Sultan of Damascus immediately appears, takes her to his "temple" (*KT*, ll. 467–68) full
of false idols, and forces her to undergo rituals of conversion to Islam.[71]

If the narrative seems unable quite to decide between color and sub-
humanness as the primary, identifying quality of the Saracen, the apparent undecidability is partly settled by the narrative's pronounced insis-

tence on the heroine's own skin color, which is of the fairest white: an in-
sistence that appears early and frames the black-white color dualism of this
romance. Since "Tars" may signify the "Tartars" or Mongols of East Asia,
"Tarsus" in Armenia Minor, a mythical "Tharsia" in "present-day
Turkestan" (*KT*, 47), or any number of possible Oriental locales,[72] to ensure we grasp that this Oriental princess is *really* an authentic European
Christian princess, like the romance Constance, and not an Oriental
Christian princess (like the historically marked Constance doppelgänger
in the source background), the *King of Tars* depicts its heroine from the
very beginning as the archetypal true European beauty of romance, whose
skin is "white as the feather of a swan" (*KT*, l. 12), with a complexion rosy
as a "blossom on a briar" (*KT*, l. 14), and with the traditional gray eyes
(*KT*, ll. 15, 941), sloping shoulders, and white neck (*KT*, l. 16) of conventional beauty in medieval European literature—an image culled from
rhetorical treatises and repeated ad infinitum in manuscript illuminations.
Just as the whiteness of the princess of Tars—attesting to her Western Europeanness, whatever her father's nominal title and territorial suzerainty—
equates with ideal beauty, the Sultan's blackness equates with the foulness
and loathliness of racial difference.[73]

The romance's pairing of religion with skin color, and subhumanity, is
instructive. For the Sultan's conversion demonstrates that, in medieval romance, the odd notion that religion might trump ontology also erupts *within* a more clearly defined moment of racial marking, in which visual evidence specifically pivoting on skin color and a hierarchical aesthetic of color,
is the operative determination, beyond any physiological dispositions (like a
lifeless lump of flesh) that might issue from religious essences alone. We see
thus that medieval taxonomies of difference are not simply plotted along
that cultural-theological axis assumed for the Middle Ages by later,
postmedieval generations of scholarship on race. To scholarship on race that
takes its examples from postmedieval periods, *religion*—which is always understood, in modern fashion, as an exclusively *cultural* system of customs,
gestures, and practices, and unimplicated in theories of biological
essences—is the a priori determinant in hierarchical taxonomizations of difference in the *medieval* period, just as *race*—understood in biological and essentialist terms—is concomitantly seen to function as the operative determinant in retrograde hierarchies of power within *postmedieval* periods. [74]

Complicating such assumptions of medieval innocence and freedom
from racial consciousness and racial thinking, the *King of Tars*, as a medieval artifact, supposes *the normativity of whiteness*, and of *the white racial
body*, as the guarantor of normalcy, aesthetic and moral virtue, European

Christian identity, and full membership in the human community, *in complicity with* the possession of a human essence conferred by religious discourse acting as biological determination. Neither side of that complicitous relationship, we might say, is given any exhibited priority: The recognition of racially marked differences of color and bodies is articulated through the authoritative, masterful grammar of religious difference; simultaneously, religious difference itself is articulated through the grammar of physiognomy, color, and genealogy, posited on normative bodies and the norm of human whiteness.

The explicit cultural politics of the *King of Tars*, with its unabashed color line, thus imparts an important insight into why the heroine of the Constance romances must not marry *her* Sultan—the Sultan of Syria, Barbary, or Saracenland—and produce a child with him. For though Constance's Sultan has been converted to Christianity, and the marriage would not in this instance transgress religious boundaries, conversion to Christianity is insufficient *in and of itself* to cancel out differences of race and color.[75] The marriage of a "Roman" (i.e., European) princess with a Syrian, Berber, or other species of "Saracen" Sultan, is *still* a marriage that crosses the medieval color line, conjuring the specter of racial miscegenation. In the *King of Tars*, the offspring of racial and religious miscegenation is feigned in narrative as an insensate, inanimate lump of flesh—a thing outside the human species, unrecognizable as human, and, mercifully, not alive. If we are briefly troubled by the strange resemblance here between a lifeless lump of flesh that is the product of miscegenation in romance and the pound of flesh that is later memorialized by Shakespeare in the story of Shylock the Jew—a Renaissance story with predecessors in medieval culture, from the *Cursor Mundi* to the *Gesta Romanorum*—we have good reason to be troubled indeed.

Significantly, though skin color is never explicitly raised as an issue in the other core Constance romances, which are characterized by a certain narrative tact, an elegant reticence, the Sultaness in Chaucer's *Man of Law's Tale* makes a telling joke, when she says of Constance, her prospective daughter-in-law: "Though [she] be crismed *ever so white*, / She shall have need to wash away the red, / Though she bring a font-ful of [holy] water with her" (*MLT*, ll. 355–57; my emphasis). The color-consciousness of the Sultaness's off-color joke—punning on the traditional white-and-red beauty of the European heroine's complexion, the whiteness of skin conferred by baptism in romance convention ("crismed ever so white") and the blood that will be shed in the Sultaness's intended massacre of

Christians and converts—hints at what might lie behind the narrative tact of the Constance stories' refusal of nuptials and consummation between Constance and the Sultan. Both Syria and English Northumberland might be heathenish foreign lands to a Christian "Roman" princess, but Syria—"the Barbre nacioun" (*MLT*, l. 281)—unlike England, presents the prospect of a penultimate alienness, an alienation beyond the pale, by virtue of the race and color of its constituents, even when the aliens have been Christianized.

When people do not share a race or a color deemed normatively human, a shared religion is not enough, even during the Middle Ages—a period in which, it is commonly assumed, religion is the master discourse that determines all. Unlike Syria, pagan Northumberland is never described as a "strange nacioun": the apellation that signals the truly alien race, people, community, or nation is reserved exclusively for the Eastern world. Just as the unremitting difference of race and color tacitly intervenes between Constance and the Sultan, only a temporary difference of religious faith intervenes between Constance and Aella, the pagan Saxon, and that religious difference is soon erased by Aella's conversion. When people *do* share a race and normative color in medieval literature, a shared religion will suffice to seal their commonality. Thanks to Trevet's Romanization of Constance, a strategy repeated by Chaucer and Gower, Constance is successfully retained as European, despite Donegild's curious reference to her daughter-in-law, once, as "so foreign a creature" (*MLT*, l. 700), a reminder of the heroine's original Oriental provenance. Where color is mentioned in connection with Constance in England, Constance is appropriately only "pale" with anxiety and fear (*MLT*, l. 645).

The politics of color in the *King of Tars* also helps us to understand why it is that the Sultaness in Syria defends her religion with mass slaughter, and not, say, with the simple murder of the converting agent, Constance—who is, after all, virtually the only target in the defensive strategy elected by Domild/Donegild, the Sultaness's counterpart in Saxon England. The Sultaness's resort to the extreme measure of group slaughter emotively suggests that more is staked in Syria, than in England, when religion is invoked, for the Syrian response is also explicitly triggered as an overarching defense of Islam, which, in Syria, is represented *as a race and a nation*, not merely a religion. The narrative makes this clear when it suggests that the Sultaness chooses to take the nation in a different direction from what is decided on by her son, the Sultan, when he submits his people to Christianity as a condition of his marriage to a Christian: "For she

hirself wolde al the contree lede" (*MLT*, l. 434) suggests more than merely personal ambition or "malice" (*MLT*, l. 363) on the Sultaness's part; it
suggests a divergent policy decision made on behalf of an entire nation, a
decision that is made plain in the Sultaness's disquisition to her council.
The Sultaness's determination to preserve the race and national character
of her people in this life and beyond—keeping intact the spiritual, national, racial, cultural character of the polity—is something that her council, in its unanimous response, indicates it understands (*MLT*, ll. 330–48).

Where the characterization of Syria is concerned, the Constance story
demonstrates, religion, race, and nation are categories that intimately
overlap, vanish into one another, and are ultimately inseparable. With the
example of Syria before us, we see that a compound category, then—
"race-religion"—defines the medieval subject of culture/biology, as well as
the medieval community in its cohesiveness, its quintessential group identity and meaning.

At the periphery of the Constance group of romances, in the examples
generously arranged by the *King of Tars*, we see an *explicit* exposition of
racial thinking, and how race-and-religion—"race-religion"—functions in
medieval culture as *a single indivisible discourse*. We see how, when the
Saracen Sultan converts from Islam to Christianity, his physical body is
ontologically rearranged, his color is stripped from him, and he loses his
race along with his religion. On becoming a Christian, the Sultan's bodily transformation describes his admission into another cultural-biological
formation, European Christianity, by performing (and requiring) a
change of biological essence, a change that ceremonially enacts his entrance into another race, the Christian-European race, defined as humans
who possess a white skin.

The Sultan's racial-religious translation—his transubstantiation—is
neatly counterbalanced by the absolute stability of the princess of Tars's
own skin color and race, despite the fact that *she* also performs all the ceremonial motions of conversion to another religion, Islam: Race-religion,
it would seem, is a discourse that does not operate symmetrically or even-
ly, for no equivalence exists in the narrative treatment of these two exemplars. Compared to his ritual of conversion, *hers* is, in fact, substantially
more extensive, prolonged, and elaborate, stagily teased out in detail. She
requests religious instruction, makes an avowal, ceremonially kisses all the
"idols" in a row, learns prayers, and "said them openly" (*KT*, ll. 484–506),
yet no physical change of any kind, however slight, occurs in her racial
being. The princess, who presumably remains at heart a Christian (if we

can trust what she says in some contexts, even if her words and gestures cannot be trusted in others), stays fair and white from beginning to end.[76] Since she professes Islam in word, law, custom, and deed, the only way to tell that the princess remains a Christian—omniscient narrator aside—is by the constancy of her skin color. And so we see that despite her name-lessness, the princess of Tars is Constance, after all, in her skin, a skin that speaks her name even when the text is silent.

We can choose to understand the princess's unremitting whiteness, then, in a couple of ways. If we concede the facticity of her conversion to Islam (as do censorious readers, who find the princess's opposite public and private avowals convincing only in their hypocrisy)—if we define religion as open adherence to theological law in conformity with a communal system of customs, gestures, and practices, in which the individual's private intent is unknowable and unverifiable—we must credit Christianity with superior power in this text, since the princess's entrance into the Muslim *ummah* fails to coincide with a successful conferral, upon her, of blackness, corresponding to a new religious essence. We must then conclude, from this failure of color conversion, that the power of the essence conferred a priori on the princess during her original christening at birth is able to trump any essence that might subsequently issue from Islam: And we would then be in possession of an implicit medieval theory of primary and secondary religious essences.

Or we can understand, in the dynamics of this color line, that an essence inheres in *both* Europeanness *and* Christianity. If we assume that the princess's secret adherence to Christianity is vindicated and supported by the text, we might speculate that a religious essence bestowed by Christianity at baptism continues to stabilize and guarantee the racial essence of the princess, despite the immediate environment to which she feigns conformity and to which she appears to belong. Alternatively we might equally say, with simultaneous justification, that a *racial* essence, exhibiting surface markers like skin color, outwits religious conversion to Islam—whether a technical, feigned, or valid conversion is less material in this instance—and signals the possession of an inner life that remains inviolable, thanks to the security of race.

Belonging to the right race—as signaled by the biological constancy of the princess's pure white skin—thus guarantees the stability of the princess's religious identity, whatever impositions might follow. Such a reading does not require (or disturb) a reader's trust in the solidity of the princess's protestations of her secret fidelity to Christianity, despite her embarrassing public acts to the contrary, nor that any valuation be made of her ostensible hypocrisy. Race—the whiteness and beauty of the European skin—can guarantee all. On the uncertain terrain of this romance—where conditions are volatile and shifting, where acts are disturbing and disjoined from inner reality, and where words are uttered in order not to be believed—the stability imparted by the guarantee of race is crucial.[77]

Clearly, the dependability of skin color as a true index of one's essence, whatever one might say or do, is a fantasy with vast appeal. Without the princess's constancy of color, her religious acts, after her outward conversion to Islam, would be deeply unnerving to an English Christian audience: If she prays like a Muslim, follows Islamic customs and law, and openly professes to believe in "Mahoun" (*KT*, l. 847), there is *nothing else* to distinguish her from faithful, practicing Muslims *except* her color. Fortuitously, skin color in romance is a dependable conductor of racial-religious essence, for after the Sultan converts to Christianity, it is *his* turn to feign belief in Islam—because of political safety, he tells the princess, since, were any of his people to learn of his and the princess's secret Christian faith, she would be burnt and he would be cut to pieces ("& ani it wist, heye or lowe, / þou schalt be brent & y todrawe" [*KT*, ll. 886–87])—but the princess can be reassured that despite his continued outward profession of Islam the Sultan truly is, like her, safely a Christian European inside his skin, because his new skin is now all white, like hers (*KT*, ll. 943–45). What his people make of their ruler's bleaching is, however, tactfully left unremarked by this remarkably unembarrassable romance. Predictably, soon after his conversion, with his racial-religious rebirth complete, the "Cristen soudan" (*KT*, l. 1105) begins to perform identically to a European crusading king in romance, slaughtering and conquering Saracens "blo & blac" (*KT*, l. 1226) by the thousands and advocating a religious zealotry that rivals the romance Richard Coer de Lyon's.

Other family members in the core group of Constance romances, especially the *Man of Law's Tale*, play out the discourse of race-religion operating in Syria and England in more psychologically nuanced ways than the explicit outing preferred by the *King of Tars*. In these other romances the racial priorities that distinguish between the episode in Syria and the episode in England tend to work, for instance, through a contrastive dynamic of absence and presence. For instance, the Sultaness in Syria who seeks to rescue her very foreign race/religion/nation is nameless, unlike Donegild/Domild in England, so that the distancing effect accomplished by the contestant antagonist's namelessness, coupled with the mechanical nature of the conversion in Syria, then represents religious change in the Is-

lamic nation largely as a technicality wrought by the Sultan's nuptial contract.[78] By contrast, Constance's first conversion in England, the result of
an intimately realized, affectionate, indeed intensely passionate relationship
with Dame Hermengild, in a domestic household in which Constance is
warmly received, represents conversion in England as an authentic, and not
a technical, phenomenon. Thanks to the miracles God is willing to perform in England, and His preference for direct intervention, and even
speech, in this part of the world, the conversions wrought in England seem
to have deeper and truer roots, and, to seal the heartfelt conversions in England, the symbolic Christian child born of symbolic Christian wedlock between imperial princess and local king is given St. Maurice's name, and a
reputation of being "the Cristeneste of alle" (Gower, l. 1598), as if the child
became, indeed, a saint. In England, all that remains of the aggressively active medieval discourse of race-religion, in the end, is a certain residual
irony, a queer irony, at the heart of a name, "Maurice," as color remains
residually, vestigially, *linguistically* secreted inside this strange half-Eastern,
half-Western, but all-Christian hybrid boy's name, "Maurice."[79]

For such fourteenth-century English audiences to whom, and for
whom, the Constance family of texts might speak, the availability of a
symbolic family that may serve to figure the imagined community of the
proto-nation of medieval England pivots on the palpable absence of similar family symbolizations elsewhere, especially—dramatically—in the
East. The pregnant blankness characterizing that symbolic Muslim East,
with its absence of any re-beginning from or continuity with the past, is a
generative, productive blankness, one that makes possible both an affect
and an investment elsewhere: in England. Absence, of course, is the location of meaning and the condition of possibility. The nation-that-is-not,
the land that is devoid of a signifying royal family, is a crucial enabling fiction for the nation-that-might-be, the land whose future and past can be
signaled by a traveling woman whose maternity and reproductive sexuality generate, in culture, the gendered domestic figures that are valuable to
nascent collectivities. The Constance romances, and their relationship to
the *King of Tars*, eminently demonstrate, moreover, how race-as-religion,
and religion-as-race, figure in the production of enabling fictions for the
medieval proto-nation-in-process. This family of romances opens a moment in which the racializing priorities and discourse at work in medieval
culture coincide with the instrumentalities of romance in service to the
creation of the nation in culture.

A family of texts begets a family of the nation: but only, it seems, in
racially—and pietistically—homogeneous England.

Why not focus on any culture's farthest range of travel while also looking at its centers . . .?

But it's a mistake . . . to insist on literal "travel."

—James Clifford, *Routes: Travel and Translation*
in the Late Twentieth Century

[Nothing] is more greedy than nature for what is like itself.

—Cicero, *De Amicitia*

Home has no meaning apart from the journey which takes one outside of home.

—Yi-Fu Tuan, "Geography, Phenomenology,
and the Study of Human Nature"

CHAPTER 5

৵

Eye on the World

Mandeville's Pleasure Zones; or, Cartography, Anthropology,
and Medieval Travel Romance

"WHEN LEONARDO DA VINCI moved from Milan in 1499," a noted
scholar of *Mandeville's Travels* observes, "his books included a number
on natural history, the sphere, the heavens. . . . But out of the multitude
of travel accounts that Leonardo could have had, in MS or from the new
printing press, there is only the one: *Mandeville's Travels.* At about the
same time (so his biographer Andrés Bernáldez tells us) Columbus was
perusing Mandeville for information on China preparatory to his voyage; and in 1576 a copy of the *Travels* was with Frobisher as he lay off
Baffin Bay" (Moseley, Introduction, 9).[1] Pointing to the approximately
three hundred manuscripts attesting "Mandeville's" popular dispersion
in a multitude of languages, the same scholar notes that the *Travels* also
helped to provoke the development of cartographic technology: The
first globe of the world, made at Nuremburg in 1492 and associated with
Martin Behaim, documents its debt (in a legend on the globe) to the
"würdige doctor und ritter Johan de Mandavilla" as authoritative source
(Moseley, "Behaim's Globe," 89).[2] Not for nothing has the *Travels* been
called "the single most popular European work of secular literature in
the late medieval, early modern period" (Braude, 106), a period in which
"it was regarded as the most authoritative and reliable account of the
world" (116).

Audience response at the University of Oregon in 2001, where a version of this chapter was delivered as a public lecture, helped to clarify and focus aspects of my argument. I thank Ken Cal-
hoon and Gina Psaki in particular. Most of this chapter was written in the course of a fellowship at the University of California's Humanities Research Institute, and under the auspices of
the "Theorizing 'Race' in Pre- and Early Modern Contexts" residential seminar convened by the
inimitable Margo Hendricks.

Thus we understand—thanks to the map makers, explorers, and inventors who sought out the *Travels'* view of the world from the fourteenth through sixteenth centuries—the importance of a romance of world travel that magically appears and consolidates a wealth of information at the end of a long cycle: a cycle of accumulated theoretical and practical knowledge in Europe, spanning many fields and centuries, known, retroactively, as the Middle Ages. Arriving at the end of a medieval cycle of knowledge accumulation, the *Travels* is also fortuitously perched before the opening of another long cycle of cultural accumulation—the so-called Renaissance age of discovery and exploration—which the global perspective of the *Travels,* looking backward and forward in time as it scans the world, also helps to incite.[3] *Mandeville's Travels* is a prime representative, an excellent model, of the impact and range of effects that timely, well-positioned travel romances can have on culture and history. The last destination in our long itinerary of visits to different species of romances, the *Travels* appropriately opens out the countries and regions of romance to the vast expanse of the world, and into the future.

Among its kind, the *Travels'* so-called lack of originality in what it offers by way of historical, anthropological, cosmographic, and geographical information becomes the precise condition that ensures the *Travels'* popularity and wide dispersion. A document that culls, in combination, ancient sources, the archive of medieval cultural wisdom and records, as well as contemporary, state-of-the-art scientific and geographical thinking, within a single, highly accessible, and engaging medium, works as a fine crucible and goad for instigating originality in its readers—a goad for propelling ideas and actions forward. Because "the human mind can only encompass the entirely new in terms of the old," and "the foremost geographical thinkers of the day" were also using the *Travels* as "a source of hard information," we are told that the *Travels* became "influential in shaping the world view of the generation that discovered America" and that "the response to America" is "governed, somewhere along the line, by the *Travels*" (Moseley, "Behaim's Globe," 90).

Given the cultural record of literature's volitional capacity to move and prompt, it scarcely seems to matter that the *Travels* are not only "a source of hard information" but at the same time also a prime representative of that hybrid genre of inextricably conjoined, seamlessly indistinguishable fact and fantasy we have been calling romance. Indeed, the romance character of the *Travels* becomes only too plain when the *Travels* is read alongside more historically attested, matter-of-fact, thick-descriptive records of medieval journeys to distant vistas, such as the missionary narratives of

John of Plano Carpini, William of Rubruck, or Odoric of Pordenone. Nonetheless, though the quasi-geographical *Travels* has been called a "mendacious romance," "satire," or even the "popular encyclopaedia" of a "marvel-monger" or "philosophical fabulist" (Higgins, *Writing East*, 11), the success of this travel story in mobilizing ideas, technology, and people, where other travel stories (even Marco Polo's celebrated narrative) lacked comparable momentum, argues that a document need not formally *be* an informational treatise, curricular text, or navigational map—that is to say, a self-advertised player in matters of information and accuracy—in order to function as any, or all, of these, and more.[4]

What, then, undergirds the immense appeal, and the effectiveness, of travel romance at its best, like the very medieval, very modern *Mandeville's Travels*, when travel romance is able to function both as information (whether accurate or unreliable) or as instigation (of a direct or tendentious kind)? We have seen how different species of romance act toward particular productive ends—to imagine a nationlike community across divisions or offer a vocabulary suited to conceiving the nation; to enact cultural rescue or furnish cultural authority for empire formation; even to defend against the encroachments of modernity and hold off the end of an era—what can a romance of travel do that other kinds of romances cannot, and how is it different from other romances?[5]

To begin with, quite simply, the reach of a travel romance like "Mandeville's" is global. Where the purposiveness of other romances might end at the boundaries of the nation, the interests of a particular social class aligned across nations, or, at farther limits still, the outermost borders of Latin Christendom, the project of a romance whose subject matter traverses the entire world itself, known and unknown—probing interiors and exteriors, scrutinizing peoples, flora, fauna, and topography, detailing state-of-the-art technology and techniques, discoursing on pasts and futures anywhere and everywhere—suggests a different kind of ambition. It must be observed, moreover, that the narrative structure of travel romances like "Mandeville's" (and "narrative," here, is a term of convenience, a generous fiction for purposes of enabling discussion) is fragmentary and fragmenting, even by the standards of famously episodic romance narrative structures. The *Travels* is organized like a self-interrupting network of nodules made up of anecdotes and vignettes—brief stories rumored or vouched for—profusely interspersed with digressions, observations, flashes of memory or insight; punctuated by disquisitions on instruments of measurement or location, scientific proofs and reasoning; interpolated with exhortations to go on crusade or be better Christians: so that the sum of its accretions ultimately performs a spectacular planetary survey that interconnects time, space, and culture.

If this impulse toward planetary totalization, on the part of the *Travels*, feels suspicious to our later centuries—centuries habituated to *grands récits* of the exotic functioning as the cultural correlatives of colonial movements—and if, as I suggested in earlier chapters, the cultural capital of medieval romance has, in fact, functioned historically to support projects of empire, both at the genesis of romance and through several incarnations throughout the Middle Ages, it is the fragmented character of travel romance narrative—the apparently indiscriminate tendency to collect atomized and diversely unrelated scraps of narrative bric-à-brac—that enables the creation of one of the most imaginative acts of cultural domination available in the Middle Ages. In the process, a narrative pleasure second to none among romance forms effloresces. More than in any other category of romance, travel narrative exercises its special attractions—such as the play between vast distances and close proximity, the lushly exotic and the cozily familiar—to insert its audience into an overarching system in which domination at a distance can seamlessly and seductively occur.

It is a truism that the consumption of successful travel narratives (and six-hundred-year-old travel romances that yet remain popular in the twenty-first century might count as successful) imparts tremendous pleasure. I will suggest how the pleasure system of a skilled travel romance like *Mandeville's Travels* is created and set in place; how that system operates to produce a world, and the idea of home, a center, and a periphery through its cosmopolitan ambitions; how a geographical imperium is seductively theorized and materialized that produces a reoriented world perspective in the pre-Renaissance late Middle Ages; and how, ultimately, a highly successful, late-medieval travel romance with an eye on the world, and pushing against the frontiers of scientific knowledge, ends up innovating new disciplines, knowledges, and techniques for a future world—a world in which speculative narratives of this and other kinds, edging outward the limits of knowledge, science, and technology, will become increasingly common.[6]

A VIRTUAL WORLD AS PLEASURE ZONE:
THE TECHNIQUES AND *Techne* OF TRAVEL ROMANCE

In þis land and in Ethiopy and many oþer cuntrez men and wymmen gase comounly to waters and lays þam in þam all naked fra vndrun of

þe day to it be passed none, for the grete hete of þe sonne; and þe ligg
all vnder þe water bot þe heued. And wymmen þare schamez noȝt þof
men see þam naked. (*Travels*, 81–82)[7]

In this land [India] and in Ethiopia and many other countries men and
women go commonly to waters and lie in them all naked from undern
of the day till it be past noon, for the great heat of the sun; and they
lie all under the water, but the head. And women there are not
ashamed if men see them naked.

The imagined spectacle of naked women lying in water, unashamed
and bold, displayed for all to see ("men" being the spectators invoked
here) is not only a pornographic staple of twenty-first-century mass culture: The scene also poses axiomatically as a resonant example of the kind
of narrative pleasure offered by European travel stories focusing on the exotic in different historical eras. Audiences of travelogues are conditioned,
from the proto-anthropology of Herodotus and Pliny on, to expect the ex-
otic/erotic, the forbidden/taboo, and the mildly to exorbitantly excessive
or bizarre as anticipated pleasures to be enjoyed in accounts of foreign
parts, especially foreign parts where exotic human bodies stand in vicari-
ously for exotic landscape.[8] Audience consumption of the forbidden even
has surrogate representation within the travel narratives themselves. We
witness the frequency with which faraway places (whether depicted in medieval *mappaemundi*—or world maps—or tales of colonial exploration/ex-
ploitation) typically feature cannibals who dramatically stage, in literature,
the very acts of taboo, exotic consumption that are more sedately enacted,
domestically, by the audiences of travel literature who consume at home
the taboo, salacious, foreign fare in sedentary acts of reading, listening,
imagining.

Naked, beautiful women, harems and multiple wives, Amazons and
fatal virgins; daringly utopian social habits; cannibalism of many
kinds—all these liberally effloresce throughout *Mandeville's Travels* precisely because they are such effortlessly accessible, and conventional,
placeholders for the forbidden pleasures afforded by the virtual worlds
of travel narratives. Hence we learn, in the "Egypt Gap" of the *Travels*,
that the Sultan of Babylon, when he journeys, has the fairest maidens all
around brought to him—to be inspected, selected, washed, perfumed,
decked out, and brought to his bed after supper for his (and the listening or reading audience's) delectation (20). Hence we hear also that the

women and men of "Lamary" go completely naked, and practice unrestricted sex and shared communal property relations in a species of care-
free, antifeudal communism; of course, as a delicious supplement—a
modest proposal—the natives also, alas and inevitably, like to eat children, whom they buy from merchants, fattening these youngsters till
they are plump, before killing and feasting on them, "the best and the
sweetest flesh of the world" (89).

If the different romances we have been considering from the twelfth
through fifteenth centuries seem, in toto, not to swerve very far from rev-
eling in depictions of cannibalism, and the invariable sweetness of human
flesh, travel romance, at least, can offer more glamorous fare than ho-hum
cannibalisms. There is an isle in the *Travels* where, in ancient times, virgins had snakes inside their vaginas so that husbands were stung to death
"inside the women's bodies" on nuptial nights (141). In the ripeness of
time and narrative, this led to the development of a corps of adventurous,
self-sacrificing young men called "Gadlibiriens" whose paid, risky occupation is "to take the maidenhead of a maiden" on her wedding night, in
surrogacy for the affrighted new husband (140). The *Travels* even furnishes a straightfaced account of "action . . . before the justices of the land"
against the young men should "the husband of the woman find her maid-
en on the next night following" (141). Sites of pleasurable identification
and fancy such as these abound in the *Travels*.

Retaining a handy convention from the earliest medieval romances,
travel romance attests that maidens galore are to be found in every foreign
country, niftily ready to serve in all possible configurations of primal
pleasure. The long-nailed Mandarin in the Cathay ruled by the Great
Khan has fifty damsels on hand for his bed and board, who "do what he
wills." In the best tradition of infantile fantasies, they sing to the Mandarin at mealtime, cut up his meat for him, and feed him (154). Hasan ibn
Sabah's illusory Paradise, in a tributary land of Prester John's, is also inhabited by the serviceably nubile. Here, beautiful damsels and boys,
"knafe childre" (for variety in sexual preference) "within the age of fifteen
years" promise "pleasure and dalliance" while remaining virginally intact
forever, despite sexual indulgence—ever enticing, ever desirable, ever
available, and utterly untouched by whatever time or deed might deliver
(137–38).[9] On one particular isle in the sea, luxuriant incest is the norm,
as men "wed their own daughters, and their sisters, and their women relatives," each man's wife being "common to the others" in shared communal quarters (142). So daring is this tremulously risky fantasy that it is
necessary to call these forbidden females-to-be-enjoyed "wives" (though

the sexual and family arrangements here render the term larkily meaning-less), in order to impart an aura of convention and legality, and thus reg-ulate a little the orgiastic import of this scene of widespread, casual incest.

By contrast, the harems of wives routinely attached to any man of sub-stance in any land heard of or visited by "Mandeville" almost seem tame in comparison, so frequently do we encounter such scenarios of multiple females per male. The Sultan of Babylon, the Great Khan, the King of Calanok, and even the sainted Prester John all have consorts in the plural. Prester John, befitting his now centuries-old status as fabled Oriental Christian king, is allowed to consort with his nuptial playmates in a fan-tasy amalgam that couples sexual license with ideal Christian piety, since this king beds his wives without lust, only four times a year, and "all only for to beget children," in chaste, overdetermined performances of ideal-ized sexual fantasy-as-rigorous-Christian-duty (136). Among the Tartars of Cathay, not only the Great Khan but each man has "as many wives as is pleasing to him, for some have a hundred, some forty, some more, some less" (120).

For audiences whose tastes incline toward dangerous women, the *Travels* offers the glamor of Medusa-like women with precious stones in their eyes, whose phallic gaze kills (141), the women warriors of the terri-fying Tartars (122), and, of course, that ancient to medieval to modern sta-ple, the militant sexuality of the Amazons (77–78). The exciting anecdote of the phallic virgins who harbor snakes in their vaginal passages thus neatly epitomizes, but does not exhaust, the unfettered fascinations of pleasure, danger, and female sexuality in varieties of combination. Fur-thermore, the many locales of the Orient in the *Travels*—the diverse places in "the East" where this panorama of women is to be found (a panorama that includes the dutiful widows of India who commit *suttee*, Chinese noblewomen with tiny bound feet, and the "fairest women that are in any land beyond the sea" in Manzi, or south China [141, 154, 101])—not only reconstitute the East as the locus of fantasy in sexual, gendered terms but also recapitulate the Orient as that traditional space and land-scape in which extreme forms of luridity and sensational violence can safe-ly occur, evacuated from Western culture.

For violence, like sex, is riveting to audiences of travel indulging in the consumption of exotica. Sadistic and masochistic exhibitions of the body, child sacrifice, bodily desecration with dung and urine (85), and other luridly extravagant bodily practices are thus also traditional fare on the menu of travel literature, and amply served up by the Orient. As a land-scape and territorial geography, the Orient also palpably exists as a vista of bodies on display, bodies that furnish the symbolic topography of the Orient. In "Marbaron," [Coromandel?] we are told, devotees of a massive idol mutilate themselves so that "the blood runs down from their wounds in great profusion" in ecstasies of religious worship (87). These cultists slaughter their own children before the Juggernaut and sprinkle their children's blood on the idol (87), and the devotees' excesses of self-mutilation include slicing off pieces of their own bodily flesh, and knifing themselves unto death (87). The drama of fetishistic religious exorbitance supplies an occasion for the *Travels* to comment on Christian customs, by contrast (87), even as it successfully articulates Oriental geography as a tableau of violent bodily practices. The National Geographic–like moment documents Marbaron as a landscape of self-mutilating bodies in cultural performance, the bizarre luridity of whose religious rituals, as living anthropological phenomena attested in travel literature, is also voyeuristically transfixing in itself, and pleasurably rivets audience attention in much the same way as cinematic violence and sex compel today.[10]

Because narrative pleasure imparted by forbidden behavior and the representation of landscape as bodies often involve contorted renditions of the human body—exaggerated depictions of the body's insides and outsides, anatomical regimen, demands, and appetites—cannibalisms of many varieties are shown to recur throughout the countries of the East. Polyphemos-like giants of the Geoffrey of Monmouth variety wade out to ships to eat seamen off one of the isles of India. In Tibet ("Ryboth or Gyboth"), also an "isle," sons ritually eat the boiled flesh from the heads of their dead fathers (152)—like the Issedones of Herodotus's *Histories* (6:26)—anthropopagi who are also located by the Hereford *mappamundi* in the Orient. Spontaneous and ritualistic cannibalisms are complemented by the aggressive military cannibalisms of monstrous races in Southeast Asia, where the dogheaded men of Natumeran eat enemies captured in battle (97), and the "wicked folk and cruel" of Melk glory in drinking human blood after delighting in human slaughter (97): a faint echo lingering here, perhaps, of the anti-Semitic medieval blood-libel of Europe projected onto distant climes.[11] Lamary's customary cannibalism—its people's preferred diet of sweet-fleshed children purchased from merchants (89)—rounds off the array of anthropopagy available in Oriental zones.[12] The East is a landscaped parade of human self-consumption.

Luridity and sensational extravagance identify only the most superficial forms of narrative pleasure devised by travel romances, however. An important technique of pleasure characterizing travel literature arises from the simple asymmetry of positions between the sedentary audience at home and the roving eye of the narrative as it travels around the world at large. The momentum of travel (including vicarious, imaginary travel) taps directly into the pleasures of accumulation (as places, people, and folkways are gathered up on an implied journey), and the satisfactions of onward advancement, as stages are completed, and phenomena and events are named, ordered, and located, in narrative recitation. Pleasures of this kind are intrinsic to travel narrative; they are equally intrinsic to any process of creating the external world as an object of knowledge, through any system of knowledge making that devises a hierarchy, and relations, of power.

In this context, the *Travels'* allegory of how men might comprehensively circumnavigate the globe—starting from their native countries, journeying around the world, and returning back home again, after a "long time"—is instructive (152). The trajectory plotted in this circular route—from home, to home—suggests it is the fixity of home, or one's native country, that orients the meaningfulness of global transversal. Everywhere the traveler passes, the secrets, curiosities, and adventures of the world are gathered and brought back to one's ultimate destination, home. Indeed, it is eminently possible to read the *Travels* as being interested not so much in foreign places and peoples *in and of themselves* but as invested in the prospect of bringing back these places and peoples to an audience in the West: for the purpose of telling the world, presenting the world, for domestic consumption. To a domestic audience, the retrieval of the world makes faraway places curiously mobile: sets in motion distant cultures, and centripetally transports them to domestic shores to allow for their inspection close-up from a vantage point of domestic fixity. The implications of this are many, but this segment of my argument concentrates principally on the pleasures derived from such mobilization and retrieval accomplished by the machinery of travel romance.

One of the reasons why travel narratives are enjoyable, then, involves the displacement of the world from outside to inside, as an external reality—huge and amorphous, disorderly, chaotic, in motion—is brought home and managed by being rendered internal, and possessed internally, first within the manuscript environment of a purported travelogue, and then within the mind of a listening, reading audience. To that audience, the world is not only the vast geophysical space inside which the narrator of the travelogue is presumed to travel but, more importantly, the finite space created inside (and by) the travelogue itself and inside the mind of the listening/reading audience. The outside world having thus become transformed into an archive of thrilling, virtually real particulars in manuscript and mind, that virtual world, reproduced within, registers as contained and knowable—under control—in ways that the outside world is not. In effect, the virtual world created by a vast travel account like "Mandeville's" transforms the world outside Europe—processing it through narrative—into a collection of facts, artifacts, and details, much like the collections in anthropological and natural history museums today, even as it allows an audience to become keepers and users of the collection.

If museums of natural history are epistemologically preceded by Renaissance wonder boxes and cabinets of curiosities that bring together, in the environment of a single receptacle, diverse objects and artifacts from the natural and human worlds, such Renaissance collections of phenomena are themselves preceded, and instigated, by medieval travel narratives like "Mandeville's." The *Travels* amass, within the receptacle of a single text, everything from alphabets to ants, idols and simulacra, a gravelly sea to a valley of death, astrolabes and compass points, crocodiles, chameleons, and cannibals, kings and Khanates, biblical stories, diamonds that grow and reproduce, agricultural techniques, places from Hangchow to the Earthly Paradise, political cameos of empires. Because the wonder box, the curiosity cabinet, of this travel romance is so ambitiously capacious in its reach, we see also why the narrative form assumed by *Mandeville's Travels* is exactly apt. This travel romance's fragments of facts, curious stories, and shards of insight create a narrative format that functions like a bricolage of exotica: The *Travels'* thick description of the world, and of history, *replicates narrative itself as a collection,* a vast holding of loosely gathered individual artifacts strung together with apparent contingency. The multifarious phenomena, objects, incidents, facts, and sketches that make up the narrative body of the *Travels* mimic the planet's diversity, and function like miniature windows on the world—framed views that open onto scenarios of time, place, and culture. As importantly, the exquisite collection of diversity also functions like a museum's acquisitions, assembled for a purpose and with a design.

But why would a narrative simulate a vast and various collection?

The instinct to collect, of course, tends to be urged by the idea—subliminal or conscious—that it is possible to control, and possess, vastness and variousness, through the possession of representative objects. Indeed, the vaster a collection, the greater the stakes in potential mastery and control over variety, as cultures and histories are acquired and sampled, through key shards and fragments.[13] A single example in the *Travels* of how cultures can be distilled into significant representative objects, and collected, resides in this travel romance's infamous exhibit of "alphabets" from many cultures—ostensibly Greek, Egyptian, Hebrew, "Saracen," Persian, Chaldean—a display that the narrative produces (with variants in different manuscript traditions) to summarize the varieties of Mediterranean culture by extracting and collecting their linguistic essences, purportedly in the form of distinctive alphabets. At the same time, the action of amassing significant collectibles such as alphabets transports different cultural worlds to a single location where these cultural worlds and their histories can be put on display, and contemplated.

Just as the vast holdings of the British Museum amply demonstrate the advantages of drawing the cultures of the world to a single center, so also does the manuscript or print environment of the *Travels*, gathering its vast storehouse to itself, afford particular epistemological advantage and viewing/sampling pleasure. Finally, the process of sampling, at close range and in one convenient vehicle, multiple cultures through their stories, rituals, folkways, treasures, or peoples produces conditions under which patterns can be detected across differences, across variety, so that similarities and relationships can be discovered among unlike particulars, and thus fuel or begin the process of formulating abstract principles, and universalizing generalizations, across the massive variety of available global particulars: This is a process of theorization, Bruno Latour points out, that initiates the beginnings of modern scientific method (225).[14]

A travel narrative like "Mandeville's," which articulates each far-off country on an implied or explicit scale of distance from Europe, and especially from England and France (two points the *Travels* names and to which the narrative periodically refers back), also constitutes the rest of the world as the periphery of Christian Europe (anchored by England/France), with home as the locus from which concentric circles of distance irradiate. As the late-medieval literary court of the romance King Arthur teaches us—at the Arthurian court many stories of marvels and adventures collect, and are told and retold—a center is constituted and consolidated at that very place where information which everyone finds useful or irresistible is gathered. (It is with good reason, thus, that Arthur refuses to sit down to a collective meal until he has heard a story or watched an adventure performed, since every story or adventure gathered at mealtime reconfirms the centrality of his court as the fulcrum of the surrounding human panorama.)

The geocultural model of the world and human relations produced by a narrative like "Mandeville's" thus implicitly, if enigmatically, describes those who stay at home as strong, crucially well-positioned, and knowledgeable, by virtue of being sedentary. Successful travel romance answers well to one crucial question in cultural colonization: How might it be possible to act at a distance on far-flung objects, places, peoples, and events? The answer—by bringing those distant places and peoples back home in such a way that the very process of retrieval itself would work to identify and establish "home" as a center—is the particular specialty, and province, of travel romance. Travel romance is a genre that obligingly allows an audience to sample the pleasures of movement while remaining in place, a pleasure that makes distant places and peoples mobile—mobilizes them—and conveys them home, so that "home" becomes a center that can dominate at a distance the world's far-flung ports.

Hence an audience at home, it would seem, has the advantage of seeing close at hand more variety, as Latour says, than is available to any ship's captain or traveling caravan from the experience of actual travel. Vicarious experience, offered as categorical forms of knowledge, enables the sedentary to inspect and command the world, in all its variety and complexity, once that world has been successfully constituted as an object of knowledge—a world that would otherwise dominate any individual traveler who attempts other modalities of experiencing and sampling.[15] If it seems strange that direct experience should thus appear to confer an inferior, more limited and limiting, species of knowledge than the secondary knowledge conferred by an indirect but apparently authoritative experience available to the sedentary reading audience at home, that strangeness is ameliorated when we grasp the political and cultural superiority assumed by a center in relation to its constituted cultural and geographical peripheries.

The cultural generosity of the *Travels*, which so impresses modern scholars, is therefore complexified when we consider the dynamic that obtains between a center and its peripheries. For instance, the *Travels* can readily acknowledge the so-called superior wisdom and skill of the people of Cathay ("most subtle and wise"), surpassing all other nations ("that folk are wondrously subtle of wit touching anything that they will do, before any other folk of the world. For they surpass all the nations of the world in subtlety of wit, whether it concerns ill or good; and that they themselves know well" [107]), because Cathay has already been inserted into a hierarchical relationship of marginality vis-à-vis Europe, the central locus at which the audience resides. The cultural confidence that makes this re-iteration of another's superiority possible—a confidence not diminished in the admission—issues from the given fact that the ostensibly superior Cathay only exists as a quaint novelty, a scrap of curious information in an archival circuit leading back to Europe: the center that judges, makes distinctions, categorizes, and pronounces. In bringing intriguing souvenirs from a virtual Cathay, on the periphery, back to a Europe, at the center, in the form of novel curiosities gathered for pleasurable domestic consumption, the cultural mastery of Cathay and its clever inhabitants, in the very act of being asserted, is already also being mastered with ineluctable assurance.

The variety and complexity of the world—in its human, animal, vegetable, mineral, historical, cosmological aspects—can only be miniaturized for the audience at home by being passed through mechanisms of selection and hierarchical ordering as the process of information transfer from peripheries to center occurs. The perfectly scaled diorama of the world thus produced by the *Travels*, exhibiting a chiaroscuro of the familiar interleaved with the unfamiliar, suggests how much the success of travel romance depends on discovering a principle by which alterity—otherness/difference—and distance can be processed and managed: held in active tension with what is intimately familiar and close by, so that pleasure and discovery, rather than anxiety or panic, are the dominant affects devised by narrative. To render palatable the depictions of otherness, the varieties of difference encountered in the world are self-consciously scaled to ensure that they are both intelligible to, and assimilable by, a domestic audience, and the invention of a functional mechanism of scaling is the special talent of travel romance. *Mandeville's Travels* epitomizes that seductive talent to an exemplary degree and with particular vivacity.

The *Travels* shows us that the scaling of the world can occur in two related ways. First, the narrative takes the precise measure and coordinates of objects and phenomena that differ from the range of normativity in Latin Christendom and Western Europe, a habit that thus establishes the precise relation of other to self, in a methodological procedure that amounts to a descriptive science. Second, and linked to the first, the narrational style of the *Travels* habitually alternates back and forth between the foreign and the familiar—by, say, strategically inserting a kernel of the familiar into each description of the foreign—so that an oscillation is accomplished in the pattern of narrative rhythm, a particular pulse frequently discovered in successful travelogues.

Narrative episodes often calibrate difference by a direct comparison with familiar equivalents at home, so that precise degrees of departure, as well as similarities, are noted with exactitude. Religious difference, in particular, falls under narrative instrumentation of this kind. Greek Orthodox Christianity's points of separation from Latin Christianity are explicated at length (*Travels*, 9–10).[16] Koranic divergence from, as well as convergences with, Old Testament law (36) are similarly tagged and noted, while the Koran's multiple crossovers into, and departures from, the New Testament story of Christ are also surveyed and mapped (66–68). The triangulated relationship binding Jews, Muslims, and Christians is located through commentary (68), and nodes of connection among various Eastern Christian denominations (Syrian, Greek, Jacobite, Georgian, Nestorian, Arian, Nubian, etc.) are pinpointed and put into articulation with Latin Christianity (59–60). A proximate link is even researched between the unlikely religion of the pagan "Tartars" and Latin Christians ("They believe all in [one] God, that made all things" [121]; "This emperor and all the folk of his land . . . they believe in great God, that made heaven and earth" [113]). Religious exposition seems to require accurate calibration of the exact angle of difference from the Western European, with even stray interconnections being observed and pinned down: "Syrians . . . hold a law midway between us and the Greeks. And they let their beards grow as the Greeks do, and make the sacrament of the altar of sour bread as the Greeks do, and use the letters of Greece, and shrive themselves as the Jacobines do" (59).

Remarkable in the *Travels'* survey of the religious spectrum is the evenness of voice in presenting the varieties of Christianity in the Mediterranean world. Rather than vilify and excoriate what would be classified in Europe as deviatory heresies by the norms of late-medieval Latin Christianity, the *Travels* offers variation from the Latin Christian norm as a potential source of pleasure, when the careful location of contrast and distinction, in dogma and practice, is managed: "And because the land of Greece is the nearest country that varies and is discordant in faith and letters from us and our faith, therefore I have set it in here, that you may wit the diversity that is between our truth and theirs; for many men have great pleasure and comfort to hear speak of strange things" (11). As the *Travels* ranges farther afield, moreover, pleasure is derived less from internal variation within the Christian fold and more from calibrating the difference between Christianity (flexibly defined) and non-Christianity.

Descriptions of the many religious cultures in the world are painstakingly overlaid by a grid that discloses each religious system's relation—

however slight—to Christianity and Christians; and the more foreign an object, the greater is the effort to interleave Christian markings into the object's description. In one discursus on the exotic horticultural glories of the Mediterranean Orient (in the Egypt Gap), in which bananas, melons, figs, and balm feature, and methods of growing, harvesting, and extracting balm are expounded on, we are spontaneously told, in the midst of lush foreign abundance, that "men of that country, [when it is] time that the field shall be tilled, get them[selves] Christian men for to till it and to gather it; and else the trees should bear no fruit, as the Saracens say themselves and oft-times has been assayed" (26). If this sudden self-referencing, and the unexpected efflorescence of a Christian moment within an anecdote on Saracen agriculture and Saracen precepts, is startling in its contingency, it is also well timed. In similarly reassuring fashion, we find that among the more than five thousand isles of India, where dwell bizarre others with "testicles [that] hang down to their shanks for the great violence of heat" (81), who worship the sun and snakes (82), and "make their [representations of] god half man and half ox" (82), or who are yellow and green (81), there are also cities where dwell "many good Christian men of good belief" and "many men of religion, and namely of friars" (83). Breaking through the sanguinary description of the Juggernaut in Marbaron, who requires the sacrifice of children's blood and the self-mutilation of devotees, is another such eruption of the Christian, this time in the form of an outcry: "Scarcely will any Christian man suffer half so much, not the tenth part, for the love of Our Lord Jesus Christ" (87).

Even farther away, in Cathay (or Mongol-dominated northern China), where those foreign people of superior wisdom and subtlety are to be found, who "surpass all the nations of the world," it appears that the superior inhabitants "hold Christian men most subtle and wise after themselves," for "they say that they look with two eyes and Christian men with one," accounting "folk of other nations . . . blind without eyes," as far as "knowledge and craft" are concerned (107). By this juncture we are no longer entirely surprised to learn that the emperor of Cathay, the Great Khan, has "many physicians, of which two hundred are Christian men, and twenty Saracens; but he trusts most in Christian men" (117). The nugget of proffered information on Christian physicians and converts in the Khan's entourage is lodged within a lengthy elaboration on the Khan's exotically foreign court, the clothing of nobles, different branches of science, knowledge, and philosophy at court, conjurations, minstrelsy, and dramatically staged spectacles, fabulous birds, beasts, and gems, descriptions of cities, hosts, and processions, provinces and deserts, empresses and women (114–17).

In contrast to contemporary historical narratives, the romance description of Christians in the Great Khan's Cathay shows no interest at all in distinguishing between *Latin Catholic* Christians—historically represented in fourteenth-century Cathay and Manzi (northern and southern China) by the houses and churches of the Franciscan friars—and *Nestorian* Christians, who were far more numerous in China and India, and who represented the exiled branch of Greek Orthodox Christianity that spread throughout the Far East since the deposition and exile of Nestorius, Greek Patriarch of Constantinople, after the Council of Ephesus in 431, and the subsequent expulsion of Nestorius's followers from Edessa in 489. Instead, the *Travels* offers *all* Christians in China as a single, unified category, so that Marco Polo's observation of a *Greek* chief physician in the Great Khan's entourage vanishes in the *Travels*, and a proliferation of two hundred undifferentiated *Christian men* who make up the Khan's Christian physicians is presented instead. In the face of the exorbitantly foreign, internal differences within Christianity are papered over, and familiar culture can be represented by any kind of Christian.

Reassuringly, we discover that the Great Khan, puissant emperor over a domain of innumerable countries, "doffs his hat" when he sees the Cross borne in procession by Christian religious in his realm, "bows devoutly to the cross" as the "prelate of those religious men" says prayers before him and blesses him with the sign of the Cross, and "bows to the blessing full devoutly" (120). Ultimately, in the *Travels'* roving disquisition on the strangeness of the world, we strategically learn—following the account of that exquisitely debauched long-nailed mandarin and the noblewomen with bound feet in Cathay—that "in all these lands, realms and nations . . . is no folk that they do not hold some articles of our belief. [Even] if all they be of diverse laws and diverse beliefs, they have some good points of our truth" (154).

Other than for the comfort and reassurance tendered, why do these self-reflexive intrusions occur, in which the Christian/European "I" punctually pops up in the midst of the utterly foreign? Beyond reading such moments as commonplace recuperations of otherness—the indelible prints of a colonizing impulse that domesticates all alterity by narcissistically reproducing oneself, and the image of one's culture, even while ostensibly speaking of otherness—can we detect another practice being explored by travel romance in encounters with alterity? We have seen how popular romances in the Middle Ages—such as *Richard Coer de Lyon* and *The King of Tars*, with their Christian-Moslem/black-white polarities—defend against difference by demonization and rejection, which is the strategy, also, of English nationalist history, with devastating consequences in the 1290 expulsion of the Jews. The preferred response of elite chivalric romances—such as the alliterative *Morte Arthure* and *Sir Gawain and the Green Knight*—has been self-celebration, the apotheosizing of the traditional values of the core milieu and culture under threat. Might the particular circuit of pleasure that is set in motion in medieval travel romance—a species of narrative with different reach and ambitions, we have said, from other varieties of romance—by comparison structure new imagined relations with otherness, beyond refusal?

Because encounters with the extraordinary, far and wide around the globe, are a repeating, incessant feature in travel narratives to an extent and kind beyond what is usual in other romances, the insertion of a familiar core is a necessary, indeed inevitable gesture. Confronted with the unintelligible—the absolutely foreign—where no familiar points of reference exist to determine an orientation, subjectivity and narration break down, lapse into incoherence. Before arrival at a moment of failure in comprehension, where a subject or a culture is overcome and silenced by the sheer incommensurability of what is encountered, the insertion of familiar coordinates by which to orient the encounter restores intelligibility and a position from which to speak. (In a related but not identical fashion, encounters with what is not absolutely different, but only contingently different, can also profit from such calibrated orientation.) The personified narrator of the *Travels*, then, a medieval human-subject-as-world-traveler and Latin Christianity/Western European culture's representative, is able to present himself as open to otherness—as actively participating in otherness—because "he" conjures up his familiar cultural and religious system in step with the narrated experience of otherness. The *Travels* narrates one of theirs, nimbly followed by one of ours; or presents a long description of something foreign alongside a smaller description of the familiar; or materializes a moment of domesticity in an environment of the outrageously foreign. The practice of punctual, reliable reference back to the known and familiar is so habitual that it is entirely unobtrusive.

Thus emboldened by a structure of support that materializes home and the constants of home in the instant of unsettling encounters with alterity, the narrative of the *Travels* willy-nilly plots a route through the economy of otherness that allows for a *modulated admission of otherness*, and a *participation* in otherness. Instead of the refusal, demonization, or self-idealizing narcissism staged by other varieties of medieval romance, the oscillation between distance and proximity in travel romances calibrates alterity as intermittent, not constant. One-of-theirs/one-of-ours, one-of-theirs/one-of-ours (or: ours-inside-theirs; theirs/ours) accomplishes a narrative frequency or pulse, a recitative rhythm, that substantially honors the principle of pleasure, in travel romance, and obviates potential panic, so that the unfamiliar can be safely enjoyed. Like all rhythmic repetitions that engage an audience in the interplay of expectation and surprise (different in *this* way, but similar in *that* way), the repetitive patterning cadence in the *Travels* can be enjoyed in and of itself, as well as for what it allows. Thus the pleasure of gazing on, and sampling, the foreign in travel narratives is not merely a voyeuristic pleasure—which the surrogate enjoyment of the forbidden, such as sex and tabooed forms of violence in travel narratives, would suggest—but also the complex mobility and freedom for partial identification and engagement with many possible positions, and from many possible vantage points, that the safety of calibrated, intermittent admission and participation opens up, and makes available.

Gazing on the foreign with the support of a familiar structure is, in any event, inevitable to a degree in travel literature, since "the human mind can only encompass the entirely new in terms of the old" (Moseley, "Behaim's Globe," 90). For travel romances, the calculated admission of difference is an imperative freedom, since the pleasures of otherness—the pull of exotica and immense variety, told against the recall, and reminder, of familiar orientation—are a vital propulsive force in travel accounts. Even if we decide that the narrative practice of punctuated self-referencing, and self-reflexivity, constitutes a willfully aestheticized gesture of co-optation, the regulated admission of otherness as a category to be conjured with, without the immediate necessity of refusal, devises alternative imagined relations with otherness in which partial identification with, and partial participation in, otherness can be *narratively rendered.* Despite the decadence of a Cathay marked by the unique debauchery of a long-nailed mandarin, Christians may yet exist in a relationship of conditional identification with the country's inhabitants by virtue of the superior wisdom that sets off both the communities of Cathay and Europe together, apart from the populations of the rest of the world, and makes them contingently alike (107). Similarly, the presence of Christians in the Khan's Cathay stages the mutual implication of cultures: cultures rendered mutually constitutive here by the Khan's dependence on his Christian physicians (117) and his demonstrable respect for Christian prelates, symbols, and processional rituals (120).

Travel romance's narrative frequency of intermittence, we might say, opens up a quasi-utopian interzone in which a Latin Christian/Western European subject, and culture, can encounter its other and announce a variety of negotiable positions, without rejection or falling into the trap of either/or oppositions. This limited, interzonal space that gathers up both subject and other in a kind of choreographed participation, an orchestrated dance of self-and-other, is utopian to the extent that it is a willed fabrication of travel romance, driven by the narrative's designs on pleasure and retention of safe guarantees.

Because travel romance can exercise a willfully, if imperfectly, utopian impulse—in the format of a narrative dynamic, or cadence, with utopian ambitions—does not, of course, mean that what our critical idiom today refers to as "othering" is preponderantly absent. Indeed, the recognition and admission of difference afforded by a narrative like "Mandeville's" says less about whether "othering" in fact occurs in travel romance and more about the fact that the status of otherness has changed, is different, in this species of romance. Scholars who have enjoyed *Mandeville's Travels* often intuitively, if inexpressibly, grasp that the changed status of otherness in the *Travels*—touched by some music or coloration that aspires to the utopian—makes the *Travels* feel, in fact, qualitatively different ("a turning . . . towards diversity, difference, the bewildering variety of 'marvellous things'" [Greenblatt, 29]) from literatures where the impulse to colonize goes more nakedly undisguised.[17]

It is important to reiterate that the status conferred on otherness by genres such as travel romance and ethnography—genres in which otherness, as a category, can be temporarily privileged or defended—does not necessarily prevent the domestication of alterity, even by successful exemplars, nor the depicted consignment of foreign others to a satellite position around Western European culture. The simple truism that one can never go where none has gone before, but only where the example of others (Herodotus, Solinus, Pliny, etc.) has preceded, in order that the traveling narrative eye might understand what is seen, means that would-be utopian impulses—in the Middle Ages as today—can simultaneously celebrate "multicultural diversity" while containing and managing the threats of "multicultural difference." Despite the *Travels'* orchestrated modulations of encounters with otherness, scholars have duly noted, for instance, the narrative's harsh treatment of the Jews, a handling that differs little, if any, from treatment in other romances (see Biddick; Westrem; Higgins, *Writing East*; and Greenblatt).[18] Ultimately, the freedom the *Travels* wrests for itself, in conjuring a circuit of pleasure, still enacts a lever for moving the world in the direction of Europe, and names alterity in order to articulate its place within a regime of knowledge and power that scales the world as an intelligible construct, an object of knowledge for consumption and use within Western Europe.

It may be that all narrative transactions with otherness, in travel romance or ethnography, inevitably arrive under the sign of compromise. Just as it is impossible to go where none before has ventured, it may be equally unrealizable to narrate a zone or dynamic of exchange in which self and other participate in mutual admission, implication, and constitution, unmarked by, and outside, regimes of knowledge/power. Exceptional as *Mandeville's Travels* is among romances, the scale model of the world created by and in narrative exists at the nodal intersection of pleasure with power.

HOME IS THE CENTER OF THE WORLD:
EUROPE, THE EAST, AND THE RE-ORIENTATION OF EMPIRE

Although the *Travels* pragmatically presents the world as a sphere amenable to circumnavigation (90, 91–92, 149–50, 152), the narrative's theological imagination also simultaneously insists that the earth's sphericity has a midpoint, identified as Jerusalem. Two kinds of cartographic systems, then—one representing a geoscientific, the other a theological, *weltanschauung*—jostle against each other in a single instant: "The earth and sea are round . . . it is the common word that Jerusalem is in the middle of the earth" (91).[19] From its inception, the narrative presupposes Jerusalam to be the objective of world travelers, who "may wend [by] many ways, both on the sea and on the land" since many ways "come all to one end." All roads, it seems, lead to Jerusalem (3). The *Travels'* location of Jerusalem at the center of the world is, of course, purposeful, more purposeful even than in the European *mappaemundi* created in the wake of the first crusades (and famously represented by the Ebstorf and Hereford), which also situate Jerusalem as the world's *omphalos* and the object of pilgrim desire and crusader occupation. Because the world of a travelogue is so richly various, thoroughly disorienting, and surpassingly strange, a clear cosmographical center by which to orient a world system, and still any dizzying encroachment of relativist notions, is deeply stabilizing.

But then we learn that the center itself has a center. In a concentrically narrowing focus, this inner center is the precise spot where Joseph of Arimathea, by tradition, laid the body of Christ, after it had been taken down from the cross: "A circle . . . and men say that that compass is in the mid-point of the world" (79). Radiating from inner and outer midpoints, then, the narrative circles around Jerusalem and the Holy Sepulcher, describing places, topography, and regions both close by and far off, faithfully relating folk anecdotes, biblical mythology, and stories associated with the surrounding regions culled from literary predecessors. The effect of these stories—some of which follow the *Travels'* principal source for describing the Near East, William of Boldensele, but with subtle differences—is to produce the surrounding regions, as scholars of the *Travels* have noticed, as "a marvellous reliquary" (Higgins, *Writing East*, 105), a field in which "The Holy Land [itself] is presented as a relic of sorts" (Howard, 9).[20] Medievals were obsessed with relics, of course, because relics were felt, inter alia, to carry the intimate presence and aura of the body associated with them, and to continue, and keep alive, some contact with the original body, *contra* the passage of time, in tangible, physical form.[21] The desire for relics is a desire for intimate contact with a precious sacred body, a body that is not lost but continues alive and present through what it once touched.

Like the Ebstorf *mappamundi*, in which the entire world itself is depicted as the manifest body of Christ, the Holy Land in the *Travels* embodies the presence of Christ, his mother, and the saints, in rock and stone, water and hill: a presence focused on a geographical region for a specific purpose. On the Mount of Olives, where Christ stood as he ascended into heaven, "still may men see the step [footprint] of his left foot in a stone that he stood on" (48). In the Vale of Jehosephat is a little stream, over which was laid, as a plank bridge for men to cross, "the tree that the holy cross was made of." A little distance away "is a pit in the earth; and therein is the base of the pillar to which Christ was bound that time that he was scourged" (47). Near the church of St. Nicholas are red rocks with white spots on them, because the Virgin "had too much milk in her paps, which grieved her sore, [and] she milked it out upon the red stones of marble that were there; and still the spots of the white milk are seen upon the stones" (36). "And half a mile from Nazareth is the leap that our Lord leaped from the Jews, when they led him upon a high rock to have cast him down and slain him; but he passed through them and leapt to another rock, where his steps [footprints] are yet seen" (56). Mount

Tabor, "a fair hill and a high" where Christ transfigured himself before the apostles Peter, James, and John, is a site that seals together past and future presence, the exact locus where all bodies will one day finally return, and be fully present: "and upon that same hill, and in that same place upon the day of judgement shall four angels blow their trumpets and raise all that are dead" (56).[22]

Such acts of pointing, in ostentatiously simple and direct fashion, to a particular spot—"upon *that* same hill, in *that* same place"—are imbued with a searching poignancy, and create a powerful evocation, an urgent narrative tug. We are made to see the physical literality of Christ's life when we look at the land, a rock, a tree: We see Christ's body saturating the Holy Land, whose constituent rocks and stones become extensions of his body, and other sacred bodies, when even the stains from his mother's milk can be seen and touched on a rock. Palpable in the sheer physicality intended by such pointing is a propulsive structure of desire—desire for the Lord, desire for the land in which he walked—created for the designated purpose of inducing visitation, of an imagined or actual kind. The cumulative effect of a Holy Land suffused, and replete, with the presence of Christ, his mother, and the saints, apostles, and angels, must be to make a medieval audience—an audience already attuned to the immanence of the sacred through liturgical repetition, Bible stories, sacramental rites, theology, and the cult of relics—long to visit the region.

The structure of desire that *Mandeville's Travels* taps and reinforces—a yearning for the Holy Land, intensified by the pull of Christ's life revivified—has meant that the *Travels* have been read, not unfairly, as participating in the lively culture of crusading propaganda that pervaded, and characterized, the fourteenth century, a culture especially vigorous in the first half of the century.[23] Such a reading is encouraged—indeed, is rendered unavoidable—by the *Travels'* exordium, a large part of which is patterned after a series of familiar, entirely conventional formulas urging crusading pilgrimage, formulas that had their exemplar in Urban II's crusading address at Clermont in 1095. Parroting, then, the ragbag of instantly recognizable, highly conventionalized locutions that are by now two and a half centuries old in usage, the exordium reminds Christians the Holy Land was promised as their heritage; exhorts every able-bodied male Christian to join in the region's reconquest and expel the infidel; and even castigates, as Urban reportedly did, the "pride, envy, and covetousness" of the "lords of the world" who are "more busy for to disinherit their neighbors than to challenge or conquer their rightful heritage" (2).

Immediately following the repetition of these standard urgings, the personified narrator—"I John Mandeville, Knight"—effloresces for the first time in his full persona, complete with authenticating biographical details ("born in England in the town of St. Albans, and passed the sea the year of Our Lord Jesus Christ 1332, on Michaelmas Day"), and declares that his travel narrative is "specially for them that want and are in purpose to visit the holy city of Jerusalem and the holy places that are thereabout; and I shall tell of the way that they shall hold thither" [2–3]). Rarely, in literature, has a plainer declaration of narratorial purpose and intent been so positioned.

Prompted thus in this manner, scholars have accordingly read the "marvellous piety" of the *Travels* (Higgins, *Writing East*, 95), its "marvellous affirmation of typological history linked with the glory days of the crusades" (107), and its insistence on Jerusalem's centrality as being directed (however tenuously or wistfully) toward "the Holy Land's reconquest" or "dreams of Christian re-expansion" (105). Historians, in surveying the vast, unwieldy body of fourteenth-century crusading propaganda—from letters, tracts, and advice literature to philosophical treatises and political-military prognostications—have occasionally included the *Travels* among the crusade-advocacy literature written by documented pilgrims to the Holy Land, including the *Travels'* principal source for descriptions of the Near East, the book of the German Dominican, William of Boldensele (see, e.g., Atiya, *Later Middle Ages*, 161–65). The *Travels'* selection of an English knight for its narrator is also intelligible in terms of crusading advocacy. Not only were "English pilgrims" to the Holy Lands "quite numerous" in the fourteenth century (Atiya, *Later Middle Ages*, 176) and knights prominent as leaders throughout crusade history, but historians have argued that, in the fourteenth century, English knights, in particular, were much drawn to the ideological ideals of the crusade (see chapter 3 above, and Keen, "Chaucer's Knight").

Other factors also favor rendering the narratorial persona as an English knight-adventurer. English knight-adventurers working for pay or booty were not uncommon in the fourteenth century (see chapter 3 above), so that the narrator, "Mandeville," in laying claim to soldierly employment, cuts a recognizable figure when he tells us that he worked for infidel and heathen alike: "I dwelled a long time with the Sultan [of Babylon] and was soldier with him in his wars against the Bedoynes" (18); "my fellows and I were dwelling [as] soldiers with the Great Khan sixteen months against the King of Manzi" (108). The history of Latin crusaders in the Holy

Land—a history of repeated alliances between crusaders and Muslims, ranged against other Muslims (and crusaders)—shows how little contradiction existed between "Mandeville's" narrated employment by the infidel and his calling for a crusade against the same. (After all, even Charlemagne's eighth-century invasion of Spain, famously mythologized as a holy war against the infidel by the *chanson de geste* rendition of Roland at Roncevaux, was, in fact, historically conducted to oblige one infidel in his wars against another.)

Another, important factor that favors making "Mandeville" an English knight is hinted at in an aside by the most recent major scholar on the *Travels.* Iain Higgins's astute observation that it is the vulnerable *Acre*, and not the long-lost Jerusalem (lost to Saladin in 1187 and a much-transacted pawn thereafter in Christian-Muslim-Mongol military politics and empire mongering in the Levant), which is given "pride of place" in the pair of maps made by the English historian Matthew Paris "to accompany his thirteenth-century *Chronica majora*" (Higgins, "Jerusalem," 49; Akbari, 21), argues for the active presence of a contextualized sensitivity, in late-medieval English culture, to the vulnerability of Christian places in crisis.

If the *Travels* were indeed created, and began to circulate in England and France, around the mid-fourteenth century, as editorial tradition agrees, the loss of Acre, the last crusader-controlled city-port in the Levant, in 1291, would have had half a century to weigh on the minds of the pious, mingled with the sedimented affects of other territorial losses, including symbolic Jerusalem: "Jerusalem" being the shorthand name, in the medieval Christian imagination, for all the lost territories of the crusader East that Latin Christianity had failed to recover, despite concerted attempts. But it is not only "Jerusalem" (or lost crusader territory) that figures as a problem place in the *Travels,* requiring rescue, reconfiguration, and restoral. The *Travels'* survey of Christendom, I want to suggest, identifies for attention *a set of key places,* specially vulnerable in the fourteenth century, that function as the sedimented locations of Christian identity and Christianity's critical "homes": the invested nodal points in a field of meaning that anchors, and shores up, the coordinates of an intelligible Christian identity in the Middle Ages.

In part because the narrative poses as a travel account—touches on the process of traveling, describes issues and phenomena associated with a location—*Mandeville's Travels* is able to show itself acutely sensitive to the *problem of place,* the urgencies posed by key locations and places in Christendom of the fourteenth century. If, as a travelogue, the *Travels* is well positioned to be sensitive to the *crisis of place* which is much in evidence in the century's first half, then as travel romance it is equally well positioned to devise an overarching answer available specifically to this form of narrativized cartography, demonstrating, in the process, that cartography-as-narrative is what travel romance—whose contents issue a global view of the world, and global ambitions—is.

English versions of the *Travels* (Egerton, Cotton, Defective) contain an interpolation at the end that has puzzled scholars, an interpolation in which the personified narrator, the knight "John Mandeville," on his way home to England, visits the Pope in Rome and shows the Holy Father the book of the *Travels* he has written, which ostensibly recounts his long journey; the Pope, in turn, then shows him another book, "after which . . . the *Mappa Mundi* has been made." The narrator then proclaims with satisfaction, "And so our Holy Father the Pope has ratified and supported my book in all points," asks for prayers in the style of good medieval authors, and ends his travelogue. If the *Travels* was completed around 1356 (as claimed in Cotton and Anglo-Norman Royal 20 B.X) or 1366 (claimed in Egerton and Defective), the Pope, of course, was *not* in fact resident at Rome, but at Avignon, and was the political puppet of the French monarchy, ever since Pope Clement V, former archbishop of Bordeaux, moved his see to Poitiers in 1305 and thence to Avignon in 1309, just outside the borders of France, inaugurating a papal disappearance from Rome that came to be called "the Babylonian Captivity." This crisis of absence from Rome was subsequently followed by an even worse exigency. Though Gregory XI returned to Rome in 1377, Gregory's death the year after itself ushered in what came to be called the "Great Schism," as the Roman curia elected one Pope to succeed Gregory while another was elected at Avignon, and the disastrous spectacle of two Popes (or more, at different moments) contesting the governance of Latin Christendom painfully haunted and divided medieval Latin Europe for more than a generation after, well into the fifteenth century.

The English *Travels*' desire for the Pope to be in residence at Rome in 1356 or 1366 attentively names Rome, with its empty see, as a problem site, like Jerusalem, emptied of monarch and crusaders.[24] If Jerusalem represented a sacred symbolic center for all Christians throughout Europe, Rome stood as the center from which the spiritual (and, by the Middle Ages, temporal) governance of the faithful on earth had issued since saints Peter and Paul.[25] Twin homes of Christianity fulfilling twinned purposes, Jerusalem and Rome are thus magically positioned at both ends of the

English *Travels'* narrative, at beginning and closure. We suddenly see another reason why the body of Christ must fill the Holy Land with its material imprint: Not only has all trace of Christian occupation been evacuated—made to vanish—from the Levantine homeland, since the loss of Acre, but another time-honored key home of Christian occupancy has been vacated by Christ's supreme vicar on earth. The *Travels* materializes, makes present and tangible, the body of Christ all around and in Jerusalem, and the Holy Land, *because* the body of Christ's human representative on earth is tangibly absent from Rome and the Holy See. Narrative insistence on Christ's immanence, then, in his historical homeland, set over and against his vicar's evanescence from the historical seat of ecclesiastical authority, identifies two problem places as linked in crisis: vacant homelands of Christendom from which Christian power and presence—material and symbolic—have been emptied.

Between Rome and Jerusalem, however, is another critical home in geopolitical Christian cartography. We note that soon after the beginning of the narrative, and immediately upon listing Jerusalem as the objective of all travelers, the *Travels* takes us from England, the first country listed in northwestern Europe from which pilgrim departure is imagined ("from the west parts of the world, like England, Ireland, Wales, Scotland or Norway" [4]), not, in fact, to Jerusalem, but to *Constantinople*, and, more concretely, to the church of St. Sophia, where we are made to halt before a statue of the Emperor Justinian, a statue, we are explicitly told, as the gaze of our mind's eye is arrested, that symbolizes the former imperial puissance of Eastern Christianity. Halting at this first pilgrim's stop, "Mandeville" renders a description of this famous statue that purposively calls attention to narratorial tampering and design: "[The narrator] comes out with a lie . . . describing the famous golden statue of Justinian that stood before the Hagia Sophia, he falsely claims that the 'round appell of gold in his hond' has fallen out [and when replaced will not remain] because 'this appull betokeneth the lordschipe that he hadde ouer all the world that is round'— which lordship has been broken" (Campbell, *Witness*, 144).

The *Travels'* willful insistence here that the emperor's insignia of lordship and rule is missing—when in fact it is not—evocatively registers the hollow absence of military-political power in fourteenth-century Constantinople, the third problem place in Christianity. Vanquished, pillaged, and plundered by the Latins of the Fourth Crusade in 1204, and occupied for more than half a century by Western Europe, Constantinople remained forever weak thereafter, its power hollowed out from within, even after its recovery by the Greeks in 1261. Once a puissant Christian empire holding back the tides of Islam and paganism for a millenium, Constantinople in the fourteenth century stood in the shadow of a new Turkish threat in the shape of a growing Ottoman dynastic rule, with the rise to power of Osman at the century's inception. The *Travels'* capsule sketch of the Emperor Justinian's statue outside the Hagia Sophia, then, is a fine instance of allegorical cryptonomy in brief, an encapsulation of the salient losses in the Byzantine Empire's history tendered with remarkable poignancy and concision:

> For he was wont to be emperor of Romany [Romania], of Greece, of Asia the less [Asia Minor], of Surry [Syria], of the land of Iudee [Judaea], in which is Jerusalem, of the land of Egypt, of Persia and Arabia; but he has lost all, except Greece, and that land only he holds. Men would many times have put the apple [back] into the image's hand, but it will not abide therein. This apple betokens the lordship that he had over all the world. The other hand he holds lifted up against the west, in token for to menace mis-doers [evildoers]. This statue stands on a pillar of marble. (4–5)

The statue's lonely and ineffectual vigil on its pillar of marble, one hand uplifted against the historical menace of the West, even as the emperors of Constantinople were forced in the fourteenth century to seek Western Europe's aid against the Turkish peril in the East, time and again after Constantinople's recovery, forlornly recognizes the poignancy of the Greek Empire's fragility—the inability of Christianity's once mighty traditional guardian in the Eastern and Southern Mediterranean to hold on to recovered power, even as men tried "many times [to] put the apple [back] into the image's hand"—a fragility that would eventually lead to the crusading debacle outside the walls of Greek Nicopolis in 1396 and Constantinople's eventual fall to the Ottoman Turks in 1453. Cued by the *Travels* in this fashion, we are invited to grasp the substantial cultural anxiousness in the fourteenth century over Constantinople: a city linked to Jerusalem and Rome not only by the history of the crusades from the eleventh century on but also, in *Mandeville's Travels,* by the suggestive motif of Passion relics at Constantinople—half of the crown of thorns and the spearhead of the Holy Lance (which "Mandeville" claims to have seen with his own eyes)—relics whose significant purpose is, yet again, to instantiate the suffering body of Christ at a specific locus (6–7).

If a statue's empty hand in Constantinople, and Christ's palpable immanence around Jerusalem, are canny figures of absence and presence that announce the linked relationship of three places in crisis in Christendom's homelands, the narration of such figures in the *Travels* also suggests how a travel romance responds to the exigency of places in crisis, and the concomitant erosion of security in the field of meaning and identity that symbolic sites, and centers of power and governance, enact for the homeland's community. Posted in the narrative foreground of the *Travels*, of course, are explicit calls to crusade, to be better Christians, calls even to effect conversion. Peter of Lusignan's crusade to Alexandria, in 1365 (the capture of Alexandria being strategically understood as the sine qua non of any attempt to recapture Jerusalem, in military prognostications after the Third Crusade), is one formal response by history—through the historical agent of the contemporary king of Jerusalem-in-exile—in answer to the myriad cultural urgings for the rescue of key places in Christendom. The Nicopolis crusade of 1396 is another prompted historical response. Indeed, that cultural exhortations might be answered by military ventures is a lesson of the fourteenth century: "The first half of the fourteenth century, extending roughly from 1292 to 1344, abounds in propagandist literature for the resumption of the Crusade. The second half of the century, lasting from 1344 to 1396, is a period of successive Crusading campaigns in the East" (Atiya, *Commerce*, 93).

Yet the *Travels'* description of the world's vast immensity, with its many pockets of possibility, implicitly issues a response of another, more durable, creative, and expansive kind, a response from the resourcefulness of cultural invention, and with long-lasting implications in the age of intensive exploration that succeeds the medieval period. Though travel narratives as a species share some commonalities of narration—e.g., the fondness for "lists" of marvels is a repeating feature from the Greek "Indika" travelogues of the third century B.C.E. through "Mandeville" and after—travel accounts are by no means alike in the worlds they select to present to their audiences. Marco Polo's narrative, for instance, shows scant interest in conjuring up the Holy Land and the Christian Near East in its mental world map. The narrator's attention is firmly lodged in Central and East Asia, the territories of the Mongols, northern and southern China, continental and insular Southeast Asia, and even Japan. In reverse, accounts of the Near East by imagined or actual pilgrims, including William of Boldensele, evince little curiosity over the farthest Asias, the "East" of India, Southeast Asia, Cathay and Manzi, and what might lie beyond. By contrast, "Mandeville's" evocation of the fullest possible planetary survey accomplishes several forms of attention in one vehicle. Scholars have noted, for instance, that the *Travels* stitches a meticulous description of the Christian Mediterranean (based primarily but not exclusively on William of Boldensele) to a more "speculative" description of the farthest East of the Franciscan/Dominican missions and Polo, based primarily but not exclusively on Odoric of Pordenone, and displaying some familiarity, perhaps, with near-contemporary letters and records documenting the Franciscan and Nestorian presence in Cathay and Manzi.

We might add that northwestern Europe, as a geographic and cultural entity, also exerts some pressure on the *Travels'* attention, with England and France being singled out for particular mention at intervals and presented as points of universal reference. Thus a pilgrim's journey, for the *Travels*, begins with England at the head of the countries listed as constituting the regions of the West (4); thus, also, remarkably, it seems the Sultan of Babylon and his lords speak French (108), apparently a universal language even for fourteenth century Egypt. England is also a normative yardstick by which to measure the constructs and systems of others. When discoursing on the so-called Saracen alphabet, the narrator observes that "we have in our speech in England two other letters than they have in their a-b-c-e, that is to say, þ and ȝ, which are called thorn and yogh" (71); and English miles are the *Travels'* assumed standard in measuring distance, a standard from which even other European measures are seen to deviate ("I speak not of leagues of France, Gascoyne, Provence, or Germany, where they have great miles" [58]).

In its geoscientific apprehension of the dimensions and shape of the world, the *Travels* tacitly uses England (partnered with Scotland) as a point by which to orient an understanding of the earth's sphericity, with all sphericity's attendant ramifications ("they have day when we have night, and night when we have day" [91]). Finally, in a long, extraordinary section expatiating on the earth's circumference ("20,425 miles," based on "a mile of eight furlongs, as miles are in our country"), angles and degrees of geometric calculation, and calibration of what appears to be azimuth, the *Travels* exhibits palpable concern that "England, Scotland, Wales and Ireland are not reckoned [accounted for] in the height of the earth, as it well seems by all the books of astronomy" recorded by "ancient wise philosophers and astronomers" from a substantially earlier era of discovery and mapping (91).

Thus we see that England and France are part of the story of the Holy Land by being sites of embarkation for imagined pilgrimages but, simultaneously, that other details in the *Travels'* references to these countries also place England and France *outside* the narrative of sacred spaces as well. Indeed, the mention of *England* and its ambient regions, in particular, often arises in descriptions of secular and scientific systems of measuring and viewing—contexts that exert a counter-gravitational pull to the pious narrative of religious places in crisis. Secular constructions in these contexts position alternative systems of intelligibility in viewing and understanding the world, interleaving what we might think of today as an expanding scientific perspective into the older, religious perspective. Inexorably, the counter-gravitational pull of newer ways to imagine the world opens out the traditional map of theological cartography and interposes new secular, geoscientific, and technological worlds betwixt and between the symbolic places of the old cosmos.

As modern ideas of the world and newer perspectives infiltrate and ramify, their very elaboration gives back to the old theological cosmos an altered image of itself, a recombined sense of intelligibility. Contact and interaction of this kind—between traditional places and what Foucault ("Of Other Spaces") called "heterotopian" geographies that give back the world to itself differently—exerts an action on the old traditional sites of the theological-cartographic system. When new allocations appear and are surveyed on the map of the cultural universe, old locations shift, and displace, and the cartographic imagination itself adjusts to the complication.[26]

Beyond inserting heterotopian mirrors into domestic European culture and Latin Christian *mentalités*, however, the *Travels'* most farsighted experiment in the construction of heterotopias pivots on opening up identificatory spaces in the farthest corners of the known and imagined world.[27] We are pointedly told by the narrator, "Mandeville," that through all the fabled heterogeneity of the five thousand isles of India, the vastness of the Khan's Cathay, Prester John's fabulous realm, or the glamorous decadence of southern China, we should "understand that in all these lands, realms and nations . . . is no folk that they do not hold some articles of our belief. [Even] if all they be of diverse laws and diverse beliefs, they have some good points of our truth. And generally they believe in God that made the world" (154). The *Travels'* remarkable embrace—more than mere tolerance—of heterogeneity in matters of faith is vividly captured in this eloquent articulation of narratorial position: a dynamic embrace of plurality and heterogeneity that stands in pronounced contrast to the persecutions of heretical opinions and movements within late medieval Latin Christian Europe itself.

The *Travels'* active and generous welcome is the more extraordinary when contrasted historically with the bitter vilifications of the Francisan friars against their Nestorian Christian counterparts and spiritual competitors in the farthest East—the lands where Mandeville is supposed to have sojourned—as recorded in the fourteenth-century archive of letters, travelogues, and chronicles, including the *Travels'* most important source on Eastern matters, Odoric of Pordenone's travel narrative. Rather than rejoice in the presence of Christian houses in Tana, for example, Odoric's record names and identifies those houses as deviant in the instant of their acknowledgment as Christian. They are "Nestorian" houses, which is to say "schismatics and heretics" ("scismatici et heretici" [Yule-Cordier, 2:284], "most worthless and most vile" [2:297]), whose deviancy is immediately shown up by the 1321 martyrdom, at Tana, of friars of Odoric's own Franciscan order, who are on their way to join the mission of John of Monte Corvino, Archbishop of Khanbalik (Peking). Dwelling on this Franciscan martyrdom at length in a lovingly conventional exercise of descriptive hagiography, Odoric's travelogue takes pains to underscore and shore up doctrinal Latin Christian orthodoxy (Yule-Cordier, 2:284–94) in the face of heterodox Nestorianism.

In Cathay itself the second letter of John of Monte Corvino, dated January 8, 1305, inveighs in detail against the "slanders" of "Nestorians [who] both directly and by the bribery of others have brought the most grievous persecutions upon me . . . so that I was often brought to judgment, and in danger of a shameful death" (Dawson, 224–25). The century before, one of the most important Franciscan missionaries from Europe to the East, William of Rubruck, had been no less scathing of Nestorian prevarication, in describing Nestorian exaggeration of a Kerait ruler's legacy in order to co-opt the magical aura attained by the Western myth of Prester John, a figure with whom the Kereit was linked: "They used to tell of him ten times more than the truth. For the Nestorians coming from these parts do this kind of thing—out of nothing they make a great rumor" (Dawson, 122).[28] The *Book of the Estate of the Great Khan*, possibly authored by John of Cora, c. 1330, merely sums up, then, the ordinary Latin Christian response in the fourteenth century to the "schismatic Nestorians" when it condemns these "false Christians and miscreants" as responsible for preventing John of Monte Corvino from converting all of China "to the Christian and catholic faith" (Moule, 250).

The *Travels'* celebration of a flexible, heterogeneous community sharing some tenets of the Christian faith in common is thus a romance gesture that sheds the historical record of fractious condemnation and division within the many nonidentical Christian constituencies of the
fourteenth century, at home and abroad, in favor of theorizing a nominal
Christianity that is cosmopolitan and ubiquitous, existing anywhere and
everywhere in the far-flung world. This optimistic hypothesis of a cosmopolitan Christianity beyond the borders of Europe presents both the
Christian faith and Christians as adventurously mobile, and ubiquitously
omnipresent: indeed, the claim attractively represents the whole world—
reorients the world—as Christianity's oyster.[29]

Thus we see that in deliberately attaching a cartographic narrative of the
Near East (the Holy Land and symbolic cities in crisis) to a cartographic
narrative of the farthest East discoverable (where Christian articles of faith
and Christian truths are located), the *Travels* accomplishes an astonishing
survey of the entire global structure that at once corrects and remakes extant
mappaemundi: compiles a planetary survey that visualizes a vast geographical imperium that is potentially the habitation of *all* Christian subjects.
This, then, is the other face of quasi-utopian identifications with otherness.

The *Travels'* strategy of stitching together two kinds of maps in language arises, of course, from that classic *romance* strategy of boldly and
seamlessly merging accepted, known reality (here in the form of established
old worlds) with theoretical, speculative fantasy (in the form of spectacularly foreign cultures, territories, and mindscapes). Conducive to seamless
continuity is the initial deformation of the traditional map of Latin Christendom from within, in small degrees, by the germinative introduction of
technological, scientific, and secular points of viewing that reshape a sense
of inner configurations within Europe. Beyond that first step of suggesting
the permeability of old worlds to strangeness, the *Travels* extrapolates a reverse hypothesis: that the strange new worlds it discovers might also, equally, be susceptible to contamination, might also be reconfigured from within, but this time by germinative pockets of familiar European culture in the
form of (an unproblematic) Christianity. For, you see, there are articles of
the Christian faith, and Christian truths, everywhere in the human world:
"There is no place that has not some measure of our creed." From the visualization of an internally de-familiarized Latin Christendom, then, to the
visualization of strange foreign lands that have been equally susceptible to
a reverse process of hybridization is but a small step in the evolution of a
cartographic hypothesis.

It is important to note that the global cartography visualized by the *Travels* differs significantly from depictions of the world produced by actual *mappaemundi* in the period. Though scholars have observed the resemblance of the *Travels* to medieval maps (see, e.g., Higgins's thoughtful hint that the *Travels* resembles, in verbal form, both a portolan chart and a *mappamundi* ["Jerusalem," 49–50]), the *Travels'* deliberate identification of Christian traces, creeds, peoples, and communities in far-flung corners of the world effectively marks, for the travelogue's audience, these extreme geographic reaches with Christian tags, and in fact reorients, shifts, the cartographic imagination. In depicting distant, highly exotic regions, the thirteenth-century Hereford world map might insert a legend attesting the existence of anthropopagi. The more forward-looking Catalan maps—like the 1375 Catalan Atlas or mid-fifteenth century Catalan-Estense—might intrude a visual representation of a camel and dark-skinned kings such as the Mansa Musa to identify Africa, or an elephant to identify India. By contrast, we can understand the *Travels'* visualized map to set down, instead, a series of *Christian marks* for *its* depictions of faraway regions, so that an audience can see that distant, exotic lands are not so exotic as to be wholly foreign, nor so distant as to be untouched by familiar Christian culture. As narrative cartography, the *Travels* thus creates a radical modification of the world map, of the world *as* map.

Ironically, the romance gesture of sidestepping history—ignoring late-medieval attitudes to heresy and heterodoxy, at home and abroad—by claiming an unproblematized Christian presence of some kind everywhere, in a world genially suffused by universal Christian traces, is also paradoxically faithful to history in significant ways. For one, the desire in the West for Christianity to exist, and proliferate, over the world has a momentum that repeats itself throughout the entire history of the medieval West. Concomitantly the medieval belief that pockets of Christian communities are to be found in distant lands, especially "India"—a name that stretches to signify, at different times, Asia, Africa, and even the Near East[30]—also has historical durability. Both that repeating desire and belief during the Middle Ages suggest why magicalized accounts of what are very likely rumors retold many times of successful Nestorian missionizing in the East, particularly in "India," periodically arrive in the West in the guise of charismatic fables and are received with more enthusiastic conviction than skepticism. Over the centuries Latin Europe duly absorbed, inter alia, the tradition of St. Thomas's conversions and martyrdom in "India"; rumors of a visit to Rome by either a Patriarch or "Indiae archiepiscopus" during the Papacy of Calixtus II in 1122 (Beckingham, "Achievements," 9); and the continually metamorphosing legend of Prester John, variously emperor of India, Edessa, or Ethiopia, from the mid-twelfth through the sixteenth centuries. The *Travels'* tagging of distant lands with Christian marks on its narrative map is truer, then, to historical forces in motion, and historical understanding, than might at first appear.

From the last quarter of the thirteenth century through the third quarter of the fourteenth, moreover, the cartographic imperative seen in the *Travels* answers to far more than merely desire and faith in Europe for an expansive Christianity to exist in extreme geographic reaches of the globe. From 1274 to 1288, in response to earlier Latin missions of the mid-thirteenth century and brief possibilities of military alliance between Mongols and Latins against Muslims in Syria and Palestine, two Mongol Khans—Abaga and his son, Arghun—sent three successive formal embassies to the countries of the West. The third and most famous of these official embassies, conducted in 1286–88 under the leadership of the Nestorian monk, Rabban Sauma—a close friend of the reigning patriarch of the Nestorian church—met with Pope Nicholas IV, Edward I of England, and Philip IV of France: "[In Rome] Rabban Sauma celebrated the East Syrian liturgy in the presence of the Pope and cardinals, and received communion from the Pope. And at Bordeaux, he did the same and Edward I received communion from him" (Dawson, xxix):

> When the cardinals expressed surprise that a Christian priest, attached to the patriarchate, should have come as an envoy from "the King of the Tartars," Rabban Sauma replied, "Know ye that many of our fathers in times past entered the lands of the Turks, the Mongols and the Chinese and have instructed them in the faith. To-day many Mongols are Christian. There are queens and children of kings who have been baptised and confess Christ. The Khans have churches in their camps. They honour Christians highly and there are many and faithful among them. (Dawson, xxix)[31]

Although the rumor that Christians existed among the ruling Mongols of Central Asia had circulated in Europe since the first quarter of the thirteenth century—thus helping substantially to fuel thirteenth-century versions and uses of the Prester John myth—the public phenomenon of Christian monks expressly sent to Western Europe's leaders by the Mongols in the late thirteenth century spectacularly ratified the now unquestionable existence of Christians of some variety in Central Asia.

Soon afterward, in 1294, Pope Nicholas IV sent John of Monte Corvino to Kublai Khan's (and his successor, Timur's) Cathay, where John, according to his second letter (dated 1305) subsequently built a church at the city of "Cambaliech" (a Nestorian archbishopric had been established at Khanbalik/Peking since 1275), baptized six thousand people, bought and trained forty acolytes, and strategically converted from Nestorianism a key personage, an Ongut princeling called by the Franciscans "King George," who was said to be "of the family of . . . Prester John" (Dawson, 225).[32] By his third letter (1306), John of Monte Corvino, who was eventually made Archbishop of Khanbalik, has built two churches in the city and a new Franciscan house "before the gate of the Lord Chaan" (229). The 1326 letter of Andrew of Perugia, from Zaitun, records that the friars inherited a cathedral church, and built a new church and house at Zaitun, near Amoy, in Fukien Province in south China, where Andrew became Bishop.

Odoric of Pordenone's travelogue confirms the existence of two houses of Minorites at Zaitun (Yule-Cordier, 2:310), the presence of friars in Kansai—the capital of Manzi/south China (2:314)—and another Franciscan house in Yamzai, where Odoric also notes the presence of three Nestorian churches (2:317). In Khanbalik itself, Odoric observes with satisfaction that the Minor friars have a place assigned to them at the Khan's court, "and it always behoves us thus to go and give him our blessing" (2:321). West of Cathay, moreover, in Central/West Asia, or "Tartary," Odoric reports that "our friars baptise a great many" (2:331).

In 1338 John Marignolli of Florence was sent from Avignon (during the papacy's "Babylonian Captivity") to Cathay, in answer to a request from the Alans in Cathay for a bishop, after the death of John of Monte Corvino, and arrived in 1342, bearing gifts, including a massive war horse from the Pope to the Khan, a destrier whose impressive size made it worthy of being recorded in Chinese annals as a "celestial horse" (translated as "supernatural horse"; Moule, 256). John Marignolli's chronicle, which mentions "three very beautiful" Minorite churches in Zaitun (Moule, 259), strikingly recounts anecdotes that have echoes in *Mandeville's Travels*. In one, John describes a ceremonial procession that he himself led into the Khan's palace, a procession in which John, singing the *Credo,* with a "beautiful cross which went before me" ended the chant by giving "a full benediction which [the Great Khan] received with humility" (Moule, 257).[33]

If the English *Travels* was written and circulated in 1356 (the date of composition offered in Cotton), the Franciscans were still active in Cathay and Manzi at the time of "Mandeville's" cartographic evocation of Christianity in distant lands: an evocation that—in the Khanate of East Asia, at least—is thus uncannily faithful to historical conditions. Not until 1362 would the last Catholic bishop of Zaitun, James of Florence, be killed when the Chinese recovered the city from the Mongols; and not until 1369 (Egerton and Defective offer 1366 as the *Travels'* date of composition) would Christians be expelled from Peking, not to return before the arrival of the Jesuits in the sixteenth century. Like a good romance narrative, however, the *Travels*, of course, also exceeds the historical record of Christian presence and activity in distant reaches of the world. Where Odoric finds four hundred "idolators," eight Christians, and one Saracen (Yule-Cordier, 2:321) among the Great Khan's court physicians, the *Travels* must enthusiastically announce the presence of "two hundred" physicians who are "Christian men, and twenty Saracens; but he trusts most to the Christians" (153). And where the historical record takes care to distinguish punctiliously between Nestorian Christians and Latin Catholic friars, the *Travels'* romance detection of Christian presence everywhere takes care to ignore serious divisions and rampant hostilities among the Christian kind.

We see, then, the shape of an overarching romance design being sketched through narrative cartography. Once identified, the historical crisis of place, which is a story of some anxiety in the *Travels*, is inserted into a cartographic fantasy, a spatialized framework, that narrates a widening multitude of Christian spaces existing in an expanding world, an enlarging global structure. Some of these spaces, of course—from the centuries' long missionizing of Nestorians and the dedicated commitments of the mendicant friars in the thirteenth and fourteenth centuries in Central, South, and East Asia—genuinely deserve to bear the signs of Christian marking, whereas others are fantasmatic creations of narrative desire.

In sum, the multitude of Christian spaces theorized by the *Travels* allows for the possibility of new identificatory relations for a late-medieval audience threatened with the slow (or rapid) dissolution of old identity structures supported and anchored into place by invested traditional symbols of Christendom and undone by corrosive crises in Christian Europe. The expanding series of Christian spaces discovered in the *Travels'* cartography does not substitute for any of the traditional investments of location (Jerusalem, Rome, Constantinople) as much as it creates new vistas in which a Christian might move; that is, it adds the vision of an expansive world system into which a Western European, Christian subject might enter, in a search for widening structures of identity and identification.

Significantly, the *Travels'* conceptualization of a world system made up of places where a Christian European subject might not feel wholly alien—might, indeed, well feel at home *because* of religion—theorizes the possibility of relocation. It is necessary to emphasize that this modality of cultural rescue conjured up by medieval travel romance—the willed insertion of the familiar into the vastness of geographical and cultural alterity—indeed *invites* relocation: urges forth the directive to explore, expand, and even to settle. Identifications with otherness, and participation in otherness, ultimately have the secondary effect of inviting the relocation of Europeans. In this light, Moseley's acuity assumes a special resonance when he asserts that the *Travels* was "influential in shaping the world view of the generation that discovered America"; and that "the response to America" is "governed, somewhere along the line, by the *Travels*" ("Behaim's Globe," 90).

We remember that Columbus, in sailing West, not only desired to find the Khan's "India" or Cathay—Columbus's log tenaciously interprets peoples and territories encountered in the West Atlantic through a hermeneutic grid supplied by the "Grand Khan's" East (e.g., Dunn and Kelley, 125, 145, 177, 217)—but also believed that the "Grand Khan" desired Christianization and eagerly sought the absorption of his "many peoples" into the Christian fold ("many times, he and his predecessors had sent to Rome to ask for men learned in our Holy Faith in order that they might instruct him in it" (17).[34]

Revealingly, by 1492–93, a newer ideology of empire—in which the directive to reach and exploit distant lands is fueled by a genial conviction in the receptivity of these far-flung regions to Christian culture—has taken hold, while an older ideology of empire, fueled by the old crusading fervor for military-territorial conquest, is yet tenacious: Columbus also wished that his royal patrons would "undertake and prepare to go conquer the Holy Sepulcher; for thus I urged Your Highnesses to spend all the profits of this my enterprise on the conquest of Jerusalem" (291). The joint momentum of the two strains of empire is neatly discernible in the articulated ambitions of a celebrated world explorer and his royally supported and authorized project at the junction where the end of the Middle Ages crosses over into the beginnings of the Renaissance.

Pre-Columbus, in the second half of the fourteenth century, those two strains of empire find their most eloquent expression, and conspicuous meeting ground, in "Mandeville's" resuscitated persona of Prester John and his exotic Christian domain. As a fantasy about the East, the Prester John legend, scholars have noted, is, in fact, archaically outmoded by this time, when detailed European knowledge of India, China, and the Mongolian Empire, had superseded the numinous hope, centuries earlier, that an inestimably puissant and unimaginably wealthy Christian emperor who ruled one (or all) of the fabulous "Indias," could be counted on as a partner in military, trade, or missionizing projects by an appropriately eager and cooperative West. The *Travels'* investment in Prester John, moreover, is consonant with the legend's gain in popularity and momentum in cultural fantasy of the late Middle Ages.

Though scholars have debated the emergence, development, and uses of the Prester John story in the twelfth and thirteenth centuries,[35] a recognition exists that late-medieval fascination with the legend, and a late-medieval investment in proliferating the legend's fictive wonders of the East, are palpable when one contrasts the early, relatively modest Latin version of the "Letter" of Prester John from c. 1165 (the earliest surviving version of the legend as epistolary fantasy)[36]—or the even sketchier hearsay reference to Prester John in Otto of Friesing's chronicle of 1145—with the over-embellished, meticulously detailed, long and rambling late-French versions of the "Letter" composed at the end of the thirteenth, or in the fourteenth, century.[37]

Why would an archaic, twelfth-century European fantasy about the East atavistically pick up speed at a historical juncture when *more*, not less, is known in Europe about the East?

In the mid-thirteenth century, a historical witness who had traveled in the East, Friar William of Rubruck, had already deflated the aureate nimbus of Prester John's myth. William's travel record localizes the legend to tribal populations in Outer Mongolia, assigning the name "John" to a Nestorian chieftain of the Naimans, "a mighty shepherd and lord" who had "set himself up as king," and who died without an heir (Dawson, 122). Of "King John," William's travelogue dryly observes, the Nestorians "used to tell of him ten times more than the truth. For the Nestorians coming from these parts do this kind of thing—out of nothing they make a great rumour. . . . Now I passed through his pasture lands and nobody knew anything about him with the exception of a few Nestorians" (122).

William's account assigns to "King John" a "brother" by the name of "Unc" who later added the title of "Khan" to his name; Unc Khan was also a chieftain but was subsequently defeated by the Mongols under the leadership of Genghis. Medievalist historians like to note that "Ong-Khan" (transcribed phonetically into English, and variously spelled) was the customary title of the chieftain of the Kereit tribe—like the Naimans, a constituent population of Outer Mongolia—and that "King John" very likely was a Kereit leader (de Rachewiltz, 14; Dawson, 122 nn. 1, 2). Unc Khan, William informs his readers, had a daughter who was taken prisoner by Genghis and was given to one of Genghis's sons (123): a detail that would ascend in significance a century later in *Mandeville's Travels*.

By the end of the thirteenth century, Marco Polo's narrative had successfully conflated the images and names of William's two Kereit brother-chieftains into a single entity: "Ung Khan" *or* "Prester John," "of whose great empire all the world speaks" (93).[38] Though the references to "Prester John" are perceptibly colored, to a greater extent than William's skeptical account, by the twelfth-century aura of the legend, Polo's account nonetheless continues to localize the realm of Prester John to tribal Central Asia and has the priest-king decisively die in a battle with the great Genghis, whose forces indisputably conquer and dominate "Prester John's" (96) realm.

Interestingly, Polo's narrative embroiders on the marital link of a daughter/wife as the connection between a mostly fictitious Prester John and an all-too-historical Genghis Khan, by making the quarrel of the two personages the consequence of Prester John's refusal to give John's daughter in marriage to Genghis Khan, as requested by the Khan (94). This striking romance motif in Polo's embellished account (the motif is more parsimoniously signaled in the earlier William of Rubruck), where a woman stands at the nexus of war between two empires, and symbolizes—gives figural expression to—the political/military competition of two male leaders, is historicized and naturalized in the following manner by one scholar:

> Chingis Khan had actually married a niece of the Ong-khan and had sought his daughter for his eldest son, and it was the Ong-khan's refusal that had led to a war between the two chiefs. . . . In North China . . . north of the Great Wall, there lived at the time a Turkish tribe called Öngüt, whose royal family had also been converted to Nestorian Christianity. The king of the Öngüt had allied himself with Chingis Khan and the Mongol conqueror had later rewarded him by giving him his daughter in marriage. Subsequently, it had become a regular practice for Mongol princesses to marry into the Öngüt royal family. Now, Friar

William's account originates from a phonetic similarity between Unc and Öngüt, and from a garbled version of Chingis Khan's relationship by marriage with the Ong-khan and with the Öngüt ruler. . . . Marco Polo, who made his famous journey to China twenty years later (1275), was led into a similar web of errors. (de Rachewiltz, 14)

Whatever genuine historicity, or inspired inventiveness, characterizes each of the elements and twists in the varied medieval accounts of a crucial marital link—via a symbolic woman—between the empires of the Great Khan and Prester John, the idea that such a linkage exists is an extraordinarily persistent one and travels with remarkable facility down the generations.

Odoric of Pordenone's historical narrative, in the fourteenth century, is as matter-of-fact in relaying the information of that marital link as it is hootingly derisive of the exaggerated reputation of "Prester John," of which not "the hundredth part" is true, that is spoken of him "as if it were indisputable" (Yule-Cordier, 2:327). If Prester John's historical credibility has diminished in the decades between William of Rubruck's and Odoric of Pordenone's historical reports—from less than 10 percent to less than 1 percent of truth-in-telling—Odoric's travelogue nonetheless retains the salient connubial feature of the Prester John story, which it credits and reports in a quite different tone of voice: "always by covenant [Prester John] receives as wife the daughter of the great Khan" (Yule-Cordier, 2:327).

In Polo's account itself, despite the invocation of a romance motif (an invocation that we might, if we wish, attribute to the romancer Rustichello's than to Polo's narration), the "web of errors" is nonetheless careful to recognize that Prester John, offered as contemporaneous with Genghis Khan, cannot be any longer alive in the imperial reign of Polo's Khan, who is, by this time, Genghis's grandson, Kublai. Accordingly, in the reign of Kublai Khan, Polo's account informs us, "Prester John" (following the example of his *doppelgänger*, the Ong Khan) has now mutated from a person into a generic title, a title assumed now by the descendants of the original Prester John/Ung Khan; and the "personal name" of the latest title holder is "George" (105–6). The concession to the inevitability of temporal progression, and scrupulous emptying out of the character known as Prester John into a *title* that can be assumed by future generations, thus saves Prester John, and his story, for medieval posterity: both a posterity attentive to historical conditions and a posterity that prefers to traffic in cultural fantasy and romance.

Succeeding Polo in the fourteenth century, the Franciscan friars in China—historical agents all—have no difficulty grasping that any descendants of "Prester John" must be heretics, and not true Christians of a recognizable kind at all. John of Monte Corvino's letter of 1305 explicitly trumpets the friar's triumph over heretical Nestorianism, when he succeeds in converting to Roman Catholicism a princeling of the Onguts, who by now are established, along with the Kereits, as the tribal family of Prester John:

> A certain king of these parts, of the sect of the Nestorian Christians, who was of the family of that great king who was called Prester John of India, attached himself to me in the first year that I came here. And was converted by me to the truth of the true Catholic faith. And he took minor orders and served my mass wearing the sacred vestments, so that the other Nestorians accused him of apostasy. Nevertheless he brought a great part of his people to the true Catholic faith, and he built a fine church with royal generosity in honour of God, the Holy Trinity and the Lord Pope, and called it according to my name "the Roman church." This King George departed to the Lord a true Christian, leaving a son and heir in the cradle, who is now nine years old. But his brothers who were perverse in the errors of Nestorius perverted all those whom King George had converted and brought them back to their former state of schism. (Dawson, 225–26)[39]

With the tribal line of Prester John settled among the royal family of the Onguts/Kereits, and localized to the environs of Cathay, another historical agent, Odoric of Pordenone, is thus able to say, a quarter-century later, as if flatly repeating an unremarkable, received given, that he came to the land of Prester John, of which not the hundredth part is true of what is told of him as if it were indisputable (Yule-Cordier, 2:326–27).

If Prester John's legendary reputation diminishes in one cultural arena of the fourteenth century because of increased historical knowledge, the linchpin of female endogamy in the story nevertheless stays vital and worthy of repetition in historical and romance narration alike. Either "Prester John" or the Great Khan—it does not seem to matter which, for the roles switch interchangeably back and forth without loss in this matter of a connubial connection—continues to give his daughter to the other side's dynastic ruler in marriage. In Odoric's record, "Prester John," who has an existence in the present tense of Odoric's time at least as someone's honorific or title, "always by covenant receives as wife the daughter of the great Khan" (Yule-Cordier, 2:327).

In *Mandeville's Travels*, the rulers' positions are reversed, and here it is the Great Khan who "had three wives, of which the first and the principal was Prester John's daughter" (122). Indeed, the *Travels* strengthens and intensifies the intimate connection between two empires and dynasties—one of historic, the other of legendary, status—by ramifying the web of intermarriage and nubile female relatives, and establishes an equality in the interchangeability of the dual patriarchs: "This same royal king Prester John and the Great Khan of Tartary are evermore allied together through marriage; for either of them weds the other's daughter or other's sister" (134).

Yule-Cordier, who track the buoyant female marital link through Latin and French manuscripts of Odoric's travelogue, observe that the Mongol Khans did, in fact, often intermarry with the Kerait royal family: "E.g., the Christian mother of Kuyuk Khan, and Dokuz-khatun the Christian queen of Húlakú, were both princesses of the Kerait royal family, i.e., apparently of Prester John's. The mother of Húlakú was of the same family, and Chingiz, as well as several of his sons, took wives from it" (246 n. 2). Dawson reiterates the idea that the Mongol Khans also often intermarried with the royal family of the Onguts, a people that, as we have seen, were bound up with the Kereits by virtue of phonetic misattribution of a titular leader's customary honorific: "The princes of the Ongut, who were Nestorian Christians and lived on the frontiers of China by the northern loop of the Yellow River, held an exceptionally influential position in the Mongol Empire owing to their intermarriages with the descendants of Chingis Khan" (225 n. 1).[40]

Fortuitously, then, by a happy coincidence of adventitious accidents, history and romance narratives alike are able to link the powerful Mongol Khans—feared and admired rulers of a great world empire in the thirteenth and fourteenth centuries—to *Christianity,* through the fortunate gift of a woman in marriage. The accidents range from ethnic miscognition (Naimans and Kereits having been conflated) to phonetic confusion (a Kerait Unc Khan/Ong-khan having been confused with the Ongut royals), but key to the coincidence of historical and cultural narratives, and running through the tangle of fortuitous misattributions, is the success of historic Nestorian missionizing in Central and East Asia.

A strange and useful irony thus binds the cultural histories of the medieval West and East. If the Prester John myth had ever insinuated itself into Europe as a species of (presumably inadvertent) Nestorian cultural revenge on a credulous West, for the West's historic expulsion of Nestorius and his followers, then successful Nestorian missionizing in the East also inadvertently supplied the West with the material conditions for imagining a path back into the heart of the East, and the center of the Mongol Empire, through the figure of a Christian (Nestorian) Prester John and his nubile female relatives.

An influential travel romance like *Mandeville's Travels*, which strategically prefers to emphasize the older, nostalgically legendary aura of Prester John, also shrewdly prefers to underemphasize the Nestorian character of the Christianity anchored into place by the localization of the Prester John story in preceding thirteenth- and fourteenth-century historical accounts. While allowing for some variation of doctrine and practice from the Latin Church, in Prester John's empire, the *Travels* vigorously underscores the ultimately universal principles of Christianity shared in common with John's people—the most important commonalities of faith and devotion—and celebrates the piety and virtue of John's folk: "This emperor Prester John is a Christian man, and the most part of his land also, if all be it so that they have not all the articles of our belief so clearly as we have. Nonetheless they believe in God, Father and Son and Holy Ghost; and full devout men they are and true each one to the other, and there is neither with them fraud nor guile" (134).

In the *Travels*, unlike the Franciscan accounts, no accusation of heresy nor condemnation of schismatics divides (Eastern) Christian from (Western) Christian; even where variations are most explicitly acknowledged, no vilification of any kind mars the *Travels'* praise of the Christian virtue and goodness of Prester John's land: "In the land of Prester John are many good Christian men and well-living, and men of good faith and of good [religious] law" (148).[41] Instead, for the *Travels*, as Moseley astutely points out, "Prester John's kingdom is the ideal Christian state" (Introduction, 25).

By emphasizing the devout Christianity of Prester John's people, and winking at their Nestorian difference, then, the *Travels* is able to present John's empire, in its Christian ideality, as a heterotopian mirror for Europe: a mirror in which Europe might see an exotic version of itself, dressed up as a successful Christian empire that happens to be located elsewhere. Simultaneously John's domain is also conspicuously partnered with the Khan's imperial domain in such a way as to suggest that John's realm functions as a kind of Christian threshold to the Khanate, a counterpart-in-empire that mimics the Great Khan's vast imperial enterprise.

For the *Travels'* ultimate object of fascinated admiration and desire—
like Polo's narrative and the Franciscan accounts before it—is no less than
the Great Khan himself and his immense imperium: "For assuredly under
the firmament is not so great a lord nor so rich nor so mighty as is the
Great Khan of Tartary. Not Prester John that is emperor of India the less
and the more [Lesser and Greater India], nor the sultan of Babylon, nor
the emperor of Persia, nor none other may be made comparison of to him.
Certes it is much harm that he were not a Christian man" (*Travels*, 108).
"Much harm" though it may be that the supreme Oriental potentate, the
Khan, is not a Christian, there is another Oriental potentate, made cozily
familiar now by two centuries of accumulated literary tradition, who *is* a
Christian: "This emperor Prester John is a Christian man, and the most
part of his land also" (134).

In fourteenth-century medieval culture, access to the Khan and the
Khanate is granted by the legend of Prester John.

Though the *Travels* dutifully reiterates that Prester John is not the
equal of the august Khan (108),[42] we see the two personages often mentioned in the same breath, and their lands appear to share an adjacency:
"The Great Caan . . . is a great emperor, yea the greatest of the world, for
he is lord of the great Isle of Cathay and of many other countries, and of
a great part of India. His land marches with Prester John's land" (*Travels*,
21). Where the two realms do not seem to border each other geographically, they nonetheless wistfully nudge each other in recitative sequence—
materialize side by side in narrative mention—and are joined also by their
immense distance from Europe: "Cathay is not so near that it does not behove them from Venice or from Genoa or other places of Lombardy to be
travelling by sea and by land eleven months or twelve ere they may win to
the land of Cathay. And yet is the land of Prester John much farther by
many a day's journey" (133).

In other parallels, the *Travels'* description of John's kingdom, palace,
gems, and wealth nostalgically reproduce the legend's splendors so traditionally that the glories of John's realm—no mere Nestorian Ongut's
tribal domain—come to approximate the aureate glories of the Khanate,
the wonders and marvels of whose capital, Khanbalik, are similarly described in lovingly meticulous, embellished detail. Identical social habits
even seem to occur in both empires, so that a custom that is distributed
over one realm is concentrated in pinpoint fashion at the heart of the
other realm, its mirrored twin: "Throughout all the land of Prester John,

they eat but once on the day, as they do in the court of the Great Khan"
(136).[43]

John and the Great Khan alike, being Oriental potentates, have multiple wives, though John, as idealized Christian-mirror-king, only chaste-
ly beds his four times a year, without lust, and solely for engendering offspring. Most tellingly of all, the royal families of both realms are
inextricably joined at the highest levels, mingling bloodlines and genealogy through marriage and connubial women: "This same royal king Prester
John and the Great Khan of Tartary are evermore allied together through
marriage; for either of them weds the other's daughter or other's sister"
(134). Given the tissue of associative relations fashioned for the rulers and
their realms, an audience might well be forgiven for visualizing the Great
Khan, and his imperial domain, in the image of Prester John, and *his* empire. The symbolic umbilical tie of bloodlines between the two imperial
dynasties and families merely culminates, then, what the layers of associative relations of other kinds already secure.

It is crucial to remember that whatever the Prester John myth might
have signified for twelfth- and thirteenth-century Europe (historians have
noted, in particular, the myth's imbrication with the military and territorial history of the crusades),[44] by the second half of the fourteenth century, the legend—an old fantasy about the Orient, and still a way to imagine a relationship with the East—offers the West a special kind of
foothold, an imaginative purchase, on an immeasurably wealthy and foreign, all-too-historical Cathay, a supremely powerful Great Khan, and a
Mongol imperium whose geographical limits were scarcely comprehensi-
ble. If, as the *Travels* laments, "it is much harm [the Khan] is not a Christian" emperor (108), the Khan could still be visualized as intimately bound
up with a Christian emperor whose charismatic tradition had grown comfortably familiar, over the centuries, in the bosom of Western Europe.

Having circulated in Europe for two centuries, John's legend is by this
time a domesticated, much rewritten, beloved local artifact. Indeed, popular investment in the legend suggests that John, a European adoptee, is
now effectively a *European* figure more than an Oriental personage, despite his exotic coloration. Once the embodiment of European desire for
a benign Oriental Christian despot to exist, somewhere in the East, the
fictive John becomes, in the fourteenth century, a Europeanized figure of
desire for *the East itself.* The *Travels* repeatedly articulates and thematizes
the historical pressure of that desire: "Wit you well that the realm of

Cathay is greater than any realm in this world; and so is he that is Great
Khan the greatest king of all other kings and richest of gold and all manner of treasure and of greatest estate" (*Travels*, 113). Indeed, in the *Travels'*
popularity might be intuited the degree of its success in enunciating and
imaginatively treating what the late-medieval *zeitgeist* wanted and considered of value.

We see a longing for some cultural purchase on China even in the
ghost of that tenuous, fictively shared spiritual conviction: "This emperor
[the Great Khan] and all the folk of his land [Cathay], though they be not
Christian men, nevertheless believe in great God, that made heaven and
earth" (*Travels*, 113).[45] In contrast to this wistfully poignant fiction that
Latins and "Tartars" might have the same God, Prester John and his kingdom offer a superior conduit for the cultural longings of the West. As a
puissant *Christian* emperor without religious difference, John's presence
suggests the possibility of European desire moving in foreign lands,
searching out the farthest inhabited regions of the world, and being busily at work in establishing identificatory relations with the Great Khan,
Cathay, and beyond. John, a European in Oriental face, and Western Europe's cultural export to the Orient, has become an eloquent figure of the
West's imaginative designs on the East.

The exoticism of John's realm, embellished in late-medieval versions
of the legend, is also, at this juncture, a thoroughly assimilated exoticism
that serves as protective camouflage to continue the fiction that John's
realm is thrillingly elsewhere, not-Europe, and not Europe-as-the-East.
Exoticism, we note, is a simple romance mechanism that works to do-
mesticate alterity—dangerous foreignness—by presenting alterity as a
panorama of colorful, collectible particulars: marvels and curiosities that
superficially signal foreignness while being shorn of risk, and that are re-
ducible, in status, to the fascination of delightful souvenirs.[46] Unlike the
truly foreign, the exotic is designed to impart pleasure, to thrill, but conventionally: foreignness packaged and tamed into pleasurable, exciting
artifacts for markets of domestic consumption. Not looking like Europe
but announced as a devoutly Christian realm sans heretical difference—
an *exotic*, idealized Christian realm—John's kingdom can then assume an
intermediary status halfway between the West and the East, in a cultural
disguise that enables European investments to mask themselves and go
undetected.

As the West's surrogate, John's kingdom naturally exists in perfect geographical symmetry to Europe, by being in the precise location as Europe

itself (and England, in particular) on the other hemisphere of the world, a world whose pivotal center is, of course, Jerusalem:

> The land of Prester John, emperor of India, is exactly under us. . . . For our land is the lowest part of the west, and the land of Prester John is in the lowest part of the east. And they have day when we have night, and night when we have day. And, as much as a man ascends upward out of our countries to Jerusalem, so much [i.e., an equal distance] shall he go downward to the land of Prester John. (91)

Narratologically linked to the West at one end, and to Cathay and the Khan at the other, the Prester John myth—fantasy counterpart to Franciscan cosmopolitanism—thus tidily situates a romance portal that secures another location of identity, a symbol of the traveling power of Western culture. A nostalgic legend, refurbished and redeployed anew, affords another means by which the West can land in the East, suitably disguised, and collect "another world"—as Peregrine, Bishop of Zaitun, called his location in Manzi (Dawson, 232)—and the unimaginable riches, power, and territory of the Mongol imperium.[47]

John's idealized Christianity, shorn of any Nestorian coloring, argues persuasively for the mobility and cosmopolitanism of Western faith, and his marriage into the Khan's royal family lodges a vital Christian nucleus at the heart of the Mongol Empire that would facilitate a strategic line of historical reasoning later conducive to ideological justifications for the roving forays of the West. Thus culture would act on historical enterprises in cunning ways: By 1492, Columbus, in the wake of the thirteenth-century Polo and the fourteenth-century "Mandeville," could confidently recite, with no hesitation, the litany of the Great Khan's strong and repeating desire for Latin Christianization in the form of religious instruction for himself and his subjects. The *Travels'* shrewd pairing of the fictional emperor of "India" with the historical emperor of Cathay also bears other fruit in historical thinking: To Columbus, the empire of the "Grand Khan" is *both* "the lands of India" (Dunn and Kelley, 17) *and* "the city of Cathay" (125); the countries of the glittering East, along with a now composite ruler, exist, in the words of the late-fifteenth-century explorer, as a single desired objective.[48]

We see from this example that it is important not to underestimate the material force of cultural mythology nor the impact of imaginative belief in the ordering of the world's relations. In the first quarter of the

thirteenth century, when the Prester John legend yet served as a consolation and a goad to a Latin Europe in the throes of attempting to retain
military extraterritoriality in the Near East and recover lost colonies in
Jerusalem and Edessa,[49] active belief in John's existence and cooperative
agency, on the part of the ecclesiastical and military leaders of the Fifth
Crusade, directly formed military policy and shaped disastrous field tactics in the taking of Damietta in Egypt, according to the eyewitness
chronicle of Oliver of Paderborn (Peters, *Christian Society*, 90, passim).[50]

In subsequent centuries, when the Prester John myth came to figure
Latin Europe's desire for the wealth of other worlds—India, Cathay, and,
later, Africa—the cultural myth of Prester John both expressed and urged
forward the drive to open up new routes and territories: "In the fifteenth
century, a possible new route to Ethiopia was investigated by the Portuguese. When they began to explore the west African coast one of their
main hopes was to make contact with Prester John" (Hamilton, "Continental Drift," 255). Henry IV of England ("who before he became king had
been an enthusiastic crusader" [254]), felt prompted to write to "Prester
John, the powerful and magnificent prince, King of Abyssinia" (254),[51]
whose revitalized legend shaded into late-medieval Western Europe's desire
to expand relations with the world outside Europe and the Mediterranean:
"When in 1487 King Joao II of Portugal despatched Pêro da Covilhã and
Afonso de Paiva on the overland mission to find the place from which the
spices came one of their tasks was to ascertain whether Prester John *confi-
nava sopra il mare*, in the words of Ramusio" (Beckingham, 20–21).

In the fourteenth century and after, Western Europe's restless reas-
signment of the country of Prester John to different locales around the far
reaches of the globe—reassignments that were assisted, in medieval understanding, by the nebulous boundaries of "India," John's original
abode, and the two or three "Indias" that were held to exist[52]—follows the
chain of Western desire in the pursuit of trade, commerce, navigation,
routes, new knowledges, and new territorial discoveries.[53] Even as Franciscan authors were historically localizing Prester John's lineage and
stamping ground to the Onguts and Kereits of Mongolia and Cathay,
John's mythical domain was at the same time beginning to be fabulously
assigned to Africa, in the first half of the fourteenth century. Jordan Cata-
lani of Severac, Dominican missionary and Bishop of Colombo in Cey-
lon, suggested in his travelogue on Asia, written between 1320 and 1340,
that Prester John was emperor of the *Ethiopians*, a people whose country
was the Third India, a land coterminous with the Horn of Africa (Hamil-

ton, "Continental Drift," 252; Kaplan, 53; Ross, 178). Jacopo da Verona, writing in 1335, refers to "Nubians . . . who are black Ethiopians of the people of Prester John" (Kaplan, 54). "By the 1330s, then, a European writer could talk confidently of Prester John of Ethiopia. . . . The first surviving instance of an African Prester on a map occurs in the form of an inscription found southwest of Egypt on the Genoese Angelino Dulcert's Portulan of 1339" (Kaplan, 54).[54]

The addition of Africa to the catalogue of exotic locales in the world where Prester John might be sought and found signals an amplification of Western Europe's interested attention as the gaze of the West swept the world for new resources and opportunities in the late Middle Ages. Ever a lure for conniving the attractions of identification and acquisition, across geography and culture, John's legend had been persistently implicated in impulses and enterprises of empire over the *longue durée*. In the twelfth and thirteenth centuries, when Latin Europe desired to reconquer territory in Syria and Palestine, and reestablish its lost crusader colonies, Prester John, "a product of the thought-world of the crusades" (Hamilton, "Continental Drift," 256), was activated as an ideological and military goad, a spur to martial projects. In the fourteenth and fifteenth centuries, John reemerged to invite and urge on Europe's peregrinatory ambitions around the world outside the Mediterranean, as an icon of ever-widening extraterritorial projects of world discovery, trade, and settlement.[55]

Even as the reallocation of John's Christian empire to new continents fluidly expresses, then, the traveling power of Western culture and the migratory range of Europe's avid gaze, by the fifteenth century, the exportation of John's domain from Asia to Africa is ominous.[56] For as the influential *Mandeville's Travels* indicates, where Prester John goes, Europe is not far behind. With Asia as a foregoing example, we see that an Africanized Prester John, later dressed by Europe in African robes and given an Ethiopian or Nubian face, but still as Christian and as wealthy as ever, must exist to invite—beckon to, even compel—European adventurism and opportunism in the African continent.[57] *Mandeville's Travels* allows us to see how the legend of Prester John, at the close of the Middle Ages and the beginning of the Renaissance, can once again dissemble, and figure, European desire in another corner of the world: this time for Africa[58]—for the wealth of Africa's caravans, cities, minerals, gems, spices, people, and range of exploitable resources—with economic results and a cost in human lives that would tragically, and rapidly, become apparent in the course of human history.[59]

"I of the World": Worlding the Empire of Magic; or, Technologies of Past and Future

By the time of the late Middle Ages, therefore, "taking the adventure" that beckons—a centuries-old European romance motif to signal embarkation on a new opportunity for questing and self-advantage—is a project that has assumed global dimensions, and is as likely to imply corporate ventures caught up in Western European expansion in different continents of the world as it is likely to concern the knightly self-fashioning of individual elites on quests that is a staple of the discourse of opportunity in twelfth- and thirteenth-century romances. As adventurism and environments ramify, moreover, romance alters its tropes and idioms accordingly, and the exemplary *Mandeville's Travels* features in narrative both the traditional motifs of older romances and the beginnings of a nascent discourse that we would associate today with the culture of science and technology, and the premises of scientific method and scientific perspective. For in late medieval travel romance, the new magic is, of course, *science* and its marvels, a magic to support new kinds of adventures. In the *Travels*, "science" appears under its most readily recognizable aspects—state-of-the-art technology, instrumentation, and techniques—and in its more fundamental form as a discursive system in which knowledge is amassed, ordered, and manipulated in specific ways, a discourse that will increasingly, in the modern era, standardize into what we will grasp as "scientific."

The *Travels'* facility with the old tropes of medieval romance, legend, and folklore is paraded in a narrative recitation of the story of Hippocrates' daughter, a story that duly features a fair damsel in distress, enchantment, a dragon, a treasure hoard, a quest, and knights who may gain dominion over fair lady, treasure, and territory alike, on successful completion of the quest and bestowal of a requisite kiss of disenchantment on the maiden; antiquated conventions all (12–13). But simultaneously our travel romance is also eager to disseminate contemporary knowledges and wonders: the adventure of global circumnavigation, the dramatic effects of magnetism, uses of the astrolabe and the compass, and the precision of alphabet systems. The *Travels'* fascination with scientifism also coexists comfortably alongside replication of the more traditional marvels that are the lexical staple of predecessors in the travel romance genre—wonders such as monstrous races and hybridities, otherworldly landscapes, exotic flora and fauna.

A fine emblem of this happy cooperation of old and new romance in-struments is discoverable, it would seem, in Cathay, at the court of the Great Khan, and the heart of the Eastern empire, where we are presented with a team of philosophers and "great clerks of diverse sciences" who are given pride of place "at a side of the Emperor's table." Practicing an array of disciplines that shade unapologetically and indistinguishably from old magic to new science, the philosopher-scientists are learned in "astrono-my," "necromancy," "geomancy," "pyromancy," "hydromancy," and "many such other sciences." The narrative *tableau vivant* presents these mages/proto-scientists with their technical instruments emblematically displayed before them: golden astrolabes, spheres formed of precious stones, "wonderfully made" clocks, vessels filled with diverse solids (hot coals, sand) and liquids of different densities and viscosities ("water and wine and oil"), scalps of human skin, and "different instruments accord-ing to their science" (115).[60]

This very concise scene—in which men, methods, and machines are gathered to engage with time, the elements, navigation, the heavens, human beings and death, liquids, minerals and matter—supposes that what is important in the greatest empire of the world, and to the greatest ruler, is an integrated knowledge of the world and how it functions. Given pride of place at the world's grandest court is a broad slate of disciplines and practitioners able to accumulate a theory of the world: both by gath-ering empirical data through appropriate instruments, and through prac-tices that are codifiable into specialized fields of investigation. The idea that collecting and codifying information on the phenomenal, physical, and human world is of prime importance recurs in *Mandeville's Travels* under different guises and is, of course, one of the fundamental assump-tions of travel literature. We also see that another procedure by which in-formation can be distilled into its essentials, abstracted, and generalized is equally important.

When the *Travels* intrudes alphabet systems into its discussions of so-cieties—theoretically the Greek, Egyptian, Hebrew, "Saracen"/Arabic, Persian, and Chaldean alphabets—it periodically intrudes a reminder that whole systems of intelligibility can be reduced to their fundamental com-ponents of discrete, atomized units that are infinitely recombinable. In many ways, these striking alphabet systems—which have attracted the at-tention of many readers and scholars of the *Travels*—function as so many sets of data codes, distilled to their most basic, fundamental elements. In this respect, the importance is reduced of whether the *Travels'* alphabets were once authentic alphabets (that subsequently became, in the parlance of scholarship generous enough to award the narrative the benefit of the doubt, "corrupt") or were principally invented, or reinvented, for the occasion: For what the alphabets attest is the operation of a certain *mind-set* or *attitude* to how information can be amassed, systematized, and arranged within an overarching context of knowledge.[61]

Here again, old and new converge in the very traditional, very modern, cultural vehicle known as *Mandeville's Travels*. Alphabet systems themselves are ancient, yet collecting them one after another, in series, produces a data bank that facilitates recognition of similarities and variations, and the detection of principles that are likely to emerge once constituent objects are viewed in series and surveyed as an encompassing group. Inserted by the narrator when closing off a discussion of an ethnic or social system, each of these alphabets also seems to sum up a system and its lifeways in brief, like a master code, a summary key, to a particular human grouping ("Since I have told you somewhat of the Saracens' law, and of their manners and customs, now will I tell you of their letters which they use, with the names and the manner of their figures" [71]; "The folk of Chaldea have a proper language and proper letters and figures; and these are the figures of their letters" [77]). If the preceding narration of a system's lifeways and society might seem, on occasion, less than impersonal, or colorfully anecdotal, the alphabets themselves, set down again and again in a reiterative pattern, have the advantage of conveying impersonality. Narrators might appear selective and partial by virtue of their humanized personae, but codes that predictably repeat in set patterns, like modular units, are a device to convey impartiality.

Given the convergence of all these effects, what, then, are the implications—both in the immediate context of a travel narrative and in the longer term—of such acts of accumulation, in which data sets, or master codes, are compiled in a repeating series?

For one, the recurrent alphabets testify efficiently and succinctly to the universal repeatability of systems—social, human, and technological—and the accessibility of these systems to generalization and abstraction. At the same time that the alphabets seem to condense complex human collectivities into masterable codes, the accumulation of alphabets also points to how plastic and phenomenal complexities might be viewed in such a way as to extract their core meanings most reliably. To be offered one alphabet only is to be offered a close-up view of a unique and particular object—magnified, as it were, by singular attention—but the presentation of strings of similar, nonidentical objects, one after another, confers an over-all viewing position from a helicopter-like height, a master vantage point from which the whole can be surveyed intelligibly. Allegorizing the great diversity of the world, and also the repeating structural patterns found within that diversity, these sets of alphabets are invaluable in instantiating the grounds for a scientific perspective of phenomena.[62] What is science if not the ability to see new things, and to see new relations emerge, that were once invisible?

Grouped as a whole, the alphabets imply, moreover, that the scientism or scientifism in which the *Travels* participates consists less in the state-of-the-art technology and instruments, and contemporary methods of meas-urement, location, or gradation, which are actually named and paraded by the *Travels*, than in ways of viewing, analyzing, and instituting that the *Travels* performs. The narrative's contributions arise from how it config-ures perception and information into knowledge, in part by finding and privileging *sites of perception*, and in part by identifying and *universalizing a viewing subject*: and, subsequently, objectifying the authority of its prac-tices in ways generative of, and entirely familiar to, scientific discourse.

Even the overt signs of science that are conspicuously on display in the *Travels* often exist not only to advertise the *Travels'* modernity, and fasci-nation with scientific technology and techniques, but also discernibly to stage a certain optical authoritativeness, a vantage point from which to view in decisive ways. At the same time, these overt signs of scientific thinking or mechanics are also directed to the burden of proof, and to the emergence of inductive extrapolation. A brief disquisition on the Pole star, and its counterpart in the southern hemisphere, revealingly extracts an in-ductive syllogism on the sphericity of the world, which is then buttressed by objective technology, and the optical testimony of a technology-wield-ing subject who is thus armed with access to a privileged vantage point:

> Þe sterne þat es called *Polus Articus* . . . standes euen north and stirrez neuer, by whilk schippe men er ledd, for it es noȝt sene in þe south. Bot þer es anoþer sterne, whilke es called Antartic, and þat es euen agayne þe toþer sterne; and by þat sterne er schippe men ledd þare, as schippe men er ledd here by *Polus Articus*. And, riȝt as þat sterne may noȝt be sene here, one þe same wyse þis sterne may noȝt be sene þare. And þare by may men see wele þat þe werld es all rounde; for parties of þe firma-ment whilk may be sene in sum cuntree may noȝt be sene in anoþer. And þat may men proue þus. For, if a man myght fynd redy schipping

... he myght ga all aboute þe werld, bathe abouen and benethe. And þat prufe I þus, after þat I hafe sene. For I hafe bene in Braban and sene by þe astrolaby þat þe pole artyc es þare liii. degreez hegh, and in Almayne towardes Boem it has lviii. degrez, and forþermare toward þe north it has lxii. degrez of height and sum mynutes. All þis I persayued by þe astrolaby. (*Travels*, 90)[63]

The star that is called *Polus Articus* . . . stands even north and stirs never, by which shipmen are led, for it is not seen in the south. But there is another star, which is called Antarctic, and that is even against the other star [exactly opposite the Pole star]; and by that star are shipmen led there, as shipmen are led here by *Polus Articus*. And right as that star may not be seen here, in the same way this star may not be seen there. And thereby may men see well that the world is all round; for parts of the firmament which may be seen in some country may not be seen in another. And that may men prove thus. For, if a man might find ready shipping . . . he might go all about [around] the world, both above and beneath. And that I prove thus, after [according to] what I have seen. For I have been in Brabant and seen by the astrolabe that the *Polus Articus* is there fifty-three degrees high [in elevation], and in Germany towards Bohemia it has fifty-eight degrees, and further more toward the north it has sixty-two degrees of height and some minutes. All this I perceived by the astrolabe.

The "I" which speaks in the above passage on inductive and deductive "proofs" goes on at length to detail the imaginary gridding of the firmament by azimuth, and attaches a calibration of sky and earth ("in circumference [the earth] is some 20,425 miles" [*Travels*, 130]) to other "proofs" authorized by the narrator's direct experience as an observer on scientific matters.

I went toward þe south, and I fand þat in Liby seez men first þe sterne Antartyke; and, as I went ferrer, I fand þat in hie Liby it hase in height xviii. degreez and some mynutes, of whilke mynutes lx. makez a degre. And so, passand by land and by see toward the cuntree þat I spakk off are, and oþer landes and iles þat er beзond, I fand þat þis sterne Antartik had in height xxxiii. degreez. (*Travels*, 90)[64]

I went toward the south, and I found that [it is] in Libya [that] men first see the star Antarctic; and, as I went further, I found that in high [upper]

Libya it has in height eighteen degrees and some minutes, of which minutes sixty make a degree. And so, passing by land and by sea toward the country that I spoke of before, and other lands and isles that are beyond, I found this star Antarctic had in height thirty-three degrees.

Not only is an audience being asked here to accept the narrator's supposed observation of physical phenomena as creditable evidence, but a presumption of the observer's impartiality and authority in observation predominates to the extent that a little lesson in scientific measurement is parenthetically, unobtrusively, intruded by the way ("sixty minutes make a degree"). Somewhat later, after other discussions, a sizable pedagogical moment explicating how the firmament and the earth are charted and measured, using degrees and arcs, is also inserted (*Travels*, 92). This observer-narrator, we are to understand, knows something about science and its methods of measurement; the means by which workable kinds of proof are arranged; and the tone of voice to use, to be convincing, when one speaks on matters of evidence and observation.

Implicitly, the position from which the observer-narrator speaks shades imperceptibly into the place occupied by a generalized, impartial observer whose objectivity we are supposed to be able to assume, and take for granted, an observer that we would think of today as very similar to a scientist. And it matters little if the actual "science" being hedged about under these conditions is suspect, whimsical, or thoroughly idiosyncratic: for the "science" that matters, in a travel romance, is the *discursive apparatus* which determines the means by which perception of phenomena assumes the status of objective universal knowledge, and enables the human-subject-who-narrates to assume the status of impartial universal observer and codifier of knowledge.

To sum up at this point: We see that, in the *Travels*, "science" is a discursive apparatus of measurement, recording, or experiencing/witnessing (with or without the aid of instruments) by which individual perception of particulars, and local phenomena, can be transformed into universalized knowledge of the world, knowledge from which principles of generalization may be gleaned. Although the objects under investigation—the people, matter, phenomena, or events that are being recorded, measured, or experienced/witnessed—may be enigmatic or unique, the *means* of investigation as such must suggest regularity, repeatability, and availability for corroboration: requirements that can partly be satisfied by the evocation of an observer whose manipulation of the "I" attracts identification by sympathetic others (audience or readers) with the role of the observing subject; that is, others must be able to imagine themselves following in the footsteps of the observer, and repeating and corroborating his observations.[65] Methods of perception and recording must, moreover, be vindicated as impartial and objective, conveying not the whimsy or idiosyncrasy of contingent practices but the considered authority of empiricism. Finally, the amassing of data in these distinctive ways ultimately assembles a theory, an epistemology, of the world, that prefigures the emergence of more specialized disciplinary varieties of scientific discourse in the modern ages.

The focal importance of the observer and his observational point of view, in the production of a scientific apparatus, means that old conventions and new disciplinary prefigurations collide in the *Travels* at the "I" of the narratorial subject. The *Travels* is thus fortuitously able to inherit, and profit from, centuries-old conventions in the genre of travel narratives, when manufacturing an appropriate persona for the eyewitness traveler-who-narrates. Generic expectations allow for a degree of individuation in the personae of such narrators, so that the characterization of the "Mandeville" observer need not be blandly featureless (a depersonalized observer) but can be sympathetically rendered to invite identification with his position, status, and role.

Narrative traditions in travel writing also habituate an audience/readership to expect authenticating devices that attest the truthfulness of the observer's account, including that old favorite, the modesty *topos* (I cannot do a description justice in this instance, so am silent here), thus allowing "Mandeville" to deploy the traditions of authentication to good effect (155). Readers accustomed to finding the traveling observer-narrator ubiquitously present, in however outlandish an environment, may also find eminently palatable the "Mandeville" observer's intrusion into places depicted as impenetrable to all but he, whose perceptual advantage is then reified on successful penetration into proscribed places.

The "Mandeville" observer-narrator is also depicted in contemporary as well as literary terms: He is a creditably common representative of his social and occupational class, easily recognizable, and readily found in many regions of the world in the second half of the fourteenth century. "Sir John Mandeville," knight, takes military service with the Sultan of Babylon, and the Great Khan, in whose local wars and battles he strives, as a paid retainer. Not only is the knight-gentleman-mercenary a familiar figure in the latter half of the fourteenth century (see chapter 3), but the socially familiar

"Mandeville" is supported by the inherited literary motif of being offered a Saracen princess in marriage (*Travels*, 18), a romance *topos* that, as we have seen, dates back to Odoric Vitalis's provision for Bohemond in the earlier twelfth century, and Richard Lionheart's joke-in-reverse-terms to Al-Adil, in the later twelfth century (see chapters 4 and 2 above).

Structured to attract identification, "Sir John Mandeville" is represented as mobile, adventurous, lucky, part of the knightly elite, and an intimate of emperors, who is granted opportunities for many kinds of advancement—including legitimate access to exotic royal females—and the seductive prospect of seeing it all, and doing it all, from within several of the world's cultures. Finally, after experiencing at close range the glories of empires, reciting allegories of navigation and science, and surveying a range of exotic, taboo cultures, and whole taxonomies of flora and fauna, his story is ratified and endorsed, at the end of his journey, by no less a figure than the Pope himself, winning the seal of approval from the highest of church authorities. If this is insufficient to attract audience identification with "Mandeville," we also find, ineluctably, that the narrator possesses a prime relic, a thorn from Christ's original crown of thorns (*Travels*, 7), and has drunk three times from the fabled well of youth and health (*Travels*, 84).[66]

But what *new* disciplinary arrangements of a "scientific" kind does this observer-narrator prefigure? Scholars of critical (and feminist) anthropology in the late twentieth century have extensively mapped the close relations and shared common ground between ethnography and literature, in terms of narrative conventions, the personae of characters featured, plots and devices, and the agency of the author (as ethnographer or literary creator). Travelogues, in particular—as a category of literature that, like ethnography, specializes in the narrative description of exotic human subjects and communities around the world—have been investigated not only for their resemblance to the ethnographic literature that they were once held to precede, as a genre, but also for their continuing resemblance today, in significant respects, to what Malinowski, founding father of modern anthropology, called "scientific ethnography." Among travelogues, *medieval* travel narratives antedate, by three or four or five centuries, the examples of travel literature usually cited in late-twentieth-century critical discourse on anthropology. In some medieval travelogues, moreover (not, of course, in all), the role and position of the observer-narrator is configured in ways startlingly predictive of the role and position of the "scientific ethnographer" today.

"Mandeville," as observer-narrator, takes the prefiguration of the ethnographer-as-scientist in the modern age one step further. As one who observes and records from within a culture in which he participates at length, "Mandeville's" practices articulate not only the tension between subjectivity and objectivity characterizing accounts of participant-observation—a nexus of tension that will trouble ethnographic and anthropological authority in later ages—but also demonstrate how the subjectivity in such accounts might be stabilized, as well as advantage extracted from subjectivity, so that a better approximation of utopian scientifism is contrived. Modern ethnographers, who aspire to the depersonalized objectivity of the scientific method idealized in the empirical disciplines of science, are bedeviled by ethnographic reliance on "the authority of the personal experience out of which the ethnography is made" (Pratt, 33). Mary Louise Pratt argues that modern ethnographers insert personal and anecdotal narratives into their ethnographic texts as partial admission of the dependence of ethnographic report on the individual ethnographer's perceptions, experience, skill, and trustworthiness ("personal narrative persists alongside objectifying description in ethnographic writing because it mediates a contradiction within the discipline between personal and scientific authority. . . . James Clifford speaks of it as 'the discipline's impossible attempt to fuse objective and subjective practices'" [32]). Because modern ethnographers are anxious to vindicate the "scientific" objectivity of their texts—an objectivity that ideally, if impossibly, requires the erasure or suppression of all subjective viewing and recording practices on the part of the observing subject—the very presence of the observer-recorder itself becomes fraught with problems. When human communities in the field constitute the empiricist's laboratory, accomplishing ideal scientific objectivity would in effect require the transformation of the observer into a panopticonic viewing and recording machine.

Pratt suggests that travel literature often makes available ways in which some of the contradictions confronting modern ethnography may be bypassed, ways unavailable to professional ethnographers. One means by which travel narratives sidestep a central conundrum beleaguering ethnographic accounts—the structurally, if not intentionally, exploitative and asymmetrical relationship that obtains between the anthropologist (a surveying and manipulating subject) and the natives he or she is studying in the field (the objects of investigation and the anthropological gaze)—is by creating a narrator who is a castaway or captive, and thus involuntarily present in a foreign culture that may then be viewed, conveniently but innocently, from within, and at close range: "Anthropologists customarily establish a relationship of exchange with the group based on Western commodities. That is how they survive and try to make their relations with informants nonexploitative. But of course this strategy is enormously contradictory, for it makes anthropologists constant contributors to what they themselves see as the destruction of their object of study. The status of the captive or castaway, by contrast, is innocent" (Pratt, 38).

If "castaways and captives in many ways realize the ideal of the participant-observer" and "the image of the castaway mystifies the ethnographer's situation" (Pratt, 38), a participant-observer-narrator such as "Mandeville," who takes prolonged service under the ruler of a native group, furnishes a superior site for ethnographic observation of a significantly authoritative, yet unencumbered, kind. The exchange relationship simulated in "Mandeville's" context—employment—is mutually entered into by both parties in the field, and is of mutual advantage to both the ethnographer figure and the object of study, while also technically making "Mandeville" subordinate to the employers he studies. Such mutuality defuses the subject-object relationship that usually characterizes the connection of the observer to the observed, equalizing the statuses of both vis-à-vis each other in important ways, even as it inherently makes the observer into a member of the very community under observation. Instead of the artificial relationship devised by the modern ethnographer in the field—an exchange relationship often guiltily based on commodity bribery of native informants—a relationship approximating normal social and economic intercourse is improvised in the *Travels*.

Even if fictitious, the semblance of some degree of mutuality, and equivalence, that does not make the observed into an object of observation is of such importance that, until today, in studies such as Ann McClintock's on the Prostitutes of New York (PONY) or Barbara Ehrenreich's on the working poor in the United States, authors take care to characterize the communities being studied as the *subjects*, not the *objects*, of discourse: a discourse also carefully presented as issuing from, or being shaped by, the subjects of observation themselves, rather than predominantly managed by the author (Ehrenreich also takes pains to live as a low-waged worker herself, temporarily joining the community of the working poor). In the instance of "Mandeville," we note, the fictively subordinate position of the Western observer—his Eastern employer is the puissant ruler of a powerful civilization, a civilization superior to the observer's own and one that the observer can therefore neither dominate nor suborn—alibis the participant-observer's role as innocent while guaranteeing him intimate access to the civilization's lifeways and people, for purposes of observation.

Lest we are concerned that the fictiveness of medieval travel romance is effaced when we re-create "Mandeville" in the persona of a scientific ethnographer, while the facticity of field reports in anthropology is impugned when we sense a structural equivalence between professional anthropologists and participant-observers in literary texts, it is useful to recall that scholarship recognizes the ease with which ethnographic accounts can be manufactured through imaginative fabrication, by recourse to conventions and formulas, just as in literature: "Given a certain quantity of secondary material, one in fact could construct a convincing, vivid, ethnographically accurate account of life in another culture *without personal experience in the field*" (Pratt, 29). Indeed, if medieval travel romance can simulate scientific ethnography, ethnography has also been caught in the act of resembling travel romance. Examining the controversy, in academic anthropology, generated by Florinda Donner's ethnographic narrative of the Yanomamo peoples of South America, Pratt quotes a comment in the September 1983 issue of the *American Anthropologist* that describes Donner's ethnography in terms which evocatively suggest that Donner's ethnography could well have been written by the author of *Mandeville's Travels*: "Donner's ethnographic data . . . were 'rather expertly borrowed from other sources and assembled in a kind of mélange of fact and fantasy'" (Pratt, 28).

Within its own mélange of fact and fantasy, the *Travels'* pairing of the authority of subjective experience with the goals of objective description in observation is successful to a surprising degree, given the vintage of this text that precedes modern ethnography by half a millenium. The *Travels'* preferred procedure is to engage directly with the authority of *both* subjectivity *and* objectivity in the extrapolation of a perceptual hypothesis of maximum advantage. Just as the collective features of "Mandeville's" persona seem contrived to maximize potentials in attracting identification with this enterprising and mobile chivalric observer, contexts in which the "I" materializes in narrative seem improvised to suggest that the observer's subjective stances can be trusted to be fair, impartial, honest, and consistent. When describing the desert wastes of "Tartary," for example, the narrator conscientiously acknowledges hearsay report:

Þare will na gude manne dwell in þat land . . . as I hafe herd say, for I hafe noȝt bene þare. Bot I hafe bene in oþer landes þat marchez þeron,

as þe land of Russy and Nyfland and þe kingdom of Cracow and Lettow and in þe kingdom of Graften and many oþer placez. Bot I went
neuer by þat way to Ierusalem, and þerfore I may noȝt wele tell it.
(*Travels*, 65)[67]

There will no good man dwell in that land . . . as I have heard say, for I
have not been there. But I have been in other lands that march thereon
[border it], as the land of Russia and Nyfland [Livonia] and the kingdom of Cracow and Lettow [Lithuania] and in the kingdom of Graften
[Silistria] and many other places. But I never went by that way to
Jerusalem, and therefore I may not well tell of it.

Disclaimers of direct personal knowledge and experience are, of course, an
honorable tradition and serve well to balance other claims of the opposite
kind ("But I have been in other lands that border it . . . and many other
places"), so that a judicious composite of calculated admissions, told
against claims of direct eyewitness experience, results, awarding an air of
balanced truthfulness to the whole compendium of observation that bol-
sters, rather than detracts from, the authority of subjective contribution.
Discretionary reticence, when phenomenal evidence is in doubt, or controversial, produces a similar facsimile of judiciousness and reasoned re-
straint. On the whereabouts of one celebrated relic, the head of John the
Baptist, "Mandeville" pronouncedly declines judgment ("Some men say
that . . . and some say that . . . I know not; God knows" [*Travels*, 53]); the
impression of responsible impartiality is decidedly served.

Rather than deny or mitigate the participant-observer's subjectivity,
therefore, and the inevitable fusion of subjective and objective content
and practices in participant-observation, the narrator's subjective contribution to what he perceives and experiences is mined to advantage. Because the *Travels* is a medieval text, the authority of the narrator's subjectivity—in addition to being founded on qualities of impartiality and
reasoned judiciousness also valued in modern ethnography—is grounded
as well in a certain *moral* authority. In a medieval universe, a participant-
observer whose observations can be respected and universalized is also a
trustworthy moral being, one whose deepest convictions can be relied on
to conform to fundamental values and principles. Thus it is that although
"Mandeville" is generously and nobly offered a rich marriage with "a great
prince's daughter and . . . many great lordships" (an offer that fulfills important cultural fantasies in late-medieval Europe by playing to dynamics

of race and sexuality, as well as to ambitions of social and economic ad-vancement), "Mandeville" can also be depended on not to be seduced by the wealth, ease, power, and superior social status gained by such a mar-riage, when the privileges offered carry the requirement of religious con-version: "If that I would have forsaken my belief and turned to theirs; but I would not" (*Travels*, 18).

"Mandeville's" steadfastness in matters of faith, in the most fundamen-tal circumstances, and against the temptation of worldly ambitions, not only attests the moral reliability of his particular viewing-and-recording po-sition and role but also vindicates this participant-observer's tolerance of religious heterodoxy—much in evidence elsewhere—as transparently goodwilled, well-intentioned generosity, a generosity innocent of other coloration, given his demonstrated religious loyalty.[68] With the stabiliza-tion of "Mandeville's" moral, social, and personal authority, we have, then, the creation of a viewing subject who possesses both a believable local identity and a pivotal role as an impartial, universal witness (the Latin-Christian/Western-European subject as universal witness). By con-veying tolerance of variety, moreover, including variety in faith, "Man-deville's" observational position is established as nonrigid and humane; and personal experience, and the observer's subjectivity, are explored and stabilized to advantage.

As reinforcement, the process of observation itself is also configured to hint at the potentials inherent in a regime of sight, and visibility, in spe-cialized viewing of a kind that exceeds mere participant-observation. View-ing can possess unusual authority when the observer's perceptual ability is significantly extended, so that an almost mechanical perspective, in range and power, is approximated, centered on the visual acuity of a roving eye, under certain conditions.[69] If viewing of an intimate kind, at close quar-ters, occurs when the "Mandeville" participant-observer describes a partic-ular social system from a vantage point within a community, and compre-hensive viewing, from a distanced, privileged vantage point, occurs when a collection of alphabets, representing the extracted essences of various eth-nic and social systems, is compiled and available for survey as a group, an-other kind of viewing is yet available in the *Travels*. This supplemental species of viewing offers the possibility of observing more than immediate-ly meets the eye—more than what is superficially visible—within a system or about a system. The allegory of a perceptual system that *penetrates into interiors, and the unseen* within an environment, occurs when the "Man-deville" observer describes his successful penetration into a proscribed site in Muslim-controlled Jerusalem, "the Temple of Our Lord":

Þe Sarzenes will suffer na Cristen men ne Iews comme þerin. . . .
Neuerþeles I come in þare, and in oþer placez whare I wald; for I had
lettres of þe sowdan with his grete seele, in þe whilk he commaunded
straitly til all his subiectes, þat þai schuld late me see all þe placez whare
I come, and þat þai schuld schew me þe relykes and the placez at my
will, and þat þai schuld lede me fra citee to citee, if mist ware, and be-
nignely ressayue me and all my felaws, and be obeischaunt to myne
askynges in all thing þat was resounable. (*Travels*, 41)[70]

The Saracens will suffer no Christian men nor Jews to come therein. . .
. Nevertheless I came in there, and in other places where I would; for I
had letters of the Sultan with his great seal, in which he commanded
strictly to all his subjects, that they should let me see all the places where
I came, and that they should show me the relics and the [holy] places at
my will, and that they should lead me from city to city, if there were
need, and benignly receive me and all my fellows, and be obedient to my
askings in all thing that was reasonable.

The claim of unrestricted access to the Temple fulfills in the first instance,
of course, the imaginative imperatives of Western European cultural fantasy—such access answering especially to the desire for direct, personal
contact with Christian holy places despite Muslim occupation. However,
we are told that "Mandeville" also went into *other* places whenever and
wherever he wished, so that he could see "*all* the places" and the objects
he wanted, even from city to city, and under secure auspices, when he so
desired. Successful penetration of this nature, and the gaining of access
into all the interiors that one might wish, and all sites, proscribed or not,
is in excess of mere pilgrimage objectives.

Indeed, viewing of this nature suggests the sweepingly wide-range scan-
ning and inexorability of a regime of the optical-mechanical, rather than
merely human conditions of sight (though offered, of course, as the human
persona's story), and prefigures the emergence of the roving eye of a technology that later ages would associate with the regimen of the panopticon
or the dominion of the closed-circuit camera that penetrates into controlled spaces. Highly portable modes of viewing and secret viewing curiously merge in "Mandeville's" description. Although the viewer and his
companions are not *spying*, per se, their sanctioned scopophilia into all
available spaces retrieves the aura, if not the formal apparatus, of surveil-
lance. The searching power of a vision able to bring to sight what is ordi-
narily undisclosed invokes, as well, the operations of X-ray technology,

though the name for such penetration would not yet exist for several centuries. When observation means the ability to freely keep an eye on anything you wish, the empiricism that results, once the eye is given access to
unrestricted vision, confers a godlike status on the observer.

In empirical and epistemological terms, godlike access is structurally
homologous to sciencelike access (and, indeed, science and technology
have been somewhile accused of usurping the status and privileges of
God). The edifice of "science," and a sciencelike discursive apparatus,
rests, in the *Travels*, on a nexus at which the observer, privileged sites and
modes of viewing, and a flexible field of vision converge. A sciencelike perspective is depicted as yielding both comprehensive, as well as intimate,
views: allowing an observer minute, close-up scrutiny of particulars, as
well as granting overall, sweeping vision from afar. Under some conditions, observation possesses an almost mechanical power of penetration,
turning the observer virtually into an all-seeing-and-recording machine.

The modes of viewing imparted across the range of "scientific" vision
thus tacitly or overtly sketch circuits of optical and observational power:
"Mandeville," through his "I" *of* the world—an ethnographic, witnessing
"I" who invites identification, and positions reader and audience alike to
imagine the possibility of following, repeating, and corroborating his example—keeps his eye *on* the world, locally and globally, in a restlessly roving survey. The varieties of his viewing may utilize known instruments
(astrolabe, alphabets, compass, arcs and degrees, recognized systems of
measuring distance or gathering information of the physical environment)
to formalize the structures of perception. In the course of observation,
other technologies (optics, methods, apparatuses) may also suggest themselves, if they are not explicitly declared or detailed, and a basis (and rules)
of viewing are accomplished or implied. When structures of perception
are thus formalized and accrue authority, vignettes and stories become
data, information: perception is turned into knowledge of the world and
its systems and peoples, and a theory of the world is produced.

The attractiveness of *Mandeville's Travels* to explorers, mapmakers, authors, readers, and printers in the late Middle Ages and early Renaissance
consists, at least in part, in that cumulative theory of the world which the
Travels accomplishes: the narrative's apprehension of the empirical and the
inductive worlds, and its sweepingly, encompassingly thorough vision of all
it surveys. But because the *Travels is* a romance, the world theorized in the
Travels is, of course, a *romance* world, one whose phenomenality is as hypothetical, or, alternatively, as recognizably real, as any world represented

in speculative fiction today. And in medieval romance, science will still feel like magic, even if it also feels like a magic of the future, a magic whose consolidation would, in the future, bring the creation of more marvels than even medieval romance might dream of or desire.

In the *Travels'* own time and context, the peculiar blending of science, scientific authority, magic, fictiveness, and reality, which characterizes the romance of science in premodern travel literature, is wonderfully quintes-sentialized when the *Travels* speaks of the sea: that last impassable frontier of the Middle Ages, as formidable a barrier then as space today might seem to travelers. Touching on the sea around Prester John's kingdom, "Mandeville" discourses eloquently on magnetism as a "scientific" expla-nation of why mariners prefer to travel to the historical Cathay, rather than to the fictional kingdom of Prester John, Cathay's proximate neigh-bor in the country of romance:

> Þer er in many placez in þe see grete roches of þe stane þat es called Adamaunt, þe whilk of his awen kynde drawez to hym yrne; and, for þer schuld passe na schippes þat had nayles of yrne þare away by cause of þe forsaid stane, for he schuld drawe þam till hym, þarfore þai dare noȝt wende þider. Þe schippes of þat cuntree er all made of wode and nane yrne. I was ane tyme in þat see, and I sawe as it had bene ane ile of treesse and bruschez growand; and the schippe men talde me þat all þat was of grete schippes þat þe roche of þe adamand had gert dwell þare, and of diuerse thinges þat were in þe schippez ware þase treesse and þase br-usches sprungen. (*Travels*, 133)[71]

> There are in many places in the sea great rocks of the stone that is called Adamant, which of his own nature draws to himself iron; and, since there should pass no ships that had nails of iron thereabout because of the aforesaid stone (for he should draw them to himself), therefore they dare not wend thither. The ships of that country are all made of wood and no iron. I was one time in that sea, and I saw as it had been an isle of trees and bushes growing; and the shipmen told me that all that was from great ships that the rock of the adamant had caused to remain there, and from diverse things that were in the ships were those trees and those bushes sprung.

Here, then, is a scientific-technological explanation—applying contempo-rary knowledge of magnetism and staunchly vouched for by that universal subject and witness, the Western European "I" of the world—as to why a nonexistent romance country cannot be pragmatically approached by sea travel. As an image rich with mystery and possibility, the sea, of course, is to travel romance what the forest is to chivalric romance, except that Ocean sea is vaster, and unifyingly encircles the world, drawing all waters to itself, as it beckons to imaginary travelers. Following in the footsteps of literary predecessors before him, "Mandeville" then tells of yet another marvelous sea—a sea of gravel and sand—in a resonant passage that scarcely has an equal in the history of cultural fantasy for its magical feel, the sense of awe it conveys, and its simple, haunting wistfulness:

> Þare is a grete see all of grauell and sande, and na drope of water þerin. And it ebbez and flowes as þe grete see duse in oþer cuntreez with grete wawes, and neuermare standez still withouten mouyng. Þat see may na man passe, nowþer by schippe ne oþer wyse; and þerfore it es vnknawen till any man whatkyn land or cuntree es on þe toþer syde of þat see. And þof þer be na water in þat see, neuerþeles þare es grete plentee of gude fischez taken by þe see bankes; and þai er riȝt sauoury in þe mouth, bot þai er of oþer schappe þan fischez er of oþer waters. I Iohn Maundeuill ete of þam, and þarfore trowez it, for sikerly it es soth. (*Travels*, 134)[72]

> There is a great sea all of gravel and sand, and no drop of water therein. And it ebbs and flows as the great sea does in other countries with great waves, and nevermore stands still without moving. That sea may no man pass, neither by ship nor otherwise; and therefore it is unknown to any man what nature of land or country is on the other side of that sea. And though there be no water in that sea, nevertheless there is great plenty of good fish taken by the sea banks; and they are right savory in the mouth [very delicious], but they are of other shape than are the fish of other waters. I John Mandeville ate of them, and therefore believe it, for certainly it is true.

Readers may be forgiven if they do not recognize a description of the desert in this poetic depiction of a sandy sea, or if they should think they scent, minisculely, a whiff of resemblance to the imaginary worlds of science fiction narratives today. On the farthest shore of the known medieval world, "I John Mandeville" once ate a marvelous fish, from a marvelous sea of sand, whose waves ebb and flow and nevermore stand still, unpassable by ship, a sea beyond which unknown lands beckon, but can never be reached.[73] What more haunting, magical vision can either medieval romance or science fiction offer, to catch at the nature of the desire that drives exploration, expansion, science, and romance?

Close to the end of the *Travels*, "John Mandeville" revisits the subject of circumnavigation again: "Other isles there are . . . by the which men might go all about [encircle] the earth, who so had the grace of God to hold the right way, and come right to the same countries that they were of and come from, and so go all about the earth, as I have said before, by process of time. But . . . it should be a long time ere that voyage were completed" (*Travels*, 152). In the mention of the Gravelly Sea as well—a sea that appears early in the narrative when we are told that the "fosse of Mynon" seems to flow into it ("And some say that it is an outlet of the Gravelly Sea" [*Travels*, 16]), and once again near the narrative's end (*Travels*, 134)—circularity seems uncannily to underpin motion and trajectory in the *Travels*.[74] Circumnavigation, then, as described by "Mandeville," seems the very figure of romance forms of travel; while travel stories, and "Mandeville" himself, seem the very figures of medieval romance and its scenic journeys.

For like "Mandeville's" tenacious, imaginary world-sojourner, medieval romance roams freely in the countries of fact and fantasy—holding the right way, with the grace of God—and, having collected adventures and people, and encircled the multifarious world in all its guises, in overarching, all-encompassing circumnavigation, finally arrives back home, to rest, before the next cycle begins anew.[75]

Notes

ॐ

Introduction: In the Beginning Was Romance . . .

1. On the genre of the "Indika" and a suggestive discussion of ancient geography in the mode of romance, see, especially, Romm. The Alexander romances exist in many editions and translations, including, conveniently, Stoneman's in Penguin, and Kratz's. Perry comprehensively discusses the romances of antiquity. Rather than rehearse, yet again, the multitude of definitions and catalogues of "romance" that medievalists and others have attempted, over generations of scholarship, here in the introduction, I cite relevant scholarship in each chapter, as my argument unfolds, over the course of this book. In the final event, as Hornstein intimated in 1971, all definitions that attempt categorization by content, in particular, are destined for frustration, as "there will emerge only hazy borderlines where epic, saga, chanson de geste, romance, historical romance, lai, saint's life, pious legend, fabliau meet and blend" ("Middle English Romances," 69). Derrida's 1979 "Loi du genre" puts the impossibility of definitive categorization as a theoretical question that haunts *all* genres: "c'était impossible, de ne pas mêler les genres . . . logée au coeur de la loi même [est] une loi d'impurete ou un principe de contamination" (178).

2. Ganim ("Myth") not only observes that "the Middle Ages is imagined as a romance" and romance is "emplaced as the stereotypical genre of the Middle Ages," but also that "from its earliest formulations in the eighteenth century . . . critical discourse surrounding the romances first imagines the Middle Ages as a romance, and then gradually becomes a species of romance itself" (149).

3. Among moderns, however, the logic of manuscript culture's "community on the page" may perhaps be least alien to those habituated to internet communities of writing—an electronic context of group communication in which individual identity may also be withheld, and texts are added to, written over, responded to, and accrue and accumulate over time, with an implicit understanding among participants that the text is dynamic and unfinished, even as it continues to be put in play and transmitted by several hands (or perhaps more accurately, "by several fonts"). But even here, of course, the analogy between medieval and twenty-first century

communities of writing—ignoring as it does issues of ephemerality and preservation, control of and access to writing and resources, questions of authority and freedom, and the quality and kinds of text produced, among a plethora of other things—is highly imperfect and unsatisfactory.

4. The cultural politics of medieval revivals, and the instrumentality of the Middle Ages for literary and cultural movements that retrieve the past have been amply studied. Girouard, Barczewski, Fay, Agrawal, and Ragussis are examples of a range of approaches. An important skein of recent work shows how the use of the medieval past facilitates the consolidation of national identities in the eighteenth and nineteenth centuries: Ragussis's important study, which considers the role of Jews as a hinge of English nationalism, treats, among other things, Walter Scott's medievalism and the retrieval of the Spanish medieval past, while Barczewski focuses on the instrumentality of the King Arthur and Robin Hood legends for British national identity. Studies on specifically Arthurian medievalisms of later centuries, or negotiations of medieval romance in postmedieval periods, include volumes by Reid, Christopher Dean, and Johnston, while Stephen Knight's socially nuanced readings of the Arthurian legend span the historical gamut from Geoffrey of Monmouth's Arthur to Mark Twain's.

5. "*Star Trek* has mushroomed into a conglomerate of texts and inter-text, becoming nothing less than a *mega*-text: a . . . seemingly undying enterprise of televisual, filmic, auditory, and written texts. In addition to the four prime-time series, the cartoon series, and the eight films, there is a gushing current of comic books, magazines, novels, compendia, biographies, and autobiographies. . . . scholars contribute . . . courses . . . articles, dissertations, and books. . . . [F]ans . . . write and distribute thousands of original stories, known as fanzines, and disperse hundreds of thousands of comments and criticisms about the mega-text in cyber-space" (Bernardi, 7).

6. Those who remember the original *Star Trek* television series which spawned the "mega" *Trek* industry documented by Bernardi fondly remember how James T. Kirk, captain of the starship "Enterprise," invariably and enterprisingly seemed to find himself, at punctual intervals, on native planets where he would proceed to inseminate native women, and perhaps temporarily go native himself, like all good colonial subjects (even involuntary, temporary ones), despite a Prime Directive that specifically instructed the roaming starships of that benign pastoral ecumen called the "Federation of Planets" not to interfere in any way with native life or native subjects. We might understand something of the durability of what impels travel romance, if we consider that the traveling "Sir John Mandeville," six hundred years before Kirk, and also roaming with companions, was already being offered Saracen princesses during *his* sojourns in strange lands, if *he*, too, were willing to go native (which in the context of medieval travel romance meant conversion to Islam).

7. Wood seems to claim for *Camelot 3000*, as I for medieval romance, a textual strategy in which fantasy and historical phenomena collide, merge, and interanimate, in order to provide a medium for the discussion of risky subjects: "A good part of *Camelot 3000*'s success appears to have resulted from its capacity to be seen simulta-

neously as pure science-fiction fantasy and also as a vehicle through which contemporary concerns could be explored at a dispassionate distance" (Wood, 307).

8. Not only can a technology of narration—the fantasy medium of cinema—function like romance, but Robert Hamilton's review of how Japan today is represented in Western popular entertainment media suggests how even a country in real time (but located, of course, at a goodly distance away) can be configured to offer a romance-like portal to what one's own culture and society most desire. Like Prester John's kingdom or the Great Khan's Cathay, the representation of Japan, it seems, demarcates a romance space that delivers what the West wants, through what the East might be: "In her *Bad Subjects* article, 'Anime Otaku,' Annalee Newitz speculated that Western fans of Japanese animation consume it because it reflects themes and characters familiar to them through foreign films and television. . . . The creators of 'South Park' are likely among the numbers that Ms. Newitz would classify as 'otaku.' Their interest in Japanese popular culture is more than just passing. The frequency of references in the series alone is enough to raise eyebrows. . . . Japan is utilized as an ideal Other. It is the source of material, inspiration and references that are familiar to many viewers, yet distant enough to retain a strange or off-beat quality."

9. If definitional criteria in race theory tended to lag behind, the spectacle of "ethnic cleansing" witnessed in Bosnia, even before September 11, 2001, demonstrated to the world that *religion* could be understood by the perpetrators of genocide to have a definitional primacy in deciding who belonged to the same species as themselves, and thus might be allowed to live and escape mass sexual brutalization. That the religion of their victims was held by the perpetrators of genocide to confer an *essential* identity, an identity which rendered the victims innately different from the perpetrators in their own minds—exemplifying, in this, a typical line of racial thinking—should have already suggested to us that not all instances of racial behavior were based on the deployment of biological criteria. The term applied to the genocides—"ethnic cleansing"—is thus more than ironically revealing in its contradictions. The "cleansing" of communal impurity, by violent acts of blood, does mark racial logic of a biological kind, even as the adjective "ethnic" denies biology its status of paramount preeminence in defining these race-murders as advanced by racial logic of a culturalist kind. Biological thinking failed to triumph in yet another way: The rape of Muslim women, and the women's impregnation by the perpetrators of genocide, only guaranteed future racial impurity in the miscegenated bloodline of the generation to come.

10. Characterizations by phenotype, of course, also continue, and brown-skinned, Semitic-looking peoples continue to be presumed Arabs, and racially identified—even if they turn out to be South Asians. To demonstrate the sheer contingency and arbitrariness of racial classification and categories, pre–September 11, 2001, there is no finer instrument than the U. S. Population Census 2000, which candidly attested to the breakdown of workable racial definitions in the twenty-first century United States by wisely asking informants to bear the responsibility of self-identification across a range of sixty-three possible variations of categories. In Census 2000, "Arabs" had not yet entered into the official imagination as a race, to be identified and distinguished,

like African Americans, Native Americans, Pacific Islanders, Asian Americans, and others, while in 2002, official consciousness of the apartness, and difference, of those variously identified as Arabs, Arab Americans, Muslims, Middle Easterners, and Arabic-speakers is acute: one vivid demonstration of how groups of people emerge into race, under contingent historical circumstances.

I. CANNIBALISM, THE FIRST CRUSADE, AND THE GENESIS OF MEDIEVAL ROMANCE

1. I use Neil Wright's excellent and timely edition of the important Bern, Burger-bibliothek, MS 568, of the vulgate *Historia* (henceforth Wright, 1), but I also refer to his edition of the First Variant ([henceforth Wright, 2] surviving in 8 of the 217 known mss of the *Historia*), and R. E. Jones's translation of a fifteenth-century Welsh manuscript, Oxford, Jesus College, MS 61, in Griscom's edition of the *Historia*, since Griscom and Jones believe their Welsh *Brut* to represent mss that might include the Welsh text that Geoffrey claimed—in a narrative pretext that scholars today treat as a fiction—to have used as his source. Despite textual differences among the 217 known manuscripts, "a remarkable homogeneity of text" obtains among the 90 percent that comprise the vulgate (Dumville, 2), a homogeneity on which—given the lack of a reliable text history and the unpublished, unedited, and widely scattered manuscripts—any critical discussion of the *Historia*, including my own, must depend. A Second Variant is represented by 15 mss (Emanuel, 104). Still unpublished, the Second Variant is treated by scholars as an abbreviated recension of the vulgate. For a catalogue of the *Historia*'s mss see Crick's comprehensive recent volume and article; Wright (1:xlvii–li) and Dumville ("Early Text") ably rehearse the difficulty of establishing a text history. Tatlock, whose magisterial study on Geoffrey remains definitive, offers 1130–33 as the earliest possible *terminus a quo* for the *Historia* (435–36); Wright merely suggests that the work was begun "at some date before 1135" (1:xvi), and most other scholars offer dates between 1130 and 1135. The *terminus ad quem* is accepted by scholars as before January 1139, when Henry of Huntingdon was shown a copy of the *Historia* at Bec, as recounted in his letter to Warin the Briton, in Robert of Torigni's *Chronicle* and some texts of Henry's *Historia Anglorum*. Dumville believes the *terminus ad quem* of the Bern ms to be before October 1147 (21–22), and Wright "the last quarter of the twelfth century" (1:l).

2. I begin here with a rudimentary description of romance as fantastical narrative, a description I complicate as my argument develops. Though it will be obvious that there are signal differences between my evolving definition of romance and earlier definitions, my debt to the tradition of scholarship will be equally apparent. For definitive moments in the ongoing discussion of romance, see Baugh, Bloch (*Etymologies*), Bloomfield, Calin, Comfort, S. Crane, Duby, Everett, Finlayson ("Definitions"), Fleischman, Frye, Ganim (*Style and Consciousness*, "Myth"), Gravdal, Haidu, Hanning (*Individual*), Hibbard, Hume, Jackson, Jauss, Jameson, Ker, Knight, Köhler, C. S. Lewis, Mehl, Nerlich, Patterson, Parker, Pearsall, Shoaf, Strohm, Vance, and Vinaver.

3. The obligations of twelfth-century historiography are perhaps best summed up by William of Malmsbury, the most magisterial medieval historian after Bede, when he relates in *De Gestis Regum Anglorum* (On the deeds of the kings of the English, c. 1125) that he has "followed the genuine laws of history" ("veram legem secutus historiae" [2:518]), in offering nothing but what he has adduced from "truthful relators or writers" ("fidelibus relatoribus vel scriptoribus" [2:518]). On conventions governing historical writing in medieval England, see, especially, Gransden's major two-volume study, Hanning (*Vision of History*), and pertinent material in Partner, Leckie, and Fletcher. Gransden names a number of the *Historia*'s admirers (1:200, 1:208–12). The *Historia*'s popularity and wide circulation soon after its appearance is attested by the large number of surviving mss from the twelfth century alone (58 or 59 at latest count, in 1995), and manuscript provenance (on the "extensiveness of the *Historia*'s popularity on the Continent" as well as England, see Crick, "Dissemination and Reception," 216–17), and the rapid use of the *Historia* by such authors as Henry of Huntingdon, Alfred of Beverly, Robert Wace, and Geffrei Gaimar. Outrage at Geoffrey's spectacular fictions—particularly the Arthurian inventions—is famously expressed by William of Newburgh, who devotes almost the entire, oft-quoted prologue—longer than any chapter of the book that follows—of his *Historia Rerum Anglicarum* (History of English Affairs)—to a refutation and fiery castigation of Geoffrey's creative untruths. A celebrated anecdote recounted by Giraldus Cambrensis is also often quoted: "A certain Meilerius, of the region of Urbs Legionum, being possessed by devils, was by them endowed with the capacity of discovering any falsehood with which he was brought into contact. When the Gospel of John was laid on his lap, the devils vanished; but when Geoffrey's *History* was substituted, they returned in greater numbers than ever" (Fletcher, 180). In the fourteenth century Ranulph Higden's *Polychronicon* "cast doubt on the authenticity of Geoffrey's account" (Patterson, 206). William Camden, in the sixteenth century, also quotes John of Whethamstede's attack on Geoffrey's credibility, in a mid-fifteenth century work (Keeler, 81–84). Leckie observes that "ambivalence" toward the *Historia* has been "a recurring feature of the work's reception" (20), although "Geoffrey's construct provided the standard framework for historiographic depictions of early British history" (20) from the thirteenth to the sixteenth centuries, after which the *Historia*'s status as a legendary or romance history of Britain resurfaced. Ward, who suggests that twelfth-century England witnessed a clerical and court culture where "men [had] to wheedle, flatter, cousen, win favour to secure posts in a situation in which eligible claimants [were] beginning to exceed the number of places available" (68), argues for the beginning of a narrational culture that strategically inserts a break between "truth" and language, in favor of "oblique" narrational forms such as "the 'Romance-parody-satire' history of Geoffrey of Monmouth" (68).

4. Though not described as a romance, the *Historia* has been given due credit, from early in this century, for helping to usher in Arthurian romance (see, e.g., Fletcher, 56; Bruce, 1:20; Gerould, 35; Tatlock [*Legendary History*, 179]). Genuinely historical accounts, particularly of the chief occasions of insular history such as Roman invasion and occupation, the Augustinian mission, and the Saxon arrival mingle with

the *Historia*'s inventions of fantasy material for Britain's past (though Geoffrey's text is not above taking liberties with even large historical occasions). The *Historia*'s necessary dependence on major early documents of British history—its use of Gildas and Bede, and the *Historia Brittonum* has most recently been traced, with acuity, by Wright ("Gildas," "Gildas Revisted," "Bede")—makes it vulnerable, of course, to error or inaccuracy in the historical sources themselves (see, e.g., Dumville, "Historical Value," 16–20, on factual errors and legendary material in the *Historia Brittonum*), a vulnerability Geoffrey's text shares with more conventional twelfth-century histories. Thorpe's introduction also suggests the confirmation of genuine historicity in the *Historia* by modern archaeological discoveries (*History*, 19).

5. Sebastian Evans's translation, in 1896, actually translates the name "Mons Aravius" into the Welsh "Eryri" (181) within the text of the *Historia* itself. Arguing from oral traditions and archaeological survivals in Wales, saints' lives, the Welsh chronicle tradition of *Bruts*, the *Mabinogion*, and other literary materials, Celticists and others sympathetic to the search for Celtic origins have offered various Welsh sources for the *Historia*, although in the case of the Welsh chronicles, as Wright ("Bede") puts it, "the search for a Welsh source never recovered from the discovery that the Welsh *Bruts* were translations of the *Historia* rather than vice versa" (27 n. 2) and "Geoffrey's claim that the *Historia* was a Latin translation of a very ancient book written in Breton or Welsh is . . . not now generally accepted" (27). The "Continental" school of the Arthurian legend, working from economic history, materialist, cultural studies, or pyschoanalytic perspectives, reception-theory, or *ideologie-kritik*, has tended by contrast to emphasize the continental development of Arthurian material. Some notable disagreements in the two directions of scholarship—which cannot be efficiently rehearsed here—have marked medievalist scholarship of the twentieth century. Thomas Jones's article on the Welsh background of the Arthurian legend is an example of Celticist scholarship that continues to be cited. For examples of an earlier, and more recent, argument on the relationship of Welsh hagiographic literature to the *Historia*, see Tatlock ("Dates") and Rider; R. S. Loomis's compendium on medieval Arthurian literature features several articles that are still useful on Welsh sources of the Arthurian legend. In a recent article Gillingham presents important new historical evidence for the Celticist argument ("Context").

6. To an extent, unacknowledged borrowing of the work of others is a reflex of twelfth-century historical writing, but in this instance scholarship has found highly self-conscious strategies in Geoffrey's extensive, hidden manipulations (see, e.g., Wright, "Bede," "Gildas," "Gildas Revisited"). After Geoffrey, writers of medieval romance frequently deploy the fiction of an original book from which they supposedly "translate" their own work, for whose contents, then, they may assume diminished responsibility, while their texts borrow from the aura and authority of the projected "original" (see Tatlock, 424 n. 11, and Brooke, 79, for examples of fictional ur-texts).

7. The Hebraic chronicles of Solomon bar Simson, Eliezer bar Nathan, and the Mainz Anonymous movingly document the genocidal atrocities of the Popular Crusade against Jewish communities in the Rhineland, massacres that antedate the

pogroms of later European history by several centuries (see Eidelberg, and also relevant extracts from Latin chronicles, in Krey, *First Crusade*, and Peters, *First Crusade*). The slaughter of the Jewish community in Jerusalem on that city's capture is well-documented (by, among others, Prawer's invaluable chapter on the Jews in his *Crusaders' Kingdom* and his *History of the Jews*). For an overview of the impact of all the crusades on medieval Jewry, see the *Encyclopaedia Judaica* ("Crusades," 5:1136–45). Anna Comnena (311) and Albert of Aix (*Recueil des Historiens des Croisades*, series Historiens Occidentaux [henceforth *RHC*, Occ.], 4:284) record cannibalistic atrocities and torture by the Popular Crusade against what would have been a population of Eastern Christians and others in the environs of Nicaea. On the pilgrimage nature of the Crusade, see Blake (17).

8. The terms "crusaders" and "crusade" evolved gradually and were not in active circulation until the late twelfth century; I use them here out of convention and for convenience of discussion. (My use of terms like "transnational" and "race" functions in similar fashion; I contextualize and complicate such terms in subsequent chapters.) Eyewitness chronicles and contemporary documents refer to the crusaders simply as "pilgrims," "Christians," "Franks," and so forth. Anna Comnena calls the crusaders by a variety of names, including "Latins," "Normans," "Kelts," and various perjorative sobriquets. A large body of chronicle literature on the First Crusade exists, some of which remains controversial as historical evidence. I have chosen to concentrate only on the records that have been agreed on by scholarship as genuine eyewitness documents written during, or a scant few years after, the First Crusade. For that reason I omit Peter Tudebode's chronicle, which may be a derivative account (but for claims on Tudebode's behalf, see Hill and Hill's edition). Because their status as epic literature and dating (late twelfth century) render even the oldest of the crusade cycles of the *chansons de geste* problematic as historical sources, I have also chosen not to treat them. I refer selectively to non-eyewitness accounts, such as Anna Comnena's biography, Arab chronicles, and Guibert de Nogent's later history, but my argument on crusader cannibalism at Ma'arra does not depend on the evidential reliability of these accounts.

9. "Ubi obsidione per XX dies acta, famen nimiam gens nostra pertulit. dicere perhorreo, quod plerique nostrum famis rabie nimis vexati abscidebant de natibus Saracenorum iam ibi mortuorum frusta, quae coquebant et mandebant et parum ad ignem assata ore truci devorabant. itaque plus obsessores quam obsessi angebantur" (Fulcher of Chartres, *Historia Hierosolymitana*, 266–67).

10. "Fuerunt ibi ex nostris qui illic non inuenerunt sicuti opus eis erat, tantum ex longa mora, quantum ex districtione famis, quia foris nequiuerant aliquid inuenire ad capiendum, sed scindebant corpora mortuorum, eo quod in uentribus eorum inueniebant bisanteos reconditos; alii uero caedebant carnes eorum per frusta, et coquebant ad manducandum" (Hill, 80). The translation is the editor's; unattributed translations are, of course, mine.

11. "Interea tanta fames in exercitu fuit, ut multa corpora Sarracenorum iam fetentium, que in paludibus civitatis eiusdem .ii. et amplius ebdomadas iacuerant, populus avidissime comederet. Terrebant ista multos tam nostre gentis homines

quam extraneos. Revertebantur ob ea nostri quam plures. . . . Sarraceni vero et Turci econtra dicebant: Et quis poterit sustinere hanc gentem que tam obstinata atque crudelis est, ut per annum non poterit revocari ab obsidione Antiochie, fame, vel gladio, vel aliquibus periculis, et nunc carnibus humanis vescitur? Hec et alia crudelissima sibi in nobis dicebant esse pagani. Etenim dederat deus timorem nostrum cunctis gentibus sed nos nesciebamus" (Raymond d'Aguiliers, *"Liber"*, 101). I have slightly modified Krey's translation (*First Crusade*, 214).

12. Al-Qalanisi's account (see Gibb, 46), written before his death in 1160, is the most contemporary, the author having been resident in Damascus during the events of the First Crusade. Ibn al-Athir's is in volume 1 (194) and Kemal al-Din's in volume 3 (583) of the *RHC*, Historiens Orientaux series. The *RHC* has been criticized for its selection of extracts, textual errors, and inaccuracies in translating Arabic into French, but it nevertheless remains invaluable as a source. I quote from the *RHC* as a last resort, when no other more recent editions/translations are available or accessible. Ibn al-Athir on the cannibalism at Antioch: "Treize jours s'étaient écoulés depuis que les Francs étaient entres dans Antioche. Ils n'avaient plus de quoi manger; les riches étaient réduits à nourrir de bêtes de somme, et les pauvres de corps morts et de feuilles d'arbres." Kemal al-Din's thirteenth-century account appears in a history of Aleppo: "Les Francs, enfermés dans Antioche, en étaient réduits à manger la chair des cadavres et des animaux morts." Gibb's translation of al-Qalanisi refers to "carrion" rather than cadavers, and the Arabic texts point to cannibalism at Antioch but are silent on Ma'arra. The Arab documents are, of course, late texts compared to the eyewitness Latin chronicles.

13. Anna also recounts an incident of cannibalism committed by the forces of the Popular Crusade in 1096 around the outskirts of Nicaea, in Asia Minor (see n. 7 above), fully a year before the armies of the First Crusade, with their eyewitness chroniclers, had arrived in the East: "They cut in pieces some of the babies, impaled others on wooden spits and roasted them over a fire; old people were subjected to every kind of torture" (Comnena, 311). The episode is also described by Albert of Aix, whose polyglot chronicle was stitched together from heterogeneous unidentified sources more than a generation after the close of the First Crusade. The historicity and accuracy of Albert's chronicle has been controversial since the demystificatory critique of the German historian von Sybel. Some modern historians continue to cite the chronicle as evidence; others, perhaps more cautious or skeptical, eschew it altogether.

14. Paschal, it should be remembered, is the successor of the pope who had been the initiator and spiritual leader of the First Crusade, a crusade ostentatiously planned by Urban II as a holy pilgrimage as much as a holy war. This confession to Urban's successor, of cannibalism performed by his Christian pilgrims—surely never an easy task—must have been a particularly uneasy one for the signatories here, who had been Urban's special delegates. Godfrey of Bouillon, Duke of Lower Lorraine, was by the time of this letter titular "Defender of the Holy Sepulcher" in the Kingdom of Jerusalem, effectually King of Jerusalem, despite his refusal to be crowned. Raymond

de Saint-Gilles, Count of Toulouse, had spent much time with Urban in preparation for the Crusade and was the secular leader preferred by Urban. Archbishop Daimbert, who became Patriarch of Jerusalem, was the highest-ranking Latin ecclesiastic in the East, following the death of Adhémar of le Puys, the Papal Legate, and William, Archbishop of Orange, en route to Jerusalem.

15. See Frances Yates, and Mary Carruthers, on medieval training in memory, and Woods on the role of luridity in school texts in the medieval curriculum. Ironically Fulcher was absent from Antioch and Ma'arra, having accompanied Baldwin of Bolougne, whose chaplain he was, to Edessa, a fact not always remembered when considering the "specular authority" of eyewitness evidence (Munro, "A Crusader," 327; Krey, *First Crusade*, 9).

16. Runciman believes Raymond's chronicle to have been completed even earlier, in 1099, and begun during the siege of Antioch itself (1:328), although the two oldest manuscripts seem to derive from the mid-twelfth century (Hill and Hill, *Historia*, 7). In 1101 Ekkehard of Aura found a chronicle in Jerusalem that scholars agree is the *Gesta*; like many among the secondary Crusade historians, he appears to have used the *Gesta* as his source (Krey, *First Crusade*, 7; Runciman, 1:329; Peters, *First Crusade*, 5; Hill, ix).

17. The quotations from Fulcher and Raymond above are typical in their use of "gens"—race, people, or nation—to describe the multiethnic/multiracial body of Christians. Even more pointed is the example dramatized in the vision of Stephen of Valence reported by Raymond's chronicle, where Christ questions Stephen on the identity of the occupation army in Antioch: "Homo, quenam est hec gens que civitatem ingressa est?" ("Man, what race/people is this that has entered the city?"). Stephen's reply describes the multiethnic, trans-class Latin forces as a single entity: "Christiani" (Raymond d'Aguiliers, *"Liber"*, 72–73). On the importance of the Christian name in establishing a transnational and transethnic community, see Bartlett, 250–54. The Eucharist, as Bynum and many others remind us, occupied a central, symbolic place in sustaining that communal identity: "From the very beginning, the eucharistic elements stood . . . for human beings bound into community by commensality" (48); "Eating Christ's body was an inclusive act, one that created community" (49).

18. Berengar of Tours's rejection, in the mid-eleventh century, of the real presence of Christ in the Eucharist, subsequent recantation (in 1059), and oath (in 1079), and the influence of the Berengarian controversy in shaping eleventh- and twelfth-century Eucharistic theology are well-established landmarks in the history of medieval theology. My principal interest lies in the resolution of the so-called Berengarian heresy, and the doctrinal establishment, in the eleventh century, of real presence and salvific promise (and, in the twelfth century, transubstantiation), and the communicant's share in divinity. Bynum emphasizes the gendered and ecstatic aspects of sacred cannibalism; Macy, Rubin, and Paul Jones have excellent accounts of Eucharistic theology. For a medieval historian's account of the Berengarian heresy, and common contemporary belief in real presence, see William of Malmsbury's *De Gestis Regum*, c.1125 (2:338–41; 2:341–42).

19. Eating an infernal race confers special horrors since eating—as Maggie Kilgour beautifully puts it—"creates a total identity between eater and eaten" and "the law 'you are what you eat'" ensures that the identity of the cannibal becomes confounded with that of the victim (7). Interestingly, for purposes of comparison, cannibalism at Antioch—unlike Ma'arra—may have been committed on Latin or Oriental Christian cadavers, since the victims are not expressly identified in reports of Antiochene cannibalism as Muslim. One element in the horror of eating human flesh—infernal self-pollution and loss of Christian identity—may not feature in the Antiochene cannibalism. The translation from Robert the Monk is by Munro (*Urban and the Crusaders*, 6), Baldric of Dol by Krey (*First Crusade*, 33), and Fulcher's chronicle by McGinty (in Peters, *First Crusade*, 78–79).

20. Askenasy (61) records cannibalism in England in 1005 and in Europe in 1016; on cannibalism in England in 1069, see Tannahill, 47. See Sumberg, 245–46, and n. 91, on cannibalism in France in 1031.

21. In 1202 a letter from Innocent III addressed to ecclesiastics at large described the letter bearer as a confessed, repentant cannibal who had killed and eaten his daughter during a famine, at the order of his Saracen captors. The penance issued by Innocent for this "great sin" is lengthy and detailed, enjoining upon the penitent a three-year pilgrimage to the shrines of saints, unshod and clothed as the Pope required; chastisement "with rod or whip" before entering any church; exactions of fasting and prayer; prohibition from marriage, recreational entertainments, the consumption of meat, and residence in any place for more than two nights; and public exhibition of the offense to the "archbishops, bishops, abbots, and priors to whom this letter shall come." After the three years the confessed penitent was to return to the Apostolic See "to seek mercy, and take pains to observe what shall *then* be enjoined upon him" (Migne, *Patrologiae Latinae*, ccxiv, 1063; my emphasis). One might argue that if ecclesiastical culture in the person of this later medieval pope was able to negotiate the horror of cannibalism with a specific punitive regime, eating your own race might not be so unthinkable after all. Of course, one might also argue conversely: that the excited proliferation of punishments here testifies to panicked confusion as to how to establish an adequate regimen of punishment and recovery. Interestingly, the long list of exactions the Pope imagined inflicting on the penitent seems to have appeared inadequate to him even as he devised it, explaining his determination to leave open the option of future additional exactions, after the initial three years had passed. For late-medieval accounts of cannibalism that may have occurred in fourteenth-century England, during famine, see Marvin.

22. "Theophilus sees cannibalism as the most heinous charge leveled against Christians, and the most heinous act performed by pagans" (*Resurrection*, 31). "Defending Christians against charges of cannibalism, Athenagoras argues, as did Theophilus, that pagans are the real cannibals" [*Resurrection*, 33]).

23. "Heretics," in particular, "homed in on the horror of [Eucharistic cannibalism], just as Christians had once accused pagans of cannibalistic excesses" (Rubin, 360). Although the ecstatic aspects of Eucharistic cannibalism have recently been

stressed (prominently by Bynum, in her invaluable and highly influential *Holy Feast*), unease at the notion of cannibalizing the body of Christ—one of the issues that had troubled Berengar and required much ingenuity to resolve—may have continued to wind through the sporadic dissidence that accompanied the doctrinal consolidation of real presence and transubstantiation, dissidence represented at one extreme by the rejection of real presence by heretical communities such as the Cathars. Unease can be detected even among the orthodox. For Rupert, Abbot of the Benedictines at Deutz, the "externally sensed species of the bread and wine are . . . a covering, a veil taken up by Christ because of our natural repugnance to eating flesh and drinking blood" (Macy, 67). In the eleventh century Cardinal Humbert of Silva Candida and Guitmund, Bishop of Aversa, had carefully rejected the notion that any part of the species might undergo "the normal digestive processes" (Macy, 54, 49), a sign, surely, of anxiety over the implications of cannibalism. It is therefore necessary to allow for the possibility that, once real presence had been established, discomfort at the cannibalism inherent in Eucharistic ingestion might shadow all representations of cannibal figures in twelfth-century cultural texts, including the figure of the cannibalistic giant of St. Michael's Mount. That being said, it is also useful to remember that, by the twelfth century, spiritual and mystical reception of the body of Christ, alongside corporeal reception, was being accorded attention; and it is possible that in the layering over of the multiple meanings of Eucharistic ingestion, the unease toward sacred cannibalism was ameliorated or eclipsed.

24. Pallister reminds us that the mouth of hell, and the devil, in medieval illustration, are particularly apt to be figured as cannibalistic, gigantic monstrosities: "Several especially notable examples can be found in the *Hours of Catherine of Clèves* (Flemish, fifteenth century). Here we find a monstrous head with seven human beings in its gigantic, toothy mouth; it has bulging, bloodshot eyes and sheds rays, like Lucifer. . . . Satan as a giant satyr-ogre is torturing and devouring lost souls in Pol of Limbourg's 'Enfer,' a miniature found in the *Très Riches Heures du Duc de Berry*" (308).

25. Scholars tend to date confirmed reports of the blood libel from the thirteenth century, but twelfth-century incidents are listed in the *Encyclopaedia Judaica*: in England (6:747), at Norwich (1144), Gloucester (1168), Bury St. Edmunds (1181), Bristol (before 1183), and Winchester (1192), and perhaps as early as 1130 in London (11:470); in France, at Blois (1171), followed by Loches, Pontoise, Joinville, Epernay, and Bray (7:13–14).

26. "The story of Abominable's conversion and his new life as a guide and soldier of the Apostles strongly influenced the *acta* of Saints Mercurius and Christopher" (Friedman, 71). St. Mercurius was one of three phantom leaders of heavenly troops seen by the crusaders outside Antioch, swelling the thin ranks of the crusading army against Karbuqa, and aiding in the conquest of Antioch (Hill, 69). In reporting on heavenly helpers at Antioch, it is poignant that the crusade chronicles chose to specify a Saint Mercurius—whose legend is so strongly associated with the guilt of cannibalism, and the forgiveness and salvation that follow the repudiation of cannibalism.

27. See, for example, 3, 17, 28, 33, 34, 43, 61–62, 85, 89, and 90. Raymond's chronicle, the least repressed on the subject of crusader cannibalism, is also the least obsessed

subtextually with food. The *Gesta*'s words—"thirsting and craving for the blood of Turks"—also astonishingly echo the medieval blood libel against the Jews, who were often accused of requiring Christian blood for ritual practices. The blood libel can thus be read as a projective accusation by Christians, the historical basis of which lay in *Christian* rather than Jewish atrocity against cultural others: Significantly the genealogy of medieval blood libel may begin as early as the twelfth century (see note 25, above). Christian anxiety over the palpable vampirism inherent in ingesting the blood of Christ in Eucharistic reception may also underpin the twelfth-century inception of the medieval blood libel (see Dundes, and n. 23 above).

28. Raymond, who begins his history by revealing that he has undertaken the task of documentation directly in response to negative criticism of the crusade (Raymond d'Aguilers, *"Liber"*, 35), optatively expresses the hope, toward the chronicle's end, that God would punish pagans on His own initiative even if the Christians' cause was weak ("si etiam causa nostra invalida fuisset" (157)—a wishfulness that we might read, perhaps, as Raymond's acute consciousness of the worst of crusader sins, and an oblique gloss on the anxious silence that troubles what cannot be discussed at length in the chronicles.

29. Porges also emphasizes the dependence of the clergy on the military leaders of the Crusade (Raymond and Fulcher were, of course, in clerical orders): "Both the higher and lower clergy tended to group themselves around the leaders whom they had followed on crusade. They often espoused their masters' quarrels, and looked to them in turn for preferment" (8). Observing that "the power of the clergy was small" (9)—a limitation he links to the unresolved investiture struggles in Europe—Porges points to the preeminent power of the military leaders in deciding religious appointees in the East: "Raymond of Toulouse presided over the election of Peter of Narbonne as bishop of Albara. . . . the leaders chose Robert, a priest of Rouen, as bishop of Ramlah. . . . These elections reflected the investiture strife raging in Europe, and would not have met the approval of a Cluniac reformer" (20). Fulcher of Chartres, who negotiates a delicate balance between conscience and diplomacy in his chronicle, illustrates, by example, the predicament of the chroniclers in their relationship to powerful patrons. Though scrupulously reporting on the cannibalism at Ma'arra (where his patron was absent), Fulcher is tactfully silent on the unsavory conduct of Baldwin at Edessa—the Count's ruthless acquisition of Edessa from Thoros, and the slaughter of three hundred crusaders outside the city walls, who had been vengefully shut out by Baldwin—events at which the chronicler was present. After accompanying Baldwin to Jerusalem, as Baldwin's chaplain, on the Count's accession to the kingship, Fulcher may have later been promoted to Prior of the Mount of Olives (Munro, "Crusader," 327); he wrote "an eloquent tribute" to Baldwin on the king's death (Fink, 23).

30. In a symposium in 1984—"The Crusading Kingdom of Jerusalem—The First European Colonial Society?"—Prawer argues concisely and powerfully for the usefulness of analyzing the crusader states as overseas colonies of Latin Europe, and the historical existence of a *medieval* version of the modern European colonial experience, based on territorial and political domination, economic exploitation, ideological re-

production, and the evidence of a "colonial mentality" and colonial relations in the records of the occupied territories of the medieval Levant. A critical strain of scholarship on the crusades has since had little difficulty in continuing Prawer's analysis. Dissenting voices in the symposium are represented by Jonathan Riley-Smith and John H. Pryor.

31. Prawer remarks of the crusader colonies: "Here was made the first step of teaching Europe how to colonize" ("Symposium," 366). Duncalf observes that "the pope seems to have intended to have the crusaders make conquests in the Holy Land. . . . Raymond took an oath to spend the rest of his life in the East, and Godfrey disposed of his western holdings. Bohemond, we may be sure, expected to find a better principality than he could hope to acquire in Italy. . . . it is reasonable to believe that Urban did intend the westerners to keep the Holy Land" (55). Calling the crusades "partly pilgrimage and partly migrations," Russell suggests that "at their peak, the crusading states controlled about three fifths of the land and population of Syria" (56). In a study of medieval sugar production and trade, Phillips emphasizes the economic consequences of the colonial experiment of Outremer, in the long term, despite the eventual loss of all the colonies: "The Crusades may have failed in . . . physical control of colonial lands in the Meditteranean—yet in economic terms they were successful, as the West wrested economic ascendancy from the East" (403). The translation from Robert the Monk is by Munro ("Speech," 6–7), from Fulcher, Krey (*First Crusade*, 280–81).

32. Krey ("Neglected Passage") dates Guibert's history early, in 1106, for purposes of establishing his argument on the ideological use of the *Gesta* by Bohemond. John Benton dates Guibert's history to 1108 (303), and Runciman to 1109 (1:330). The secondary and tertiary historians who treat the Crusade are many, and include Baldric of Dol, Robert the Monk, Ralph of Caen, Ekkehard of Aura, Orderic Vitalis, Albert of Aix, and William of Tyre; even William of Malmsbury has a chapter on the Crusade (*De Gestis*, bk. 4, chap. 2). In general, most accede to the occurrence of cannibalism (William of Tyre is an exception) and variously express horror, defensive compassion at the extreme afflictions of famine, or a range between the two responses. These later histories, because of their dependence on uncertain or polyglot sources—some original and some not, with the authenticity of some sources being controversial—are substantially less authoritative than the eyewitness chronicles, and I do not treat them. Guibert's account is unusual, however, for its materialization of the "Tafurs"—a group whose facticity is taken for granted by some modern historians—and thus deserves special attention.

33. I follow Cook, Foulon, Trotter, Duggan, and others in reading the oldest epic in the crusade cycles of *chansons de geste*—the *Chanson d'Antioche*—as deriving from the late twelfth century. Earlier scholarship on the two crusading cycles of *chansons* had tended to emphasize an internal textual claim by Graindor de Douai that he had revised the *Antioch* from a very early original text, now presumably lost, by one "Richard le Pèlerin," supposedly an eyewitness participant of the First Crusade. Although some still subscribe to the view that the *Antioch* was written on crusade or immediately after,

and its contents depict factual history, Robert Cook has persuasively argued for the *Antioch*'s status as epic literature, demonstrating the *Antioch*'s relations to other *chansons de geste*, and concluding that it is worthwhile discussing the *Antioch* only in the form in which we currently have it: "les gens du douzième siècle ne nous parlent pas claire-ment d'une 'Chanson d'Antioche' ancienne, et leurs écrits ne semblent pas en suggér-er non plus l'existence. . . . Le texte connu d'*Antioche* est tardif; nous n'en avons pas d'autre, nous n'avons même pas de preuve qu'un autre a existé. . . . Nous n'avons vu jusqu'ici nulle raison de ne pas compter d'Antioche, avec le cycle dont il participe, comme un poème épique, comme une chanson de geste" (*Le Cycle*, 38–39; see also "Crusade Propaganda"). Cook's emphasis is persuasive for several reasons. Although *chansons de geste* do not as a rule concern themselves with the subject of the poor, the *Antioch* presents the fiction of the cannibalistic Tafurs and their "king" in more devel-oped form than Guibert's chronicle—a development that, as the most recent editor of the *Antioch* notes, represents a radical departure from the usual *chanson* concern with problems and questions of the feudal relationship of monarch and magnates ("Quant à 'la gent menue,'" observes Duparc-Quioc, "peu de poèmes épiques s'en occupent au-tant" [2:259]). The developed dramatizations of the Tafurs and their king in the *Anti-och* that we have thus seem to *follow* Guibert, giving evidence of Guibert's influence, rather than precede him. A late-twelfth-century origin for this text would also account for the *Antioch*'s presentation of a fully developed and much elaborated legend of Peter the Hermit, a historically vague figure. Furthermore, there is a strange reference, in the *Antioch*, to "the Old Man of the Mountain"—"Li Viels de la Montaigne" (*Chanson d'Antioche*, laisses CX, CXII)—whom the *chanson* presents as the lord of "Rohais" (i.e., Edessa), a reference contemporary only with the late twelfth century. The "Old Man of the Mountain" was the sobriquet applied by the Franks of the Levant to Sinan Rashid ed-Din, leader of a breakaway group of Shi'ite Muslims called the Batini, or, more popularly, the Assassins, a group famed for the sensational assassinations they conducted. Sinan's legend grew in the last decades of the twelfth century, perhaps in part because the Assassins were considering a conversion to Christianity in the 1170s (Runciman, 2:397). A late-twelfth-century origin would make the *Antioch* contempo-raneous with the rise of romance as a genre, so that the *Antioch*'s fictionalized devel-opment of the Tafurs might be seen as romance-inflected.

34. There is still no agreement as to what race of people is meant by "Tafurs" or "Trudennes," which strongly suggests Guibert's invention of the name, but a consen-sus exists that a non–Western European race is signaled by the foreign-sounding name. Sumberg offers the fullest discussion of the etymological origin of "Tafur," cit-ing Hatem's detection of an Armenian root, in "tahavor," meaning "king"; Cahen's suggestion of an Arabic derivation, from "tâfoûr," meaning "miserable"; Sauvaget's derivation from the Arabic "tafrân"; Duparc-Quioc's suggestion of a Turkish origin; and Porges's belief that the term indicated "Saracens . . . gypsies and Truands of any nationality" (226, and nn. 11, 12). Sumberg himself believes, however, that the Tafurs are probably Flemish. If Guibert had meant to indicate, by the name, a non-European racial or ethnic group—as perhaps intimated by his invocation of a "barbarian

tongue"—his association of a foreign race with monstrous behavior would only have been, as we have seen, merely conventional. Friedman emphasizes the almost reflexive equation, in medieval culture, between foreign and monstrous races, for which biblical justification is often found. Thus it is that the monstrous races of Asia are descended from the line of Ham (in some traditions), as are Moors and Saracens (in other traditions); churls—human beasts by virtue of poverty and unfree status—are descended from Cain, while "gentle" folk are descended from Seth (102–3). The *Cursor Mundi* economically has both serfs and Africans descend from the line of Ham, the accursed ("þe maledight" [R. Morris, 57:128, 130]). Guibert's identification of the poorest class of folk, who may also be of foreign ethnicity, with cannibals is thus consonant with the ideological practices of medieval culture. For Guibert, heretics are also homosexuals and cannibals (Benton, *Self,* 212–13).

35. Fulcher of Chartres, *Historia Hierosolymitana,* 301–2; Guibert: *RHC,* Occ., 4:140; Hill, 80. Munro ("Speech") compares the extant versions of Urban's address. Sumberg cites P. Paris's skepticism at the cannibalism of Guibert's Tafurs at Ma'arra: "Would the Tafurs not have already done likewise at the siege of Antioch, where the famine was infinitely worse and of longer duration?" (242). John Benton, discussing Guibert's invention of a detailed story about relics supposedly brought back to Nogent from Palestine by a "King Quilius of England," concludes that Guibert "was willing to distort history when it suited his purposes" (*Self,* 310).

36. Much has been said in scholarship about the medieval historian's inability or refusal to distinguish between fact and fiction, the relative cultural indifference of the period to distinctions of this nature, and the liberties taken in historical writing with matters of facticity. What is usually meant by such indifference is the medieval historian's assumption of the right to select, arrange, or rewrite his materials in accordance with an ideal of usefulness or truth, rather than hewing slavishly to models of factual adherence. For instance, a medieval historian would not be reluctant to put an invented speech into the mouth of a historical personage, make up additional material to support an argument of his choice, or excise what he believed to be irrelevancies in his sources—forms of tampering unacceptable to historiography today. Guibert's "Tafurs" and "King Quilius of England" are examples of such tampering, the former representing an effort at repairing the reputation of the First Crusade, and the latter designed to increase the reputation of Nogent. The adherence to "higher usefulness" over plain facticity did not mean, however, that medieval historians were naïvely unable to tell fact from spectacular fables or to value the distinction between such categories, as the varied response to Geoffrey's *Historia* demonstrates. William of Malmsbury's distinction between the historical Arthur and the "nonsense" of spurious Arthurian fables is a case in point (see n. 51 below); William's statement on historiographic practice that hews to the authentic "laws of history" and relies on trustworthy sources (see n. 3 above) responds eloquently to the modern scholarly fiction of medieval cultural indifference to distinctions of truth and fabulousness. Southern, always insightful, offers Geoffrey's *Historia* as the point of clearest departure between the fabulous and the historical: "Romance became separated from History" ("Classical Tradition," 196).

37. "Michael" recalls the East in yet another way: The standard gold coins of the Orient, in the twelfth century, were Byzantine "micheles," so-called after the last coinage by an emperor, Michael Ducas, that had undebased value. Alexius I, emperor at the time of the First Crusade, had debased the coinage, rendering "micheles" of especial value as a reliable medium of currency. Byzantines commonly referred to their coinage by the name of the emperor issuing the coins; the term "bezants," derived from the name of the empire's capitol, is the term used principally by Latins to refer to the coins. The First Crusade is also cunningly recalled by the name "Helena," memorialized here in "Helena's Tomb," since the empress Helena, mother of Constantine the Great, by tradition originally discovered the relics of the Passion, two of which—the True Cross and Holy Lance—were recovered again in the Crusade. The church that the grieving Hoel builds for his Helena, over her sepulcher, oddly recalls the Church of the Holy Sepulcher in Jerusalem, built by Constantine to commemorate his Helena's discovery of the relics. In a final round of suggestiveness that unites another Helen, Michael, and Constantine, Helena, Bohemond's sister, was bethrothed to Constantine, the infant son of Michael Ducas (Runciman, 1:68). Arthur, of course, is the royal descendant of another Constantine in the *Historia.*

38. The literature of Britain, including the *Historia,* is no exception: In the *Historia,* Albion is inhabited by giants—with whom one of Brutus's men, Corineus, derives particular pleasure in fighting—before Brutus's conquest and settlement of the island (Wright, 1:16). From Herodotus in the fifth century B.C.E., documents of discovery, anthropology, or conquest—including Renaissance literature, ethnography on the Indies and the Tropics, Columbus's log, *mappaemundi,* literatures of colonization, early American literature, and so on—have depicted foreign races or tribes as giants, cannibals, or other monstrous exotica. In the Middle Ages, the idea that giants are monsters is implicitly derived from Isidore of Seville, whose definition of "monstrum" as something outside nature, extremely large or extremely small, is influential (*Liber Differentiarum* [c.612], in Migne, 83, 56, bk. 1, item 457). Isidore facilitates the medieval narrative of othering by intimating that there are whole races of monsters: "Just as among individual races there are certain members who are monsters, so also among mankind as a whole, certain races are monsters, like the giants" (*Etymologiae,* 3.12:52). For anthropological narratives of cannibalism, see especially Arens, and Sanday; even *Lingua Franca* has entered the anthropological controversy on cannibalism (see Osborne).

39. The eyewitness chronicles' naming of Levantine territories as "Hispania" is coterminous with the cultural *mentalité* of the *chansons de geste,* in which Muslim Spain often featured. Though controversy continues over the dating of its earliest manuscript, the *Chanson de Roland* is sometimes thought to be contemporary with the First Crusade, even if the Pseudo-Turpin's *chanson*-like Charlemagne legend is now dated from the mid-twelfth century (1140–45?). William of Malmsbury's account of Hastings records that a version of the *Roland* was sung to urge on the Normans before the battle began (William of Malmsbury, *De Gestis Regum,* 2:302). Duggan wittily sums up Raymond d'Aguiliers's naming of Syria as "Hispania" as a reversal of the axiom, "if this is Spain, there must be Arabs here," into "if there are Arabs here, this

must be Spain" (308)—which is not to say, of course, that the crusaders believed themselves to be anywhere but in the Levant.

40. Eleventh- and twelfth-century medievals were familiar with the fact that Muslims did not eat pork, so that the eating of pork becomes a key marker to distinguish medieval Christian identity from its Muslim opposite: Orderic Vitalis, for example, tells us that "Turks and many other Saracen peoples" abhorred the flesh of pigs, while Christians ate the very best pork (5:372). Bohemond and Tancred antedate the *Historia*'s pork-eating giant: The *Gesta* presents them as huge pork-eaters with gigantic appetites, believed to consume "four thousand pigs at a single meal" (Hill, 56). The insulting association of Muslims with pigs occurs as early as the ninth century, when an apocryphal life of the prophet Mohammad, attributed to Alvaro of Córdoba, relates that the prophet, after dying as a drunkard, was eaten by pigs or dogs on a dung heap.

41. Though Arabia and Syria are obviously separate territories to moderns, medieval European presentation of Levantine geography is as notoriously inexact as, say, the presentation of statistical figures in medieval literature and history. A typical example is the ubiquitous use of "Chorosan" (Khurrasan) in the *chansons de geste* and crusade histories to designate, vaguely, all Persia or regions to the east of Syria. William of Malmsbury, who ranks with Bede in his stature as a historian, confuses Egypt with Arabia, and has Baldwin I of Jerusalem die in "Arabia" when Baldwin was stricken with fever in Egypt and died in Jerusalem (William of Malmsbury, *De Gestis Regum*, 2:451). A century later Oliver of Paderborn's eyewitness narrative of the capture of Damietta in the Fifth Crusade equates Syria with Arabia: It calls the territory in which the crusader castles of Kerak and Montréal are located "Arabia," instead of southern Syria or Transjordan (Peters, *Christian Society*, 86). Though Arabia gained some attention late in the twelfth century, when the notorious Reynald de Châtillon turned pirate against Muslim pilgrim caravans in the Arabian peninsula and Muslim ships in the Red Sea, earning Saladin's wrath, it is uncertain even then if territorial specifications in the Orient meant much to medievals exclusively resident in Europe. On several other Oriental place-names in the *Historia*, some of which are also discussed by Faral, see Tatlock, *Legendary History*, 112. Prime examples of Mediterranean place-names that find their way into medieval romance, to become commonplaces in medieval and postmedieval Arthurian literature, for instance, are Cilicia ("Siesia") and Ascalon ("Astolat" or "Shallott").

42. Scholars fascinated with the *Historia*'s highly memorable description of a monstrous cloak of king's beards no doubt find equally fascinating Herodotus's description, in his *Histories*, of coats made from human scalps. In *Histories*, 4:64, Herodotus tells us that the Scythians, *barbaroi* that they were, skinned the scalps off the skulls of their slain and defeated enemies, and "many of them make coats to wear by sewing the scalps together into a patchwork leather garment like leather coats" (Waterfield, 256).

43. Anna says of Bohemond: "Whether his beard was red or of any other colour I cannot say, for the razor had attacked it, leaving his chin smoother than any marble" (Comnena, 422). As late as the thirteenth century Oriental authors continue to marvel

at the beardlessness of Europeans. Al-Qazwini, in his *Athar al-bilad*, reports with disgust of the Franks: "They shave their beards, and after shaving they sprout only a revolting stubble. One of them was asked as to the shaving of the beard, and he said, 'Hair is a superfluity. You remove it from your private parts, so why should we leave it on our faces?'" (B. Lewis, 2:123).

44. Norman figures in the Bayeux tapestry, including Duke William and Odo of Bayeux, are conspicuously clean-shaven. That beardedness among Norman elites constituted a deviation from the norm in Norman court culture in Western Europe is witnessed by the strenuous clerical censure repeated in contemporary chronicles in which the wearing of a beard or long hair is typically offered as a sign of degeneracy in court circles. However, though I here suggest the association of beardedness with Orientals, note 62 below also offers the possibility that the threat figured in Ritho's cloak of beards represents the *Historia*'s understanding that the threat of cannibalistic monstrosity would redound back, eventually, to injure the ethnic and class companions of those originally marked by a share of responsibility in crusader monstrosity, since some Anglo-Norman aristocrats did, in fact, sport beards, for which they were much castigated.

45. That the economic duress of a historical king might be linked to the literary fantasy of a romance king is not as provocative as it may seem. Because economic crisis is a subject that surfaces with difficulty in aristocratic cultural discourse, romance—with its deployment of fantasy material as a language of analogy—is a medium well suited to the articulation of economic anxiety, as my discussion of the inheritance struggle in Chrétien de Troyes's *Yvain* suggests (see note 52 below). It is worth comparing the humor in the anecdote of Baldwin's beard with the putatively "Welsh" humor that Tatlock (*Legendary History*, 389) finds in the *Historia*'s anecdote of the cloak of beards. Tatlock offers a wonderfully detailed note (*Legendary History*, 388–89 n. 35) where he does his best to find parallels for the story of a cloak of beards, though none of Tatlock's parallels, in fact, bears much resemblance to the details of Geoffrey's story or is definitively earlier than the *Historia*, which strongly urges that Geoffrey invented his episode, perhaps from anecdotal details of Baldwin's story in popular circulation.

46. While I have read the giants of St. Michael's Mount and "Mons Aravius" as hallucinated figurations of European culture personifed at its demonic extreme, after the trauma of crusader cannibalism, it is possible to read the giants more simply and intuitively as merely rude figurations of Saracens. After all, it is unarguable that "throughout medieval literature there is a tendency to represent Saracens and Saxons as 'giants'" (Pallister, 304). To perform this more direct reading, we would have to understand the romance episode of the two giants as merely repeating a familiar move: scapegoating the cultural other for one's own atrocities, by projecting blame upon the enemy, who is then resoundingly defeated by a hero from one's own whitewashed culture. This reading would suggest that European culture, as represented by Geoffrey's text, enacts here both denial ('not we who have committed cannibalism, but they') and suppression—moves that exact a price, in the case of cultural trauma. My reading assigns to cultural performance a greater capacity for complexity and nuance: a ca-

pacity to acknowledge atrocity and guilt, and to negotiate, cunningly, a medium of acknowledgment and treatment that would rescue culture from its demons, without the consequences that attend denial and suppression. That Saracens and cultural enemies are often rendered as giants in medieval literature—just as powerful women are rendered as enchantresses—does not disturb my preferred reading. The permeability of such figures as giants—their capacity to figure diverse, contradictory meanings, and to tip over from one extreme referent to another (what Pallister calls "the floating nature of such symbols" [321])—is hinted at by medieval literature itself, in the person of that complex, multivalent giant-knight, in the Middle English romance, *Sir Gawain and the Green Knight*: a giant at once familiar and foreign, friend and foe, domestically grown, and ineluctably alien, and whose color is the color of Islam as well as the color of the lush vegetation of native England.

47. The *Historia's* dedications to opposing camps speak volumes for the volatile political climate of its day, and are less extraordinary when situated in the context of contemporary behavior: Fulk of Anjou and Jerusalem, for example, married a daughter each to the sons of *both* Henry I *and* Robert of Normandy, the warring royal offspring of the Conqueror. Though earlier scholarship on the *Historia* tended to focus on the apparent contradictions of the dedications, more recent work has noticed shared denominators of class and ethnicity among the dedicatees. For the distribution of manuscript dedications, see Crick, "Dissemination and Reception," 113–20; on the relationship of the *Historia* to the politics of royal succession, issues of patronage, and manuscript dedications, see, particularly, Gerould, 38–40; Tatlock, 288, 426–30; Shichtman and Finke, 15–28; Gransden, 1:204; and Noble, 162.

48. Elizabeth Salter reminds us that "twelfth-century England was decidedly international in its political and cultural temper. Under Norman and Angevin rule, historians, poets, theologians, philosophers, and mathematicians moved easily between England and the Continent—and further, too: For the ties between the royal houses of England, northern France, and Norman Sicily were strong, and encouraged free interchange in many spheres of activity. . . . English painters imitated the colours and the designs of Byzantine mosaics, which they may have easily seen for themselves . . . or which they found, at one remove, in pattern-books, brought to northern Europe along the crowded trade and pilgrimage routes" (21–22).

49. Indeed, Waleran of Meulan, one of the dedicatees of the *Historia*, would soon be a baronial leader in the calamitous Second Crusade. See Tyerman's excellent *England and the Crusades*, on Anglo-Normans and Anglo-Saxons in the different crusades.

50. Although I once agreed with textual editors of the *Historia Brittonum* who felt that it would have been an absurd impossibility for Arthur to have carried an image of the Virgin "super humeros suos" into his eighth battle and emerged victorious thus encumbered, and that therefore the phrase had to be a scribal error requiring emendation to "on his shield" (Heng, "Feminine Knots," 511 n. 15), I have since come around to the opinion that it is not at all impossible for a victorious Arthur to have carried into battle an image of the Virgin Mary on his shoulders—if, that is, the image had been *sewn* on a mantle or tunic, like the cross of the crusaders.

51. Written material in which Arthur features that can be conclusively proven to antedate the *Historia* is scarce, and I have discussed the uncontested sources here. In an early article Tatlock also considers five Welsh and two Breton saints' lives in which Arthur minimally features, some of which preexist the *Historia*; he concludes, however, that even where the hagiographic texts antedate the *Historia*, the Arthur that appears in their narratives—an "uncontrolled and tyrannous" Arthur ("Dates," 345), a "silly and unstable Arthur" (352), "an unstable potentate submissive to the church" (351)—is ignored by Geoffrey, whose history, Tatlock decides, owes nothing to the influence of such figuration. Nonetheless, stories of Arthur must have circulated in culture, beyond the sketchy annalistic and chronicle record: William of Malmsbury, in his *De Gestis Regum Anglorum* of 1125, makes a distinction between an Arthur of false fables ("fallaces . . . fabulae") or nonsense ("nugae") and the Arthur of authentic history (1:11). While rejecting the supposition that *developed* stories of Arthur might have antedated Geoffrey's text, Tatlock seems finally to accept that the *name* of Arthur, at least, was culturally meaningful in some way: "The plain fact is . . . there is no evidence for a largely developed Arthur-saga anywhere whatever before Geoffrey. . . . Outside [the *Historia Brittonum*], the *Annales Cambriae*, and the saint's lives, nearly all the evidence for the vogue of Arthur before Geoffrey relates merely to the Briton hope in Wales and Brittany for his messianic return; which no more proves an active cycle of stories about him than American popular observances about Santa Claus prove the familiarity of stories about him" (357–58).

52. Key examples occur in Chrétien's *Yvain*. In one episode a younger and an elder sister quarrel acrimoniously over property inheritance, the elder insisting on a strict application of primogeniture and the younger seeming to plead for a modified system of *parage*, in which a younger sibling might hold a fief of an elder, to whom the younger would then perform vassal homage. Though the problematics of primogeniture are arguably of urgent concern to male elites of the twelfth century, this romance ostentatiously constructs inheritance rights as a *women's* problem: a problem, moreover, that is chivalrously resolved when the sisters' champions, Yvain and Gauvain, outdo each other in generosity, courtesy, and affection, when each knight insists that the other is the victor of the judicial duel in which both participate on the sisters' behalf. Typically, a problem assailing male elites is presented in romance as an occasion of feminine vulnerability, necessitating male intervention and rescue, the resolution of which then splendidly vindicates the ideological values and institution of chivalry, uniting knights. A similar dynamic operates in the episode of the sweatshop maidens at Pesme Avanture: Gentlewomen are exploited by an entrepreneurial class figured as sons of the devil, who expropriate the surplus labor of the female aristocratic silkworkers whom they keep confined and miserably underpay. If, as Eugene Vance suggests, the threat to *nobiles* in the twelfth century issues from the "power of capital" (129), and the exploited silkworkers in *Yvain* figure the "nascent textile industry lying just to the west of Champagne in Flanders" (146), it is pointedly noble*women* here who are made to represent the seigneurial interests imagined as under threat by the aggressive entrepreneurialism of an emergent middle class (figured, of course, as de-

monic spawn). The symbolic manumission that Yvain's rescue of the noblewomen enacts then confirms the supremacy, humanity, and, most important, the *efficacy* of the chivalric system and its institutions, the episode allowing not only the anxiety of male elites to be expressed in safely distanced fashion but also exorcised and banished by the proven supremacy of the male elite system functioning in perfect form.

53. Arguing from local topography, the distances traveled, and time taken by Arthur and his companions, Thorpe convincingly shows Geoffrey's lack of familiarity with the real Mont Saint-Michel—a place chosen by Geoffrey, I have suggested, for its association with pilgrimage, and the name of St. Michael, patron saint of warriors. Thorpe argues that Geoffrey's onomastic explanation for "Helena's Tomb," was invented by Geoffrey, since "tumba" in the region referred not to a "sepulchre," as Geoffrey would have it, but to a hill ("tumba veut dire 'hauteur, éminence' dans le pays, non pas 'sépulcre'") ("Le Mont Saint-Michel," 381), and "Tumba Helene"— Geoffrey's formulation (Wright, 1:119)—was a corruption of "tumbellana," referring not to the tumulus of a maiden called Helena but to the topography of Mont Saint-Michel: "*Tumbellana* est un diminutif de *tumba*, disons *tumbella* (cp. *tumbella* dans le *De Laudibus Virginilatis* d'Aldhelmus, évêque de Salisbury, écrit au commencement du VIIIe siècle), mot auquel on avait ajouté un suffixe *-ana*, avec le sens de: petite colline qui appartient à une colline plus grande" (382). "Il y a dans la baie du Mont Saint-Michel deux collines, que l'on appelait *Duae Tumbae*. . . . Geoffroi de Monmouth ne les a jamais visitées; mais il en a entendu parler, car elles étaient des centres de pèlerinage et, comme on sait, en 1135–1136, l'abbé Bernard était sur le point de construire une nouvelle église sur le rocher de Tombelaine et il érigeait un prieuré dépendant à St. Michael's Mount en Cornouaille" (382); "l'étymologie populaire *Tumba Helenae,* souvent attestée après 1136, ne semble pas antérieure à cette date" (380). "Helena," of course, is a name that Geoffrey might choose to memorialize for several reasons, as I suggest in note 37 above. In Arthurian romance, the name "Helen" evolves into "Elaine" and becomes attached to Lancelot, whose eventual displacement of Arthur, in chivalric prominence, is signaled by the presence of three different Elaines in Lancelot's life, by the time of Malory, toward the close of the Middle Ages.

54. It will be plain to many that I borrow extensively here from Foucault—though Foucault was not, of course, speaking of romance in his theorization of "genealogy" and "genesis." Equally plain is that a Foucauldian perspective of history underpins my argument in this paper.

55. In Orderic's history, Fatima, the daughter of Ali, king of the Medes, is one of the wives of the captor of Baldwin II, King of Jerusalem; she plays a large role during Baldwin's captivity and is assigned key speeches by Orderic (5:116–20).

56. Scholars have long distinguished the romance features of the Arthuriad from preceding modalities in the *Historia*. The courtly love relationship of Uther and Ygerne is palpably different from the varieties of heterosexual desire featured earlier: Uther *courts* Ygerne—rather than simply taking possession of her, as predecessor kings in the *Historia* had done with women they desired—sending food and drink to her (by contrast, it

is Renwein, Hengist's daughter, who had earlier courted Vortigern [Wright, 1:67]); Ygerna is married, and the triangulation of desire so typical of courtly romance comes into focus; Uther suffers the "lover's malady," with stereotypical symptoms; and the eventual union of Uther and Ygerne is touted as a relationship of equals as well as a love relationship. (For a discussion of courtly love, see Andreas Capellanus, Benton, Boase, Kristeva, Lacan, C. S. Lewis, Newman, de Rougemont, and Wack.) Other romance elements include Arthur's coronation at the romance age of fifteen years, tournamentlike occasions of single combat between champions such as Arthur and Frollo, and the opulent culture of the plenary court at Caerleon, convocated by Arthur at Pentecost, the iconic festive season of Arthurian romance. This plenary court is an ostentatiously international affair: There is no prince of any note "on this side of Hispania" (Wright, 1:111) who does not come when invited, and its religious, ceremonial, gustatory, and recreational events are staged with sumptuous, lavish romance magnificence, in an ecstatic display of the puissance and material superabundance of the imperial monarch. The opulence and glory of the massed companions become reflexive in later romances, as does the already distinctive behavior here between the sexes. Men perform in tournamentlike mock combats, and women incite and inflame them with flirtatious attention. The ethicizing fiction of the courtly romance relationship also appears—we are told that women in Britain give their love only to those thrice-proved in battle, and in setting these standards become chaste and finer creatures, as knights, for their love, correspondently increase in excellence—along with the lineaments of gender identity that form the basis of courtly romance.

The gilded wonders of this emblematic occasion, however—an occasion at which Arthur and his queen ceremonially wear their crowns in state, signifying dominion of the Western world—arrive in romance as a species of magical theater borrowed from the East. Tatlock shows how the *Historia*'s so-called ancient "Trojan" custom of separate coronations for the king and queen, with separate church services and feasts for the men and women in attendance—a "tradition" religiously paraded here as a treasured pedigree of ancient lineage—is a simulacrum of the segregational customs observed and practiced in twelfth-century Constantinople (*Legendary History*, 273–74). Sex-segregated feasting was also the Norman custom in southern Italy and Sicily and, indeed, was a custom in the Near East in general from biblical times on. William of Malmsbury clearly records Constantinople's influence on meals in the Anglo-Norman court of Henry I: Robert, Count of Meulan—father of Waleran of Meulan, one of the *Historia*'s dedicatees—introduced into Anglo-Norman England Alexius I's custom of only one meal a day (William of Malmsbury, *De Gestis Regum*, 2:483). Gransden (1:206) and Gillingham (*Richard*, 135) also remark that sex-segregated meals occurred in Anglo-Saxon courts (though in literature we see Queen Wealtheow feasting with Hrothgar and his thanes in *Beowulf*). The *Historia* itself winks at the origin of some of its Arthurian customs, when it hints that Caerleon, with its gilt-plastered pediments, imitated "Rome" (Wright, 1:110)—a name, I have suggested, that retrieves a vision of Constantinople, "the most brilliant and civilized society" of Geoffrey's era (Tatlock, *Legendary History*, 273). The description of Arthur's principal seat—"Caerleon" eventually metamorphoses into "Camelot"—thus likely derives from fabled Constantinople/Byzantium, the imaginative model for Caerleon/Camelot.

57. Merlin's prophecies make frequent references to the Orient, so that their exotic context adds weight to a reading of his "montem Aravium" as "the Arabian mountain." It is also Merlin who tells Vortigern that Stonehenge comes from Africa (Wright, 1:91), brought by giants. Merlin's ability to relocate the rocks then presents him as a latter-day giant of sorts, like the original movers of the "Giants' Ring" and may suggest an Oriental patina for Merlin's arts. A recent article by Shichtman and Finke that usefully reconsiders a number of scholarly concerns on the *Historia* identifies the Saxon invasions and the entrance of Merlin as the textual moments that "signal the shift in Geoffrey's narrative from a conventional medieval chronicle history to history encoded as romance" (13).

58. Merlin and his author might have been pleased to learn of Arthurian romance's vigorous popularity with a changing variety of audiences for nine hundred years and—with the advent of electronic media—the likelihood of Arthur's survival well into the twenty-first century. In 1998 alone, when NBC broadcast its two-part Arthurian romance named for the magus, on April 26–27, the astonishing results were recorded in the *New York Times*: "With an audience that NBC estimated at a total of 70 million for Sunday and Monday nights, 'Merlin' took a broadsword to the competition. . . . It was especially strong with the younger viewers—those between the ages of 18 and 49—that NBC values most. It was also the first program in several years to put a dent in the almost unshakeable audience for Fox's 'X-Files' on Sunday night, sending that show to its lowest rating in almost three years. It dwarfed the ratings for the big box office theatrical movie 'Apollo 13'" (Carter, B8). For a list of Arthurian films, see Harty (203–47); on the popularity, genres, and audiences of Arthurian romance in the Renaissance, eighteenth century, and Victorian England, see Dean, Johnston, and Girouard, respectively.

59. The triangulated relations between Queen Melisende of Jerusalem, the youthful and dashing Hugh Le Puiset, lord of Jaffa, and Fulk of Anjou, King of Jerusalem, has uncanny echoes for the Guenevere-Mordred-Arthur and Guenevere-Lancelot-Arthur triangles. Hugh's dalliance and reputed adultery with his kinswoman, Melisende, became a scandal that resulted in the division of the court into the king's party and the count of Jaffa's; Hugh was charged with treason, challenged to judicial combat, and exiled; the gossip and sensation brought the Kingdom of Jerusalem to the brink of civil war (see, e.g., Runciman, 2:187–93). Significant elements resemble those of later Arthurian romance: a king of mature years and doting attachment to his queen; an atmosphere of courtly intrigue, scandal, and division; a handsome and noble retainer who is a younger rival; enmity between the king's faction and the retainer's; and the queen's domination of her doting older husband. The time frame—the early 1130s—coincides with the period of the *Historia*'s composition, and it is possible that the scandalous and sensational features of the story later influenced Chrétien and subsequent Arthurian romancers, since there were close ties between the courts of Champagne and Jerusalem. Chrétien's patroness, Countess Marie of Champagne—

who, Chrétien claimed, prompted the writing of his romance, *Lancelot*—was the mother of Henri II of Champagne, de facto King of Jerusalem-in-exile, on his marriage to Isabella of Jerusalem, after Jerusalem had been lost to Saladin. Marie's husband, Count Henri I of Champagne, had died on crusade to the East. Chrétien's romances display knowledge of the Orient: The romance *Yvain* invokes Nuraldin, Saladin's predecessor and master, by name, and Mabonagrain's enclosed habitat, in the Joie de la Cort episode of Chrétien's *Erec et Enide*—a feminized space, where there is pleasure, but not freedom—much resembles, as Seth Lerer once remarked in conversation, an Oriental harem. The definitive volume on Chrétien's relationship to the crusader East, as Sherron Knopp once observed, has yet to be written.

60. The words in the vocative "you, who need to submit far-distant kingdoms to your own authority" also recall Urban's crusading address. For the *Historia*'s invention of an African invasion from a phrase in *De Excidio*, see Wright, "Gildas," 11. Tatlock discusses the relationship between this episode in the *Historia* and the *chanson Gormont et Isembart* (*Legendary History*, 135–39). The behavior of the Africans in Britain not only recalls the Saxon invasions but also the behavior of the crusaders in the Orient. Interestingly, in the catalogue of horrors is the mention that the Africans convert the nephew of the king of the Franks away from Christianity. Hugh of Vermandois, younger brother of the French king, and Stephen of Blois, brother-in-law of the English king, were among the leaders who turned back, away from the Christian crusading mission. European documents (e.g., Joinville, *Histoire de Saint Louis*, 215–17) sometimes record the conversion of captive children and others to Islam, as do, of course, the Arab chronicles.

61. The symbolic reenactment of the saving gestures of Eucharistic sacrifice fulfills other useful ends. The comforting invocation of Eucharistic ritual also helps to dispel any anxiety residually attaching to sacred cannibalism (see n. 23 above), since the glowing affirmation of the life-giving and health-giving nature of the generous sacrifice enacted here serves as a blanket reassurance and vindication of Eucharistic function. Furthermore, Brian's sacrifice—his production of himself as food—eerily fulfills Merlin's earlier prophecy that King Arthur would also be food ("cibus") "in the mouths of peoples" (Wright, 1:74), thus linking together the two romances featuring cannibalism in the *Historia*. Both these good cannibalisms constitute positive literary examples reinforcing the valorization of sacred (Eucharistic) cannibalism.

62. Historians have, from the nineteenth century on, argued vigorously over the reputed homosexuality of William Rufus and Robert Curthose, evidence for which turns on the interpretation of chronicle material, and especially Orderic Vitalis, who refers in passing to sodomy, and to a Venus of Sodom—though, unfortunately, as John Boswell wryly remarks, "it seems that Ordericus did not attach very specific connotations to 'sodomiticus'" (229–30 n. 71). A scholarly consensus appears nonetheless to be emerging that these sons of the Conqueror were likely to have been, at the very least, bisexual, and that they inhabited courts notorious for their wide spectrum of profligate sexual transgressions, courts that the chroniclers, including Orderic, also castigate for effeminacy and excesses of fashion and appearance. Significantly, among

the horrors listed by the chroniclers was the keeping of *beards*, by courtiers, as an affectation: Though presumably not contributing to the problem of effeminacy, this wearing of beards was sufficiently countercultural to warrant Bishop Serlo's barbed association, at Carentan, of bearded courtiers with goats or Saracens, as Orderic reports (see p. 38 above). Since clean-shaven male faces seemed to function for Norman culture as signifiers of normalcy, psychosexual discipline, and good social order, the cloak of beards collected by the giant Ritho might wittily have indexed a second layer of reference. Crusader monstrosity can thus be read as injuring both the bearded Saracen enemy and a set of local Anglo-Norman court elites identifiable in contemporary contexts by their hirsute affectations. Boswell suggests that the trope of hunting, perhaps by association with Ganymede, was a frequent medieval figure for homosexuality (253), which adds another dimension to Brian's hunt for flesh with which to satisfy the king. I am indebted to Martha Newman for calling my attention to a photograph in Boswell (plate 13) of a statue of John lying tenderly in the bosom of Christ that strangely echoes Geoffrey's tableau of Brian/Cadwallo, since Brian pointedly functions as a Christ figure in the homoerotic romance that follows.

63. If, in a twelfth-century family romance, cannibalism is the trope that enables sodomy to find analogical expression—in a form of "symbolic thinking, where one . . . [stands in] for another" (Crain, 26)—Caleb Crain's discussion of homosexuality and cannibalism in Melville suggests that a tropological substitution of this kind operates just as effectively in nineteenth-century America, whose dominant culture had a name, and a discourse, for cannibalism but not for homosexuality. I am indebted to Sam Otter for drawing Crain's article to my attention.

64. As early as the mid-eleventh century Peter Damian's *Liber Gomorrhianus*, addressed to Pope Leo IX, had inveighed in an extended tract against sodomitical practices among the clergy, and in 1049 "a local synod excommunicated certain unnamed Gallican heretics along with 'sodomites'" (Goodich, 7). Even before the Council of Nablus's passage of the death penalty into law, "scriptural glossators grouped around Anselm of Laon linked heresy and sodomy as forms of sacrilege punishable by death" (Goodich, 7). Though Boswell argues that a vigorous, short-lived homosexual subculture existed among select Norman clerics of the early twelfth century—as evinced by the survival of homoerotic verse as a minor strain in their poetry—it would seem likely that a subculture of this kind would have been required to negotiate the currents of dominant culture, resorting perhaps to literary ruses like Geoffrey's where necessary. We do not know what relationship Geoffrey had, if any, to the subculture or its literature: though Baldric of Dol (Baudri of Bourgeuil, later Archbishop of Dol) wrote a history of the First Crusade (which Geoffrey may or may not have read), as well as homoerotic verse. Boswell notes that Baldric, who was closely attached to the Anglo-Norman royal court—Adela of Blois, sister of Robert Curthose and supporter of Bohemond of Antioch, also supported Baldric's candidacy for the archbishopric of Orléans (Goodich, 6)—was "twice driven from office by mysterious scandals" (Boswell, 246) and eventually disclaimed his poetry, insisting that no "evil love" had ever touched him (246), and even created literary personae attacking

sodomitical practices (246 n. 14). Many have noticed that despite the *Historia*'s immense popularity and cultural usefulness to Norman aristocracy Geoffrey was only rewarded with the minor bishopric of St. Asaph. For exemplary discussions of medieval homosexuality, including shifting definitions of "sodomy," see Goodich, Boswell, Bullough, Stehling, and Jordan.

65. Hutson offers support for my reading: "There is some evidence that Geoffrey knew a man named Brian. This was Brian Fitz-Count, whom William of Malmsbury calls the son of Robert of Gloucester. He was more probably the son of Alan, count of Brittany. Brianus (Brient, Brienius, Brientius) *filius comitis* appears often with Robert of Gloucester, Waleran, Count of Mellant, and Alexander, bishop of Lincoln (all of whom were friends or patrons of Geoffrey), as a witness to various charters in the years from 1130 to 1141. Together with Robert he supported the claims of Matilda against Stephen from 1138 until Geoffrey's death in 1147. All this evidence goes to show that Geoffrey was probably flattering a friend by including his name in the *Historia* as the name of a very brave and gallant young knight."

66. In the *Vita Mahumeti*, composed perhaps as early as 1040 by Hildebert, Bishop of Mayence (1057–1134), the Prophet Mohammad is also rendered as a "magus" who introduces a corrupting and threatening culture (Melitzki, 201–2). Indeed, the image of Mohammad as an enchanter was so popular, Melitzki notes, that more than three hundred years later it would dominate "one of the most rational discussions of Islam in medieval literature [i.e., Langland's]" (202) and might well shadow the literary representation of other magi, like Pellitus and Merlin.

67. Provocatively, Brian's public assassination of Pellitus resembles the assassinations for which the Batini, or Assassins—a breakaway Shi'ite Muslim group of Ismailites—were famed in Syria in the early twelfth century. Batini enmity toward Sunni Islam, and their targeting of Sunni princes for assassination, often furthered the Christian cause by eliminating Sunni political and military enemies of the Latins: an accidental conflation of purposes that earned the Batini the suspicion of the Sunni Muslims dominating Syria, who suspected that the Assassins were either secretly pro-Christian or even really Christians in disguise. A Christian writer, Arnold of Luebeck, has the Assassins "eat swine's flesh against the law of the Saracens" (Melitzki, 223). The first Assassin leader in Syria who appeared in Aleppo in the twelfth century, the Persian al-Hakim al-Munajjim, was, like Pellitus, an astrologer (and a physician). Curiously, a number of assassinations in the *Historia*, including Brian's, have at least some of the hallmarks of Batini-style killings: The assassinations are conducted in public, at great personal risk (sometimes certain death) to the perpetrator; involve disguise, including assuming the costume or dress of the enemy; require time spent in the company of the intended victim, to allay suspicion; and even, in one episode of the *Historia*, the shaving of beards in order that the would-be assassins might pass for Britons. Melitzki points out that the oldest attested appearance of the Assassins in European literature is in "five Provençal poems" (223) and that "the Western public got its first knowledge of the Assassins from the Crusaders" (223).

68. Matheson, Fletcher, Ernest Jones, and Keeler provide exemplary accounts of the afterlife of the *Historia* and its later influence. In a tribute to both Geoffrey and Chrétien, Rabelais in the sixteenth century winks knowingly at the Oriental origins of Arthurian romance by having the giant parents of his benevolent giant-figure, Gargantua, created not "in France, but on the highest mountain of the Orient" (Stephens, 52)—a nod in the direction of "Mons Aravius." The body of Gargantua's father, Grant-Gosier, is derived from "the bones of a male whale and the blood of Lancelot" and that of his mother, Galemelle, from "the bones of a female whale and the nail-parings of Guinevere" (Stephens, 52). Stephens shrewdly notices that "Gargantua's feats in the service of Arthur very closely mimic those of Corineus for Brutus in Geoffrey of Monmouth's chronicle (which was printed twice at Paris during the first two decades of the sixteenth century)" (Stephens, 54). With consummate humor, Rabelais has Grant-Gosier create Mont Saint-Michel and Galemelle create Tombelaine, so that his two giants are responsible for creating the Arthurian romance site and monument that the *Historia* creates for its own two giants who are Grant-Gosier's and Galemelle's predecessors. Rabelais's understanding of Geoffrey's subtle wiles extends to his making Gargantua a "harmless or at least inadvertent" cannibal, in a humorous incident where "205 'Irish/Dutch' soldiers fall into Gargantua's mouth while he is asleep, and he unwittingly drowns them when he awakes and drains a river to slake his thirst" (Stephens, 55). Indeed, Gargantua economically reenacts both Cadwallo and Arthur, since he is an involuntary cannibal and a giant-killer, whose feasting is celebrated in the *Chroniques* by "joyous description" (Stephens, 56).

69. Most scholars believe that the First Variant was written immediately after the *Historia*'s appearance and before the *Roman de Brut*, and that Wace used both the vulgate and variant versions for the *Brut*, although a suggestion also exists that the First Variant's author might have followed and used Wace's text rather than the other way around (see, e.g., Dumville 2:xii–xv).

2. The Romance of England: *Richard Coer de Lyon* and the Politics of Race, Religion, Sexuality, and Nation

1. *RCL* survives in seven manuscripts and two early printings. Brunner's edition (henceforth *RCL*) traces two lines of descent, "A" and "B" versions, with the oldest extant mss—the Auchinleck and Egerton, from the early and later fourteenth century—represented in B. Scholarship has sometimes argued that B is "closest to the 'original'" (Finlayson, "Richard," 179), a lost Anglo-Norman ur-text from the thirteenth century ("Entstehungszeit der Dichtung ist . . . das 13. Jahrhundert anzusetzen" [Brunner, 11]). I follow editorial tradition in reading the romance as emerging in the thirteenth century (while bracketing the existence of a French original whose contents are irretrievable, despite the lure of an occasional internal narrative hint or fiction), but whose text required the next centuries of collective authorship by copyists, redactors, and editors to complete. Lineation and numbering are Brunner's. The first cannibalism is not in all the mss (the text in the Auchinleck is a mere fragment); the sec-

ond cannibalism is in the Egerton, and both versions of narrative descent; the well poisoning is represented also in A and B.

2. European chroniclers of the tenth century use "Saracen," as well as "Agarene" (i.e., a descendant of Hagar) to signify Arabs, and "in pre-Islamic Greek usage 'Saracen' is synonymous with 'Arab' (Daniel, *Arabs*, 53). "The Greek word 'Saracen' . . . is of unknown etymology, and was thought to imply a claim to descent from Sarah, so that 'Agarene' was often used as a corrective. . . . 'Agarene' and 'Ismaelite' [i.e., a descendant of Ismail] are more specific than 'Saracen,' which would ultimately come to be used as a portmanteau word with no clear significance, as when a group is said to contain Arabs, Turks, and Saracens. Then it means an unspecified residuum of Arabic-speaking Muslims. . . . from the twelfth century onwards . . . 'Saracen' in many contexts . . . meant 'Muslim' . . . 'Saracen' is never used to refer to a Christian Arab. . . . No mediaeval writer seems ever to have realized that 'Saracen' has no Arabic equivalent form" (Daniel, *Arabs*, 53). In the twelfth-century *Alexiad*, the Byzantine princess Anna Comnena uses all three terms—"Agarenes," "Ishmaelites," and "Saracens"—to signify Muslim Orientals, without reference to their linguistic use of Arabic specifically (i.e., as opposed, say, to the use of Persian). In medieval literature thereafter a "Saracen" is generally just a Muslim Oriental: "Saracen," that is, is a *racial and religious*—not a linguistic—marker. I read the "old knight" in *RCL* as a residual figure from the First Crusade. In the long history of European crusades to the East, the First and Third Crusades are often held to be successful, and thus thought to resemble each other, since territory was wrested from the Muslims in the First and held or partially regained in the Third, by the Latins, whereas all the other crusades are usually thought to have been disastrous to various degrees.

3. To recapitulate: I argued in chapter 1 that historical cannibalism performed by Latin Christian crusaders on Turkish Muslim cadavers at Ma'arra an-Numan in Syria, in 1098, during the First Crusade (and perhaps a few months before at Antioch) issued in a cultural trauma that required strategies of attenuation, displacement, and transformation supplied by a hybrid genre of cultural fantasy, with the emergence of the literary legend of King Arthur one generation later, in Geoffrey of Monmouth's fabulous *History of the Kings of Britain* (*Historia Regum Britannie*), thus eliciting the genesis of the magical genre we call medieval romance. The literary ancestry of the cannibalism in *RCL* can be traced back to the *Historia's* negotiation of trauma in the First Crusade: to the *Historia's* tacit memorialization of the cannibalism, followed by the transformation of the cannibalistic memory into romance event through the heroism of King Arthur. The *second* romance action in the *Historia*, which further transforms the thus-attenuated memory of historical cannibalism, is *precisely the kind of restorative cannibalism that occurs in RCL*: Cadwallo, King of Britain, is restored to good health by his retainer Brian, who turns the king into an inadvertent cannibal in order to heal the king's malady.

The cannibalistic episode in *RCL* thus has a literary genealogy of predecessor moments that makes possible its production as a joke. Guibert de Nogent's crusade history in the first decade of the twelfth century half-admits that certain Christians might

eat Saracens under certain conditions ("secretly and rarely," Guibert says, if at all)—
when, that is, the Christians involved are "Tafurs," wild men who are desperately
poor, ragged, and possibly foreign: "Tafurs" being Guibert's invented name for a subaltern group of impoverished, useful underclass folk in the Christian army designed
to shoulder exclusive responsibility for accusations and rumors of cannibalism directed at the Christian forces of the First Crusade. Late in the twelfth century the *Chanson d'Antioche* embroidered on the guilt of "Tafurs," who are depicted by the *Antioche*
as unabashedly eating boiled and roast Turk openly, to the amusement of the barons
of the First Crusade (*Chanson d'Antioche*, laisses CLXXIV, CLXXV). We note that
the *Antioche*'s contribution appeared only *after* Geoffrey's *Historia*, in the first third
of the twelfth century, had already interpolated the good, healing cannibalism of the
British king Cadwallo. The *Antioche*'s principal addition to the genealogy of Christian cannibalism, then, was to insert *laughter* as an ingredient: to suggest that when a
Christian underclass—the dregs or human debris of the crusading army—turns cannibal, laughter by seigneurial onlookers is an appropriate response (laisse CLXXV).
Finally, an essential link between cannibalism and military conquest in war was intruded very early, when Raymond d'Aguiliers's eyewitness chronicle of the First Crusade in the opening years of the twelfth century half-consciously recognized that the
Latin crusaders' depraved reputation for anthropopagy is tied to their reputation as
successful conquerors of Antioch.

4. This discourse functions differently from other treatments of cannibalism in
medieval culture/history in that the cannibalizing subjects are not monstrous races or
variously demonized others who are marked off as different from Western European
Christians (cannibalistic others being commonplace staples in anthropological and
travel literature, and literatures of conquest and colonization, including the medieval).
Instead, the discourse on cannibalism positioned in the time elapsing between the two
polar examples of horror and elation I describe concerns itself with cannibalisms inflicted *by* Europeans and Christians *against* cultural others, and organizes the depiction of European cannibalism into specific patterns of intelligibility and meaning, patterns traversed by desire, purpose, duration, and direction. *RCL* is one such instance
of discursive patterning.

5. An important exception is the African invasion: Unlike others before them, the
Africans do not become part of the assimilated heterogeneity of Britain's population
since they are not mentioned again as occupants of insular Britain (Wright, 1:133).
Membership in the Christian community and a tribal origin in Europe seem the essential conditions, in the *Historia*, for the successful assimilation of immigrants in the
island *domus*: conditions that will have key implications for a definition of medieval
England as nation, both in history and romance. A reader attuned to discourses of difference in medieval culture might also suspect that color may play a role in the nonas-
similation of the *Historia*'s Africans, who remain unaccounted for in Britain's heterogeneous population.

6. Henry of Huntingdon, according to John Gillingham, is one of the earliest
chroniclers to document the Anglo-Norman assumption of an English identity. "In

answer to the question of the date at which the descendants of those newcomers who settled in England in the wake of the Norman conquest began to think of themselves as English, historians have often said, 'by the end of the twelfth century.' However, I am convinced that it was 1140, at the latest" (Gillingham, "Foundations," 54). Koht concurs with Gillingham:

> In the crusade of 1147, Normans and English [from England] formed a single group, separate from, although allied with, Flemings, Scots, and forces from Cologne. . . . A little later, one of the highest officers of the kingdom, the royal treasurer, Richard FitzNeal, felt that he could say that frequent intermarriages had to such a degree brought about a mingling of [Normans and Anglo-Saxons] that, in the class of free men, it could scarcely be ascertained who was English and who Norman. The Anglo-Norman chroniclers of the twelfth and the thirteenth centuries uniformly gave the whole population of England the common name *gens Anglorum* without differentiating between conquerors and conquered. (270)

And, according to Clanchy:

> By the end of the twelfth century the Normans had been absorbed by intermarriage. This is specifically stated in the *Dialogue of the Exchequer* and it is also indicated by the way charters are no longer addressed to both French and English but simply to all faithful persons. . . . nationalist [feeling] is explicit even in an official document from 1217, which looks forward to the 'English' (*Anglici*) recovering their lands in Normandy. (*England*, 252)

Renan's classic essay on the formation of nations describes the "fusion of . . . component populations" as an essential stage of nation formation (10).

7. "In the account of the life of Edward the Confessor in the later thirteenth-century prose narrative, the *Livere de Reis de Engletere*, Edward has a dream just before he dies which the narrator interprets as being about the future of England. . . . In this dream sequence and its interpretation, we can identify an amalgamation of certain commonplaces in the representation of a political community in twelfth-century England. The community is a realm; it is metonymically represented in the person of its king" (Johnson, 125). The "sovereign . . . embodies in him the idea of the nation" (Koht, 269). As king of England, Richard Lionheart not only symbolizes the English polity but lends his name to his people, when, in *RCL*, English Christians become like lions ("as lyouns" [l. 5108]).

8. *RCL* depicts Richard's principal foe in Christendom as a "Mordard," a name that recalls Arthur's betrayal by Mordred. Richard and Arthur are also positioned identically in the narrative, when each in turn is recalled from foreign invasion by untimely domestic betrayal and insurgency. Enemy ambassadors to both Richard and Arthur are old men, to point up the aggressive virility of the two legendary kings. The *Historia*'s Arthur, like Richard, is a military conqueror with, as Tatlock puts it, "the nimbus of a crusader"(*Legendary History*, 262). *RCL*'s citation of the Brian-Cadwallo romance in the *Historia* is even more direct: Richard and Cadwallo are kings who fall

gravely ill, desire meat that is unavailable, and are served human flesh instead by a retainer who restores them to health through cannibalism; and both are instated, by the kindly deception practiced, as involuntary, unconscious cannibals.

9. Derek Pearsall's is the most succinct sketch of the process by which a popular medieval romance like *RCL* collects as a series of aggregative acts laid down over time: "The existence of such texts demands from us a special kind of understanding, one which recognises a fluidity in the nature of a popular romance. . . . After the writing down of the original poem, individual texts crystallize moments in the poem's existence, in a process of change. . . . each romance lies in a network of intersecting developments" ("English Romance," 59) since even "the work of copying is . . . often a work of re-composition" (58). See also Clanchy (*Memory*), Stock, Gellrich. To varying degrees *all* medieval literary work, of course, including signed work, like Chaucer's, is a collective repository of complex mediations (see, e.g., Lerer). And even after the advent of print culture, complex textual mediations continue (see, e.g., Marcus, on Renaissance texts). Moderns might understand, in a strictly limited fashion, what a micrological "community on the page" might look like in twentieth-century terms by considering, say, the history of how the text of T. S. Eliot's "The Wasteland" was aggregatively compiled: Though, of course, the degree and extent to which a medieval text truly sediments a "community on the page" bears little comparison with modern literatures, given worlds of difference in reproduction, centuries-long processes of retranscription, redaction, and revision, and divergent cultural and mental attitudes toward authority, fidelity, adaptation, signature, and so on, between the medieval and modern eras. Pearsall reminds us, nonetheless, that even through the centuries of a medieval popular text's creation, certain core essentials are likely to continue, since the very fact of a romance's repeated re-composition, as demonstrable with *RCL*, "argue[s] for a continuity of taste, in which [a] few specific directions can be isolated" (61).

10. By contrast, the epic, Diane Speed argues, is a narrative genre that runs counter to nationalist discourse, because the "chain-reaction of destruction" in epic thematizes social disorder, chaos, and extralegality, all antithetical to national formations (146). Medieval epics have usually been treated in scholarship as tribal, rather than national, narratives. An important subspecies of epic, the *chanson de geste*, has been seen as particularly obsessed with the relationship of the monarch to his greatest magnates/tenants-in-chief (see, e.g., Duparc-Quioc, 2:259). For a key argument on the relationship between vernacular prose historiography and epic and romance in France, see Spiegel.

11. William of Newburgh recounts Richard's famous joke on his willingness to sell off London, if he could only find a buyer (1:306) and Richard's celebrated jest that he had made a new earl out of an old bishop, after inducing Hugh, Bishop of Durham, to purchase the earldom of Northumberland from the crown (1:305; also Roger of Wendover, 1:168). A joke expressing Richard's crafty diplomacy is recorded by Saladin's biographer, secretary, and confidant, the imam Beha' ed-Din. To drive a wedge between Saladin and his younger brother and trusted lieutenant, al-Adil, Richard provocatively suggested to al-Adil that al-Adil should marry Joanna,

Richard's widowed sister, the former queen of William II of Sicily, and that the conjugal couple be given Jerusalem to govern, by Saladin, as king and queen, together
with the territory commanded by Latins and Muslims on the Levantine coast and in
the interior. That Saladin recognized Richard's trick is borne out by the emir's ready
acquiescence to the unthinkable match and his certainty that the English king had
no intention of carrying out his proposal (Beha' ed-Din, 310–11; Gabrieli, 227;
Runciman, 3:59–60). For a romance rethinking of the unthinkable in the form of
this particular royal joke, see the discussion of the Constance saga, in chapter 4.

12. The Latin kingdom of Jerusalem fell to Saladin in 1187. Thereafter, the kingdom briefly and temporarily passed through Latin hands, transacted as pawn in political and diplomatic maneuvers when it was given back to Christendom in 1229 by
Saladin's nephew, al-Kamil, in his complex diplomatic, cultural, and affective relationship with the Mozarabic Hohenstauffen emperor, Frederick II. Subsequently,
Jerusalem was captured by the Mongols, and shortly thereafter recaptured for Islam.
In 1268, the Latin principality of Antioch fell to the Egyptian Mamluk sultan, Bay-
bars. In 1291, Acre, the last stronghold, fell to the sultan Khalil, permanently ending
the almost two-centuries-long crusader occupation of the Levant.

13. Lateran III in 1179 issued twenty-seven canons; Lateran II in 1139 thirty canons,
and the First Lateran Council in 1123 a mere twenty-two canons. Some of the impulses
I identify as characterizing the epistemic formation of the "thirteenth century" may of
course be nascent in the mid-to-late twelfth century as well, history producing jagged,
rather than neat, epistemic edges.

14. Though one should, strictly speaking, refer to medieval "inquisitors" rather
than an "inquisition"—there having been no centralized authority called the "Inquisition" constituted in the Middle Ages—inquisitional procedures and ideology rapidly formalized a body of models, practices, documentation, and authorizations that was
remarkably coherent and distinctive, in structure and institutional culture. It is that
totality of practices and apparatuses that is referred to here as the "inquisition" (see Peters, *Inquisition*, 56–68).

15. Paradoxically the range of instruments that became available in the epistemic
culture of the thirteenth century also enabled the formation of Europe as an overarching idea and entity, in tandem with the rise of individual medieval nations, so that
"by 1300 Europe existed as an identifiable cultural entity" (Bartlett, *Making of Europe*,
291). The complex relationship of Christendom to the rise of "Europe" is comprehensively argued by Barlett. The inquisition, of course, never took root in England.

16. The use of enemy skulls in drinking (if not in dining), as well as the boastful exhibition of such skulls of the defeated and slain, is a subject that is also treated in
Herodotus's *Histories* to characterize a community of *barbaroi* (Scythians) whose bloodthirsty bellicosity in war extends to the aggressive display of defeated enemies as trophies
during celebratory consumption. In 4:64–65 of the *Histories* Herodotus tells us:

> Here is how they conduct themselves in war. When a Scythian kills his first man, he
> drinks some of his blood. He presents the king with the heads of those he kills in bat-

tle. . . . The way a Scythian skins a head is as follows: he makes a circular cut around the head at the level of the ears and then he picks it up and shakes the scalp off the skull. . . . As for the actual skulls . . . they saw off the bottom part of the skull at the level of the eyebrows and clean out the top bit. . . . a rich Scythian . . . gilds the inside and then uses it as a cup. Also, if a Scythian falls out with one of his relatives, they fight to the death in the presence of their king, and the winner treats the loser's skull in the way I have just described. When he has important visitors, he produces these skulls and tells how they made war on him, but he defeated them. This they call courage. (Waterfield, 255–56)

Herodotus's ethnography, and Richard's romance, in other words, both offer consumptive practices and strategic exhibition of dead enemies as characteristic observances that define the collective identity of the group: The difference, of course, lies in the implicit critique of one community (as *barbaroi*) and the vaunted celebration of the other community (as triumphant English Christians).

17. "Whyl any Sarezyn quyk bee / Lyuande now in þis cuntree, / Ffor mete wole we noþyng care: . . . Into Yngelond wol we nouȝt gon, / Tyl þay be eeten euerylkon" (ll. 3555–62). Maggie Kilgour notes that cannibalism is "the most demonic image for the impulse to incorporate external reality and get everything inside a single body, be it physical, textual, or social" (16). I am indebted to Carol Pasternak for her insight that a joke is also an *aide-mémoire*, like the luridity of cannibalism, and thus the one is a conducive medium for the other.

18. The plucking and shaving of Richard's aristocratic and royal victims recall, of course, the Arthurian giant's cloak of defeated kings' beards in the *Historia*—linking Richard to Arthur on yet another level—and suggest *RCL*'s winking comprehension of the historical meaning of beardlessness, and the loss of facial hair, for masculine identity among Levantines. See chapters 1 and 3 for discussions of the cloak of beards.

19. As Freud points out, "jokes . . . are highly suitable for attacks on the great, the dignified and the mighty" (8:149). Arab and Latin chronicles both alike honor Saladin's memory and reputation. Runciman cites William of Tyre and Ernoul as Christian sources for the story of how Saladin, while attacking the fortress of Kerak, where the marriage of the castellan's son was taking place, chivalrously forebore to bombard the tower where the nuptial couple was housed, despite the fact that the castellan, the abominable Reynald de Châtillon—detested by both Latins and Muslims—was an enemy Saladin had sworn to kill by his own hand, after Reynald's gratuitous raid on a pilgrim caravan in which Saladin's sister had been traveling. In gratitude, the bridegroom's mother, the Lady Stephanie, "herself prepared dishes from the bridal feast which she sent out to Saladin" (Runciman, 2:441). When the emir recaptured Jerusalem from the Latins, his conduct was equally humane, self-restrained, and honorable: "Where the Franks, eight years before, had waded through the blood of their victims, not a building now was looted, not a person injured. By Saladin's orders guards patrolled the streets and the gates, preventing any outrage on the Christians" (Runciman, 2:466). Runciman remarks: "At the Horns of Hattin and the gates of Jerusalem . . . he had shown how a man of honour celebrates his victory" (2:473). The

most moving testimony of Saladin's life and conduct is recorded by the imam and kadi Beha' ed-Din, Saladin's biographer, secretary, and chronicler, who relates how his master's characteristic generosity had emptied the royal coffers, so that at Saladin's death "we were obliged to borrow money to purchase everything necessary for the funeral, even down to things that cost but a halfpenny" (407). "I had often heard people say," Beha' ed-Din reflects with pathos, "they would lay down their own lives for that of someone very dear to them, but I thought it was only a manner of speaking, from which a good deal must be deducted in reality; but I swear before God, and I am sure that had we been asked that day, 'Who will redeem the Sultan's life?' there were several of us who would have replied by offering his own" (407).

20. Within the field of nationalism, as Etienne Balibar notes, there is "the nationalism of the dominant" and "that of the dominated." A consequence of anticolonial and anti-imperialist movements is that modern postcolonial nations emerge from a "nationalism of liberation." Medieval nationalisms, implicated in war with border countries and cultural and political others, may be constituted as a "nationalism of conquest" (Balibar, 45).

21. The medieval European discourse on color is, of course, unstable, unevenly distributed across socio-regional divides, and riven with contradictions. However, what is essential to understand is that blackness is *not neutral*, but typically negatively valenced, in the epistemic culture I describe. That a racializing discourse exists in which color is positioned instrumentally, from the thirteenth century on, is inescapable: The attention given to blackness, and variations on blackness, in cultural texts ranging from romances like the *King of Tars, Moriaen*, and *Parzival* to the statuary of St. Maurice, and visual representations of the Queen of Sheba and Lady Fortune (in which characters are black, piebald, mottled, split into black-and-white halves, etc.) suggests a discursive system in place to guide responses to characters and narratives from cues supplied by color. Nonetheless, the prime role of religion in the medieval period means that culture can function like biology: In literature, for instance, baptism can whiten the skin color of blacks and partial blacks, indicating that the spiritual essence conferred by religion can work on the genetic essence conferred by the biologism of color (a black St. Maurice, moreover, is also patently acceptable under limited local and regional conditions). That religion might be understood to impart an essence is a special feature of the medieval moment in racial discourse. But to grasp that religion locates an essence is only partially to grasp the specificities of the medieval racializing apparatus. Disbelief and suspicion toward Jewish *conversos* in the period suggests that, even after conversion to another religion, something is felt to continue, as a remainder—a core essence—within the once Judaic body, that religious conversion, however essential, cannot erase: a remainder that can only be racially named. In chapter 4, I pick up and develop the thread of the argument on medieval racial thinking begun in this chapter. For visual representations, see, especially, volume 2 of Devisse, *Image of the Black in Western Art*.

22. *Faces*—an important index of shared humanity—are also pivotal in the recognition of racial apartness from the Western European norm, alongside color contrast.

In *Moriaen, Parzival*, the *Song of Roland*, inter alia, Moors and blacks are identified by their possession of a black face and white teeth, while the product of miscegenation between the fair, white princess of Tars and the black, loathly Sultan of Damascus, in the *King of Tars*, is presented as a lump of flesh without a face (or torso or limbs). Glenn Burger aptly remarks, in his study of the Armenian Hetoum of Korikos's *La Fleur des Histoires de la Terre d'Orient*, that "most Western observers" of the Mongols in the thirteenth and fourteenth centuries "comment on the ugliness of Mongols' Asiatic facial appearance as a way of underscoring an often essentializing racial difference" (77). Richard's automatic designation of a black face as indicating a "deuyl" is merely the latest example of a centuries-long, inherited tradition that Dorothy Verkerk's important study of blackness in the late-sixth-century Ashburnham Pentateuch situates as beginning in the late-antique/early-medieval period: a period when "a paradigmatic shift from the Roman black barbarian to the Christian black demon" (59) picks up and develops the uses of color in patristic exegetical tradition. "The illustration of the tenth plague [in the Ashburnham Pentateuch] shows a transitional moment where the representation of blacks, playing upon the fears of sixth-century Christians, acquires sinister associations, laying the groundwork for later depictions of blacks as demons" (59). Though in this "intermediate stage" of the late-antique/early-medieval period, "the conventions [on color] are not [yet] fully worked out but are in flux" (60), patristic allegoresis cumulatively and over time puts in place ideas linking sin, non-Christianity, and blackness, so that by this period "the sinful non-Christian . . . has a face and it is black" (63).

23. Peter the Venerable's letter to Louis VII of France, on the subject of the Second Crusade, savagely opined that Jews were worse than Saracens, and the "only reason they should not be wiped off the face of the earth is that God wishes them to live a fate worse than death" (A. Abulafia, "Bodies," 130). Like Saracens, Jews were often represented in medieval manuscript illuminations as dark-skinned and bearded. The diptych of Moses expounding the law to a heterogeneous group, in the Bury St. Edmunds Bible of 1125–37, depicts Jews—including Moses himself—as both dark-skinned and hirsute, whereas the clean-shaven men (including redheads) among his listeners are presumably European Christians (Ford, plate 5). Many have written on the deterioration in the treatment of the Jews in Europe, from a relative tolerance influenced by Augustinian tradition, earlier in the Middle Ages, to the harsh persecutions and libels of the thirteenth century (see, e.g., R. I. Moore, Chazan). Jeremy Cohen, in particular, powerfully tracks the role of the mendicant orders, and the growing consolidation of Latin Christendom itself, in the spread, intensification, and renovation of anti-Judaism in the thirteenth and fourteenth centuries (*Friars*, "Jews").

24. Jewish chronicles document genocides at Mainz, Worms, Speyer, Cologne, Regensburg, and elsewhere during the Popular Crusade; the Second Crusade also occasioned the sacrificing of medieval Jewries (see Eidelberg). Crusades are linked to the punishment of Jews also through legalized *fiscal* extortions: Peter the Venerable suggested that Jews should be made to finance the cost of the Second Crusade (A. Abulafia, "Bodies," 130); and English monarchs, of course, plundered Jews through

tallages during the many crusades declared in the twelfth and thirteenth centuries (Roth, *History*, 17 n. 2, 44, 46, 67; Richardson, 162, 163, 214; Tyerman, 79).

25. Attacks took place also at Lincoln and Winchester, where, however, the local Jewish populations were able to escape extermination. Attacks may also have occurred at Colchester, Thetford, and Ospringe (Roth, *History*, 21). The massacre and ritual suicides of more than 150 Jews at York on March 16 and 17, 1190, were followed the next day by a massacre of 57 Jews at Bury St. Edmunds. Roth notes that for the first time "Jewish historians incorporated the sufferings of the communities of England in their martyrologies" (*History*, 25).

26. Boswell notes, for instance, that in the thirteenth and fourteenth centuries, Jews, Muslims, heretics, traitors, and sodomites, tended to be lumped together by association, as were lepers, Jews, and witches, although each group was "disliked by the majority for entirely different reasons. . . . There was certainly no single cause for such varied expressions of public hostility, but it is difficult to view them as wholly unrelated. However different the immediate circumstances . . . they all drew support from widespread fears of alien and disruptive social elements, fears which could easily be focused on vulnerable or little-understood minority groups" (272). Bullogh traces ideological constructions linking together homosexuality-heresy-witchcraft/sorcery-transvestism ("Heresy"). Analogical thinking is quickly reinforced when contingent alliances among enemy (or outcast) communities seem to occur, although the historicity of some putative collusions continues to be debated, including that of the so-called Lepers' plot of projected well poisoning, which, in 1321, conveniently attaches lepers to Jews at the instigation of Granada (see Menache, "Expulsion," 369–70).

27. Although blood-libel *imagery* occurs in twelfth-century documents (e.g., in William of Newburgh's *Historia*), confirmed blood libels are apparently thirteenth-century phenomena. Dundes's anthology on the blood libel contains several excellent articles; on the relationship of Jews to blood and human sacrifice, see Strack. Langmuir's work on the ritual murder libel is incomparable ("Thomas of Monmouth," "Knight's Tale"; see also Roth, *Ritual Murder*). On the libel of Host desecration, see Langmuir ("Tortures"), Rubin, and Jeremy Cohen.

28. "Already in the 630s, the very decade of the Arab invasion of the Christian Middle East, the Byzantine Christians associated Jews with, and considered them agents of, the Muslims" (Cutler and Cutler, 90): "In the tenth century Hasdai ibn Shaprut, the powerful Jewish vizier of two caliphs of Cordova, Abd ar-Rahman III (912–961) and his successor Hakam II (961–976), definitely assisted his Muslim masters against the Christians of Spain. . . . that the Fatimid caliphs of Egypt employed Jewish viziers in the second half of the tenth century may have contributed to the fact that the Jews of Western Europe were blamed when the Fatimid caliph destroyed the Holy Sepulchre in Jerusalem" (Cutler and Cutler, 93). In the medieval association of Jews with Muslims, emphasis need only fall on Christian *perceptions* of collusion: "There is . . . an eleventh-century tradition that the Jews betrayed Toulouse to the Arabs circa 756–788. . . . Toulouse never fell to the Arabs; rather, it fell to the Normans in 848. This tradition that the Jews betrayed Toulouse may reflect an earlier

ninth- or tenth-century . . . charge that the Jews betrayed Marseilles to the Arabs in 848" (Cutler and Cutler 91).

29. See Shroeder (584). The relationship of Jews and Muslims might derive from the early days of Islam, with partial Jewish acceptance of the political authority of Mohammad, after his flight from Mecca to Medina. Three Jewish tribes were originally considered part of the *ummah*, or Islamic nation, because they submitted to Mohammad's political authority, without converting to Islam, an important historical precedent for later Jewish-Islamic relations. In *RCL*, Richard I has a demon-queen, curiously named "Cassodorien" of Antioch, instead of Eleanor of Aquitaine, for his mother. The name "Cassodorien" oddly echoes *Cassiodorius*, who had an early Christian account of the Jewish murder of a Christian boy translated into Latin:

> An "accusation against Jews in antiquity is the charge against the Jews of Inmestar (Syria) about 415 in connection with the celebration of Purim. . . . about 415, drunken Jews of Inmestar allegedly took a Christian boy, tied him to a cross in place of an effigy of Hamman, and so mistreated him that he died. Our only evidence for the incident is a contemporary Christian historian, Socrates. . . . Socrates' story of the Inmerstar incident was available to the Latin West during the Middle Ages in the work known as the *Historia tripartita*, the translation of the histories of Theodoret, Sozomen, and Socrates commissioned by Cassiodorius. Manuscripts of the work were widely disseminated . . . of the 138 known manuscripts . . . two early ones are found in England, and they date from the late twelfth or early thirteenth century." (Langmuir, "Thomas," 826)

"Cassodorien's" father's name, "Corbaring," is an echo from the First Crusade, since Karbuqa, the atabeg of Mosul whose army ringed crusader-occupied Antioch before the city was fully won by the Latins, is variously referred to in eyewitness Latin chronicles as "Corbaras" (Raymond d'Aguiliers), "Curbaram" (the *Gesta Francorum*), and so forth. By making "Cassodorien" the daughter of "Corbaring," *RCL* is able to intimate, perhaps, that Saracens are linked to Jews in a kind of filial and familial relationship.

30. Kedar cites Roger of Howden, the *Gesta Henrici* (83), and William of Tyre (82 n. 112) on conversion. Historically it is *Spain*, not the Holy Land, that is the locus of conversion efforts:

> None of the extant papal summons to later crusading expeditions, which call for the defense or recovery of Jerusalem and the Crusading Kingdom, presents Saracen conversion as a goal of the crusade. Neither does any of the extant papal letters to the prelates of the Crusading Kingdom dictate the conversion of the infidel as one of their main duties, as do the exhortations of Urban II, Paschal II, and Hadrian IV to the archbishops of Toledo. Nor does any rule of the military orders established in the Crusading Kingdom contain a clause similar to that of the Spanish Order of Santiago that prompts the brethren to lead the Saracens to the practice of Christianity. (Kedar, 60)

Kedar shows that it is Albert of Aix—one of the most notoriously unreliable of sources on crusading history—that most often mentions Muslim conversion, and even in Albert's chronicle the mention seems sporadic (see the chapter, "Christian Re-conquest and Muslim Conversion," in Kedar). The forcible conversions that Kedar notes occur most frequently in the context of Jews in Europe. Interestingly, he also points out that "while fragments of an account of conversion by a twelfth-century Christian who became a Jew . . . and a full-fledged report by a twelfth-century Jew who became a Christian . . . are extant, no contemporary record of a Muslim's con-version to Catholicism has ever come to light" (84). Cutler's "First Crusade" is an un-usual instance of an opinion that goes against the grain of scholarly views that the con-version of Saracens in the Holy Land is not a twelfth-century historical phenomenon (see Burns, and Waltz, *contra* Cutler).

31. For overviews of forcible conversion of medieval Jews throughout the countries of Europe, see the *Encyclopaedia Judaica*; Beinart's *Atlas of Medieval Jewish History* maps demographic distribution. For England, Roth's account is still authoritative (*History, Oxford*); see also Lipman. A famous incident of conversion in twelfth-century England occurred during Richard I's coronation, on September 3, 1189. Dur-ing the attack on the Jews at Westminster, the wealthy financier, Benedict of York, escaped death by agreeing to convert to Christianity.

32. Jewish moneylenders who realized the pledge of property as security could take seisin, and receive the fealty of tenants, but because they could not hold land in fee simple, would sell the acquisition after holding it long enough to establish claim of ownership (Roth, *History*, 107). There were rare exceptions in which Jews possessed land in fee simple in England, but the more common practice was to transfer mort-gaged land to buyers:

> Creditors of no other class were incapable of acquiring a freehold interest in land while acquiring the right to dispose of land. This circumstance, and their predominance for a time as private moneylenders caused the Jews to become the vehicle . . . for the trans-fer of land. Before the expulsion of the Jews, repeated attempts were made to curb their dealings in land or to mitigate the consequences. (Richardson, 108)

Roth observes that one complaint "specifically ventilated at the Parliament of Oxford in 1258 was that the Jews sold lands pledged to them to the great magnates of the realm, who took possession and subsequently refused to accept payment of the debt if it were offered" (*History*, 60).

33. Mundill cites Langmuir's description of Jewish intermediaries as "'real estate agents'" and quotes Maitland and Pollock on the impact of land transfer: "'land is being brought to the market and feudal rights are being capitalized'" (37), partly through "'ecclesiastical business acumen' [that] extended the lands of abbeys, priories and individuals in the late twelfth and early thirteenth centuries" (Mundill, 36, quot-ing Hatcher and Miller). Finally, "'Jewish money-lenders introduced abbeys, lay mag-nates and [also] the growing race of stewards and royal clerks to the opportunities of investment in the property of indebted knights'" (Mundill, 37, quoting Harding). Roth observes that Crown tenants were forbidden, from 1234, to borrow from Jews on the security of their estates, a provision extended in 1238 to "all who held their

property by military service" (52). See also Walter Map's *De Nugis*, which particularly criticized the Cistercians for their land acquisitions.

34. "Jews and Christians lived cheek by jowl with each other" (Stacey, 264); "Jews lived in 'open' rather than 'closed' Jewries. There were no ghettos in England" (Mundill, 33). Roth (*Oxford*) and Lipman document the lived intimacy of particular Jewish and Christian communities in Oxford and Norwich. Among the variety of relations between Jews and Christians, sexual intimacy, of course, was the most proscribed: Boswell notes that a thirteenth-century legal text specified that those who had sexual intercourse with Jews were to be buried alive (292).

35. Historical scholarship has amply and ably argued for the formative role played by England's military, political, and cultural relations to the Irish, Scots, Welsh, and French in the shaping of an English national identity. My focus here, on an *internal* minority uniquely identified by its religious and racial difference from the English communal majority, does not, of course, disturb the older and continuing understanding of the critical importance of England's traditional rivals, border colonies, and subject populations in the emergence of a medieval English nation. Rather, it augments the perspective of England's invasions, wars, and conflicts with external others, with a perspective of English manipulation of internal others. See, for a representative sample of scholarship on England's colonial relations with its neighbors, Frame, Gillingham ("Foundations"), R. R. Davies (*Domination and Conquest*), Clanchy (*England*), Biddick, and articles in Lydon. Ingham treats English (Arthurian) romance and the subject of Wales, Rambo discusses Ireland and medieval English literature, and Ambrisco discusses English nationalism of the fifteenth century and *RCL*'s manipulation of the French.

36. Because Jewish immigration into England, from Rouen in the eleventh century, first came in the wake of the Conquest and was encouraged by the new ruler of England, English Jews were also aliens initially associated with the Norman elites who ruled England, and marked by linguistic differences from the local population:

> The majority of Jews were probably trilingual in Latin, Norman-French and Hebrew. The Jews' legal language and the language of contracts was Latin. . . . they also spoke and wrote in French and it is possible that the majority preferred to use it as their everyday language [since letters from Jews written in French survive]. . . . But it was not the Jews' ability to converse and write in both Latin and Norman-French which set them apart from society. As Professor Michael Clanchy has observed: "At all social levels except that of the King's court native French speakers seem to have rapidly and repeatedly assimilated into the local population. The only exception to this rule are the Jews who remained separate because of their different religion and scriptural language and not because of their French origins." The major linguistic difference between Jew and Gentile was the Jews' use of Hebrew. This was widely used and is found in epitaphs and grafitti as well as in transactions made between Jews, and their own signatures. . . . The Edwardian Jew [also] actively perpetuated an intellectual and literary culture that set him apart from Christian society. The Jews' linguistic ability, literature, nomenclature, diet and laws all separated them from Gentile society. (Mundill, 28–29)

37. Some disagreement exists over the accuracy of the sum of £60,000—the Guildford tallage—cited by Gervase of Canterbury (Tyerman, 79), a figure best read perhaps as "no more than a symbol for a very large sum, [though] we may be sure that the tallage was heavy and that it was imposed on the whole of the Jewry" (Richardson, 162). Historians generally agree that, around 1180, Henry II abandoned his practice of borrowing from Jewish financiers in favor of a policy of general and special tallages on English Jewry, which, though levied on the community, must have been disproportionately borne by the wealthier Jews. Subsequent monarchs followed Henry's preference for taxation rather than loans.

38. "In consideration of a cash payment of £1,000 in 1269, the king pledged himself that no further tallage should be imposed [on the Jews] for the next three years, unless he or his son should go on crusade" (Roth, *History*, 64). The fiscal resources of English Jewry were also affected by the crusades in other ways, such as the crusading privilege of waiver of interest on debts borne by crusaders.

39. "The Jew was Crown property. Bracton gave the contemporary view: 'Truly the Jew can have nothing which belongs to himself, because whatever he acquires he acquires not for himself but for the king'" (Mundill, 54–55). On the subject of Jews as the king's chattel, Menache, citing the *Calendar of Close Rolls Preserved in the Public Record Office, 1251–1253*, wryly observes: "The king's treatment of the Jews *tanquam proprium* was clearly manifested by the royal decision of 1253 'that no Jew should remain in England unless he does some service to the king and that, as soon as possible after birth, whether male or female, every Jew should serve us in some way.' Declarations of this sort seemingly corroborate Ramsay's conviction that 'the crown regarded the Jews as domestic animals to be milked and used'" ("Anglo-Jewry," 142).

40. In *RCL*, the romance "Marquis Ferraunt" villainously converts to Islam and treacherously betrays Jerusalem to Saladin. Historically, Conrad, the Marquis of Montferrat, is the victor who *saves* the great coastal city of Tyre *from* Saladin—after the emir's decimation of the combined Latin forces of the Levant at the Horns of Hattin—thus securing a santuary at Tyre for Christian refugees. Conrad's subsequent marriage to Isabella of Jerusalem, moreover, made him the de facto (if uncrowned) king of Latin Jerusalem-in-exile. That the "Marquis Ferraunt" is a *renegade* in *RCL* stems from the fact that the historical Richard's preferred candidate for the kingship of Jerusalem was Guy of Lusignan, whose military ineptitude had resulted in the Latin defeat at Hattin. Conrad, it is true, undertook diplomatic negotiations with Saladin—as did Richard—and Richard and Conrad were both competitively offering Saladin their separate terms for peace when Conrad was mysteriously murdered, a sudden development that one rumor attributed to Richard's agency. In *RCL*, the re-conversion back to Christianity of the renegade at Orgulous is a direct romance contrast to the wealthy financier Benedict of York's historical re-conversion back to Judaism, an event recorded in several medieval chronicles.

41. Some of the prohibitions of 1287—such as the injuction against Jews holding public office, going outdoors in the last days of Holy Week, and the requirement of

the badge—simply repeated conciliar prohibitions of Lateran IV in 1215. However, in 1286 Pope Honorius IV sent a letter to the archbishops of Canterbury and York, expressing deep anxiety over the intermingling of Jews and Christians: in banquets and feasts, in the Jewish use of Christian wet-nurses and servants, Jews giving Christians gifts or inviting Christians into synagogues, Christians reading the Talmud, and so on. The letter, directed at English clergy, led Archbishop Pecham of Canterbury to act at the Council of Exeter in 1287 (Mundill, 272).

42. Christian Europe's cultural and intellectual dependence on Jewish mediations in the Middle Ages is unarguable: "During the later eleventh and early twelfth centuries Jews had been among the intellectual leaders of the 'twelfth-century renaissance,' contributing not only many of the translations of Graeco-Arabic science and philosophy which filtered into the rest of Europe from Spain but also the content of much religious and philosophical thinking of the time" (Boswell, 273). In England, commingling and interdependence between Christians and Jews was at once characterized by intimacy and difference: "What was remarkable about a Jewish *commune* was that it existed within, and yet apart from, an urban *commune*: in the words of a royal letter of 1218, the Jews were accustomed to have *communam inter Christianos* or, as it is elsewhere expressed, *communam cum eis*" (Richardson, 134). In discussing the occasional resistance to treating anti-Semitism as a racial project, Balibar identifies two varieties of racism, an "internal" kind, applicable to Jews, and an "external" kind, applicable to the colonies subject to European rule: The "internal" kind works on "an internal minority which is not merely 'assimilated,' but constitutes an integral part of the culture and economy of the European nations since their beginnings" while external racism functions "to exclude a . . . minority from citizenship and from the dominant culture" (42). We see that medieval Jews thus function *both* like Jews *and* like colonized subjects of European empires under the varieties of racism named by Balibar.

43. "Probably from their arrival, the Jews had their own individual royal charter of rights. H. G. Richardson observed that a charter may have existed in Henry I's reign" (Mundill, 54). The earliest surviving general charter of protections and rights was issued by Richard I at Rouen on March 22, 1190. In 1201 John reconfirmed the charter (Mundilll, 56–57). Historians of Jewish history in England often agree that a turning point for English Jewry occurred after the first years of Henry III's reign, with a "growth of the spirit of intolerance and persecution" hardening in the reigns of Henry III and Edward I (Richardson, 167)—a period in which other scholars such as Turville-Petre also see the rise of English nationalism. In general, historians understand the thirteenth century as the beginning of a period "bent on restraining, contracting, protecting, limiting, and excluding" and that its culture of regimentation and discipline coincides with the rise of "absolute government. . . . and corporatism throughout Europe" (Boswell, 270).

44. In England "Archbishop Pecham . . . carried out a very active campaign for . . . wholesale conversion" (Mundill, 47). The English church's role in urging conversion

also gained momentum when economic advantages accruing to the church were ended by the Provisions of Jewry: "The prevention of land alienation by the Provisions of 1269 . . . put a stop to the Church making gains from Jewish usury. Now that the Church no longer gained materially from Jewish business activities, it was ready to make a more enthusiastic attack on the Jews to demand conversion" (Mundill, 44). As early as 1213 the prior of Bermondsey had opened a school for converted Jews (Mundhill, 49). In its economic restrictions even the *Statutum de Judeismo* of 1275 seemed designed to convert the Jew into an economic subject that resembled a Christian one, albeit one shorn of a Christian's rights and privileges.

45. "In parallel, we learn about the royal decision to sustain converted Jews in religious houses all over the country. In 1247, only fifteen years after the opening of the *Domus,* the *Close Rolls* provide a list of about seventeen *conversi* whom the king had decided to send to fourteen religious houses in various parts of the realm. In 1255, probably a peak year in the history of Anglo-Jewry's conversions, 150 converts were assigned to some 125 religious houses, and there is sufficient evidence of the allocation of places for *conversi* during the remaining years of Henry III's reign" (Menache, "Anglo-Jewry," 145).

46. Modern nationalism, in this respect, functions much like medieval nationalism: "According to [Hans] Kohn, modern nationalism took three concepts from Old Testament mythology: 'the idea of a chosen people, the emphasis on a common stock of memory of the past and of hopes for the future, and finally national messianism.' If the concept of superiority ('chosen people') characterizes the outlook of the European . . . it is the Hebraic underdog, the sense of being an outcast people, that characterizes the other" (Brennan, 59). Menache ("Expulsion") exemplifies a newer emphasis, in scholarship, on the ideological use of the expulsion. (For other scholarship on the expulsion, see, e.g., Abrahams or Mundill.)

47. The first three "discourses that signify a sense of 'nationness'" cited by Homi Bhabha in *Nation and Narration* are, provocatively, "the *heimlich* pleasures of the hearth, the *unheimlich* terror of the space or race of the Other," and "the comfort of social belonging" (2). Balibar, always extraordinary on the subject of race and nationalism, recalls that "the racial-cultural identity of 'true nationals' remains invisible, but it can be inferred (and is ensured) *a contrario* by the . . . visibility of the 'false nationals': the Jews, the 'wogs,' immigrants, Pakis, natives, Blacks" (60). Balibar's formulation of the relationship of race to nation is finely precise: "Racism is not an 'expression' of nationalism, but a *supplement of nationalism* or more precisely a *supplement internal to nationalism,* always in excess of it, but always indispensable to its constitution and yet still always insufficient to achieve its project, just as nationalism is both indispensable and always insufficient to achieve the formation of the *nation* or the project of a 'nationalization' of society" (54).

48. As the multivolume *Image of the Black in Western Art* pertinently observes: "There was probably no time when the image of the black . . . was so insistently, intimately, and essentially present to the Christians of the Occident as it was in the centuries during which they were cut off from Africa" (Devisse, pt. 1, 2:35). Sylvia Tomasch's preference for her coined term—"virtual Jew"—over "notional Jew" and

other descriptions that name the phenomenon of Jewish presence in late-medieval English culture and literature after the expulsion of actual Jews (252) is also useful in suggesting how "absent presence" functions ("Jewish absence is likely the best precondition for virtual presence" [253]).

49. Jewish physicians were invited into England by Edward II in 1309, by Richard Whittington, the mayor of London, in 1409, and by Henry IV in 1410 (Roth, *History*, 132–33).

50. In medieval romance, a range of examples exist of knights and knights, as well as knights and ladies, sharing the same bed (and in the Constance romances that I discuss in chapter 4, two noblewomen, linked by love, share the same bed). In general, heterosocial bed sharing in romance is highly charged and sexualized, usually occurring in a context of seduction (or attempted seduction, as Chrétien's *Lancelot*, for instance, evinces), while homosocial bed sharing is more ambiguous (perhaps deliberately so: Homoeroticism, as I suggested in chapter 1, is a vibrant sub-theme in romance, and a perilous subject). The larger-than-life historical Richard tended to behave like a figure in courtly romance (as his surviving poetry and music attest), and the veiled references by Roger of Howden, as well as the events of Richard's life, suggest at the very least a spectrum of sexual behavior on Richard's part, though the interpretation of that spectrum remains controversial. Gillingham, for instance, is a representative of the scholarly school that vigorously rejects the notion that Richard was any kind of "homosexual." More recently Jaeger has resuscitated the notion of "passionate love" of an ennobling and exalted, nonsexual, kind between medieval men. David Halperin's example, in his discussion of classical Athens, is perhaps still the most useful in considering sexuality in premodern societies. Halperin unexceptionably points the way when he says, "certain kinds of sex *acts* could be individually evaluated and categorized, and so could certain sexual tastes or inclinations, but there was no conceptual apparatus available for identifying a person's fixed and determinate sexual *orientation*, much less for assessing and classifying it" (423). Whether Richard was a *homosexual*—i.e., a member of a more or less stable category of persons—as Gillingham and others would have it, is therefore a distinctly modern way of putting the question. By contrast, medieval penitentials specify penances for *acts*, or sins against nature, committed by individuals, rather than positing groups of persons with essential sexual orientations, identities, or natures.

51. Spencer, in an unattributed reference, cites "a young knight, a crusader, one Raife deClermon, whom [Richard] freed from Saracen captivity" as another of Richard's lovers (111). In the Auchinleck manuscript—the anthology that lodges the earliest surviving fragment of *RCL*—the stories of Richard I and Edward II (another English king to whom rumors of sodomy were notoriously attached) sometimes appear together in a single text, or in quick succession. The *Liber Regum Anglie* in the Auchinleck *both* incorporates material from *RCL and* ends with a brief account of Edward II, while *The Simonie*, a satirical poem positioned after *RCL* in the manuscript, meditates on "the disastrous reign of Edward II" (Finlayson, "Richard," 163), a reign sensationally marked by Edward's scandalous attachment to Piers Gaveston, among other favorites.

52. Mark Jordan's excellent discussion of the etymology and dissemination of the term traces the origin of "sodomia" to Peter Damian, who was able to coin the neologism, Jordan argues, after a long cultural process in which the meaning of the biblical story had been thinned and condensed ("That complicated and disturbing story was simplified until it became the story of the punishment of a single sin, a sin that could be called eponymously the sin of the Sodomites" (29): a process that selected one strain in the biblical story's range of possible meanings over others, and had involved scribal error in tenth-century recopying of Gregory the Great (29–44). Once settled, the association of Sodom and Gomorrah with sodomitical acts was retained through the Middle Ages: "Guy de Roye . . . archbishop of Tours and Reims, in 1388 in *Manipulus curatorum* . . . opined: 'Of the vice of sodomy Augustine declares how detestable it is, saying that the sin is far greater than carnal knowledge of one's own mother, as shown by the punishment inflicted on the Sodomites who perished in fire and brimstone from heaven'" (Johansson and Percy, 174). Sodomy, of course, was not the only form of sexuality considered deviant and pernicious in a religious culture whose early history identified asceticism and chastity as the ideal; indeed, all nonprocreative forms of sexuality—including recreational heterosexual and nonprocreative sexual acts or excessive passion between married heterosexuals—would be considered evils. Documentation indicates, however, that in the wide spectrum of sexual evils, sodomy attracted special attention.

53. The "bulk of the charges [against the Templars] were drawn by Philip's chief advisor Guillaume de Nogaret, and his assistants, from the standard cases of heresy of the last two or three centuries. Some of the details can be traced back to the eleventh century, while the charges made against a group of German heretics in 1233 by Pope Gregory IX are very similar to those against the Templars" (Barber, 124). The link between sodomy and heresy (and, occasionally, sorcery) is implicit even as early as the twelfth century. See, e.g., Guibert of Nogent's *De sua vita* (Benton, *Self and Society*, 212; Bullogh "Heresy," 184, 188–89, 191).

54. As a weapon used by Richard against Saladin, Richard's tree vengefully brings back, in another register, the True Cross that had been lost to Saladin at Hattin. In romance, lost objects tend to be re-found in surprising ways, returning in other guises. The spearhead of steel, in *RCL*, which no armor can resist and that comes from heaven, recalls that other Passion relic, the Holy Lance—found and discredited in the *First* Crusade but resurrected here in another form, to be directed against the *Third* Crusade's most formidable Islamic enemy, Salah ad-Din Yusof. The massive head of the ax that Richard wields should, in fact, have become *smaller* by Richard's day, as the great axes wielded by Anglo-Saxons, Scandinavians, and Normans evolved: "During the twelfth [century] a lighter axe-blade became fashionable . . . the whole head was lighter" (Oakeshott, 257).

55. The Middle English "cuyle" here is obscure, though the *Oxford English Dictionary* glosses "cuyl(l)" or "cule" as "fundament." Turville-Petre translates this line colloquially as, "You'll get it up the arse" (*England*, 123).

56. The joke, and the English-language pun, thus operate a dynamic that Kruger, building on Freud, associates with "the logic of the fetish" (202): a dynamic that simultaneously allows for disavowal and denial of the dangerous (Richard's taint of sodomy), and partial acknowledgment, through a form of daring celebration (thanks to the resourcefulness of the English language and a great English warrior-king). For an exploration of how fetishistic logic operates in medieval texts, see Kruger, "Fetishism, 1927, 1614, 1461."

57. Richard's failure to conquer Jerusalem and restore Christian domination of the Levant—the avowed purpose of the massively costly mobilizations of the Third Crusade—deeply troubles all historical narratives of the period. The footnote to his failure is the English king's capture, en route home, by Leopold of Austria and his subsequent prolonged imprisonment by the German emperor Henry VI, whose extortionate, illegal ransom demands were heavily borne by the English national community en masse. Predictably *RCL* undercuts the humiliation of Richard's capture by making the capture precede, not follow, the adventure of the Crusade; by transforming the king's imprisonment into a glorious, courtly-heroic romance adventure of love, prowess, and grand opportunity; and by telling us that the ransom money was returned. The historical Richard's reputation did not suffer much from the captivity; it was Henry and Leopold who were excommunicated for detaining a returning crusader-king, and modern historians have shown that Richard conducted excellent diplomacy in the strategic politics of Western Europe while Henry's prisoner (see, e.g., Gillingham, *Richard Coeur de Lion*). But the vast disappointment of Richard's failure to retake Jerusalem does resound through chronicle history, and even *RCL*'s attempt at cultural rescue is riven with symptomatic unease, registering its own sense of an anticlimax as the Crusade concludes in a truce with the enemy, and the narrative offers a multiplying series of explanations for Richard's failure, none of which on its own seems either to convince or to suffice. In the century to follow, a telling anecdote that became attached to Richard's legend would express Richard's poignant sense of his own failure, the pathos of which would be endlessly retold (see, e.g., Brundage, Broughton, Norgate, and Gillingham [*Richard Coeur de Lion*]). The romance's failure to find adequate accounting for *RCL*'s failure is paralleled in the chronicles, where efforts are also made, if with less ample and less fabulous narrational resources. See, for example, Richard of Devizes (82), who has Richard admit and lament his failure, while others are blamed for his truce with Saladin. Military insufficiency, of course, is seen as feminizing a warrior, and chapter 1 discussed denigrating accounts of the enemy's military failures: a militarily inferior foe—especially Oriental enemies such as Byzantines and Turks—is gendered as female, while the virility of one's own triumphal forces is hootingly trumpeted.

58. "Cassodorien," the Antiochene romance demon-queen who replaces the historical Eleanor of Aquitaine, is perhaps *RCL*'s way of hinting that the historical Eleanor, with her appetites, machinations, visits to the East, and large role in the lives of two kings of England and a king of France, was also perhaps herself a demon of

sorts. Antioch, Cassodorien's domicile, is where Eleanor putatively had her notorious affair with her uncle, Raymond of Tripoli—so well publicized by the chroniclers—while she was on crusade in the Levant with her husband, Louis of France. The original story of a demon bride—a countess—is associated with a lengendary Angevin ancestor, Fulk Nerra, and recounted by Gerald of Wales (8:301).

59. That Jews in medieval England used Christian wet-nurses, as Christians used Jewish wet-nurses, materializes fascinatingly in documentation, especially when least expected: for example, in the receipts of the sheriff of Kent, Reginald of Cobham, for payments that Jews, who had to pay for the right to employ Christian wet-nurses, made in the years 1251–54 (Mundill, 33–34). On the Kentish mss of *RCL*, see L. H. Loomis, *Mediæval Romance*. "In 1240, Bishop William de Cantilupe of Worcester decreed that no Christian woman should be employed as a wet-nurse by the Jews" (Mundill, 50); yet in "1256, the bishop of Salisbury complained bitterly that the prohibition that stopped Christian women from acting as wet-nurses to Jewish children was not being observed and threatened future transgressions with excommunication" (Mundill, 50). Henry III's edicts of 1253 to the justices of the Jews also expressly forbade Jews to employ Christian wet-nurses (Mundill, 58), and the subject of Christian wet-nurses in Jewish employment is obsessively broached again in Pope Honorius IV's letter to the archbishops of Canterbury and York (Mundill, 272).

60. The field of meaning, for the terms "nation" and "state," in medievalist scholarship, differs to varying degrees from the field of meaning retrieved in postmedievalist cultural and social theory on nations and nation-states. The crusader colonies, for instance, are often called "crusader states" by medievalist scholars—with "state" here perhaps functioning in the Weberian sense as the agency within society possessing the monopoly of legitimate violence—whether or not the panoply of a state apparatus, as understood in our contemporary sense of a centralized totalization of power, supervision, and control, existed in Outremer. For the historian Strayer, "medieval states" existed as "sovereign states" and "law-states," while the Oxford historian R. R. Davies's plenary address at the Medieval Academy annual meeting of 1998, made a difficult "maximum case" for a *nation-state* as existing from as early as the mid-eleventh century in England. Apparatuses of governmentality and ideology in the Middle Ages were, of course, feudal, not modern, and thus less thoroughly pervasive, routinized, and in control than state apparatuses in the modern period, and the modern state, are held to be. Like Davies, Clanchy (*England*, 249) and Harding also refer to "nation-states": "At the end of the [thirteenth] century, the kings of England, France and Scotland faced one another as heads of nation-states, though they still argued in feudal terms when it suited them" (Harding, 322), and Ambrisco cites V. H. Galbraith on the "European nation state" of the fourteenth century (527 n. 43).

Though medieval states and administrative culture are not co-identical with modern states and state culture, if we accept the Foucauldian hypothesis that the two definitive functions of the state are to "see" (through, e.g., an apparatus of counting, location, and identification, such as a population census) and to "police" (through, e.g., a legal system), then signs of the state would include the eleventh-century census of the Domesday project and the consolidation of English law and the law courts. "The most important events in the thirteenth-century making of an English state," Harding notes, "were 'Bracton's' compilation of The Laws and Customs of England and the continuation of the work of the law-book writers in semi-official registers of writs and collections of statutes" [322]). For Kaeuper, "the movement toward the Western form of state which was so evident across the twelfth and thirteenth centuries in France and especially in England . . . was toward public authority vested in a sovereign and exercised theoretically for the common good" (195). John Bowers, discussing Chaucer's administrative activities in the fourteenth century, points out that "tax collecting, accountancy, and financial transactions of the sort Chaucer conducted [on behalf of the crown]" were part and parcel of the "uniform practices" and "centralization" that went into "the process of state-making" (59). The articles in Maddicott and Palliser consider a range of features and types of medieval "states" from the early through the late Middle Ages in Europe. I am deeply indebted to conversations with Penn Szittya on the subject of medieval nations and states.

With "nation," the usage by medievalists is often closer to the meaning of the term as it first arose in medieval culture—to signify the linguistic communities in residence at medieval universities—though here, too, a range of meaning also exists, and there is disagreement on when medieval "nationalism" arose. Halvdan Koht argues for the existence of an early "primitive nationalism" and identifies the twelfth century as the stage for "the first expressions of European nationalism" (266), whereas Kathleen Davis already finds "national writing" in existence in ninth-century Anglo-Saxon England. Beth Bryan finds "figurations of nation" in Laȝamon's post-Norman, thirteenth-century *Brut*, while the articles in Bjørn, Grant, and Stringer's, and Forde, Johnson, and Murray's, excellent anthologies traverse the range of national dispositions and time periods. Speed, Turville-Petre, and Bowers, who emphasize late-medieval England and Middle English texts, perhaps come closest, in their view of history, language, and culture, to a rapprochement with postmedievalist critical and cultural theory. For a representative range of postmedieval theoretical work on nations and nationalisms, see B. Anderson, Renan, Bhabha (*Nation and Narration*), Gellner, J. Armstrong, and Breuilly.

61. "In all the maps Scotland and Wales are included, but are at the same time distinguished with rubrics describing their peoples as different in origin and character" (Turville-Petre, *England*, 2). Clanchy makes the point that "in the thirteenth century . . . England became territorially distinct from Scotland and Wales because they too were developing into nation states" (*England*, 249). "In Matthew's illustrated account [of the struggle with Louis of France], the sea-battle off Sandwich on St. Bartholomew's Day in 1217 becomes a struggle to save England from the invader. 'If these people enter England unopposed,' says the English leader in Matthew's text, 'she will be lost without doubt.' In the accompanying drawing, a bishop surveying the battle says 'I absolve those who are about to die for the liberation of England'" (Turville-Petre, *England*, 3). "Although a variety of people fought on both sides in 1217, Louis' defeat was seen in retrospect as a victory for England over France: 'Thus the Lord

struck his enemies who had come to destroy the English people,' the chronicler Ralph of Coggeshall commented" (Clanchy, *England*, 252). Matthew Paris's maps can be seen as *productive*, as well as *descriptive*. Ben Anderson's *Imagined Communities*, in the second edition, thoughtfully quotes Thongchai Winichakul on the performative character of mapping: "A map was a model for, rather than a model of, what it purported to represent" (173).

62. The "concept of [a] chosen people, taken from the Jewish heritage" or an "'Israel of the spirit' would serve to express the uniqueness and superiority of the English people over other nations" (Menache, "Expulsion," 360). The "proud new Hebrews [were] the English. . . . The Hundred Years' War served as a catalyst for this process. The contrast between the English and their enemies was pointed out to posterity in several examples derived from the concept of 'Israel of the spirit'" (Menache, "Expulsion," 362).

63. Like other crusaders, Fulcher of Chartres in the First Crusade (Phillips, "Sugar," 395) and Oliver of Paderborn in the Fifth Crusade remark on the presence of the "honey cane" and its amazing sweetness. The crusader colonies and Cyprus later began sugar cane plantations; Spain, Crete, and eventually Sicily were also sugar producers. Phillips ("Sugar") reads "the transmission to the West of the techniques of cultivation, production, and refining of sugar" (393) as an example of how *translatio imperii* functioned, as "the West wrested economic ascendancy from the East" (403), a point implicit also in Ashtor (206–8). On the subject of nationalist emblems in *RCL*, Finlayson points out that even Richard's siege engine, the Mategriffin, is "made out of 'embre of Englonde' (1850)" ("Richard," 171). R. S. Loomis observes that the Auchinleck manuscript has an illustration of Richard with a large ax in his hands (folio 326) and identifying insignia on his surcoat (523). If medieval English culture produces symbols of nation, so does French medieval culture (see Beaune).

64. "It is precisely during the thirteenth century that scholars discern the first appearance of nationalism and patriotism in Western Europe, in the law and the propaganda of the period. By the end of the century . . . *patria* denoted specific national entities like England and France. Yet the notion of the *patria* and devotion thereto (patriotism) had always constituted important motifs in the theology of the Church. . . . the emergence of feelings of patriotism on behalf of one's polity also derived from the current tendency to view Christendom as a corporate *corpus mysticum*" (Jeremy Cohen, *Friars*, 254). Bartlett, as already observed, also discusses the church's implicit grasp of, and ability to tap, impulses and momentum that also drive nationalist modalities, symbolizations, and unificatory practices. Menache, as noted above, sees "the Biblical heritage, so deeply rooted in the medieval mentality" as "an important propaganda tool in molding . . . national consciousness," so that eventually, useful biblical *topoi* of community, like an "Israel of the spirit," are secularized by nationalizing discourses ("Expulsion," 374).

65. Brennan, who discusses substantially later historical nationalisms, puts it this way: "The 'national idea' . . . flourished in the soil of foreign conquest. Imperial con-

quest created the conditions for the fall of Europe's universal Christian community, but resupplied Europe with a religious sense of mission and self-identity that becomes *universal*" (59).

66. "It seems to have been understood virtually from the beginning that these poems constituted a distinct corpus: there is substantial intertextuality amongst the various romances, frequently involving the recurrent use of generic conventions, sometimes apparent borrowing from one work to another, and explicit reference" (Speed, 144). The case for a textual community of romances in England performing cultural work specific to the land, and distinguishable from the work of romance on the continent, is first made by Susan Crane, whose important argument on behalf of an "insular" group of Anglo-Norman and Middle English romances critically facilitates the later arguments of Turville-Petre (*England*), Speed, and others on the distinctive commonality of Middle English romances.

67. "The use of English was a precondition of the process of deepening and consolidating the sense of national identity by harnessing the emotive energy of the association between language and nationalism" (Turville-Petre, *England*, 10). Writing of a later period in England than that in which *RCL* first arose, Bowers refines the argument on the English language and nationalist impulses by stressing the ascension of a predominant English dialect, and the role of *London* English in the consolidation of national feeling. "Since commonality is achieved only when the center is able to assert its superiority over the rest of the country, the universality of the Latin language actually worked against this process. Only the ascendancy of a single regional dialect would spell success. . . . vernacular [English] writings such as Chaucer's would become essential for the cultural construction of nationhood as a form of social and textual affiliation" (59).

68. Although *RCL* specifically cites as its audience the "unlearned men" who know no French, "among a hundred scarcely one" ("Lewed men cune Ffrensch non, / Among an hondryd unneþis on" [ll. 23–24]), the romance *Of Arthour and of Merlin* makes the point that "many nobles" know no French either: "Mani noble ich haue yseiȝe / þat no Freynsche couþe seye" (ll. 25–26). The solution is clear: "The net can be spread widest by the use of English" (Salter, 32). Salter (32) quotes the author of "one of the most popular of fourteenth-century religious poems, the *Speculum Vitae*": "Bothe lered and lewed, olde and yonge, / Alle understonden english tonge" ("Both learned and unlearned, old and young, / All understand [the] English tongue").

69. "An argument used in the English parliaments of 1295, 1344, 1346, and 1376 for support in the wars against France was that French victory would annihilate the English language" (Fisher, "Language Policy," 1169). "Langland's constant complaint about foreign Cardinals, and his identification of the Devil as a 'proud prikere of Fraunce' tap sources of resentment already plentiful in the poetry of the first half of the fourteenth century. Not only Mannyng and Minot, but a number of anonymous verse writers express, in crude but pungent English their pride in 'Inglis lede of Ingland'" (Salter, 30).

70. We note, in this anti-Jewish, pro-nationalist text hostile to the French, that the Norman invasion is also the occasion of Jewish migration to England. William I invited Jews from Rouen in the late eleventh century, and English Jews, like the Anglo-French elites with whom they were associated by provenance, might have used French as well as Latin and Hebrew. Some, like Mundill, believe that French was perhaps even the "preferred . . . everyday language" of the Jews of England (28). If "denying and forgetting are . . . the very grounds of cognition and assertion" (Fish, 241), the desire to forget the Norman invasion is thus an overdetermined species of nationalist desire.

71. Barnie quotes Froissart's observation that in the peace negotiations of 1393 the leaders of the English embassy were painfully conscious that "the French which they had learnt at home during their childhood was not of the same nature and condition as that of France" and had to ask for clarification "of any language that was obscure and hard or difficult for them to understand" in the written French of the proposals the English received. Noting that "such eminent princes" as the dukes of Gloucester and Lancaster were the leaders of the English embassy, Barnie extrapolates the likely humiliation among the *haute noblesse* of "speaking an uncouth provincial dialect" (100). Thus the "forgetting" Renan finds essential for the "creation of a nation" (11) notably includes the ironic "forgetting, by the conquerors, of their own language" (10). Salter observes, more delicately, that "from the late thirteenth century onwards . . . while the status of French, as a spoken and written medium, was still very high, some effort was needed to keep it up, even in the households of gentlefolk" (27).

72. "The Auchinleck collection [in which the earliest text of *RCL* appears] is not an unlikely product of these active and ambitious classes: it admits the status of English as a suitable medium for verse to be read by a substantial, and influential, section of Englishmen. It conveys a sense of the utility of English, its wide intelligibility, sharpened by some growing sense of independence of, even hostility to French" (Salter, 31–32). Salter, who observes that "the Auchinleck Manuscript is forward looking" in "its single-minded dedication to English for the poetry of England" (33) goes on to note that "the gradual emergence of a new multi-faceted class of readers, with sufficient power to create their own market for poetry . . . had important consequences for the stabilization of English as the dominant literary vernacular" (34).

73. My discussion of the relationship of the English language to English nationalism in multilingual late-medieval England is necessarily a foreshortened one in a chapter of many moments. For a discussion of the complex linguistic contest, and the implications of multilingualism, in late-medieval English culture, see for example, Fisher, Hussey, Clanchy (*Memory*), Kibbee, Rothwell, Yeager, Bowers, and the chapter "Conditions and Status" in Salter. Salter cautions that "the takeover, by English, as the favoured literary vernacular of the fourteenth century was not a simple, forward-driving process" (29) but observes that, by the late-thirteenth century, "a type of reader" was "beginning to be a force in English literature—as also in English politics: the secular middle-class citizen, urban, literate or partly-literate, aspirant, yet not entirely imitative of the tastes and criteria of his social superiors. The stirring events of the sixties, when the citizens of London backed Simon de Montfort against Henry

III, and helped to secure, in the *Mise of Lewes*, the dismissal of his foreign relatives and dependents, were warnings of this new force operating in a political field. It could not be long before it operated in the field of literature. Not surprisingly, when it did, it showed itself only partly satisfied with [Anglo-Norman] which was a reminder, not only of social hierarchies, but also of some 'foreign' resentments and antipathies" (28). That both the *Cursor Mundi* and *RCL* explicitly represent themselves as addressing audiences who know no French suggests to Thompson that "both the poet of *Richard* and the *Cursor*-poet . . . self-consciously draw attention to the timeliness of their decisions to write French-style narratives in English" and "a range of different writers in the period were aware of the relative merits of writing in English for an English audience"(115). On the "Lancastrian project" of English linguistic nationalism, Ambrisco quotes Lee Patterson's agreement with Fisher ("Language Policy") that the crown made use of English as part of a "state-generated linguistic nationalism" (514).

74. Revealingly the French use "wylde fyre" against their enemies (l. 1902)—that is, "Greek fire," the fabulous incendiary so terrifying to Latin crusaders—a weapon not historically used by Western Europeans and that usually identifies the enemy as Levantine, either Muslim or Byzantine, and thus an association insulting in the extreme. In another association of the French with Saracens, a Saracen dromond bearing "wylde ffyr" (l. 2477) claims to belong to the king of France. At Messina the "Frensshe" and "Gryffons" (French and Greeks) are said to have despised the "nacyons" of the English (ll. 1847–48). Ambrisco's fine article discusses the role of the French in *RCL* at length, in the context of fifteenth-century England.

75. A necessary if not sufficient benchmark of a romance's popularity is, of course, its number of surviving manuscripts. Pearsall, who lists *RCL* as one of the top 8 most popular Middle English romances out of about 95 surviving verse romances (by his count), considers "5 or more" mss an indication of popularity ("English Romance," 58). *RCL, Bevis,* and *Siege* each has 7 mss. Hudson ("Theory"), who counts more than 120 surviving ME romances, also seconds Brewer's observation "that for each remaining copy, there were once at least five more" copies of a medieval text (x). A "popular" medieval audience might include knights, esquires, petty aristocrats, gentry, civil servants and administrators, burgesses, *haute et petite bourgeoisie,* and a wide variety of townspeople and others who might listen to the reading or narration of a romance, as well as a wide range of reading publics. Sir John Paston, for instance, a representative of fifteenth-century gentry, had *RCL* among the books in his library (Gairdner, 3:300, item 869). Recent scholarship, such as Justice's on the peasant rebellion of 1381, has also suggested that literacy in late medieval England was more widespread than formerly supposed. Indeed, only royalty and *haute noblesse* of magnatial rank, whose library holdings seem to indicate a preference for Latin and Anglo-French rather than English texts, have been excluded from considerations of possible reading audiences, though obviously not from audiences for recitation in English, if Chaucer's and Gower's experience offers ground for extrapolation. The two print copies of *RCL,* from 1509 and 1528, were published by Wynkyn de Worde, who "saw the future of

commercial printing" in markets of increasingly "larger and less exclusive" audiences (Pearsall, "English Romance," 83).

76. The Auchinleck manuscript, in which the earliest fragment of *RCL* appears, "tells us that the middle classes were, by 1340, showing a growing preference for poetry in English" (Salter, 36). Pearsall also stresses the relationship between the Auchinleck and the London merchant elite of the 1330s (see Pearsall and Cunningham's facsimile of the Auchinleck, with an introduction). "Middle class demands could guarantee a steady flow of works in the English vernacular—however little they were acknowledged in bequest form. English metrical romances, produced in such numbers from the later thirteenth century onwards, must no doubt be seen in a particular context, catering for a 'class of social aspirants who wish to be entertained with what they consider to be the same fare, but in English, as their betters.' . . . The solid mass of romance translations, made between 1275 and 1340, and the almost equally solid mass of religious translations . . . must have a close connection with the solid achievements of the urban middle classes over those years" (Salter, 41–42).

77. The new social realities thus ensured that denotational language originating from commercial craft spread its umbra, so that "mystery" expanded its range of meaning to capture the more general sense of *any* occupation. By the time of the Statute of Additions of 1413, it was specified that "in all indictments and writs . . . 'additions' should be included, identifying the 'estate or degree, or mystery' of the person indicted" (Keen, "Esquires," 96).

78. Where Shonk, Pearsall, L. H. Loomis, Richmond, Salter, and others stress the role of mercantile and urban interests in their reconstructions of readership, Coss suggests that Middle English romances drew an audience from among rural gentry, while Meale ("Audiences") also considers women as readers of Middle English romances. Meale, who warns that the audiences of romance ultimately "resist generalisation and easy classification, just as the genre itself does" ("Audiences," 225), argues for the widest possible audience and audience interests:

> That merchants should have collected and read romances does not imply a simple form of literary and social aspiration, whereby they wished to emulate the tastes of those in a different position within the social hierarchy. Rather, it suggests that those facets of English romances which literary critics have singled out as distinguishing them from works in French—elements of didacticism, a reduction in the attention paid to the refinements of "courtliness," and an interest in history, whether authenticated or not— attracted an increasingly broad selection of readers. . . . This is not to say, of course, that members of the gentry, who might be assumed to have a more intimate connection with the values upheld by a martial élite, did not form an important constituency for romance. ("Audiences," 220)

79. In a complaint in Chancery about clerical schoolmasters, one schoolmaster was accused of offending "a draper's apprentice by sending him into the kitchen 'to

washe pottes pannes disshes and to dighte mete'" (Thrupp, 159). Leveling fantasies across social class can be detected in more than one Middle English romance: The Middle English *Sir Degarré*, for instance, would have it that anyone, including burgess or churl ("Be he burgeis, be he cherl" [l. 483]), might succeed in winning a king's daughter for his bride. The most prominent example, however, besides *RCL*, is perhaps *Havelok*: a romance in which a king is also depicted as cheerfully undertaking menial labor alongside the common subjects of the realm (and is even raised in servile conditions in early life). Like *RCL*, *Havelok* is a romance also characterized by a certain robust humor, an implied address to the widest possible audience, and a common linguistic audience-community of Anglophones. In *Havelok*, "interranks of society play a central part in the action through the career and the person of Havelok himself, as he moves through the social hierarchy from poverty to power, from 'cherles sone' . . . to king, carrying fish, swilling dishes, and inheriting two thrones. The poem ends with a vision of harmony throughout society, as people not only of different ranks but also of different ethnic origins witness the coronation in London" (Turville-Petre, "Havelok," 134). Delany suggests that Havelok's occupational progression "from lowest to highest social class" is specifically designed to display the attitude most appropriate to each occupational class, and thus teaches appropriate class conduct—"whether cheerful acquiescence or valiant self-defense"—even as it supports the fantasy that "Havelok's experience of all classes will enlarge his political sympathies when he is king, and teach him the needs of his entire population" (*Medieval Literary Politics*, 70). If Delany is correct in suspecting that *Havelok* is ultimately a romance which subserves the interests of those exercising hierarchical power—by specifying appropriate behavior for the rank and file—we note that throughout Havelok's occupational sojourns we are not allowed to forget that he is of royal blood, even as the romance plays with the *bel inconnu* tradition of chivalric romance. Delany warns, moreover, that although "Havelok is presented as an ideal worker . . . we must acknowledge that he is an ideal worker only from the point of view of an employer. He is extremely competitive with other workers, works for nothing [but his keep], gladly works to the point of exhaustion, and never complains but always smiles. None of this behaviour could be considered either realistic or admirable by an audience of ordinary workers, though it would suit the taste of their urban employers or manorial supervisors" (*Medieval Literary Politics*, 69).

80. Bowers, writing of Chaucer's contribution to medieval England's experiment of nation making, has the last word:

> Unlike some modern nationalisms, the nationalist movement in late medieval England was an 'inside job' undertaken by members of the ruling elite itself, Chaucer included. The goal was the extension of a sense of collective belonging from the *polis* to the *patria*, from the face-to-face society of the city to the abstract community of the nation. The key to such ambition was commonality: a common territory, a common language, a common culture, a common religion, and a common history. (57)

As for the genre of romance: the "history of romance," as Meale points out, "is one of participation in cultural change and upheaval" ("Audiences," 225).

3. Warring against Modernity: Masculinity and Chivalry in Crisis; or, The Alliterative *Morte Arthure*'s Romance Anatomy of the Crusades

1. Like its elite counterpart thematizing other aspects of chivalric ideology, *Sir Gawain and the Green Knight*, the *Morte* survives in only one manuscript, Lincoln Cathedral Library MS. 91, also known as the "Thornton MS," after its scribe, Robert Thornton, lord of East Newton in the North Riding of Yorkshire, a gentleman amateur copyist whose name appears at the end of the poem (on the life and milieu of the scribe, see Keiser, "Lincoln"). I use Mary Hamel's very fine, relatively recent edition (henceforth *Morte*), and consult Krishna's. The Thornton manuscript is dated to "about 1440" (Patterson, "Historiography," 12; *Negotiating the Past*, 211), and, "given the watermark dating of the MS of 1420–1450, one may infer that the MS was transcribed earlier in this period rather than later, i.e., in the 1430's if not the 1420's" (Hamel, *Morte*, 3). The core text of the *Morte* is dated to the late fourteenth or very early fifteenth century, "though the poem may have been *begun* much earlier" (Hamel, *Morte*, 56). My reading in this chapter understands the core text to have arisen after the failure of the Nicopolis Crusade in 1396, as my argument below will make plain.

2. Calling the *Morte* a "linguistic omnivore" (Hamel, *Morte*, 30), Hamel marvels at its "extraordinary lexical resources" (31), including "words of great rarity, some of them in fact unique in English," a "large number of French loanwords," borrowings from Old Norse, words "otherwise recorded only in Scots texts," as well as "precise technical language in a number of fields": "two nautical scenes," "heraldry," "law, diplomacy, and bureaucracy," and "exotic cookery . . . well-attested in contemporary recipe-books and feast-menus" (30). On law and diplomacy in the *Morte*, in particular, see Vale. To the subjects of "dress, diplomacy, language, geography, and chronology," Patterson adds the *Morte*'s fidelity to "both map and calendar" ("Historiography," 13; *Negotiating the Past*, 212). We are forced to conclude that, among romances of any kind, the *Morte* is the nonpareil in exemplifying the axiom that romance is a cannibalistic genre.

3. A divide separates scholars who argue that the *Morte* is an antiwar tract from scholars who argue the reverse. Matthews perhaps best represents the view that the *Morte* sediments an exhaustion with warfare in medieval England of the later fourteenth century (a disenchantment and resistance toward war arising from English reverses in the Anglo-French Hundred Years War, overtaxation, and opposition to the king's principal advisers. See Göller's "Summary of Research" and anthology, for the differences of view. On the relationship between the Anglo-French War and the *Morte*, and the *Morte*'s relation to contemporary history, monarchs, politics, and geography, see, especially, Patterson; Finlayson, "Date"; L. D. Benson; and Keiser, "Edward III." The *Morte*'s engagement with English strategies and politics in the Hundred Years War during the time of Edward III, and/or its commentary on the

usurpation of the throne of Richard II by Henry IV, has been debated by these critics, who read the *Morte*, very reasonably, as an allegory of history.

4. Göller, remarking on the *Morte*'s "pathos, humour and realism" ("Summary," 7), hardly exaggerates when he avers that "the *AMA* has been classified by literary critics as a romance, an epic, and a *chanson de geste*, as well as a tragedy, an exemplum of the virtue of fortitude, and a *Fürstenspiegel*" as well as "an anti-romance" ("Reality," 15). One might add, given the *Morte*'s ostensible framing structure, that it is also an oddly foreshortened form of imitation chronicle, peculiarly memorable for its "very twisted . . . bawdy . . . grotesqueness" (Göller, "A Reassessment," 22). Patterson ("Historiography," 13–14; *Negotiating the Past*, 213), who reiterates that "critics have considered the poem an anti-romance, an epic, and a pseudo-chronicle," also notes the *Morte*'s encouragement of attention to its generic promiscuity: "It recognizes that there are two streams of Arthurian writing, 'romaunce' (3200, 3440) and 'cronycle' (3218, 3445), but locates itself at the source of both by designating them as later developments and calling itself a history: 'herkenes now hedyrwarde and herys this storye'" ("Historiography," 25).

5. The wittily memorable phrase, "cannibalism as command performance" is Sam Otter's (16). For an absorbing study of giants in medieval literature, including Geoffrey's and the *Morte*'s cannibalistic giants, see J. J. Cohen, *Of Giants*.

6. Critics have wondered at the *Morte*'s extensive use of the metaphor of pilgrimage but have appreciated the romance's mordant wit in suggesting that a visit to a cannibalistic monstrosity is best couched in figures of pilgrimage, when the monster resides at St. Michael's Mount, a traditional pilgrimage site. Arthur calls the cannibal a "saint" (l. 937), to whom Bedivere should make an offering (l. 939); Bedivere also refers to the cannibal as a "saint" and mentions his "holy bones" and relics enclosed in silver (ll. 1163–65, 1168–69). References to signing oneself with the sign of the cross, as if at a shrine, occur (ll. 966, 969), and Arthur also specially signs himself before the giant fight (1042). The memory of a different kind of pilgrimage—the crusade as pilgrimage—effloresces, however, with the mention of martyrdom and the making of martyrs (ll. 1066, 1221); and the fact that the giant has killed *Christians* receives special play (l. 1187). See chapter 1 for a discussion of themes of martyrdom and pilgrimage in crusade history.

7. Hamel's finely conceived suspicion that "jerodyn," in Arthur's "jupon of jerodyn," might be a place-name is right on the mark: "[the jupon's] material ("jerodyn") has not been identified, though it may be a corrupted place-name to correspond to Acre and Basel" (*Morte*, 288 nn. 900–913). Before Hamel, Krishna, who capitalizes "Ierodyn," also suspects, in her edition of the *Morte*, that "Jerodyn" is a place-name: "*Ierodyn*. Unknown. Very likely a place; see *Acres*, line 103"(177 n. 905). Of course, "Jerodyn" can signify *both* a place (Jordan) *and* a kind of fabric, like muslin from Mosul, another city in the Levant that gives its name to a prime export ("shallots"—small red onions from Ascalon—are an example of an agricultural export that takes its name from its provenance). I thank Laura Hodges for the timely reminder that cloth, in particular, often assumes the name of its provenance (e.g., cambric from Chambrai, "veil of Valence" from Valencia, double-worsted from Worsted, etc.).

8. Contamine's survey of scale armor (187–88) also finds it linked to Turks (187 n. 32). Hamel (*Morte*, 288 nn. 906–11) contemplates a known historical equivalent of European scale armor in the dress armor of Ferdinand I of Portugal (d.1383). The 1423 Bedford Book of Hours also depicts the Merovingian Clovis receiving the fleur-de-lis blazon while armed in overlapping steel plates, a newly fashionable fifteenth-century style of armor (British Museum Add. Ms. 18850.f.288b, quoted by Marina Warner, *Joan of Arc*, 168). Arthur's carefully elaborated, beautiful armor also has other odd features—his bacinet and aventail are strange in "having both crest and coronal . . . being decorated with heraldic figures . . . having a visor that opens in an unusual way" (Hamel, *Morte*, 288 nn. 906–11). The purpose of the bacinet and aventail is to suggest ornamental, dress armor evocative of ceremonial occasions rather than battle gear suited to a rough-and-tumble struggle with a brutal antagonist, and to suitably materialize the male military body in a ritualized, sumptuously memorable fashion. The inutility of Arthur's armor quickly becomes apparent in the giant-fight, when Arthur's "creest and coronall"—offering superb biting surfaces in battle—are the first casualty in the opening moments of the giant-fight (l. 1108–9). *Sir Gawain and the Green Knight*, a late-medieval chivalric companion to the *Morte*, also has an elaborate arming episode. My discussion of why chivalric romance investigates knighthood through the bodies of knights (see, below, the section "The Unmaking and Making of Men") discusses armor's simulation of a masculine military body in its carapace.

9. If the medieval-colonial *RCL*'s culinary experiment of Saracen's head stewed in broth precedes, by some centuries, the later-colonial British interest in "curry," I have been provocatively reminded that the description of the cannibal giant's cuisinary arts in the preparation of boys, in the *Morte*, might well be the ancestral forebear of Jonathan Swift's dishes in the "Modest Proposal." I quote from Jim Garrison: "The 'economic sign-system of cannibalism [in "Warring against Modernity"] reminded me in some of its details of Swift's Modest Proposal, especially the 'artful preparation and consumption' (cf. Swift's 'whether stewed, roasted, baked, or boiled, and I make no doubt that it will equally serve in a fricasee or a ragout')" (personal communication, August 16,1999). Postmedieval literary cannibalisms, of course, constitute vivid examples of cultural repetitions-with-difference over time. For the precise pleasures of stories about eating children, see Marina Warner's "Fee fie fo fum" in Barker, Hulme, and Iversen's useful volume, *Cannibalism and the Colonial World*. Bartolovich's study, in the same volume, suggests that "cannibals have been, and are, obliged to be a site of negotiation of specifically capitalist crises in appetite even prior to the dominance of the capitalist mode of production" (211).

10. "He grennede as a grewhounde with grysly tuskes; . . . And owte of his face, fome ane halfe fote large; / His frount and his forheude all was it ouer / As the fell of a froske, and fraknede it semede; / Huke-nebbyde as a hawke, . . . Harske as a hunde-fisch, . . . So was þe hyde of þat hulke hally all ouer. . . . Flatt-mowthede as a fluke, . . . And the flesche in his fortethe fowly as a bere. . . . Crassede as a mereswyne . . . Ilke wrethe as a wolfe-heude, . . . Bulle-nekkyde was þat bierne, . . . Brok-brestede as a brawne, with brustils full large; . . . Lym and leskes full lothyn,

. . . Schouell-fotede was þat schalke, . . . Thykke theese as a thursse, . . . Greesse-growen as a galte, full grylych he lukez" (He grinned like a greyhound with grisly tusks; . . . And out of his face came foam a half foot long; / It was all over his front and his forehead / Like the skin of a frog, and spotted it seemed; / Hook-nosed as a hawk, . . . harsh as a dogfish, . . . Thus was the hide of that hulk wholly all over. . . . Flat-mouthed as a flounder, . . . And the flesh around his front teeth horrible as a bear . . . Fattened as a sea-pig . . . Each fold like a wolf-head, . . . Bull-necked was that creature . . . Badger-breasted as a wild boar, with bristles full large; . . . Limb and flanks full hairy, . . . Shovel-footed was that creature, . . . Thick thighs as a demon, . . . Growen over with grease like a boar, full grisly he looks" [ll. 1075–1101]).

11. To keep the memory of that first rape fresh in our minds, lines 1030–32 offer the information that the three women who turn the roasting spits are also raped and that, indeed, the giant's sexual appetite is as enormous as his other kind of appetite, so that another "such four should be dead within four hours" (1031) before he is sated. The *Morte*'s sexual voyeurism testifies to its fascination with all kinds of interiors—including the "inner life," the private, and the secret—some late-medieval manifestations of which have been recently theorized by Spearing. The *Morte*'s urgent absorption with the somatic body, moreover, implies that continuity might exist between forms of disclosure, suggesting that the secrets of bodies, once disclosed, might lay bare other secrets in the body's "inner life." On the scopic regime in medieval texts, see Stanbury.

12. "I faght noghtenwyth syche a freke þis fyftene wyntyre, / Bot in þe montez of Araby I mett syche anoþþer— / He was þe forcyere by ferre. Þat had I nere funden, / Ne had my fortune bene faire; fey had I leuede!" (I have not fought with such a creature these fifteen winters, / But in the mountains of Arabia I met such another— / He was the more powerful by far [of these two comparable giants]. That I had never found, / Had not my fortune been fair; I had been left dead" [ll. 1174–77]).

13. To facilitate Arthur's displacement of, and substitution for, the giant, the *Morte* has the Roman senator-emissary to the Arthurian court say, before the giant-killing, that Arthur is not interested in money, a lack of interest ostensibly meant to link Arthur to the wealthy giant capitalist (ll. 538–39), though it is palpably not true, as Arthur's repeated interest in feudal rent attests (e.g., in lines 2405, 3215, 3526, 3571, 3587).

14. Historically, in the fourteenth century, knighthood was "a social distinction shared by kings, princes and earls . . . In every shire there were [also] established knightly families . . . The wealthiest . . . enjoyed a standing and estates which hardly distinguished them from the less wealthy barons. Correspondingly, [their] social and economic position . . . had become sharply differentiated from that of the poorer knights who, if they had been obliged to dispose of land, might often have a level of prosperity not greatly above that of a well-to-do freeman-peasant. It was usually from the better-off knightly families that men were chosen for the administrative, jury, tax-assessing and tax-collecting functions. In addition, there were the king's household knights . . . who were rewarded with land for service at court. . . . knighthood generally had come to be the mark of a kind of minor aristocracy, much occupied with administration . . .

'knights of the shire' . . . assisted the standing of the House of Commons within Parliament. . . . [though] paradoxically [some of] the 'knights' at Parliament . . . were of comparatively modest estate; others were not in fact knights at all" (Butt, 253).

15. In the Arthurian legend's evolution, it is La3amon, in the thirteenth century, who begins the replacement of "Britain" with "England" and facilitates the transfer of the legend's use for contemporary English interests. La3amon alters the myth of Arthur's return, so that the once British or Celtic Arthur is prophesied to return to the people3e of *England*, not of Britain (*Brut*, ll. 14295–97): "Bute while wes an wite3e Mælin ihate; / he bodede mid worde—his qui0es weoren so0e— / Þat an Ar0oour sculde 3ete cum Anglen to fulste" (But once there was a wise man called Merlin; / he predicted with words—his sayings were true— / That an Arthur should yet come to help the English).

16. The use of the term "knight," in the *Morte*, to describe elites ranging from great magnates and crown tenants-in-chief to newly dubbed men of deserving status derives from the term's historical capacity to stretch as a social category. Historians emphasize that "there was no sharp social dividing line between peers [i.e., lords, barons, earls, greater aristocracy] and the knights whose representative role was the foundation of the House of Commons and who were the origin of that class later known as the gentry" (Butt, 252), a class from whom the author and audience of the *Morte* are sometimes thought to derive. As a formal category, the term "gentleman" is attested from 1384, "when Richard II granted to one of his servants a pension of 7l/2d. [7.5 pence] a day 'to enable him to support the estate of a gentleman to which the king has advanced him,' though not until the early fifteenth century does the term seem to have come into widespread usage" (Given-Wilson, 70). The *Morte* also often uses "commons," a term no doubt borrowed from Parliament, to denote, presumably, common people who are freemen, burgesses, yeomen, *valetti* (though not "churls," a term of abuse in the *Morte*, and not clergy, who are, like "churls," differentiated by this text).

17. "The banneret was a battlefield commander who would normally bring with him a larger retinue than a knight, was entitled to the use of a square banner rather than the triangular pennon of the knight, and received wages while on campaign of 4s. [4 shillings] a day rather than the knight's 2s [2 shillings]. In royal wardrobe account books of the early fourteenth century, for example, there are separate lists of *baneretti* of the household, and *milites simplici* of the household" (Given-Wilson, 189 n. 15). "Bannerets were leaders of squadrons and paid at twice the rate of knights; their arms are represented on banners rather than the normal shields" (Harding, 183).

18. "The knightly families [by 1300] were the ones that remained when the growing cost of being dubbed a knight, the expense of providing for an excess of daughters and younger sons, and probably most of all failure to meet the challenge of 'the managerial revolution' which began late in the twelfth century, had weeded out the rest. . . . Enough examples of declining families have been given to suggest a 'crisis of the knightly class' in the thirteenth century" (Harding, 196). "Many knights had very small estates and merged into the ranks of the peasant farmers" (Harding, 199).

19. "Both Henry III and Edward I had issued writs for the distraint of knighthood, requiring any man . . . who held land in knight's fee worth at least the traditional £20 to be knighted and to provide the due service or money. . . . Edward I had instituted a further change by relating the obligation to become a knight to the value of land held rather than to the notion of the knight's fee. The property qualification for obligation to knighthood varied from time to time, but it had settled at £40 annually. These remedies, however, had not produced a sufficiency of knights" (Butt, 253).

20. Maurice Keen ("Esquires"), studying legislation from the fourteenth and fifteenth centuries, shows how the legislative record "appears to confirm that esquires . . . were considered as belonging with knights and other persons of superior grade to that upper tranche of society that could be distinguished as *gentilz*" (96). The ascent of squires up the social hierarchy of the *gentilz* is striking, as seen in their right to possess and display arms: "In the second Dunstable Roll of 1334, as in the Parliamentary Roll of Arms, esquires are notable by their absence. The rolls of the later fourteenth century, however, like Sir George Calveley's book, the County Roll, and the Norfolk and Suffolk Roll, do blazon the arms of substantial numbers of men who were not knights. Sir Robert Laton's Roll (c. 1370, now lost), which according to his testimony in the *Scrope v. Grosvenor* dispute he wrote down at his father's dictation, blazoned the arms of all the 'kings, princes, dukes, earls, lords, knights and esquires' that his father could remember"(99). Departing from Coss, who stresses the significance of lesser landowners of non-knightly rank in local administration and office holding, Keen suggests that the "heraldic 'rise' of the esquires, their recognition specifically as armigerous, would . . . seem to have been connected . . . with the very significant part that men of their status had come to play in the great campaigns of the fourteenth century. In indentures of the mid-fourteenth century the words 'esquire' and 'man at arms' are used more or less interchangeably, denoting the mounted troops superior in military status to the archers, and as Andrew Ayton has recently shown, very large numbers of such men served in some of the greater hosts of the mid-century. There were perhaps as many as 4,000 men at arms at the siege of Calais (1346–7), and over 3,000 in the host that Edward III led to France in 1359" (99). This expansion of the ranks "to embrace a wider range of people," Keen suggests, created something like a *petite noblesse*: "The fourteenth-century esquires, for the most part, came of landowning families, as did the knights; they served and fought alongside knights in campaign retinues; locally and regionally, they played their part in administration as stewards, keepers of the peace and jurors, as knights did, though most often in somewhat humbler capacities" (100). Noting that the "extension of the range and the greater refinement of the degrees of those capable of being armigerous reflects heraldically a growing preoccupation with gradation which was a striking feature of English social history in the later Middle Ages" (95), Keen points out that by the end of the Middle Ages, "'mere' gentlemen . . . too were recognised as armigerous" (101).

21. Squires acting as knights were also found in Parliament: "Edward II had been obliged to receive esquires as the representatives from several counties, and in 1325 only twenty-seven of the knights in Parliament had been belted. In the first years of

Edward III, several attempts had therefore been made to ensure the return of 'belted' knights, but in 1350 the writ for Parliament in the following year recognized that ordinary country gentlemen would have to do instead. . . . Even so, efforts were continued to ensure that only real knights were sent to Parliament in order to keep up the standing and quality of the Commons" (Butt, 254).

22. If the Syrian king's inquiry issues from the third through fourth quarters of the fourteenth century, when bannerets (knights whose rank was military, often accruing from campaigns in which the knights had distinguished themselves, rather than attached to significant estates) were yet being distinguished from peerage and barony, then the query also performs the secondary function of distinguishing bannerets from nobles. However, "gradually the distinction between barons and bannerets evaporated. By about 1425, they were all just 'peers'" (Given-Wilson, 62).

23. Edward III created the first dukedom in England, that of Cornwall, for the Black Prince in 1337, later adding Lancaster (in 1351 and 1362), and Clarence (1362). Richard II made the first marquis—the marquis of Dublin—ranking higher than an earl but lower than a duke, in 1385 (Given-Wilson, 45, 48). Edward III, of course, also made his heir the first Prince of Wales.

24. The importance of administration as an avenue of advancement had, of course, been growing from at least the twelfth century, though twelfth-century administrators and officers tended to issue from the clerical class. The expansion of lay literacy, by the late Middle Ages, however, means that administrative, shire, and household officials in the *Morte*'s time often came from the social stratum that also supplied the ranks of knights and squires, many of whom performed military *and* administrative service for the lords or monarch they served: "The 3,000 or so knights and esquires . . . were not just soldiers, they were also . . . serving both king and baronage in a variety of offices . . . within the spheres of their administration . . . they had come to be regularly involved in the judicial and financial administration of their shires . . . serving as jurors, tax assessors, military arrayers, escheators, coroners and sheriffs. For the magnates, they served as stewards and councillors. . . . As Mr. Denholm-Young once remarked, 'if every baron was a politician, it may be added that most knights were administrators'" (Given-Wilson, 16–17).

25. Edward III also made Sir William "Chief Baron of the Exchequer" (Bourne, 43). Sir William's "eldest son, Michael, contemporary with Chaucer . . . became an especial favourite with Richard the Second," while the fourth earl of Suffolk in the line, also named William, was made the first duke of Suffolk: "the direct line of succession from Sir William de la Pole, merchant of Hull" did not end till the sixteenth century, when the only child of the last male heir, a daughter, became a nun (Bourne, 47). "The increase in the number of citizen knights . . . was symptomatic of the city's [i.e., London's] growing wealth. From the days of Sir Richard de la Pole [brother of Sir William] and Sir John Pulteney to those of Sir Thomas Seymour, Sir Richard Gresham, and Sir Thomas Kitson, London fortunes provided more and more recruits for the landed nobility. A formidable list could be quoted" (McFarlane, *Nobility*, 14).

26. These are not bannerets but "the children of the king's chamber" (l. 1821), either fosterlings-at-court or *milites camere regis*, a late-fourteenth century designation, attested in the 1360s and after, and associated mostly with the courts of John of Gaunt and Richard II for household knights. It is this that Gawain claims to be in the Priamus episode (see "The Unmaking and Making of Men," below). Interestingly, many great nobles were also newly created and thus were "new men" in the fourteenth century, since the lack of male heirs thinned the ranks of baronial dynasties through extinctions: "Of the thirteen English earls and dukes in 1362, only three (Arundel, Warwick and Oxford) were primogenitary descendants of men who had held the same titles in Edward II's reign. The rest were new men" (Given-Wilson, 45).

27. Historians generally follow McFarlane's dictum that "there can be no question that the ranks of the nobility were thinnner at the top in 1400 than a century earlier" (*Nobility*, 15). Political power soon accrued to those with ability and economic means, as David Wallace reminds us: "Merchants came remarkably close to the center of political power in the last years of Edward III and the first years of Richard II. London merchants such as John Pecche, fishmonger, Adam de Bury, skinner, and Richard Lyons were frequently to be seen in and around the court circle of the elderly Edward III" (187). In the contest for definition and power, however, "the merchants could not think of themselves as lords for long without being challenged by the established 'seigneurs,' the magnates who saw the military and political guidance of the realm as their own rightful business. John of Gaunt was evidently not thrilled to learn that Philpot's fleet was covering itself with glory while his own military expedition to Brittany was making little headway" (Wallace, 188).

28. If indeed the Scrope versus Grosvenor trial of 1386 *is* being alluded to in Clegis's remarks, then Clegis's contemptuous calling of the Saracen "earl" a "cowntere" and "auditor" is specially pointed, since the father of Richard le Scope, the plaintiff in the trial of 1386, had been "chief baron of the Exchequer from 1330 to 1336" (Keen, "Chaucer's Knight," 51)—that is, the Scropes of Bolton, represented by Sir Henry, father of Richard, are indeed descended from an auditor and counter par excellence. While Chaucer testified on behalf of the Scropes (Keen, "Chaucer's Knight," 50), we might say that Clegis's sentiments, in the *Morte*, are ranged on the side of Grosvenor.

29. "Bastard feudalism," according to McFarlane, was a term coined in 1885 by Charles Plummer ("Bastard Feudalism," 23). McFarlane develops the concept, positing the late thirteenth century as the earliest emergence of the phenomenon; later economic historians have pushed the *terminus a quo* back ever earlier (Hicks to as far back as 1140). McFarlane sees Edward I as the first monarch to extend the practices of bastard feudalism "systematically to his English troops" ("Bastard Feudalism," 24), with Edward's barons initiating subcontracts with their own contingents ("The oldest known example of such a sub-contract in writing, one between Edmund Mortimer and Peter Maulay, was sealed at Wigmore in the summer of 1287; and a very few more have survived from the last years of the thirteenth century" [25]). In the "written or oral contract . . . secured by salary in the form of cash annuity" emphasis fell on "the voluntary

and contractual nature of the new association [and] worked against the exclusivity of the vertical ties that bound a person in service to his lord" (Strohm, *Social Chaucer*, 14).

30. Among the best known surviving indenture records have been John of Gaunt's. A prime example is the contract "drawn up at the Savoy palace on 10 November 1369 between John of Gaunt, duke of Lancaster, and Sir John Neville, lord of Raby. The latter agreed to serve the duke 'before all others in the world' except the king wherever it pleased the duke, in peace and in wartime, except for express royal prohibition. In return he was to receive for life 50 marks a year on the revenues of two manors in the county of Richmond. He would have *bouche en court* whenever he visited his lord. . . . In wartime John de Neville was to serve with 20 men-at-arms (including five knights) and 20 mounted archers. In exchange he would receive annually for his fee 500 marks and the usual wages. . . . For war in Scotland he would furnish up to 50 men-at-arms and 50 archers" (Contamine, 151).

31. "Alongside contracts drawn up between the leader of an expedition and his captains, sub-contracts allowed the captains to recruit their own contingents. In 1381 Sir Thomas Felton agreed to serve in Brittany for six months with 500 men-at-arms and the same number of archers. Fifteen sub-contracts in which he figures have also been preserved, assuring him of the service of 178 men-at-arms and 181 archers" (Contamine, 152).

32. Strohm, citing Nigel Saul's "remarkable finding that in the fourteenth century between half and two-thirds of Gloucestershire gentry were retained by local magnates" (*Social Chaucer*, 18), lucidly specifies the social implications of retaining:

> Granting that retaining by indenture sought in some ways to perpetuate older values (such as continuity of service to a single lord), the fact remains that it represents a new system of social organization. As a contract rather than a sworn oath, the indenture permits a degree of voluntarism not possible . . . within the system of vassalage. . . . the agreement to serve and to compensate service is made subsequent to a rational calculation of each party that his profit will be served. No sanctified agreement or earthly replication of the heavenly hierarchy, the indenture is entered into as a transaction between two persons, each seeking to advance his own interests. (17–18)

33. "Militarily, the feudal levy was being eclipsed by a profession of 'soldiers,' so-called from the wages they received; for a *miles solidarius* these rose from 8d. [8 pence] a day in 1162 to 2s. [2 shillings] in John's reign; for a mounted sergeant they then stood at 4d. or 6d., for an infantryman at 2d. or 3d. Politically, raising an army became largely a wrangle about how wages were to be paid" (Harding, 188).

34. The *Morte*'s emphasis on "rents" also points to the expansion of an agriculture-based monetary economy through lease-farming, a system to which landlords reverted in periods when the price of crops fell and/or the cost of labor rose, and demesne-farming, a system in which landlords farmed their own lands with the help of work-service from tenants, which proved less profitable than the leasing out of those lands. "Rents" from lease-farming guaranteed a regular income, and cash flow, in periods of uncertainty or instability, and testify to the presence and operations of an

agricultural monetary economy that is acceptable to the *Morte*, in contrast to the cash relations undermining military feudalism.

35. "A landmark in the history of archery was reached in Henry III's Assize of Arms of 1251. After ordering that the richer yeomanry who own a hundred shillings in land should come to the host with steel cap, gambeson, lance and sword, that document commands that 'all who own more than forty or less than 100 shillings in land come bearing a sword and a bow with arrows and a dagger." There is a special clause at the end of the paragraph providing that even poor men with less than forty shillings in land and nine marks in chattels should bring bow and arrows if they have them (Oakeshott, 294–95). In the fourteenth century, demands and restrictions involving archery intensify:

> The *London Calendar Book* for 1337 to 1352, covering the period of the Battle of Crécy, asks for 500 archers from London. Nor were commanders necessarily satisfied with mere numbers. There were complaints about the physique of men provided. There were also fears that the French would emulate the English achievement with archery, and in an attempt to prevent this development, proclamations in 1357 and 1369 forbade the export of bows and arrows, and in 1365 archers were forbidden to leave England without royal licence. In 1341, before any major land battle had been fought in the Hundred Years' War, Edward III ordered the collection of 7,700 bows and 130,000 sheaves of arrows. The Tower of London was the major storage centre. The country was scoured for these weapons. In 1356, the year of Poitiers, it was claimed that no arrows could be found in all England, since the king had taken them all. (Bradbury, 94).

36. Recognition of the importance of the longbow continues in the following century: in 1456, football and golf were proscribed as sports, in favor of archery, to ensure the maintenance of skill in the longbow (DeVries, 39). Because of the expense involved, it was merchants in particular, who "took a lead in local efforts to cultivate skill in use of the longbow" (Thrupp, 168). On the comparative use of the longbow and the crossbow, see Bradbury. The vulnerability of horses meant that English horsed archers from the mid-fourteenth century onward rode to battle, but dismounted for combat, an option not available to mounted knights: "The mounted archers of the Hundred Years' War almost certainly dismounted to shoot their bows on foot, but their horses gave them valuable mobility on campaign. At the siege of Calais Edward III had 20,076 archers, and 4,025 of them were mounted" (Bradbury, 95).

37. "Neilson's argument that the battle in the vale of Sessoynes (1963–2385) embodies a large-scale allusion to Crécy implies that the poet's audience would recognize references to the English strategy at the battle. To assume that an English audience would know of the English victory at Crécy is certainly reasonable. To assume that the same audience, unless we have clear evidence that it included the king or his generals, would be familiar with the strategy is considerably less reasonable. And if the poet were writing at some considerable length of time after the battle at Crécy, the possibility that the audience was familiar with the strategy is very remote" (Keiser, "Edward III," 39). Matthews, Keiser ("Edward III"), Finlayson ("Date"), inter alia,

nonetheless agree that the "*Morte Arthure* abounds in place-names which were important in Edward III's wars" (Finlayson, "Date," 628).

38. "With flonez fleteredé þay flitt full frescly þer frekez, / Fichene with fetheris thurghe þe fyne maylez— / Siche flyttnge es foule þat so þe flesche derys, / That flowe o ferrome in flawnkkes of stedez" (ll. 2097–2100).

39. "Almost certainly at Crécy (1346), as Villani's *Chronicle*, the *Grandes chroniques de France* and Froissart's *Chroniques* attest in unison, the English 'fired off some cannons which they had brought to the battle to frighten the Genoese'" (Contamine, 198–99). In 1387 the English mercenary, Sir John Hawkwood, captaining the Paduan army at the battle of Castagnaro, "positioned cannons in an ambush prepared for Veronese forces" (Contamine, 199).

40. "Western methods of war . . . proved to be inferior to those of the Turks'. The shock tactics of the iron-clad knight lost their deadly effect in the face of the elusive mobility of the light Turkish steed which harrassed the flanks of the Christian line and the extraordinary Turkish skill in the use of the arrow" (Atiya, *Later Middle Ages*, 449). Philippe de Mézière's analysis of Nicopolis, in his letter to the Duke of Burgundy whose son had been a leader of the crusaders, also addresses the heart of the problem: "The campaign had failed because the army was lacking in good government and in the essential rules of discipline, obedience and justice" (Atiya, *Later Middle Ages*, 153). Atiya's *Crusade of Nicopolis* extensively treats the causes of defeat, and tracks the quarrels of the knights and barons of the van, chief among whom were the French, English, and Germans (86). Although chivalric folly was dramatically and repeatedly the bane of French knighthood in the late Middle Ages, it was by no means exclusive to them, as English examples testify: "Sir Hugh Calveley. . . . almost lost the battle of Auray for the English by refusing to take command of the rearguard on the grounds that it was dishonourable and an insult" (Barnie, 90).

41. "The response of many Englishmen to the [Anglo-French] war was characterized by a growing chauvinism, but as the actions of . . . French and English knights suggest, this was not the case with the aristocracy. The main reason for this was the intense caste solidarities they possessed. Aristocrats like Henry of Grosmont and knights like Sir John Chandos considered themselves members of a chivalric élite which transcended national boundaries and which was governed by an internationally recognized code of honour" (Barnie, 82). Family kinship among aristocrats and royals contributed to the sense of class solidarity: "The tendency to honour . . . kinsmen and great knights who were at the same time one's enemies suggest[s] the extent to which the English and French royal houses regarded themselves as members—if exceptionally elevated ones—of an élite which transcended boundaries of allegiance and nationality" (Barnie, 83).

42. Hugh de Payens, a knight from Champagne, formed the Order of the Temple in 1118—so-named because the monk-knights were quartered in the vicinity of the Temple, occupying what had been al-Aqsa mosque before the Latin capture of Jeruslam, a site that had been given over to their use by Baldwin I—with a Rule

written for them by the *abbé* of Clairvaux, St Bernard. The monks of the Hospital were originally keepers of a hostel-hospice for pilgrims at Jerusalem, "dedicated to St. John the Almsgiver, the charitable seventh-century Patriarch of Alexandria" from 1070. Around the time of the Templars' formation, the Knights of St. John, or Hospitallers, were constituted as a military-monastic Order (Runciman, 2:156–57). The Teutonic knights were also initially organized as keepers of a hospice—for Germans at Acre, at the time of the Third Crusade—and were constituted as a military Order in 1198 (Runciman, 3:97–98). Their principal field of action eventually shifted from the Levant to "crusades" of conversion in northeastern Europe. Barnie notes that in the fourteenth century, "for some who found themselves with conflicting loyalties during the Hundred Years War, the crusade provided an honorable solution. During the fighting in Aquitaine after the renewal of the war in 1369 Sir Aymenion de Pommiers found himself in this predicament. He resolved it by declaring that while the war lasted he would take arms for neither party. Instead he went as a pilgrim-crusader to Cyprus, the Holy Sepulchre 'and on many other fair voyages'" (87).

43. The vernicle, by tradition the cloth with which St. Veronica wiped the face of Christ, on the *via dolorosa*, and that takes its name from the saint, appears, significantly, in both the *Morte* and the *Siege of Jerusalem*, a poem that Hamel, in a fine article, reads as a crusading poem ("Siege").

44. "The Great Schism in the church made it possible for Despenser's expedition to Flanders in 1383 and Gaunt's attempt to conquer Castile in 1386–87 to rank technically as crusades, in that the Roman Pope granted indulgences to those who served in these two campaigns against people whom he regarded as schismatic because they obeyed the Pope of Avignon" (Keen, "Chaucer's Knight," 46).

45. As the chronicle of Ibn Wasil (1211–1231) observes, "the [Roman] Emperor [Frederick II] was a sincere and affectionate friend of al-Malik al-Kamil, and they kept up a correspondence until al-Kamil died . . . and his son al-Malik al-'Adil Saif ad-Din succeeded him. With him too the Emperor was on sincerely affectionate terms and maintained a correspondence" (Gabrieli, 276). When al-Kamil handed over Jerusalem to Frederick peaceably, without bloodshed to either Muslims or Christians, Arab chronicles fondly relate how Frederick's visit to Jerusalem was tactfully designed to honor his Muslim hosts. Ibn Wasil relates that "when the time came for the midday prayer and the muezzins' cry rang out, all [Frederick's] pages and valets rose, as well as his tutor, a Sicilian with whom he was reading [Aristotle's] *Logic* in all its chapters, and offered the canonic prayer, for they were all Muslims" (Gabrieli, 275). One anecdote, in particular, resounds to indicate the extent of Frederick's Arabization, and his saturation in Islamic culture. On the second night of the emperor's stay in the Holy City, the Qadi of Nablus instructed the muezzins of Jerusalem, at al-Kamil's orders, not to issue the evening call of the faithful to prayer, as a sign of respect accorded to the visiting Holy Roman Emperor of the Christians. The following day, Frederick—who had nostalgically missed hearing the call to prayer—chastized the Qadi for silencing the muezzins: "'You did wrong to do that,' he said: 'My chief aim

in passing the night in Jerusalem was to hear the call to prayer given by the muezzins, and their cries of praise to God during the night'" (Gabrieli, 271, 275).

46. Ibn Wasil documents Frederick's attempts to discourage St. Louis from leading the Seventh Crusade:

> When the King of France, one of the great Frankish kings, attacked Egypt, the Emperor sent him a message in which he tried to dissuade him from the expedition and warned him of the consequences of his action, but the French king did not take his advice. . . . Frederick had sent . . . a secret embassy to al-Malik as-Salih Najm ad-Din Ayyub to tell him that the King of France had decided to attack Egypt and to put him on his guard and advise him to prepare to resist the attack, which al-Malik as-Salih did. . . . When al-Malik as-Salih died and the King of France met the fate he deserved—the defeat and destruction of his army by death and capture, his own capture by al-Malik al-Mu'azzam Turanshah, his release after al-Malik al-Mu'azzam was murdered and his return home—the Emperor sent to remind [the King of France] of the advice he had given him and of the sorrow he had brought upon himself by his obstinacy and disobedience, and reproached him harshly for it. (Gabrieli, 276–77)

47. In particular, Frederick's correspondence with al-Kamil's vizier, Fakhr ad-Din—a favorite friend of Frederick's—is especially revealing for the emperor's utter ease and familiarity with Arabic cultural conventions and his fluent deployment of fulsome Arabic literary figures to express his tender regard:

> In the name of God, the merciful, the forgiving . . . We departed, and left behind us our heart, which stayed (with you) detached from our body, our race and our tribe. And it swore that its love for you would never change, eternally, and escaped, fleeing from its obedience to me. If we set ourselves to describe the great desire we feel and the sorrowful sensations of solitude and nostalgia we endure for the high excellency of Fahkr ad-Din—may God lengthen his days and extend his years, and make his feet firm in power, and keep the affection He has for him and do him honour, and give his desires fulfilment, and direct his actions and his words and heap him with abundant graces, and renew his safety night and morning—we should exceed by far the limit of an exordium and err from the path of reason. For we have been smitten, after a time of tranquility and ease, with a bitter anguish, and after pleasure and peace with the torment of separation; all comfort seems to have fled, the cord of strong-mindedness is cut, the hope of meeting again turned to despair, the fabric of patience slashed. (Gabrieli, 280–81)

If Frederick's epistolary figures—so reminiscent here of European courtly love talk—are startling, when addressed to an Arab companion who is technically an antagonist of Christendom, the Roman Emperor's correspondence with his Latin royal brother-in-Christ, Henry III of England, is brisk, imperially dignified, and deploys appropriately Christian rhetoric and formulas:

> Frederick, by the grace of God, the august emperor of the Romans, king of Jerusalem and Sicily, to his well-beloved friend Henry, king of the English, health and sincere af-

fection. Let all rejoice and exult in the Lord, and let those who are correct in heart glorify Him . . . for in these few days, by a miracle, rather than by strength, that business has been brought to a conclusion [the Latin re-acquisition of Jerusalem], which for a length of time past many chiefs and rulers of the world amongst the multitude of nations, have never been able till now to accomplish by force, however great, nor by fear. (Peters, *Christian Society*, 162)

48. Echoes in the *Morte* selectively recall the Third Crusade and its English leader, Richard Coeur de Lion: "Sessoyne," for instance, is a place-name that occurs in both the *Morte* and the romance of *RCL* (where "Cessoyne" is near "Araby" [l. 4970]), and Arthur kills an enemy on the battlefield in the *Morte* (ll. 2206–8) in a fashion that drolly duplicates Richard's identical anatomization of one of Saladin's sons in *RCL* (ll. 7127–28). In *RCL* Richard kills the son by cutting him in half, so that half the victim's body falls off his horse, while the other half continues in the saddle, which is the precise treatment meted out by Arthur to the giant Golapas in the *Morte*. Arthur's physical fearlessness, and sense of his own bodily invulnerability to arrows and such, also recalls the historical Richard's own similar sense of physical invulnerability. Conrad, Marquis of Montferrat—who had saved Tyre from Saladin, and was himself a crusading hero—is vilified in *RCL* as a renegade apostate who treacherously betrays Jerusalem to Saladin ("traytour, Markes Fferaunt" [*RCL*, ll. 1307–10]), a traitor who fights against Richard's crusading Christians as Saladin's ally ("Markes Manferaunt" [*RCL*, l. 2713]; "Markys Feraunt" [*RCL*, l. 2721]) and whom Saladin wants to make king of Syria (*RCL*, l. 3248). The *Morte*, to recall the Third Crusade, also happens to feature "One sir Feraunt" (l. 2760) whose father is cursed as a "fiend" (l. 2761) and who had been "fostered in Farmagusta" (l. 761)—that is, on the island of Cyprus, captured by Richard en route to crusade—and who wars against Arthur's crusading knights. The *Morte* also features, as an enemy, a "Raynalde of . . . Rodes . . . rebell to Criste" (l. 2785), who is the *Morte*'s version of *RCL*'s traitorous "Eerl Roys" (l. 1298).

Historically, both Conrad of Montferrat and Richard Lionheart entered into competitive diplomatic negotiations with Saladin in 1191–92, each striving to outmaneuver the other diplomatically. Richard is sometimes credited with Conrad's sudden murder (Runciman, 3:65; see also my chapter 2); after Conrad's murder, moreover, Richard's nephew, Henry of Champagne (the son of Chrétien de Troyes's patroness, Countess Marie of Champagne), marries Isabella of Jerusalem and, following Guy's death, becomes de facto king of Latin Jerusalem-in-exile. Interestingly, in the early 1360s, the English mercenary knight, Sir John Hawkwood, "was part of the 'Great Company' of the marquis of Monferrat in the service of the counts of Savoy against the Visconti of Milan" (Contamine, 159); I discuss the *Morte*'s interest in the Viscontis below in the section "Priamus, Fortune's Wheel, and Genoese Giants." See Hamel (*Morte*, 332–33 n. 2421) and Matthews (49) for alternative characterizations of the *Morte*'s "sir Feraunt."

49. The *Morte*'s repeated mention of boy children—not only as the victims of the giant of St. Michael's Mount but also as hostages from Rome to Arthur (which draws

another parallel between Arthur and the giant)—may point in some fashion to the Children's Crusade of 1212–13, which ended in death or slavery for many "crismed children" of Europe, especially boys.

50. Peter I of Cyprus, of the Lusignan dynasty of kings of Jerusalem in exile, was another Priamus-like figure, disinherited by the loss of Jerusalem and traveling to "the princes of the West" for "close on a year and a half, with great dangers, [hard] work, and expense, constantly asking for assistance" (Housley, 85–86) after Pope Urban V proclaimed Peter's crusade, in 1363, according to the famed crusading propagandist of the late Middle Ages, Philippe de Mézières.

51. Constantine the Great, the emperor who married Christianity, a pacific religion, to the might and organization of the Roman Empire, by his conversion to Christianity, might seem a logical choice for a Christian imperial conqueror to name as one of Arthur's predecessor authorities, and Geoffrey's Arthur sensibly cites Constantine in his list. That the *Morte*'s Arthur should deliver "Baldwin" as *his* preferred choice instead must have seemed unaccountable to many. The *Morte*'s latest textual editor, Hamel, has inserted an emendation that replaces the Thornton manuscript's *Morte*'s original formula, "and Baldwin was the third" ("and Bawdewyne the thyrde") with the Winchester Malory's later account of the same story ("that were born in Britain"), so that Baldwin is effaced by editorial emendation, and Arthur is only left with two predecessor kings, not three: an emendation that is unnecessary, once the crusading context of the romance is grasped. "Baldwin" is a resonant name in crusading history: four kings of Jerusalem were named "Baldwin," and Baldwin III selected as his own successor Fulk of Anjou—father of the Plantagenet Geoffrey, who married the empress Matilda, and sired Henry II, thus founding the Plantagenet dynasty in England that was named for Geoffrey's sobriquet. The *Morte*'s punning "and Bawdewyne the thyrde" therefore economically points in two directions at once, butressing the authority of Arthur, as king of Britain/England, in more than one way.

52. A little knot of numbers coincidentally knits together contemporary accounts of the Christian forces at Nicopolis and Arthur's war in the *Morte*. According to Johan of Schiltberger, an eyewitness participant who was sixteen years old at Nicopolis, sixteen thousand crusaders were at the battle. In the *Morte* Rome has sixteen kings on its side, along with the Sultan of Syria (l. 608); Idrus has sixteen knights (l. 1491); Arthur's fleet is ready in sixteen days (l. 634); and takes 160 papal hostages in "togas" from "Tars" (l. 3189)—a possible reference to Tharsia, in Armenia. By a coincidence, in Greater Armenia, there happens also to be a "Nicopolis" (Atiya, *Nicopolis*, 181 n. 66).

53. "Travellers came back from the Levant with tales of suffering, sacrilege and misery; but perhaps the most potent of reminders were the wandering princes of Christian Kingdoms, now extinct or on the verge of extinction at the hand of the Saracen" (Atiya, *Later Middle Ages*, 15); "the wanderings of august kings and emperors among the peoples of Western Europe could not but inflame the ardour of men and women among whom the crusade was still a living memory" (Atiya, *Later Middle Ages*, 16). Priamus's name conveniently recalls Priam and Troy, pointing to a Greek provenance. A "Priamon" also exists among the Saracen knights of the *Chan-*

son de Roland (l. 65). Malory's rendition of Priamus's christening (*Works*, 1:241)—a clear point of divergence between the Thornton *Morte*'s and the Winchester Malory's accounts—emphasizes that Malory's Priamus, unlike the *Morte*'s, is *not* a Greek Christian.

54. See chapter 1, note 59, on the relationship between Champagne and Jerusalem, and Chrétien's allusions to, and possible knowledge of, the Levantine East. Alice Lasater's and Dorothee Melitzki's well-known volumes on literary and cultural exchanges in the Middle Ages between Western Europe, Spain, and the Levant have descriptive chapters treating romances, while Menocal's influential volume on East-West medieval cultural exchange specially treats the phenomenon of courtly love. Lasater identifies Catalonia, in particular, as implicated "in the interchange between Oriental materials and Arthurian and other European matter in European romance" (147), while observing that "many critics have commented upon the large number of Oriental figures and stories in Arthurian romance" (195). In Middle English literature, Lasater traces the figure of the Green Knight in *Sir Gawain and the Green Knight* to "al-Khadir, 'the Green One,' of Arabic and Persian lore" (195) and locates "al-Khadir" also in an analogue of Chaucer's *Squire's Tale* (193). Though Melitzki's chapter on "the making of medieval romance" specifically concentrates on "Oriental" romances in Europe (the "matter of Araby"), she notes that "the making of medieval romance falls into a period when there was not only the most intimate personal contact with Islam that Europe has ever experienced but when there was considerable knowledge about Islam" (247). Ganim ("Native Studies") also specifically identifies the Orient as one of the contact zones of medieval romance.

55. "There were not, perhaps, many houses as large and splendid as the palace built . . . by the Ibelins at Beirut, with its mosaic floors, its marble walls and its painted ceilings, and great windows looking, some westward over the sea, and others eastward over gardens and orchards to the mountains. . . . There were carpets and damask hangings, elegantly carved and inlaid tables and coffers, spotless bed-linen and table-linen, dinner-services in gold and silver, cutlery, fine faience and even a few dishes of porcelain from the Farther East. In Antioch water was brought by aqueducts and pipes to all the great houses from the springs at Daphne. Many houses along the Lebanese coast had their own private supplies. In Palestine, where water was less abundant, the cities had well-organized storage tanks; and in Jerusalem, the sewerage system installed by the Romans was still in perfect order. The great frontier-fortresses were almost as comfortably appointed as the town-houses. . . . They had baths, elegant chambers for the ladies of the household and sumptuous reception halls. . . . The clothes of the settlers soon became as Oriental and luxurious as their furnishings" (Runciman, 2:316–17).

Balian, lord of the great Ibelin family of Outremer, was the leader of the small defensive force at Jerusalem when the city was besieged by Saladin, surrendering the city after a desperate, short-lived, and futile struggle. By an odd coincidence, Balian of Ibelin's name resounds curiously against the name of that fateful knight in Malory, who deals the dolorous stroke that creates the Wasteland—"Balin"—a knight who has an alter-ego and brother of almost identical name, "Balan." It is not, perhaps, overly fanciful to think of the loss of Jerusalem to Saladin—a calamity for which Balian of Ibelin might be held accountable, if unreasonably, in cultural fantasy—as inaugurating a spiritual wasteland for Christendom. Scholars have sometimes observed that the legend of the Quest of the Holy Grail assumed special urgency and vivacity after the loss of Jerusalem and that holiest of Passion relics, the True Cross, to Saladin. The Grail—variously a platter, or green stone, or something else in Arthurian tradition—crystallized definitively in literary tradition as the chalice of the Last Supper, and hence a genuine (if invented) relic, once Jerusalem, and the True Cross, had been lost. We have already noted that what is lost in the register of history may, curiously, be rediscovered in the register of cultural fantasy.

56. The switching back-and-forth of alliances between Latin crusaders and their ostensible foes began to occur very early in the history of Outremer, as strategic interests dictated the usefulness of contingent alliances with individual antagonists, sometimes even in conflicts expressly against fellow crusaders. Thus it is that in 1109 Tancred of Antioch—while regent for his captive uncle, Bohemond I—allied himself with Ridwan of Aleppo, and against Tancred's fellow crusaders, Baldwin, Count of Edessa, and Baldwin's nephew, Joscelin of Tal Bashir, crusaders who were themselves ranged on the side of Jawali, a Turkish emir who had conquered Mosul. The chronicle of Ibn al-Athir documents one of these quirky shifts of loyalty:

> Tancred . . . set out from Antioch with six hundred cavalry sent by Ridwan. When Jawali heard the news, he sent to Baldwin of Edessa to ask for his help. . . . Baldwin left Edessa and met Jawali at Manbij. . . . In the battle that followed the men from Antioch charged the Count of Edessa, and after some violent fighting Tancred forced the enemy's [*sic*] centre to retreat. But Jawali's left wing charged the infantry from Antioch. (Gabrieli, 22–23)

Ibn al-Qalanisi records an alliance in 1140 between Damascus, under attack by Zengi, the atabeg of Mosul, and the Frankish crusaders of Outremer: "The Franks agreed to give Damascus support and help in driving Zengi back and prevent his getting what he wanted. The agreement was sealed with a solemn oath, and each side gave guarantees that it would honour its obligations" (Gabrieli, 45–46).

57. "Life amongst the Frankish colonists was uneasy and precarious. They were in a land where intrigue . . . flourished and enemies lay in wait. . . . infant mortality was high, especially among the boys. Fief after fief fell into the hands of an heiress, whose inheritance might lure gallant adventurers from the West; but too often great estates lacked a lord at the hour of crisis, and every marriage was a matter of dispute and of plotting" (Runciman, 2:323–24). The Kingdom of Jerusalem was particularly vulnerable to female succession. Its second king, Baldwin II, left four daughters but no sons; and a consort had to be imported from Europe for Melisende, the eldest (on the odd resemblance of the triangulated relationship of Melisende, her husband, Fulk of Anjou, and the young Hugh le Puiset, lord of Jaffa, to Arthurian legend, see chap. 1 n. 59). Alix, Melisende's sister who became princess of Antioch, also produced a sole

daughter as heir. On the death of her husband, Bohemond II of Antioch, Alix, be-having like a character in romance, intervened in the geopolitics of the Levant by of-fering Zengi, the atabeg of Mosul, homage, if he would but confirm her possession of Antioch, and sent him a magnificent charger, "splendidly caparisoned," as a chivalric gift (Runciman, 2:183). Even after the loss of Jerusalem, heiresses continued to be a focal point in the survival of Latin Jerusalem-in-exile, as the quarrel between Richard Lionheart and Philip Augustus, on the Third Crusade, over the right candidate for marriage to Isabel of Jerusalem, demonstrated.

58. An audience or reader to whom the *Morte*'s quotation of "Mandeville's" de-scription of the Emperor Justinian's statue outside the Hagia Sophia is meaningful—that is, an audience or reader familiar with *Mandeville's Travels*—will also be cued in advance to anticipate Arthur's fall from power, in the *Morte*. For *Mandeville's Travels* says that Justinian's statue "*was wont*" to have the apple of rule in its hand, but the apple had fallen out, and, despite the best efforts of men to put the symbol of ruler-ship and imperial dominion back into the statue's hand, the apple would not remain there, by any means. *Mandeville's Travels*, like the *Morte* and other cultural texts of the late Middle Ages, has Constantinople on its mind and in its field of vision, but the *Travels*' anxiety is focused more specifically on Constantinople's contemporary weakness in the face of Muslim threat, since, to the *Travels*, Constantinople's old glo-ries of imperial dominion were over (as signaled by the apple that would not remain in Justinian's hand). For a fuller discussion, see the second section of chapter 5, "Home is the Center of the World."

59. Fortune curiously mentions Frollo in line 3345, when Frollo is a character who does not appear in the *Morte*, though his battle with Arthur is depicted in the *Historia*. Hamel observes that "it appears that the poet assumes his audience would be fa-miliar with Wace or Geoffrey" (*Morte*, 364 n. 3345).

60. In Malory's romance, Arthur's sword is also from a woman, the Lady of the Lake, to whom the sword has to be returned upon his death (*Works*, 1:65). Lancelot's sword, in both the Old French Prose *Lancelot* and Malory, is closely associated with Guinevere: In the *Lancelot*, Guinevere supplies Lancelot's sword (Sommer, *Vulgate*, 3:131, 137), while in Malory it is "lapped . . . in [Guinevere's] trayne" (*Works*, 2:1058). In Malory, Balin's sword also comes from a woman (*Works*, 3:65); while in the *Morte* itself—where Fortune gives Arthur a sword—Guinevere gives Mordred Arthur's sword, Caliburn. At the very least, the many symbols of phallicism that can be traced back to women in chivalric romance register a double-edged apprehension that women position the material instrumentality that undergirds masculine agency in the world, and feminine support of masculine identity and power surfaces in the form of female characters' responsibility for supplying gifts or alibis to male elites. Whether the women in question are goddesses like Fortune, enchantresses, fays, or magical women like the ladies of the lake, or courtly wives and mistresses like Guinevere, is scarcely material, since the mystification of all varieties of women who display power of any kind in chivalric romance—a mystification that ensures their larger-than-life aura—emphasizes a commonality of status and usefulness in narrative. Fortune, in

particular, is a favorite source of blame and accusation in medieval literature and culture. As God's vicar in the world, one of the roles of Fortune—like Nature—is to absorb resentments and blame that cannot be directed toward God himself: the ultimate diversion in gender politics. On Fortune in the Middle Ages, see Patch.

61. Egypt had been the geopolitical base of Ayyubid power (the short-lived dynasty of kings named for Saladin's father, Ayyub) from the time that Saladin ended the Fatimid caliphate in Egypt and established his suzerainty there, ostensibly in the name of his master, Nuraldin. Strategically Egypt was also the supply point for Syria and the Holy Land—the next objective of the crusaders of the Fourth Crusade, once Egypt had been taken. Richard Lionheart had become convinced, after the failure of the Third Crusade, that it was necessary to capture Egypt first, before the Holy Land could be successfully reconquered, and Egypt subsequently became the objective of the Fourth, Fifth, Seventh, and Eighth Crusades (the last two being St Louis's crusades). The Venetian redirection of the Fourth Crusade away from Eygpt, and to Constantinople, meets with hearty approval, all around, in the Arab chronicles of the period. With the Venetians ranged against Constantinople, the rivals of Venice, the Genoese, naturally allied themselves with the Greeks, from whose recapture of Constantinople, in 1261, the Genoese then substantially profited. Following 1255, in their war with the Venetians in Syria, the Genoese counted Greek Christians among their allies (Byrne, 177–78). Historically the English tended to range themselves with Genoa's fiercest competitors, the Venetians and Pisans.

62. "In the thirteenth century, the Genoese were especially active in the slave trade. They had participated in the First Crusade, and thereafter they maintained a steady commerce with Muslim Egypt. Until the second half of the thirteenth century, they played a secondary role to Venice, whose doge persuaded the leaders of the Fourth Crusade to divert their armies to the conquest of Constantinople from the Byzantines. As a consequence, the Venetians received favored trading rights in the Byzantine Empire and easier access to the Black Sea. When Michael Paleologus drove the Westerners from the Byzantine Empire in 1261, the Genoese, thanks to a previous treaty with the new Byzantine ruler, replaced the Venetians in the eastern imperial trade and received a near monopoly on trade to the Black Sea. In Pera, a suburb of Constantinople, and in Tana and Caffa on the north side of the Black Sea, the Genoese merchants maintained commercial posts, from which they obtained slaves among other goods, until the fifteenth century. During the second half of the thirteenth century, Genoa regularly supplied Mamluk Egypt with slave recruits for its army, due in large part to the fact that the normal overland caravan routes from the Black Sea across Anatolia to Egypt were cut" (Phillips, *Slavery*, 104). Genoese slaves included Slavs, Circassians, Serbs, Slovenes, Albanians, Armenians, Mongols, Turks and Turcomans, and Kurds (Atiya, *Commerce*, 182–83; Phillips, *Slavery*, 104–5).

63. "This important Christian-Muslim trade was vigorous, despite papal attempts to limit it by forbidding exports of arms, materiel, and slaves to the Muslims. R.-H. Bautier, however, believed that 'the blockade does not seem to have been very effective since in 1154 Pisa undertook to deliver precisely those forbidden commodities to

the sultan [of Egypt].' In Genoa the slave market seems to have come into full flowering around 1190. Before that there had been only sporadic sales of slaves" (Phillips, *Slavery*, 103).

64. In fourteenth-century Europe "an escalating series of disasters caused a severe decline in population [and] there [was] a substantial rise in demand for slaves" (Phillips, *Slavery*, 104); in particular, the "Black Death . . . created a heightened demand for slaves" (105). By "1363 the Florentine government allowed the unrestricted importation of slaves from outside Italy, stipulating only that they be of non-Christian origin" (105). Phillips, Huppert, et alia note that slaves imported *into* Europe itself by the Genoese tended to be girls: "In the late fourteenth century, when the free work force was decimated by disease [i.e., by the Plague], wages were high, so that the purchase of a slave could be viewed as a rational investment. The price of a slave girl was about the same as that of a mule, equivalent, roughly, to eight years' wages for a free servant" (Huppert, 114).

65. "Christians were not permitted to be enslaved. Violations of this rule occurred with some regularity, as impious slave dealers passed off Greek Orthodox and even foreign Catholic slaves as non-Christians" (Phillips, *Slavery*, 101). Phillips, moreover, tracks an important change in Genoese slave trafficking—representing the general Italian pattern—away from the taking of Muslim slaves, and toward increased commerce in Christian slaves, or people who had been Christianized before being auctioned off in the Genoese slave markets:

> Thirteenth-century slave recruitment in Genoa illustrates the common Italian pattern. In the first three-quarters of the century, Muslims made up around 75 percent of the slave population, reflecting the well-established trading links with Iberia and North Africa. The Aragonese conquest of the Islamic kingdom of Valencia in the 1230s placed numerous Muslims on the market, and many of these found their way to Italy. . . . In the final quarter of the thirteenth century, the situation began to change dramatically, as the primary area of recruitment shifted to the Black Sea. In 1275 the first recorded Russian slave, a man named Balada, appeared in Genoa. . . . Their numbers grew rapidly when the Genoese set up trading stations in Pera beginning in 1281 and in Caffa around 1289. Most of the slaves brought in from the Black Sea reached Genoa after having been baptized. This set the pattern for the fourteenth and fifteenth centuries. (104–5)

Finlayson ("Giant") is among those who note that "what is important about the giant is that he is an enemy of Christendom and not merely an abductor of young women" (114).

66. The *Morte*'s solicitude over *boy* children, in particular, runs counter to the historical fact that most of the human consumables in the Italian slave markets were female. Of 357 slaves sold in Florence, Phillips notes, fully 329 were female, "either women or young girls, while only 28 were males" (*Slavery*, 105). The *Morte*'s solicitude thus exemplifies the usual trajectory of gender anxiety in chivalric romance. Among the small quantity of male stock, however, boys did predominate over men:

"Only 28 were males, and only 4 of them were over the age of sixteen" (Phillips, *Slavery*, 105).

67. "The urban *conjuratio*, founding pact of the commune and one of the nearest actual historical approximations to a formal 'social contract,' embodied a new principle altogether—a community of equals. It was naturally hated and feared by nobles, prelates and monarchs: the *commune* was a 'new and detestable name' for Guibert de Nogent in the early 12th century. . . . Communes on the Italian model never became universalized in Europe: they were the privilege only of the most advanced economic regions" (P. Anderson, 194).

68. "In the course of two centuries the Genoese had created and thrived upon an imposing commercial empire in the Levant. In the Syrian colonies they conducted a series of experiments in administration which passed through a succession of steps reflecting the evolutionary process through which the commune itself had passed: from feudal control by privileged families through a stage of communal administration by a loosely knit system of consular agents several in number reflecting the plural executive at home with a tendency toward election of officials in the colonies, to the final stage of concentration of power in the hands of a single executive corresponding to the podestà in Genoa who had long since displaced the consuls. Upon the basis of these colonies and the trade therewith, Genoa rose to such wealth and power . . . as to give even Venice pause" (Byrne, 182).

69. Variously glossed by historians as hostelries, warehouses (D. Abulafia, 439), bazaars (Byrne, 141), or markets, *funduqs* were defended at all cost by the Italians as the arteries keeping open the routes, supplies, and flows of East-West trade that supported the vast wealth of the Italian republics.

70. Gold coinage reappeared in England when Edward III had gold coins struck in 1343–44; interestingly, gold's emergence in English currency meant attention to florins in particular: "for England in the 1340s, there were additional reasons for the introduction of gold coins. The most common unit of currency used in international trade was the Florentine gold florin, and Italian merchants were artificially maintaining its value at 3s. [3 shillings] when it was worth only 2s.6 1/2d. [2 shillings, 6.5 pence]. So Edward III issued his leopards of 108, 54 and 27 grains in weight" (Bolton, 75).

71. The behavior of the Venetians in the Fourth Crusade was only the most notorious example of hard bargaining between the Italians and knightly crusaders. Philippe de Mézière's account of the Alexandria crusade of 1365, closer to the *Morte*'s time, repeats the standard attitude to the merchant states: "Because the deadline had passed, the Venetians were legally released from their previous offer [of ships], and the knights dispersed sadly, with downcast faces, despairing of the crusade. Then the wicked merchants rejoiced and mocked the passage" (Housley, 85); a Cypriot-Genoese dispute also posed a particular threat to the Alexandria crusade.

72. There were some sixty-nine Italian firms in later-thirteenth-century England, which took over "the upper end of the market" from the Jews (Bolton, 340). Circumventions of laws against usury took many ingenious forms. In most instances,

[interest] simply went underground. In the later Middle Ages the chief instrument for recording debts was the bond obligatory. In this no mention was made of interest because the sum it was made out for comprised both principal and interest, or in other words more was repaid than was borrowed. . . . Interest could be paid in a whole variety of ways, by 'gifts', by grants or favours, licences to export wool duty free, keeperships of royal manors, or, as with the chief lender to Henry V and VI, Cardinal Beaufort, virtual control of the customs revenues of a great port over a number of years. (Bolton, 342)

73. By contrast to romance, Genoese citizens in Syria historically "were exempt from the ordinary *cours des bourgeois* in most of the important towns, and had the right to hold their own court" *under their own law* (Byrne, 156, 178–79). In Tyre the Genoese court "had both civil and criminal jurisdiction" (179), another way in which Genoese might be imagined as "lingering outside the law" of the Latins of Outremer. English knights, of course, also functioned as officers with judiciary duties: "They had come to be regularly involved in the judicial and financial administration of their shires, meeting every forty days in the county court, serving as jurors, tax assessors, military arrayers, escheaters, coroners and sheriffs" (Given-Wilson, 16).

74. After 1385 Gian Galeazzo was the Sire of Milan, "with hegemony over Como, Piacenza, Ponet, Pontremoli, Pavia, and (after 1399) Pisa (cf MA 3134–44). The peculiar hostility expressed against this figure in the poem seems to reflect the Visconti's popular reputation, echoes of which are found in Chaucer's Monk's account of the murder of Giangaleazzo's uncle Bernabò, and in Froissart's excoriation of his atheism, treachery, and complicity in the defeat of the Christian knights at Nicopolis in 1396" (Hamel, 54). Interestingly, the titular identification "Visconti" was also generic nomenclature among Genoese: "The dominant group of feudal families in Genoa [were] known generally as the visconti, descendants of the Ligurian viscounts who represented the margraves of the preceding centuries" (Byrne, 145). In the crusader colonies of Outremer, *vicecomites et consules* were local titles of officers of administration whose duties included the judicial (Byrne, 165–69).

75. Hamel's acute observation that lines 2053–57—which describe the "Vicount's" arms as a dragon swallowing a dolphin—are a reference both to the Visconti arms ("a serpent swallowing a naked man") and, more punningly, to Gian Galeazzo's quarrel with France over his daughter's putative poisoning of the child dauphin ("dolphin") in 1396, is entirely persuasive (Hamel, 317 n. 2054), and partly recounts the complex relationship of the Viscontis to French and English royal families in the fourteenth century. In the English royal family, Lionel, Duke of Clarence, younger son of Edward III, also married a Visconti—Violante, niece of Bernabò and sister of Gian Galeazzo—as did the highly successful mercenary-knight-brigand, Sir John Hawkwood. Hamel's emendation in line 864, favoring the manuscript of the Winchester Malory over the Thornton *Morte*, in the reference to the noblewoman-victim of the giant of St. Michael's Mount, is then probably unnecessarily zealous. The Thornton

MS refers to the victim as Arthur's "wyfes cosyn," and Hamel substitutes the Winchester Malory's "cousyns wyff," in order to firm the original identity of Helen, kinswoman of Hoel of Brittany, Arthur's "cousin," or nephew, in the older Arthurian tradition. But if the Visconti is a late-medieval referent in the giant's figuration, the *Morte* might be less interested in securing the features of the victim as once originally British (or Breton) in tradition—an identification already dutifully, if cursorily, made in line 852, in any event—than in implying that she also figures a contemporary *French* prize, a child princess of tender years who is the "flour of all Fraunce" (l. 869). The *Morte*'s palpable neglect of Helena's name—despite the mention of Troy later (l. 887)—shows its lack of interest, as we have said, in retaining or exploiting the old potentials inherent in Helen's original identity. To have the giant's female victim Arthur's "wyfes cosyn," moreover, injures Guinevere more than Arthur, and is fully consonant with this romance's summarily harsh handling of its women characters, and relative indifference to female injury.

76. At the end of a detailed discussion on the identity of the *Morte*'s author and audience, Hamel speculates that, given the author's erudition, and the supposition that "a poem so complex implies a sophisticated audience" (*Morte*, 61), the author might well have been attached to the household of a magnatial aristocrat of the highest rank, perhaps even a royal: "*If* he was a man of Lincolnshire, and *if* he was attached to a magnatial household, his lord *might* have been John of Gaunt, his son Henry of Bolingbroke, or Thomas Mowbray, Duke of Norfolk, the men who dominated the county in the late 14th century" (*Morte*, 62). If Hamel's speculation is sound, the *Morte*'s author would likely be familiar, at close range, with the doings of the Viscontis, and their relationship to the extended royal family of England, from the subject of the French king's ransom promised to the crown, to the marriage of the Duke of Clarence to one of the Visconti daughters.

77. The crusading history that I have argued constitutes the frame of the *Morte* does not, of course, preclude the *Morte*'s depiction as well of historical phenomena from the Hundred Years War nearer home. Cultural texts are rooted in overlapping realities in the contexts they inhabit and invariably sediment multiple realities simultaneously. Scholars have noted, for instance, that Arthur's *chevauchées* are very like the campaigns and raids of the free companies, one of whose infamous leaders, Sir Robert Knollys, was said to have had the head of a giant. Sir John Hawkwood, another larger-than-life leader of the companies, who married an illegitimate daughter of Bernabò Visconti and became wealthy in Milan, ended his days in comfortable retirement in England, where he could also have served as inspiration for lurid figures in literature (Contamine, 158–59).

78. On the body's relationship to the soul, in particular, see, especially, Bynum ("Why All the Fuss about the Body?," *Resurrection*). "The *exempla* of preachers and the stories of hagiographers make soul unabashedly somatomorphic" (*Resurrection*, 319), and "the idea of person, bequeathed by the Middle Ages . . . was a concept of self in which physicality was integrally bound to sensation, emotion, reasoning, identity" (*Resurrection*, 11). Bynum notes that "the years around 1300 saw enthusiastic

prying into the body—studying it, severing it, distributing and scattering it" (*Resurrection*, 327).

79. Even the *chanson*-style vertical and horizontal slashing in the *Morte* displays specialized details and an eye for culling elaborate possibilities of ingenuity and humor. Arthur's Richard Lionheart-like slicing of a man in half, for example, has the bottom half of the man's trunk still galloping off on the man's horse (ll. 2206–8); and Arthur's killing of the giant Golapas offers a two-step horizontal division of the giant that slices the giant into three sections (Arthur first cuts him off at the knees, then beheads him [ll. 2125, 2129]), suggesting that with the very tall enemy, such as giants, the standard *chanson*-style horizontal slashing does not suffice and must be elaborated.

80. "sweltand knyghtez— / Lyes wyde opyn welterande one walopande stedez— / Wondes of wale men, werkande sydys; / Facez feteled vnfaire in filterede lakes, / All craysed, fortrodyn with trappede stedez: / The faireste-fygured felde that fygurede was euer— / Alls ferre alls a furlange, a thosande at ones!" (*Morte* ll. 2146–52).

81. Richard, who had been "instrumental in bringing [the crossbow] into general military use in France" (Brundage, 223)—after it had been forbidden as a weapon against Christians, by Canon 7 of the Lateran Synod of 1097 and Canon 29 of the Second Lateran Council of 1139—died from gangrene arising from the crossbow wound in his shoulder. Before Richard, William Rufus is another celebrated example of an English king felled by a crossbow shot, while hunting. Thus history demonstrates the exact *opposite* of what Arthur says here: Annointed kings are, in fact, as vulnerable as anyone else, and technology does not respect nobility or social class. With the historical examples of English kings in mind, the *Morte* may well be commenting here on Arthur's bravura rashness and arrogance. Contamine also notes that cannon artillery was as dangerously undiscriminating as archery:

> Even the lives of captains and war-leaders were directly threatened by the new weapon. One of the first examples of an identified victim is provided by Froissart from the siege of Ypres in 1383: 'There Louis Lin a very brave English esquire was killed by a cannon shot.' Among others who can be mentioned later are Louis Paviot killed at the siege of Meulan (1423), the earl of Salisbury at the siege of Orléans (1428), the earl of Arundel (1434), Pedro of Castille (1438), the Admiral Prigent de Coëtivy and Tugdual de Bourgeois, both at the siege of Cherbourg (1450). . . . Not even princes and kings were safe from danger; James II of Scotland 'mair curieous nor becam him or the majestie of ane King . . . unhappely (was) slane with ane gun, the quhilk brak in the fyring' at the siege of Roxburgh on 3 August 1460; the arquebus which killed Tanguy du Chastel nearly carried off Louis XI. (206)

82. The necessity for clarification registered in this encounter between Gawain and Priamus mimes a similar social necessity in the historical period. Maurice Keen ("Esquires") details the repeated efforts made in the late Middle Ages precisely to have the categories come clear, and be as distinct and separate from one another as possible, and thus ward off unease of exactly the kind that haunts Gawain here. The statuses

"knight," "esquire," "gentleman," and "yeoman" were carefully delineated, so that differences in social class might be secured and stabilized. "Yeoman," as Gawain's alarm suggests, was a degree below "gentleman"and three degrees down from "knight": so that by the fifteenth century "the statute of 1445 which regulated eligibility to represent a shire in parliament bluntly rejected as ineligible any man 'which standeth in the degree of Yeoman and under'" (97). Although yeomanry "could include men who were distinctly substantial in economic terms. . . . A yeoman was not, however, of sufficient status to speak for his shire in the community of the realm assembled in parliament. That was reserved for a different sort of people: knights, notable esquires and gentlemen" (97). Legislation of the fourteenth and fifteenth centuries, Keen remarks, is particularly "illustrative of the preoccupation with precise social gradation . . . characteristic of late medieval England" ("Esquires," 96).

83. Affective family relationships of all kinds—except among the military family of warriors—are shown, by this romance, to fail. Guinevere is depicted by the *Morte* as cowardly, saving herself by taking the veil (ll. 3916–18) rather than saving her children, as Mordred had instructed her to do (l. 3907), a betrayal of maternity that mime's Fortune's earlier betrayal of Arthur as favorite son. Indeed, children do not fare well in this romance. Where they are not crammed into tubs, to be eaten at leisure by a cannibal giant—or born under conditions of treachery and betrayal, only to be abandoned—they are destined to be killed at King Arthur's order. The infanticide that Arthur orders here, on dynastic grounds, damns him by the covert illegality of the projected homicides, and Arthur's words ("go like a man to . . .") ironically mock him in the very act of their utterance. Echoes of Herod's order of infant slaughter, the child Moses's escape by water, inter alia, lead us to suspect that the project that Arthur orders is also likely doomed to failure.

84. Matthews is an example of critics who, following the *Morte*'s overt cues, duly read Gawain as "a type of sinless Christ" (150), whereas Hamel more suspiciously notes that Arthur "honors not Christ's teachings but chivalry" (*Morte*, 385 n. 3986) in his actions. To ensure that the military emphasis is not lost among the religious metaphors, Arthur stores the blood of his dead nephew and retainer in his *war helmet* (l. 3995).

85. Even when Arthur weeps over the news of the giant's victims, he weeps for pity of his people, rather than over the Duchess's plight per se ("Thane romyez the ryche kynge for rewth of þe pople" [l. 888]).

86. If the sectarian interests of chivalry and knights run counter to the impetus of imagining a national community binding together different social classes and categories of peoples, Kaeuper suggests that chivalry also concomitantly obstructed the process of medieval state formation: a process in which the centralization and vestment of public power in the *sovereign* was crucial. "The chivalric ethos easily made kinglets of knights," Kaeuper observes—a process we have seen dramatized in this chivalric romance, inter alia, in Arthur's passionate avowal that his greatest accomplishments are really owed to his kingly chivalry—"chivalry by and large represented a countermovement to the movement toward the Western form of state which was so

evident across the twelfth and thirteenth centuries in France and especially in England" (195). Kaeuper also remarks that "maintaining the peace in the emerging medieval state was a problem of significant dimensions because of the existence and the idealization of a noble code of violence; it is the violence of the powerful and privileged classes which so sharply differentiates the medieval from the modern problem of order" (188).

4. Beauty and the East, a Modern Love Story: Women, Children, and Imagined Communities in *The Man of Law's Tale* and Its Others

1. The oldest version of the Constance story in the core English group is in Trevet's *Les Cronicles*, authored in Anglo-Norman, c. 1334, with nine extant manuscripts surviving from the fourteenth and fifteenth centuries (eight from the fourteenth and one from the fifteenth). Trevet, an English Dominican who taught at Oxford in the early fourteenth century, is thought to have issued "at least two and probably three redactions" (R. J. Dean, "Manuscripts," 97). The dedication in four of the manuscripts, including the two earliest, is to Princess Mary of Woodstock, fourth daughter of Edward I and Eleanor of Castile, and sister of Edward II, "a nun of Amesbury, one of the English cells of the abbey of Fontevrault" (R. J. Dean, "Nicholas Trevet," 339). Trevet's "Life of Constance" appears in a useful anthology, *Sources and Analogues of Chaucer's Canterbury Tales*, edited by W. F. Bryan and Germaine Dempster, in which Trevet's text is edited by Margaret Schlauch (in 1941). I use Bryan and Dempster's volume in referring to Trevet and Gower's texts (while also consulting Edmund Brock's 1872 edition of Trevet's "Life of Constance" in the nineteenth-century anthology by F. J. Furnivall, Edmund Brock, and W. A. Clouston, *Originals and Analogues of Some of Chaucer's Canterbury Tales*; henceforth cited as Furnivall); for Chaucer's *Man of Law's Tale*, I use the *Riverside Chaucer*, edited by L. D. Benson (henceforth *MLT*). That the versions of the Constance story in Chaucer's *Canterbury Tales* and Gower's *Confessio Amantis* traveled well, and found audiences of various kinds through their recensions and large numbers of manuscripts, need not be belabored.

For *Emaré*, extant in only one manuscript, Cotton Caligula A.ii, from the early fifteenth century, I use the text in Laskaya and Salisbury's *The Middle English Breton Lays*. The fourteenth-century *King of Tars* (*KT*) is preserved in three famous compendia-manuscripts, the Auchinleck, Vernon, and Simeon; Judith Perryman's edition, based on the Auchinleck, is used in all references to *KT* in this chapter. *Florence of Rome* is attested by seven manuscript versions (one English, five French, and one Spanish, spanning the late thirteenth through fifteenth centuries). The manuscript of the Middle English *Le Bone Florence of Rome* probably descends from the late fifteenth century; I refer to it in passing and use Heffernan's edition. Consensus exists that Trevet is Chaucer's and Gower's source for the Constance story, but the relationship of Chaucer's and Gower's versions to each other was once contested (scholars today agree, *contra* Skeat and Macaulay, that Gower wrote earlier than Chaucer, and thus the literary debt is Chaucer's, where borrowing or adaptation is found (see Correale,

135, 155 n. 11, for a brief account); the relation of *Emaré* to Chaucer's *Man of Law's Tale* continues to be debated. On Trevet's *Cronicles*, see, especially, R. J. Dean ("Manuscripts," "Nicholas Trevet") and, more recently, Correale; on Chaucer's *Man of Law's Tale* and *Emaré*, see Hanks. L. H. Loomis ("Chaucer") treats the relation of Chaucer to the Auchinleck's Breton lays in general, and Hornstein considers the relationship of *Tars* to Trevet's Constance. Perryman's edition of *KT* and Heffernan's edition of *Florence* contain excellent, detailed introductions on their romances and on the Constance saga. Schlauch's volume on Constance (*Chaucer's Constance and Accused Queens*) and introduction to the Constance texts in Bryan and Dempster still offer the most comprehensive account of the story's widespread literary, folkloric, and historical relations (but see also A. B. Gough's *Constance Saga*). References to Chaucer's *Clerk's Tale* are also to the *Riverside Chaucer*. Critical studies on individual romances in the Constance story are cited elsewhere in the notes to this chapter.

2. In their volume Furnivall et al. adduce the tale "Merelaus the Emperor," from the *Gesta Romanorum* (1350), and an excerpt from Matthew Paris's "Life of Offa the First" as analogues of the Constance/Florence story, since some motifs from the Constance story appear in the *Gesta* and in Matthew Paris (57–84). The motifs, however, are only randomly and haphazardly organized in these two adducements, and, given that the story of the "calumniated queen" is widespread—with the folkloric elements, in particular, having all manner of European and Asian literary relations and antecedents, including perhaps Sanskrit, Persian, Turkish, and Arabic narratives (Heffernan, 3–4)—usually in the form of a motif here, or a convention there, I concentrate specifically on the core group of Constance stories in England that are closely identified by the linked integrity of their shared details and purposefulness, as described below. Farther-ranging than Furnivall et al. is Schlauch's survey, in her *Chaucer's Constance and Accused Queens*, of the story's folkloric prehistory and widest possible range of cultural relations. Schlauch's volume not only recovers a matrix of motifs, themes, and plots from folklore and legend, but it considers numerous literary analogues in Europe, some with highly attenuated features of the Constance story, like a fifteenth-century Flemish play, *Esmoreit*, which centrally features a male, not a female, character, but happens to have an accused queen in the plot (who is not herself noticeably a Constance figure). The narratives Schlauch surveys include stories involving heroines without children, heroines persecuted by their husbands, and postmedieval stories. *Emaré* and *Florence of Rome* are touched on (*KT* appears in a footnote), but the closest analogue to the Constance story of Trevet-Chaucer-Gower, in Schlauch's volume, is the mid-fifteenth-century *La Belle Hélène de Constantinople*, written half a century later on the continent, and thus chronologically and regionally removed from the core group of Constance texts I consider.

3. Perhaps the most dramatic example of transgendered mimicry in medieval romance is offered by the character Silence in the *Roman de Silence*, a character whose chivalric transvestism is ramified in the many heroines of renaissance romances like the *Faerie Queene*, the *Orlando Furioso*, and *Gerusalemme Liberata*. For a feminist analysis of what Silence's transgendered performance means, in the politics of medieval feudal

lineage, see Kinoshita ("Heldris"). Hudson ("Construction of Class"), following Lee Ramsey, prefers the term "domestic romances" to describe "the appearance in fourteenth-century England of a new type of romance that concerned family conflict" where "the greatest threats to the family are seen to come from within the family," including "threats of incest and other taboos" (83). Since many of these late Middle English romances involving family relations explore the central taboos identified by Freud many centuries later while retaining the sociohistorical markings of their contexts, my preference is for the term "family romances," given the term's punning ability to retrieve the affective and erotic lineaments (and the sexual politics) of later Freudian models of family romance, while still retaining a specifically medieval contextuality.

4. Scholars have long noted the many points of convergence between saints' legends and romances. Bloomfield, who observes that "some saints are even warriors" (118), recalls that, like romance, "marvel is of course the stock in trade of the saints' lives" (118) and that "the atmosphere of both romance and saint's life can be very similar" (119). Dieter Mehl notes, in particular, the Constance romances' resemblance to saints' legends, and Brewer remarks, of saints' legends and the *Man of Law's Tale*, that "Chaucer raised what had been a semi-popular genre to literary status" (221). Wogan-Browne points to convergences of other kinds: "Recent work on manuscripts and on social history emphasizes at least overlap, and frequently identity, among medieval *audiences* and *social contexts* for romance and hagiography. . . . Books most plausibly seen as household books, like . . . the Auchinleck manuscript . . . include saints' lives as well as romances while romances are included among monastic manuscript holdings" (85–86; my emphasis). The term "hagiographic romances" (*romans hagiographiques*)—a naming that captures succinctly both the borrowed hagiographic aura and the fantastical-historical nature of this species of imaginary narrative—is advocated by Delehaye (Mehl prefers the term "homiletic romances"). For the relationship of hagiography to romance, see also Childress; Hurley; Pearsall ("Capgrave"); and Wogan-Browne. *Florence of Rome*, in which the Constance story is relatively attenuated, is only occasionally referred to in this chapter.

5. Unlike Orderic, who had never been to the Levant, but ingeniously awards the Saracen-princess love episode to Bohemond (a famed crusading hero in Europe by the time of Orderic's *Historia Ecclesiastica*), chroniclers writing in the East—Fulcher of Chartres, Raymond d'Aguiliers, the author of the *Gesta Francorum*, and Anna Comnena—who might reasonably be expected to notice high-ranking Muslim conversion to Christianity, recount Bohemond's captivity by Danishmend with no mention of a Saracen-princess love episode whatsoever, nor the enactment of any conversion by an amorous "Melaz." That Orderic has a certain fondness for the motif of treasonous Muslim princesses is seen when he subsequently offers yet another disloyal Muslim queen, Fatima, who inveighs against her own royal husband, "Belek" or "Balad," and who also eagerly desires Christian conversion. Orderic tells readers that Fatima speaks on behalf of the other wives of Belek, all of whom also wish to be christened, and are dismayed at being released from Christian captivity and returned to their husband (11:118–20). F. M. Warren's 1914 article on the depiction of treacherous (and libidinous) Oriental woman,

always royals, in Western medieval literature, is an oft-cited classic. More recently feminist scholarship discussing the phenomenon includes the important work of Melitzki, Kinoshita ("Courtly Love," "Pagans"), Weiss, and de Weever. Cutler speculates that the historical "Zaida, the daughter-in-law of al-Mutamid of Seville, whom al-Mutamid gave as a concubine to King Alfonso VI of Castile (1065–1109) to cement a political alliance" and who was christened "Elizabeth," may well have been the model for the *Prise d'Orange*'s lovely Muslim renegade: "Zaida-Elizabeth may well be the source of Orable-Guibourc, the [*sic*] famous Muslim woman of the *chansons de geste* who converted to Christianity and married the great southern French hero, William of Orange" (58 n. 9).

6. Since conversion is a prime trope expressing successful conquest, the depiction of conversion—whether forced, semi-coerced, or voluntary—is, of course, to be found in some degree, to some extent, in narratives of cultural fantasy that feature the conquest of communities marked by religion-and/as-race in any period (including literatures of colonization in the modern era). However, *mass* conversion *because* of a woman's sexuality—a sexuality that can be defined as simply her desirability to men in power—is not an obsession of medieval narratives before the late Middle Ages. The overblown sexuality of some of the Muslim queens and princesses who convert also bears witness to the sexual politics of courtly love and exists on a continuum with depictions of aggressive European courtly mistresses in medieval romance. Melitzki, Kinoshita ("Courtly Love," "Pagans"), Weiss, and de Weever detail the implications of the marriage of East and West, Islam and Christianity, through gendered figures.

7. Although scattered, individual conversions occasionally occur in locales where religious-cultural systems and groups collide in unequal relations of power (as among Jews and Christians in medieval England before the Jewish expulsion or in Islamic-Christian Spain), conversion as a systematically articulated, actively pursued communal goal in Christendom is a phenomenon that begins in what I called, in chapter 2, the "long thirteenth century": "In the thirteenth century 'the overall strategy of Christendom underwent modification': the battle now was 'not only military but doctrinal'"(Burns, 1387). "At the opening of the thirteenth century the great Pope Innocent III, inclining to a popular belief that the world might end around 1284, envisoned a final crusade effort in East and West to prepare the mass conversion both of Jews and Muslims. Jacques de Vitry, preaching and baptizing converts in the crusader Holy land, informed Europe from 1217 to 1221 that 'many' Muslims, 'if they heard sound doctrine, would easily be converted'" (1390). "In the 1260s Roger Bacon hungrily eyed the multitudes of Muslims, Mongols, Buddhists, and pagans ripe for conversion. . . . Thirteenth-century crusading popes like Honorius III, Gregory IX, and Innocent IV encouraged conversion of Muslims by persuasion [and] from time to time the program tended to focus on a promising princely candidate" (1391). Burns usefully details two directives in conversion programs, which focused on the development of philosophical disputation and the creation of *language schools* that prepared missionaries, especially Dominican friars, for conversionist preaching: "As early as 1235 the master-general [of the Dominicans], writing from Milan to all the order, called for men 'prepared to learn Arabic, Hebrew, Greek, or some other outlandish language'" (1402).

Trevet, a Dominican, characterizes his Constance in the early fourteenth century as a missionary who had been educated in multiple languages.

8. Atiya (*Crusade in the Later Middle Ages*), for one, surveys the more prominent crusading propagandists of the fourteenth century and their detailed recommendations. Early in the century Ramon Lull's *Liber de Fine*, which discusses the tactical advantages of different routes to the East and the importance of language, medical, legal, and surgical skills, also suggests how a new order of crusading knights might be financed and created, even specifying what their habit should look like ("a black habit for penitence with a red cross for humility and triumph, and as a mark of sorrow all have to wear their beards long" [Atiya, *Later Middle Ages*, 79]). Burcard's *Directorium ad Philippum Regem* reflects on routes, expands the list of enemies to include many communities of Eastern Christians, and makes recommendations utterly demonstrating a lack of geographical pragmatism and familiarity with current events (Atiya, *Later Middle Ages*, 96–110). Marino Sanudo's *Liber Secretorum Fidelium Crucis*, which views the economic and military suppression of Mamluk Egypt as the sine qua non of successful recapture of the Holy Land, is also, commodiously, "a work of exceptional value for . . . the history of commerce, of medieval economics as well as navigation, geography and cartography . . . a pioneer of scientific geography and economics . . . even . . . the origin of all statistical studies" (Atiya, *Later Middle Ages*, 123).

Among late-fourteenth-century crusading propagandists, Philippe de Mézière is perhaps best known. "A dreamer and a mystic pilgrim," who had been chancellor of the Kingdom of Cyprus and close companion to the Papal Legate, Pierre de Thomas, during the failed crusading venture in Alexandria in 1365, Philippe de Mézière not only conceptualized a new order of chivalry, the Order of the Passion ("Militia Passionis Jhesu Christi"), but in his advice literature to his pupil, Charles VI, the *Songe du Vieil Pèlerin*, Philippe devotes attention to the groundwork of necessary diplomacy and the right moral ethos before the launching of a crusading enterprise, admonishing the kings of England and France to make common cause, bury differences, establish peace, and encourage pious rather than decadent courtly cultures (Atiya, *Later Middle Ages*, 139–46). Philippe would have different nations of crusaders travel by different routes, specifies the appropriate kind of naval craft for the sea journey ("craft of middle size, especially the 'taforesse' and the 'nef moyenne' in preference to the ordinary armed galley, for reasons of speed, efficiency and economy" [148]), and considers questions of climate in military engagement. Dates of sailing are precisely defined, the problem of congestion onboard ship is addressed, and provision is even made for women to accompany their husbands in order to avoid scandal (147–49). After the debacle of Nicopolis in 1396, and the massive defeat of the last crusading army of any size, Philippe de Mézière, in 1397, sent "a lengthy epistle . . . to console the Duke of Burgundy whose son had led the crusaders," again theorizing the usefulness of creating a new order of chivalry along with his specifications for the order (153).

9. At a seminar at the University of Oregon where part of this chapter was read, Ann Marie Rasmussen contributed a timely reminder that the Baltic "crusades," conducted

by the Teutonic knights, in Prussia, Lithuania, and the easterly interiors of continental
Europe, is the sole example of later-medieval "crusading" that, unlike the crusades to the
Holy Lands and Near East, accomplished *both* military success *and* cultural conversion.
Such wars of conversion in *Europe*, she went on to note, produced *chronicles* rather than
romances. Aggressions against the Albigensians, and assorted English military expedi-
tions were also sometimes dubbed "crusades" in the later Middle Ages.

10. "Et la cite de Ierusalem abaundona a la seignurie des Cristiens pur enhabiter,
e ffraunchises as euesques Cristiens e a lour clergie de precher, e enseigner les genz de
sa terre la dreite foy, e de baptizer e deglises fere, e les temples de maumetz destrure"
(Bryan and Dempster, 166). Chaucer's Man of Law conspicuously underscores the
warlike nature of Custance's advance into enemy territory, when he likens Custance's
arrival to imperial Caesar's, observing, with satisfaction, that the "triumph of Julius
[Caesar]" was not any more royal or any more elaborate (*MLT*, ll. 400–403).

11. "fraunche passage de aler fraunchement e marchaunder, e pur visiter les seintz
luz del sepulcre, e del mount de Caluerie, e de Bethleem e de Nazareth e del val de
Josaphat e tous autres [lieux] seyns" (Bryan and Dempster, 166). Cultural fantasy thus
circumvents the strategic military problem of Jerusalem's indefensibility, after Saladin
had had the city's walls destroyed, and subsequent developments in military and
strategic negotiations between Latin and Muslim forces prevented the rebuilding of
the walls, thus rendering the Holy City, in the opinion of the Templars and Hospitallers who would have had to conduct any required defense, impossible to defend
successfully for any duration, even in the eventuality of the city's successful military
recapture. Constance's peaceful takeover of the coveted Holy Places, by contrast, ensures a harmonious and noncontentious, rather than fractious and hostile, environment in which Christians might safely encompass both commercial and religious
ends: the precise reasons, and expressed in practical terms here, for the recovery of the
coveted lands.

12. As the goal of domination by cultural means gained momentum, pro-crusading
tracts enjoyed imagining the ways that successful conversion of the enemy might be encompassed. The key role played by *gender* in this project is specifically addressed by
Pierre Dubois's early-fourteenth-century polemical tract, which outlines the role that
can be usefully played by Constance-like women, in the imperial ideological adventure
of conversion:

> Pierre Dubois accorded girls an equal place with boys in the schools which he proposed
> should be founded for the education of a generation which should convert the East, and
> so recover the Holy Land. Like the boys, the girls were to be highly educated in the lan-
> guages which they would need for everyday converse, as well as in Greek and Latin.
> These girls [would be] trained in medical skills, more especially in those skills needed
> to deal with women's ills, so that they might then proceed to their conversion. To make
> this conversion feasible, the girls were also to be trained in theology, since they would
> need to be able to instruct the women in the tenets of the Christian faith. But Dubois
> gave these girls . . . no say in their own fate. As missionaries they were to carry out their

allotted task whether as the wives of Eastern clergy, or in whatsoever capacity they should find themselves, serving the cause of Christianity. This was a very different set of values from that which seemed to be so hopefully emergent toward women crusaders in the last quarter century before the fall of Acre [in 1291]. (Purcell, 61)

The coincidence in Trevet's Constance's resemblance to Dubois's ideal women missionaries—who, like Constance, should be skilled in several languages, make *rapprochements* with native women, marry when and where needed, and be sent forth without a "say in their own fate"—is difficult to overlook (see following note).

13. Trevet's Constance is herself a convert (and perhaps thus doubly zealous), before she converts others, and acquires Christianity along with her diverse languages and knowledges, including "the seven sciences, which are logic, physics, morality, astronomy, geometry, music, perspective" ("lez sept sciences, que sount logicience, naturel, morale, astronomie, geometrie, musique, perspectiue" [Bryan and Dempster, 165]). Trevet's accomplished heroine, who well realizes Pierre Dubois's ideal woman missionary, encompasses not only the conversion of the East but, more importantly, that of pagan Northumberland/England by being able also to speak Saxon ("E ele lui respoundi en Sessoneys . . . come cele questoit aprise en diuerses laungages"; "And she replied to him in Saxon, as one who was learned in diverse languages" [Bryan and Dempster, 168]). When Hermengild, the Saxon chatelaine who loves Constance, tells Constance several times a day that she would do whatever Constance wanted of her, Constance exploits the rapport she has with the native woman by having Hermengild convert to Christianity, since "there is nothing that you will not do at my will" ("'rien ne est,' dist ele, 'qe vous ne freez a ma volunte'" [Bryan and Dempster, 169]). Attacked at sea by the knight who boards her vessel and would rape her, the valiant missionary even has the presence of mind, and the rhetorical skills, to resist the attacker by reasoning with him, using the presence of her child as a pretext to suggest that they should wait to have intercourse on land; Constance subsequently distracts the attacker's attention and shoves him into the sea, where he drowns (Bryan and Dempster, 175–76).

14. Gower's *Confessio* describes Constance weeping and crying from sheer fright when the Sultan's mother has every Christian and Christian convert slain at her feast, except for Constance, who stands there "dead for fear" ("ded for feere" [l. 696]). Gower's Constance is also a tender mother who decides not to die when she is set on the waters a second time, despite her grief, because she must ensure her son's survival, and nourish and protect him (ll. 1066–83), for "motherhood and for tenderness" ("moderhed and for tendresse" [l. 1073]). This Constance suckles her child, and sings and rocks him to sleep, a gentle picture of earnest motherhood. Wetherbee, who makes the salient case on the "wholly passive exemplarity" of the Man of Law's "Custance" (74), a character who appears to be merely "a sort of icon in a series of tableaux," observes that Gower's Constance and her husband, Aella ("Allee"), Saxon king of Northumberland, by contrast, share a conjugal intimacy (72, 79). Gower's is a Constance who "hadde a gret part of [the king, her husband's] wille" (l. 1047). Childress, citing examples from the Constance group of romances, suggests that "the

passive protagonist is especially evident in those works that are concerned with the trials and hardships of a pious heroine, *Le Bone Florence of Rome*, *Emaré*, and the *King of Tars*" (318)—presumably because passivity creates a heroine who is a superior conduit of the divine will. Wetherbee's comparative analysis of Gower's and the Man of Law's Constance, however, reveals distinctive differences *within* characterizations in the group of so-called passive pious heroines, differences that call for explanation.

15. The argument formulated here emerged after a key conversation with Pete Wetherbee on Gower's nationalism and Wetherbee's characterization of Chaucer's Constance as "icon-like" rather than human (Wetherbee, 71). A subsequent conversation with Betty Sue Flowers, on the mythology of the "American Dream," yielded insight into how narratives solicit and the importance of non-elaboration. Wetherbee's insight that Gower's nationalism should not be underestimated, and Flowers's perception that narratives, when elaborated, shut out, rather than invite in, an audience, thus underpin the thinking both here and in my argument on the importance of mother-and-child figures in the nationalistic imaginary. What is true of Constance is also true of Griselda, another cipherlike figure in her saintly, uncomplaining patience, despite the relentlessly vicious, sadistic "tormentyng" devised by Griselda's husband, Walter.

16. The extent of culture's dependency on gendered figures, and the politics of gender relations, to express the intimate relationship of settlers and land is captured with curious vivacity in medieval Irish literature in the story of the debilitating labor pains that are putatively visited on the men of Ulster: Ulstermen, it seems, are rendered cyclically vulnerable (every nine months) to reproducing the original birth pangs of Macha, the legendary woman for whom their capital is eponymously named, because Macha was forced to run a race, thanks to the folly of a boastful husband, close to the time of her birth pains. The twins she births, in the course of the race, a son and a daughter, onomastically award the capital of Ulster its name, Emain Macha ("the twins of Macha").

17. As Saladin's secretary and chronicler, 'Imad ad-Din, makes plain, Jerusalem is a woman not only to Urban and the West. The Islamic rhetoric of counter-crusade issues similarly gendered figures as masculine military zeal is incited to recapture Jerusalem from crusader occupancy: "Islam wooed Jerusalem, ready to lay down lives for her as a bride-price, bringing her a blessing that would remove the tragedy of her state, giving her a joyful face to replace an expression of torment" (Gabrieli, 147). Quoting Saladin, 'Imad ad-Din has the emir say, of the captive city, "And who knows that God will not, by means of us, restore her to her former beauty, as He honours her by mentioning her among His most noble creations" (Gabrieli, 152).

18. "The story of Constance, as told by the Man of Law, is in the main enacted in the setting of Syria and Rome, 'Rome' originally being Constantinople, as known by its Arabic designation of *rūm*. The name of the heroine, Constance, first found in Trivet, reveals its Byzantine origins. Trivet seems to have synchronized a historical Aella of Northumberland (d. 580 [*sic*]), the second husband of Constance, with the

reign of the sixth-century Eastern Emperor, Tiberius Constantius, father of a daughter named Constantina" (Melitzki, 153–54).

19. Both in report and direct address, the desirability and beauty of Rome (the city) and Florence (the woman) are closely identified: "The effect of Rome Y haue yow tolde . . . But of þe feyrenes of þe maye / I can not telle" (*Le Bone Florence of Rome*, ll. 346–50); "Syr, wyth þis dynte Y chalenge Rome, / And þy doghter bryght as blome" (*Florence*, ll. 685–86). As if to underscore the heroine's association with Latin realms and Latin Christianity, Florence's name also inevitably evokes her namesake Italian city. By contrast to Florence/Rome, the old Greek Empire, and site of schismatic Eastern Christianity—Constantinople—is exemplified by its aged emperor, the repellent Garcy, whose lecherous desire for conjugal union with Florence perhaps allegorizes how Greek desire for union with, and domination of, Latin Christian Rome (a union that would end centuries of Schism between Latin and Greek Christianity) might be fearfully imagined. For fourteenth-century Greek and Roman efforts to end the Schism between Eastern and Western Church, see Atiya (*Later Middle Ages*, chap. 11). *Florence* also rather ostentatiously features periodic appearances by the Roman Pontiff, who is ostensibly *not* the Avignonese Pope of the late-medieval Schism. Historical markings of this nature in the romance do not seem to detract from what Lee calls the "coherence and realism of the English version" of *Florence* (351).

20. Male desire for Emaré, including her own father's incestuous desire, tends to erupt when Emaré is specifically displayed in the cloak. On the first occasion that Emaré dons the cloak, after it has been fashioned from the Oriental cloth-of-gold, her father the Emperor exclaims: "Dowghtyr, y woll wedde the, / Thow art so fresh to beholde" ("Daughter, I will wed thee, / Thou art so fresh to behold" [ll. 248–49]). After Emaré washes up on the shores of Wales ("Galys") and is taken in by the king's steward, Sir Kador (a good, traditional Arthurian name), Emaré's appearance before the king, at Sir Kador's feast—dressed again in the glittering, embroidered treasure—renders the king instantly abject with desire and unable to eat, "so anamered of that syghth" (l. 400) was he. On these occasions where the masculine gaze falls upon the luminous woman from the East, swathed in her luminous raiment, the glory of both the woman and the luxurious prize mutually enhance each other, so that Emaré appears "unearthly," extraordinary beyond the pale. Two objects of desire merge in the rapturous descriptions, and an imperial or royal monarch's desire for the beauty from the Orient becomes indistinguishable from desire for the Orient itself. For a fuller account of Emaré's relation to her cloak, needlework, and craft, see Katherine Oldmixon's dissertation on exoticism in the Middle English Breton lays. Donovan also discusses the relationship of the cloak to Emaré, and Arthur reads the object's meaning as a sign.

21. The Man of Law vilifies the Sultaness as a "Virago" and a second Semiramis ("Semyrame the secounde," *MLT*, l. 359), naming the militant Babylonian queen as the Sultaness's predecessor in masculinized militancy and political leadership. More recently than Semiramis, however, the historical record gleams with depictions of Muslim royal and noble women who defend Islam, and Syrian and Egyptian territory, both in military and political contexts. Ousama Munkidh, a princeling of Shaizar,

describes militant Islamic warrior women in his early-twelfth-century *Autobiography*, one of whom, "wearing a coat of mail and a helmet, and bearing a sword and shield," turns out to be the mother of Ousama's cousin's relative (*Autobiography*, 163). Ousama's own mother "distributed my swords and my padded tunics" (164), and "an old woman named Fanoûn, who had served my grandfather, the emir Aboû 'l-Hasan 'Ali . . . on this day covered her face with a veil, seized a sword and rushed into the fight. She did not stop until she saw us get the upper hand and triumph over our enemies" (164–65). Best known among Muslim queens, perhaps, who were decisive in crisis and in the aftermath of exigency, is the mid-thirteenth-century Shajar ad-Durr, "Tree of Pearls," the widow of the last Ayyubid sultan of Saladin's line, who effected a seamless transition of power when her royal husband died in untimely fashion during a war with Louis of France's crusaders. The chronicler Ibn Wasil notes:

> From that time she became titular head of the whole state; a royal stamp was issued in her name with the formula "mother of Khalil," and the *khutba* [the address from the pulpit, at Friday prayer, in the mosque of the capital city] was pronounced in her name as Sultana of Cairo and all Egypt. This was an event without precedent throughout the Muslim world: that a woman should hold the effective power and govern a kingdom was indeed known; there was for example the case of Daifa Khatūn, daughter of the Sultan al-Malik al-'Adil, who governed Aleppo and its province after the death of her son al-Malik al-'Aziz for as long as she lived, but in this case the *khutba* was pronounced in the name of her grandson al-Malik an-Nasir. (Gabrieli, 297–98)

22. Trevet's Domild stresses Constance's foreignness and unknown lineage ("qi lynage lui nestoit pas conu") as well as her royal son's forsaking of his first faith, "the religion that all his ancestors had loyally and entirely kept" ("sa primere ley gwerpi, quele touz ses auncestres auoient leaulment e enterement gardes" [Bryan and Dempster, 172; Furnivall, 25]). Domild's response is thus explicitly represented, first and foremost, as a nationalist (or xenophobic) reaction—a concern to preserve both native royal descent/the unbroken purity of the native royal bloodline, and the integrity of the religious community of faith, whose continuity is disrupted with the king's conversion to Constance's religion—before the reaction is also inevitably naturalized, in a conventional, gendered accusation of the older woman's "envy" toward a younger, more popular, and more admired female rival (Bryan and Dempster, 172; Furnivall, 25). Following Trevet's example, Chaucer's Man of Law also makes Donegild reject the foreign creature who is Constance ("vne femme estraunge" [Bryan and Dempster, 172; Furnivall, 25]; "so strange a creature" [*MLT*, l. 700]).

23. Schlauch (*Chaucer's Constance and Accused Queens*, 62) notes that a repeating feature of the "accused queen" motif, in folklore and *märchen*, is the gender of the accusing persecutor: an older female in the family not linked to the Constance-like victim by blood kinship and often a mother-in-law or stepmother figure (sometimes a sorceress). Even as the Constance romances in England offer Domild and the Sultaness as symbolic defenders of religious communities and homelands, therefore, the narratives also tap an old reliable trove of cultural response to familiar,

conventional stereotypes of the dangerous older female relative. Trevet, Chaucer, and Gower cannot resist naturalizing the women's motives by reference to the personal (echoing, thus, the folkloric antecedents). Trevet's "Deumylde" has her heart wounded by "great envy" ("graunt enuye" [Bryan and Dempster, 172; Furnivall, 25]) of her daughter-in-law because of universal admiration for Constance. The Man of Law cites the "malice" of both the Sultaness and Donegild (*MLT*, ll. 36, 779), and the *Confessio* stresses the "envie" of the Sultan's mother (ll. 641, 684). Correale points out that "Gower even changed his source in [Constance's] first exile scene . . . so that the wicked mother of the Souldan, and not her navy, is directly responsible for putting Constance on the 'wawes wilde'" (140).

24. Although her argument and interest point in other directions, Bullón-Fernández (retroping Patricia Eberle's use of Brian Tierney's concept) makes a similar observation on this palimpsestic regraphing of conversion historiography in England:

> The story of Constance is a "story of origins," that is, a story that attempts to legitimize a certain form of authority. Constance, according to the tale, brought Christianity to England. She is in this sense the origin, the spiritual mother who gave birth to the authority of the Christian monarchs of medieval England, and the one who thus validates royal authority. It is significant, of course, that a woman sent by an emperor . . . should function as the symbolic origin of the English state, rather than a man sent by the pope (as was historically the case with Augustine's conversion of the English). (141)

The Constance story's displacement of the Augustinian mission onto *women* goes so far as to attribute one of Augustine's miracles, described by Bede (*Historia Ecclesiastica*, 2:ii)—the giving of sight, in God's name, to a blind Angle who is brought to Augustine (Plummer, 1:82)—to Dame Hermengild, Constance's convert who gives sight to a blind Briton imploring her help in God's name, a miracle that goes on to spread the chain of conversion in Northumbria.

25. An important critical study of how commerce, money, and cash/credit relations profoundly affect the representation of knightly identity in late-medieval English literature is Shoaf's classic, *Poem as Green Girdle* (see also his *Currency of the Word*). Shoaf implies that a subtextual association exists between women and money in the *Man of Law's Tale*, through their shared properties as instruments in circulation (women in literary texts, money in socioeconomic contexts) and as instrumental media: "The Man of Law is obsessed with retention . . . he is anxious about circulation, afraid of the flow of things, of media, be they money or women or words" ("Unwemmed Custance," 293).

Karen Jambeck, who discusses several famous, wealthy women who happened to be literary patrons in fourteenth- and fifteenth-century England, also implicitly suggests why late-medieval *authors*, in particular, might be especially alive to the possibilities of representing women as the source of money, treasure, and other forms of capital such as vast estates, in late-medieval literature, and be keenly alert to the reasons for depicting women as supplying the means, opportunities, and resources for men, noble and non-noble, who are making their way in the world. Jambeck notes that Blanche of Lancaster's "inheritance of the vast Lancaster fortunes upon the deaths of her father (1361) and her sister, Maud (1362)" publicly brought John of Gaunt "the title of Duke of Lancaster and made him one of the wealthiest men of the realm" (235). Among the many prominent and highly visible women of great fortune and vast resources in the period who were the patrons of authors, with influence over literary productions, Jambeck names Joan FitzAlan, countess dowager of Hereford, Eleanor of Bohun, co-heir of the Bohun fortune, Anne of Woodstock ("perhaps the wealthiest woman in England"), Joan Beaufort (who "opened great opportunities" to her husband), Anne Neville Stafford, dowager duchess of Buckingham, Alice Chaucer, an "heiress in her own right" who married the Earl of Salisbury and Duke of Suffolk, and afterward "lived as a wealthy and esteemed widow for a quarter of a century," and Maud Burghersh, who not only brought her husband, Thomas Chaucer, "substantial land holdings but increased "her properties in Oxford, Cambridge, Essex, Hampshire, and Suffolk" through inheritance and skillful negotiations (236–44).

26. Shulamith Shahar's elaboration of women as a "Fourth Estate," amplifying the traditionally recognized system of three estates in medieval society, follows Jill Mann's insight that "women were recognised as a separate class in estates lists" (121), and pivots on the anomalous and slippery, inside-outside position of women within the estates system. Work by feminist historians on women book owners and women cultural patrons in the late Middle Ages also thoughtfully suggests ways that women might be associated in the authorial imagination with the mobility of culture, and with cultural, symbolic, and economic capital. Citing the contents of libraries, behests and wills, commissions, and statistical tables of book ownership, Susan Groag Bell constructs a persuasive argument for the role of book-owning and book-commissioning aristocratic women in the transmission of culture, as these women circulated through diverse lands, in the course of sometimes serial marriages: "That these women and their books originated in diverse European locations, while they often journeyed across the Continent and the English Channel on marriage, suggests important trends in the diffusion of medieval culture" (139) since "medieval marriage customs . . . forced women to move from their native land to their husbands' domains. Medieval marriage bestowed upon women a role of cultural ambassador that it did not bestow upon men who remained on their native soil" (156).

Bell notes, for example, that the "Winchester style" of manuscript illumination "traveled from England, to Bavaria, and thence to Tuscany" in the eleventh century, when Judith of Flanders brought work she commissioned at Winchester (during her marriage to Tostig, Earl of Northumbria) to Bavaria, in her later marriage to Welt of Bavaria; the Winchester-illustrated Gospels subsequently traveled to Tuscany, as Judith's wedding gift to her daughter-in-law (156). In "the age of Wycliff and Chaucer," Anne of Bohemia's marriage to Richard II of England in 1382 meant the movement of Anne's books, and Bohemian book illustrators in her entourage, to England, where the "influence of Anne's books and illustrators on English art [became] clearly established" (158). "Anne's uninhibited ownership of multilingual Gospels in England"— pointed to by Wycliff to justify English translations of the Bible from Latin—also meant that "the cultural exchange that Anne initiated from Prague to London also encouraged the reverse: the influence of Wycliffe and other English reformers on Hussite Bohemia accelerated" (159).

If medieval women of means thus facilitated the mobility of culture and mediated the movement of cultural capital—in the form of books and cultural artifacts they commissioned from authors and artists—it is scarcely remarkable that the authorial imagination might seize on female figures to symbolize cultural transactions and exchange, and to figure the transmission and reproducibility of culture, with such characters as Constance. Constance as a reproducer of culture abroad has her historical counterparts in traveling queens and noblewomen who bring culture (if not culture as religious conversion) with them. Similarly Constance, as an intimate reproducer of culture at home, domestically, in the education her young son, Maurice, in his early childhood, also has historical counterparts in the queens and noblewomen who taught their young children at home to read or who read to them (Bell, 148–51). Discussing "the collaborative involvement of women in the act of reading, and perhaps compilation," Meale ("Audiences") speculates that the Vernon manuscript—in which the *King of Tars*, a Constance romance, as I show below—might also have been "commissioned for a community of women, whether secular or religious" (222).

27. On the typicality of economically successful female figures like the Wife of Bath, see Thrupp (172–73), Robertson (discussing successful women workers in the rural textile industry), and Huth's Ph.D. dissertation on women and the professionalization of female labor as depicted in late-medieval English literature. Hudson's "Construction of Class," on the relationship between Middle English "domestic romances" (what I have been calling "family romances") and the gentry, suggests that "a major function of English gentry women" was to administrate family estates—another means, perhaps, by which women might be publicly associated with capital assets in the fourteenth and fifteenth centuries (89–90). The argument on Noah's wife is made by Huth, in her Ph.D. dissertation.

28. Kowaleski and Bennett, building on the cornerstone work of Marian Dale's historical study of medieval London textile workers, reiterate both the highly skilled nature of silk work and its profitability:

> Silkworking was a true "mystery" . . . a skilled craft with secrets of production and trade passed on only from mistress to apprentice. The women who worked in this craft had many of the attributes associated with high-status work: they had valued skills, ran workshops and trained apprentices, invested large amounts of money in purchases of raw materials and trading ventures, and stayed in the same craft throughout their working lives. They also banded together for mutual aid. On six occasions between 1368 and 1504, the London silkworkers sought protection of their craft and trade through petitions (presented to either Parliament or the mayor of London), and most of their requests were granted. (17–18)

Though feminist historians duly note that Englishwomen in the textile trade did not organize themselves into formal guilds, and lament this strategic error in medieval labor relations, they nonetheless also note the relative wealth of the silk workers and their "large and lucrative contracts" (17), and that female textile workers in medieval Paris, Rouen, and Cologne *did* organize themselves into "exclusively female or female dominated" guilds (18), in which "ties between women might have been more important . . . than ties between women and men" (19). Significantly, the seven known women's guilds in Paris, the five in Rouen, and the three in Cologne all profitably concentrated on work in luxury textiles, thread, yarn, embroidery, purses, headgear, silk, lace, and intricate handwork of the kind at which the romance Emaré excels.

29. Despite Urban II's injunction at Clermont in 1095 that women, as noncombatants, not go on what became known in Europe as the First Crusade, "the anonymous author of the *Gesta Francorum* . . . pays warm tribute to the women who, in the Battle of Dorylaeum, were of great help in the dire straits in which the army found itself, acting on the occasion as water-carriers" (Purcell, 57). At the seige of Antioch, during the same crusade, more than one eyewitness chronicle noted that women crusaders (among whom, presumably, were camp followers and prostitutes who invariably accompanied medieval military forces on campaigns of any duration) were put out of the camp, away from male combatants, on occasions when continence was advised by crusading clergy to ensure the success of military skirmishes, and God's approval. Some crusader barons were also accompanied by their wives: "Fulcher of Chartres refers to the wife of Raymond of St. Gilles as having been left behind at Laodicea. . . . Albert of Aix records the death of Baldwin of Boulogne's wife, Godvere of Tocsin [Godehilde of Tosni] at Marash" (Purcell, 57).

Before the advent of the crusade as armed pilgrimage, nuns already journeyed on pilgrimage, as the infamous anecdote of the abbess who died, after having been gang-raped during the great German pilgrimage of 1064–65 (recounted in the *Life of Bishop Altmann of Passau*) suggests. Inevitably the names of the women crusaders that descend to us were those of noblewomen and royal wives such as Eleanor of Acquitaine (with an entourage of Amazons, according to the Greek chronicler Nicetas Choniates [*RHC, Historiens Grecs*, 1:250–51]): "Numerous chroniclers record the setting out in [the crusade of] 1101 of a great number of women among whom we know the names of Ida, margravine of Austria, widow of Leopold III, and Corba, wife of Geoffrey Burel" (Purcell, 58). That Richard I of England found it necessary to forbid the presence of all women but laundresses on the Third Crusade, however, suggests that non-noble women crusaders might have been relatively common. On the side of the Arab chroniclers, Saladin's secretary, 'Imad ad-Din, offers what also appears to be a description of a warlike Eleanor and her knights in battle (Gabrieli, 207), as well as an account of European women crusader warriors of all ages, including old women acting in the familiar medieval gender role of goad to warriors:

> Among the Franks there were indeed women who rode into battle with cuirasses and helmets, dressed in men's clothes; who rode out into the thick of the fray and acted like brave men although they were but tender women . . . clothed only in a coat of mail they were not recognized as women until they had been stripped of their arms. Some of them were

discovered and sold as slaves; and everywhere was full of old women. . . . They exhorted and incited men to summon their pride, saying that the Cross imposed on them the obligation to resist to the bitter end, and that the combatants would win eternal life only by sacrificing their lives, and that their God's sepulchre was in enemy hands. (Gabrieli, 207)

'Imad ad-Din also offers a lurid, near-pornographic account of European camp followers and prostitutes, rendered in his characteristic purple prose, and rich with *double-entendres* and sexual metaphors (Gabrieli, 204–6).

30. Herlihy remarks that "the Holy Family itself was viewed as a trinity, which in some ways replicated on earth the Blessed Trinity in heaven" ("Medieval Family," 128). On the proliferation of female saints, which occurs from the thirteenth century, Herlihy cites Weinstein and Bell (*Medieval Households,* 207 n. 5).

31. Sheingorn, tracing the intimacy of mother-child relations in late medieval culture as represented in the visual arts, reiterates that "both in medieval Europe and in our own society women have primary responsibility for the parenting of babies and young children. The many representations of the Holy Kinship, that is, of Saint Anne and her daughters surrounded by their children, provide visual analogues" (83). Sheingorn also persuasively argues that it is the transcendent "God the Father who, from the Annunciation onward, remained a steady presence in Mary's life" (86) rather than the Virgin's earthly husband, Josesph: "As Ruth Mellinkoff puts it in her recent book, *Outcasts* . . . 'Joseph was belittled as a doddering old man, a grumbling, disgruntled husband, a fool, a cuckold and comic, a crude rustic' . . . Mellinkoff cites many examples in which Joseph is denigrated by the denial of a halo, even when minor figures such as a nursemaid have them, as in a painting of the Nativity dated about ca. 1390" (84). McLaughlin in turn makes the point that "in a military and expansionist society" the father was often "virtually absent from the child's early life" (128) and that from the eleventh through thirteenth centuries, and possibly beyond, "the demands of a military life, as well as distant pilgrimage and crusade, helped to create, as Herlihy suggests, a 'woman's world at home,' a world in which women played a particularly active role in the administration of feudal households and in the early rearing and training of children" (135). Hale, who reiterates that "the Joseph cult did not begin to flourish until the fifteenth century" (103), as "a creation of such churchmen as Pierre d'Ailly, Jean Gerson, Bernadino de Siena, Bernadino de Feltre and Isidore Isolanis" (107), discusses popular representations of Joseph in "plays and rituals" (107) before the fifteenth century that "appropriated and adapted elements and features associated with a cult of . . . Mary as mother of Jesus" (102).

32. Bynum's classic study discusses the phenomenon, in twelfth-century Cistercian writing, of imagery conceptualizing Jesus as a mother, in which Christ's vicars also conceptualized themselves as engaged in mothering: "Maternal imagery was applied in the Middle Ages to male religious authority figures, particularly abbots, bishops and the apostles, as well as to God and Christ" (*Jesus*, 112). Though Bynum first discusses the subject in the context of twelfth-century religious culture, her insights have been extended to later periods, even if the High Middle Ages remains a fertile

ground of recovery for maternal imagery: "His biographer speaks of the 'almost moth-
erly affection' of Hugh of Lincoln, and in the last illness of Ailred of Rievaulx, we are
told, his monks used to visit him, 'lying about his bed and talking with him as a little child prattles with its mother'; it is reported that his dying words to them were 'I
love you as earnestly as a mother does her sons." (McLaughlin, 132). "To a delinquent
monk [Bernard of Clairvaux] wrote: 'And I have said this, my son, . . . I begot you in
religion by word and example. I nourished you with milk. . . . You too were torn from
my breast, cut from my womb. My heart cannot forget you.' Male writers thus linked
their own 'motherhood' . . . with that of Christ" (Bynum, "'. . . And Woman His Humanity,'" 264).

33. Trevet mentions Constance's own death a year after the mother-son dyad resumes on the death of Aella (Bryan and Dempster, 181; Furnivall, 53), a death that is
necessary, perhaps, to bring the tale to chronicle-style narrative closure, as well as, perhaps, out of a certain narrative tact and delicacy, for Trevet's Maurice is a young man
of some eighteen years, and not a child. Narrative decorum, therefore, presumably requires that some gesture be made to close off the perilously incestuous-seeming dyadic
pair of mother and son who have lived together for eighteen years. By interesting contrast, Chaucer's *Man of Law's Tale* has Constance and Maurice, and the old emperor,
live together, as a triangulated family of parents and children, "til deeth departeth hem"
(*MLT*, l. 1158): a queer description of family relations in a formula that echoes the marriage ceremony's liturgy. The *historical* Constance—daughter of the Byzantine Emperor Tiberius II (578–582)—was, of course, *married* to Maurice ("Mauritius,"
582–602), a general of Tiberius II who succeeded to Tiberius's imperial throne through
marriage to Constantina (i.e., "Constance"), so a historical shard is secreted within the
seemingly incestuous relations of the romance Constance-and-Maurice dyad.

34. A blessed ambiguity is thus available when Chaucer's Custance says to the
Constable, who is about to strand her and Maurice on their vessel at sea, "kys hym
ones in his fadres name!" ("kiss him once in his father's name"): Whether Constance
means that the Constable should kiss the infant in the name of Aella, Maurice's biogenetic father by whose presumed will the heinous deed is about to be committed, or
whether Constance is adverting to a more kindly divine father remains ambiguous
here (*MLT*, l. 861).

35. Chaucer's Alla momentarily attempts to claim his son with a comparison of
similitude between the boy and himself ("Maurice my sone" [*MLT*, l. 1063]) in their
guiltlessness, but in the same moment has to admit the lack of difference between
mother and child, by which he is so strongly struck ("so lyk youre face" [*MLT*, l.
1063]). In *Emaré*, metaphors of clothing and fabric delineate the space of identity resemblance between mother and child: Emaré's child is described as "worthy unthur
wede" (ll. 736, 988) while the mother herself is "lufsumme . . . unthur lyne" (l. 864).
In Trevet, as we have said, Maurice is fully eighteen years old and a young man, not
a child any longer, when he meets his genetic father for the first time. Maurice's intimate closeness to his mother, in Trevet's version, is thus peculiarly colored by his
youthful male adulthood. (Orme, like others, notes that "seven, or the seventh year,

seems to have been a traditional point for noble children to pass from the care of women to tuition by males. . . . Fourteen was the age . . . at which . . . in the poll taxes of 1377–81, children became adults and subject to be charged" [7].)

In general, however, critics of the Constance story are inclined to neglect the hints of an odd, seemingly incestuous relationship between Constance and her son in favor of the incest suggested between Constance's father, the emperor, and Constance herself, as daughter—an incest that is narratively played out only in the *Emaré* version of the Constance story (but see Bullón-Fernández [137] on Gower's incestuous pair)— or, alternatively, to note instead, when discussing queer parent-child emotions, the Sultan's and Aella's mothers' intense possessiveness over their adult sons (see, e.g., Dinshaw, *Chaucer's Sexual Poetics*; C. David Benson, "Incest"; Archibald, "Flight from Incest; and Shoaf, "Unwemmed Cuctance").

As a pair, Constance and Maurice's retrieval of the image of Madonna and child protects them, to an extent, from intimations of incest ("Not only does the Man of Law use language that associates [Constance] with the Virgin Mary (she is a "queen," "unwemmed"); Constance herself . . . makes her own Marian role explicit" [Dinshaw, *Chaucer's Sexual Poetics*, 111]). Hints of mother-son incest, like father-daughter incest, can, however, be readily found in Middle English romances (e.g. *Sir Degaré* and *Sir Eglamour* both feature sons who win their mother's hand and marry her, though carnal relations are averted at the eleventh hour). Archibald ("Appalling Dangers"), who suggests that "mother-son incest seems to be the worst possible crime, the discovery of which changes the course of the protagonist's life and propels him toward sanctity" in medieval literature (160), reminds us that Semiramis took her own son, Ninus, as lover (158)—and Semiramis, of course, is a queen to whom Chaucer's Man of Law pointedly likens the Sultaness (*MLT*, l. 360).

36. "The Aristotelian view of woman's role in conception, as accepted by the Middle Ages, is pertinent here: a female only passively receives the active male principle, contributing to prenatal development only the matter shaped by the active male principle and the environment in which the fetus is nourished" (Parsons, "Pregnant Queen," 48). "Genesis 1:28 defines the purpose of woman's creation (in 1:27) as generative, Augustine argues. Woman was created to help Adam beget children, and woman's role in generation is passive, opposite from and inferior to man's active role" (Schibanoff, 67). See also Bullough ("Medical and Scientific Views"), Borresen, and Allen.

37. Kolve's discussion of Constance's journeys by ship offers the most thorough and detailed exploration of the vessel's symbolism, and is supplemented by extensive reference to the visual arts. Kolve suggests that in Constance's first two ship journeys the vessel is unmistakably "the Ship of the Church," and the first voyage's "purposiveness and splendor," with a "large and significant company" accompanying Constance, specifically draws on iconographic tradition (308–9). "The rudderless boat of Custance's second journey, in which she drifts for three years before arriving at the coast of Northumbria, gives precedence to a different meaning . . . but it remains a Ship of the Church as well, whose voyage will convert another kingdom" (Kolve, 316). The second ship's rudderlessness suggests that "it is as *Lord* of Fortune, the shaping

intelligence and moral coherence behind the apparent anarchy of human life, that God is invoked, at once rudder to Constance's boat and shipman to her soul" (330). Finally, "the third journey resumes the second, emphasizing the continuity of the whole *peregrinatio* and linking the two in ways that can be read anagogically, as the unitary death voyage of the soul" (349). Trial, isolation, endurance, divine agency, and providential resolution are implicitly or explicitly evoked when individuals are cast on the waters: "Persons were most often set adrift for one of three reasons: when guilt could not be conclusively determined by human investigation, when men wished to combine severity with some possibility of mercy, or when, as in the case of Custance, society wished to expel an unwanted person from its midst" (326).

38. Trevet's narrative discloses its sympathies through a gently rueful irony, when it describes Maurice as an infant who "learnt seamanship young / at a youthful age" (Furnivall, 33). To advocate an ideal maternity, Catherine of Cleves's Book of Hours has an illustration depicting the Virgin "with milk spurting from her breast" standing on one side of the cross, as Catherine is depicted on the other (Bell, 147). Besides the Virgin, "the Bible offered the examples of Sarah, Hannah . . . as women who nursed their own children" (Orme, 11). "For all classes the mother who nursed her own children reflected the ideal maternal image. Celebrated in contemporary representations of the *Virgo lactans*, the nursing mother of Christ, and in the poignant Eve nursing her child portrayed on the bronze doors of Hildesheim, and later at Verona, this essential maternal function was emphasized and extolled in literary and didactic works of various kinds. Praising it on both scientific and emotional grounds, Bartholomew of England explained that 'while the foetus exists in the womb it is nourished on blood, but at birth nature sends that blood to the breasts to be changed into milk" (McLaughlin, 115). Because of "the general conviction that the formative influences of milk affected the character as well as the physical constitution of the infant" (116), the traditional explanation of why Eustace, the younger brother of the crusader barons Godfrey of Bouillon and Baldwin of Boulogne, the first two rulers of the Latin Kingdom of Jerusalem, never rose to the celebrated heights of his accomplished brothers, is that Eustace, unlike Godfrey and Baldwin, had been nursed by a wet nurse, rather than their noble mother, and had not received the qualities of character imparted through an aristocratic mother's milk. Like Constance in the Constance stories, the two examples cited by Orme, of noblewomen in medieval romances depicted as nursing their own babies, also stem from the late Middle Ages: Sir Ector's wife in Malory, and prince Blanchardyn, in Caxton's *Blanchardyn and Eglantine* (Orme, 11).

39. Chaucer and Gower also explicitly make the leader of the punitive "Roman" forces Constance's uncle/relative, a development that reinforces, in the saga, the symbolization of family as religious community. Thus the Sultaness's form of resistance itself is represented as ironically determining Christendom's strategy of domination, as her violence is punished with violence, and becomes the occasion for a crusade-style punitive military expedition wreaked on the Islamic nation by Constance's father, the Christian emperor, and his surrogates: a military fantasy that, following on the heels of a woman's success in converting through feminine sexuality, is no doubt satisfying

to imagine. Delany observes: "Woman isn't *eternally* Other; the infidel is" ("Geographies," 28). Wetherbee, who calls the Sultaness and Domild "spokeswomen for their cultures" (78), also observes that the Sultaness's exhortation of her people constitutes "a kind of anti-crusade" (77). Because the People of the Book—Jews, Christians, Muslims—share a common matrix of sacred texts, figures, and traditions, despite doctrinal differences, these religious communities also share a kind of intimate relationship to one another that seems familylike, with all the concomitant problems of tension, heritage, incestuousness, and sanguinary competitiveness so often seen, historically, among large, disparate family-and-clan structures. The intimate relationship interlinking the communities of the Book perhaps irresistibly solicits the use of family metaphors and figures in cultural representation.

40. Lest we are momentarily tempted to read the name of the sixth-century Aella (or Aelle) of Deira as somehow implicated in the Islamic family/nation of Islam— "Allah," after all, is the Arabic designation for God, as every modern reader knows, since September 11, 2001, and the name "Aella," in one Constance story, the Man of Law's, appears as "Alla," even as the *Confessio Amantis* refers to the king as "Allee"— we should remember that Middle English literature usually invokes the Islamic divine through the name of His prophet, "Mahoun," or "Makomete" (*MLT*, l. 333), or through a fictitious pantheon of Gods ("Mahoun," "Tervagant," "Apollo/Apollin," etc.), inherited no doubt from the *chanson de geste* tradition (see note 71, below), or simply as "God" (*MLT*, l. 334), even when Middle English texts name the Muslim holy book as "Alkaron" (*MLT*, l. 332). Indeed, the Man of Law directly refers to the Islamic deity as "grete God," rather than as "Allah," names "Makomete" or "Mahoun" as "Goddes message[r]," and renders Islam as "Makometes lawe," rather than Allah's (*MLT*, ll. 333–34, 336, 340). We should, of course, distinguish between familiar terms that we as moderns take for granted and terms that habitually appear in Middle English as their equivalents.

There is one intriguing instance in *Mandeville's Travels* in which "alla" phonetically appears in a given string of "Saracen" syllables, in the Middle English Egerton and Cotton manuscripts: a moment where the narrator, as he is describing the "Saracen" alphabet, purportedly offers a rough transcription of the centuries-old Islamic avowal, "There is no God but God, and Mohammad is His prophet" (rendered in the *Travels* as "There is no God but one, and Mohammad his messenger"). Egerton renders the avowal as "La elles ella sila Machomet rores alla hec" (G. F. Warner, 71), and Cotton as "La ellec olla syla Machomet rores alla" (Hamelius, 1:92). Though the narrator's corruption of the Arabic ("Saracen") attestation is missing one reference to Allah ("La illaha illa Allah, wa Muhammad rasul [messenger] Allah" would be the correct rendition), Denise Spellberg, my colleague in medieval Arab and Islamic history who supplied the Arabic, accepts the "Mandeville" narrator's derivation of the prayer—probably, she speculates, via Spain—as a proximate, if condensed and garbled, transliteration.

Unlike *Mandeville's Travels*, however, the *Man of Law's Tale* shows no equivalent grasp of any formulaic prayer or, indeed, any ambient context in which God's Arabic name might accrue meaning for a reader of Middle English. "Makomete," however, is accurately represented as "God's messenger," and Islam appears monotheistic, even if, like Old Testament Judaism, Islam requires "sacrifices" (*MLT*, l. 325). Manuscript study suggests that Chaucer's orthographic use of "Alla" for the king's name (except in l. 725, where it is "Alle," for the rhyme) points to Chaucer's consultation of manuscripts of Trevet's *Cronicles* from the B family of texts, in which the scribes use "Alla" when narrating events up to and until the king's pilgrimage to Rome (and "Alle" for the remaining narrative), whereas Gower's name for the king, "Allee," suggests that the name came from an A family manuscript, since the scribes of the A manuscripts consistently spell the king's name "Alle" (see Correale, 149), even if Gower's text more closely resembles the manuscripts of family B in other respects (Correale, 150). Nicholson adds that Gower's "Allee" might also derive from "another scribe's variation of 'Alle' that could have occurred in a manuscript of either 'A' and 'B'" (92). Trevet's selection of Aella of Deira to illustrate the success of Constance's missionary efforts in England is a resonantly canny decision: Bede's *Historia Ecclesiastica* (2:i) relates a story about Gregory the Great—a story that makes Gregory definitively decide to send missionaries to convert England—in which Gregory, on discovering that some beautiful slaves are from "Deiri," a province ruled over by "Aelli" ("Aelle," "Elle"), decides that Deirans must be instructed from wrath ("de ira") and called to the mercy of Christ ("et ad misericordiam Christi uocati") punning on their king's name, to make the land praise God the Creator, in singing "*Alle*-luia" (Plummer, 1:80).

41. Constance shows how well she understands the symbolic relationship of her affective-biological family to the family of Christendom when she pleads with her father, on her return home, "Sende me namoore unto noon hethenesse" (*MLT*, l. 1112). That families should represent collectivities is part of the cultural logic of medieval life: "In the medieval period," as Keith Stringer notes, "collective activity of all kinds was permeated by the ideas and values of family life, and the family, that central organ of social cohesion, for long remained at the core of community action and experience" (12). The crucial symbolic logic invoked in depicting whole societies and communities as families is thus able to override and suspend the impossibilities of historical time, as Olson, who succinctly captures the tale's historical contradictions, wryly notes: "The fictive Constance's period must be the late 500s. Chaucer, Trivet, and Gower all picture a Christian Roman empire still alive and governed from Rome, an Islam that has already captured Syria, and an England about to be re-Christianized" (95).

42. Religious cultures and communities, imagined as families, are also, as Olson points out in his discussion of why it is a Man of Law who is chosen to tell the story of Constance in the *Canterbury Tales*, systems of *law* that aptly represent those communities: In Syria, Islamic law is "characterized . . . as so contrary to Christian law that no marriage treaty is possible. . . . The Islamic ruler's mother-in-law, perceiving a threat to the 'olde sacrifice' required by Islamic law, feigns conversion . . . to protect Islamic law defined as, first, sacrifice like that of Old Testament Judaism . . . second, the rule of the Koran and Mohammad's commands . . . and third, a law promising

hell to Islamic converts to Christianity and encouraging killing the infidel without mercy. . . . This episode defines the Man of Law's theme in the relationship between a country's religion and its law" (94). By contrast, "in Northumbria, neither religion nor law exists. The period is dark. . . . Briton Christianity has gone underground" (93–94). By this reckoning, then, Constance's arrival and successful missionizing simultaneously births the nation of England as a Christian nation *and* affirms the English nation as a nation of law in which the king, Aella, functions as a locus of justice and protection under the law (despite Donegild's temporarily disruptive machinations). Olson contrasts the Sultan of Syria—a "consultative monarch" who, by electing to undergo conversion, makes a "consultative decision foolishly" when he misinterprets his privy council's advice—with Aella, whose judgment is judicious and whose acts of law are those of "a good king" and confirmed by "supernatural intervention" (99–100).

43. I elaborate this argument elsewhere, using a contemporary postcolonial nation-state as an example (see Heng and Devan, "State Fatherhood," and Heng, "'A Great Way to Fly'").

44. National convulsion, in the United States, over the recent untimely death of John F. Kennedy Jr. dramatized with particular visibility the deep public investment in the Kennedy family (a family often described as a "clan," with a clan's suggestion of longevity and duration) *as a family that symbolizes the nation to itself:* a family that articulates the nation's profoundest ideals and optimism, as demonstrated through the Kennedys' immigrant history, successful capital accumulation (wealth, glamor, and fame), and distinguished family record of public service and leadership. National fascination with the Kennedys is plainly more than mere voyeuristic absorption in the lives and scandals of the rich and famous, for the Kennedys issue as a model of demographic, economic, and social success of the kind on which national mythology crucially depends. Thus when journalists, public commentators, and scholars alike suggest that the Kennedys constitute the "royal family" of the United States (with the *National Enquirer* referring to JFK Jr., in postmortem mourning, as "America's Son"), they point to the Kennedy family as offering the nation a romance image of the nation itself: a family always seen through the eyes of *a communal desire that imagines the country's national narrative as a romance.* Effortlessly marrying the image of a royal family with the image of an intimately domestic family, the patrician and yet deeply personable Kennedys dramatize an ideal romance family able to represent the family of the nation and to render the drama of the nation *as* romance.

Part of the horror in the fearful projection of a "Kennedy curse"—a specter periodically raised by media journalists—is then the subliminal suspicion that the national narrative, as played out in the human drama of this symbolic family that phantasmagorically represents the nation at its immigrant best and most ideationally aspirational, might really belong to the mode of *tragedy*, rather than to the mode of romance. (Tragedy, as we know, is not a mode that encourages the collective optimism necessary to secure a country's projected momentum into the future.) Jacqueline Kennedy Onassis's canny representation, to the journalist William Manchester, of her husband's administration as reinstating the "brief shining moment" of a new, reinvigorated "Camelot" that in some fashion resembled the old "Camelot" of King Arthur and his knights is only ironic, then, for those of us who read the implication of the original Arthurian "Camelot" in projects of empire alongside the involvement of JFK's America in Vietnam.

For medievalists, the presidential widow's representation of JFK as Arthur and JFK's America as a revivified Arthurian realm resuscitates a medieval insight into the symbolic and representational possibilities of the ruler for the characterization of communal identity and constitutes an inspired, productive moment in which the national story is specifically identified and narrated as a romance.

45. Gough, in tracing the Constance saga's variants, observes a feature of some importance. Although the Constance story is "spread all over Europe, not only in *märchen*, but also in literary versions, which date from the 12th century to the 19th," in all the centuries of the story's existence, and through the many cultural variants rendered in different languages, "Trivet's chronicle contains the only existing version of the Constance saga in which the hero is identified with any historical personage. . . . The heroine of Tr[evet] marries King 'Alle' of Northumbria, i.e. Aella of Deira, who died in 588" (34). Gough may be forgiven for imagining that Aella, and not Constance, is the "hero" of the Constance story, when we consider his acuity in recognizing that, in fourteenth-century England, it has become important to link Constance to a historical local king. Trevet's attachment of Constance's centuries-old legend to a historical king is, I have been arguing, deeply meaningful in the context of a fourteenth-century England that is nationalizing as a community. That Chaucer and Gower—two other prominent fourteenth-century authors participating in the cultural project of imagining England—also retain and foreground the link between the imperial Constance and the local Aella, is key to an understanding of how national-cultural projects function aggregationally.

46. Eberle, following Brian Tierney's account of stories of "origin" narrated to "lend legitimacy" to authority, emphasizes Christian rulership in this newly remade English community: "All three versions of the story, by Trevet, Gower, and Chaucer, present it as the story of the origins of Christian rulership in Saxon England, and all the main events of the plot are designed to further this purpose. Constance is responsible for the conversion of Alla, the pagan king of Northumbria; she marries Alla and bears him a son, Moris, who succeeds her father and is named 'the most Christian emperor,' thus linking the Roman empire with the English royal line" (126). The reunion of Alla with Constance and her son later "not only confirms the Christian conversion of England but leads to the close association of England with the Christianized Roman empire, since the child of Alla and Constance is to become the 'most Christian' emperor" (127).

47. The break and re-beginning, for a community, which also requires an assertion of continuity, commences, Fradenburg reminds us, at the point of the political marriage itself: "Marriage is a site of crossover, between change and fixity, identity and difference, freedom and constraint, pleasure and sacrifice. Marriage impels the cross-

ing of thresholds, movement from the familiar to the strange, union with new worlds: the refiguration of bonds and loyalties. . . . Precisely because of the adventurousness, even at times the imperial expansiveness of marriage—particularly of what Bourdieu calls 'extraordinary' political marriage—marriage has the potential to threaten with change the stability of the very social and political structures it works to extend" ("Sovereign Love," 82).

48. Ben Anderson's remark that "*amor patriae* does not differ in this respect from the other affections, in which there is always an element of fond imagining" (154), has led to an understanding of how "fantasy and desire, 'fond imagining,' are crucial to the articulation of a national identity" (L. Moore, 15–16).

49. The slaying of Hermengild, while she is asleep in the same bed with Constance, and the subsequent false accusation of Constance that enables the heroine to be miraculously vindicated, both economically advances the plot and neatly closes off any suggestion of an unlawful circuit of desire between the two women. Despite the covert articulation of same-sex desire or homoeroticism that we have seen in historical romances like Geoffrey's *Historia* and chivalric romances like the Alliterative *Morte*, romance is also, as Dinshaw puts it, "one major narrative form whose ostensible task is to promote heterosexuality against all odds . . . [including] the homosexual potential of bonds between men and plots between women . . . [that] imperil heterosexual fulfilment" ("Chaucer's Queer Touches," 86).

Trevet's description of intensely passionate love felt by the Western woman, Hermengild, for the Eastern woman, Constance, implicitly suggests, then, if it does not explicitly announce, why Hermengild must die. It would be difficult not to notice that Hermengild, "taunt fu de samour supprise" (Bryan and Dempster, 169), is implicitly positioned by the narrative in the classic role of the female native on the island who is won over by the foreigner whose arrival changes everything in her culture—a popular heterosexual romance trope of intercultural relations—so that Hermengild's attachment to Constance means she is willing to do anything for the strange newcomer. Not all the Constance romances, moreover, are equally forward in their depiction of one woman's love for another. The circuit of desire by the native for the foreigner is most strongly realized in Trevet's version, and perhaps least realized in Chaucer's, so that feminist readings queering Chaucer have thus far tended to overlook the *Man of Law's Tale* in favor of, say, the Pardoner's characterization (see, for instance, Dinshaw's splendid chapters in *Chaucer's Sexual Poetics* and *Getting Medieval*). For how intimate associative relations—amatory, erotic, or platonic—*between women* might allegorize nationalist relations, see Lisa Moore's *Dangerous Intimacies*.

50. David Aers notes that "major historical studies of recent years . . . document the emergence of fully articulate theories of *limited* monarchy in the later Middle Ages in which the ruler was viewed as the servant of a community where individuals . . . were to be the prime beneficiaries of government. They trace the *desacralization* of secular power together with the supersession of the hierocratic thesis of sovereignty in which all secular authority, law and government derived its legitimation from God through the ruler rather than through the community" (172). The late-medieval idea

that the ruler is the *servant* of the community and derives his legitimation from *the community itself,* rather than from God, is one key moment in the stages of the na-tionalist impulse. As Schlauch puts it, "Rulers were instituted for the sake of peoples, not peoples for rulers. Some writers even went so far as to state explicitly: the right of lordship is based on the consent of the governed" ("Chaucer's Doctrine," 134). Eber-le cites the 1386 statement of Parliament, in Henry Knighton's *Chronicon,* which re-sponds to the high-handedness of Richard II, as the historical background of caution and implied threat against which we might usefully read the fictive critique of Aella in the Constance group:

> They maintained that if, either because of evil counsel or . . . his own wilfulness, the
> king should alienate himself from his people, and should be unwilling to be governed
> and ruled by the laws . . . and praiseworthy customs of the realm . . . but instead, on
> the basis of his own foolish opinions, should stubbornly insist on making his own in-
> dividual will the basis of his rule, then it is lawful, on the basis of the common . . . con-
> sent of the people of the kingdom, to depose the king from his royal throne and to raise
> to the throne someone else of royal blood. (115)

51. Eberle, in deploying Walter Ullmann's classification of medieval authority as "descending" from the English monarch or "ascending" from the populace through their parliamentary representatives, correctly reads Trevet's account as being most critical of any view which implies that authority should "descend" downward, from the king. Chaucer's *Man of Law's Tale* and *Prologue,* she suggests, also "offer a critique of the 'descending' theory of political authority" (147), and, "in his reply to the Host, the Man of Law endorses a view of authority that has a good deal in common with the 'ascending' view of the 1386 Parliamentary statement" (143). By contrast, Eberle observes, Gower (who dedicated the 1392 version of his *Confessio Amantis* to Richard II, the patron commissioning the work), offers a carefully nuanced position on a monarch's authority that emphasizes "not the ruler's absolute authority over those be-neath him but [the ruler's] absolute dependence on and duty of obedience to the God who is above him as the source of his power" (132). In the context of this diplomatic displacement of authority (from the human monarch to the divine monarch) that Eberle detects in Gower, we note in passing that Gower's version, when depicting the injustice first done to mother and child, offers a particularly memorable and striking figure to express popular grief, a figure that later accrues resonance by being reem-bedded in a configuration of justice, with the reinstitution of rightful authority. When injustice is visited first on Constance and her babe—an injustice caused, it is thought, by the king—popular grief is expressed by a remarkably memorable image: "So great a sorrow they begin, / As they their own mother seen / Burnt in a fire before their eyes: / There was weeping and there was woe" ("So gret a sorwe thei beginne, / As thei here oghne moder sihen / Brent in a fyr before here yhen" [ll. 1046–49]). When justice is later correctly visited on the king's mother for her heinous "treason" ("tre-soun" is repeated three times in rapid succession) to the maternal Constance and the young princeling/heir to the throne, the king has a fire made and has his mother cast

in it so that she is *literally* burnt to death in a fire before *his* eyes: "And then she was to death brought / And burnt before her son's eyes" ("And tho sche was to dethe broght / And brent tofore hire sones yhe" [ll. 1292–3]). Thus the image of grief first mentioned at Constance's victimization—supposedly by an unjust king—is fulfilled later as literal justice, when blame for her victimization has been correctly reassigned and the king has been vindicated.

52. In one of the Constance stories—Chaucer's—the ascription of the tale to a Man of Law perhaps intrudes the suggestion that law is one of the instruments mediating between coercion and consent in a medieval community, as Elizabeth McCartney pointed out during a seminar discussion of this chapter. McCartney also added the reminder that the power of law to exercise the will of a community on a monarch (and, by repeated exercise of the collective will, to project an imagined community) is palpable as early as Magna Carta, when a community of barons visibly enacted their collective will into law. Historians of medieval political theory stress that "within the feudal function of kingship, law, as the vehicle of government, was arrived at by counsel and consent, hence by cooperation leading to team work" (Ullmann, 148) and "law as a joint effort was made and not given . . . and made it was by the king and the barons or other corporate body (parliament)" (152).

Law, as the codified power of the community to which even the king was subject ("What Magna Carta expressed in chapter 39 was contained in Bracton's famous statement, 'The king was to be under God and the law'"), was arrived at by "common consent" and collective making (Ullmann, 152). In political thought the shaping power of law also functions usefully in mystificatory symbolism. Ernest Kantorowicz quotes Sir John Fortescue, "England's greatest jurist of the Lancastrian period" (223), on how the laws of England, like the nerves of the human body, unify and hold together the collective or corporate body: "The law by which a *cetus hominum* is made into a *populus* resembles the nerves of the physical body; for just as the body is held together by the nerves, so is the *corpus mysticum* [of the people] joined together and united into one by the Law" (224).

If the people of England are historically united by the common possession of law—common law, the "Laws of the English"—medieval romance in the form of the Constance story ensures we remember that the English are also united by religious faith—"lawe"—canon law, sacred literature, catechism, exhortations, and creed, "creance," that bind each community, Christian and Islamic alike, into union ("The hooly lawes of Alkaron" [*MLT*, l. 332]). While the Anglo-Norman manuscripts of Trevet refer to faith ("fei," "foi") and law ("ley," "loi") interchangeably, as synonyms for religious belief, and Gower uses "feith" rather more frequently than "lawe," the Man of Law, true to the vocabulary of his profession, evinces a preference for describing both Christianity and Islam as systems of law (e.g., in ll. 221, 237, 332, 337, 376, 572) rather than of "creance" (ll. 340, 915). The trope of "law" in one of the Constance stories would thus seem to resonate on many levels.

53. Griselda's story, like Constance's, has precedents in folktale and was retold in Italian, Latin, French, and English. Appearing in Italian as the concluding tale in

Boccaccio's *Decameron* in 1353, it was retold by Petrarch in Latin in 1373–74 (*Seniles*, 17.3), and by Giovanni Sercambi in Italian circa 1374 (in his *Novella*). Thence the story was renarrated in French prose translations of Petrarch, by Philippe de Mézières (1384–89)—whose version found its way into *Le Ménagier de Paris* (c. 1393)—and by an anonymous author. In 1395 a French play, *L'Estoire de la Marquise de Saluce*, also based on De Mézières's version, presented the story once again. A version in Latin verse, based on Petrarch and represented by the unique manuscript MS 93, fol. 96v, at the Bibliothèque de Poitiers, was adapted by Pierre de Hailles. Severs's study of the literary relations of the *Clerk's Tale* notes Chaucer's use of Petrarch's Latin version and the anonymous French prose translation, while disputing dependence on the *Decameron* and *Le Ménagier* (see *Literary Relationships* and "Introduction" to the *Clerk's Tale* in Bryan and Dempster, 288–95).

54. Griselda is expressly depicted as a shepherdess and spinner, like the medieval Virgin (l. 223), and, when she is first introduced, her simplicity and purity are outlined in scenes that recall details from the Annunciation and Nativity. When Walter arrives and calls for her, for instance, "she set down her water pot at once, / Beside the threshold, in an ox's stall, / And down upon her knees she began to fall" (ll. 290–92). The first mention of Griselda and her father underlines their extreme poverty and simplicity, while intruding the suggestion that they are specially blessed and chosen by God for attention: "Among these poor folk there dwelt a man / Who was held the poorest of them all; / But high God sometimes can send / His grace into a little ox's stall . . . A daughter had he" (ll. 204–7, 209). The ox's stall, and the will and intentions of God, are recalled a third time after Griselda is newly dressed in finery, so that the symbolic background does not stray far from the mind: "God has such favor sent her of his grace / That it did not seem by appearance / That she was born and fed in humble lowness, / As in a hut or in an ox-stall" (ll. 395–98). While the *contexts* in which Griselda's purity and innocence are emphasized may be ironized to make a point (Walter is scarcely the archangel Gabriel, although the maidenly innocent will indeed endure much, following the visitation), the pathos that the *Tale* arranges does not swerve from its determined purposefulness: In saying farewell to her firstborn child, whom Griselda believes Walter means to put to death, the Cruxifixion is emotively retrieved, as Griselda and her child form a pièta-like affective tableau before the occurrence of the human sacrifice. She marks her child with the sign of the cross (l. 556), blessing and recalling the savior "who for us died upon a cross of tree [wood]" (l. 558) and addresses her infant as if another sacrifice similar to Christ's is about to occur: "Little child . . . this night shall thou die for my sake" (ll. 559–60).

55. Walter loftily informs Griselda that it pleases her father and Walter himself that he should wed her, magnanimously adding, as an afterthought, that he supposes she also wishes it ("and eek it may so stonde, / As I suppose, ye wol that it so be" [ll. 346–47]). In the same instant of his casual assumption that Griselda's desire would follow his, however, Walter nonetheless takes care to solicit her verbal, technical assent to "demands" he specifies: "But these demands I ask first. . . . /Will you assent . . . ?" (ll. 348, 350). Walter's demand is simply for Griselda's total, unquestioning, and

absolute obedience to his will—whatever his will might be, in whatever circum-stances—by her every word, deed, attitude, and facial expression (ll. 351–56): "Swear this," he concludes, "and here I swear our alliance" (l. 357). In answer, Griselda in-stantly swears, on pain of death, that she will "never willingly, / In work nor thought . . . disobey" her lord (ll. 362–63). Such a depiction of the overarching context of power and control in which Griselda's conformity is sought and voiced comments critically on the character of the feudal contract—expressed here, in a late-medieval Chaucerian text, in totalizing, absolute terms—if we read Walter's and Griselda's roles and characters allegorically, as I have been suggesting we do. The Clerk's rendi-tion of the marital contract's approximation of the feudal contract is not, of course, the only instance of such treatment in the *Canterbury Tales*. Where the *Clerk's Tale* delivers the marital-feudal allegory in the mode of high political and moral serious-ness, the *Merchant's Tale* delivers it in the mode of winking, bawdy satire. It would take too long, and delay overmuch, the Merchant declares, to tell of every writ and bond by which May, a young woman of "smal degree" like Griselda, was enfeoffed in her elderly knight-husband's land, through her marriage to him ("it were to longe yow to tarie, / If I yow tolde of every scrit and bond / By which that she was feffed in his lond" [ll. 1697–98]).

56. Ernst Kantorowicz, who recalls that "Augustine compared matrimony to a 'political' government" (217) suggests that "the secular marriage metaphor . . . became rather popular in the later Middle Ages when, under the impact of juristic analogies and corporational doctrines, the image of the Prince's marriage to his *corpus mys-ticum*—that is, to the *corpus mysticum* of his state—appeared to be constitutionally meaningful" (212). Kantorowicz goes on to note that "the analogy of the *corpus mys-ticum* served to clarify the relations between the estates of the body politic and their king, and the marriage metaphor served to describe the peculiar nature of the fisc" (218). Aers reminds us, further, that metaphoricity is a "two-way" street, and "do-mestic relations could be seen in terms of political ones": "It may not be far-fetched to wonder whether the long-lived metaphor in which the marriage of man and woman is used to examine political questions concerning sovereignty and responsi-bility could have been an element in Chaucer's treatment of the ruler and his wife in the *Clerk's Tale*. . . . [A]ccording to M. Wilks's investigations this metaphor had ac-quired an anti-absolutist meaning by Chaucer's day in which the ruler's authority ceases at the point it becomes harmful to the community of individuals symbolized by his wife" (172).

57. Schlauch points out that one focus in the late-medieval critique of tyrants—a critique in which Chaucer participated—is the ruler's irresponsible pursuit of his own pleasure: "It emerges, then, that a tyrant seeks his own weal, not the common weal; he pursues his own pleasure (*delectabilia*)" ("Chaucer's Doctrine," 139–40); "tyrants were said . . . to pursue 'delit' (*delectabilia*) rather than the common welfare" (154). We are told by the Clerk that Walter, as marquis, lives *precisely* for pleasure and has done so of old ("Thus in delit he lyveth, and hath doon yoore," [l. 68]), so much so that Walter is explicitly critiqued for neglecting the responsibilities of a ruler: "But on

his lust present was al his thoght, / As for to hauke and hunte on every syde. / Wel nigh alle othere cures let he slyde" ("But on his immediate pleasure was all his thought, / So as to hawk and hunt everywhere [at every opportunity]. / Well nigh all other duties he let slide" [ll. 80–82]).

That Walter descends from the lineage ("lynage") of Lombardy ("Lumbardye") is thus no accident but highly meaningful—as the editors of the *Riverside Chaucer* observe, this detail is not in Chaucer's sources (881 n. 72)—when we consider Queen Alceste's discourse, in the Prologue to the *Legend of Good Women*, on the righteous ruler: "This shulde a ryghtwys lord han in his thought, / And not ben lyk tyraunts of Lumbardye, / That usen wifulhed and tyrannye" ("This should a righteous lord have in his thought, / And not be like tyrants of Lombardy, / That employ wilfulness and tyranny" [*Legend* G text, ll. 353–55]. If Walter should be seen as the latest in a long line of "tyrants of Lombardy," the depiction of Griselda in her role as the ideal ruler who accomplishes the "commune profit," in lines 430–41, is also deeply meaningful, since Griselda's advocacy of the common weal is precisely a mark of the good ruler, as self-indulgence is a mark of the tyrannical ruler: "The *bonum commune*, objective of a true king, is several times mentioned by Chaucer" (Schlauch, "Chaucer's Doctrine," 153). Rewriting its source, the Petrarchan story of Griselda, "Chaucer's phraseology brings [the meaning] closer to political theory. He uses the English equivalent of *bonum commune* in place of [Petrarch's] vague *salus publica*" (153).

58. John Parsons suggests that medieval queenship traded on the intercessory role of the medieval Virgin Mary to authorize the mediatory status of historical queens as useful, "given the expansion of royal bureaucracy that distanced the king from his subjects" ("Pregnant Queen," 40). By interceding with their royal husbands on behalf of the populace, "queens could (and did) exploit their intercession for their own ends—to win supporters, to create networks of mutual obligation and . . . to shape popular opinions of themselves and the king" (48). Pregnant queens, in particular, offered a public image of touching and wondrous fecundity that enhanced their intercessory roles, so that the intercession and pregnancy of queens found its way to ritual expression and ceremony. In England, where "no queen after 1066 exercised full sovereign powers as regent" and "the tendency in English ritual was to dissociate the king's wife from his authority" ("English Medieval Queenship," 64), Parsons carefully notes the limits of the queen's intercessory potential. (Before Parsons's formulation, Jane Chance's classic *Woman as Hero*, on the representation of Anglo-Saxon women as "peace-weavers" between men of power, and between male elites and the communities they ruled, offered an earlier model akin to Parsons's.) Still, if historical queens during the Middle Ages "effectively claimed power through their active participation in matrimonial diplomacy" ("Mothers, Daughters," 76), Griselda's public role, then, does not seem abhorrently monstrous when depicted by Chaucer's clerk.

However, Griselda's de facto assumption of surrogacy for Walter, in his absence, far exceeds wifely intercession with her husband on the people's behalf, of the kind assembled by Parsons's historical examples. Chaucer's text describes Griselda acting in the ruler's place, rather than merely interceding with her husband, and she is not described as pregnant when the paen of praise for her rulership appears in the *Clerk's Tale*. Indeed, David Aers notes that Henry IV, addressed by Chaucer in his "Complaint of Chaucer to his Purse" (l. 22), "pledged himself to pursue the 'commune profyt' and to preserve the laws above his self-will. In this, significantly enough, he [Henry IV] was promising to rule as Griselda did in Walter's absence, not like Walter" (172).

59. Even when Griselda bears a daughter, and not a son and heir, to their ruler in marriage, the people—in their partiality and attachment—rejoice, because, we are told, the birth proves that Griselda is not barren, and a boy might soon follow: a fondly generous, poignantly optimistic interpretation of the circumstances of not securing an heir (ll. 445–48). When the anticipated son and heir is finally born, all the country is "merry" over the child (l. 615).

60. David Wallace's acuity is timely: "The commons are roundly condemned for their fickleness with Chaucer's text, but this critique is voiced by another part of the same social body across a line of rupture drawn by the tyrannical Walter himself. The people criticize the people since Walter stands beyond open criticism: "O stormy peple! unsad and evere untrewe! / Ay indiscreet and chaungynge as a fane! / Delitynge evere in rumbul that is newe" (4.995–97). Such lines suggest unease at the voice of the commons without quite disowning it as a political force" (291). David Aers's analysis of the meaning of the Wife of Bath's rebellion against, yet conformity with, dominant ideology speaks resonantly also to the Clerk's description of a labile commons who act, finally, against their own: "[Chaucer] discloses the complexities involved in opposing dominant social and ideological forms. He dramatizes . . . an aesthetic representation of the way subordinate groups or individuals may so internalize the assumptions and practices of their oppressors that not only their daily strategies of survival but their very acts of rebellion may perpetuate the outlook against which they rebel. Their penetration of dominant ideology and practice is distorted and displaced into a significant conformity with the established values which they are opposing" (147).

Florence Scott, who follows Chaucer's attendance at the Parliament of 1386, as a Knight of the Shire from Kent, and his subsequent withdrawal from public office until 1389, as he retired to "the seclusion of his beautiful country, where he engaged in writing the *Canterbury Tales*" (85), on having "seen his king [Richard II] defeated and his colleague [Simon Burley] beheaded by the Parliament he had attended," sympathetically suggests why a discourse at once of critique and containment might be active in the *Canterbury Tales*: "The reason why so little of contemporary life is reflected in Chaucer's writings becomes increasingly clear . . . in the light of the records. Titanic events like these could not . . . be safely communicated in the greater reality of the *Canterbury Tales*. . . . Chaucer's few guarded references emerge with greater poignancy against this background" (85).

61. Walter's pusillanimous reference to peasant freedom, when he tells Griselda, "I may nat doon as every plowman may" (l. 799), represents laborers as "free" to follow animal-like drives, while nobles are constrained by deep responsibilities to the social polity: "It was a seigneurial maxim that villeins possessed *nihil extra ventrem*—nothing

outside their own bellies" (Justice, 142). The "freedom" of the plowman, smirkingly invoked by Walter, is thus "the grasping of an unregulated [will] . . . the peasant has only will, without mind or notion" (143), unlike the aristocracy, whose representative here is claiming moral rationality by belatedly repudiating his wife. The status of plowmen and gentles is precisely the focus of the famed couplet featured in John Ball's inflammatory sermon of June 13, 1381, "to the rebellious peasants on Blackheath menacing London" (A. B. Friedman, 213), a couplet that first appears in English in a recension of Thomas Walsingham's *Chronica Maiora:* "Whan Adam dalf and Eve span, / Who was þan a gentil man?" The proverb "in Latin is found in a sermons preached in 1374 and 1377 by Thomas Brinton, bishop of Rochester, a diocese which furnished a large number of the Kentish agitators . . . his abbreviation is . . . evidence that the lines were common knowledge. . . . Hope E. Allen is led to conjecture that Ball 'may have caught up and adapted a folk-saying long current" (A. B. Friedman, 214).

Because the plowman as an image of rectitude, and social and theological virtue, is widespread at this historical moment, as we see from Langland's *Piers,* anonymous songs, anticlerical tracts, and literature of various kinds ("Pierce the Plowman's Crede," "The Plowman's Tale," "Gode, Spede the Plow," etc.), Walter's invocation of plowman and noble in this self-serving context is also significant for its rebuttal of public discourse that redistributes moral authority among social classes, and that cites an originary equivalence of status, with a mealy mouthed aristocratic fantasy of reversal, in which the laboring class is offered as already liberated, while seigneury is bound in lifelong bondage. Griselda, identified early as a spinner (l. 223)—like the medieval Virgin, and, more pointedly in context, like Eve in John Ball's couplet—is interpolated into Walter's fantasy on the side of plowmen and laborers, and her role in the *Clerk's Tale* as the representative of an underclass is thus reinforced. Justice's extraordinarily fine study of writing, literacy, and the Rebellion of 1381 suggests that the threat of "lay rural workers" at this time resides, in part, in a blurring of social and class boundaries, since "lay rural workers had begun to write and were taking part in the culture of literacy" in the late fourteenth century (25).

62. Griselda's pointing to her "maydenhede" also recalls her identification with the Virgin. The relation of the lowborn to culture, if Griselda's example might be cited, is demonstrated by a poignant trust in the feudal contract, among the lowborn, and in their unreliable contractual partners in feudalism represented by the nobility. That Walter—Knapp calls him "a curious sadist" (134), Olson "a tyrant" (99)—discloses his abominable ruses in the end and belatedly restores Griselda's children to her does not eradicate the memory of his abominations, though it suggests that nobles might behave humanely, after they have fulfilled a certain quota of sadistic behavior. Walter's theft, from Griselda, of the experience of her children's childhood also robs her of a portion of her maternity—to the extent that she is deprived of mothering beyond the nursling stage until the moment when her children are returned—which has led feminist scholars such as Newton to decry the disappearance of maternity in the tale, and the triumph of patriarchy.

63. Walter's malice, in slyly exhorting his faithful wife to take back the "dowry" she had bestowed on him—a malice apparently residing in the confident belief that Griselda had, indeed, entered the marriage with nothing, not even the clothes on her back— holds open the prospect that a naked Griselda would, Godiva-like, be exposed to the public gaze as she made her way back to her paternal home. Indeed, the public exhibition of her body, and the sacrifice of her privacy and dignity, to prurient voyeurism might be yet another satisfying strategy in the "tormentyng" to which Walter subjects his loyal wife. Griselda's quiet request for a simple smock with which to cover her nakedness, in payment for the real dowry she had brought Walter, her hymen, thus counters that potential voyeurism by invoking the traditional respect for the female body—a body otherwise registered as sexual—when the female, sexual body is specifically seen and understood as *maternal*, a body that has borne children and whose hymen ("maydenhede" [ll. 837, 866, 883]) has been freely given so that children might lie in the womb and be born ("thilke wombe in which youre children leye" [l. 877]).

Knapp points to "the moving detail of Griselda's now ill-fitting old coat" (137), kept for her by her father, Janicula, as a poignant detail that specifies the irreplaceability of Griselda's lost maidenhead and the change of her figure through maternity: "The *olde coote* does not fit. . . . the woman is older. Perhaps her fuller figure is the result of Griselda's child-bearing. She can never have back her only dowry, her maidenhead, as she says herself" (135). The reproductive sexuality to which Griselda deliberately refers—and that effortlessly translates a potentially voyeuristic gaze into a respectful glance at traditional maternity—is also, of course, humanly represented by Constance and sublimely represented by the Virgin.

64. Barbara Newman shows how Griselda's *imitatio Mariae* is part of what she calls a "'marternal martyr' paradigm [which] emerges as a . . . literary convention that duplicates tendencies in the cult of Mary. . . . By the fourteenth century, when this hagiographic type has become well established, we begin to see 'secular saints' like Griselda as romance heroines—'good women' who will establish their virtue by sacrificing their children" (77).

65. "Although enacted publicly, at court, this is a wholly private moment from which (as Griselde swoons) Walter is hopelessly excluded. The next narrative moment, in which Griselde's children are drawn from her body with great care and difficulty (4.1102–3), has all the physical intensity of childbirth" (Wallace, 292).

66. For John Bowers, the *entire Canterbury Tales*, as a corpus, is an expression of "Chaucer's English nationalism" (56). Bowers quotes Ben Anderson ("The idea of a sociological organism moving calendrically through homogenous, empty time is a precise analogy of the idea of the nation") in order to show how precisely the *Tales*, in their structure, details, and totality, conform to theoretical criteria for a literary analog of the nation:

> The *Canterbury Tales* is set not in the liturgical time of Easter but in the calendrical month of April. Its chronology is not teleological but a true in-between time . . . the

open road deployed as a discontinuous somewhere between London and Canterbury. . . . As true members of an "imagined community" [Chaucer's pilgrims] are possessed of a radical contingency that emerges from anonymity . . . The sum of the Canterbury fragments represents "the collective voice of the people as a performative
discourse of public identification," just as Homi Bhabha discovers in the realistic novel,
which has been privileged as the literary analog to the larger social discourse of nationhood. (60)

Bowers, observing that "Anderson has argued that 'pilgrimage' provides a powerful
organizing trope for the unification of a community *e pluribus unum*," emphasizes:
"The fact that Chaucer's pilgrims never reached their goal accords better with the narrative of a nation, which is always unfolding and never fulfilled. . . . The one-way pilgrimage provided an even more specific metaphor for the careerism of those state
functionaries like Chaucer himself whose efforts, although steadily self-serving, drove
the machinery of nation-building" (61).

    67. Three Christian youths who are part of Constance's entourage escape ("treis
vallez Cristiens eschaperent") and bring news of the slaughter back to Constance's father, the emperor (Bryan and Dempster, 167; Furnivall, 11). The segregation of the
sexes during ceremonial feasting—with the men, Christians and Saracens alike, dining together at the Sultan's banquet and the women separately feasting *en groupe* in
the Sultaness's hall—is a realistic detail that accurately reproduces Meditteranean sex
segregation (Bryan and Dempster, 167; Furnivall, 11). I suggested, in chapter 1, that a
similar custom of festive and ritual sex segregation at King Arthur's court was likely
derived from, and imitated, the Byzantine Emperor's celebrated court, where feasting
and ritual were also segregated by sex.

    68. Lillian Hornstein argues that Trevet's tale of Constance derives, in fact, from
the plot featured in *KT* ("Trivet's Constance," 354–55), an argument that renders intelligible stray details in both romances: Hornstein notes, for instance, that "Trivet
has his heroine born on St. John's day; this has no significance in his tale, whereas in
the *King of Tars* the monstrous child is baptized on the saint's day and named John"
[356]). Judith Perryman's edition of *KT*, the best and most recent, dates the genesis of
the story's main plot between 1280, when key details of the plot first appear in chronicles, and 1330 (or 1330–40), when the romance, as we largely have it, appears in the
Auchinleck manuscript (17). Hornstein narrows the margin to "soon after 1300,"
when she believes the story reached England ("Trivet's Constance," 354). *KT*, that is,
seems to have emerged in the same period as *RCL*, which also has a prominent discourse on blackness and color, and is also a crusading romance (both are also thought
to have had a lost French original, but appear, in their earliest extant romance incarnations, in the English vernacular, as items in the Auchinleck). In the Auchinleck and
the two later sister compendia in which *KT* is also featured, namely, the Vernon and
Simeon manuscripts (which share scribes and substantial overlap of content, and date
from 1380 to 1400), the romance is classed among religious items. In the Auchinleck
the fourteenth-century number vii, in the middle of the top margin of ff 9r, 10r, and

11r, indicates that *KT* was to have been the seventh item in the manuscript, following *The Legend of Pope Gregory* and preceding *The Life of Adam and Eve*. In the Vernon, *KT* follows the *Sayings of St Bernard* and precedes the *Proverbs of the Prophets, Poets, and Saints* (Perryman, 9–26).

69. Such a theory of religious essences, in which certain privileged religions—Christianity is, of course, the prime example; Judaism, by virtue of ancient pedigree and predecessor status, is another—are held to confer, or are postulated as conferring, an essence so powerful that it can override and determine biology would thus, I repeat, seem to constitute a theory of difference that appears specifically medieval: a theory of difference whose explanatory power derives from a historical period in which religion is the dominant discourse, the master discourse, in culture. But the terrain of the Middle Ages is more complex than what straightforward hypotheses allow for. Rather than understand that culture, in the form of religion, is allowed to trump biology, by the power of hypothesized religious essences, one can as easily say here that since religion is shown to confer an essence, in this line of hypothetical thinking, religion is assumed not only to the domain of culture, as such, in the Middle Ages, but also to the domain of biology, in the medieval hypothesis of difference, a notion I will address below.

70. Another Middle English text from the first half of the fourteenth century, the *Cursor Mundi* (c. 1325), also features a Saracen bleaching. When four Saracens, "blac and bla als led" ("black and blue-black as lead," l. 8072) meet King David, and the king holds forth three rods blessed by Moses for them to kiss, the Saracens transform from black to white on kissing the rods, taking on, we are told, the hue of those of noble blood: "als tite / Als milk thair hide becom sa quite / And o fre blode thai had the hew, / And al thair scapp was turned neu" ("at once / Their hide became as white as milk / And they had the hue of noble blood, / And all their shape [appearance] was turned new" [ll. 8119–22]). The *Cursor Mundi*, which participates in the racial thinking of the *King of Tars*, suggests that romance is not the only medium in which color transformations—entry into a new class of human beings—might occur; nor is the Christian sacrament of baptism specifically required for such transformation and admission. Moreover, we see in this example that the appropriate color for those of high-born blood, is white: Whiteness is a marker of class, as well as race-and-religion.

71. The depiction of Islam in medieval European literature is not consistent or homogeneous. For instance, the fiction that Islam is idolatrous and polytheistic—a fiction found in *chanson de gestes* and *chanson*-like romances—contrasts with, but coexists placidly alongside, a medieval Christian argument, attested in chronicles and tracts since Petrus Alfonsi's early-twelfth-century *Disciplina Clericalis*, that Islam was really a Christian heresy and thus (as Oliver of Paderborn optimistically confides, in one chronicle reference) Muslims could be brought eventually to the Roman Catholic faith the more readily. Schibanoff follows the spoor of the belief that Islam was a heresy (69–76), whereas Bellamy discusses the names of the so-called Saracen pantheon of paganlike "gods" in the *Chanson de Roland*, with special attention to the fascinating etymology of "Tervagan." By the time "the *chanson de geste* had run its course

in the sixteenth century," Bellamy notes, monotheistic Islam had been provided with about a dozen deities in the *chanson* tradition (268–69). On visual depictions of so-called Saracen gods, in manuscripts and carvings, see Camille's chapter, "Idols of the Saracens." *Mandeville's Travels*, as I note above, like the *MLT* depicts yet another understanding of Islam as monotheistic, a religion with only one God, and Mohamad ("Machomet") as God's "messenger" (G. F. Warner, 71; Hamelius, 1:92): a distinctly accurate representation of Islam. Olson, as noted above, also suggests Islam's resemblance to Old Testament Judaism, in the *MLT*, in the matter of "sacrifice" (94).

The princess's feigned conversion to an Islam depicted here as idolatrous and polytheistic, immediately after her dream of traumatization by a black hound who turns into a man in white, might usefully be contrasted to St Perpetua's "vision on the eve of her martyrdom in which she fights with a 'foul' Egyptian who is the devil" (Verkerk, 64). Whether one reads this hagiographic romance's citation of hagiography admiringly (as a daring depiction of an apparent conversion to Islam) or critically (as commentary on female Christian cowardice and failure to accept martyrdom), *color* tellingly features in both the traumatic visions to characterize negatively the religious-racial antagonist/oppressor.

72. Perryman, who traces the range of possible locales indicated by the name "Tars" (42–48), concludes: "Whichever way the romance writer understood his king of Tars, as the historical Tartar Ghazzan, as an Armenian king from Tarsus, or as a king from Tharsia, all these geographical areas were under Mongol domination at the time of the poem's conception. So from a historical viewpoint 'king of Tartars' is a fair gloss for *king of Tars*" (48). Four decades before Perryman, Hornstein, who identifies *Tars* as a garbled story about the Ilkhan ("el-khan") Ghazan ("Cassanus," in European chronicles), grandson of Abaga Khan, and son of Arghun, who ruled over the Persian Khanate in the far-flung Mongol Empire of interlocking khanates, had come to a similar conclusion:

> The probability suggests itself that by the King of Tars in the English version is to be understood a king of the Tartars. French, German, and Latin chronicles contain numerous references to a miraculous conversion of Cassanus, King of the Tartars. . . . *Tars* . . . was formerly thought to refer to *Tarsus*, but is now believed to mean *Tartary* or *Tabriz*. . . . [E]ven if the title *Tars* was . . . associated with the cities Tarsus or Tauris (the modern Tabriz), it is legitimate to consider the king a Tartar, for in the thirteenth and fourteenth centuries both cities were under Tartar domination. Tauris was considered by the Persian khans as one of their principal cities, and Tarsus was important for military reasons. There are, moreover, contemporary references in 1299 in which the Tartar king is called 'the king of Tars.'" ("Historical Background," 405–6)

Kaplan suggests that "Tharsis," originally linked to "a region of the Levant" was "in the thirteenth century usually identified with Tartary" (64). Despite the romance's exoticized fable of a foreign locale and history, however, the romance's simultaneous insistence that the princess of Tars is a classic Western European beauty whose whiteness of skin, along with her Christianity, should be repeatedly paraded, prevents any muddying or expansion of the human color palette of races.

73. Dorothy Verkerk's important article on the illustrations of the tenth plague, in the late-sixth-century Ashburnham Pentateuch, where blackness is used to depict and characterize the enemies of Moses and the Israelites, argues that the manuscript's color symbolism suggests that the early medieval period comprises "a transitional moment in the emergence of the perjorative representation of blacks in medieval art" (60). "In this intermediate stage," she notes, citing parallel examples of other manuscript depictions of blackness in late-antique, early-medieval periods, "the conventions are not fully worked out but are in flux" (60). However, because "the association of blackness, or darkness, with the devil and sin is a repetitive theme found throughout the biblical text and patristic thought" (64), and because patristic exegetes repeatedly linked "blackness with spiritual corruption . . . black skin now becomes a metonym for evil. . . . [And] the sinful non-Christian now has a face and it is black" (63). If, in this pre-Islamic, early period "dark skin suggests a dark spirit, a state of being before becoming one of God's people" (63)—a "world of images, where the color of skin can be indicative of an interior spiritual state" (71)—we have a nucleus of racial thinking in the making that will emerge in later-medieval discourses such as those we see operating in the *King of Tars*, discourses that, as Tom Hahn puts it, "draw . . . upon established medieval conventions and emerging mentalities" (15).

These later-medieval discourses on race are significantly distinguishable from earlier, nascent antecedents of the kind offered by Verkerk, and, usefully, by J. J. Cohen in musing on the color allegoresis of the early Church Fathers ("Saracen Enjoyment," 118), in possessing a key pivotal feature: the crucial emergence of *whiteness* as a normative and central category of European Christian identity. The princess of *Tars*, as we see here, is a prime example of the stabilizing centrality, the sheer normalcy, of whiteness; other cultural examples from the long thirteenth century include the "whitened" Saracen princesses discussed by de Weever, Saracen women who are magically evacuated of color in order to make them valued objects of desire for purposes of successful circulation in, and assimilation into, European contexts of identity and culture. Herzeloyde (whose whiteness and fairness are the intent focus of an obsessive, pleasurable erotic voyeurism) and Gahmuret (who is "love's color") in Wolfram von Eschenbach's *Parzival* also aver and proclaim the centrality of whiteness in later-medieval European Christian identity.

The ascension of whiteness to a position of centrality, out of the array of human somatic colors found across Greek and Latin texts, is long in the making, before whiteness consolidates as a definitive, indispensable, and vaunted category of use in *identity making*, quite apart from a general positive valuation of whiteness over color in Western culture (Hahn, who notes that the "beauty of blackness" in Bernard of Clairvaux's sermons "is always grounded in whiteness as the default category of perfection" also notes that "blackness and whiteness as terms of racial difference [were] . . . less stable in the twelfth century" [20, 24]). Although discourses on blackness—

discourses that were positively, negatively, or neutrally valenced—had existed throughout the Greek and Roman eras and into the early and high Middle Ages (as repeatedly attested by a range of arguments among classicists with differing views, from Frank Snowden through Martin Bernal, and as Hahn's reading of Bernard of Clairvaux's sermons and Peter Abelard's letters specifies for the twelfth century), developed racial discourses manipulating color as a critical category of definition emerged when *whiteness*, consolidated as a central criterion, was applied to European Christian identity.

74. Though magisterial in every respect, even Bartlett's pivotal study, *The Making of Europe*, thus also implicitly seems to understand race in terms made familiar by postmedieval race discourse—which supposes culture and biology to be separate and distinct—when the study says that "while the [medieval] language of race—*gens, natio*, 'blood', 'stock', etc.—is biological, its medieval reality was almost entirely cultural" (197). However, in addressing the "medieval reality" of race discourse, and racial behavior, *The Making of Europe* easily recognizes racial *practices* that assume religious identity (i.e., the "cultural") to be inextricably linked to ontological and essential nature, and Bartlett also unswervingly supports medievalist scholarship on race:

> Many scholars see in the later Middle Ages a tendency for racial discrimination to become sharper and racial boundaries to be more shrilly asserted. The hardening of anti-Jewish feeling between the eleventh and the fifteenth centuries is recognized by all who work on the subject and they disagree only on their dating of the crucial change for the worse: the pogroms associated with the First Crusade, the Talmud trials of the mid-thirteenth century, the expulsions and persecutions of the 1290s, the ominous massacres in cosmopolitan Spain in 1391. There is, at any rate, no doubt that the Christian Europe of 1492, the year of the expulsion of the Jews from Spain, had a starker and grimmer attitude to its minorities than had been the case 400 years earlier. (236)

More recently Bartlett's "Medieval and Modern Concepts of Race and Ethnicity" revisits the subject in order to complicate and extend his earlier study. Bartlett's recent article allows for the fundamental importance of "descent groups," birth, and genealogy in medieval categories of selection and prioritization, an importance that conduces to a medieval understanding of "race" in biological terms: "Some of the key terms of medieval Latin usage, such as *gens* and *natio*," Bartlett reiterates, "imply, etymologically, a concept of races as descent groups" (42); "such words as *gens* and *natio* fit in well with what can be called the genealogical idiom of much medieval thinking. This was a world in which blood and descent were seen as fundamental. A noble was *generosus* or *gentle* or *gentil*—'well born.' A serf was a *nativus*—'born unfree'" (44). However, though Bartlett goes on to cite the later-medieval Bartolomaeus Anglicus and Albertus Magnus to show how Bartholomew's and Albert's climatological determinisms formulate explanations of skin color that are linked to the origins and characters of racial communities (46–47), such determisms, for Bartlett, do not in fact constitute racial discourse, as such, but instead undermine racial thinking by citing "environmental influence" (45). Commenting on Bartlett's reasoning in *The Making of Europe*, J. J. Cohen ("Saracen Enjoyment") suggests that "dermal and physiological difference, the most familiar markers of embodied race, play no role in Bartlett's formulation because he overlooks race's humoral-climatological (that is, medical and scientific) construction" (115); ultimately, Cohen suggests, "the erasure of embodied race in . . . Bartlett is traceable to the fact that [he focuses his] attention silently and almost exclusively on the *Christian* body" (116).

75. The problem of a fertile sexual union that produces a child is thus explicitly a problem of the color line, not a problem of the plot line: In terms of plot, any child begotten of Constance and the Sultan can easily be disposed of, in allowing Constance to journey on to England; indeed, poignancy can be profitably milked, plot-wise, from the child's imagined disposal. Nor is even a Christian-Muslim marriage *in itself* an insuperable obstacle to sexual-conjugal union, since, historically, Christian-Muslim marriages were known to occur, and one is even a historic royal project strategically proposed by Richard Lionheart to Saladin's brother, al-Adil, as part of a diplomatic master joke (see chapter 2, above). The color line is what must not be crossed in the specter of miscegenation that haunts interracial encounters offered as interreligious encounters: biology and physiognomy in race matters.

An important exception to later-medieval (thirteenth-century and after) European discourses on race and color is posed, interestingly, by Germany, where a black St. Maurice in statuary and painting makes an appearance from the mid-thirteenth century through the early Renaissance, and where black and black-and-white (indeed, piebald) characters can be represented in Arthurian romance as performing creditably, even if their treatment bespeaks occasional ambiguity (Wolfram von Eschenbach's *Parzival* is the prime example, with its characters of Belacane and Feirefiz). Such German exceptionalism is able to exercise, on occasion, some regional influence (e.g., *Parzival* seems to influence the Middle Dutch Arthurian romance, *Moriaen*, in the Dutch romance's treatment of its titular black protagonist; and black Maurices are found as far north as Roskilde, Denmark, where their "fantasy" treatment suggests that they are a welcome exotic puzzle [Devisse, 2:175]). Germany's exceptionalism, in this regard, might be traced at inception to the politics of its empire and to the cultural role played by key German emperors—especially Frederick II, who is thought to have introduced the black St. Maurice to Magdeburg in the mid-thirteenth century (Devisse, 2:160, 164; for a differing opinion, see Suckale-Redlefsen)—whose possession of Sicily, a pivotal contact zone for Western Europe's encounter with the Near East/Mahgrebi Africa, underscored the uneven dissemination of cultural contact with black Africa, and black African Christians, by Western Europeans. However, except for Germany, and a limited German influence on the treatment of blackness, later-medieval discourses on blackness are negative (for a discussion of intricate twelfth-century theological and allegorical uses of blackness, see Hahn's reading of St. Bernard, Peter Aberlard, et al. [20–23]). I am currently elaborating the parameters of late-medieval discourses on race and color in a project in progress, "The Races of England."

76. The mention, in line 568, that the princess, in pregnancy, "chaunged ble" thus refers to complexional change (increased rosiness or a heightened glow) in pregnancy

or anatomical change—which confirms she is indeed pregnant—and does not advert
to color change as a result of (false) conversion, despite the equivocating potential of
"ble." The context of her pregnancy, the deliberate reiteration of her fairness just two
lines preceding the reference, and the sultan's joyful response, in the two lines succeeding the reference, work to stabilize the meaning here: "Þat leuedi, so feir & so fre,
/ Was wiþ hir lord bot moneþes þre / Þan he gat hir wiþ childe. / When it was geten
sche chaunged ble; / Þe soudan himself þat gan se / Iolif he was & wilde" ("That lady,
so fair and noble, / Was with her lord but months three / When he got her with child.
/ When it was begot, she changed appearance; / The sultan himself that did see / Gay
he was and exuberant" [ll. 565–70]). By contrast, the references to the sultan's own
color change are unmistakable: "His hide, þat blac & loþely was, / Al white bicom,
þurth Godes gras / & clere wiþouten blame" ("His skin, that black and loathly was, /
All white became, through God's grace / And clear without taint" [ll. 928–30]).

77. Hornstein makes the important observation that the princess's feigned embrace of Islam is *unique to the Middle English romance*, despite the wide dispersion of
analogues of the very popular story ("in Italian and German chronicles and in a number of Latin MSS in England, France, Germany, and Spain"): "The motif of religious
hypocrisy is peculiar to the *King of Tars* and does not occur in its analogues" ("Trivet's Constance," 355–56). I have attempted to suggest at length here what cultural
work might be performed by this romance's unique depiction of feigned conversion
in the discourse of race-and/as-religion.

78. That the Sultaness is depicted as nameless, taking her honorific from her son's
royal office, rings curiously true to history. Shajar ad-Durr, the first Sultaness of
Egypt, an extraordinary personage who had the Friday sermon from the pulpit of
Cairo's mosque pronounced in her name, assumed the title, "mother of Khalil"
(Khalil being the name of a son who had died in infancy), for the royal stamp issued
in her name, when she came to power (Gabrieli, 298).

79. None of the Constance stories teases us with the etymological possibilities of
Maurice's name, neither by pointing to color nor provenance, in "Mauro," the Moor,
nor by gesturing, through the name, at the phenomenon of the black St. Maurice in
Germany. Yet the stories' emphasis on Maurice's exemplary Christianity ("the
Cristeneste of alle"), imperial status, and provenance in the East, and the mission of
conversion to which Constance submits as meekly as a martyr, are all gestures of a
kind that work, on us, to tease. Devisse, who notes the arrival of the Maurician cult
in England where, he says, it was not destined to have any significant development
(2:152), follows the martyr's odd development as a military saint and, eventually, "an
'imperial' saint" (2:154) closely associated with, and supported by, emperors and archbishops, and interests of empire, until Maurice becomes a symbol of conversion by
military means—"symbol of the Germanic offensive against the Slavs" (2:154) and
"patron saint of the empire . . . protector of the imperial army" (2:154). The subsequent colorization of St. Maurice, Devisse thoughtfully speculates, is likely to have
been linked to crusading failure of a military kind in the thirteenth century—whereas the Constance stories, I have suggested, are linked to crusading failure of a military

kind in the fourteenth: "Egypt was the land that drew the attention of Western Christians, Crusaders and merchants alike, in the thirteenth century. If he could not conquer the country, Frederick [II] could at least demand that it furnish him the geographic, and then the ethnic, origin of St. Maurice" (2:160). Whatever we think of this representation of Frederick II's intentions, the Constance stories seem to function, in one respect, at least, oddly like the St. Maurice legend and cult they do not mention—that is, as a species of compensation and fantasmatic, exotic fulfillment, which accomplishes useful local work and serves the cultural politics, and political culture, of their location.

5. Eye on the World: *Mandeville's* Pleasure Zones; or,
Cartography, Anthropology, and Medieval Travel Romance

1. "We know of [Columbus's] familiarity with *Mandeville's Travels* from Andrés Bernáldez, *Memorias del reinado de los Reyes Católicos*, ed. M. Gómez Moreno and J. de Mata Carriazo (Madrid: Real Academia de la Historia, 1962), 270, 307, 315, 319. Columbus's son, Fernando, also wrote that among the reasons that led his father to undertake his voyage were the works of 'Marco Polo, a Venetian, and John Mandeville'" (Greenblatt, 156–57 n. 1). In their 1576 voyage, Michael Lok and Christopher Hall—Martin Frobisher's companions—describe the Inuit they encounter as "Anthropologi, or deuourers of mans fleshe" at least in part through the influence of *Mandeville's Travels*: "Before the despatch of the 1576 voyage, the adventurers had purchased a copy of Mandeville's *Travels* as though it were capable of providing useful information on what the voyages should expect. Such late-medieval works . . . were still, on the whole, regarded as reliable" (McDermott, 185).

2. Scholars agree that *Mandeville's Travels* was first written in French, though they divide on whether the *Travels* first arose in England or in France. Despite the *Travels'* long and tangled text-history, almost all agree that the Insular and Continental Versions of the *Travels* best represent the author's initial work. Among the manuscripts of the Insular Version, the most commonly cited and used in literary criticism is perhaps British Library MS Cotton Titus c. xvi, in part perhaps because its inclusion among the series editions of the Hakluyt Society (in a two-volume 1953 edition by Letts) and the Early English Text Society (in a two-volume 1919–23 edition by P. Hamelius) grants easy access to the contents and use of Cotton. Along with Cotton (which is missing three leaves after folio 53), British Library MS Egerton 1982 is the other fine, well-rendered, and relatively complete manuscript among the English *Travels*, though Egerton is less readily suited to use, being available only in a large, nineteenth-century limited edition, beautifully produced (with twenty-eight facsimile miniatures from British Library MS Additional 24189), by the Roxburghe Club, and edited by G. F. Warner. Egerton, however, corresponds more precisely than Cotton to the Anglo-Norman manuscripts of the Insular Version, and to the earliest extant dated manuscript of the *Travels*: the important Paris, Bibliothèque Nationale MS nouv. acq. fr. 4515, copied in 1371, and representing the Continental version. I use Egerton in this chapter (henceforth *Travels*); and, where long passages from Egerton

are quoted, reproduce equivalent passages from the Paris text, and Anglo-Norman
British Library Harley 4383 and Royal 20 B.X, both from the late fourteenth century
and representing the Anglo-Norman Insular manuscripts (Warner's edition offers MS
Harley 4383 till chapter 22 and replaces the lost latter half of Harley 4383 with the very
closely related MS Royal 20 B.X thereafter), so that detailed correspondences can be
seen at a glance, and also Cotton if it deviates in important ways from Egerton. All
references to the text of the *Travels* are to G. F. Warner's edition.

Claims have also recently been made for the English manuscripts grouped under
"Defective" (so-called because a section of the *Travels*, usually referred to as the
"Egypt gap," is missing from the narrative, among several other omissions: "Defective," for example, features only two of the famous alphabets in the *Travels* whereas
Egerton features six). Kohanski points out that "Defective" represents thirty-eight
manuscripts, whereas Egerton and Cotton exist only as single copies, and that the
popular dispersion of "Defective" likely meant that the *Travels* reached its widest English readership in this abridged form. "Defective" is also the version from which
Richard Pynson made his 1496 printing, abridged and edited, into the edition that became the basis of subsequent English printed copies till 1725. The Early English Text
Society also has editions of the Bodley and Metrical versions of the English *Travels*
(usually thought to be further removed than Cotton and Egerton from the author's
work), edited by M. C. Seymour, with studies that recapitulate the *Travels*' text history in England. Iain Higgins (*Writing East*), who offers the most substantial and important recent criticism on the *Travels*, notes that "within about fifty years of 1356,
The Book was circulating widely on both sides of the English Channel in a total of
eight languages—French, Czech, Dutch, English, German, Italian, Spanish, and
Latin and within about fifty years more it would be available in another two: Danish
and Irish" (6). Higgins goes on to observe that, after the book made the transition to
print, it reached sixty printings by 1600 (8). I refer to "Mandeville" without, of course,
assuming the facticity of "Sir John Mandeville's" persona (see also Higgins's response,
in *Writing East*, to the fictional author; however, Josephine Bennett's chapter, "The
English Mandevilles," discusses numerous historical candidates in the fourteenth century who went by the name of "John Mandeville"). In continuing to refer to "*Mandeville's Travels*," over other possible ways to refer to this work, my preference continues the tradition of signaling this work as a species of travel narrative (however
fictional).

3. "[The *Travels*] . . . looks back toward an earlier synthesis of theology and geography as much as it looks ahead toward the expanded and revised physical geography that eventually undermined medieval conceptions of the earth" (Higgins,
"Defining," 50).

4. Donald Howard, who also calls "Mandeville" "an encyclopaedist" (1) puts it
this way: "Mandeville was trying to write a new kind of work, a summa of travel lore
which (a) combined the authority of learned books and guidebooks with the eyewitness manner of pilgrim and travel writers; (b) combined the pilgrimage to the Holy
Land with the missionary or mercantile voyage into the Orient; and (c) combined the

curious and vicarious intentions of some such works with the thoughtful and devo-
tional intentions of others" (2). Higgins, too, renders the hybridity of the *Travels* succinctly: "[*Mandeville's Travels*] is not just two books at once, but several: a piece of intermittent crusading propaganda; an occasional satire on the religious practices of
Latin Christians; an implicit treatise on right rule in both the Christian and the non-
Christian worlds (a kind of mirror for Christian princes); a proof of the earth's
sphericity, the existence of inhabited antipodes, and the possibility of circumnavigation; a demonstration that most non-Christians have a "natural" knowledge of the
One, True God; a framed collection of tales and diversities, both exemplary and entertaining; and the desultory memoirs—the travel lies, in fact—of a 'verray, parfit
gentil' English Knight Errant" (*Writing East*, 13).

5. The "romance of travel" (the term is Josephine Bennett's) has a time-honored
literary genealogy:

> Mandeville was writing in a literary genre which has a long history, from the *Odyssey*
> and the lost *Arimaspeia* of Aristeas, through Ctesias, Megasthenes, and parts of
> Herodotus, Strabo, Aelian, Photius, and the lost novel of Antonius Diogenes about the
> wonders beyond Thule. Pliny collected these travelers' tales indiscriminately, and Soli-
> nus, perhaps Mandeville's closest forerunner, made a selection from Pliny of choice ge-
> ographical wonders. Lucian travestied the genre in his *True History*, but St. Augustine
> included a chapter on the fabulous races of men in his *City of God*. In his day, the ro-
> mance of Alexander was beginning its long history with the *Pseudo-Callisthenes* and the
> Epistle of Alexander to Aristotle about the marvels of India. In the seventh century
> Isidore of Seville repeated much of this lore, and shortly afterwards the pseudo-
> Aethicus produced his *Cosmographia*, which shows the same disregard for the changes
> wrought by time, and the same appropriation of other people's experiences complained
> of in Mandeville. . . . [B]etween the third and seventh centuries a letter was invented
> which purported to be from "Fermes" to the Emperor Hadrian, describing a journey
> to the East on which the writer saw all the traditional marvels of strange beasts and
> stranger men. A book of *Marvels of the East* was made, mostly out of "Fermes." It is pre-
> served in both a Latin and an Anglo-Saxon text. At the opening of the thirteenth cen-
> tury, Gervase of Tilbury included all of "Fermes" in his *Otia Imperialia*. . . . [A]bout
> 1165, the *Letter of Prester John* appeared and circulated widely. In the thirteenth centu-
> ry, when Europeans had an opportunity to visit China, they reported not only what
> they saw, but what they expected to see. (Bennett, 39)

6. Higgins's recent *Writing East* joins others in identifying the *Travels'* principal
sources as "the German Dominican William of Boldensele's *Liber de quibusdam ul-
tramarinis partibus* [Book of certain overseas regions] (1336), a tidy and detailed narrative of its author's pilgrimage to Egypt and the Holy Land, and Friar Odoric of Pordenone's *Relatio* (1330), a dictated account of wonders seen and heard about during
the friar's decade-long missionary wanderings in India and China" (9), especially the
versions of Odoric "translated into French in 1351 by Jean le Long of Ypres, monk of
Saint-Bertin at Saint Omer" (9). *Writing East* seconds Christiane Deluz's account of

the *Travels'* "extensive use of nearly two dozen texts" and selective consultation of "another dozen," including Josephus, Orosius, Macrobius, and Isidore of Seville. The range of sources also include "other pilgrimage and travel writings (John of Würzburg, *Descriptio Terrae Sanctae* [c. 1165], Thietmar, *Peregrinatio* [1214]); historical works (Jacques de Vitry, *Historia Orientalis* [early 13th century]; Hayton, *Flor des estoires de la terre d'Orient* [1307]); encyclopedias (Vincent of Beauvais, *Speculum historiale, Speculum naturale* [c. 1256–59]; Brunetto Latini, *Li Livres dou Tresor* [1260s]); religious writings (the Bible; Jacobus de Voraigne, *Legenda aurea* [before 1267]; William of Tripoli, *Tractatus de statu Saracenorum* [1273]); literary works that many medieval readers considered historical (*Littera Presbyteris Johannis* [late 12th century]; *Roman d'Alexandre* [mid-12th century]); and a single scientific treatise (Johannes de Sacrobosco's *De sphera* [c. 1220])" (9).

7. This passage in the Paris text reads: "En ce pays et en Ethiope et en maint autre pays les gens gisent toute iour ens es riuages des eaues, hommes et femmes tous ensemble, de leure de tierce iusques a basse nonne; et gisent tous dedenz leaue fors que la face pour le grant chaut quil y fait, si que a peine le peut nulz endurer. Et si nont les femmes point de honte des hommes, mais gisent tous priueement tant que la chaleur est abessiee" (Letts, 2:322). The Anglo-Norman is only minisculely more terse (lacking only the extra emphasis of "si que a peine le peut nulz endurer"): "En ceo pais et en Ethiope et en mointe autre pais les gentz gisent touz nuz as riuages deawes, hommes et femmes touz ensemble, de tierce du iour iusqes a basse nonne; et gisent totdys deins leawe forsqe la face pur la grant chaud qil fait. Et si nont les femmes point de honte des hommes, mes gisent tot apertement lez a lez tanqe la chaleure soit abaisse" (G. F. Warner, 81–82). On exotic pleasures, and the uses of clothing (or lack thereof) in travel writing, see, especially, Campbell's chapters, "Travel Writing and Ethnographic Pleasure" and "My Travels to the Other World" in her *Wonder and Science*.

8. Outside travel romance—a genre that offers what Akbari pithily calls "a luxurious Orient, characterized by sexual and economic surplus" (19)—more matter-of-fact medieval descriptions exist of even extreme forms of cultural difference in the behavior of the sexes. In direct contrast to the *Travels'* depiction of an Afro-Asian, trans-Asiatic luxuriance in wet nakedness, ("in this land and in Ethiopia and many other lands"), for instance, is the straightforward report of a Franciscan friar, Bartholomew Custos of Tarbriz, as relayed by Menentillo of Spoleto, on the lack of clothing worn by men and women in India: "The women as the men go barefoot and naked, wearing a towel around the loins. The boys and girls up to 8 years wear nothing but grow up and go naked just as they come from the mother's womb. [These people] do not shave the beard. They wash themselves many times a day" (Moule, 201).

9. As with some other depictions of the voyeuristically sensational, the *Travels'* account of Hasan ibn Sabah's illusory paradise follows Odoric of Pordenone's account in his *Descriptio Orientalium Partium* (henceforth *Descriptio*) in outline but embellishes details selectively. Friar Odoric, for instance, does not specify the tender years of the "virgines" ("fifteen") in the false paradise of the "Senex a Monte," nor does his narrative dwell on the pleasure and dalliance they represent or the promise of the

young people's perpetual virginity (Yule-Cordier, 2:330). Marco Polo's account (70–72) also refrains from the explicit offer of bisexual pleasures, nor does it focus on the perpetual youth of the pleasure givers. Olschki, who traces these exotically fulsome late-medieval cultural depictions of the Assassins' stronghold of Alamut to accounts by Polo and a 1263 Chinese source (372), points out the irony of such fanciful depictions of the austere, messianic, political-religious zealots who constituted the breakaway Shi'ite-Ismaeli group of the Batini, popularly known in Europe as the Assassins.

Though the depictions might represent ironic departures from history, however, such erotic-aesthetic exoticisms as are favored by late-medieval narratives like Polo's, Odoric's, and the *Travels* usefully convey something of European cultural speculations about the forbidden, and about the East, as well as indicate how late-medieval excitement over the exotic typically functioned. (E. San Juan Jr., quoting John Steadman on postmedieval Orientalisms, suggests that Europe's perception of Asia, and the Orient, transhistorically "functioned as an 'equivoque' that mixed belief and imagination, fact and fiction, resulting in the fabrication of a 'geographical fantasia . . . as unreal as the landscape of a dream'" [34]). Ultimately the depictions, of course, tell us more about European desire and fascinations in the period than about Alamut and its residents. J. J. Cohen, following Alain Grosrichard and Mladen Dolar, suggests that "Orientalist dreams of distant, copious indulgence provide a necessary support for the West's sacrificial systems of nationhood and identity in that they maintain the fantasy that a potentially recoverable full enjoyment is in fact located somewhere, even if it is not possessed by 'us'" ("Saracen Enjoyment," 125): "What motivates such fantasies, Dolar argues, is that they provide a 'subject supposed to enjoy,' a figure who consumes and hoards the enjoyment that 'we' as Westerners have renounced *in order to be Westerners*" (125).

Another way of putting this, perhaps, is to say that *because* Western identity is implicitly or explicitly posited on a notion of civilizational maturity understood to be based on sacrifice, discipline, and degrees of austerity, Oriental cultures and identity are required, in turn, to be linked to the plenitude and polymorphous pleasures associated with human infancy and pre-maturity. Late-medieval Western fantasy about the opulent licentiousness and extravagance of the East—particularly when the fantasies recur as individual Latin Christian societies begin the long process of nation making—thus offers the possibility that, despite the sacrifice, renunciation, and discipline that mature adult identity, individually and societally, requires, the pleasures and plenitude that have been renounced, or left behind, have not been completely lost in a prior, irrecoverable time but are still somewhere available in geographical space that coexists simultaneously with mature Western civilization and mature Western time. For historical accounts of the Batini, see Olschki, *Marco Polo's Asia*; Nowell, "Old Man"; and B. Lewis, "Sources."

10. Odoric of Pordenone's *Descriptio* (sometimes also referred to as the *Relatio*), the *Travels'* most important source for material on South, Southeast, and East Asia, also relates native self-desecration with dung and urine, self-mutilation in "Mobar"

5. Eye on the World

(the *Travels*'"Marbaron") before an idol of gold ("totum de auro"), ritual suicide and self-sacrifice by the devotees, and the burning of the sacrificial bodies afterward (Yule-Cordier, 2:295–96, 297–99). However, though the *Travels* seems to follow its source closely in the description of the self-consuming bodies on display in Marbaron, it also palpably embroiders on the spectacle by adding that parents kill their children by sacrificing them to the idol, and sprinkle the blood of these innocents on their false god. Indeed, the *Travels* seems particularly alive to the effects that can be milked from the depiction of children who are abused in ingenious ways by native adults. For instance, though the cannibalism of "Lamary" ("Lamori" in Odoric) follows Odoric's account (Odoric relates that merchants come to this island from a distance, bringing children [or, variously, men, or fat men] with them to sell to those infidels there, who buy and slay them and eat them [Yule-Cordier, 2:300]), it is the *Travels* that insists the children are fattened till they are plump, before being killed and eaten, with the child flesh, presumably after the tending, being the "best and sweetest flesh of the world" [*Travels*, 89]). Wittkower suggests that the *Travels* was also particularly attentive to varieties of adult luridity: "If Marco Polo was satisfied with the generic denomination 'wild race' . . . [b]y contrast to Marco Polo, Mandeville enumerates, of course, all the marvellous races of the East one by one, nor does he forget the people who have faces in their breasts" (162).

11. Biddick's article on how the *Travels* detemporalizes medieval Jews links together several important arguments related to the representation of Jews in the *Travels*. One of these arguments treats the *Travels'* resemblance to *mappaemundi* and "the growing tendency" in the "textual and pictorial tradition of *mappaemundi* in the twelfth century" to associate "Jews with stories of the enclosed peoples of Gog and Magog" and the unclean nations that would break forth in the last days to threaten Christendom (275–76). On Biddick's linkage of the anti-Semitic blood libel with eschatology, and Gog and Magog, see, especially, 292 n. 17. Westrem, who notes that "Gog or Magog appears in map legends [on the approximately 1,100 extant *mappaemundi*] with remarkable infrequency" (59), tracks the developments through which an association between Jews and the enclosed monstrous races is consolidated. In Matthew Paris's cartography, for instance, Westrem observes, "the people confined by a semicircular sweep of mountains in the northeast corner of his three extant maps of the Crusader Kingdom are Jews whose escape Matthew describes as a future danger" (59). The association becomes fully consolidated in the *Travels*:

> The most direct claim I know of that European Jews were complicit in a plot against Christians is found in *The Book of John Mandeville* (circa 1360), a text whose genial treatment of Muslims, Hindus, and animists is offset by one astonishing anecdote. It begins by identifying Gog and Magog with the Ten Lost Tribes of Israel, which we have seen literalists in western Europe already doing in the twelfth century. In the mountains of the Caspian region, *The Book*'s author claims, "are enclosed the Iewes of the ten tribes [ligniees] whom one calls Goth and Magoth"; their incarceration was effected by Alexander, who "chased" them into a natural trap, and then, though he him-

self was a pagan, successfully prayed that God would miraculously cause the mountains to close. Alexander thus resembles one of *The Book*'s Brahmans, who are ignorant of Christian revelation but nevertheless demonstrate moral virtue and so win divine favor. Jews, on the other hand, are regularly excluded from this celestial Jerusalem. (68–69)

My discussion in this chapter of the *Travels'* conscientious project of relative tolerance for differences within Christianity and Christendom, and its calibrated negotiation of the difference and alterity it finds in the variousness of the world, must thus be read, and weighed against, the *Travels'* unremitting virulence toward Jews, a people who seem to constitute, for the *Travels*, the one species of otherness to which no humane generosity can be shown: Jews being the ultimate scapegoat that subtends the *Travels'* other recuperations of difference.

12. Citing the *Travels* as an example, Campbell warns against any straightforward assumption that we plainly know what is meant whenever cannibalism is depicted in varieties of travel literature:

> The scene of cannibalistic feasting is . . . the master scene of ethnography, and in straight travel writing or accounts of exploration, whatever its particular nuances of context, it always means one thing: they (the Others) are not really Human. They are functionally animals, even if genealogically human. . . . Its closeness to the symbolism of the eucharist, however, makes it satirically usable for the different purpose of mocking European cultural arrogance; it is used this way famously in *Mandeville's Travels* and Montaigne's essay "Of Cannibals." (*Wonder and Science*, 173–74)

13. Though Susan Stewart's discussion of "collections" in her marvelous volume, *On Longing*, has postmedieval economies of exchange and consumption in view, her description of how a shard stands in for the whole is keenly apposite:

> There are two movements to the collection's gesture of standing for the world: first, the metonymic displacement of part for whole, item for context; and second, the invention of a classification scheme which will define space and time in such a way that the world is accounted for by the elements of the collection. . . . [T]he museum of natural history allows nature to exist "all at once" in a way in which it could not otherwise exist. Because of the fiction of such a museum, it is the Linnaean system which articulates the identity of plants, for example, and not the other way around. (162)

14. As will be obvious to many, the discussion in this entire first section of my chapter is substantially shaped by Bruno Latour's thinking in *Science in Action*. James Clifford, who asks, "What is the proper balance between scientific analysis and public display?" (*Predicament of Culture*, 221) meditates on the relationship between collecting and identity: "Identity, whether cultural or personal, presupposes acts of collection, gathering up possessions in arbitrary systems of value and meaning" (217). By way of elaboration, Clifford also quotes and extrapolates from Susan Stewart's *On Longing*: "She shows how collections, most notably museums, create the illusion of adequate representation of a world by first cutting objects out of specific contexts

(whether cultural, historical, or intersubjective) and making them 'stand for' abstract wholes—a 'Bambara mask,' for example, becoming an ethnographic metonym for Bambara culture" (220). Stewart's work, along with others, Clifford concludes, "brings collecting and display sharply into view as crucial processes of Western identity formation" (220). Ethnography (a theme I treat later in this chapter) is also a modality of collection, to both Stewart and Clifford: "To see ethnography as a form of culture collecting (not, of course, the *only* way to see it) highlights the ways that diverse experiences and facts are selected, gathered, detached from their original temporal occasions, and given enduring value in a new arrangement" (Clifford, *Predicament of Culture*, 231).

15. "The collection," Stewart notes, "is often about containment on the level of its content . . . those great civic collections, the library and the museum, seek to represent experience within a mode of control and confinement. One cannot know everything about the world, but one can at least approach closed knowledge through the collection" (161). Craig Clunas's "China in Britain," which considers collections of Chinese artifacts in the British Museum and the Victoria and Albert Museum, suggests how "the framing of Chinese objects in these institutions conditions their viewing as expressive of discourses of national and imperial identity" in the British homeland (43). Control and domination of the far-away (and/or long-ago), through the acquisition of representative objects, is Clunas's focus: musing on the great carved lacquer throne of the Chinese emperor Ch'ien-lung, in the Victoria and Albert Museum, Clunas observes: "The throne was there, and the Emperor of China sat on it. Now it is here, and you the visitor view it. Do not ask how it got here. . . . You are here to engage with 'China,' not 'Britain,' so do not ask what the throne of the emperor of China might tell you about 'Britain,' and its narratives about 'China'" (41). See also the other studies on museum collections, objects, and empires, in Barringer and Flynn's *Colonialism and the Object*.

16. Consider the following quotation from the *Travels*:

> And if all it be so þat the Grekes be Cristen, ȝit þai vary fra oure faith. For þai say þat þe Haly Gaste commes noȝt oute of þe Sonne, bot anely of þe Fader; and þai er noȝt obeyand to þe kirke of Rome, ne to þe Pope. And þai say þat þaire Patriarke has als mykill power beȝond þe Grekis see as oure Pope hase on þis syde. And þerfore þe Pope Iohn þe xxii. sent letters to þaim schewand þam how þat the cristen faith schuld be all ane, aud þat all cristen men schuld be obeyand to a pope, whilke es Cristez vicar in erthe, to wham Godd gaffe full powere for to bynd and to louse; and þerfore þai schuld be o[be]dient til him. . . . Þe Grekes also makes þe sacrement of þe autere of leuaynd breed; for oure Lord made it of leuaynd breed, when he made his maundee. And þai say we erre þat makes þe sacrement of tharf breed. And on þe schire Thursday make þai þat breed in a takenynge of þe maundee, and dries it at þe soune, and kepez it all þe ȝere, and giffez it to seke men in steed of howsill. And þai make bot ane vnccioun, when þai cristen childer, ne dippes þaim bot anes in þe fount. Þai anoynt na seke men; and þai say þer is na purgatory, and þat saules sall nowþer hafe ioy ne payne before þe

day of dome. Þai say also þat fornicacion es na dedly bot a kyndely thing, and þat men
and wymmen schuld noȝt be wedded bot anes, and, wha so weddes ofter þan anes, þaire
childer er bastardes and geten in synne. Þer prestes also er wedded. And þai say þat oker
es na dedly synne. Þai sell benificez of haly kirk, and so duse men in oþer places; and
þat is grete sclaunder and grete harme. For now is symony kyng corouned in haly kirk.
Godd may amend it, when his will es. Þai say also þat in lentyn men schuld noȝt synge
messe bot on þe Setirday and on þe Sonounday. And þai fast noȝt þe Seterday na tyme
of þe ȝere, bot it be ȝole euen or pask euen. Þai suffer na man þat commes fra þis syde
of þe Grekes see syng on þaire awters; and, if it fall þat þai do, þai wasche þe awter al-
sone with haly water. And þai say þat þer schuld bot a messe be sungen at ane awter on
a day. Ouer þat þai say þat oure Lorde ete neuer bodily mete, bot he made signe of
etyng and feyned as he had etyn, schewand taken of manhede. Þai say we synne dedly
in þat we schaue oure berdes, for þai say þat þe berde es taken of manhede and þe gifft
of Godd. And þa þat schafes þaire berdes, þai do it all anely for to plese þe werld and
þaire wyfes. Þai say also þat we synne dedly in etying of bestez þat ware forbedd in þe
alde lawe, as swyne, hares and oþer bestez þat chewez noȝt cudde. Also þai say þat we
synne in etyng of flesch in þe three days before Ask Wedensday, and also in etyng of
flesch on Wedensdays, and when we ete whitmete on Frydays. And þai curse al þase þat
etes na flesch on þe Saterday. Also þe emperour of Constantynople makes þe patriarkes,
ercebischopes, and bischopes, and he giffes all þe digniteez of haly kirk in þat cuntree;
and he pryues þaim þat hym think vnworthy. And so he es þare lorde bathe of tem-
peraltee and of spiritualtee.

And if albeit so the Greeks be Christian, yet they vary from our faith. For they say that
the Holy Ghost comes not out of the Son, but only of the Father; and they are not obedient to the church of Rome, nor to the Pope. And they say that their Patriarch has as
much power beyond the Greeks' sea as our Pope has on this side. And therefore the
Pope John XXII sent letters to them showing them how that the Christian faith should
be all one, and that all Christian men should be obedient to a Pope, which is Christ's
vicar in earth, to whom God gave full power for to bind and to loose, and therefore
they should be obedient to him. . . . The Greeks also make the sacrament of the altar
of leavened bread; for our Lord made it of leavened bread, when he made his Maundy
[his Last Supper]. And they say we err who make the sacrament of unleavened bread.
And on the Shere-Thursday they make that bread in a tokening of the Maundy [Last
Supper], and dry it at the sun, and keep it all the year, and give it to sick men instead
of housel. And they make but one unction, when they christen children, nor dip them
but once in the font. They anoint no sick men; and they say there is no purgatory, and
that souls shall neither have joy nor pain before the day of judgment. They say also that
fornication is no deadly, but a natural, thing, and that men and women should not be
wedded but once, and, whoso weds oftener than once, their children are bastards and
gotten in sin. Their priests also are wedded. And they say that usury is no deadly sin.
They sell benefices of holy church, and so do men of other places; and that is great slan-
der and great harm. For now is simony crowned king in holy church. God may amend

it, when [it] is his will. They say also that in Lent men should not sing mass but on the
Saturday and on the Sunday. And they fast not the Saturday [at] any time of the year,
except it be Yule eve or Paschal eve. They suffer no man that comes from this side of
the Greeks' sea [to] sing [mass] on their altars; and, if it happen that they do, they wash
the altar at once with holy water. And they say that there should but [one] mass be sung
at one altar on a day. Over that, they say that our Lord never ate bodily meat, but he
made sign of eating and feigned as [though] he had eaten, [for] showing token of manhood. They say that we sin deadly in that we shave our beards, for they say that the
beard is token of manhood and the gift of God. And they that shave their beards, they
do it all only for to please the world and their wives. They say also that we sin deadly
in eating of beasts that were forbidden in the old law, as swine, hares and other beasts
that chew not the cud. Also they say that we sin in eating of flesh in the three days before Ash Wednesday, and also in eating of flesh on Wednesdays, and when we eat white
meat on Fridays. And they curse all those that eat no flesh on the Saturday. Also the
emperor of Constantinople makes the patriarchs, archbishops and bishops, and he gives
[i.e., issues] all the dignities of holy church in that country; and he deprives them who
seem to him unworthy. And so he is their lord both of temporality and of spirituality.
(*Travels*, 9–10)

17. Greenblatt offers a modulated description of this utopian impulse: "Mandeville's open and lively interest in the customs of exotic peoples, his refusal to invoke demonic causality for unfamiliar or even repellent practices, and his willingness to im-
pute internal coherence to superficially irrational behavior is not tolerance but rather
an early instance of what Hans Blumenberg calls 'theoretical curiosity.' Yet in the
fourteenth century such curiosity . . . is itself heterodox" (46). Higgins concurs: "It is
hard to deny that *Mandeville's Travels* often displays an almost un-medieval capacity
to imagine lives radically different from those known within fourteenth-century Latin
Christendom, and to do so sympathetically" ("Imagining Christendom," 96). "The
Book does in fact promote . . . and celebrate the world's marvellous diversity" (Higgins, "Defining," 40). Bynum adds a caveat, however: "Marvelling at the world's diversity can be the prelude to appropriation" (*Metamorphosis*, 69).
18. Higgins's *Writing East* emphasizes the *Travels'* "generally sympathetic portrayal of even the most radically different beliefs and practices" but draws attention to
"the one striking exception to that sympathy: the depiction of the Jews" (27). Despite
the *Travels'* crusading exordium, Higgins notices that the narrative suggests possible
co-amity between Christians and Muslims, by scapegoating Jews: "After mentioning
the Saracen practice of fasting, the text returns to a theme dear to the Mandeville-
author's heart: Jewish wickedness and waywardness . . . a move that makes Christians
and Saracens potential allies" (114). Greenblatt, who "honor[s] the generosity of *Mandeville's Travels*," similarly recoils at its treatment of Jews, and finds an explanation in
the postulation that Jews "are at once rivals in [the *Travels'*] dream of repossession and
rivals in the dream of wandering" (51). Linda Lomperis indicts the *Travels* as "one
more demonstration of the way in which European Christian identity tried to estab-

lish its own coherence and stability largely at the expense of the Jews, who are rele-
gated to a position of social marginality, contained and sustained in a fantasmatic
identity construct determined by the binary opposition between Christians and Jews.
There is indeed a strong desire encoded in this text to keep the Jews entirely separate
from all other racial groupings, as witnessed by the narrator's inclusion of the story of
the Jews of the Ten Lost Tribes, Gog and Magog, who are entirely held at bay from
the rest of the world in the impenetrable hills beyond the land of Cathay" (162).

19. Hamilton ("Continental Drift") very reasonably points out that the geoscientific *weltanschauung* has conventional practices that are as arbitrary as those of the theological *weltanschauung* and that "the cartographic convention, inspired by the
prophet Ezekiel, of placing Jerusalem at the center of the earth is no more arbitrary
than that of running the meridian through Greenwich" (239). Indeed, though at first
glance the decision to offer a location as the center of the world appears illogical, and
counterintuitive to an understanding of the earth's sphericity—appears, that is, wholly ideological—the *convention* of a center that allows an organization of the world as
an intelligible system is also a calculably logical practice and antedates Judaeo-
Christian thinking. Donald Lach notes that Eratosthenes, in his *Geographica* (lost but
summarized by Strabo), "took the island of Rhodes as his center and calculated distances along two lines which intersected there" in order to extrapolate the measurement and placement of known territories on the earth, an earth that he postulates as
spherical and that he "measures and divides into zones" (1 [book 1]: 10). The *Travels'*
location of Jerusalem as the midpoint of the world thus expresses not only theological but also *cartographic* investments in locating the zones, geographical interrelations,
and borders of the known world, oriented by a stable, familiar, and conventional location of a center of some variety.

20. Greenblatt, whose chapter on *Mandeville's Travels* argues that the *Travels* is
about "what it means not to take possession, about circulation and wandering as an
alternative to ownership, about a refusal to occupy" (27), modifies what he believes to
be the *Travels'* disinterest in possessing and collecting the world when the palpable
object of narrative desire is the Holy Land: "He [the narrator] wants the land in which
Jesus Christ was born and lived and traveled and died, and in particular he wants
Jerusalem" (28).

21. The power of relics, and the inexorable pull exerted by the sacred topography
of the Holy Land did not end with the Middle Ages. A *New York Times Book Review*'s
description of James Carroll's recent new history of the Church's relationship to Jews
relates Carroll's encounter with sacred geography in Jerusalem: "In general, Carroll was
disgusted by the commercialism and grubbiness of many of the holy places. But then
'a skeptical old Frenchman' took him to an excavation site where he pointed out a large
stone slab. 'This was the threshold stone of the city gate at the time of Jesus,' he said.
'It was buried in the rubble of the Roman destruction and is only now being uncov-
ered. It is certain'—the Frenchman had used this expression of nothing else he had
shown me—'that Jesus of Nazareth would have stepped on this stone as he left the city
for Golgotha.' Carroll kneels and kisses the stone. It is a deeply Catholic moment—its

physicality, its sacramental simplicity, its faith that . . . the living Jesus can still be found and felt and loved" (Sullivan, 6).

22. The many vestiges and imprints of a sacred, divine body distributed, ex post facto, around the Holy Land, attest, Bynum suggests, a medieval concept of the body that assumes "some kind of material continuity between Christ's body in the *triduum* and in heaven" (*Resurrection*, 319) and the power of an eschatology "that bestows on the risen body all the organs and senses—even the scars—of earthly experience" (*Resurrection*, 319). All bodily parts, Bynum notes, not only recall a bodily totality but imply that totality: "Fourteenth-century images implied the part . . . to be the whole. In vision, in art, and in literary metaphor, soul was sometimes self. Body was sometimes self. But finger or toe was also sometimes self" (*Resurrection*, 319). "The assumption that the material body we occupy in this life is integral to person was reflected in legend, folktale, and even 'science.' Many stories that circulated in the Middle Ages implied that the body was in some sense alive after death" (*Resurrection*, 326). In addition to eschatological reasoning, Beckwith also urges a "late medieval identification with Christ" impelling pilgrimage, ritual, and pious performance that understood "Christ's body . . . as both image *and physical presence*"(my emphasis), "both an image and a physical, experiential, felt presence" (60–61). The impact of the material environment of the Holy Land also derived from resemblance, in the Apocalypse of John, between an extant, historical Jerusalem and the anticipated spiritual New Jerusalem to come: the "real, historical, earthly" Jerusalem, Emmerson observes, "even as an earthly city . . . seems to resemble John's heavenly one" (316).

23. Atiya's survey of the more prominent crusading propagandists of the fourteenth century (in his *Crusade in the Later Middle Ages*) is summarized in chap. 4 n. 8, above. Travel literature and geographical lore were, of course, conducive narrative contexts for exhortations to crusade. Moreover, Glenn Burger's study of the Armenian Hetoum of Korikos's *La Fleur des histoires de la terre d'Orient* reminds us that the call to crusade not only infected travel narratives of the late-medieval Latin West but also the geographical writing of even Eastern Christians of Cilician Armenia (72).

24. The English versions of the *Travels* are particularly attentive to Rome. Higgins (*Writing East*) emphasizes the "radical overwriting" of the exordium by the Metrical version, with its intense focus on Rome: "Hardly has 'this little treatise' sent Sir John off 'atte Dover' than it takes its lords and ladies to Rome, 'chief of alle cristiante / And also hede of holi church, / . . . *Roma caput mundi tenet imperium mundi*.' By the time the nameless narrator announces that 'here of Rome I make an eende,' the audience has received some four hundred lines of historical and topographical material adapted from the twelfth-century *Mirabilia Urbis Romae*. This displacement of Jerusalem—and Constantinople, *The Book*'s first stop—by Rome, and of prose by verse, represents the most radical overwriting of the exordium" (61–62). Egerton, Cotton, and Defective, as noted, contain that interpolation in which "Mandeville" describes himself presenting his book to the Pope in Rome, and the Pope's ratification

and confirmation of the book (an interpolation also present in a late-fifteenth-century Latin manuscript that follows either Egerton or Defective).

Higgins, who repeats the suggestion that the interpolation is original to the Insular version, is undoubtedly correct in concluding that Cotton's reference to "the Pope *of Rome*" is a partisan English declaration against the Avignonese pope aligned with the French crown, in the Schism: "The interpolated account of Sir John's visit to Rome on his return journey in order to have the pope legitimate his 'tretys' looks like a conscious and not altogether simple-minded attempt to enlist the English Knight and his book on behalf of the pro-Roman camp by showing him and the pope endorsing each other's authority—a gesture that authenticates the book in the process" (*Writing East*, 255). Cotton, Higgins properly suggests, emphasizes "the pope as . . . *spiritual* head" (*Writing East*, 255), an emphasis that would implicitly identify the Roman see as a problem site.

Where Cotton emphasizes the Pope (Cotton, but not Egerton, depicts "Mandeville" confessing to the Pope and being shriven), Egerton's interpolation directly emphasizes *Rome itself* as a critical center: For Egerton, Rome is *both* the place where the Pope and curia are/should be located *and* a world center, a meeting point for all the nations of the world: "Diverse folk . . . are in Rome, for there are evermore dwelling men of all nations of the world" ("diuerse folke . . . er in Rome, for þare er euermare dwellande men of all naciouns of þe werld" [*Travels*, 156]). Egerton's singular awareness of an international world, and the importance of fixing key Christian orientations in a global structure, partly drives my discussion in this chapter. Moseley ("Implications") suggests that the English *Travels* might also well have added the interpolation in order to establish 1377 (before the Great Schism of 1378–1417) as the *terminus post quem* of the English *Travels*.

25. If, for the *Travels*, all roads explicitly lead to Jerusalem, and inferentially to Rome, Chaucer's "Treatise on the Astrolabe" axiomatically makes Rome the destination of all paths: "Diverse pathes leden diverse folk the righte way to Rome" (l. 40). If late-medieval literary texts seem to point to one or the other holy city as sites of arrival, we note that Jerusalem and Rome, of course, are *both* key pilgrimage destinations *and* Christian places in crisis in the second half of the fourteenth century.

26. We might also see the narrator's cumulative references to *England*, in particular (the originating point for pilgrimage, and a country whose miles are a benchmark by which to measure distance, and whose alphabet has special, extra letters) as a way to put England, specifically, on the (world) map, since the narrator seems palpably troubled by the fact that England does not appear in ancient (i.e., Greek) systems of mapping the world. The insertion of heterotopian spaces that complicate old traditional views of the world also constitutes a moment, as Greenblatt suggests, when a "horizontal, secularizing metonymy" imagines "a world in which every point has an equal and opposite point" (42–43), a world with an infinitely mobile horizon.

27. Burger's reading of Hetoum of Korikos's *La Fleur des Histoires de la Terre d'Orient* suggests that Hetoum's hybrid geographical-historical narrative—written out

of the Near East/West Asia, and with Armenian interests in mind, but addressed to Latin Europe—might also offer another geographical-cultural perspective from the period that serves a heterotopic function of the kind I describe here, and work "to change the European worldview, to realign it" (78). Burger suggests that,

> Hetoum's text maps Jerusalem as one destination among many, sees it in a geographical context quite different from the usual European one: on the periphery of Asia, *strategically*, not *conceptually*, in the center of Egyptian, Mongol, Frankish, Armenian geopolitical interests. This Jerusalem therefore does not define a whole and originary *Christianitas* (and with it a supreme Latin Europe) by acting as mirror and *translatio*. In a more "standard" crusade or travel account from a European perspective, in "naturally" ending in Jerusalem one thereby proves who one truly is, that is, a Christian subject, and proclaims the centrality of that "I" and the inherent superiority of its point of view. Hetoum's methodology is metonymic . . . a bringing close together into productive contiguity a variety of differences rather than a process of othering. . . . His Asia thus becomes a productive place of contiguity rather than orientalizing spectacle, part of the multiplicity of crosscultural identifications that *La Fleur des histoires* inscribes and encourages. (78)

28. Nestorian Christian missionaries had preceded Latin Christian missionaries to the East by six to eight centuries. Nowell notes that "a Nestorian named A-lo-pen arrived in China to preach as early as 635" and "the Asiatic Christian historian, Bar Hebraeus, [records] that in 1007 the powerful Mongol tribe of the Kereits was baptized en masse into the Nestorian faith, and . . . evidence exists to show that this people remained Christian, at least in part, until the thirteenth century" ("Prester John," 443). Ross observes that the "two principal tribes [in Central Asia] who carried on the faith were the Kereits and the Onguts . . . tribes . . . converted to Nestorian Christianity by the influence of Nestorian merchants, and priests sent to them by the Metropolitan of Merv" (182). After the condemnation and degradation of Nestorius, the Greek Patriarch of Constantinople, for heresy, by the Council of Ephesus in 431, and the expulsion of his followers from Edessa in 489, the Nestorians moved to Persia, along the trade routes, and thence to India, China, Mongolia, and Manchuria. Rumors of successful Nestorian missionizing intermittently filtered back to Europe through East-West commercial routes, Constantinople, and Syria. "The apocryphal account of St. Thomas preaching in India," one historian remarks, "is almost certainly related to the work of the Nestorian missionaries in southern India, which eventually led to the establishment of the Syro-Malabar Church still active today" (de Rachewiltz, 3). Prester John's legend appears to be another inadvertent beneficiary of Nestorian Christianizing, which made available in the West knowledge of Christian Oriental communities that existed far to the East of Persia and Armenia, knowledge the West urgently needed to fuel its hopes for military aid, at an exigent moment in the twelfth century, when the legend arose: "The Prester John legend must . . . be regarded as being fathered by the Nestorians and mothered by the Christian nations of the West" (de Rachewiltz, 8).

29. Linda Lomperis offers a slightly different perspective on the heterogeneous ubiquity of Christian traces, in paraphrasing the Sultan's accusation in the so-called Egypt Gap:

> European Christians merely pass as Christians, and they do not do a very good job of it at that: they transgress their own laws, they are swollen with pride and vainglory, and their priests are poor practitioners of the faith . . . European Christians are shown by the *Travels* to be "Christians" in name only, not at all as embodiments of some sort of essential Christian identity. Indeed, the rest of the text strongly suggests that there is no such thing as essential or authentic Christian identity insofar as all sorts of "others" in this text can and do indeed effectively pass as Christian. Witness, for example, the pious half-man/half-goat that the narrator encounters in the deserts of Egypt. And witness, of course, all of the so-called virtuous pagans in this text, many of whom, though manifestly not Christian, strike one nonetheless as more Christian than the so-called real Christians. (155)

My argument here—that the *Travels* is manifestly anxious about stabilizing the structures of late-medieval Christian identity and, as part of that process, is invested also in finding identificatory spaces for the expansion of Christian identity—is consonant with my argument in chapter 4 that late-medieval literature intensely desires and believes Christianity to possess an essence, one that be seen to function when it confers an essential identity upon baptism. Elsewhere in her article, Lomperis more closely approaches my argument here, when she describes the *Travels* as "a kind of Christian, colonialist fantasy . . . as Mandeville's *Travels* as a whole demonstrates, all the world is quite literally a stage for Christianity, insofar as everyone in this text seemingly has the potential to pass as a Christian," adding, moreover, that "the text of Mandeville's *Travels* . . . with the sense that it conveys of a world entirely filled with Christians and others wishing to be Christian, can be understood as a significant testament to the power and longevity of this fantasy within the imagination of Latin Christendom" (161–62).

30. "The three Indias were Nearer or Lesser India, Further or Greater India, and Middle India. Nearer or Lesser India meant, approximately, the north of the subcontinent, Further or Greater India meant the south, Malabar and Coromandel. . . . [F]or some European peoples at certain times the south of India was more interesting, more important, and more accessible than the north. The monsoon winds made it easy to reach from the Arabian and East African ports; its pepper and other exports and reexports were far more worth obtaining than the products of Gujerat and Kathiawar. Its fertility, its wealth, the presence of a Christian community, however small and politically uninfluential it may have been, above all its role in the oceanic trade of Asia justify the preference given to it over the north. In comparison Nearer India seemed forbidding and unproductive. What Europeans knew about it, or supposed they knew, was commonly ascribed to Alexander the Great. Middle India was, of course, Ethiopia" (Beckingham, "Achievements," 15). Beckingham notes that two Indias, "India Major and India Minor occur as early as the fourth century . . . [but] three Indias appear for the first time in 1118 in a manuscript of Guido Pisano" (17).

Beckingham shows, moreover, that Syrian *Edessa* and India also sometimes overlap. Citing the fifteenth-century Pilgerfahrt of Arnold von Harff, Beckingham points out that, for Arnold, Lesser India is not northern India but Malabar in southern India, while "Greater India is Prester John's domain, with its capital at Edessa, to which [John] had removed the head of St. Thomas after forcing the King of Moabar [Malabar] to pay tribute. . . . It is its association with St. Thomas that has brought Edessa into India" (Beckingham, "Achievements," 19). To suggest the range of geographical associations, Lach points out that Marco Polo also called south China ("Mangi") "'Upper India,' a term that was still current as late as the seventeenth century" (40). Conceding that the confusion of India and Ethiopia, in particular, "dates back to at least the time of Homer" (225 n. 38), Kaplan sums up the fluid geographical placement of "India" neatly: "The medieval placement of the many Indias—first, second, third, major, minor, upper, lower, near, middle, furthest—is extremely variable" (64). From the fourteenth century on, especially, "the third India was often associated with East African regions" (Kaplan, 64): "Ethiopia was regarded in the Middle Ages as one of the Three Indias, though it was not known exactly where it was" (Ross, 178).

31. Budge, in his *Monks of Kublai Khan*, tracks the progress of Nestorian missionizing in Central Asia and the Far and Near East, with specific chapters on Nestorian conversion in Turkestan and China, and an appendix on the Mongols and Christianity. A key role in Mongol Christianization, it would appear, seems to have been played by royal mothers and wives who were themselves Nestorian Christians: conducing, perhaps, to the Christianization of princes and princelings, and to the transmission of hearsay, far afield, of the substantial presence of Christians among the Mongol ranks. Budge notes that Hulagu Khan, brother of Kublai and founder of the Il-Khan dynasty ("Western Khans") that ruled over Persia, Syria, and the Near East, was a Christian (as was his mother, Sarkuthani Bagi) and proved "a fanatical adversary of the Muslims" (106). Hulagu's wife, Dakuz (or Tokuz) Khatun, was also a Christian, and his son and successor, Abaga (Abhaka), also had a Christian wife, "the great Queen Kuthai Khatun," who may have been Mary, a daughter of Michael VIII Paleologus (107–8). Abaga's son, Arghun (Arghon) "had at least two Christian wives, and some of his children were baptized" (108). Kaikhato and Kazan, Arghun's sons, who succeeded him, in turn, also seem to have been Christians (108–9).

Montgomery speculates on what Arghun might have become: "Had Arghon, following in the track of statesmanlike popes, won over the West to his plan of a Crusade against the Mamluk power, the centre of Islam's resistance, he might have become the Constantine of his Mongols. His grand idea perished, unsupported, and despite the favorable attitude towards the Christians of his immediate successors, Gaykhatu, Baidu, Ghazan, Islam triumphed" (17). Montgomery emphasizes the persistence of Nestorian missionizing across six to seven centuries in Central and East Asia: "A Nestorian monument with an inscription in Chinese and Syriac at Singanfu . . . in the province of Shen-si, is the earliest local record of Christian missions in China. The stone was erected, according to its dating, in 781 A.D., and records the bringing of the Faith into that capital of the empire in 636. Subsequent records prove the continued zeal and success of the Nestorians, and it looked fair for a time that Christianity might become the religion of the empire" (15).

32. Although John's first church at Khanbalik—the capital of the Mongol Khans in the ancient northern Chinese capital of Peking/Beijing—had been duly sought, by later eras, in China, Donald Lach, citing N. Egann's article, "Olon-Sume et la dé-couverte de l'église catholique romaine de Jean de Montecorvino," reports that the "remains of this first Roman Catholic Church" have apparently been discovered at a site "between Inner and Outer Mongolia" rather than in China (1 [book 1]: 39 n. 125). Discoveries, or rather suggestions of yet unverified residues, of Franciscan activity in China continue: "Some years ago (1935), . . . the Danish architect Johannes Prip-Møller, pointed out how astonishingly like an Avignon basilica was the ruined Ling ku ssu, situated to the east of Nanking, built about the years 1324–27, with its beam-less brick hall, its bell tower on the west and not the east side, its lack of a drum tower, and its measurements of 150 pieds du roy by 102 pieds, etc. . . . [J]ust last year John Foster has published in the *Journal of the Royal Asiatic Society* (London) many fresh indications of Franciscan residence in the great Yüan city of Ch'üan-chou" (Goodrich, 2).

33. Compare the account in the *Travels*:

> And, if Cristen men of religioun dwell nere whare he schall passe, as þai do in many citeez in þat land, þai go agayn him with procession with crosse and haly water, syngand with a hye voice, *Veni, Creator spiritus*. And, when he seez þam comme, he commaun-dez þe lordes þat rydez nere him to make way þat þe men of religioun may comme to him. And, alssone as he seez þe crosse, he doffez his hatte . . . And þan he lowtez deuote-ly to þe crosse; and þe prelate of þase religious men saise twa orisouns before him and giffez him benysoun with þe crosse, and he lowtes to þe benisoun full deuotely.

> And, if Christian men of religion dwell near where he shall pass, as they do in many cities in that land, they go toward him in procession with cross and holy water, singing with a high voice, *Veni, Creator spiritus*. And, when he sees them come, he commands the lords that ride near him to make way [so] that the men of religion may come to him. And, as soon as he sees the cross, he doffs his hat . . . And then he bows devoutly to the cross; and the prelate of those religious men says two orisons before him and gives him benison with the cross, and he bows to the benison full devoutly. (*Travels*, 119–20)

Yule-Cordier (333–4) offers an addendum to Odoric's narrative, in some manuscripts, by Friar Marchesino of Bassano, who relates that it was *Odoric* (like John Marignolli in his own account, and the "Cristen men of religioun" in the *Travels'*) and his broth-er friars who raised the cross to the Khan, singing *Veni, Creator Spiritus*, etc, and be-fore whom the Khan made his devout reverences to the cross.

A subject also strikingly repeated through different travel accounts of Cathay, like the above account, is the anecdote of animals with human souls. John Marig-nolli's account is decisively skeptical, savagely discrediting the Buddhist notion of the transmigration of souls after death: "There are also certain animals almost of human shape . . . in the garden of Campsay, in that most famous monastery where there are so many monstrous animals which they believe to be souls of the dead. But I learnt of certain knowledge that they are unreasoning animals, except that the devil uses them as once the serpent's tongue. . . . I conclude that these monsters are not men, though they may seem to have some [human] actions, but are like monkeys which, if we had never seen, we should suppose to be men" (Moule, 260). Odoric's account suggests Odoric disputed with the local religious who leads him to the animals, but gives up the quarrel when the man insists that the souls of noble men enter the animals that are noble, and so on (Yule-Cordier, 315). Though of course skeptical of the phenomenon of transmigration, the *Travels'* account is mild in tone and tolerant by comparison (Egerton: "and þat es fully þaire belefe, and þer may na man turne þam fra þat opinioun" [and that is fully their belief, and there may no man turn them from that opinion (*Travels*, 102)]). The transmigration of human souls into animal bodies is not a common subject in travel literature, and specifically characterizes these accounts of China, but the subject of hybrid creatures who are part-human and part-animal is a staple of travel literature, with examples variously ranging from the "dog-headed" men exotically featured among the monstrous races of antiquity, to Gerald of Wales's wolf-man and wolf-woman, and half-ox/half-man in his *Topographia Hibernica.* Tuplin observes that "'Dog-head' can mean baboon . . . so the dog-heads of Libya or India" might be intended to suggest simian or apelike barbarian peoples (50 n. 15).

34. "The Holy Father had never provided them; and thus so many peoples were lost, falling into idolatry and accepting false and harmful religions" (Dunn and Kelley, 17). The stipulated desire of the Mongol Khans for religious instruction, noted alike by Marco Polo in the thirteenth century (120), and Columbus in the fifteenth, is consonant with the Khans' historically noted respect for education, and the Khans' curiosity and interest in the uses of learning. Goodrich points out that "Kodon, 2nd son of Ogedei" instituted an imperial examination system to separate out the "scholar class" from "the masses," in order "to secure their services for the conquering invaders": "The following year (1238) . . . 4,030 of the literati were adjudged successful [in the examination] and absorbed into the new bureaucracy" (3). "Foreigners," Goodrich notes, "were in demand in the China of Mongol times: in the bureaucracy, in the army, in business, and even in the arts. The country was prosperous, especially in the reign of Kublai (1267–94), and there seems to have been little prejudice against people of other faiths and cultures" (2). By the end of Kublai's reign, there was "flourishing interest in education" in the empire, with 24,000 schools and 143 private academies in 1288 (3). The *Travels'* mention of the Khan's foreign physicians, including Christian ones, and its description of philosopher-scientists at the Khan's court, should thus be read in the historical context of a thriving culture of learning in Mongol China, in which foreigners, as well as locals, participated.

35. In 1122, almost as a prologue to the inception of the Prester John legend, an Archbishop John of "India" was reported, in an anonymous tract, to have arrived at

the court of Pope Calixtus II in Rome, in the company of papal envoys returning from Constantinople, and "gave a colorful account of the power and riches of the Christians who guarded the shrine of the Apostle Thomas. Reports of his visit were popular and circulated widely" (Hamilton, "Continental Drift," 237). Odo, abbott of St Rémi at Rheims, was also in Rome at the time and mentions, in a letter, the embassy of John of "India." Slessarev, Beckingham ("Achievements," 8) and Hamilton ("Continental Drift," 236, 258 n. 3) suggest that this Archbishop John, if his visit occurred, likely hailed from Syrian Edessa, a locale that, like India, was associated with St. Thomas, whereas the description of India, with the capital at Hulna was, like the later India of Prester John, a fable. The first mention of a *Prester* John, who was also a *king* and military leader, then, occurs as reportage and hearsay, appearing in Book VII, chapter 33, of the chronicle of Otto, Bishop of Friesing, the *Historia de Duabus Civitatibus.* Otto reports that in 1145, visiting the court of Pope Eugenius III, he met at Viterbo Bishop Hugh of Jabala, who "related that not many years ago a certain Iohannes, a king and a priest, living in the Far East, *in extremo Orientale,* beyond Persia and Armenia, who like all his people was a Christian though a Nestorian, made war on the brothers, the kings of the Persians and Medes, the Samiardi, and stormed the capital of their kingdom, Egbattana. . . . [T]hey fought for three days. . . . At last Presbyter Iohannes—for so they are in the habit of calling him—was victorious, putting the Persians to flight with most bloodthirsty slaughter" (Beckingham, "Achievements," 2).

In 1165 the famed *Letter* of Prester John, an anonymously authored, fictitious epistle declaratively from Prester John, King of India, and addessed to Emmanuel, Prince of Constantinople (Manuel Comnenus), materialized in Europe. The celebrated and much-discussed contents of the *Letter*—describing a vast utopian empire of ideal social and ethical order, flowing with milk and honey, and encompassing great wealth, masses of gems, exotic phenomena and palatial architecture, processional rituals with crosses, and tributary kings, and prominently featuring a crusading promise to conquer the enemies of Christ with an immense army—are now readily available in the volume by Beckingham and Hamilton, which reprints the texts edited in the late nineteenth century by Friedrich Zarncke. In 1177 a letter from Pope Alexander III, dated September 27, 1177, from the Rialto in Venice, and addressed to "John, his dearest son in Christ, illustrious and magnificent king of the Indians" ("karissimo in Christo filio Iohanni, illustri et magnifico Indorum regi") was sent through Philip, physician and member of the pope's household: a letter that has been read by some modern scholars as the Pope's reply to Prester John (for informed and well-reasoned disagreements, however, see Hamilton, "Three Kings," 189; and Beckingham, "Achievements," 9–13).

The dominant strain of historical scholarship on how the Prester John legend arose—an argument dating from the late nineteenth century, initiated by Gustav Oppert and Friedrich Zarncke—interprets the story attributed to Hugh of Jabala as a garbled account of the military victory of the proto-Mongolian Khitan conqueror, Yeh-lü Ta-Shih, founder of the Central Asian Empire of Kara-Khitay (an empire lending its name, "Khitay," to "Cathay," the northern China ruled over by the Mongol Khans), over the Seljuk Sultan of Persia, Sanjar, at Qatwan, near Samarkand, in September 1141. Hugh of Jabala's visit to Europe in 1145, scant months after the crusader county of Edessa had fallen to Zengi of Mosul, was concerned, as many have noted, with rousing the West to the "perilous situation" of the crusader colonies (Beckingham, "Achievements," 6), and it is possible to see how a successful, mighty enemy of Seljuk Muslims, a conqueror who dealt a deathblow to the Seljuk Empire, might be optatively hailed, by an ecclesiastic, as a Christian conqueror, for, as the Arab chronicle of Ibn al-Athir lamented, "a greater and bloodier defeat for Islam never before happened in Khorasan" (Nowell, "Prester John," 442). If the mid-twelfth-century military success of Yeh-lü Ta-Shih (who took the title of Gur-Khan) offered a historical kernel around which the early legend of Prester John was able to coalesce, the early-thirteenth-century military conquests in Central Asia of Genghis Khan and his familial line were even better placed to fuel the development of the Prester John legend, since Nestorian Christians were prominently found in the imperial families and generals of the Mongol Khans: "'Yuhanan,' the Syriac for John," de Rachewiltz (6) remarks, was even "one of the most common Nestorian names" to be found (for the *Relatio de Davide*'s account of Genghis Khan's campaign of 1219–21 against the Khwarazm Shah, an account that helps to develop the legend of John, see Jean Richard). Among scholars, de Rachewiltz, Olschki (*Marco Polo's Asia*), and Hamilton ("Continental Drift"), in particular, offer detailed, historically contextualized accounts of the thirteenth-century elaboration of John's legend in Central Asia and European travel narratives.

A second strain of scholarship suggests that Prester John's legend remembers, in veiled fashion, the existence of Christian kings in Africa:

> The African hypothesis comes from Constantine Marinescu . . . who announced it in 1923. . . . Prester John . . . was the monarch of Ethiopia, a land whose conversion to Christianity began in the fourth century and which later was cut off from communication with Europe by the Arab conquest of Egypt and the Sudan. In spite of this Ethiopian isolation, persistent rumors floated westward of a Christian ruler beyond the outer fringe of Islam. Subjects of his occasionally visited Jerusalem and other holy places, where now and then they met and conversed with Europeans. An exaggerated notion of Ethiopia, lacking any geographical orientation, gradually took shape in the occidental mind, until finally, says Marinescu, it emerged in concrete, if imaginary, form in the Prester John letter. (Nowell, "Prester John," 437)

In support of this thesis, Nowell remarks, "Ethiopia alone had priest kings in the Middle Ages. . . . [And] in both Geez and Amharic, the religious and aristocratic languages of the country, the word for 'king' or 'majesty' is one that can be written *Zan* . . . and pronounced somewhat like the French 'Jean' or the Italian 'Gian,' both of which stand for John" ("Prester John," 438; see also Ross). The African thesis continues to be suggestive (Kaplan, e.g., repeats the argument of linguistic phonology and priest-kings), though twelfth-century Europe appeared to have thought of Ethiopians as Muslim (Kaplan concedes that "the twelfth-century West had some awareness of Christian Nubia, but very little if any of Christian Ethiopia" [49]). Ross suggests that Abyssinia (where "Christianity is said to have been introduced . . . about the middle of the fourth century by a certain Frumentius" [185]) is meant by "India," rather than Ethiopia (184–85). Scholars who discuss Prester John in Ethiopia tend to focus on the legend's African contexts in the fourteenth century and later (see, e.g., Beckingham, "Ethiopian Embassy," "West Africa"; and also Ross). "Yet a third theory was put forward by the Russian scholar Bruun in 1876, who suggested that Prester John might be found among the kings of Georgia, but this theory . . . is summarily dismissed by Zarncke, who declares that it does not furnish an atom of probability" (Ross, 184).

A final argument in source scholarship is represented by Leonardo Olschki, who, in 1931, suggested that the *Letter* had "no historical prototype" at all but was a utopian document describing "an ideal society, frankly imaginary, yet not utterly beyond the power of mankind to achieve," with the Oriental wonders in the *Letter* "included as a bait to catch readers" (Nowell, "Prester John," 437). The mid-twelfth-century provenance of the *Letter* aimed, then, at addressing the "destructive conflict between Empire and Papacy, then personified by Frederick Barbarossa and Alexander III, which, in 1165, had reached a particularly bitter stage" (Nowell, "Prester John," 438). The *Letter*'s "barbed remarks" and "doubts about Western devotion to the faith" ("Prester John," 438) would thus function as pointedly ironic commentary on the status quo (a version of this argument is perhaps also expressed by de Rachewiltz: "I cannot help feeling that it was written with tongue in cheek from beginning to end" [7]). Hamilton ("Three Kings") also discusses how the *Letter* might have been an instrument of use in the late-twelfth-century political contest between papacy and empire, since the *Letter* presents "an ideal Christian society in which the church hierarchy is subordinate to the secular ruler" (188). Hamilton concludes: "Belief in Prester John may have been deliberately promoted by Rainald of Dassel . . . to aid Frederick Barbarossa in his struggle against Alexander III" (184). We might note, perhaps, that the highly overdetermined usefulness of the *Letter* might well render the historical explanations mutually compatible, rather than mutually exclusive.

36. The appeal of the twelfth-century *Letter*, as scholars have noted, consisted, in part, of the fact that the *Letter*'s contents were so traditional—and fulfilled cultural expectations and understanding in the Latin West—rather than that the contents were astonishingly original or newly exotic: "Malcolm Letts has shown that almost all the sources used by the author of the letter were available in the west in the 1160s. The most important were the Alexander Romance, the apocryphal Acts of St. Thomas, the anonymous account of John of India's visit, Otto of Freising's *Chronicle*, the Vulgate and standard Latin commentaries on it, the works of Solinus and Latin bestiaries and lapidaries" (Hamilton, "Three Kings," 185). Hamilton adds:

> The author also used some Jewish sources, either oral or written, as is seen from his account of the Ten Lost Tribes and from his use of the name Samarkand for the city which classical writers had called Macaranda. Only one phrase in the letter has no

known western source: Prester John complains "we have few horses and they are wretched," which apparently was the only defect in his otherwise perfect kingdom. It was indeed difficult to rear horses in medieval south India and no western European could have had direct knowledge of this in 1165 [Marco Polo's thirteenth-century narrative mentions the same difficulty], but Slessarev has pointed out that western merchants trading in the Crusader States could have picked up this information from Muslim contacts. ("Three Kings," 185)

37. Slessarev traces the genealogy of the elaborate French vernacular versions, in their older and younger traditions, in his volume (see, especially, the chapter "The French Versions") and offers the text of a fifteenth-century example for comparison with the original in Zarncke (Zarncke's text is in Beckingham and Hamilton's volume of texts, interpretations, and historical material).

38. One scholar sums up the chain of knowledge on "Prester John" thus: "Jean du Plan Carpin crut qu'il s'agissait du souverain musulman du Khwarezm, car il était en effet vassal de l'empereur des Karakhitaï et participa aux campagnes de ce souverain contre Sandjar; Rubruck pense qu'il s'agit du souverain des Naiman, ces Turco-mongols de Mongolie occidentale, dont les rois était nestoriens; pour Bar-Hæbreus, le Prêtre Jean était Ong-khan des Kèrèyit, car un souverain des Kèrèyit se serait converti au début du XIème siècle par l'intervention miraculeuse de Saint Serge. Il est donc naturel que Marco Polo ait crut qu'il s'agissait également du souverain des Kèrèyit" (Hambis, 184).

39. Interestingly the Nestorian princeling, "George," converted by John of Monte Corvino, appears to have been simultaneously Christian and "Confucian" in his cultural practices. Goodrich thus questions the authenticity of "George's" conversion to Latin Christianity, though Confucianism, rather than understood to constitute a religion, might also well be understood as a system of belief centrally belonging to moral, social, and political philosophy, and thus primarily a part of social and ethnic—rather than religious—culture:

> Was Prince George really a Christian? Professor Ch'en Yüan doubts it, and shows how Chinese records—the tablets of Yen Fu (1236–1312) and Liu Min-Chung (1243–1318), the biography in the *Yüan shih*, and the local history of Chi-an (Kiangsi)—dwell on his adherence to the Chinese culture around him. Prince George, we learn from these records, was a brave man, well versed in military matters, and especially devoted to Confucian ideals. He built a library housing ten thousand volumes in his palace; also temples and schools. Every day he was wont to discuss with scholars the Confucian canon, histories, ethical principles, and the masculine and feminine principles of divination. With one literatus in particular, Wu Tsou of Chi-An, he took up the study of the *I* (*The Changes*) and was responsible for making the woodblocks of Wu's book the *Chou I chu*, or Annotations of the *I*, in ten *chüan*, at P'ing-yang, the chief printing center of those times. (7–8)

40. "The privileged situation of the Nestorians among all the Christians of Asia under Mongol domination depended upon the well-known fact that several female

members of the imperial family . . . belonged to that sect" (Olschki, *Guillaume Bouch-er*, 15). Historically, various elite, highly literate, and ethnically diverse women from a range of religious and ethnic/tribal genealogies seem to have been recorded as resident in Mongol China, including women from the Onguts and other tribes: "One lady remembered for her poetry, painting, and calligraphy was Li Shun-hsien, a Persian. Another, Chao Ting, the daughter of Chao Shih-yen, was an Öngüt, who at the early age of eight could recite from memory the *I*, *Lun yü*, and *Meng tzu* (*Changes, Analects, and Mencius*). She was skilled in divination and astrology and could play the harp. The daughter of Kuan-yün-shih (native of Pei-t'ing, or present day Urumchi) too received a good Chinese education in literature and calligraphy. A fourth well educated lady of Manichean background, named Yüeh-lun-shih-hu-tu (Ügrünc-quduy?), married into the Ch'i family, who were Turks of Kao-ch'ang. Her husband was one of five brothers awarded the *chin-shih* degree, and she is credited, along with her husband, with educating their son in Chinese letters, so that he too achieved the highest degree (in 1345). A fifth was Yüeh-e, daughter of Jamal al-Din, of Moslem origin. She was so literate that in her hand was placed the education of her younger brother Ting-hao-nien, later to distinguish himself as a superior craftsman in Chinese poesy. When the Ming revolutionaries attacked her city she and her daughter, together with eight other women, committed suicide by drowning" (Goodrich, 19).

41. There is a calculated admission, by the *Travels*, of *some* variations:

> And þai hafe prestez amanges þam þat singez þam messez; bot þai make þe sacrement of leuaynd breed, as þe Grekez dose. And also þai say noȝt þaire messez in all thingez as oure prestez duse; bot þai say all anely þe *Pater Noster* and þe wordes of þe conse-cracioun with whilk þe sacrament es made, as sayne Thomas þe apostill taght þam in alde tyme. Bot of þe ordynauncez and addiciouns of þe courte of Rome whilk oure prestez vsez can þai noȝt. (148)

> And they have priests among them that sing them masses; but they make the sacrament of leavened bread, as the Greeks do. And also they say not their masses in all things as our priests do; but they say all only the *Pater Noster* and the words of the consecration with which the sacrament is made, as Saint Thomas the apostle taught them in old time. But of the ordinances and additions of the court of Rome which our priests use they know nothing.

42. "Vnder þe firmament es noȝt so grete a lorde ne sa riche ne na sa myghty as es þe Grete Caan of Tartre. Noȝt Prestre Iohn þat is emperour of Inde þe less and þe mare, ne þe sowdan of Babiloyn, ne þe emperoure of Pers, ne nan oþer may be made comparisoun off till him" (*Travels*, 108). Cotton has an additional instance of such re-iteration that is missing from Egerton, where the manuscript intones in nearly identical terms: "Vndre the firmament is not so gret a lord, ne so mighty, ne so riche, as is the Grete Chane; nought Prester Iohan, þat is emperour of the highe Ynde, ne the sowdan of Babyloyne, ne the emperour of Persye" (*Travels*, 120). Historians like Lach also emphasize the emperor of Cathay's superiority to the emperor of India, in the

Travels: "Cathay for Mandeville is Utopia, and his hero is the Great Khan. The ruler of Cathay is far more impressive to him than Prester John, whose 'land is good and rich, but not so rich as the land of the Great Caan'" (1 [book 1]: 79).

43. This ethnographically striking custom that is claimed for the two Asian empires—Prester John's and the Great Khan's—not only links together India and China but also links these two Far Eastern places to the Near Eastern/West Asian/Mediterranean Empire of Byzantium, and thence to England. For William of Malmsbury explicitly records the transplantation of Constantinople's customs into the Anglo-Norman court of Henry I, through the introduction into English court life of the social habit of a single diurnal meal: Robert, Count of Meulan, it seems, imported into Anglo-Norman England the Greek emperor Alexius I's practice of only one meal a day (*De Gestis Regum*, 2:483). That far-flung places on the globe, and a chain of empires, can be thus linked up and connected to England, by a single, memorable anthropological feature shared among them all, is extraordinary: the economy, and powerful efficiency, of a cultural symbol is attested at the same time that a fantasy of imperial convergence and continuity is also witnessed, as intimated by the shared cultural symbol. Since Constantinople epitomized the glories of imperial culture for Western Europe over centuries before contact with Mongol China (see Lach 1 [book 1]: 41 n. 130, e.g., on how descriptions of medieval cities are influenced by Constantinople's image), it scarcely surprises that China's and India's wonders are presented by the *Travels* in the image of Constantinople, so to speak—especially when, as I have said, a sense of Constantinople's intensifying fragility drew attention in the historical period. However, despite my naturalization, here, of an uncanny chain of associations, it is still dizzying—in the way suggested by Foucault's "heterotopias"—to think of the court of the Great Khan in Cathay as connected to the court of Norman England, via Constantinople.

44. The original *Letter* of Prester John, appearing circa 1165 (or at least no earlier than 1143 or later than 1180), specifically raises up the image of a massive crusade from the East and couches the military threat in the entirely conventional terms and locutions of crusade rhetoric, when the writer, "Prester John," thunderingly avers that he means to visit "the sepulcher of the lord" with the greatest army, "to humble and conquer the enemies of the cross of Christ and his blessed name to exalt" ("humiliare et debellare inimicos crucis Christi et nomen eius benedictum exaltare" [Zarncke, "Prester John's Letter," 78]). Slessarev, following Olschki's 1931 suggestion that the original *Letter* be read as positing an exemplary Utopia for twelfth-century Christendom and Europe to imitate, also reminds us that the idea of an Indian Utopia was begun by the Alexander legend and its example of earlier territorial conquests:

> There is a school of thought, initiated by Leonardo Olschki in 1931 and vigourously supported ever since, which views the *Letter* as a piece of Utopian literature. It claims that the message of Prester John did not intend so much to baffle contemporary readers as to instruct them by depicting the high moral standards of the Indians and by contrasting the perpetual discord between the Church and the Empire in the West with

the ideal theocracy of Prester John's realm. . . . India was traditionally known to be a country of a strict moral code. . . . The famous correspondence between the King of the Brahmans, Dindimus, and Alexander must have furnished the *Letter* with a substantial part of its high ethical content. (Slessarev, 39–40; see also Nowell, "Historical Prester John," 437)

Since the vast power, wealth, and resources fantasized in the original *Letter* specifically served the protection of Christians within John's far-flung empire, with its seventy tributaries—an empire free, it seemed, of the avarice, adultery, thievery, and vice that bedeviled the success of so many crusading enterprises, as was often claimed in crusade literature—it is possible to see how the utopian fantasy of the *Letter* might subserve crusade ideals and hopes beyond the most immediate appeal of an Oriental Christian potentate's military aid to the Latin Christian West.

45. An example of European fascination with Oriental difference and the resources of the East can be seen in the attentive, detailed interest in the odd phenomenon of paper money. Paper money—a glimpse of the world's financial future—was introduced into Szechuan at the beginning at the eleventh century, Abu-Lughod notes, and adopted in northern China by the end of the century. By 1280 "only paper was accepted for trade" and precious metals were not allowed to circulate. "Thus, at the end of the thirteenth century, Marco Polo could write that the ordinary money in Cathay was a piece of cotton paper stamped with Mangu's (Möngke) seal. . . . This was confirmed by Ibn Battuta who [wrote] about the 1340s" (334). The use of such money, Abu-Lughod adds, intensified China's wealth and power: "By increasing the velocity of money, it stimulated economic growth . . . by requiring everyone to use the same currency, the state was able to regulate the foreign exchange rate and thus become the indispensable intermediary between foreign and local merchants" (334–35). In representing the phenomenon of paper money, the *Travels* is by turns naïve, precise, and agog with fascinated attention:

> Þis emperour may dispend als mykill as him list spend, for he makez na monee bot owþer of lether, or of papire, or of barkez of treesse. And, when þis monee waxen alde, and þe prynte þeroff defaced by cause of vsyng, it es broȝt to þe kynges tresoury, and his tresourer giffez new for alde. Þis monee es prynted on bathe þe sydes, as monee es of oþer cuntreez, and it gase thurgh all þe Grete Caan landes. For þai make na monee þare of gold ne siluer, when it es broght þider fra oþer landes by diuerse naciouns, bot þe emperour gers enourne his palace þerwith and gers make þeroff oþer necessaries at his awen list. (*Travels*, 117)

> This emperor may spend as much as it pleases him to spend, for he makes no money but [except] either of leather, or of paper, or of barks of trees. And, when this money is waxen old, and the print thereof defaced because of using, it is brought to the king's treasury, and his treasurer gives new for old. This money is printed on both the sides, as money is of other countries, and it goes through all the Great Khan's lands. For they make no money there of gold nor silver, when it [gold or silver] is brought thither from

other lands by diverse nations [peoples], but the emperor has his palace adorned therewith [with the gold or silver] and has other necessaries made at his own pleasure.

Cotton omits the mention of "barks of trees."

46. As a cultural response, the late-medieval European fascination with exoticism,
in a period of expanded travel and missionizing, is thus highly instructive. Lorraine
Stock's work on representations of wild men and wild folk, for instance, urge the conclusion that forms of alterity meeting with fear and loathing in the *early* Middle Ages,
were, by the *late* Middle Ages, welcomed, incorporated for individual, family, and social use, and manipulated for public attestations of identity.

> In the early Middle Ages the Wild People were considered monstrous examples of oth-
> erness to be feared and loathed [but] in the Late Middle Ages the attitude toward the
> Wild People exhibited by the cultural elite included both identification with and im-
> personation of them. Identification was revealed in the incorporation of the Wild Peo-
> ple in heraldic shields, family crests, and other signifiers of personal identity and in vi-
> sual depictions of Wild People interacting with civilized humans, usually aristocrats. As
> exemplified in the Bal des Ardents, impersonation took the form of representation of
> Wild People by civilized humans, such as a king, publicly enacted in ritual performance
> and pageantry. (138–39)

The late-medieval period's desire for the exotic was elaborated along a range of objects, stories, styles, and arts. Black Saracen heads made an appearance in heraldic sig-
nification, alongside wild folk, for instance, and *morescas* were danced "as often as possible" in fifteenth-century courts: "The opulence and exotic color of the Islamic world
were highly valued in Western court circles and exercised a fascination. . . . Besides
fancy dress, actors were recruited; 'black Moors' and 'white Moors,' in the terminol-
ogy of the day, were the African slaves frequently to be found in countries bordering
the Mediterranean, but also present in more northerly countries" (Piponnier and
Mane, 145). The late-medieval elaboration of Prester John's archaic twelfth-century
letter thus exists on a continuum with other exotic investments in the period.

47. History and romance alike are agog at the Khan's wealth and the vastness of
the Khanate. In the midst of that passage expatiating optimistically on the Khan's
demonstrable respect for Christian rituals, because the Khan doffs his hat before the
Cross, the *Travels* cannot resist momentarily describing the value of that imperial hat:
"whilke es made full richely with perlez and precious stanes, and þai say þare þat þat
hat es worthe a kyngdom" ("which is made full richly with pearls and precious stones,
and they say there that that hat is worth a kingdom" [*Travels*, 120]). The 1326 letter
of Andrew of Perugia, Franciscan Bishop of Zaitun in southern China, tries with difficulty to impart some idea of the munificence of the Khan, on whose charity Andrew
(who receives an imperial stipend) subsists: "I live on the bounty of the Emperor
which . . . according to the estimate of the Genoese merchants, may amount to the
value of a hundred gold florins or thereabouts" (Dawson, 236); "I forebear to speak of
the wealth and magnificence and glory of this great Emperor, of the vastness of the

empire and the number of its cities and their size; and of the government of the empire, in which no man dares to draw sword against another; for it would be too long to write and would seem unbelievable to my hearers. For even I who am on the spot hear such things that I can hardly believe them" (Dawson, 235). If the modesty *topos* glimmers in Andrew's disclaimer, Odoric of Pordenone attempts a multifaceted description of a single city, Kansai (Hangchow), in southern China, to give some idea of its urban immensity, city divisions, lakes and twelve thousand bridges, population size and density, taxes, use of paper money, ample provisions of food and wine, and sheer abundance (Yule-Cordier, 2:312–14).

In the thirteenth and fourteenth centuries the cities of the glittering East—Hangchow is a revealing example—beckoned powerfully:

> Built between the shores of an enormous artificial lake (West Lake) and the banks of the Che River leading to the sea, the city of Hangchow and its suburbs covered an area of some seven to eight square miles. It was surrounded by walls pierced by "five gateways through which camels passed, and by thirteen monumental gates." . . . By the thirteenth century, the suburban zone outside the walls was even more extensive than the walled city itself. The city . . . was planned so that the major "imperial way" traversed the city from north to south. . . . The southern hill region contained the imperial palace, around which were the residential zones of the rich—the high officials and "the merchants who had made their fortune in the maritime trade." . . . [O]n the paved Imperial Way, three miles long and 180 feet wide(!), there were carriages drawn by tiny horses or by men. . . . As in Venice, canals played a major part in transport. . . . There were at least ten markets in the city as well as the fish market near the lake and the wholesale market outside the city. Merchants were therefore numerous and rich. They entertained guests at the many tea houses and restaurants of the city . . . or hired boats and musicians to cruise on West Lake. . . . One entire quarter of the city housed foreign, mostly Muslim, traders. In the early fourteenth century Hangchow grew even larger. . . . According to Ibn Battuta . . . who visited Hangchow in the 1340s, it was still "the largest [city] on the face of the earth." (Abu-Lughod, 337–39)

The *Travels* duly calls Hangchow ("Cassay")

> . . . the greatest city of the world . . . as mighty . . . as the City of Heaven. This city is of fifty miles circumference, and there is wondrous mighty folk therein. This city has twelve great gates; and before each gate . . . is a great town and a good. This city is built in the same manner that Venice is built; and there are therein twelve thousand bridges and more. And on each bridge is a good tower at either end, and men of arms in them for to keep the town against the Great Khan, for it marches upon his land. And upon one side of the city runs a great river along the length of that side of the city. And there dwell many Christian men and many merchants of diverse nations, for the country is wondrous plentiful and good and full of all manner of riches.

> . . . þe maste citee of þe werld . . . als mykill . . . as þe Cytee of Heuen. Þis citee es of l. myle vmgang, and þer es wonder mykill folk þerin. Þis citee hase xii. grete ȝates; and

before ilke a ȝate . . . es a grete toune and a gude. Þis citee es bigge on þe same manere þat Venice es bigged; and þer er þerin xii^m brigges and ma. And on ilke a brigg es a gude toure at ayther end, and men of armes in þam for to kepe þe toune agayne þe Grete Caan, for it marchez apon his land. And apon a syde of þe citee rynnes a grete ryuer endlang the citee. And þare dwellez many Cristen men and many marchandes of diuerse naciouns, for þe cuntree es wonder plentifous and gude and full of all maner of ricches. (*Travels*, 102)

48. Patricia Parker ("Fantasies"), who notes the "European appetite or hunger for report" of the world through travelers' tales in the Renaissance, shows how even half-belief or skeptical unbelief in such reports as *Mandeville's Travels* did not stint the greedy eagerness of domestic consumption of exotic fare in an age driven to explore and exploit. Parker shows how the world created by travelogues such as "Mandeville's" creates the world view in Europe that makes possible the racial discourse in Shakespeare's *Othello* against the titular character (*"Othello* has long been linked with . . . Mandeville's 'fabulous' reports" [91]). Othello, Shakespeare's invented Moorish adventurer, inhabits the very world theorized by "Mandeville" as real, and sought as real by Columbus, the historical adventurer-discoverer.

49. "Prester John was in part the product of the thought-world of the crusades. He symbolized the hope of embattled Christians that they were not alone in their fight against powerful Islamic enemies; that in other parts of the world there were strong Christian rulers who would help them" (Hamilton, "Continental Drift," 256). Hamilton insists: "It is no coincidence that Prester John first appeared in 1145, a few months after the holy city of Edessa had fallen to Zengi of Mosul. This was the first serious loss of territory which the Franks in the East had suffered, and so severe was the psychological shock to western Christendom that it led to the preaching of the Second Crusade" (238). The "certain knowledge" of "western Christians in the twelfth century . . . that there were in the lands beyond Islam Christian communities who might potentially be useful allies . . . focused [hopes] on the region where allies were most needed, the lands to the east of Mosul, whose Zengid rulers were threatening the crusader states" (238). Prester John's later relocation to an Ethiopia confirmed in the fourteenth century as Christian might similarly feature in fourteenth-century hopes that Ethiopia could become an ally in Latin Christendom's late-medieval crusades, when Egypt became a crusading focus of the fourteenth century, as Edessa had been in the mid-twelfth:

> During the first third of the fourteenth century . . . a series of treatises . . . desperately plead for yet another Crusade in the Levant. Newly aware of Ethiopia, these authors almost always mention that nation as a possible ally. For Guillelmus Adam (1317), Ethiopians are Christians who would like to help the West exterminate Islam. For Etienne Raymond (1332), the Christian Ethiopians of Nubia have already gained several triumphs over the Sultan of Egypt and many more are foretold. . . . [N]either of these writers directly brings in Prester John. The Venetian Marino Sanudo the Elder is the first of this group to do so, sometime just before 1321. (Kaplan, 53)

Kaplan also cites "an Italian letter addressed to Charles the IV shortly after 1370" (56) and the letter from Henry IV of England, dated October 20, 1400 (57), both of which associate Prester John with the hope of crusading alliances between Europeans and African Christians against Islam. The usefulness, then, of Prester John's twelfth-century legend for territorial crusading survived late into the Middle Ages, into the fifteenth century, even as new uses for the legend had begun to appear. Nowell sums up the multipurpose, mutating usefulness of the legend:

> From the twelfth century until well after the discovery of America, he was an estab-lished part of the European pattern of thought. As a potential Christian ally in the rear of the Moslem foe, he figured in plans for the later crusades and thus had a place in Eu-ropean ideas of world strategy. By entering the calculations of both Henry the Naviga-tor and Columbus, he helped to inspire the great geographical discoveries. Still later, amid conditions that had ceased to be mediaeval, he was a factor in the hopes and plans of Emperor Charles V. ("Prester John," 435)

50. Edward Peter's editorial note on Oliver's narrative summarizes in brief the per-ilous error of the crusaders:

> When Damietta was conquered in 1221, the victors spread a report that in the East, King David, either the son or the nephew of Prester John, had started with three strong armies against the Mohammedans. An Arabic prophecy foretold that Islam would be abolished when Easter fell on April 3. When this happened in 1222, many thought that King David (referred to here by Oliver) and his forces would join the expected army of Frederick II [Frederick, on friendly terms with Egypt, did not make an appearance]. Enthusiasm over this hope helped lead to the premature outbreak against Cairo and the defeat of the crusaders. (*Christian Society*, 90 n. 2)

Three texts intersecting at the powerful legend of Prester John influenced the cru-saders into their disastrous military decision. The book written in Arabic mentioned by Oliver of Paderborn (Peters, *Christian Society*, 89–90)—the *Prophecies of Hanan*, "an update of the work of a ninth-century Nestorian scholar, Hunain Ibn Ishak" (Hamilton, "Continental Drift," 243)—"related that an army would come from the West, led by a tall man with a lean face, which would conquer Damietta and occupy Egypt. It went on to tell how a king would then come from beyond the mountains and capture Damascus, while the King of the Abissi [i.e., Abyssinia, sometimes con-flated with Ethiopia in the medieval period] would invade Arabia, attack Mecca and scatter the bones of Mahomet" (Hamilton, "Continental Drift," 243; Oliver of Pader-born's chronicle refers to a king of "Christian Nubians" [Peters, *Christian Society*, 90]). Before the capture of Diametta in 1219, the Papal Legate, Cardinal Pelagius—a dominant figure who, despite his ecclesiastical status, asserted tactical field leadership and authority over the military leaders of the Fifth Crusade—had been shown a copy of the *Prophecies of Hanan*, and his enthusiasm for the work led the Eastern Christians of Damietta in 1221 to present Cardinal Pelagius with "another prophecy written in Arabic, *The Book of Clement*" (Hamilton, "Continental Drift," 246), which confirmed in part what the earlier prophecy had foretold but went further: "The fall of Damietta would mark the beginning of the total collapse of Islam, which would be completed by the arrival of two kings, one from the East and the other from the West, who would meet in Jerusalem in a year when Easter fell on April 3rd" (Hamilton, "Continental Drift," 246).

By a coincidence, in the early months of 1221, a message from Prince Bohemond IV of Antioch had also reached Jacques de Vitry at Damietta, reporting how "spice merchants coming from the East had brought . . . a written account of the deeds of David, King of the Indies, who was commonly called Prester John, but who in fact was the Priest King's great-grandson" (Hamilton, "Continental Drift," 244). This account, also in Arabic, the *Relatio de Davide*, in fact describes the rise of the Mongol Empire, ending with the campaign of Genghis Khan against the Khwarazm Shah in 1219–21 (Hamilton, "Continental Drift," 245). Jean Richard notes that when the Bishop had a Latin translation made of the *Relatio*, "Jacques de Vitry points out that the common people (*vulgus*) called the King of the Indies Prester John although his real name was David" (147). Stressing that "the identification of David with Prester John is . . . the Franks' work," Richard observes that a letter from King Andrew II of Hungary to Pope Honorious III, cited by the chronicler Richard of San Germano under the year 1223, also "reports how *Davit*, a king 'commonly called Prester John,' had left India seven years before" (148).

This insistent belief in the Prester John legend—that Prester John/King David was an actual Christian King from the Orient/India, and not a misconception arising from a garbled narrative of Mongol military and imperial ascent—had tragic consequences for the crusaders. Cardinal Pelagius, identifying himself as "the tall man with the lean face" mentioned in the *Prophecies of Hanan*, and believing that "the King from the West was clearly the Emperor Frederick II whose arrival was imminently expected [and the] King from the East was equally clearly King David, about whom James of Vitry had just received such encouraging news," thought that the fulfillment of prophecy was at hand, especially as "Easter would fall on 3 April in 1222 and then not for another eleven years" (Hamilton, "Continental Drift," 246).

> If Jerusalem was to be restored to Christian rule by Easter 1223, then the crusade should not hesitate to play its part in bringing this about by marching on Cairo immediately. Pelagius therefore assembled the army and either had the *Book of Clement* read to them in translation, or else . . . had a sermon preached to them about the prophecy. In either case, he persuaded the crusade to set out for the south on 17 July 1221. His decision to ignore the timing of the Nile floods led to the surrender of the army to the Sultan of Egypt a few weeks later. (Hamilton, "Continental Drift," 246)

51. "On 20 October 1400, an Italian cleric named John, described as 'Archiepiscum Orientalis ac Aethiopiae' and possibly the archbishop of Sultaniyeh in Persia, was entrusted with a letter to 'magnifico et potenti Principi Regi Abassiae [Abyssinia, i.e., Ethiopia] sive Presbitero Johanni.' The sender of this missive,

which again proposed an alliance against Islam, was none other than King Henry IV of England. We have no way of knowing whether this letter reached the ruler of Ethiopia" (Kaplan, 57).

52. Beckingham, who discusses at length the mobile geographical location of the two or three medieval Indias, points out, as we have said, that although two Indias, "India Major and India Minor occur as early as the fourth century . . . three Indias appear for the first time in 1118 in a manuscript of Guido Pisano" ("Achievements," 15). "Otto of Freising himself [in whose chronicle survives the earliest mention of Prester John] speaks of only two Indias. When the apostles dispersed to evangelize the world, Thomas and Bartholomew, he tells us, went to the two Indias, *utrasque Indias*; Matthew went to Ethiopia" (18). Beckingham concludes that, for Otto, "Nearer India" meant the northern part of the Indian subcontinent visited by Alexander, and "Further India" was "Ethiopia" (18). However, for the *Letter* of Prester John, which specifies three Indias, the geography necessarily shifts. "Further India" would now designate the southern part of the Indian subcontinent, especially "Malabar and Coromandel" (Beckingham, "Achievements," 17), and *Middle* India, Beckingham concludes, would now be Ethiopia: "I do not think that the use of Middle India as a synonym for Ethiopia, itself a vague term, implies that twelfth and thirteenth century geographers necessarily supposed Ethiopia to lie in the middle between Lesser and Greater, Nearer and Further, North and South India. . . . By Middle India I think we should understand not the middle of India, but rather Intermediate India, half way to India in fact [i.e., Ethiopia]. There had been times when the navigation of the Red Sea and western Indian Ocean was at least partly under Ethiopian control and at such times this usage would not be difficult to understand" (Beckingham, "Achievements," 19).

Whether one subscribes to a part-Ethiopian origin for the twelfth-century Prester John legend, "in the fourteenth and fifteenth centuries, 'Indian' was frequently employed as a synonym for Ethiopian in its narrower sense, due to a long-standing confusion about the dimensions of 'India,' a realm often believed to include East Africa" (Kaplan, 4). Kaplan (who is among those interested in the possibility of a twelfth-century Ethiopian localization of the legend) suggests that John's relocation to Africa was also supported by other serendipities: "The Ethiopian word *zan*, meaning emperor, sounds similar to 'John,' and may explain the origin of that half of his title. The term 'prester' (priest) also suggests Ethiopia, where the sovereign was usually ordained and had wide ecclesiastical as well as secular powers. Furthermore, the emphasis on processional and talismanic crosses found in the 1165 letter is reminiscent of Ethiopian practice, at least in subsequent centuries" (46). Nubia, known to be Christian at least to some in the West as early as the last quarter of the twelfth century (Kaplan, 48–49) is also associated with India in Marco Polo's narrative, by being "a land where St. Thomas preached and made converts before going on to India" (Kaplan, 51).

53. A figure from an ethos of crusading culture, Prester John well expresses the persistent continuity of a chain of European desire because crusading—a modality of expansionist activity from the late eleventh century—also helped to push the development

of trade in directions farther East, an impetus that fueled subsequent forms of commercial expansionist desire:

> The Crusades had helped to extend the horizons of Europe and had given the growing
> population of southern Europe a commercial frontier in the eastern Mediterranean region. The returned crusaders also added their names to the customer lists of those selling Oriental and African commodities. . . . growing demand in Europe was accompanied by increased purchasing power won from moneylending, piracy and the looting of
> Muslim towns. Much of the capital so accumulated apparently was used to buy spices,
> raw silks, and furs from Asia. . . . [I]t is not to be wondered at that the European merchants were quick to take advantage of the land routes opened by the Mongol conquests. In their drive to gain direct access to the emporiums of Asia, the Genoese apparently led the way. . . . Practically all the Christian missionaries, as well as the Arab
> traveler, Ibn Batuta, agree that Genoese merchants were active in India and China during the first half of the fourteenth century. Boccaccio refers to the Genoese as the best
> witnesses to consult in verifying one of his stories that allegedly happened in China.
> (Lach, 1 [book 1]: 44–45)

In addition to the Genoese, Venetians are also mentioned in the handbook of the Florentine merchant Francesco Balducci Pegolotti (written between 1310 and 1340), in discussing the route from the Levant to Peking and the appropriate "merchandise to carry for sale in China. For example, 'anyone from Genoa or Venice wishing . . . to make the journey to Cathay should carry linens with him.' Pegolotti . . . gives the prices in Genoese currency that the merchant might expect to pay for silk in China" (Lach, 1 [book 1]:45). In a moment that oddly parallels the Florentine merchant's handbook, *Mandeville's Travels* also assumes a point of departure from the Italian ports, when indicating Cathay's distance from Europe: "Cathay is not so near that it does not behove them from Venice or from Genoa or other places of Lombardy to be travelling by sea and by land eleven months or twelve ere they may win to the land of Cathay" (133). Significantly, in this same description that conceives of a route to Cathay from mercantile Italy, the figure Prester John is not far behind: "And yet is the land of Prester John much further by many a day's journey" (133).

54. "By 1300 the more advanced and reliable writers had already begun to turn to Ethiopia as the Prester's land" (Kaplan, 48). Kaplan suggests that Prester John's legend might have been assigned to Ethiopia at the very beginning of the fourteenth century: Giovanni da Carignano, a Genoese cleric and cartographer, reports an Ethiopian embassy in 1306, a report in which "Prester John is clearly Emperor of Ethiopia" (Kaplan, 52). Ross remarks that in 1316, "eight Dominicans, sent by Pope John XXII, arrived in Abyssinia, and made a number of converts to Catholicism. Abyssinians even entered the Dominican Order, the most notable being the famous Tekla Haymanot. Among the earliest true accounts of Prester John must be reckoned the story told in 1391 to King John I of Aragon by a priest who had spent several years at Prestor John's court" (192–93).

John's charismatic ability to figure a European desire that seamlessly assumes the local coloring of the moment continues to do service well into the eighteenth century: Srinivas Aravamudan dryly remarks that "depicted as a chivalric European king but colored black, the Ethiopian emperor known as 'Prester John' is not all that different from Oroonoko" (203). Indeed, Prester John is an exemplary instance of a medieval idea with significant uses in the modern period, constituting one of the continuities-with-difference that, as Steven Kruger observes of certain categories of cultural objects, "not only *survives into* but *constitutively shapes* 'modernity'" (202)—in John's case by urging on the opening up of exploration and discovery that supposedly newly characterizes the advent of the Renaissance. Uebel, on the utopian potential of the gifts mentioned in the *Letter* of Prester John, concludes that "coinciding with the structure of imperial fantasy and fetishistic pleasure . . . Prester John functioned as the fetish par excellence of medieval and early modern imperialism. He became the symbolic ground upon which problems of cultural exchange could be negotiated" (272).

55. Braude's detailed and attentive study supports Kaplan and Ross in suggesting that Prester John is reassigned to Africa, from Asia, as part of a twofold move in late-medieval Europe's (re)discovery of Africa. On the one hand, Italian contact with Christian Ethiopians conduced to an understanding that Christians were to be found in Africa:

> Ethiopian envoys reached Venice in 1402. Ethiopian pilgrims made their way perhaps as far as Rome in 1408. An Italian, Pietro Rombulo, was in Ethiopian service for most of the first half of the fifteenth century. The Ethiopian community in Jerusalem sent regular missions to Rome. And in 1441, two Ethiopians were present at the Council of Florence. Around this time or slightly earlier began the gradual movement, in European fantasy, of Prester John, the mythic Christian ruler on the other side of Islam, from India to Ethiopia. (126)

Concomitant with benign transmigratory movements, on the other hand, was a grimmer species of contact:

> At a slightly slower pace, a very different image of the so-called black African was [also] emerging. . . . It originated through European contacts in West Africa, not East Africa, among pagans and Muslims, not Christians, and among states that offered little potential alliance in the struggle with Islam. The initial constructors of this image were Iberian adventurer-explorers in search of booty, human or otherwise, not priests, pilgrims, and envoys. They set forth in a series of expeditions under the patronage of Prince Henry the Navigator of Portugal from 1415 until his death in 1460. . . . As is well known, the Portuguese engaged not only in exploration but also in slaving. . . . [A] cargo of West African slaves had been shipped to Portugal for the profit of Prince Henry, who received them with delight. (127)

Braude, whose remarkable study carefully specifies the precise linkages between Jews, Africa, and blackness, and the sons of Noah, in different exegetical traditions across two millenia, calls the *Travels* "arguably the most important single work for the study of the European conception of the Other in the late medieval-early modern period" (115), observing that the *Travels* "not only represents a summa of medieval European knowledge and prejudice about the rest of the world, but . . . is . . . essential for tracking the transformation of European understanding of the Other" (116).

56. The traveling power of Western culture, and the ingenuity of European desire, might be better understood if we grasp how Prester John's fourteenth-century relocation from Asia (back?) to Africa is prepared for, in thirteenth-century culture, when John is allocated a famous half-African ancestor who is, by virtue of birth and desire, half-European and half-African, and who is, accordingly, half-white and half-black. Significantly, at the end of Wolfram von Eschenbach's Middle High German romance, *Parzival*, the piebald Feirefiz of Zazamanc, son of the European Arthurian knight Gahmuret and African queen Belacane, and famed half-brother to a famed Parzival, is baptized and migrates to India with his European wife, Repanse de Schoye, and produces there a son whom people came to call Prester John, with all subsequent kings in India being given that name. We might say that thirteenth-century fantasy thus thoughtfully supplies a retroactive "prequel" to the absorbing twelfth-century fantasy of an Oriental Christian king: a "prequel" that explains John's Christianity as really originating in Europe after all. Of course, the thirteenth-century structure of desire that would assert Europe's responsibility for a Christian king in Asia through the paternal line—a fantasized colonization that makes Indian territory really Europe's—also tacitly acknowledges that the Asian potentate, who is not really Asian at all but three-fourths European, is a prime figure for the peregrinatory power of European desire—a desire also embodied by the sojourning Arthurian knight Gahmuret, who sires Feirefiz out of a cooperatively pliant Africa.

Europe's work in formulating Prester John as a transcontinental racial-genetic-cultural hybrid (one fourth black/three fourths white) comes to fulfillment, then, across the centuries, as a powerful volitional nexus randomly searching out and serving multiple purposes. Twelfth-century cultural desire materializes John out of the hopes and anxieties of a crusading Europe; thirteenth-century desire attaches a European blood-presence in India and Africa, through John's legend, annexing foreign places through a fantasized dynastic bloodline; fourteenth-century desire transplants the bloodline back from Asia to Africa, while simultaneously annexing the legend of John to China and the great Khan. By the fifteenth century and after, European desire, forcing new routes in the world, purports, ironically, to be *following* John, rather than insistently producing him: a phantom whose legend, solicited by desire, is now represented as soliciting European desire to explore and "discover" the many places and faces attributed to him, in a world where rich varieties of colonization conveniently beckon.

57. In the fourteenth century the gold of African kingdoms served as a tantalizing lure, as Fernández-Armesto notes of the fame of Mali, one of whose rulers, the Mansa Musa, undertook a spectacular pilgrimage to Mecca in 1324, "which spread his renown far and wide" partly because of the Mansa's lavish distribution of gold en route

(146). In Egypt, where the Mansa stayed for three months, the Mali ruler magnanimously "gave 50,000 dinars to the sultan and thousands of ingots of raw gold to the shrines which received him and the officials who entertained him," causing the value of gold to fall by 10 percent to 25 percent, with the sudden glut, and inflation to develop: "The image of the Mansa's splendour reached Europe. In Majorcan maps from the 1320s, and most lavishly in the Catalan Atlas of 1375, the ruler of Mali is portrayed like a Latin monarch, save only for his black face. Bearded, crowned, and throned, with panoply of orb and sceptre, he is perceived and presented as a sophisticate, not a savage: a sovereign equal in standing to any Christian prince" (Fernández-Armesto, 147). If the Catalan's depiction of the Mansa Musa seems strangely to coincide and resonate with the fourteenth-century wish for an African Prester John, Fernández-Armesto reminds us that "in the fourteenth century, Mali projected an enthralling image for European gold hunters. It was the gold that particularly appealed to the Mediterranean 'public.' 'So abundant is the gold which is found in his country,' said the Catalan Atlas of Mali's ruler, 'that this lord is the richest and noblest king in all the land.'" Fernández-Armesto observes that since the "Maghribi emporia were the termini of the gold trade," new attempts, "mounted from within Latin Christendom in the middle and late fourteenth century, to make conquests in Barbary may have been inspired in part by a desire to wrest more of the [gold] trade" (147).

58. "In 1402, for the first time in nearly a hundred years, Ethiopian emissaries are known to have arrived in Europe. These ambassadors . . . led by a Florentine, one Antonio Bartoli, are described in Venetian documents as representatives of 'Lord Prester John, lord of the regions of India,' but all scholars agree that the embassy was from Ethiopia. With this renewal of actual contact between Ethiopia and Western Europe, the introductory phase of the Africanization of Prester John comes to an end. In the fifteenth century the black [African] version of Prester John is the norm, and it would be tedious to cite every example of his appearance in European culture" (Kaplan, 57).

59. Frye notes that sixteenth-century England witnessed a continuing attention to African gold and luxury commodities: "English merchants were simply after a share in the profits to be gained from African gold, ivory, and pepper. The Portuguese had been hogging this lucrative West African trade for more than 100 years" (5), and "Englishmen were not to start trafficking in slaves" till 1563 (5). Historians such as David Abulafia stress, however, that for many countries in Europe, African slaves were well established as an exploitable resource in the Middle Ages:

> The most important commodity to come out of black Africa, after gold, was probably slaves. Spain, Sicily and Naples drew large numbers of Berber and black captives out of Africa . . . [and] in the fifteenth century Naples was a major 'consumer.' . . . [I]n Christian lands they tended to perform domestic functions or, in Valencia, agricultural work. They were also something of a prestige symbol, to judge from the possession of eighty black slaves by the Jewish treasurer of Castile, Don Samuel Abulafia (1320–60). The slaves were often traded for horses, sent from North Africa. . . . [A]nd there was still a link between the two commodities when Leo Africanus visited black Africa in about 1500. (469)

Fernández-Armesto also identifies the appearance of *slave-based plantations* in the fifteenth century, off the shores of West Africa:

> In the Cape Verde islands . . . in the 1460s, a new model was introduced: the slave-based plantation economy [in the sugar industry], unprecedented in European experience since the ancient *latifunda*. Cape Verde offered an inhospitable environment in which European immigrants were hard to come by and ill adapted to survive. . . . The islands possessed no indigenous population, but were close to sources of black slaves in west Africa. By the 1480s the demand for slaves on the island of Santiago was . . . so great . . . [that] the settlers of Cape Verde [claimed] that the slaves were essential to them for the very maintenance of life. The plantation economy of this remote frontier was a world apart from that of the metropolis, where slaves formed an essentially domestic labour force. (200–201)

English participation in the African slave trade only began with John Hawkyns's first triangular run in 1562–63, which garnered at least three hundred captives from the Guinea coast (Fryer, 8), who were sold in the Americas, and established a pattern in which slaves unsold in the New World returned with slavers to England (Walvin, *Black and White*, 7; see also Walvin, *Black Presence*). "Though it would be another 100 years before English merchants were trafficking in slaves in a really organized way, and longer still before they succeeded in dominating the slave trade . . . African slaves were brought to England from the 1570s onwards" (Fryer, 8), so that "towards the end of the sixteenth century it was beginning to be the smart thing for titled and propertied families in England to have a black slave or two among the household servants" (Fryer, 7). Prester John's firm location in Africa shines like a beacon through it all: "As more and more Englishmen went to Africa [and] were surprised and impressed by the riches and living standards of the rulers and merchants they met, [they] started publishing their findings in travel books . . . that contained matter-of-fact reports providing accurate details of the Africans' houses, manners, dress, crops, and crafts . . . [yet also] gave equal weight to the fabulous Prester John, King of Ethiopia" (Fryer, 6).

60. The *Travels'* fascination with science is, of course, replicated in late-medieval culture. The library, at Caister, of Sir John Falstoff, one of the richest landowners in England when he died in 1456, included five volumes on science, "Liber Geomancie cum iiij aliis" (H. S. Bennett, 111). The *Travels'* attraction to the allure of science and technology also means that it rewrites predecessor travelogues' accounts of *magical enchantments*, rather than science, that occur at the Khan's court.

61. Letts, who believes that the alphabets "range from genuine Greek, through unrecognisably corrupt Egyptian, Hebrew, Saracen, Persian, Chaldean, Tartar-Russ and Cathayan to an incredible production called Pentexoire, the language of Prester John's empire," notes that the alphabets "have been despaired of by former commentators. Warner says that they are 'too corrupt to be worth reproducing.' Hamelius (in his edition of the Cotton version, vol. II, p. 22) suspects them to be a set of codes for the use of opponents of the papacy" (*Sir John*, 151–52). Though "the possibility remains that the alphabets were fabrications . . . introduced in order to increase the atmosphere of

wonder and mystery which surrounds the whole book" (*Sir John*, 152), Letts traces the *Travels'* "Egyptian" alphabet to Coptic, its "Saracen" alphabet to "runic forms," and its "Persian" and "Chaldean" to a "corrupt version of Nestorian-Syrian" (*Sir John*, 155–58). "Tartar-Russ"—only found in one manuscript, von Diemeringen's translation—is a "ghost" alphabet, "manufactured from . . . Saracen names and Cathayan forms" while "Cathayan and Pentexoire"—occurring in von Diemeringen's version and Brussels 10420 ("Pentexoire" also occurs in Paris 24436)—are pure inventions (*Sir John*, 158–59). Though the Greek alphabet's letters are named correctly, and in order, and Letts and Howard agree on the authenticity of the Egyptian/Coptic (Howard, 8), Josephine Bennett suggests that the "'Egyptian,' 'Jewish,' 'Saracen,' 'Persian,' and 'Chaldean' range from unrecognizable to purely fanciful" (65). She adds: "The invention of them was not Mandeville's" (65).

"[G. F.] Warner points out that similar alphabets occur in Hrabanus Maurus, *De Inventione Linguarum*, and some are printed (in J. G. Eccard's *De Origine Germanorum*), which are said to derive from a Ratisbon manuscript of the eleventh century. . . . The alphabets were evidently an attractive feature of the *Travels*, for the second redactor added alphabets for the Chinese and for the land of Prester John. One was invented for the Old Man of the Mountain. A Dutch version, copied in 1430, has no less than seventeen alphabets. Two subsequent visitors to the Holy Land, Breydenbach and Von Harff, in the sixteenth century, included alphabets in their itineraries and borrowed other things from Mandeville. Sir Thomas More provided an alphabet for his Utopians very much in the manner of Mandeville" (Bennett, 65–66). Higgins, who calls these alphabets "multipurpose punctuation mark[s]," echoes the tradition that they are at least "partly fabricated" (*Writing East*, 71). For an arresting example of how hearsay and fabrication might mingle and combine in these alphabet productions ("virtual alphabets"), see chap. 4 n. 40, above, on Aella of Deira, and the invocation of the Islamic deity, in the avowal, "There is no God but God, and Mohammad is His prophet" (given in Egerton and Cotton as "There is no God but one, and Mohammad his messenger"). The *Travels'* Egerton renders the Arabic ("Saracen") as "La elles ella sila Machomet rores alla hec" (*Travels,* 71), and Cotton as "La ellec olla syla Machomet rores alla" (Hamelius, 1:92). Though both these accounts resemble, at best, garbled simulacra of the Arabic attestation—"La illaha illa Allah, wa Muhammad rasul Allah"—yet syllables and half-syllables coincide at points, and evoke a suggestion of almost recognizable meaningfulness: It is that evocative specter of something linguistically familiar-sounding, dangling at the edge of intelligibility and recognizability, which so provokes scholars attempting (impossibly) to decide if the alphabets are genuine (but corrupt) or sheer inventions.

62. Biddick makes the critical point that the alphabets are by no means benign, especially when applied to Jews:

> The *Travels* uses the medium of the alphabet to exclude Jews from its model of human diversity. . . . The *Travels* uses a geography of the alphabet as one of its chief ploys to exclude Jews. It traces the forms and names of the letters of an alphabet when it finally

comes to the borders of a region. Such topographical edges and their alphabets occur along Mandeville's route in the following order: Greek, Egyptian, Hebrew, Saracen, Persian, and Chaldean. (277)

Biddick concludes: "[The] Hebrew alphabet is mapped in the *Travels* at a border in the west while the Hebrew language is located in the space of the apocalypse. Thus, the narrator casts Hebrew as a language of conspiracy, a technology of Antichrist" (279). Westrem explores the issue of a linguistic "conspiracy" by showing how the *Travels* represents the role of Hebrew in the threat against Christians in the last days: "The Book's author mentions that the people of Gog and Magog are entrapped by the Hebrew language itself. He observes first that 'they know no language but their own language, and thus they cannot get out.' This limitation turns out to be less absolute than it first seemed" for in the last days, when the enclosed tribes of Jews emerge, "they will be aided by a fifth column of supporters, with whom they share a language. . . . With uncanny subtlety, the Mandeville-author has managed to turn 'les Iuys' of central Asia into 'other Jews' of Flanders, the Rhineland, Bohemia, and Iberia: these constitute the real danger of Gog and Magog" (69).

63. The Paris and Anglo-Norman texts closely parallel the methodical reasoning here, in proving sphericity through observation and instrumentation, emphasizing slightly more, if anything, the traveling individual who experiences and calibrates ("pare experience et subtille indicacion"). Paris has:

> [L]estoille tremontaine, cest lestoille de mer qui ne se muet point, qui est vers bize. Mais on voit vne autre, qui est au contraire de celuy, vers mydi, que on appelle Antartique. Et tout aussi que les maronniers prennent aduis yci et se gouuernent par ceste estoille vers bise, aussi font les maronniers de la par ceste estoille deuers mydi, la quelle ne appartient point a nous, et ceste deuers bise ne appartient point a eulz. Pour quoy on puet apperceuoir que la terre et la mer sont de ronde fourme; car la partie du firmament appartient a vn pays qui ne appartient point a autre. Et ce peut on apperceuoir pare experience et subtille indicacion, que se on trouuoit passage de nef . . . on pourroit aler a nauie tout entour le monde, et desseure et dessoubz. La quelle chose ie preue selon ce que ie ay essaie, car ie ay este par les parties de Braibant et par le signe de lastrolabe ie treuue que la tresmontaine estoille est liii. degres de haut, et en Alemaigne vers Rome elle a lviii., et plus auant vers les parties de septentrion elle a lxii. degres de haut et aucuns minus auec; car ie meismes lay mesure a lastrolabe. (Letts, 2:331)

The Anglo-Norman is virtually identical though it substitutes Bohemia for Rome:

> Lestelle transmontane . . . est lastelle du mer qi ne se moet point, qi est vers byse. Mes homme veoit vne autre qi est al contrarie de celle, qi est vers mydy, qe homme appelle Antartike. Et si come ly maryners preignent auis icy et se gouernent par celle esteille vers byse, ensy fount ly mariners de la par celle esteille vers mydi, la quelle ne y piert poynt a nous, et ceste deuers byse napiert poynt a eux. Par quoy homme poet aperceyuoir qe la terre et le mer sount de rounde fourme; qar la partie de firmament y piert en vne pays qi napiert mie en vn autre. Et poet homme bien trouer par experience

et par subtile indagacioun qe, si homme troueroit passage des niefs . . . lem purroit aler
a nauie tout entour le mounde, et dessure et dessouz. La quelle chose ieo proue ensy,
solonc ceo qe iay veu. Qar iay este vers les parties de Braban et regarde al astrolabre qe
la transmontane est liii. degrez de haut, et plus auaunt en Almaigne et Beome elle est a
lviii. degrez, et plus auant vers lez parties septemtrionels elle ad lxii. degrez de haut et
ascuns menues, qar ieo mesmes lay mesure al astrolabre. (G. F. Warner, 90)

64. The Paris text has an added minor directional detail ("in high Libya toward
Ethiopia") and an added sixteen minutes of elevation:

Ie suy ale vers les parties meridionelles, cest vers mydi, et ay trouue vers la haute Libie
que on voit premierement lestoille Antartique. Et tant comme ie alay plus auant en
celles parties, tant trouuai ie celle estoille plus haute, si que plus auant en la haute Libie
vers Ethiope elle a xviii. degres de haut et aucuns minus auec, dont les lx. minus font
vn degre. Et en alant vers ce pays dont ie parle, et en es autres ylles et pays oultre, ie
trouuay lantartique de xxxiii. degres de haut et xvi. minus. (Letts, 2:331–32)

Anglo-Norman:

Ieo su ale vers les parties meridionels, ceo est vers le mydy, et ay troue qe en Lybie
homme veoit primes lesteille Antartike; et, taunt ieo alay plus auaunt en celles parties,
taunt trouay celle esteille plus haut, si qe vers la haute Lybie il y ad xviii. degrez de haut
et ascuns menutz auqes, dont lx. menutz fount vn degree. Puis, en alant par mer et par
terre vers ces parties dont ieo parle, et as autres isles et terres en outre ceo pais, ieo
trouay lantartik de xxxiii. degreez de haut et plusours menutz. (G. F. Warner, 90)

65. Note, for instance, the orderly stages of the empirical experiment that the
Travels describes, on how to test a diamond for authenticity and power—using gems
and metals, and verifying with magnetism—an experiment that cites an ongoing body
and history of tests and testing, and suggests the repeatability and verifiability of the
entire exercise:

Take þe dyamaund and rubbe it on þe saffir or on cristall or sum oþer precious stanez
or on clene burnyscht stele. And seyne take þe adamand, þat drawez þe nedill til him,
by þe whilk schippe men er gouerned in þe see, and lay þe dyamaund apon þe adamaund
and lay a nedill before þe adamaund. And, if þe dyamaund be gude and vertuous, þe
adamand drawes noȝt þe nedill to him, whils þe dyamand es þare. (*Travels*, 80)

Take the diamond and rub it on the sapphire or on crystal or some other precious
stones or on clean burnished steel. And afterward take the adamant, that draws the needle to him [to itself], by which shipmen are governed in the sea, and lay the diamond
upon the adamant and lay a needle before the adamant. And, if the diamond be good
and virtuous [i.e., full of power], the adamant draws not the needle to him [to itself],
while the diamond is there.

Wittkower notes that even Marco Polo's narrative makes observations and distinctions that would later be important for the natural sciences and anthropology, for

instance, when Polo identifies the great apes: "There is a reference in the land of Comari to 'great apes of such build that they have the appearance of men,' an extraordinarily acute statement. In fact, this passage is the first intimation by a European that the difference between man and anthropoid ape had been noticed" (162).

66. Prominent English knights were among the *Travels'* readers: Among the possessions of Sir Thomas Urswyck, Recorder of London and Chief Baron of the Exchequer, in 1479, for instance, were the *Travels*, Chaucer, Froissart, and law books (Salter, 39).

67. The Paris text reads: "Et vraiement nul preudons ny deuroit demourer en ce pays. . . . Ie nay point este par ce chemin; et si ay este aus autres terres marcissans a ce coste, comme en la terre de Russie, en la terre de Niflam, et ou royaume de Craco et de Leto, et ou royaume de Rastem, et en pluseurs autres lieux en celles marches. Mais ie nalay conques par ce chemin a Iherusalem, pour quoy ie ne le pourroie bien deuiser" (Letts, 2:301). The correspondent passage in the Anglo-Norman is virtually identical: "Et verayment nul prodhomme ne doit demorrer en ceo pais. . . . Ieo nay point estee par cest chemyn; et si ay estee as autres terres marchisantez a ceste, come en la terre de Russie et en la terre de Niflan et el roialme de Crako et de Leito et en le roialme Daresten et en plusours autres lieux en celle marche. Mes ieo nalay vnqes par ceste chemyn a Ierusalem, pur quoy ieo ne le purroie bien deuiser" (G. F. Warner, 65).

68. Following in the wake of the Alexander tradition on India/the Brahmans, and roaming over a diverse population in the proximate domain of the nominally Christian Prester John, the *Travels*, for instance, advocates generous and careful tolerance: "Despise no men for the diversity of their laws. For we know not whom God loves nor whom he hates; and therefore, when I pray for the dead and say my *De Profundis*, I say it for all Christian souls and also for all the souls that are to be prayed for. And of this folk I say thus much, that I believe they are fully acceptable to God, they are so true and so good" ("Despise na men for þe diuersitee of þaire lawes. For we wate noȝt wham Godd luffez ne wham he hatez; and þerfore, when I pray for þe deed and sayse my *De profundis*, I say it for all Cristen saules and also for all þe saulez þat er to be prayed fore. And of þis folk I say þus mykill, þat I trowe þai er full acceptable to Godd, þai er so trew and so gude" [*Travels*, 146]). It is important to observe that the *Travels'* attested and much-remarked tolerance of Christian heterodoxy—a tolerance that exists in such pointed contrast, as critics have noted, to the travelogue's hostility to Jews—has a *historical parallel* in Edward I's pointed magnanimity to Rabban Sauma, the Nestorian missionary to Europe from whose hands Edward, the monarchic zealot responsible for the expulsion of the Jews from England, received the Eucharist. Whether it is political and military diplomacy that prompts Edward I to act with gracious generosity to the Nestorian Christian—when Nestorians, as we have seen, were vilified as heretics in other contexts—or whether it is that Christian heterodoxy can be papered over when a prime scapegoat of a non-Christian variety, such as Jews, can be found on which a Christian unity might be piously established and

celebrated, Rabban Sauma's biography informs us that Edward's acceptance of all Christians as one body, confirming only one faith, despite differences of practice, was enacted in both word and deed:

> And the king commanded Rabban Sawma to celebrate the Eucharist, and he performed the Glorious Mysteries; and the king and his officers of state stood up, and the king partook of the Sacrament, and made a great feast that day. . . . And the king [said], "Thus shall ye say to King Arghon and unto all the Orientals: We have seen a thing than which there is nothing more wonderful, that is to say, that in the countries of the Franks there are not two Confessions of Faith, but only one Confession of Faith, namely, that which confesseth JESUS CHRIST; and all the Christians confess it." (Budge, 186–87)

69. Akbari's discussion of how late-medieval *mappaemundi* shift from an easterly to a northerly orientation also accords importance to the postulate of a perceiving, traveling observer in the late Middle Ages. Akbari concludes that "the transition from East to North is a transition from the primacy of the sacred object [Jerusalem, at the center of the world in older *mappaemundi* oriented East] to the primacy of the seeing subject" (31). The late-medieval reorientation of the world, in which a hot zone of the south is assumed to the Orient, while a cold zone of the north is assumed to the Occident, produces, Akbari says, a two-directional "dichotomy of Orient and Occident" that underpins modern world views and enables the emergence of Orientalism as a phenomenon. Concident, then, with the rise of the "seeing subject"—if I understand Akbari correctly, and am not overextending her argument—is also the rise of the West as an idea: "The 'West,' as we know it, appears to be an invention of the fourteenth century" (31).

70. As usual, Egerton corresponds fairly closely to the Paris text, but Paris omits mention of the Sultan's great seal:

> Les Sarrazins ny laissent entrer ne Crestiens ne Iuyfz. . . . Mais ie entray la et autre part ou ie vouloie, par la vertu des lettres au Soudan, enz es quelles il auoit commandement a touz les subgiez a moy laissier veoir tous lieux, et a laissier entrer par tout, et a moy deuisier les lieux et les misteres de chascun lieu, et a conduire de cite a autre, se il estoit mestier, et moy benignement a receuoir et moy et ma compaignie, et a encliner a toutes mes requestes raisonnables. (Letts, 2:272)

The Anglo-Norman is almost identical to Paris:

> Ly Sarazins ne lessent entrer ne Cristiens ne Iuys. . . . Mes ieo y entray la, et autre part ou ieo voloie, par vertue des lettres del soudan, en les quels il y auiot especial mandement as touz ses subgitz a moy lesser veoir touz les lieux et a moy deuiser les lieux et les mesteirs de chescun lieu et a conduire de cite en autre, sil estoit mestiers, et a benignement resceuier moi et ma compaigne et a encliner a touz mes requestes resonables. (G. F. Warner, 41)

71. As is usual in romance, the whimsically fantastical treatment of reality—here, the scientific phenomenon of magnetism—is erected on a shard of historical fact: Arab ships without nails did, in earlier times, coast along the shores of India (the domain originally assigned to Prester John), Arabia, and Persia. Citing G. F. Hourani's *Arab Seafaring in the Indian Ocean in Ancient and Medieval Times,* Donald Lach describes these nail-less and iron-less Arab ships as "sewn together with hemp made of coconut fibers" (1 [book 1]: 11). The Paris text on the description of magnetism's maritime dangers reads:

> Il a en moult de lieux grandes roches de pierres daymant, qui trayent a eulz le fer de leur propre nature. Et pour ce, sil y passe nulle nef ou il ait clous ne bendes de fer, tantost ces roches la traient a elles, ne nen pourroient iamais partir. Ie meismes vi en la mer de loing ainsi comme vne grande ylle, ou il auoit arbrissiaux, espines, ronces et herbes a grant foison; et nous distrent les maronniers que cestoient toutes nez, qui estoient la ainsi arrestees pour les roches daymant. Et de la pourreture qui estoit dedenz les nefz estoient creus et naissanz ces arbrissiaux, ces ronses et celle herbe a si grant foison, comme on le pouoit veoir adont. (Letts, 2:383–84).

The Anglo-Norman reads:

> Il y a en mointz lieux en la mer roches grandez de piere daymant, qi de sa proprete tret a ly le fer. Et pur ceo, si il y passe nulle nief ou il y a claus ou bendes de fer, tantost ces roches les traient a elles et iames ne pourroient departer de illeoqes. Ieo mesmez vy en celle mer de loins auxi come vn grant isle, ou il auoit arbresseaux et espines et rounses grant foisoun; et nous dissoient ly mariners qe ceo estoient toutz niefs qi estoient ensi arestez pur lez roches daymont, et de la purretture de ceo qi estoit deins niefs croissent ces arbresseux et espines et rounces del herbe grant foysoun. (G. F. Warner, 133)

72. The delicately poetic and conclusive touch in Egerton, where "I John Mandeville" materializes, declaring that he has eaten fish from the sandy sea, "and therefore believe it, for it is true," is in neither the Paris text nor the Anglo-Norman (nor, indeed, in Cotton). Paris is content to end the description of the gravelly sea with the deliciousness of the fish:

> La est la mer areneuse, qui est toute plaine de arene et de grauelle senz goute deaue, et va et vient a grandes ondes tout aussi bien comme fait lautre mer, et nulles fois et nulles saisons ne se tient quoye ne napaise. Et ne peut on passer celle mer par nauie ne autrement; et pour ce ne puet on sauoir quelle terre il a oultre celle mer. Et combien quil ny ait point dyaue, neentmoins si treuue on aussi bien des bons poissons aus riues que on fait en lautre mer, mais il sont dautre facon quil ne sont en lautre mer; et si sont de bon gouste et moult dilicieus a mangier. (Letts, 2:384–85).

The Anglo-Norman passage also concludes with the claim that the fish from the gravelly sea are good to eat, without personal attestation by "I John Mandeville":

En soun pais est la mer arenouse, qest tout dareine et de grauell saunz deauwe. Et vait et vient as grandes vndes auxi come lautre mer fait, et nulle foitz ne nul saisoun ne se tient toy ne paisible. Et ne poet homme passer celle mer, ne par nauie nautrement; et pur ceo ne poet homme sauoir quel terre il y a outre cel mer. Et, come bien qil nait point deawe, nient moinz lem troue des bons pessons sour les riuers de autre manere et dautre facioun qe homme ne troue en lautre mer; et sount de bone gust et delicious de manger. (G. F. Warner, 134)

73. By contrast to the whimsical claim of "I John Mandeville," narrator of the Egerton manuscript, to have eaten a marvelous fish, from an extraordinary sea of sand, Odoric, in a more down-to-earth and homely moment, claims to have eaten, in the Malay archipelago of Southeast Asia, not delicious fish ("riȝt sauoury in þe mouth") from sandy waters, but what appears to be very good bread ("panem multum bonum") baked from sago flour extracted from tree sap (a process Odoric describes). If Odoric's claim of exotic food (sago) in exotic lands (the Malay archipelago) takes comfortably quotidian form (bread), whereas "Mandeville's" has a certain speculative wildness (what kind of edible animal swims and breathes in a sandy sea?), the Friar nonetheless vouches for truth-and-goodness-in-tasting in similar fashion to "Mandeville" ("I Iohn Maundeuill ete of þam"): "de quo ego frater Odoricus jam comedi" (Yule-Cordier, 2:302).

74. Lomperis puts it thus:

Circumnavigation . . . is much more than merely an important theme . . . it is also another name for the text's structural make-up and readerly effects, highlighting as it does the many circularities and round-about turns of the narrative itself. Certainly the experience of reading Mandeville's *Travels* can be accurately characterized as one which produces a sense of going around and around. No sooner does the narrator approach the entry point proper to Jerusalem, for example, than he moves into a long, ostensibly digressive discussion of the customs, practices, and sights to be seen in Egypt, the realm controlled by the Sultan of Babylon. The journey toward the Christian center of the world thus takes a decidedly asymptotic turn, never quite concluding at the place to which it ostensibly was heading. All throughout this narrative, moreover, the experience of going to a manifestly *new* place tends to represent itself, paradoxically enough, as an experience of turning back once again to an *old* place, a place where one has already been. . . . No matter where one goes in Mandeville's *Travels*, one always seems to travel in a circle back to the place from which one started. The journey out, the journey away from home is circularly linked to the journey back, the journey toward home. (152)

75. Medieval travel writing, romances, and diverse documentary matter on foreign lands are suggestively gathered in manuscript collectanea that attest the mutual interrelationship of these bodies of texts in the minds of those who make, commission, and use medieval manuscripts. Wittkower discusses the manuscript assemblages of MS. 2810 at the Bibliothèque Nationale, MS. 264 at Oxford, and MS. Royal 19. D. I of

the British Museum, to hint at a late-medieval *mentalité* that links travel and romance marvels and adventures to projects of crusading, exploration, and discovery in intricate ways that have yet to be fully studied:

> Collectanea are very common in which Marco Polo's *Milione* appears together with romances, mainly Alexander texts or Colonna's *Historia Trojana*, with the fantastic journeys of Odoric and Mandeville, and the spurious epistle of Prester John. The famous MS. 264 at Oxford consists of the Alexander romance and Marco Polo's book. . . . MS. Royal 19. D. I of the British Museum . . . contains a French Alexander followed by the journeys of Marco Polo, Odoric, and John of Plano Carpini. To these are added what has been called the crusaders' handbook to the Holy Places attributed to Burchard of Mount Sion, further a chapter on miracles of the French king St. Louis with an account of his last crusade, and finally extracts from the *Bible Historiale* concerning battles of the kings of Israel. It has been suggested that such a collection was meant to whet the appetite of potential crusaders. (170)

WORKS CITED

❧

Abrahams, B. L. *The Expulsion of the Jews from England in 1290*. Oxford: Blackwell, 1894.

Abulafia, Anna Sapia. "Bodies in the Jewish-Christian Debate." In *Framing Medieval Bodies*, ed. Sarah Kay and Miri Rubin, 123–37. Manchester: Manchester Univ. Press, 1994.

———. "Christian Imagery of Jews in the Twelfth Century: A Look at Odo of Cambrai and Guibert of Nogent." *Theoretische Geschiedenis* 16 (1989): 383–91.

Abulafia, David. "Asia, Africa, and the Trade of Medieval Europe." In *The Cambridge Economic History of Europe*. Vol. 2: *Trade and Industry in the Middle Ages*, ed. M. M. Postan and Edward Miller, 402–73. Cambridge: Cambridge Univ. Press, 1987.

Abu-Llughod, Janet L. *Before European Hegemony: The World System, A.D. 1250–1350*. Oxford: Oxford Univ. Press, 1989.

Aers, David. *Chaucer, Langland, and the Creative Imagination*. London: Routledge, 1980.

Agrawal, R. R. *The Medieval Revival and Its Influence on the Romantic Movement*. New Delhi: Abhinav, 1990.

Akbari, Suzanne Conklin. "From Due East to True North: Orientalism and Orientation." In *The Postcolonial Middle Ages*, ed. Jeffrey Jerome Cohen, 19–34. New York: St. Martin's, 2000.

Allen, Prudence. *The Concept of Woman: The Aristotelian Revolution, 750 B.C.–A.D. 1250*. Montreal: Eden, 1985.

Ambrisco, Alan S. "Cannibalism and Cultural Encounters in *Richard Coeur de Lion*." *Journal of Medieval and Early Modern Studies* 29, no. 3 (1999): 499–528.

Ambroise. *L'Estoire de la Guerre Sainte*. Edited by Gaston Paris. Paris: Imprimerie Nationale, 1897.

Anderson, Benedict. *Imagined Communities: Reflections on the Origin and Spread of Nationalism*. London: Verso, 1991.

Anderson, Perry. *Passages from Antiquity to Feudalism*. London: NLB [New Left Books], 1974.

Andreas Capellanus. *The Art of Courtly Love*. Translated by John Jay Parry. New York: Columbia Univ. Press, 1990.

Aravamudan, Srinivas. *Tropicopolitans: Colonialism and Agency, 1688–1804*. Durham, N.C.: Duke Univ. Press, 1999.

Archibald, Elizabeth. "'The Appalling Dangers of Family Life': Incest in Medieval Literature." In *Medieval Family Roles: A Book of Essays*, ed. Cathy Jorgensen Itnyre, 157–71. New York: Garland, 1996.

———. "The Flight from Incest: Two Late Classical Precursors of the Constance Theme." *Chaucer Review* 20 (1986): 259–72.

Arens, William. *The Man-Eating Myth: Anthropology and Anthropopagy*. New York: Oxford Univ. Press, 1979.

Armstrong, John. *Nations before Nationalism*. Chapel Hill: Univ. of North Carolina Press, 1982.

Armstrong, Nancy. *Desire and Domestic Fiction: A Political History of the Novel*. New York: Oxford Univ. Press, 1987.

Arthur, Ross G. "Emaré's Cloak and Audience Response." In *Sign, Sentence, Discourse: Language in Medieval Thought and Literature*, ed. Julian N. Wasserman and Lois Roney, 80–92. New York: Syracuse Univ. Press, 1989.

Ashtor, Eliyahu. *Levant Trade in the Later Middle Ages*. Princeton, N.J.: Princeton Univ. Press, 1983.

Askenasy, Hans. *Cannibalism: From Sacrifice to Survival*. Amherst, N.Y.: Prometheus, 1994.

Atiya, Aziz Suryal. *Crusade, Commerce, and Culture*. Bloomington: Indiana Univ. Press, 1962.

———. *The Crusade in the Later Middle Ages*. London: Methuen, 1938.

———. *The Crusade of Nicopolis*. London: Methuen, 1934.

Balakian, Peter. "A Memoir across Generations: Baby-Boom Suburbs, the American Genocide, and Scholarly Corruption in America." *Chronicle of Higher Education*, June 12, 1988, B6.

Balibar, Étienne. "Racism and Nationalism." In *Race, Nation, Class: Ambiguous Identities*, ed. Étienne Balibar and Immanuel Wallerstein. London: Verso, 1992.

Barber, Richard. *The Knight and Chivalry*. Ipswich, N.Y.: Boydell, 1974.

Barczewski, Stephanie. *Myth and National Identity in Nineteenth-Century Britain: The Legends of King Arthur and Robin Hood*. Oxford: Oxford Univ. Press, 2000.

Barker, Francis, Peter Hulme, and Margaret Iversen, eds. *Cannibalism and the Colonial World*. Cambridge: Cambridge Univ. Press, 1998.

Barnie, John. *War in Medieval English Society: Social Values in the Hundred Years War, 1337–99*. Ithaca, N.Y.: Cornell Univ. Press, 1974.

Barringer, Tim, and Tom Flynn, eds. *Colonialism and the Object: Empire, Material Culture, and the Museum*. London: Routledge, 1998.

Bartlett, Robert. *The Making of Europe: Conquest, Colonization, and Cultural Change, 950–1350*. Princeton, N.J.: Princeton Univ. Press, 1993.

————. "Medieval and Modern Concepts of Race and Ethnicity." *Journal of Medieval and Early Modern Studies* 31.1 (2001): 39–56. Special Issue on Race and Ethnicity in the Middle Ages, ed. Thomas Hahn.

Bartolovich, Crystal. "Consumerism; or, the Cultural Logic of Late Cannibalism." In *Cannibalism and the Colonial World*, ed. Francis Barker, Peter Hulme, Margaret Iversen, 204–37. Cambridge: Cambridge Univ. Press, 1998.

Beaune, Colette. *The Birth of an Ideology: Myths and Symbols of Nation in Late-Medieval France*. Edited by Fredric L. Cheyette. Translated by Susan Ross Huston. Berkeley: Univ. of California Press, 1991.

Beckingham, Charles F. "The Achievements of Prester John." In *Prester John, the Mongols, and the Ten Lost Tribes*, ed. Charles F. Beckingham and Bernard Hamilton, 1–24. Aldershot: Variorum, 1996.

————. "An Ethiopian Embassy to Europe, c. 1310." In *Prester John, the Mongols, and the Ten Lost Tribes*, ed. Charles F. Beckingham and Bernard Hamilton, 197–206. Aldershot: Variorum, 1996.

————. "Prester John in West Africa." In *Prester John, the Mongols, and the Ten Lost Tribes*, ed. Charles F. Beckingham and Bernard Hamilton, 207–11. Aldershot: Variorum, 1966.

Beckingham, Charles F., and Bernard Hamilton, eds. *Prester John, the Mongols, and the Ten Lost Tribes*. Aldershot: Variorum, 1996.

Beckwith, Sarah. *Christ's Body: Identity, Culture, and Society in Late Medieval Writings*. New York: Routledge, 1993.

Beha' ed-Din. *Saladin; or, What Befell Sultan Yusuf (1137–1193)*. Lahore: Islamic Book Service, 1976.

Beinart, Haim. *Atlas of Medieval Jewish History*. Translated by Moshe Shalvi. New York: Simon and Schuster, 1992.

Bell, Susan Groag. "Medieval Women Book Owners: Arbiters of Lay Piety and Ambassadors of Culture." In *Sisters and Workers in the Middle Ages*, ed. Judith M. Bennett, Elizabeth A. Clark, Jean F. O'Barr, B. Anne Vilen, and Sarah Westphal-Wihl, 135–61. Chicago: Univ. of Chicago Press, 1989.

Bellamy, James A. "Arabic Names in the Chanson de Roland: Saracen Gods, Frankish Swords, Roland's Horse, and the Olifant." *Journal of the American Oriental Society* 107, no. 2 (1987): 267–77.

Bennett, H. S. *The Pastons and Their England: Studies in an Age of Transition*. Cambridge: Cambridge Univ. Press, 1922.

Bennett, Josephine Waters. *The Rediscovery of Sir John Mandeville*. New York: Modern Language Association of America, 1954.

Benson, C. David. "Incest and Moral Poetry in Gower's *Confessio Amantis*." *Chaucer Review* 19 (1984): 100–109.

Benson, Larry D. "The Date of the Alliterative *Morte Arthure*." In *Medieval Studies in Honor of Lillian Herlands Hornstein*, ed. Jess B. Bessinger Jr. and Robert K. Raymo, 19–39. New York: New York Univ. Press, 1976.

Benton, John F. "Clio and Venus: A Historical View of Medieval Love." In *Culture, Power, and Personality in Medieval France*, ed. Thomas N. Bisson, 99–121. London: Hambledon, 1991.

———. "The Court of Champagne as a Literary Center." In *Culture, Power, and Personality in Medieval France*, ed. Thomas N. Bisson, 3–43. London: Hambledon, 1991.

———. *Culture, Power, and Personality in Medieval France*, ed. Thomas N. Bisson. London: Hambledon, 1991.

———, ed. *Self and Society in Medieval France: The Memoirs of Abbot Guibert of Nogent*. Toronto: Univ. of Toronto Press/Medieval Academy of America, 1984.

Bernardi, Daniel Leonard. *Star Trek and History: Race-ing Toward a White Future*. New Brunswick, N.J.: Rutgers Univ. Press, 1999.

Bhabha, Homi K., ed. *Nation and Narration*. New York: Routledge, 1990.

Biddick, Kathleen. "The ABC of Ptolemy: Mapping the World with the Alphabet." In *Text and Territory: Geographical Imagination in the Middle Ages*, ed. Sylvia Tomasch and Sealy Gilles, 268–93. Philadelphia: Univ. of Pennsylvania Press, 1998.

Bjørn, Claus, Alexander Grant, and Keith J. Stringer, eds. *Nations, Nationalism, and Patriotism in the European Past*. Copenhagen: Academic Press, 1994.

Blake, E. O. "The Formation of the 'Crusade Idea.'" *Journal of Ecclesiastical History* 21, no. 1 (1970): 11–31.

Bloch, Howard. "The Economics of Romance." In Howard Bloch, *Etymologies and Genealogies: A Literary Anthropology of the French Middle Ages*, 159–97. Chicago: Univ. of Chicago Press, 1983.

———. *Etymologies and Genealogies: A Literary Anthropology of the French Middle Ages*. Chicago: Univ. of Chicago Press, 1983.

Bloomfield, Morton W. "Episodic Motivation and Marvels in Epic and Romance." In Morton W. Bloomfield, *Essays and Explorations: Studies in Ideas, Language, and Literature*. Cambridge, Mass.: Harvard Univ. Press, 1970.

Boase, Roger. *The Origin and Meaning of Courtly Love: A Critical Study of European Scholarship*. Manchester: Manchester Univ. Press, 1977.

Bolton, J. L. *The Medieval English Economy, 1150–1500*. London: Dent, 1980.

Borresen, Kari Elisabeth. *Subordination and Equivalence: The Nature and Role of Women in Augustine and Thomas Aquinas*. Translated by Charles H. Talbot. Washington, D.C.: Univ. Press of America, 1981.

Boswell, John. *Christianity, Social Tolerance, and Homosexuality: Gay People in Western Europe from the Beginning of the Christian Era to the Fourteenth Century*. Chicago: Univ. of Chicago Press, 1980.

Bourne, H. R. Fox. *English Merchants*. London: Chatto and Windus, 1898.

Bowers, John M. "Chaucer after Smithfield." *The Postcolonial Middle Ages*, ed. Jeffrey Jerome Cohen, 53–66. New York: St. Martin's, 2000.

Bradbury, Jim. *The Medieval Archer*. New York: St. Martin's, 1985.

Braude, Benjamin. "The Sons of Noah and the Construction of Ethnic and Geographical Identities in the Medieval and Early Modern Periods." *William and Mary Quarterly* 54 (1997): 103–42.

Brennan, Timothy. "The National Longing for Form." In *Nation and Narration*, ed. Homi K. Bhabha, 44–70. New York: Routledge, 1990.

Breuilly, John. *Nationalism and the State*. Chicago: Univ. of Chicago Press, 1985.

Brewer, D. S. "The English Chaucerians." Introduction to *Chaucer and Chaucerians: Critical Studies in Middle English Literature*, ed. D. S. Brewer, 201–39. London: Nelson, 1966.

Brooke, Christopher. "Geoffrey of Monmouth as a Historian." In *Church and Government in the Middle Ages*, ed. C. N. L. Brooke et al., 77–91. Cambridge: Cambridge Univ. Press, 1976.

Broughton, Bradford B. *The Legends of King Richard I Coeur de Lion: A Study of Sources and Variations to the Year 1600*. The Hague: Mouton, 1966.

Bruce, James Douglas. *The Evolution of Arthurian Romance from the Beginnings Down to the Year 1300*. Vol 1. Baltimore: The Johns Hopkins Univ. Press, 1923.

Brundage, James A. *Richard Lion Heart*. New York: Scribner's, 1974.

Brunner, Karl, ed. *Richard Coer de Lyon. Der Mittelenglische Versroman Richard Löwenherz*. Leipzig: Wilhelm Braumüller, 1913.

Bryan, Elizabeth J. "Laȝamon's Four Helens: Feminine Figurations of Nation in the Brut." *Leeds Studies in English* (New series) 26 (1995): 63–78.

Bryan, W. F., and Germaine Dempster, eds. *Sources and Analogues of Chaucer's Canterbury Tales*. New York: Humanities Press, 1958.

Budge, E. A. Wallis. *The Monks of Kublai Khan, Emperor of China*. London: Religious Tract Society, 1928.

Bullón-Fernández, María. "Engendering Authority: Father, Daughter, State, and Church in Gower's 'Tale of Constance' and Chaucer's 'Man of Law's Tale.'" In *Re-Visioning Gower*, ed. R. F. Yeager, 129–146. Asheville, N.C.: Pegasus, 1998.

Bullough, Vern L. "Heresy, Witchcraft, and Sexuality." *Journal of Homosexuality* 1, no. 2 (1976): 183–201.

———. "The Sin against Nature and Homosexuality." In *Sexual Practices and the Medieval Church*, ed. Vern L. Bullough and James Brundage, 55–71. Buffalo, N.Y.: Prometheus, 1982.

Burger, Glenn. "Cilician Armenian *Métissage* and Hetoum's *La Fleur des Histoires de la Terre d'Orient*." In *The Postcolonial Middle Ages*, ed. Jeffrey Jerome Cohen, 67–83. New York: St. Martin's, 2000.

Burns, Robert I., S. J. "Christian-Islamic Confrontation in the West: The Thirteenth-Century Dream of Conversion." *American Historical Review* 76, no. 5 (1971): 1386–1434.

Butt, Ronald. *A History of Parliament: The Middle Ages*. London: Constable, 1989.

Bynum, Caroline Walker. *Holy Feast and Holy Fast: The Religious Significance of Food to Medieval Women*. Berkeley: Univ. of California Press, 1987.

———. *Jesus as Mother: Studies in the Spirituality of the High Middle Ages.* Berkeley: Univ. of California Press, 1982.

———. *Metamorphosis and Identity.* New York: Zone, 2001.

———. *The Resurrection of the Body in Western Christianity, 200–1336.* New York: Columbia Univ. Press, 1995.

———. "Why All the Fuss about the Body? A Medievalist's Perspective." *Critical Inquiry* 22 (1995): 1–33.

———. "'And Woman His Humanity': Female Imagery in the Religious Writing of the Later Middle Ages." In *Gender and Religion: On the Complexity of Symbols,* ed. Caroline Walker Bynum, Stevan Harrell, Paula Richman, 257–88. Boston: Beacon, 1986.

Byrne, Eugene H. "The Genoese Colonies in Syria." In *The Crusades and Other Historical Essays,* ed. Louis J. Paetow, 139–182. New York: Crofts, 1928.

Calin, William. *The French Tradition and the Literature of Medieval England.* Toronto: Univ. of Toronto Press, 1994.

Camille, Michael. *The Gothic Idol: Ideology and Image-making in Medieval Art.* Cambridge: Cambridge Univ. Press, 1989.

Campbell, Mary Baine. *The Witness and the Other World: Exotic European Travel Writing, 400–1600.* Ithaca, N.Y.: Cornell Univ. Press, 1988.

———. *Wonder and Science: Imagining Worlds in Early Modern Europe.* Ithaca, N.Y.: Cornell Univ. Press, 1999.

Capellanus, Andreas. *The Art of Courtly Love.* Translated by John Jay Parry. New York: Columbia Univ. Press, 1990.

Carruthers, Mary. *The Book of Memory: A Study of Memory in Medieval Culture.* Cambridge: Cambridge Univ. Press, 1990.

Carter, Bill. "Merlin Sparks Ratings Magic." *New York Times,* April 29, 1998. B8.

Chance, Jane. *Woman as Hero in Old English Literature.* New York: Syracuse Univ. Press, 1986.

Chaucer, Geoffrey. *The Riverside Chaucer.* Edited by Larry D. Benson. Boston: Houghton Mifflin, 1987.

Chazan, Robert. "The Deteriorating Image of the Jews: Twelfth and Thirteenth Centuries." In *Christendom and Its Discontents: Exclusion, Persecution, and Rebellion, 1000–1500,* ed. Scott L. Waugh and Peter D. Diehl, 220–33. Cambridge: Cambridge Univ. Press, 1996.

Chibnall, Marjorie. *The Empress Matilda: Queen Consort, Queen Mother, and Lady of the English.* Oxford: Blackwell, 1991.

Childress, Diana T. "Between Romance and Legend: 'Secular Hagiography' in Middle English Literature." *Philological Quarterly* 57 (1978): 311–22.

Chrétien de Troyes. *The Knight with the Lion, or Yvain (Le Chevalier au Lion).* Edited and translated by William W. Kibler. Vol. 48, Series A, Garland Library of Medieval Literature. New York: Garland, 1985.

Christine de Pisan. *Treasure of the City of Ladies, or the Book of the Three Virtues* [*Le Livres des Trois Vertus, or Le Trésor de la Cité des Dames*]. Translated by Sarah Lawson. Harmondsworth: Penguin, 1985.

Clanchy, M. T. *England and Its Rulers, 1066–1272: Foreign Lordship and National Identity.* Oxford: Blackwell, 1983.

———. *From Memory to Written Record, England 1066–1307.* Oxford: Blackwell, 1993.

Clifford, James. *The Predicament of Culture: Twentieth-Century Ethnography, Literature, and Art.* Cambridge, Mass.: Harvard Univ. Press, 1988.

———. *Routes: Travel and Translation in the Late Twentieth Century.* Cambridge, Mass.: Harvard Univ. Press, 1997.

Clunas, Craig. "China in Britain: The Imperial Collections." In *Colonialism and the Object: Empire, Material Culture, and the Museum,* ed. Tim Barringer and Tom Flynn, 41–51. London: Routledge, 1998.

Cohen, Jeffrey Jerome. *Of Giants: Sex, Monsters, and the Middle Ages.* Minneapolis: Univ. of Minnesota Press, 1999.

———. "On Saracen Enjoyment: Some Fantasies of Race in Late Medieval France and England." *Journal of Medieval and Early Modern Studies* (Special Issue on Race and Ethnicity in the Middle Ages, ed. Thomas Hahn) 31, no. 1 (2001): 113–46.

———, ed. *The Postcolonial Middle Ages.* New York: St. Martin's, 2000.

Cohen, Jeremy. *The Friars and the Jews: The Evolution of Medieval Anti-Judaism.* Ithaca, N.Y.: Cornell Univ. Press, 1982.

———. "The Jews as the Killers of Christ in the Latin Tradition, from Augustine to the Friars." *Traditio* 39 (1983): 1–27.

Comfort, W. W. "The Essential Difference Between a '*Chanson de Geste*' and a '*Roman d'Aventure*.'" *Publications of the Modern Language Association* (*PMLA*) 19 (1904): 64–74.

Comnena, Anna. *The Alexiad of Anna Comnena.* Translated by E. R. A. Sewter. London: Penguin, 1969.

Contamine, Philippe. *War in the Middle Ages.* Translated by Michael Jones. Oxford: Blackwell, 1984.

Cook, Robert Francis. *"Chanson d'Antioche," Chanson de Geste: Le Cycle de la Croisade est-il Epique?* Amsterdam: John Benjamins, 1980.

———. "Crusade Propaganda in the Epic Cycles of the Crusade." In *Journeys Toward God: Pilgrimage and Crusade,* ed. Barbara N. Sargent-Baur, 157–75. Kalamazoo, Mich.: Medieval Institute, 1992.

Correale, Robert M. "Gower's Source Manuscript of Nicholas Trevet's *Les Cronicles.*" In *John Gower: Recent Readings,* ed. R. F. Yeager, 133–57. Kalamazoo, Mich.: Medieval Institute, 1989.

Coss, Peter. "Aspects of Cultural Diffusion in Medieval England: The Early Romances, Local Society, and Robin Hood." *Past and Present* 108 (1985): 35–79.

Crain, Caleb. "Lovers of Human Flesh: Homosexuality and Cannibalism in Melville's Novels." *American Literature* 66 (1994): 25–53.

Crane, Ronald S. *The Vogue of Medieval Chivalric Romance during the English Renaissance.* Menasha, Wis.: George Banta, 1919.

Crane, Susan. *Insular Romance: Politics, Faith, and Culture in Anglo-Norman and Middle English Literature.* Berkeley: Univ. of California Press, 1986.

Crick, Julia. *The Historia Regum Britannie of Geoffrey of Monmouth III. A Summary Catalogue of the Manuscripts.* Cambridge: Brewer, 1989.

———. *The Historia Regum Britannie of Geoffrey of Monmouth IV. Dissemination and Reception in the Later Middle Ages.* Cambridge: Brewer, 1991.

———. "Two Newly Located Manuscripts of Geoffrey of Monmouth's *Historia Regum Britannie.*" In *Arthurian Literature XIII,* ed. James P. Carley and Felicity Riddy, 151–56. Cambridge: Brewer, 1995.

Curley, Michael J. *Geoffrey of Monmouth.* New York: Twayne, 1994.

Cutler, Allan. "The First Crusade and the Idea of Conversion." *The Muslim World* 58, no. 1 (1968): 57–71, 155–64.

Cutler, Allan Harris, and Helen Elmquist Cutler. *The Jew as Ally of the Muslim: Medieval Roots of Anti-Semitism.* Notre Dame, Ind.: Univ. of Notre Dame Press, 1986.

Daniel, Norman. *The Arabs and Medieval Europe.* London: Longman, 1975.

———. *Islam and the West: The Making of an Image.* Edinburgh: Edinburgh Univ. Press, 1960.

Dante Alighieri. *Divina Commedia: Inferno.* Translated by Alan Gilbert. Durham, N.C.: Duke Univ. Press, 1969.

David, Charles Wendell. *Robert Curthose: Duke of Normandy.* Cambridge, Mass: Harvard Univ. Press, 1920.

Davies, R. R. *Domination and Conquest: The Experience of Ireland, Scotland, and Wales, 1100–1300.* Cambridge: Cambridge Univ. Press, 1990.

———. "Good Order and 'Sweet Civility': The Cultural Parameters of the Medieval English State." Plenary address, Annual Meeting of the Medieval Academy of America, March 27, 1998.

Davis, Kathleen. "National Writing in the Ninth Century: A Reminder for Postcolonial Thinking about the Nation." *Journal of Medieval and Early Modern Studies* 28, no. 3 (1998): 611–37.

Dawson, Christopher, ed. *Mission to Asia.* Toronto: Univ. of Toronto Press, 1980. *Medieval Academy Reprints for Teaching* 8.

Day, Mabel, and Robert Steele, eds. *Mum and the Sothsegger.* London: Early English Text Society (o.s., vol. 199), 1936.

de Rachewiltz, I. *Prester John and Europe's Discovery of East Asia.* Canberra: Australian National Univ. Press, 1972.

de Rougemont, Denis. *Love in the Western World.* Translated by Montgomery Belgion. Princeton, N.J.: Princeton Univ. Press, 1983.

De Vries, Kelly. *Medieval Military Technology.* Lewiston, N.Y.: Broadview, 1992.

de Weever, Jacqueline. *Sheba's Daughters: Whitening and Demonizing the Saracen Woman in Medieval French Epic.* New York: Garland, 1998.

Dean, Christopher. *Arthur of England: English Attitudes to King Arthur and the Knights of the Round Table in the Middle Ages and Renaissance.* Toronto: Toronto Univ. Press, 1987.

Dean, Ruth J. "The Manuscripts of Nicholas Trevet's Anglo-Norman Cronicles." *Medievalia et Humanistica* 14 (1962): 95–105.

———. "Nicholas Trevet, Historian." In *Medieval Learning and Literature: Essays Presented to Richard William Hunt,* ed. J. J. G. Alexander and M. T. Gibson, 328–52. Oxford: Clarendon Press, 1976.

Delany, Sheila. "Geographies of Desire: Orientalism in Chaucer's Legend of Good Women." *Chaucer Yearbook* 1 (1992): 1–32.

———. *Medieval Literary Politics: Shapes of Ideology.* New York: Manchester Univ. Press, 1990.

Derrida, Jacques. "La Loi du Genre/The Law of Genre," *Glyph* 7 (1980): 176–232.

Devisse, Jean. *The Image of the Black in Western Art.* Vol. 2. New York: Morrow, 1979.

Dinshaw, Carolyn. "Chaucer's Queer Touches/A Queer Touches Chaucer." *Exemplaria* 7, no. 1 (1995): 75–92.

———. *Chaucer's Sexual Poetics.* Madison: Univ. of Wisconsin Press, 1989.

———. *Getting Medieval: Sexualities and Communities, Pre- and Postmodern.* Durham, N.C.: Duke Univ. Press, 1999.

Donovan, Mortimer J. "Middle English *Emaré* and the Cloth Worthily Wrought." In *The Learned and the Lewd: Studies in Chaucer and Medieval Literature.* ed. Larry D. Benson, 337–42. Cambridge, Mass.: Harvard Univ. Press, 1974.

Douglas, David C., and George W. Greenaway, eds. *English Historical Documents, 1042–1189.* Vol 2. London: Eyre and Spottiswoode, 1953.

Duby, Georges. "Youth in Aristocratic Society." In *The Chivalrous Society,* trans. Cynthia Postan, 112–22. Berkeley: Univ. of California Press, 1977.

Duggan, Joseph. "Medieval Epic as Popular Historiography: Appropriation of Historical Knowledge in the Vernacular Epic." In *Grundriss der Romanischen Literaturen des Mittelalters,* ed. Hans Robert Jauss and Hans Ulrich Gumbrecht. Vol. 11, no. 1: *La Littérature Historiographique des Origines à 1500,* 285–311. Heidelberg: Carl Winter, 1986.

Dumville, David. "An Early Text of Geoffrey of Monmouth's *Historia Regum Britanniae* and the Circulation of Some Latin Histories in Twelfth-Century Normandy" In *Arthurian Literature IV,* ed. Richard Barber, 1–36. Totowa, N.J.: Barnes and Noble, 1985.

Duncalf, Frederic. "The Pope's Plan for the First Crusade." In *The Crusades and Other Historical Essays,* ed. Louis Paetow, 44–56. New York: Crofts, 1928.

Dundes, Alan, ed. *The Blood Libel Legend: A Casebook in Anti-Semitic Folklore.* Madison: Univ. of Wisconsin Press, 1991.

Dunn, Oliver, and James E. Kelley Jr., trans. *The Diario of Christopher Columbus's First Voyage to America 1492–1493.* Norman: Univ. of Oklahoma Press, 1989.

Duparc-Quioc, Suzanne, ed. *Chanson d'Antioche. La Chanson d'Antioche.* 2 vols. Paris: Paul Geuthner, 1976–82.

Eberle, Patricia J. "The Question of Authority and the Man of Law's Tale." In *The Center and Its Compass: Studies in Medieval Literature in Honor of Professor John Leyerle,* ed. Robert A. Taylor, James F. Burke, Patricia J. Eberle, Ian Lancashire, and Brian S. Merrilees, 111–149. Kalamazoo, Mich.: Medieval Institute, 1993.

Ehrenreich, Barbara. Foreword to Klaus Theweleit, *Male Fantasies,* ix–xvii. 2 vols. Translated by Stephen Conway. Minneapolis: Univ. of Minnesota Press, 1987.

Eidelberg, Shlomo, ed. and trans. *The Jews and the Crusaders: The Hebrew Chronicles of the First and Second Crusades.* Madison: Univ. of Wisconsin Press, 1977.

Ellis, Alexander J., ed. *The Only English Proclamation of Henry III.* London: Transactions of the Philological Society, n.d.

Emanuel, Hywel D. "Geoffrey of Monmouth's *Historia Regum Britannie:* A Second Variant Version." *Medium Aevum* 35, no. 2 (1966): 103–10.

Emmerson, Richard K. "The Apocalypse in Medieval Culture." Introduction to *The Apocalypse in the Middle Ages,* ed. Richard K. Emmerson and Bernard McGinn, 293–332. Ithaca, N.Y.: Cornell Univ. Press, 1992.

Encyclopaedia Judaica. 17 vols. Jerusalem: Keter, 1972(?)–82.

Evans, Sebastian, trans. Geoffrey of Monmouth, *Histories of the Kings of Britain.* London: Dent, 1912.

Everett, Dorothy. "A Characterization of the English Medieval Romances." In *Essays on Middle English Literature.* ed. Patricia Kean, 1–22. Oxford: Clarendon, 1955.

Fabre-Vassas, Claudine. *The Singular Beast: Jews, Christians, and the Pig.* Translated by Carol Volk. New York: Columbia Univ. Press, 1997.

Fay, Elizabeth. *Romantic Medievalism: History and the Romantic Literary Ideal.* Houndmills, United Kingdom: Palgrave, 2002.

Fernández-Armesto, Felipe. *Before Columbus: Exploration and Colonisation from the Mediterranean to the Atlantic 1229–1492.* London: Macmillan, 1987.

Fink, Harold S. Introduction to Fulcher of Chartres's *A History of the Expedition to Jerusalem 1095–1127,* ed. Harold S. Fink, trans. Frances Rita Ryan, 3–56. Knoxville: Univ. of Tennessee Press, 1969.

Finlayson, John. "Arthur and the Giant of St. Michael's Mount." *Medium Ævum* 33 (1964): 112–20.

———. "Definitions of Middle English Romance." *Chaucer Review* 15 (1980–81): 44–62, 168–81.

———. "*Morte Arthure:* The Date and a Source for the Contemporary References." *Speculum* 42 (1967): 624–38.

———. "Richard, *Coer de Lyon*: Romance, History, or Something in Between?" *Studies in Philology* 87 (1990) 156–80.

Fish, Stanley. *There's No Such Thing as Free Speech*. New York: Oxford Univ. Press, 1994.

Fisher, John H. "Chancery and the Emergence of Standard Written English in the Fifteenth Century." *Speculum* 52 (1977): 870–99.

———. "A Language Policy for Lancastrian England." *PMLA* 107 (1992): 1168–80.

Fleischman, Suzanne. "On the Representation of History and Fiction in the Middle Ages." *History and Theory* 22 (1983): 278–310.

Fletcher, Robert Huntington. *Arthurian Materials in the Chronicles*. [Harvard] *Studies and Notes in Philology and Literature* 10 (1906).

Ford, Boris, ed. *Medieval Britain*. Cambridge: Cambridge Univ. Press, 1992. *Cambridge Cultural History of Britain*, Vol. 2.

Forde, Simon, Lesley Johnson, and Alan V. Murray, eds. *Concepts of National Identity in the Middle Ages*. Leeds: Leeds Texts and Monographs (n.s., 4), 1995.

Foucault, Michel. "Nietzsche, Genealogy, History." In *Language, Counter-Memory, Practice: Selected Essays and Interviews by Michel Foucault*, ed. Donald F. Bouchard, 139–64. Ithaca, N.Y.: Cornell Univ. Press, 1977.

———. "Of Other Spaces." *Diacritics* 16 (1986): 22–27.

Foulet, Alfred. "The Epic Cycle of the Crusades." In *A History of the Crusades*, Vol. 6. ed. Harry W. Hazard and Norman P. Zacour, 6:98–115. Madison: Univ. of Wisconsin Press, 1989.

Fradenburg, Louise Olga. "Sovereign Love: The Wedding of Margaret Tudor and James IV of Scotland." In *Women and Sovereignty*, ed. Louise Olga Fradenburg, 78–100. Edinburgh: Edinburgh Univ. Press, 1992.

Frame, Robin. "Overlordship and Reaction, c. 1200–c. 1450." In *Uniting the Kingdom? The Making of British History*, ed. Alexander Grant and Keith J. Stringer, 65–84. New York: Routledge, 1995.

———. *The Political Development of the British Isles 1100–1400*. Oxford: Oxford Univ. Press, 1990.

Freud, Sigmund. *The Standard Edition of the Complete Psychological Works of Sigmund Freud*. Ed. and trans. James Strachey. 24 vols. London: Hogarth, 1960.

Friedman, Albert B. "'When Adam Delved . . .': Contexts of an Historic Proverb." In *The Learned and the Lewd: Studies in Chaucer and Medieval Literature*, ed. Larry D. Benson, 213–30. Cambridge, Mass.: Harvard Univ. Press, 1974.

Friedman, Jon Block. *The Monstrous Races in Medieval Art and Thought*. Cambridge, Mass: Harvard Univ. Press, 1981.

Frye, Northrop. *The Secular Scripture: A Study of the Structure of Romance*. Cambridge, Mass.: Harvard Univ. Press, 1976.

Fryer, Peter. *Staying Power: The History of Black People in Britain*. London: Pluto, 1992.

Fulcher of Chartres. *Historia Hierosolymitana (1095–1127)*. Edited by Heinrich Hagenmeyer. Heidelberg: Carl Winters, 1913.

————. *A History of the Expedition to Jerusalem, 1095–1127*. Edited by Harold S. Fink. Translated by Frances Rita Ryan. Knoxville: Univ. of Tennessee Press, 1969.

Furnivall, F. J., Edmund Brock, and W. A. Clouston, eds. *Originals and Analogues of Some of Chaucer's Canterbury Tales*. London: Trubner, 1872–87.

Gabrieli, Francesco, ed and trans. *Arab Historians of the Crusades*. London: Routledge, 1969.

Gairdner, James, ed. *The Paston Letters: 1422–1509 A.D.* 3 vols. London: Arber, 1872–75.

Ganim, John M. "The Myth of Medieval Romance." In *Medievalism and the Modernist Temper*, ed. R. Howard Bloch and Stephen G. Nichols, 148–66. Baltimore: The Johns Hopkins Univ. Press, 1996.

————. "Native Studies: Orientalism and Medievalism." In *The Postcolonial Middle Ages*, ed. Jeffrey Jerome Cohen, 123–34. New York: St. Martin's, 2000.

————. *Style and Consciousness in Middle English Narrative*. Princeton, N.J.: Princeton Univ. Press, 1983.

Gantz, Jeffrey, trans. *Early Irish Myths and Sagas*. Harmondsworth: Penguin, 1981.

Gellner, Ernest. *Nations and Nationalisms*. Ithaca, N.Y.: Cornell Univ. Press, 1983.

Gellrich, Jesse. *The Idea of the Book in the Middle Ages: Language Theory, Mythology, and Fiction*. Ithaca, N.Y.: Cornell Univ. Press, 1985.

Gerald of Wales. *Geraldi Cambrensi Opera*. Edited by George F. Warner. Rolls series 21. 8 vols. London: Longman, 1861–91.

Gerould, Gordon Hall. "King Arthur and Politics." *Speculum* 2 (1927): 33–52.

Getz, Faye. *Medicine in the English Midle Ages*. Princeton, N.J.: Princeton Univ. Press, 1998.

Gibb, H. A. R., trans. *The Damascus Chronicle of the Crusades: Extracted and Translated from the Chronicle of Ibn Al-Qalanisi*. London: Luzac, 1932.

Gildas. *De Excidio Britanniae*. Edited and translated by Michael Winterbottom. London: Rowman and Littlefield, 1978.

Giles, J. A., trans. Geoffrey of Monmouth, *Geoffrey of Monmouth's British History. Six Old English Chronicles*, 89–292. London: Bell, 1900.

Gillingham, John. "The Context and Purposes of Geoffrey of Monmouth's *History of the Kings of Britain*." *Anglo-Norman Studies* 13 (1990): 99–118.

————. "Foundations of a Disunited Kingdom." In *Uniting the Kingdom? The Making of British History*, ed. Alexander Grant and Keith J. Stringer, 48–64. New York: Routledge, 1995.

————. *Richard Coeur de Lion: Kingship, Chivalry, and War in the Twelfth Century*. London: Hambledon, 1994.

————. "Some Legends of Richard the Lionheart: Their Development and Their Influence." In *Richard Coeur de Lion in History and Myth*, ed. Janet L. Nelson, 51–60. London: King's College, Centre for Late Antique and Medieval Studies, 1992.

Girouard, Mark. *The Return to Camelot: Chivalry and the English Gentleman*. New Haven: Yale Univ. Press, 1981.

Given-Wilson, Chris. *The English Nobility in the Late Middle Ages: The Fourteenth-Century Political Community.* New York: Routledge, 1987.

Göller, Karl Heinz., ed. *The Alliterative Morte Arthure: A Reassessment of the Poem.* Cambridge: Brewer, 1981.

———. "Reality versus Romance: A Reassessment of the *Alliterative Morte Arthure.*" In *The Alliterative Morte Arthure: A Reassessment of the Poem,* ed. Karl Heinz Göller, 15–29. Cambridge: Brewer, 1981.

———. "A Summary of Research." In *The Alliterative Morte Arthure: A Reassessment of the Poem,* ed. Karl Heinz Göller, 7–14. Cambridge: Brewer, 1981.

Goodich, Michael. *The Unmentionable Vice: Homosexuality in the Later Medieval Period.* Santa Barbara, Calif.: ABC-Clio, 1979.

Goodrich, L. Carrington. "Westerners and Central Asians in Yuan China." In *Oriente Poliano,* 1–21. Rome: Istituto italiano per il Medio ed Estremo Oriente, 1957.

Gough, A. B. *The Constance Saga.* Berlin: Mayer and Müller, 1902.

Gower, John. *Confessio Amantis.* Edited by Russell A. Peck. Toronto: Univ. of Toronto Press, 1980.

Gransden, Antonia. *Historical Writing in England.* 2 vols. Ithaca, N.Y.: Cornell Univ. Press, 1974.

Gravdal, Kathryn. "Chrétien de Troyes, Gratian, and the Medieval Romance of Sexual Violence." *Signs* 17, no. 3 (1992): 558–85.

Greenblatt, Stephen. *Marvellous Possessions: The Wonder of the New World.* Chicago: Chicago Univ. Press, 1991.

Griscom, Acton, and Robert Ellis Jones, ed. *The Historia Regum Britanniae of Geoffrey of Monmouth with Contributions to the Study of Its Place in Early British History.* London: Longman, 1929.

Guibert of Nogent. *Gesta Dei per Francos.* Recueil des Historiens des Croisades. Vol. 4. Paris: *Académie des Inscriptions et Belles-Lettres. Historiens Occidentaux,* 1844–1895.

Hagenmeyer, Heinrich, ed. *Die Kreuzzugsbriefe aus den Jahren 1088–1100.* Innsbruck: Verlag der Wagnerschen Universitäts-Buchhandlung, 1901.

Hahn, Thomas. "The Difference the Middle Ages Makes: Color and Race before the Modern World." *Journal of Medieval and Early Modern Studies* (Special Issue on Race and Ethnicity in the Middle Ages, ed. Thomas Hahn) 31, no. 1 (2001): 1–37.

Hale, Rosemary Drage. "Joseph as Mother: Adaptation and Appropriation in the Construction of Male Virtue." In *Medieval Mothering, Medieval Motherers,* ed. John Carmi Parsons and Bonnie Wheeler, 101–116. New York: Garland. 1996.

Halperin, David. "Is There a History of Sexuality?" In *The Lesbian and Gay Studies Reader,* ed. Henry Abelove, Michèle Aina Barale, and David M. Halperin, 416–31. New York: Routledge, 1993.

Hambis, Louis. "Le Voyage de Marco Polo en Haute Asie." In *Oriente Poliano,* 173–91. Rome: Istituto italiano per il Medio ed Estremo Oriente, 1957.

Hamel, Mary, ed. *Morte Arthure: A Critical Edition.* New York: Garland, 1984.

————. "The Siege of Jerusalem as a Crusading Poem." In *Journeys Toward God: Pilgrimage and Crusade*, ed. Barbara N. Sargent-Baur, 177–94. Kalamazoo, Mich.: Medieval Institute, 1992.

Hamelius, P., ed. *Mandeville's Travels.* 2 vols. Early English Text Society, o.s., vols. 153 and 154. London: Kegan Paul, 1919.

Hamilton, Bernard. "Continental Drift: Prester John's Progress through the Indies." In *Prester John, the Mongols, and the Ten Lost Tribes*, ed. Charles F. Beckingham and Bernard Hamilton, 237–69. Aldershot: Variorum, 1996.

————. "Prester John and the Three Kings of Cologne." In *Prester John, the Mongols, and the Ten Lost Tribes*, ed. Charles F. Beckingham and Bernard Hamilton, 171–85. Aldershot: Variorum, 1996.

Hamilton, Robert. "Empire of Kitsch: Japan as Represented in Western Pop Media." *Bad Subjects*, no. 60 (April 2002).

Hanks, D. Thomas. "Emaré: An Influence on the Man of Law's Tale." *Chaucer Review* 18 (1983): 182–86.

Hannaford, Ivan. *Race: The History of an Idea in the West.* Baltimore: The Johns Hopkins Univ. Press, 1996.

Hanning, Robert W. *The Individual in Twelfth-Century Romance.* New Haven: Yale Univ. Press, 1977.

————. *The Vision of History in Early Britain: From Gildas to Geoffrey of Monmouth.* New York: Columbia Univ. Press, 1996.

Harding, Alan. *England in the Thirteenth Century.* Cambridge: Cambridge Univ. Press, 1993.

Hartley, Sir Percival Horton-Smith, and Harold Richard Aldridge, eds. *Johannes de Mirfeld of St. Bartholomew's, Smithfield: His Life and Works.* Cambridge: Cambridge Univ. Press, 1936.

Harty, Kevin J., ed. *Cinema Arthuriana: Essays on Arthurian Film.* New York: Garland, 1991.

Heffernan, Carol Falvo, ed. *Le Bone Florence of Rome.* Manchester: Manchester Univ. Press, 1976.

Heng, Geraldine. "Feminine Knots and the Other Sir Gawain and the Green Knight." *PMLA* (May 1991): 500–514.

————. "'A Great Way to Fly': Women, Nationalism, and the Varieties of Feminism in Southeast Asia." In *Feminist Genealogies, Colonial Legacies, Democratic Futures*, ed. M. Jacqui Alexander and Chandra Talpade Mohanty, 30–45, 364–66. London: Routledge, 1996.

————. "A Woman Wants: The Lady, *Gawain*, and the Forms of Seduction." *Yale Journal of Criticism* 5, no. 3 (1992): 101–34.

Heng, Geraldine, and Janadas Devan. "State Fatherhood: The Politics of Nationalism, Sexuality, and Race in Singapore." In *Nationalisms and Sexualities*, ed. Andrew Parker, Mary Russo, Doris Sommer, and Patricia Yeager, 243–64. London: Routledge, 1991.

Herlihy, David. "The Making of the Medieval Family: Symmetry, Structure, and Sentiment." *Journal of Family History* 8 (1983): 116–30.

———. *Medieval Households.* Cambridge, Mass.: Harvard Univ. Press, 1985.

Hibbard, Laura A. *Mediæval Romance in England: A Study of the Sources and Analogues of the Non-Cyclic Metrical Romances.* New York: Oxford Univ. Press, 1924.

Hicks, Michael. *Bastard Feudalism.* London: Longman, 1995.

Higgins, Iain Macleod. "Defining the Earth's Center in a Medieval 'Multi-Text': Jerusalem in *The Book of John Mandeville.*" In *Text and Territory: Geographical Imagination in the European Middle Ages,* ed. Sylvia Tomasch and Sealy Gilles, 29–53. Philadelphia: Univ. of Pennsylvania Press, 1998.

———. "Imagining Christendom from Jerusalem to Paradise: Asia in *Mandeville's Travels.*" In *Discovering New Worlds: Essays on Medieval Exploration and Imagination,* ed. Scott D Westrem, 91–114. New York: Garland, 1991.

———. *Writing East: The "Travels" of Sir John Mandeville.* Philadelphia: Univ. of Pennsylvania Press, 1997.

Hill, Rosalind, ed. *Gesta Francorum et Aliorum Hierosolymitanorum.* Oxford: Clarendon, 1962.

Hornstein, Lillian H. "The Historical Background of the *King of Tars.*" *Speculum* 16:4 (1941): 404–14.

———. "Middle English Romances." In *Recent Middle English Scholarship and Criticism: Survey and Desiderata,* ed. J. Burke Severs, 55–95. Pittsburgh: Duquesne Univ. Press, 1971.

———. "Trivet's Constance and the *King of Tars.*" *MLN (Modern Language Notes)* 55 (1940): 354–57.

Housley, Norman, ed. and trans. *Documents on the Later Crusades, 1274–1580.* New York: St. Martin's, 1996.

Howard, Donald. "The World of Mandeville's Travels." *The Yearbook of English Studies* 1 (1997): 1–17.

Hudson, Harriet. "Construction of Class, Family, and Gender in Some Middle English Popular Romances." *Class and Gender in Early English Literature: Intersections,* ed. Britton J. Harwood and Gillian R. Overing, 76–94. Bloomington: Indiana Univ. Press, 1994.

———. "Middle English Popular Romances: The Manuscript Evidence." *Manuscripta* 28, no. 2 (July 1984): 67–78.

———. "Toward a Theory of Popular Literature: The Case of the Middle English Romances." *Journal of Popular Culture* 23, no. 3 (1989): 31–50.

Hume, Kathryn. "The Formal Nature of Middle English Romance." *Philological Quarterly* 53 (1974): 158–80.

Huppert, George. *After the Black Death: A Social History of Early Modern Europe.* Bloomington: Indiana Univ. Press, 1986.

Hurley, Margaret. "Saints' Legends and Romance Again: Secularization of Structure and Motif." *Genre* 8 (1975): 60–73.

Hussey, Stanley. "Nationalism and Language in England, c. 1300–1500." In *Nations, Nationalism and Patriotism in the European Past*, ed. Claus Bjørn, Alexander Grant, and Keith J. Stringer, 96–108. Copenhagen: Academic Press, 1994.

Huth, Jennifer Mary. "'For I Have Tools to Truss': Women, Work, and Professionalism in Late Medieval Literature." Ph.D. diss., Department of English, University of Texas at Austin, 1996

Hutson, Arthur E. "British Personal Names in the Historia Regum Britanniae." *University of California Publications in English* 5 (1944): 1–160.

Ingham, Patricia Clare. *Sovereign Fantasies: Arthurian Romance and the Making of Britain*. Philadelphia: Univ. of Pennsylvania Press, 2001.

Jackson, W. T. H. "The Nature of Romance." *Yale French Studies* 51 (1974): 12–25.

Jacobs, Joseph. *The Jews of Angevin England*. London: D. Nutt, 1893.

Jaeger, Stephen C. *Ennobling Love: In Search of a Lost Sensibility*. Philadelphia: Univ. of Pennsylvania Press, 1999.

Jambeck, Karen K. "Patterns of Women's Literary Patronage: England, 1200–ca. 1475." In *The Cultural Patronage of Medieval Women*, ed. June Hall McCash, 228–265. Athens: Univ. of Georgia Press, 1996.

Jameson, Fredric. "Magical Narratives: Romance as Genre." *NLH (New Literary History)* 7:1 (1975) 135–63.

Joinville, Jean de. *Histoire de Saint Louis*. Edited by Natalis de Wailly. Paris: Firmin Didot, 1874.

Johansson, Warren, and William A. Percy. "Homosexuality." In *Handbook of Medieval Sexuality*, ed. Vern L. Bullough and James A. Brundage, 155–189. New York; Garland 1996.

Johnson, Lesley. "Etymologies, Genealogies, and Nationalities (Again)." *Concepts of National Identity in the Middle Ages*, ed. Simon Forde, Lesley Johnson, and Alan V. Murray, 125–36. Leeds: Leeds Texts and Monographs (n.s., 4), 1995.

Johnston, Arthur. *Enchanted Ground: The Study of Medieval Romance in the Eighteenth Century*. London: Athlone, 1964.

Jones, Ernest. "Geoffrey of Monmouth, 1640–1800." *University of California Publications in English* 5 (1940–44): 357–439.

Jones, Paul H. *Christ's Eucharistic Presence: A History of the Doctrine*. American University Studies, series 7, vol. 157: *Theology and Religion*. New York: Peter Lang, 1994.

Jones, Thomas. "The Early Evolution of the Legend of Arthur." *Nottingham Mediaeval Studies* 8 (1964): 3–21.

Jordan, Mark D. *The Invention of Sodomy in Christian Theology*. Chicago: Univ. of Chicago Press, 1997.

Justice, Steven. *Writing and Rebellion: England in 1381*. Berkeley: Univ. of California Press, 1996.

Kaeuper, Richard W. *War, Justice, and Public Order: England and France in the Later Middle Ages*. Oxford: Clarendon, 1988.

Kantorowicz, Ernst H. *The King's Two Bodies: A Study in Mediaeval Political Theology*. Princeton, N.J.: Princeton Univ. Press, 1957.

Kaplan, Paul H. D. *The Rise of the Black Magus in Western Art*. Studies in the Fine Arts: *Iconography*, vol. 9. Ann Arbor: UMI Research, 1985.

Kedar, Benjamin Z. *Crusade and Mission: European Approaches toward the Muslims*. Princeton, N.J.: Princeton Univ. Press, 1984.

Keeler, Laura. *Geoffrey of Monmouth and the Late Latin Chroniclers 1300–1500*. Berkeley: Univ. of California Press, 1946.

Keen, Maurice. "Chaucer's Knight, the English Aristocracy, and the Crusade." In *English Court Culture in the Later Middle Ages*, ed. V. J. Scattergood and J. W. Sherborne, 45–62. London: Duckworth, 1983.

———. *Chivalry*. New Haven: Yale Univ. Press, 1984.

———. "Heraldry and Hierarchy: Esquires and Gentlemen," In *Orders and Hierarchies in Late Medieval and Renaissance Europe*, ed. Jeffrey Denton, 94–108, 184–87. London: Macmillan, 1999.

Keiser, George R. "Edward III and the Alliterative *Morte Arthure*." *Speculum* 48 (1973): 37–51.

———. "Lincoln Cathedral Library MS 91: Life and Milieu of the Scribe." *Studies in Bibliography* 32 (1979): 158–79.

Ker, W. P. *Epic and Romance*. New York: Dover, 1957.

Kibbee, Douglas A. *For to Speke Frenche Trewely: The French Language in England, 1000–1600*. Amsterdam: J. Benjamins, 1991.

Kilgour, Maggie. *From Communion to Cannibalism: An Anatomy of Metaphors of Incorporation*. Princeton, N.J.: Univ. of Princeton Press, 1990.

Kinoshita, Sharon. "Heldris de Cornuälle's *Roman de Silence* and the Feudal Politics of Lineage." *PMLA* 110, no. 3 (1995): 397–409.

———. "'Pagans Are Wrong and Christians Are Right': Alterity, Gender, and Nation in the *Chanson de Roland*." *Journal of Medieval and Early Modern Studies* 31, no. 1 (2001): 77–109.

———. "The Politics of Courtly Love: *La Prise d'Orange* and the Conversion of the Saracen Queen." *Romanic Review* 86, no. 2 (1995): 265–87.

Knapp, Peggy. *Chaucer and the Social Contest*. New York: Routledge, 1990.

Knight, Stephen. *Arthurian Literature and Society*. New York: St. Martin's, 1983.

Knighton, Henry. *Chronicon*. Edited by J. R. Lumby. 2 vols. London: Rolls, 1889–95.

Kohanski, Tamarah Malley. "Uncharted Territory: New Perspectives on *Mandeville's Travels*." Ph.D. diss., University of Connecticut, 1993.

Koht, Halvdan. "The Dawn of Nationalism in Europe." *American Historical Review* 52, no. 2 (1947): 265–80.

Köhler, Erich, ed. *Der Altfranzösische Höfischer Roman*. Darmstadt: Wissenschaffliche Buchgesellschaft, 1978.

Kolve. V. A. *Chaucer and the Imagery of Narrative: The First Five Canterbury Tales*. Stanford: Stanford Univ. Press, 1984.

Kowaleski, Maryanne, and Judith M. Bennett. "Crafts, Gilds, and Women in the Middle Ages: Fifty Years after Marian K. Dale." *Sisters and Workers in the Middle Ages,* ed. Judith M. Bennett, Elizabeth A. Clark, Jean F. O'Barr, B. Anne Vilen, and Sarah Westphal-Wihl, 11–38. Chicago: Univ. of Chicago Press, 1989.

Kratz, Dennis M., trans. *The Romances of Alexander.* New York: Garland, 1991.

Krey, A. C. "A Neglected Passage in the *Gesta* and Its Bearing on the Literature of the First Crusade." *The Crusades and Other Historical Essays,* ed. Louis Paetow, 57–78. New York: Crofts, 1928.

———, ed. and trans. *The First Crusade: The Accounts of Eye-Witnesses and Participants.* Princeton, N.J.: Princeton Univ. Press, 1921.

Krishna, Valerie, ed. *The Alliterative Morte Arthure: A Critical Edition.* New York: Burt Franklin, 1976.

Kristeva, Julia. "Stabat Mater." In Julia Kristeva, *Tales of Love,* 234–63. New York: Columbia Univ. Press, 1987.

Kruger, Steven F. "Fetishism, 1927, 1614, 1461." In *The Postcolonial Middle Ages,* ed. Jeffrey Jerome Cohen, 193–208. New York: St. Martin's, 2000.

Lacan, Jacques. "God and the *Jouissance* of the Woman." In *Feminine Sexuality: Jacques Lacan and the école freudienne,"* ed. Juliet Mitchell and Jacqueline Rose, 138–48. New York: Norton, 1982.

Lach, Donald F. *Asia in the Making of Europe.* Vol. 1, Book 1: *The Century of Discovery.* Chicago: Univ. of Chicago Press, 1965.

Laȝamon. *Brut. Laȝamon: Brut.* Edited by G. L. Brook and R. F. Leslie. 2 vols. Early English Text Society, vols. 250 and 277. London: Oxford Univ. Press, 1963, 1978.

Langmuir, Gavin. "The Knight's Tale of Young Hugh of Lincoln." *Speculum* 47, no. 3 (1972): 459–82.

———. "Thomas of Monmouth: Detector of Ritual Murder." *Speculum* 59, no. 4 (1984): 820–45.

Lasater, Alice. *Spain to England: A Comparative Study of Arabic, European, and English Literature of the Middle Ages.* Jackson: Univ. of Mississippi Press, 1974.

Laskaya, Anne. "The Rhetoric of Incest in the Middle English *Emaré.*" In *Violence against Women in Medieval Texts,* ed. Anna Roberts, 97–113. Gainesville: Univ. of Florida Press, 1998.

Laskaya, Anne, and Eve Salisbury, eds. *Emaré.* In *The Middle English Breton Lays.* Kalamazoo, Mich.: Medieval Institute, 1995.

Latour, Bruno. *Science in Action: How to Follow Scientists and Engineers through Society.* Cambridge, Mass.: Harvard Univ. Press, 1987.

Leckie, R. William, Jr. *The Passage of Dominion: Geoffrey of Monmouth and the Periodization of Insular History in the Twelfth Century.* Toronto: Univ. of Toronto Press, 1981.

Lee, Anne Thompson. "*Le Bone Florence of Rome:* A Middle English Adaptation of a French Romance." In *The Learned and the Lewd: Studies in Chaucer and Me-

dieval Literature, ed. Larry D. Benson, 343–54. Cambridge, Mass.: Harvard Univ. Press, 1974.

Lerer, Seth. *Chaucer and His Readers: Imagining the Author in Late-Medieval England*. Princeton, N.J.: Princeton Univ. Press, 1993.

Letts, Malcolm. *Sir John Mandeville: The Man and His Book*. London: Batchworth, 1949.

———, ed. *Mandeville's Travels: Texts and Translations*. 2 vols. London: Hakluyt Society, 1953.

Lewis, Bernard, ed. and trans. *Islam: From the Prophet Muhammad to the Capture of Constantinople*. 2 vols. New York: Harper and Row, 1974.

———. "The Sources for the History of the Syrian Assassins." *Speculum* 27 (1952): 475–89.

Lewis, C. S. *The Allegory of Love: A Study in Medieval Tradition*. New York: Oxford Univ. Press, 1958.

Lipman, Vivian D. *The Jews of Medieval Norwich*. London: Jewish Historical Society of England, 1967.

Loomis, Laura Hibbard. "The Auchinleck Manuscript and a Possible London Bookshop of 1330–1340." In Laura Hibbard Loomis, *Adventures in the Middle Ages: A Memorial Collection of Essays and Studies*, 150–87. New York: Burt Franklin, 1962.

———. "Chaucer and the Breton Lays of the Auchinleck MS." *Studies in Philology* 38 (1941): 14–33.

———. *Mediæval Romance in England: A Study of the Sources and Analogues of the Non-Cyclic Metrical Romances*. New York: Oxford Univ. Press, 1924.

Loomis, Roger Sherman, ed. *Arthurian Literature in the Middle Ages: A Collaborative History*. Oxford: Clarendon, 1959.

———. "*Richard Coeur de Lion* and the *Pas Saladin* in Medieval Art." *PMLA* 30 (1915): 509–28.

Lomperis, Linda. "Medieval Travel Writing and the Question of Race." *Journal of Medieval and Early Modern Studies* 31, no. 1 (2001): 149–64.

Lydon, James F., ed. *The English in Medieval Ireland*. Dublin: Royal Irish Academy, 1984.

MacCannell, Dean, and Juliet Flower MacCannell. "The Beauty System." In *The Ideology of Conduct: Essays in Literature and the History of Sexuality*, ed. Nancy Armstrong and Leonard Tennenhouse, 206–38. London: Methuen, 1987.

Macrae-Gibson, O. D., ed. *Of Arthur and of Merlin*. 2 vols. Early English Text Society, vols. 268 and 279. London: Oxford Univ. Press, 1973, 1979.

Macy, Gary. *The Theologies of the Eucharist in the Early Scholastic Period*. Oxford: Clarendon, 1984.

Maddicott, J. R., and D. M. Palliser, ed. *The Medieval State: Essays Presented to James Campbell*. London: Hambledon, 2000.

Malory, Sir Thomas. *The Works of Sir Thomas Malory*. Edited by Eugene Vinaver. Revised by P. J. C. Field. 3 vols. Oxford: Clarendon, 1990.

Mann, Jill. *Chaucer and Medieval Estates Satire: The Literature of Social Classes and the General Prologue to the Canterbury Tales*. Cambridge: Cambridge Univ. Press, 1973.

Marcus, Leah S. *Unediting the Renaissance: Shakespeare, Marlowe, Milton*. London: Routledge, 1996.

Marvin, Julia. "Cannibalism as an Aspect of Famine in Two English Chronicles." In *Food and Eating in Medieval Europe*, ed. Martha Carlin and Joel T. Rosenthal, 73–86. London: Hambledon, 1998.

Matheson, Lister M. "King Arthur and the Medieval English Chronicles." In *King Arthur Through the Ages*, ed. Valerie M. Lagorio and Mildred Leake Day, 1:248–74. New York: Garland, 1990.

Matthews, William. *The Tragedy of Arthur: A Study of the Alliterative "Morte Arthure."* Berkeley: Univ. of California Press, 1960.

McDermott, James. *Martin Frobisher: Elizabethan Privateer*. New Haven: Yale Univ. Press, 2001.

McFarlane, Kenneth B. "Bastard Feudalism." In Kenneth B. McFarlane, *England in the Fifteenth Century: Collected Essays*, 23–43. London: Hambledon, 1981.

———. *The Nobility of Later Medieval England*. Oxford, Clarendon, 1973.

———. "War, the Economy, and Social Change: England and the Hundred Years War." In Kenneth B. McFarlane, *England in the Fifteenth Century: Collected Essays*, 139–49. London: Hambledon, 1981.

McLaughlin, Mary Martin. "Survivors and Surrogates: Children and Parents from the Ninth to the Thirteenth Centuries." *The History of Childhood*, ed. Lloyd deMause, 101–81. New York: Psychohistory, 1974.

Mead, William Edward, ed. *The Squyr of Lowe Degre*. Boston: Ginn, 1904.

Meale, Carol M. "'Gode me/Wiues maydnes and alle men': Romance and Its Audiences." In *Readings in Medieval English Romance*, ed. Carol M. Meale, 209–25. Cambridge: Brewer, 1994.

———. *Readings in Medieval English Romance*. Cambridge: Brewer, 1994.

Mehl, Dieter. *The Middle English Romances of the Thirteenth and Fourteenth Centuries*. New York: Barnes and Noble, 1969.

Melitzki, Dorothee. *The Matter of Araby in Medieval England*. New Haven: Yale Univ. Press, 1977.

Menache, Sophia. "Faith, Myth, and Politics: The Stereotype of the Jews and Their Expulsion from England and France." *The Jewish Quarterly Review* 75, no. 4 (1985): 351–74.

———. "Matthew Paris's Attitudes Towards Anglo-Jewry." *Journal of Medieval History* 23 (1997): 139–62.

Menocal, Maria Rosa. *The Arabic Role in Medieval Literary History*. Philadelphia: Univ. of Pennsylvania Press, 1987.

Migne, J.-P., ed. *Patrologiae Latinae Cursus Completus.* 221 vols. Paris: Garnier, 1844–64.

Modeleski, Tania. "The Incredible Shrinking He(r)man: Male Regression, the Male Body, and Film." *differences* 2, no. 2 (1990): 55–75.

Montgomery, James A, trans. *The History of Yaballaha III, Nestorian Patriarch, and of His Vicar, Bar Sauma.* New York: Columbia Univ. Press, 1927.

Moore, Lisa. *Dangerous Intimacies: Toward a Sapphic History of the British Novel.* Durham, N.C.: Duke Univ. Press, 1997.

Moore, R. I. *The Formation of a Persecuting Society: Power and Deviance in Western Europe 950–1250.* Oxford, Blackwell, 1987.

Moorman, Charles. "Literature of Defeat and of Conquest: The Arthurian Revival of the Twelfth Century." In *King Arthur through the Ages,* ed. Valerie M. Lagorio and Mildred Leake Day, 1:22–43. New York: Garland 1990.

Morris, John, ed. and trans. *Historia Brittonum. Nennius: British History and the Welsh Annals.* London: Rowman and Littlefield, 1980.

Morris, Richard, ed. *Cursor Mundi: A Northumbrian Poem of the Fourteenth Century.* Early English Text Society, o.s., 57, 59, 62, 66, 68, 99, 101. London: Oxford Univ. Press, 1991–96.

Morrison, Toni. *Playing in the Dark: Whiteness and the Literary Imagination.* Cambridge, Mass.: Harvard Univ. Press, 1992.

Moseley, C. W. R. D. "Behaim's Globe and 'Mandeville's Travels.'" *Imago Mundi* 33 (1981): 89–91.

———. Introduction to *The Travels of Sir John Mandeville.* Edited and translated by C. W. R. D. Moseley. Penguin: Harmondsworth, 1983.

———. "Sir John Mandeville's Visit to the Pope: The Implications of an Interpolation." *Neophilologus* 54 (1970): 77–80.

Moule, A. C. *Christians in China before the Year 1550.* New York: Macmillan, 1930.

Mundill, Robin R. *England's Jewish Solution: Experiment and Expulsion, 1262–1290.* Cambridge: Cambridge Univ. Press, 1998.

Munro, Dana Carleton. "A Crusader." *Speculum* 7 (1932): 321–35.

———. "The Speech of Pope Urban II at Clermont, 1095." *The American Historical Review* 11 (1906): 231–42.

———. *Urban and the Crusaders.* Translations and Reprints from the Original Sources of European History series, vol. 1, no. 2. Philadelphia: Univ. of Pennsylvania, 1895.

Murray, Alan V. "Ethnic Identity in the Crusader States: The Frankish Race and the Settlement of Outremer." In *Concepts of National Identity in the Middle Ages,* ed. Simon Forde, Lesley Johnson, and Alan V. Murray, 59–73. Leeds: Leeds Texts and Monographs (n.s., 4), 1995.

Nerlich Michael. *Ideology of Adventure: Studies in Modern Consciousness, 1100–1750.* 2 vols. Translated by Ruth Crowley. Minneapolis: Univ. of Minnesota Press, 1987.

Newman, Barbara. *From Virile Woman to WomanChrist: Studies in Medieval Religion and Literature.* Philadelphia: Univ. of Pennsylvania Press, 1985.

Newman, F. X., ed. *The Meaning of Courtly Love.* Albany, N.Y.: State Univ. of New York Press, 1968.

Newton, Allyson. "The Occlusion of Maternity in Chaucer's *Clerk's Tale.*" In *Medieval Mothering, Medieval Motherers,* ed. John Carmi Parsons and Bonnie Wheeler, 63–75. New York: Garland. 1996.

Nicholson, "Chaucer Borrows from Gower: The Sources of the *Man of Law's Tale.*" In *Chaucer and Gower: Difference, Mutuality, Exchange,* ed. R. F. Yeager, 85–99. English Literary Studies Monograph series, 51. Victoria, British Columbia: Univ. of Victoria, 1991.

Nirenberg, David. *Communities of Violence: Persecution of Minorities in the Middle Ages.* Princeton, N.J.: Princeton Univ. Press, 1996.

Noble, James. "Patronage, Politics, and the Figure of Arthur in Geoffrey of Monmouth, Wace, and Laȝamon." In *The Arthurian Yearbook II,* ed. Keith Busby, 159–78. New York: Garland, 1992.

Norgate, Kate. *Richard the Lion Heart.* New York: Russell and Russell. 1924.

Nowell, Charles E. "Historical Prester John." *Speculum* 28 (1953): 435–45.

———. "The Old Man of the Mountain." *Speculum* 22 (1947): 497–519.

Oakeshott, R. Ewart. *The Archaeology of Weapons.* New York: Praeger, 1960.

Oldmixon, Katherine. "Otherworlds/Otherness: The Cultural Politics of Exoticism in the Middle English Breton Lays." Ph.D. diss., Department of English, Univ. of Texas at Austin, 2001.

Olschki, Leonardo. *Guillaume Boucher: A French Artist at the Court of the Khans.* Baltimore, Md.: The Johns Hopkins Univ. Press, 1946.

———. *Marco Polo's Asia.* Translated by John A. Scott. Berkeley: Univ. of California Press, 1960.

Olson, Paul A. *The Canterbury Tales and the Good Society.* Princeton, N.J.: Princeton Univ. Press, 1986.

Orderic Vitalis. *The Ecclesiastical History of Ordericus Vitalis.* Edited by Marjorie Chibnall. 6 vols. Oxford: Clarendon, 1969–80.

Orme, Nicholas. *From Childhood to Chivalry: The Education of the English Kings and Aristocracy, 1066–1530.* London: Methuen, 1984.

Osborne, Lawrence. "Does Man Eat Man? Inside the Great Cannibalism Debate." *Lingua Franca* 7, no. 4 (1997): 28–38.

Otter, Samuel. *Melville's Anatomies.* Berkeley: Univ. of California Press, 1999.

Ousama Munkidh. *The Autobiography of Ousama.* Translated by George Richard Potter. London: Routledge, 1929.

Pallister, Janis L. "Giants." In *Mythical and Fabulous Creatures: A Source Book and Research Guide,* ed. Malcolm South, 293–324. New York: Greenwood, 1987.

Parker, Patricia. "Fantasies of 'Race' and 'Gender': Africa, *Othello,* and Bringing to Light." In *Women, "Race," and Writing in the Early Modern Period,* ed. Margo Hendricks and Patricia Parker, 84–100. New York: Routledge, 1994.

———. *Inescapable Romance: Studies in the Poetics of a Mode.* Princeton, N.J.: Princeton Univ. Press, 1979.

Parkes, James. *The Jew in the Medieval Community*. New York: Hermon, 1976.

Parsons, John Carmi. "Mothers, Daughters, Marriage, Power: Some Plantagenet Evidence, 1150–1500. In *Medieval Queenship*, ed. John Carmi Parsons, 63–78. New York: St. Martins, 1993.

———. "The Pregnant Queen as Counsellor and the Medieval Construction of Motherhood." In *Medieval Mothering, Medieval Motherers*, ed. John Carmi Parsons and Bonnie Wheeler, 39–61. New York: Garland. 1996.

———. "Ritual and Symbol in the English Medieval Queenship to 1500." *Women and Sovereignty*, ed. Louise Olga Fradenburg, 60–77. Edinburgh: Edinburgh Univ. Press, 1992.

Partner, Nancy F. *Serious Entertainments: The Writing of History in Twelfth-Century England*. Chicago: Univ. of Chicago Press, 1977.

Patch, Howard R. *The Goddess Fortuna in Mediaeval Literature*. Cambridge: Harvard Univ. Press, 1927.

Patterson, Lee W. "The Historiography of Romance and the Alliterative *Morte Arthure*." *Journal of Medieval and Renaissance Studies* 13, no. 1 (1983): 1–32.

———. *Negotiating the Past: The Historical Understanding of Medieval Literature*. Madison: Univ. of Wisconsin Press, 1987.

Pearsall, Derek. "The Development of Middle English Romance." In *Studies in Medieval English Romance: Some New Approaches*, ed. Derek Brewer, 11–35. Cambridge: Brewer, 1988.

———. "The English Romance in the Fifteenth Century." In *Essays and Studies 1976*, ed. E. Talbot Donaldson, 56–83. London: John Murray, 1976.

———. "John Capgrave's *Life of St. Katherine* and Popular Romance Style." *Medievalia et Humanistica* (n.s., 6) (1975): 121–37.

———. "Middle English Romance and Its Audiences." In *Historical and Editorial Studies in Medieval and Early Modern English*, ed. Mary-Jo Arn, Hanneke Wirtjes, and Hans Jansen, 37–47. Groningen: Wolters-Noordhoff, 1985.

Pearsall, Derek, and I. C. Cunningham, eds. *The Auchinleck Manuscript: National Library of Scotland, Advocates' MS 19.2.1*. London: Scolar, 1977.

Perry, Ben Edwin. *The Ancient Romances: A Literary-Historical Account of Their Origins*. Berkeley: Univ. of California Press, 1967.

Perryman, Judith, ed. *The King of Tars*. Heidelberg: Carl Winter, 1980.

Peters, Edward, ed. *Christian Society and the Crusades, 1198–1229*. Philadelphia: Univ. of Pennsylvania Press, 1971.

———, ed. *The First Crusade: The Chronicle of Fulcher of Chartres and Other Source Materials*. Philadelphia: Univ. of Pennsylvania Press, 1971.

———. *Inquisition*. New York: Collier Macmillan, 1988.

Phillips, William D., Jr. *Slavery from Roman Times to the Early Transatlantic Trade*. Minneapolis: Univ. of Minnesota Press, 1985.

———. "Sugar Production and Trade in the Mediterranean at the Time of the Crusades." In *The Meeting of Two Worlds: Cultural Exchange between East and West during the Period of the Crusades*, ed. Vladimir P. Goss and Christine Verzár

Bornstein, 393–406. *Studies in Medieval Culture*, vol 21. Kalamazoo, Mich.: Medieval Institute, 1986.

Pipponier, Françoise, and Perrine Mane. *Dress in the Middle Ages.* Translated by Caroline Beamish. New Haven: Yale Univ. Press, 1997.

Plummer, Charles, ed. *Venerabilis Baedae Historiam Ecclesiasticam Gentis Anglorum, Historiam Abbatum, Epistolam ad Ecgberctum, una cum Historia Abbatum Auctore.* 2 vols. Oxford: Clarendon, 1896.

Pollins, Harold. *Economic History of the Jews in England.* East Brunswick, N.J.: Associated Univ. Presses, 1982.

Porges, Walter. "The Clergy, the Poor, and the Non-Combatants on the First Crusade." *Speculum* 21 (1946): 1–23.

Potter, K. R., ed. *Gesta Stephani.* Oxford: Clarendon, 1976.

Pounds, Micheal C. *Race in Space: The Representation of Ethnicity in "Star Trek" and "Star Trek: The Next Generation."* Lanham, Md.: Scarecrow, 1999.

Pratt, Mary Louise. "Fieldwork in Common Places." In *Writing Culture: The Poetics and Politics of Ethnography*, ed. James Clifford and George E. Marcus, 27–50. Berkeley: Univ. of California Press, 1986.

Prawer, Joshua. *The Crusaders' Kingdom: European Colonialism in the Middle Ages.* New York: Praeger, 1972.

———. *The History of the Jews in the Latin Kingdom of Jerusalem.* Oxford: Clarendon, 1988.

———. "The Roots of Medieval Colonialism." In *The Meeting of Two Worlds: Cultural Exchange between East and West during the Period of the Crusades*, ed. Vladimir P. Goss and Christine Verzár Bornstein, 23–38. *Studies in Medieval Culture*, vol. 21. Kalamazoo, Mich.: Medieval Institute, 1986.

Purcell, Maureen. "Women Crusaders: A Temporary Canonical Aberration?" *Principalities, Powers, and Estates: Studies in Medieval and Early Modern Government and Society*, ed. L. O. Frappell, 57–64. Adelaide: Adelaide Univ. Union Press, 1979.

Radway, Janice. *Reading the Romance: Women, Patriarchy, and Popular Literature.* Chapel Hill: Univ. of North Carolina Press, 1984.

Ragussis, Michael. *Figures of Conversion: "The Jewish Question" and English National Identity.* Durham, N.C.: Duke Univ. Press, 1995.

Rambo, Elizabeth L. *Colonial Ireland in Medieval English Literature.* Selinsgrove: Susquehanna Univ. Press, 1994.

Raymond d'Aguiliers. *Historia Francorum Qui Ceperunt Iherusalem.* Translated by John Hugh Hill and Laurita L. Hill. Philadelphia: American Philosophical Society, 1968.

———. *Le "Liber" de Raymond d'Aguilers. Historia Francorum qui ceperunt Iherusalem.* Edited by John Hugh Hill and Laurita L. Hill. Paris: Paul Geuthner, 1969.

Recueil des Historiens des Croisades. Paris: *Académie des Inscriptions et Belles-Lettres.* Series *Historiens Grecs.* 2 vols. 1875–81.

Recueil des Historiens des Croisades. Paris: *Académie des Inscriptions et Belles-Lettres.* Series *Historiens Occidentaux.* 5 vols. 1844–95.

Recueil des Historiens des Croisades. Paris: *Académie des Inscriptions et Belles-Lettres.* Series *Historiens Orientaux.* 5 vols. 1872–1906.

Reid, Margaret J. C. *The Arthurian Legend: Comparison of Treatment in Modern and Mediaeval Literature. A Study of the Literary Value of Myth and Legend.* New York: Barnes and Noble, 1938.

Renan, Ernest. "What Is a Nation?" In *Nation and Narration,* ed. Homi K. Bhabha, 8–22. New York: Routledge, 1990.

Richard of Devizes. *Cronicon Richardi Divisensis de Tempore Regis Richardi Primi. The Chronicle of Richard of Devizes of the Time of King Richard the First.* Edited by John T. Appleby. Toronto: Thomas Nelson, 1963.

Richard, Jean. "The *Relatio de Davide* as a Source for Mongol History and the Legend of Prester John." In *Prester John, the Mongols, and the Ten Lost Tribes,* ed. Charles F. Beckingham and Bernard Hamilton, 139–158. Aldershot: Variorum, 1996.

Richardson, H. G. *The English Jewry under Angevin Kings.* London: Methuen, 1960.

Richmond, Velma Bourgeois. *The Popularity of Middle English Romance.* Bowling Green: Bowling Green Univ. Popular Press, 1975.

Rider, Jeff. "Arthur and the Saints." In *King Arthur through the Ages,* ed. Valerie M. Lagorio and Mildred Leake Day, 1:13–21. New York: Garland 1990.

Robert de Clari. *La Conquête de Constantinople.* Edited by Philippe Lauer. Paris: Champion, 1956.

Robertson, D. W., Jr. "'And for My Land Thus Hastow Mordred Me?': Land Tenure, the Cloth Industry, and the Wife of Bath." *The Chaucer Review* 14, no. 4 (1980): 403–20.

Roger of Howden. *Chronica Magistri Rogeri de Houedene.* Edited by William Stubbs. *Chronicles and Memorials of Great Britain and Ireland during the Middle Ages,* 4 vols., no. 51. London: Longman, 1868–71.

Roger of Wendover. *Rogeri de Wendover Liber qui dicitur Flores Historiarum ab Anno Domini MCLIV annoque Henrici Anglorum regis secundi primo.* Edited by Henry G. Hewlett. *Chronicles and Memorials of Great Britain and Ireland during the Middle Ages,* 3 vols., no. 84. London: Longman, 1886–89.

Romm, James S. *The Edges of the Earth in Ancient Thought: Geography, Exploration, and Fiction.* Princeton, N.J.: Princeton Univ. Press, 1992.

Ross, Sir E. Denison. "Prester John and the Empire of Ethiopia." In *Travel and Travellers of the Middle Ages,* ed. Arthur Percival Newton, 174–194. New York: Knopf, 1926.

Roth, Cecil. *A History of the Jews in England.* Oxford: Clarendon, 1941.

———. *The Jews of Medieval Oxford.* Oxford: Clarendon, 1951.

———, ed. *The Ritual Murder Libel and the Jew: The Report by Cardinel Lorenzo Ganganelli (Pope Clement IV).* London: Woburn, 1935.

Rothwell, William. "The Teaching of French in Medieval England." *Modern Language Review* 67 (1968): 37–44.

———. "The Trilingual England of Geoffrey Chaucer." *Studies in the Age of Chaucer* 16 (1991): 45–67.

Rubin, Miri. *Corpus Christi: The Eucharist in Later Medieval Culture.* Cambridge: Cambridge Univ. Press, 1991.

———. "The Eucharist and the Construction of Late Medieval Identities." In *Culture and History, 1350–1600: Essays on English Communities, Identities, and Writing,* ed. David Aers, 43–63. New York: Harvester Wheatsheaf, 1992.

Runciman, Steven. *A History of the Crusades.* 3 vols. Cambridge: Cambridge Univ. Press, 1951.

Russell, Josiah. "Demographic Factors of the Crusades." In *The Meeting of Two Worlds: Cultural Exchange between East and West during the Period of the Crusades,* ed. Vladimir P. Goss and Christine Verzár Bornstein, 53–58. *Studies in Medieval Culture,* vol 21. Kalamazoo, Mich: Medieval Institute, 1986.

Salter, Elizabeth. *Fourteenth-Century English Poetry: Contexts and Readings.* Oxford: Clarendon, 1983.

Sampson, Kathryn Ann. "The Romantic Literary Pilgrimage to the Orient: Byron, Scott, and Burton." Ph.D. diss., University of Texas at Austin, 1999.

Sanday, Peggy Reeves. *Divine Hunger: Cannibalism as a Cultural Construct.* Cambridge: Cambridge Univ. Press, 1986.

San Juan, E., Jr. "Symbolic Violence and the Fetishism of the Sublime: A Metacommentary on David Hwang's *M. Butterfly.*" *Journal of Intercultural Studies* 23, no. 1 (2002): 33–46.

Schibanoff, Susan. "Worlds Apart: Orientalism, Antifeminism, and Heresy in Chaucer's Man of Law's Tale." *Exemplaria* 8, no. 1 (1996): 59–96.

Schlauch, Margaret. *Chaucer's Constance and Accused Queens.* New York: New York Univ. Press, 1927.

———. "Chaucer's Doctrine of Kings and Tyrants." *Speculum* 20, no. 2 (1945): 133–56.

———. "The Man of Law's Tale: Introduction." In *Sources and Analogues of Chaucer's Canterbury Tales,* ed. W. F. Bryan and Germaine Dempster, 155–64. New York: Humanities Press, 1958.

Schroeder, H. J. *Disciplinary Decrees of the General Councils: Text, Translation, and Commentary.* St. Louis, Mo.: Herder, 1937.

Scott, Florence R. "Chaucer and the Parliament of 1386." *Speculum* 18, no.1 (1943): 80–86.

Severs, J. Burke. *The Literary Relationships of Chaucer's "Clerkes Tale."* New Haven: Yale Univ. Press, 1942.

Seymour, M. C., ed. *The Bodley Version of Mandeville's Travels.* Early English Text Society, n.s., 253. London: Oxford Univ. Press, 1963.

———, ed. *The Metrical Version of Mandeville's Travels.* Early English Text Society, n.s., 269. London: Oxford Univ. Press, 1973.

Shahar, Shulamith. *The Fourth Estate: A History of Women in the Middle Ages.* New York: Methuen, 1983.

Sheingorn, Pamela. "The Maternal Behavior of God: Divine Father as Fantasy Husband." In *Medieval Mothering, Medieval Motherers.* Ed. John Carmi Parsons and Bonnie Wheeler, 77–99. New York: Garland, 1996.

Shichtman, Martin B., and Laurie A. Finke. "Profiting from the Past: History as Symbolic Capital in the *Historia Regum Britanniae.*" *Arthurian Literature XII,* ed. James P. Carley and Felicity Riddy, 1–35. Cambridge: Brewer, 1993.

Shoaf, R. A. *Dante, Chaucer, and the Currency of the Word: Money, Images, and Reference in Late Medieval Poetry.* Norman: Univ. of Oklahoma Press, 1983.

———. *The Poem as Green Girdle: Commercium in Sir Gawain and the Green Knight.* Gaineswille: Univ. of Florida Press, 1984.

———. "'Unwemmed Custance': Circulation, Property, and Incest in the Man of Law's Tale." *Exemplaria* 2, no. 1 (1990): 287–302.

Shonk, Timothy A. "A Study of the Auchinleck Manuscript: Bookmen and Bookmaking in the Early Fourteenth Century." *Speculum* 60 (1985): 71–91.

Siberry, Elizabeth. *Criticism of Crusading, 1095–1274.* Oxford: Clarendon, 1985.

Slessarev, Vsevolod. *Prester John: The Letter and the Legend.* Minneapolis: Univ. of Minnesota Press, 1959.

Sommer, Doris. *Foundational Fictions: The National Romances of Latin America.* Berkeley: Univ. of California Press, 1991.

Sommer, H. Oskar, ed. *The Vulgate Version of the Arthurian Romances.* Vol. 3. Washington, D.C.: Carnegie Institution, 1910–12.

Southern, R. W. "Aspects of the European Tradition of Historical Writing: 1. The Classical Tradition from Einhard to Geoffrey of Monmouth." *Royal Historical Society Transactions.* 5th series, 20 (1970): 173–96.

———. "Aspects of the European Tradition of Historical Writing: 4. The Sense of the Past." *Royal Historical Society Transactions.* 5th series, 23 (1973): 243–63.

Spearing, A. C. *The Medieval Poet as Voyeur: Looking and Listening in Medieval Love-Narratives.* Cambridge: Cambridge Univ. Press, 1993.

Speed, Diane. "The Construction of the Nation in Middle English Romance." In *Readings in Medieval English Romance,* ed. Carol M. Meale, 135–157. Cambridge: Brewer, 1994.

Spencer, Colin. *Homosexuality: A History.* London: Fourth Estate, 1995.

Spiegel, Gabrielle. *Romancing the Past: The Rise of Vernacular Prose Historiography in Thirteenth-century France.* Berkeley: Univ. of California Press, 1993.

Stacey, Robert C. "The Conversion of Jews to Christianity in Thirteenth-Century England." *Speculum* 67, no. 2 (1992): 263–82.

Stanbury, Sarah. *Seeing the Gawain-Poet: Description and the Act of Perception.* Philadelphia: Univ. of Pennsylvania Press, 1991.

Stehling, Thomas. "To Love a Medieval Boy." *Journal of Homosexuality* 8 (1983): 151–70.

Stephens, Walter. *Giants in Those Days: Folklore, Ancient History, and Nationalism.* Lincoln: Univ. of Nebraska Press, 1989.

Stewart, Susan. *On Longing: Narratives of the Miniature, the Gigantic, the Souvenir, the Collection.* Baltimore, Md.: The Johns Hopkins Univ. Press, 1984.

Stock, Brian. *Listening for the Text: On the Uses of the Past.* Philadelphia: Univ. of Pennsylvania Press, 1990.

Stock, Lorraine. "Froissart's *Chroniques* and Its Illustrators: Historicity and Ficticity in the Verbal and Visual Imaging of Charles VI's *Bal des Ardents.*" *Studies in Iconography* 21 (2000): 123–80.

Stoneman, Richard, trans. *The Greek Alexander Romance.* London: Penguin, 1991.

Strack, Hermann L. *The Jew and Human Sacrifice: Human Blood and Jewish Ritual.* New York: Benjamin Blom, 1971.

Strayer, Joseph R. *On the Medieval Origins of the Modern State.* Princeton, N.J.: Princeton Univ. Press, 1920.

Stringer, Keith. "Social and Political Communities in European History: Some Reflections on Recent Studies." In *Nations, Nationalism and Patriotism in the European Past,* ed. Claus Bjørn, Alexander Grant, and Keith J. Stringer, 9–34. Copenhagen: Academic Press, 1994.

Strohm, Paul. "The Origin and Meaning of Middle English *Romaunce.*" *Genre* 10, no. 1 (1977): 1–28.

———. *Social Chaucer.* Cambridge, Mass.: Harvard Univ. Press, 1989.

———. "*Storie, Spelle, Geste, Romaunce, Tragedie*: Generic Distinctions in the Middle English Troy Narratives." *Speculum* 46 (1971): 348–59.

Stubbs, William, ed. *Itinerarium Peregrinorum et Gesta Regis Ricardi.* London: Longman, 1864.

Sullivan, Andrew. "Christianity's Original Sin." *New York Times Book Review,* January 14, 2001, 5–6.

Sumberg, Lewis A. M. "The 'Tafurs' and the First Crusade." *Mediaeval Studies* 21 (1959): 224–46.

Symposium. "The Crusading Kindom of Jerusalem—The First European Colonial Society?" In *The Horns of Hattīn,* ed. B. Z. Kedar, 32–366. Jerusalem: Variorum, 1992.

Tannahill, Reay. *Flesh and Blood: A History of the Cannibal Complex.* London: Abacus, 1996.

Tatlock, J.S.P. "Certain Contemporaneous Matters in Geoffrey of Monmouth." *Speculum* 6 (1931): 206–24.

———. "The Dates of the Arthurian Saints' Legends." *Speculum* 14 (1939): 345–65.

———. *The Legendary History of Britain: Geoffrey of Monmouth's Historia Regum Britanniae and Its Early Vernacular Versions.* New York: Gordian, 1974.

Theweleit, Klaus. *Male Fantasies.* 2 vols. Translated by Stephen Conway. Minneapolis: Univ. of Minnesota Press, 1987.

Thompson, John J. "The *Cursor Mundi*, the 'Inglis tong,' and 'Romance.'" In *Readings in Medieval English Romance*, ed. Carol M. Meale, 99–120. Cambridge: Brewer, 1994.

Thorpe, Lewis, trans. *Geoffrey of Monmouth, History of the Kings of Britain*. New York: Penguin, 1966.

———. "Le Mont Saint-Michel et Geoffroi de Monmouth." In *Millénaire Monastique du Mont Saint-Michel*, 2:377–82. Paris: P. Lethielleux, 1967.

Thrupp, Sylvia. *The Merchant Class of Medieval London, 1300–1500*. Chicago: Univ. of Chicago Press, 1948.

Tomasch, Sylvia. "Postcolonial Chaucer and the Virtual Jew." *The Postcolonial Middle Ages*, ed. Jeffrey Jerome Cohen, 243–60. New York: St. Martin's, 2000.

Tompkins, Jane. *West of Everything: The Inner Life of Westerns*. Oxford: Oxford Univ. Press, 1992.

Trotter, D. A. *Medieval French Literature and the Crusades (1100–1300)*. Histoire des Idées et Critique Littéraire. Vol. 256. Geneva: Droz, 1988.

Tudebode, Peter. *Historia de Hierosolimitano Itinere*. Edited by John Hugh Hill and Laurita L. Hill. Paris: Paul Geuthner, 1977.

Tuplin, Christopher. "Greek Racism? Observations on the Character and Limits of Greek Ethnic Prejudice." In *Ancient Greeks West and East*, ed. Gocha R. Tsetskhladze, 47–75. Leiden: Brill, 1999.

Turville-Petre, Thorlac. *England the Nation: Language, Literature, and National Identity, 1290–1340*. Oxford: Clarendon, 1996.

———. "*Havelok* and the History of the Nation." In *Readings in Medieval English Romance*, ed. Carol M. Meale, 121–134. Cambridge: Brewer, 1994.

Tyerman, Christopher. *England and the Crusades, 1095–1588*. Chicago: Univ. of Chicago Press, 1988.

Uebel, Michael. "Imperial Fetishism: Prester John among the Natives." *The Postcolonial Middle Ages*, ed. Jeffrey Jerome Cohen, 261–82. New York: St. Martin's, 2000.

Ullmann, Walter. *Medieval Political Thought*. Harmondsworth: Penguin, 1975.

Vale, Juliet. "Law and Diplomacy in the Alliterative *Morte Arthure*." *Nottingham Medieval Studies* 23 (1979): 31–46.

Vance, Eugene. *Mervelous Signals: Poetics and Sign Theory in the Middle Ages*. Lincoln: Univ. of Nebraska Press, 1989.

Verkerk, Dorothy Hoogland. "Black Servant, Black Demon: Color Ideology in the Ashburnham Pentateuch." *Journal of Medieval and Early Modern Studies* (Special Issue on Race and Ethnicity in the Middle Ages, ed. Thomas Hahn) 31, no. 1 (2001): 57–77.

Vinaver, Eugène. *The Rise of Romance*. Oxford: Clarendon, 1971.

Wace. Roman de Brut. *Le Roman de Brut de Wace*. Edited by Ivor Arnold. 2 vols. Paris: Société des Anciens Textes Français, 1938.

Wack, Mary Frances. *Lovesickness in the Middle Ages: The Viaticum and Its Commentaries*. Philadelphia: Univ. of Pennsylvania Press, 1990.

Wallace, David. *Chaucerian Polity: Absolutist Lineages and Associational Forms in England and Italy*. Stanford: Stanford Univ. Press, 1997.

Walsingham, Thomas. *Chronicon Angliae*. Edited by Edward Maunde Thompson. London: Longman, 1874.

Waltz, James. "Historical Perspectives on 'Early Missions' to Muslims: A Response to Allan Cutler." *The Muslim World* 61 (1971): 170–86.

Walvin, James. *Black and White: The Negro and English Society, 1555–1945*. London: Allen Lane, 1973.

———. *Black Presence: A Documentary History of the Negro in England, 1555–1860*. New York: Schocken, 1972.

Ward, John O. "Gothic Architecture, Universities and the Decline of the Humanities in Twelfth Century Europe." In *Principalities, Powers, and Estates: Studies in Medieval and Early Modern Government and Society*, ed. L. O. Frappell, 65–75. Adelaide: Adelaide Univ. Union Press, 1979.

Warner, George F., ed. *The Buke of John Maundeuill*. London: Roxburghe Club, 1889.

Warner, Marina. "Fee fi fo fum: The Child in the Jaws of the Story." In *Cannibalism and the Colonial World*, ed. Francis Barker, Peter Hulme, and Margaret Iversen, 158–182. Cambridge: Cambridge Univ. Press, 1998.

———. *Joan of Arc: The Image of Feminine Heroism*. New York: Vintage, 1982.

Warren, F. M. "The Enamoured Moslem Princess in Orderic Vital and the French Epic." *PMLA* 29 (1914): 341–58.

Waterfield, Robin, trans. Herodotus. *The Histories*. Oxford: Oxford Univ. Press, 1998.

Watt, W. Montgomery, and Pierre Cachia. *A History of Islamic Spain*. Edinburgh: Edinburgh Univ. Press, 1965.

Weiss, Judith. "The Wooing Woman in Anglo-Norman Romance." In *Romance in Medieval England*, ed. Maldwyn Mills, Jennifer Fellows, and Carol M. Meale, 149–61. Cambridge: Brewer, 1991.

Westrem, Scott D. "Against Gog and Magog." In *Text and Territory: Geographical Imagination in the Middle Ages*, ed. Sylvia Tomasch and Sealy Gilles, 54–75. Philadelphia: Univ. of Pennsylvania Press, 1998.

Wetherbee, Winthrop. "Constance and the World in Chaucer and Gower." In *John Gower: Recent Readings*, ed. R. F. Yeager, 65–93. Kalamazoo, Mich.: Medieval Institute, 1989.

White, Lynn, Jr. *Medieval Technology and Social Change*. Oxford: Oxford Univ. Press, 1962.

William of Malmsbury. *De Gestis Regum Anglorum*. Edited by William Stubbs. 2 vols. London: Rolls, 1887–89.

————. *Historia Novella*. Edited by K. R. Potter. London: Thomas Nelson. 1955.

William of Newburgh. *Historia Rerum Anglicarum. Chronicles of the Reigns of Stephen, Henry II, and Richard I*. Edited by Richard Howlett. Rolls series, 82:1. London: Longman, 1964 [1884].

William of Tyre. *A History of Deeds Done Beyond the Sea*. Translated and edited by Emily Atwater Babcock and A. C. Krey. Vol. 1. New York: Columbia Univ. Press, 1943.

Wittkower, R. "Marco Polo and the Pictorial Tradition of the Marvels of the East." In *Oriente Poliano*, 155–72. Rome: Instituto italiano per il Medio ed Estremo Oriente, 1957.

Wogan-Browne, Jocelyn. "'Bet . . . to . . . rede on holy seyntes lyves . . .': Romance and Hagiography Again." In *Readings in Medieval English Romance*, ed. Carol M. Meale, 83–97. Cambridge: Brewer, 1994.

Wood, Charles T. "*Camelot 3000* and the Future of Arthur." In *Culture and the King: The Social Implications of the Arthurian Legend: Essays in Honor of Valerie M. Lagorio*, ed. Martin B. Schictman and James P. Carley, 297–313. Albany, N.Y.: State Univ. of New York Press, 1994.

Woods, Marjory. "Rape and the Pedagogical Rhetoric of Violence." In *Criticism and Dissent in the Middle Ages*, ed. Rita Copeland, 56–86. Cambridge: Cambridge Univ. Press, 1996.

Woodward, David "Medieval Mappaemundi." In *The History of Cartography Vol 1: Cartography in Prehistoric, Ancient, and Medieval Europe and the Mediterranean*, ed. J. B. Harley and David Woodward, 286–370. Chicago: Univ. of Chicago Press, 1987.

Wright, Neil. "Geoffrey of Monmouth and Bede." In *Arthurian Literature VI*, ed. Richard Barber, 27–59. Cambridge: Brewer, 1986.

————. "Geoffrey of Monmouth and Gildas." In *Arthurian Literature II*, ed. Richard Barber, 1–40. Cambridge: Brewer, 1982.

————. "Geoffrey of Monmouth and Gildas Revisited." In *Arthurian Literature IV*, ed. Richard Barber, 155–63. Cambridge: Brewer, 1985.

————, ed. *The Historia Regum Britannie of Geoffrey of Monmouth*. Vol. 1: *Bern, Burgerbibliothek, MS 568*. Cambridge: Brewer, 1985.

————, ed. *The Historia Regum Britannie of Geoffrey of Monmouth*. Vol. 2: *The First Variant Version: A Critical Edition*. Cambridge: Brewer, 1988.

Yates, Frances. *The Art of Memory*. Chicago: Univ. of Chicago Press, 1966.

Yeager, R. F. "Learning to Read in Tongues: Writing Poetry for a Trilingual Culture." In *Chaucer and Gower: Difference, Mutuality, Exchange*, ed. R. F. Yeager, 115–29. English Literary Studies Monograph series 51. Victoria, British Columbia: Univ. of Victoria, 1991.

Yewdale, Ralph Bailey. *Bohemond I, Prince of Antioch*. Princeton, N.J.: Princeton Univ. Press, 1924.

Yule, Sir Henry, ed. and trans.; Cordier, Henri, rev. *Cathay and the Way Thither: Being a Collection of Medieval Notices of China.* 4 vols. Vol. 2: *Odoric of Pordenone.* London: Hakluyt Society, 1913–16.

Zarncke, F. "Alexander III's Letter to Prester John." In *Prester John the Mongols and the Ten Lost Tribes,* ed. Charles F. Beckingham and Bernard Hamilton, 103–12. Aldershot: Variorum, 1996.

———. "The Patriarch John of India and Prester John." In *Prester John, the Mongols, and the Ten Lost Tribes,* ed. Charles F. Beckingham and Bernard Hamilton, 23–38. Aldershot: Variorum, 1996.

———. "Prester John's Letter to the Byzantine Emperor Emanuel, with a Note by B. Hamilton on Additional Latin Manuscripts of the Letter." In *Prester John, the Mongols, and the Ten Lost Tribes,* ed. Charles F. Beckingham and Bernard Hamilton, 39–102. Aldershot: Variorum, 1996.

INDEX

❧

CPSIA information can be obtained
at www.ICGtesting.com
Printed in the USA
JSHW040053191120
9677JS00001B/2

9 780231 125277